AN INTRODUCTION TO THE STUDY
OF THE SHAKESPEARE CANON

AN INTRODUCTION TO THE STUDY

OF THE

SHAKESPEARE CANON

PROCEEDING ON THE PROBLEM OF "TITUS ANDRONICUS"

BY

J. M. ROBERTSON

GREENWOOD PRESS, PUBLISHERS
WESTPORT, CONNECTICUT

Originally published in 1924 by
E. P. Dutton, New York
and George Routledge & Sons, Ltd., London

First Greenwood Reprinting 1970

Library of Congress Catalogue Card Number 70-100200

SBN 8371-3744-6

Printed in United States of America

CONTENTS

	PAGE
PROLEGOMENA	I
PROLOGUE TO THE FIRST EDITION	41
I. THE CRITICAL SITUATION	43
II. THE EXTERNAL EVIDENCE	56
APPENDIX : The Stage History of the Play	83
III. SHAKESPEARE'S EARLIER WORK	87
IV. THE ALLEGED INTERNAL EVIDENCE	92
§ 1. Alleged Shakespearean Parallels	92
§ 2. Alleged Shakespearean Poetry	104
§ 3. Alleged Shakespearean Legal Allusions	116
V. REAL SHAKESPEAREAN PARALLELS	121
VI. THE PROBLEM INDUCTIVELY CONSIDERED	167
§ 1. Preliminary Scientific Tests	168
§ 2. The Traces of Peele	176
§ 3. Peele's Vocabulary in " Titus "	190
§ 4. " Titus " compared with " Locrine "	198
§ 5. Greene and Kyd in " Titus "	216
§ 6. Marlowe in " Titus "	239
§ 7. Lodge's Vocabulary in " Titus "	246
VII. PEELE'S UNSIGNED WORK	249
§ 1. Fleay's Ascriptions	249
§ 2. " Alphonsus, Emperor of Germany "	252
§ 3. " The Troublesome Raigne of King John " ..	278
§ 4. The Old " King Leir "	287
§ 5. Kyd's " Spanish Tragedy " and " Soliman " ..	293
§ 6. The Altered Plays of Marlowe	295
§ 7. " Edward III "	305

PAGE

VIII. Greene's Unsigned Work 311
    § 1. " Selimus " 312
    § 2. " Edward III " 326
    § 3. " Arden of Feversham " 338
    § 4. " Edward III " (continued) 343
    § 5. " Soliman and Perseda " 350
    § 6. " Edward III " (continued) 352
    § 7. The Versification of " Edward III " 368
    § 8. Summary 375

IX. The Unsigned Work of Marlowe, Kyd, and Lodge 378
    § 1. " Edward III " 379
    § 2. " Leir " 385
    § 3. " A 'Larum for London " 392
    § 4. " The Troublesome Raigne of King John " .. 400
    § 5. " Arden of Feversham " 403
    § 6. " A Warning for Faire Women " 406
    § 7. Other Lodge Clues 411

X. The Tests of Metre, Versification, and Diction .. 416
    § 1. Metre 416
    § 2. Rhythm 431
    § 3. Diction 444

XI. The Tests of Plot, Structure, and Substance .. 457

XII. Summary 478
    Epilogue 481
    Index 487

PROLEGOMENA

I

Planned on a smaller scale, this work appeared nineteen years ago under the title " Did Shakespeare write TITUS ANDRONICUS ? " The excuse for a greatly expanded edition of such a book is that the primary inquiry implicates a whole series of problems that are all more or less preparatory to a comprehensive treatment of the Canon of Shakespéare, a work upon which I have long been engaged. We shall never settle with precision the authorship and origination of the composite Shakespeare plays until we have not only compared them narrowly with the signed but traced with some completeness the unsigned work of his immediate predecessors and contemporaries. In SHAKESPEARE AND CHAPMAN (where a number of the suggestions were avowedly tentative) and more advisedly in Parts I and II of THE SHAKESPEARE CANON, I have attempted investigations of the same kind. The research now republished, with an alteration of title in keeping with the extension of the field, covers the ground that seems to me to call for special examination with a view to the laying of sound foundations for a Canon. During eighteen years it has been substantially rewritten ; and I do not doubt that other students, bringing open minds and fresh perceptions to the matter, will be able to reach fuller and clearer knowledge than I can now hope to compass. I am content to have attempted some pioneering.

The course of criticism since the first issue of the work has been such as to leave me satisfied of the soundness of its main positions, as well as of the continued necessity for affirming them. Its publication brought me from

a number of scholars and critics assurances of agreement which seemed to me to outweigh contrary deliverances of a general kind, argument apart. Enlarged
research has yielded new light, and competent criticism
has shewn grounds for doubt on some issues ; but the
main thesis has not suffered. At the same time, the
persistence of the traditionary view in certain quarters[1]
has moved me to revise and expand my case, which is
now strengthened by many fresh literary proofs, and,
I trust, rectified at a number of points of subsidiary
investigation. In particular, I have been able, after a
fresh examination, to recognise in the play under
dispute a larger amount of work fairly ascribable to
Kyd and Marlowe than had before seemed probable.
It may be that this correction of estimate will further
facilitate a consensus of opinion, the Marlowe theory
having always had adherents among good judges.
Further, I have been led to the view that the general
editorial trimming by Shakespeare may have been
somewhat more assiduous than I had previously
inferred.

II

Even the revision of such an undertaking as the
present would seem to be vetoed in advance by the
pronouncements of Mr. E. K. Chambers in the Introduction to TITUS (1907) in his " Red Letter " edition
of the Shakespeare plays. That learned editor, com-
plaining that in the long debate over the play no one
has " convinced " everybody else, declares that not
only have all critics alike abstained " from any attempt

[1] Quite a number of English professors seem latterly to have capitulated
to the argument from external testimony. Thus, in addition to those dealt
with in this introduction and in the following chapters, we have Raleigh deciding, on the strength of the Folio, that *Titus* is Shakespeare's and " a work of
youthful bravado " (*Shakespeare*, p. 125) ;   and Professor McCallum of
Sydney (*Shakespeare's Roman Plays*, 1910, p.177) pronouncing that " the
flame-tipped welter of *Titus Andronicus*, the poignant radiance of *Romeo and
Juliet*, belong to Shakespeare's pupilage and youth." The Professors have
indeed in this matter a sad record.

to think out and apply a logical method of investigation," but the " considerable " labour required to do this is " only to be faced by the co-operation of many scholars." As he does not offer the slightest ground for supposing that such an act of co-operation will ever take place, every individual attempt is thus apparently barred ; and Mr. Chambers concludes by pronouncing that unless what he feels to be " convincing arguments as to style, derived from such an induction " as he ostensibly prescribes, are forthcoming, even " scepticism " as to the authority of the evidence supplied by Meres and the Folio editors is not " permissible."

On these somewhat minatory decisions, of which the last echoes Professor Churton Collins of Birmingham University, I take leave to comment that as Mr. Chambers has flatly transgressed his own final veto, exhibiting plain scepticism on his own part, he may be held open to further contradiction. Early in his introduction he writes : " Not yet has Shakespeare, *if it was* Shakespeare who prepared this meal of horrors, learnt the authentic touch upon pity and upon fear " ; and again he defines the nature of " the arguments to be weighed in investigating Shakespeare's share, *if any*, in the play." His introduction as a whole, indeed, indicates that, disturbed (with good reason) by his dubious task of editing as Shakespeare's every play in the Folio, he has thought to indemnify himself by blaming all previous critics for not having so swayed the mass of opinion as to save him the trouble of making up his mind. They appear to be discredited, in his opinion, either because they have not " convinced " a reading world which has paid them little attention, or failed individually to convince each other. An editor tied to the task of editing every play in the Folio as " by Shakespeare " is indeed entitled to some sympathy, though his trouble is of his own making. No man is bound to undertake such a task. But he labours ill to preserve sympathy when he resorts to an indiscriminate denunciation of all critics who have taken any pains to show reason for doubts which he himself visibly shares. It would have been more seemly to note and weigh some of their reasons, and leave the problem open ; or else to proceed to a separate investigation on his own account. Mr. Chambers has done neither of these things. Remarking with asperity on the "small extent to which . . . the literary history of England has come into contact with the scientific spirit," he suggests that this may be "*primarily* due to the fact that it has never, at the more important universities, become a matter of literary discipline." This may or may not mean that the less important universities cannot initiate any useful literary discipline—a question not to be pronounced upon by a mere layman. Remembering, however, that neither Young nor Darwin,neither Dalton nor Joule, neither Faraday nor Franklin, neither Priestley nor Croll, seems to have received any important propaedeutic from our universities ; remembering too that the universities do not yet seem to have trained many students to deal efficiently with the problem of the disputed Dialogues of Plato, one may venture to doubt whether scientific study of literary history must really wait indefinitely for an official impulse from Oxford or Cambridge.

According to Mr. Chambers, those of us who have presumed to enter "the void thus left"—that is, to meddle with the Titus problem without an academic impulse—are "a crowd of journalists and idle antiquaries, who have come to their task with an imperfect equipment of training, and have pursued it under the stimulus rather of partisanship than of research." This seems a cavalier treatment of the late Professor Churton Collins, even if he did hold a chair in one of the less important universities ; it is an unworthy attack on Professor Schröer, and on Charles Crawford, whose defence of tradition might have been turned without such cheap vituperation ; and it is, I may add, a sorry fling at Fleay,[1] who was no more "idle" than Mr.

[1] Of whom Mr. Chambers writes, in the introduction to his "Warwick" edition of *Hamlet :* " I may add that for this [a sketch of the probable working-up of the play] I am largely indebted to the suggestive work of Mr. Fleay."

Chambers. As one of the "crowd of journalists," I have nothing to say for the crowd in the mass, save that, to my knowledge, it includes one or two men who have studied the Elizabethan drama with the independent vision for differences of style which Mr. Chambers appears to lack. But, even under the disability of having had to build up my own imperfect equipment, in the lack of recent assistance from the other crowds, in one or other of which Mr. Chambers may happen to be included, I am unfortunately driven to say that his extensive equipment as an antiquary has left him, in this connection, an inadequate exponent of " the scientific spirit."

His demand for a wholesale "convincing" of Shakespearean students, to begin with, is idle. Theses in this as in many other branches of speculative inquiry normally and necessarily take many years to win general assent even if they be ultimately regarded as sound. Only such things as a new and successful drug, a working invention, a new fossil, an unearthed monument, make instant and universal " conversions." Shakespearean editors cannot be saved from the onus of making their own decisions by any all-swaying argument from internal evidence, since such arguments carry conviction only relatively to the accessibility and the receptivity of the mass of readers ; and the editors are among those concerned in receiving and conveying critical impressions. Conversion on such an issue can only be gradual and cumulative. Each new treatise is read, as a rule, by but a few hundreds of people ; and of these only a percentage are likely to be specially listened to if they proclaim their assent. There is no Œcumenical Council for any department of Æsthetics ; no " co-operation of many scholars " on questions of authorship of disputed plays. The fit course for Mr. Chambers would have been to investigate for himself and offer at least a tentative opinion. He has preferred to disparage all who do.

Professing to make only a general charge, but indicating no exceptions, he pronounces that the twofold

" crowd " of his animadversion start either from the
sentiment of conservatism or from that of Shake-
speariolatry, " which resents the ascription to ' our
Shakespeare ' of anything which the sentimentalist
chooses to consider unworthy work." It was after this
fulmination that Mr. Chambers published (1908) his
edition of PERICLES, his introduction to which sets out
with the declaration (italics ours) :—

> " Quite *unmistakeable* is the cleavage in PERICLES . . . between
> the work of Shakespeare and the work of another ; nor is
> there any literary experience so *immediate* in its *conviction of style,*
> as that of passing from the *tedious commonplace* of the first two
> Acts to the magnificent opening of the third. . . ."

And in his introduction to TIMON, in the same year, he
assures us that " the *instinct* is a right one which refuses
to accept TIMON OF ATHENS as a complete and jointed
Shakespearean whole."

Here, then, " the sentimentalist " finds it perfectly
proper to found once for all on *his* sentiment as to what
he " chooses to consider unworthy work," without a
suggestion of the need for a preliminary enquiry as to
what are valid evidences of style. An " instinct "
about either style or structure is validated as such
without more ado ; and an " immediate conviction "
about style is given unchallenged status.[1]

In the TITUS introduction this happy state of
" immediate conviction " as to style is not only not
conceived of : it is banned. Not for a crowd of
journalists and antiquaries are the franchises which
Mr. Chambers reserves for himself in his subsequent
inquiries.

> " They frame," he goes on, " such an hypothesis as the senti-
> ment may suggest to them ; and proceed to support it with that
> combination of rhetorical appeal and unconscious manipulation of
> evidence which the theologians have elaborated into a system
> under the title of apologetics. Meanwhile the inductive method,

---

[1] If, then, one should declare that on " instinct " or " immediate conviction "
one flatly denies Mr. Chambers's assertion (*The Elizabethan Stage*, 1923, ii,
129) that there is " no reason to doubt " Shakespeare's authorship of the Talbot
cenes in *I Henry VI*, it does not appear that Mr. Chambers could protest.

PROLEGOMENA

7

of which it is of the very essence that it is disinterested and leaves
the hypothesis to be suggested by the facts themselves, is neglected,
or is regarded as an instrument belonging to the natural sciences
and somewhat beneath the dignity of literature."

If " the scientific spirit " permits of all this heat in an
introduction which resolutely ignores the numerous
inductions that have been pressed upon its author, it
may perhaps warrant the suggestion that an editor
committed to the task of editing TITUS as a work of
Shakespeare is not exactly disinterested ; and that he
may be moved by a " sentiment " of annoyance at his
own predicament. His charges are as it were exple-
tives. In its original form, in which it incurred Mr.
Chambers's censure with the rest of the literature on the
subject, the ensuing research certainly resulted from a
procedure which " left the hypothesis to be suggested
by the facts themselves," even at the preliminary stage
at which I avowed myself as having been " always
unable to see that TITUS exhibited any of the characteristics of Shakespeare's work." And, letting the
facts do their suggesting to my groping perceptions, I
passed gradually from hypothesis to hypothesis, finally
seeking to strike a balance by what I regarded as loyal
induction from the data. The fling about " senti-
mentalists " is a resort to the very kind of nugatory
rhetorical device which the critic charges on the theo-
logians. He appears to consider it an argument when
he is impugning other people's views. The inability
to see a Shakespearean play in TITUS is an expression
of primary *æsthetic* judgment, in which an impression
from style and versification and an impression from
substance coincide ; and the course taken in the following treatise was and is to test the impression by a comparative analysis of the phenomena. That is an inductive procedure.

Mr. Chambers, however, seems to have reached—and
he assuredly cannot have done it by induction—the
singular position (p. 13) that a serious critical investigation about TITUS can be carried-on only " in abstraction from each and all of the particular difficulties which

its results may ultimately help to clear up." This
astonishing proposition, which is utterly flouted in his
own treatment of TIMON and PERICLES, quadrates with
another (p. 11), to the effect that such an investigation
as the present is to be condemned because it "attempts
to proceed upon grounds of style without any *preliminary* enquiry as to what elements of style are evidential and what are not." As a matter of fact, in
Chapter V of my original treatise (Ch. VI of the present
volume), under the heading, "The Problem Inductively Considered," there *is* a section on "Preliminary
Scientific Tests." But for Mr. Chambers this section,
apparently, was not, so to speak, preliminary enough,
having been preceded by some concrete handling of
concrete issues. This, it appears, is fatal, from the
standpoint reached by Mr. Chambers in his editorial
dilemma, and in the absence of the necessary but non-
existent university discipline. But the rest of us also
have standpoints. I have myself had to animadvert
rather frequently on the paralogistic character of much
of the orthodox apologetics concerning TITUS ; and I do
not remember to have noted there any dogmatic
deliverance more gratuitously illogical, or more
belatedly unscientific, than the two last cited. As
already noted, they receive no support from Mr.
Chambers's own procedure in regard to PERICLES and
TIMON, where he offers neither a preliminary investigation as to what is valid evidence nor a single concrete
indication of what evidence he has in view. It might
suffice, then, to note how he plays fast and loose with
principles, and dismiss his dicta. But it may be useful
to indicate the nullity of his negative rulings in themselves.

To demand, in an enquiry as to the authenticity of a
given literary work, a *preliminary* decision as to what
are evidential elements of style, before notation of any
of the style elements which can set up debate, is to
prescribe a procedure which no scientific enquiry ever
followed, and which Mr. Chambers, if he should try it,
can follow only to his own stultification. It would be

something much more barren than the " formal logic " of the schools, so often dismissed as fruitless, but, after all, really a result of much concrete debate. It is only after doubts have arisen *from* apparently incongruous style elements in a given case that the question as to what is validly evidential in such a case can arise ; and to prescribe either an à priori or an abstract decision as to what elements are evidential in general—as if there were in existence a built-up science of Pseudepigraphics, with an exhaustive body of classifications—is only the more preposterous when it is professedly done in the name of induction. Denouncing every spontaneous *impression* (on the part of other people) as " sentimental," the editor-critic proposes to substitute for them a preliminary decision as to what is valid evidence before the impressions are critically traced to their concrete sources. Ostensibly repelling à priori methods in æsthetics, he proposes to instal one. In the demand —or command, for that is its form—that the investigation of the style as a means of ascertaining the authorship of TITUS must proceed " in abstraction from each and all of the difficulties which its results may ultimately help to clear up," I can discover nothing but a desperate attempt to justify Mr. Chambers's editorial abstinence from examination of the TITUS problem on literary lines, and an indignant but otherwise unconfirmed conviction of the necessary superiority of his own mental processes. As a delimitation of the inquiry, it tells only of failure on his own part to realise its purport. The natural and the practical course in an æsthetic dispute is to examine the current theses, test their supports, and through the examination of these reach the reasoned conclusion which Mr. Chambers proposes to reach *in abstracto*. The rational inference as to what is validly evidential in style can be drawn only in the process of weighing the conflicting claims.

Thus fatally infirm in his most general critical positions, Mr. Chambers is even more surprisingly so in detail. He does not scruple to allege (p. 9) that " those who question Shakespeare's authorship have *exhausted their energies* in *endeavouring to suggest* that Meres may have been ignorant, and Heminges and Condell dishonest. This is abusing the plaintiff's attorney with a vengeance." The very wording here tells of a temper that excludes reflection. The energies which get " exhausted " in " endeavouring to suggest " the simple propositions here cited are surely not worth countering ; and the specification of Meres and the player-editors as " the plaintiff's attorney " is one more unfortunate excursion into abstract reasoning. These are the *witnesses*. But it is something worse. It is not only another rhetorical recourse to those discredited theological methods which Mr. Chambers has himself condemned, inasmuch as it uses the pejorative adjectives " ignorant " and " dishonest " to cloud the issue : it entirely misses the vital fact that the two authorities cited really amount to but one, to wit, the assignments of the theatre management. For there is not the least reason to believe that Meres got from any higher source his list of twelve plays, assigning to Shakespeare in 1598 six comedies, and (with obvious difficulty) six tragedies. Meres lays no claim to personal acquaintance with Shakespeare, though he has heard of, and may have seen, some of his " sugred sonnets," and would be likely to meet him *after* acclaiming him. And inasmuch as our inquiry takes it for granted that, for the purposes of the theatre-company, *any* revision by Shakespeare of a play by other hands constituted it his,[1] and by commercial sequence theirs, the citation of Meres as an authority external and additional to the theatre-company is quite uncritical. To reason as above is not to call Meres " ignorant " and the players " dishonest " : it is to do dispassionately what Mr. Chambers calls for and does not perform.

So much may suffice by way of general vindication, against a generalised attack, of the critical method of my treatise of 1905, which, nonetheless, I have seen occasion greatly to revise and to expand. That there

---

[1] Mr. Chambers himself puts it (p. 9) that the reviser was " in some sense" the author.

was much lacking in the procedure by which matter that set up the impression of being alien to Shakespeare was assigned to other hands, (though I trust there was never the resort to mere oracular assertion which satisfies Mr. Chambers over TIMON and PERICLES) I very readily concede, having, in fact, all along regarded such processes of proof as reaching only " probable " truth— a term which might perhaps usefully be held to connote both " probe-able " and "likely." But seeing that that is after all the logical status of a great deal of what ranks as rational " science," and seeing further that my main hypotheses seem to strengthen rather than to weaken inasmuch as they are tested and better delimited, I am fain to hope that, even in the absence of the desirable sanction of the more important universities, we may gradually widen the consensus as to what are and what are not Shakespearean characteristics. Behind the ill-considered deliverances of Mr. Chambers as to the logical method required, there lay, no doubt, the perception that there is difficulty about the *discrimination* of style elements, as such, especially if you feel editorially bound to suppose, in the absence of à priori disproof, that Shakespeare wrote whatever rubbish the Folio may contain—save in the case of TIMON.

Even Mr. Chambers will perhaps finally realise that style *differences* can be cognised only by comparison of all apparently relevant instances—relevant, that is, to a given problem, not in abstraction from all particular problems. And while I think, and indeed trust, that style tests will in course of time be developed to a degree of academic precision not yet attained, I do not see how that is to come about save as a result of much concrete inquiry, outside the universities, over interesting individual problems. As Mr. Chambers avows, very little original work in this field has been done in our universities, though a good deal has been done in American. Others must venture where our academics fear to tread. So far as I can see, *all* " elements of style " separately cognisable as such *may* for me be

evidential ; until I am able to mark off some as universal
and some as individual. And I suspect from first to
last that much trouble is involved in the manifold possibilities of imitation among the minor men, though I am
moved to dismiss as fantastic· the apparently common
assumption that Shakespeare above all others assidu-
ously imitated every style in sight, every order of taste,
every man's tics and tags, and every man's versification,
for years after he had formed or indicated a style, a
taste, and a versification of his own. Holding these
views, I can but revise, with what vigilance I can compass, the series of investigations originally grouped
under the title " Did Shakespeare write TITUS ANDRON-
ICUS . " [1]

III

The most important of all the recent discussions of
the play which have come to my notice, the essay of my
friend Professor T. M. Parrott on " Shakespeare's
Revision of TITUS ANDRONICUS,"[2] appeared only after
I had given much revision to this book. It was all the
more interesting to go over the central problem again,
on the tracks of the accomplished editor of Chapman's
plays, though he had felt bound to accuse me of
" neglecting or suppressing facts in favour of Shakespeare's authorship," while himself denying that authorship. Despite some ambiguities of expression, and some
antagonisms on vital details, his position on the central
issue is substantially that of this treatise—that Shakespeare was *not* the author of TITUS, but merely made a
" superficial revision " of an old play. Such a result of
a professional survey of the entire discussion, which

---

[1] Mr. Chambers soundly if confusedly observes (pp. 7-8) that ours " is not
really an isolated problem but a mere [but why " mere " ?] fragment of one
far wider [? isolated, or not ?], which embraces a large mass of anonymous
dramatic work produced in the decade preceding 1594." It was and is so
regarded and treated by me, in the sense of the fundamental proposition which
Mr. Chambers verbally entangles.

[2] *Modern Language Review*, Jan., 1919.

claimed to be the first judicial application of right
method to the subject, could not but be encouraging ;
and the recent work of other students on other issues,
dealt with in detail in the following chapters, appears to
me to promise new discovery which will render future
literary chronicling in regard to the Elizabethan period
much more satisfying. At the same time the antagonisms involved in some of Professor Parrott's conclusions,
involving as they do some acutely interesting problems
as to Shakespeare's earliest literary work, call for careful
discussion. They will be considered generally at the
close of this introduction, fully in an additional chapter,
and in detail in the various sections of the book upon
which they bear. But I will first note another pronouncement which goes some small way in Professor
Parrott's direction.

Among the communications called forth by the first
edition was the following from the late Dr. Richard
Garnett :—

" You seem not to be acquainted with my observations on the
play in the History of English Literature which I wrote conjointly
with Mr. Gosse. I there remark—probably not for the first time,
though I have not met with the observation—that the scene
following the death of Saturninus (Act V, Sc. ii) contains two
undoubted lines of Shakespeare's occurring with little alteration
elsewhere in his works :—

Do shameful execution on herself.

But soft, methinks I do digress too much.

From this circumstance, and from the fact that the scene at
the end of the play is in a different style to the rest of it, containing
nothing crude, offensive, or unworthy of Shakespeare, I am
inclined to accept the tradition that he finished a piece left incomplete by the original author or authors. I entirely agree with you
that he cannot be the author of the whole. In the History I gave
some reasons for conjecturing the original author to have been
Marlowe, but you have convinced me that the play is more likely
to have been the production of Peele and Greene."

Any opinion of so ripe and scholarly a critic as was
Dr. Garnett is entitled to the most anxious attention ;
and I am the more concerned to weigh impartially the

claim put, inasmuch as I seem to have induced Dr. Garnett to make too little of his own original case for Marlowe. Marlowe was indeed not the "original author" of TITUS, in any of its forms, but there is enough in it of his apparent work as well as of marked imitation of him by Peele to account reasonably for the long current ascription of it to him. I have therefore dealt fully with Dr. Garnett's suggestion in the fifth chapter, which is entirely new.

Reviewing the whole play very carefully, and seeking for the traces of redaction by Shakespeare which I admit are reasonably to be looked for, I find indeed general reason for believing him to have metrically (though not rigorously) revised the whole, and a small number of single lines which may be of his re-writing, but no entire speech that seems to me to be his. I am free to say that the tissue of the verse is throughout closer and firmer than that of almost any signed play by Peele or Greene or Kyd.[1]

As to Peele, the quality of all his verse, dramatic and non-dramatic alike, is as it were dilute, the amount of meaning to the square inch being scanty. He thus makes tedious reading. In TITUS, the mere verbiage, the waste tissue, though bulky, is *relatively* small, in speeches where we can be quite sure that the matter is his. And so with the Greene portions : there seems to have been a sweating down of the material, a girding of the loins of the diction, so that we have less of mere rhetoric and discursiveness and more of concrete force than is normal with him. The whole play, in fact, has been in a sense " keyed " and metrically levelled up by the hand of one fully alive at once to dramatic effect and to the popularly effective element in declamation, so that every speech tells somehow for its purpose. It is thus quite intelligible that the play as revised should have had a prolonged stage success. But there is not

---

[1] None of whom, however, save Peele (in the *Arraignment of Paris* and *David and Bethsabe*) seems to have published a supervised dramatic text ; unless *Locrine*, in which Peele can be shown to have shared, was supervised by him as well as by " W.S." See below, ch. vi.

a scene, not even a speech, that in general conception rises above the Kyd-Peele-Greene level of dramatic imagination, unless we are to give that praise to Marlowe's work on Aaron.

The late James Thomson (" B.V."), a critic of uncommon power, gave the opinion that Shakespeare penned the lines (III, i, 12-13) :

> For these, these, tribunes, in the dust I write
> My heart's deep languor and my soul's sad tears ;

but, to say nothing of the mechanical duplication of idea, these lines occur in a context that is quite Peelean, the physical prostration of Titus being exactly in the manner of that of David in DAVID AND BETHSABE. I would rather surmise the young Shakespeare's handiwork in some of the lines of Lavinia :

> Some say that ravens foster forlorn children . . .

> For 'tis not life that I have begg'd so long :
> Poor I was slain when Bassianus died.

But " poor I " is a tic of Peele's ; and there can be no certainty in the matter. Here the touch of superiority lies in the pathos. Elsewhere we may seem to find it in an unusual concision, as in the speech of Titus (III, i, 193) despatching his severed hand :

> Now stay your strife : what shall be is despatch'd
>   . . . . let him bury it ;
> More hath it merited : that let it have.

But the next speech is also in the concise style, yet without appeal. There are a number of such *possible* lines ; but I repeat, no complete Shakespearean speech ; and though Shakespeare may have retrenched and solidified the speech of Marcus after the fourfold slaying in the fifth Act, it remains, I think, unmistakeably Peelean in much of its phrasing.

Of the two passages put forward by Dr. Garnett, with which I have dealt at length in the fifth chapter, one appears to me a possible touch of Shakespeare, though

far from being " Shakespearean " as we commonly
understand that term : the other, though of more
literary importance, seems to me to belong to the order
of current apophthegms of the period, and to be
probably Peele's. That, however, is a small matter :
the important point is that Dr. Garnett, after having
supported the Marlowe theory, came round, like Fleay,
to the view that Peele and Greene were the likeliest
main authors of the recast play as it stands, and
remained doubly convinced that it was not a work of
Shakespeare's. It has to be confessed, indeed, that
insofar as such a case was made out without due recognition of the (probably prior) share of Kyd in the play,
it was defective. But the general negative case is none
the less strong.

This conclusion continues to be ignored or resisted
by a number of students. The authorship of TITUS
ANDRONICUS is still pronounced upon with uncritical
confidence by ostensibly qualified critics who, unlike
Mr. E. K. Chambers, do not so much as recognise that
there is a problem. Thus Dr. W. D. Briggs, in his very
scholarly introduction to Marlowe's EDWARD II,
declares without hesitation that " in TITUS ANDRONICUS
we sup full of horrors, but the drama is merely the *tour
de force* of a clever youth who does not realise that he is
playing with fire."[1] Very similar is the tone of a writer
on " The Elizabethan Playwright " in the *Edinburgh
Review*, January, 1912, who affirms (p. 50) that the
young Shakespeare, " so soon as he has gained a little
courage by botching up other people's plays and writing
may-be a good part (!) of ARDEN OF FEVERSHAM,"
" tries " in TITUS ANDRONICUS to imitate Marlowe, and
does it " on the whole deplorably ill," though the
beginner " does not quite forget the simple wood-notes
of his own Warwickshire," and " at one time speaks
finely enough, in the high strain of Marlowe :

" As when the golden sun salutes the morn
And having gilt the ocean with his beams,

[1] *Marlowe's " Edward II,"* 1914, p. cxiv.

> Gallops the zodiac in his glistening (*sic*) coach,
> And overlooks the highest-peering hills,
> So Tamora. . . ."

The passage here not unjustifiably cited as Marlowesque is, as will be shown hereafter, a markedly mannered echo of several passages in Peele's signed play DAVID AND BETHSABE, where the " As " and " So " form of period occurs over a dozen times. As Peele in that play openly echoes himself, it is an obviously reasonable question whether, granting the possibility of the intervention of Marlowe, Peele may not be the author of the passage in TITUS, of which so much else is in his manner. But the writer under notice has no idea that there is any question to raise. He knows something of Marlowe, remembers nothing of Peele, and, placidly ignoring the historic issue as to whether TITUS is Shakespeare's work at all, declares him to be copying his greatest contemporary when, in much of the rest of the play, if it is he who is writing, he is demonstrably copying others of much lower gift. Similarly the problem of the authorship of ARDEN is dealt with in a parenthetical *obiter dictum* without so much as a glance at the evidence.

In this fashion English Shakespearean criticism continues to be largely conducted. In place of critical tests and reasoned analysis we continue to get arbitrary pronouncements by writers who, however diligent in other directions, will here take no trouble to ascertain or prove anything. The most striking illustration of the temper in question is the handling of the problems of authorship in the chapter by Professor Saintsbury on " Shakespeare : Life and Plays " in the fifth volume of the Cambridge History of English Literature. This is how the Professor disposes of the TITUS problem :—

> " *Titus Andronicus*, as we have it, has been denied to Shakespeare, but this denial really passes the bounds of all rational literary criticism. The play, we know, was *acted and published* in 1594 ; it is included with Shakespeare's by Meres in 1598 ; it is included in the folio by Shakespeare's intimates and dramatic

associates in 1623. If we are to disregard a *three-fold* cord of evidence like this, the whole process of literary history becomes a mere absurdity—a game of All Fools, with the prize for the craziest topsyturvyfier, as Thackeray would say, of actual fact. It is, of course, possible—almost everything is possible—that the wrong play got into the folio, that Meres was mistaken, that the play acted and printed in 1594 was not Shakespeare's ; but it is also possible that all the world is mad, except the inhabitants of lunatic asylums. As it happens, too, there are reasons given for the denial ; and these reason are valueless. *Titus* is the one play of Shakespeare which is assuredly of the Marlowe school ; the one play, too, which is almost wholly what is called ' repulsive ' throughout ; the one play in which (see below) the stiff, ' single-moulded ' blank verse line hardly ever—but not never[1]—ruffles itself and grows social. Granted : but this is exactly what we should expect as one very probable result of the novitiate in such a case as Shakespeare's. Considering the shreds and patches in the same style which are actually to be found in his work up to *Macbeth* and *King Lear*, not to say *Hamlet ;* considering, further, the genuinely Shakespearean character of Aaron, and the genuinely Shakespearean poetry of more than one or two passages— the internal evidence would be strong. Joined to the external it is irresistible. But the novitiate on another side is equally unmistakable here : though the novice, scholar, tiro, explorer (call him what you will) is in a different mood. He is playing a particular game—the game of the tragedy with horror as its main motive and a stately but monotonous and verbally ' bombasted ' blank verse as its vehicle. In a certain sense it is the complement of *The Comedy of Errors* and might be called *The Tragedy of Horrors*—outrage and bloodshed taking the place of horseplay and buffoonery for stuff, rhetorical and conceited diction that of word-play, and coarseness for language. And, as there, so here, the novice, though he cannot keep his identity and quality wholly invisible, cramps and curbs them in order to play somebody else's game.''

So we are actually to believe that Shakespeare, after writing the blank verse of the first scene of the COMEDY OF ERRORS, or of LOVE'S LABOURS LOST, deliberately wrote that of TITUS, '' cramping and curbing '' all his powers in order to '' play a particular game.'' Professor Saintsbury, who disposes of the

---

[1] This notable piece of syntax, grammatically construed, would read :=
'' the one play in which the stiff . . . line *ever* ruffles itself.'' But the '' hardly ever '' would seem to exclude that interpretation. The Professor would seem to have meant to affirm that in *Titus* the rigid line is *seldomer* departed from than in any other Shakespeare play.

weighed objections of a long line of notable critics for a hundred and fifty years, including Johnson, Malone, Coleridge, Lamb, Hazlitt, Swinburne, Browning, Sidney Walker, Bathurst, Craig, Aldis Wright, Garnett, and Dr. Greg, as " passing the bounds of all rational literary criticism," puts forward an æsthetic theory which comes as near fulfilling that description as anything ever published outside the propaganda of the Baconians.

Without any attempt to specify the passages which he alleges to constitute internal evidence, the Professor declares that they, with the " genuinely Shakespearean character of Aaron," are " irresistible " when joined to the external evidence, which he had already affirmed to be such as could not be rationally challenged. He also posits as part of his " three-fold cord " of exernal evidence the fact that " the play was acted *and published* in 1594 "—as if simple publication, *without any author's name*, were evidence for anything whatever save that the authorship was unknown to the publisher. The remaining " strands " of the " cord " are Meres's mention and the inclusion in the Folio. But the Folio also includes the HENRY VI trilogy, of which the second and third parts can be ascribed to Shakespeare as wholes only by assigning to him the authorship of the two foundation plays separately published, which they embody. Of those plays, and of the bulk of the SHREW, thousands of competent readers are unable to conceive as either originated or rewritten by Shakespeare. The last strand of the cord, the list in Meres, is simply an outsider's report derived from the theatre. The " cord" is thus really of one strand. To say that Meres could not possibly have been misled is as idle as it would be to credit Shakespeare with all the spurious plays published under his name. But for Professor Saintsbury it is as unthinkable as that all the people in the asylums are sane, and all those outside mad.

It seems unfortunate that in academic circles this fashion of presenting history and estimating evidence should continue to be thought adequate to modern needs, as recognized in the "Cambridge History of English Literature." The data which the Professor declares to exclude all rational doubt were perfectly well known to all the critics who have doubted ; and they in turn founded their doubts upon data which the Professor industriously ignores. In other provinces of enquiry in which "rational" tests are professedly recognized, the method of simple brow-beating has passed more or less out of use ; and it seems improbable that it can be conducive to truth in literary criticism. The authority of the Cambridge History on Shakespearean matters, in fact, is commonly felt to rest on the more studious and scholarly contributions of writers who are content to rely on research and argument.

Even these at times leave something to be desired in point of completeness of investigation. So candid a scholar as Mr. Gregory Smith, in his otherwise excellent chapter on "Marlowe and Kyd," is content to dismiss in a footnote, as "not convincing," Mr. Charles Crawford's exact and compulsive demonstration of Kyd's primary authorship of both ARDEN OF FEVERSHAM and SOLIMAN AND PERSEDA. While differing radically from Mr. Crawford as to TITUS, I do not hesitate to say that his argument as to the authorship of ARDEN OF FEVERSHAM is in large part a convincing demonstration, though it fails to prove that the play is absolutely homogeneous. I can only suppose that Mr. Gregory Smith met with it after his chapter was written, and lacked time to weigh it. Professor Moorman, again, in his interesting chapter in the same volume on "Plays of Uncertain Authorship attributed to Shakespeare," roundly declares that the author of ARDEN "stands as a man apart, neither owning allegiance to the recognised masters of English tragedy, Kyd and Marlowe, nor claiming fellowship with the rising genius of Shakespeare"—this without a reference to Mr. Crawford's essay, which Professor Moorman evidently had not seen.

His general difficulty clearly arose from the failure

to realise that Kyd could develop in power and method, in his way and degree, just as did Marlowe and Greene. That once recognized, the facts become fairly clear. Fleay first put the proposition, and I indicated some fresh grounds in support. Mr. Crawford, going quite independently to work, supports by irresistible evidence his point that " there are at least thirty passages in ARDEN OF FEVERSHAM that were directly inspired by EDWARD II."[1] The only alternative inference would be that Marlowe himself had a hand in the play. The passages cited by Mr. Crawford are absolute echoes and repetitions, which rebut Mr. Moorman's denial of any sign in the play of " allegiance " to Marlowe.[2] No less irresistible, however, are the multitude of absolute parallels of phrase between ARDEN and SOLIMAN, and between SOLIMAN and EDWARD II ; and the lesser number of equally decisive parallels between ARDEN and THE SPANISH TRAGEDY, and again between ARDEN and Kyd's pamphlet on THE MURDER OF JOHN BREWEN. Professor Moorman's suggestion (an old one) that LOCRINE is the work of Kyd, is an arguable proposition, though not finally tenable : his judgment as to ARDEN must simply be cancelled. As to his treatment of the problem of the authorship of the Countess episode in EDWARD III, where he makes no attempt to deal with the case for Greene, I leave the reader of the following treatise to his own judgment.

Mr. Gregory Smith and Mr. Moorman, being open-minded scholars, will doubtless[3] rectify their over-sights. Professor Saintsbury's methods are beyond rectification, and simply serve to exhibit to the readers of the Cambridge Literary History how literary history ought not to be written. Be it noted that the Professor had previously committed himself to this pronounce-ment :—

---

[1] *Collectanea*, First Series, p. 114.
[2] Mr. Dugdale Sykes has still further fortified the case in his *Sidelights on Shakespeare*, 1919.
[3] I leave as it was written this sentence, by way of tacit tribute. Mr. Moorman met an untimely death some years ago.

"I do not know an unnatural character or an unnatural scene in Shakespeare, even among those which have most evidently been written to the gallery."[1]

Then in Professor Saintsbury's opinion Tamora, hounding on her sons to a rape, is not an unnatural character, and neither that scene nor that in which she is made to eat her sons' baked heads is an unnatural scene. Let the lover of Shakespeare appraise the eulogy. And let him note, further, that after labelling TITUS as "the one play of Snakespeare which is assuredly of the Marlowe school" (p. 179), the Professor declares (pp. 184-5) that RICHARD II may be classed *with* TITUS " as exhibiting the Marlowe influence more strongly than anything else, save some parts of HENRY VI."[2] Such are the consistencies of our academic dictators.

IV

If it be necessary to censure such misleading of Shakespeare-study, it is a still clearer duty to award praise for better guidance. In the preface to the first edition, I avowed a special debt to the late F. G. Fleay, the most original of our pioneer students of the un-assigned Elizabethan drama. I am now moved to reassert his claims. In the first edition, differing from him as to the hypothesis of Shakespeare's presence in EDWARD III, I dissented from his further assignment of the rest of the play to Marlowe. To-day, though more than ever satisfied that he was wrong as to Shakespeare, and that the author (or rewriter) of the Countess episode as well as of some other parts of the play is Greene, I recognize that he was right in assigning a primary share in the play to Marlowe, who may, I think, even have drafted the Countess episode. The

[1] *Elizabethan Literature*, ed. 1910, p. 172.
[2] *Richard III.* being thus excluded from the group of Marlowesque plays.

evidence for Greene, I believe, I have greatly strengthened ; but there is much work in the play that on a
strict induction cannot properly be assigned to him ;
and here I think Marlowe's share can now be proved.
And that is not all. Portions of the play are either
by Kyd or by someone closely and deliberately copying
Kyd's early manner and diction ; and the natural
presumption is for the first alternative. Such a discovery vetoes confidence in any complete assignment ;
but the argument against the claim for Shakespeare
seems to me stronger than ever.

It was doubtless Fleay's deference to the opinion
of Tennyson that biassed him to the Shakespeare
hypothesis, which cannot be squared with the evidence.
On the whole, I am increasingly disposed to respect
his ascriptions. He was the first to assign ARDEN to
Kyd ; and the late Mr. H. C. Hart, who after Mr.
Crawford's independent demonstration assented to
that assignment, has also accepted Fleay's ascription of
JACK STRAW to Peele. In regard to other surmises
of Fleay's, it will be seen below, I have found fresh
grounds for agreeing with him. On yet other grounds
I am fain to claim for Fleay a fuller meed of recognition
than he has received. Like every other pioneer, he
made mistakes ; but in reissuing a treatise in which a
number of mistakes have had to be rectified, I may be
permitted to urge that that is the fate of all explorers.
Many of his mistaken surmises Fleay himself corrected;
others are rectified by those who follow in his steps and
profit alike by his research and by his speculations.
But even where he erred, he is full of fruitful suggestion ;
and no man, I think, has contributed so large a number
of really illuminating ideas to the investigation of the
field of literary history with which we are here concerned.[1] His handling of the problems of TIMON and
PERICLES brought them appreciably nearer the stage
at which they may be solved.

[1] I am glad to find that Mr. E. H. C. Oliphant, who has done so much
original investigation in the old drama, paid a similar tribute to Fleay as long
ago as 1889.

V

But it would still be rash to speak of any of these problems as thoroughly solved. Every new orientation brings out new aspects in them ; and this is notably the case with the essay of Professor Parrott[1] on " Shakespeare's Revision of ' Titus Andronicus,' " before referred to. Pronouncing decisively against Shakespeare's authorship of the play, Professor Parrott ascribes to him no less confidently certain speeches and parts of speeches which had not previously been so assigned by those critics who saw merely revision work by Shakespeare in the play, grounding his ascriptions partly on parallels of idea and diction in the VENUS and the LUCRECE, and partly on his unfortunate assumption that Shakespeare " led the way " in double-endings. It is in respect of those items that I understand him to lay his charge against me of " neglect or suppression of facts in favour of Shakespeare's *authorship*." As he himself denies Shakespeare's authorship, save in a sense of that term which is objectionably inexact, the term " revision," I suppose, should be taken as intended. It is quite true that in the first edition, assuming that such traditionists as Professor Churton Collins had pretty fully traced the parallels from the poems as well as from the plays, I did not try to supplement their case. Later re-reading of the poems, which are clearly of special importance in this connection, disclosed to me some of the parallels noted by Professor Parrott, and I had been dealing with them in my revision. Such was the extent of the " suppression " or " neglect " of those data which had not been put forward by previous critics, strikingly relevant as some of them are. Even Professor Parrott " neglects or suppresses " a parallel which, from his point of view, though not from mine, strongly supports his own case, occurring as it does in an early play.

---

[1] *Modern Language Review*, Jan. 1919.

And the full consideration of these items seems to me to raise problems which Professor Parrott has not recognised. He stresses, for instance (p. 29), a parallel between the " Sorrow concealed " passage in TITUS (II, iv, 36) and that in the VENUS (331 sq.), ending his quotation of the latter before it deviates in its application, and dismissing as mucn less close those parallels cited by me from Greene. Yet in these the identity of diction is so close that if Shakespeare wrote the TITUS passage he must be admitted to have deliberately used a common Greene tag, or set of tags ; while in the other parallel passage in the TWO GENTLEMEN which the Professor overlooks he must on the same grounds be held to have penned a third imitation. Now, we can conceive of the young Shakespeare, when rapidly composing his two long poems for the market in a time of closed theatres, echoing many current tropes, as he did in his sonnets. But to conceive of him as using the same trite tropes three times over about the same period in his revision of plays by old hands is for me much more difficult. Seeing that Greene *admittedly* had a hand in TITUS, it seems much more economical to credit him with the tags found there as well as in the TWO GENTLEMEN, which he had used a dozen times before.

And so with regard to certain ascriptions founded by Professor Parrott on passages in other early plays concerning which there are strong grounds for inferring that they were not of Shakespeare's origination, but are adaptations by him from plays framed by his predecessors. All such issues Professor Parrott ignores, save as regards the HENRY VI plays, treating the early comedies and the two RICHARDS as homogeneous and unchallenged. But when the thesis of Marlowe's origination of RICHARD II and RICHARD III is involved in the dispute, to prove from these plays Shakespeare's presence in TITUS is merely to support one disputed claim by another.

Professor Parrott's method in these matters, I think, calls for revision. While accusing me of unjudicially neglecting or suppressing facts in favour of Shakespeare's authorship, he never once mentions the surely significant fact that not one of the three editions of TITUS published in Shakespeare's lifetime bears his name. But that is not all. He writes (p. 20) that Meres's " famous list of twelve plays includes all that can by any possibility be conjectured as in existence before 1598 "—apparently taking it for granted that the SHREW is the LOVE's LABOUR's WON of Meres's list. Yet in the same paragraph he notes that " Meres omits mention of the HENRY VI trilogy, possibly because he knew that Shakespeare's share in these plays was small." Now, Professor Parrott believes that Shakespeare's share in TITUS was small. Yet he treats Meres's inclusion of TITUS in his list of twelve (so hard to eke out, as to the tragedies) as an almost decisive evidence for the " small share," and this without asking whether Shakespeare's share may not have been small in other plays in the list—RICHARD III, for instance. Thus, while blaming my " attempt to discredit the external evidence," he is really discrediting it himself to the same degree, and only formally treating it as valid. To say that " if any men in 1623 *knew what plays Shakespeare had written*," they were Heminge and Condell, and then to say on the same page (21) that whether a Folio play was an adaptation, a revision, a collaboration, or an original play, " *mattered not at all to them* "—this is at once to acclaim and to discredit the evidence in question. It in fact reduces the testimony of the Folio to complete dubiety. Meres and the Folio are evidence for Shakespeare's " authorship " of TITUS, and the Professor rejects that ascription. To say that they give ground for ascribing to Shakespeare only a revision—and that was my own position— is to discredit them *pro tanto*, exactly as I have done.

All Professor Parrott's ascriptions of passages to Shakespeare are separately considered hereinafter. On such points I cannot hope to see critical unanimity attained. It is impossible to prove that Shakespeare never inserted tasteless passages in his early adapta-

tions. But we can on the one hand watchfully apply
the tests of style ; and on the other we can find guidance
in a careful notation of metrics and rhythm.   These
things, unfortunately, Professor Parrott has not done.

What seems to me the most astonishing error in his
argument, however, is his confident assumption (p.24)
that "from the very first" Shakespeare "quite
outranked all his predecessors in the frequency with
which he employed" the double or feminine ending
in his blank verse. This pronouncement appears to
me to overlook (or, as the Professor would say, to
suppress) all the essential facts. Noting only a few
of the best-known pre-Shakespearean plays, saying
nothing of the CONTENTION and the DUKE OF YORK,
or of the Countess episode in EDWARD III, or of
ALPHONSUS EMPEROR OF GERMANY, or of ARDEN or
SOLIMAN AND PERSEDA, the Professor alleges that
"Shakespeare's minimum (5%) exceeds the maximum
of his predecessors."[1] Citing as he does the SPANISH
TRAGEDY, he appears to assume that because Kyd
has hardly any double-endings in his early play, he
never resorted more freely to them ; and perhaps, on
that presupposition, the Professor would deny Kyd's
authorship of ARDEN OF FEVERSHAM. But, whoever
wrote the play, there it is ; and, published in 1592, it
reaches in one scene (III, vi) a double-ending percentage
of 18.6 (28 in 150 lines of blank verse). As to SOLIMAN
AND PERSEDA there is the difficulty that the earliest
dated quarto is issued in 1599 ; and that no year has
yet been assigned for the undated one ; but Kyd's
main authorship is not much disputed. In that play
we have these percentages :—Act I, sc. iv, nine double-
endings in the first 52 lines (17.3) ; in I, vi (Chorus),
ten in 36 of blank-verse (27.7) ; in II, i, twelve in the
first 75 lines ; in III, i, after 60 lines with three double-
endings, eleven in 80 lines ; in IV, i, forty-four in 260
lines (17%) ; in IV, ii, eight in the first 29 (27.5) ; and
in V, iv, twenty-three in 153 lines of blank-verse (15%).
When we note that in his version of CORNELIA, finished

[1] Essay cited, p. 24.

in 1593, Kyd has no less than twenty-three double-endings in the last 58 lines of blank-verse (nearly 40 per cent.) it is not reasonably to be disputed that he could have reached the percentages in SOLIMAN as early as 1592, when the play was entered for publication. Fleay's conjectural date of 1583 clearly cannot stand ; but 1592 very well may. Even Peele in his SPEECHES TO QUEEN ELIZABETH AT THEOBALD'S, written in 1591, has eight double-endings to 109 blank-verse lines, or 7 per cent.

Marlowe, again, actually has in the Second Part of TAMBURLAINE nine double-endings in a scene (II, i) of 61 blank-verse lines (ten if we count ' power '), which is 14.9 per cent. This scene was probably an addition made after the first production ; but the play was printed with it in 1590. In EDWARD II, again, in a scene (III, i) of 183 blank lines there are 17 double-endings ; and in a scene-section of which part appears to be an addition, but still Marlowe's (IV, ii, from the Queen's " Ah, boy " to " But who are these ? "), there are eleven double-endings in 80 lines. Even in THE JEW (I, ii) we find nine double-endings in 65 lines, nearly 14 per cent.

Apart from these plays, Marlowe had certainly reached in or before 1593 the rate of 17 per cent. of double-endings in his translation of the first book of LUCAN (26 in the first hundred lines : 23 in the last) ; and if Professor Parrott admits the smallness of Shakespeare's share in the three HENRY VI plays, I do not see how he can deny to Marlowe a main share in bringing up the percentage in the Roses scene of Part I (27), and in the second and third Parts, where the rates are so much higher than those of the DREAM, the LABOUR, ROMEO, and KING JOHN. Accepting the double-ending test as a general mark of evolution, he in effect (though he repeatedly flinches from his own thesis) assigns to Shakespeare's revision the higher percentages in parts of TITUS, in the face of the fact that the blank-verse of I HENRY IV and KING JOHN with its low percentages (5 and 6 respectively), is in every way superior to the best verse in TITUS. On Professor Parrott's view, the young Shakespeare used many double-endings for poor stuff in TITUS ; then went to a very low percentage in much better work in the DREAM, JOHN, and I HENRY IV, then returned to the high percentage of the verse of his prime. This crux is vital to the TITUS problem, and the Professor—I will not say, has ignored or suppressed—has not seen it.

Equally arresting is the problem set up by the first and second scenes in the COMEDY OF ERRORS, the first, surely early-Shakespearean, with three double-endings in 155 lines, the second with 24 in 100 lines of much poorer verse. To say that Shakespeare wrote both because of the testimony of Meres and the Folio is merely to burke a problem, when it has been expressly avowed that the Folio editors did not care whether a given play was written or merely revised by Shakespeare. If he wrote both scenes of the ERRORS at the same date, we need hardly worry over TITUS at all. As Professor Saintsbury might say, anything in that case is possible. To say that Shakespeare wrote the second scene towards the end of the decade, and the first towards the beginning, would be again to defy the critical sense. The verse and the substance of the second scene are alike, for him, flat and poor. To admit that the second scene is early, but not Shakespeare's, is to admit that other men reached a high percentage of double-endings long before he did. And to admit this is to destroy Professor Parrott's proposition, upon which, he tells us, his ascriptions are " based in the main." He has not really followed his false clue consistently, else his results would have been worse ; but he has founded on it often enough to go far astray.

The resort to the datum of double-endings in TITUS is not only vain as a production of evidence for Shakespeare's intervention : it is a lead to a contrary inference. If we seek for Shakespeare's early blank-verse style we must turn to such indisputable work as we find in the DREAM, the LABOUR, the opening scene-

section of the Two Gentlemen, the first scene of the
Errors, the best of Romeo, and the whole of John
and I Henry IV ; and in none of these do we find 8.6
per cent. of double-endings—the figures for Titus as a
whole. In so characteristic a part of the Dream as the
Oberon-Titania-Puck dialogues in Act ii, sc. i, the
percentage is only 4.6 ; in Mercutio's speech on Queen
Mab there is not one double-ending in the 44 lines ; and
the percentage for the whole play is only 7.3. In a
word, one or two years after the printing of Titus,
Shakespeare has gone less far with the double-ending
than Marlowe, Kyd, and Greene had gone before.

Sooth to say, the total problem is more complicated
than Professor Parrott has realised ; though he has
handled one side of it with force and freshness. His
pronouncement on the order of precedence in the use
of double-endings is a vital error, which on the face
of the case vitiates his whole reasoning as to Titus,
and cancels his claim to have applied a right method.
As having overlooked some of the data in my first book,
written at what I now see to have been a too early stage
of investigation, though after years of labour, I take
my full share of blame for imperfect solutions. But
this crux of the double-endings I did posit at the outset,
and I have not yet seen it reckoned with by any other
critic since Fleay unfortunately shelved it with an
untenable formula.

While the double-ending test, critically applied, thus
tells fatally against Professor Parrott's assumption and
argument, they are no less clearly rebutted by two other
tests of similar importance. The points of versification
in which Shakespeare *did* demonstrably lead the way
or hasten the pace are run-on lines, with variations of
pause, and the ending of speeches on a short line—the
latter, with the pause variation, being his most marked
advance. While in the early non-Shakespearean and
composite plays such speech-endings are very few (only
.5 in I Henry VI ; .6 in the Errors ; 2.9 in Richard
III ; 3.6 in the Shrew) we find in such admittedly
early Shakespearean work as the Labour ten per cent. ;

and in the DREAM 17.3. But in TITUS there are only
2.5. So with run-on lines. The revised SHREW has
only 8.1 ; but in I HENRY IV, with only 5.1 of double-
endings, we have 22.8 of run-ons ; in the earlier DREAM
13.2 ; in ROMEO 14.2 ; in JOHN 17.7, in the LABOUR,
frequently reckoned the earliest of all, 18.4.[1] But in
TITUS there are only 12 per cent., as against a higher
rate of double-endings than in any of these five plays.
Of all this, Professor Parrott takes no account—as if
these were not " metrical characteristics."

It is necessary, then, to insist once more on the
impossibility of reconciling any chronology and any
theory of metrical progression with the traditional
canon of the plays ascribed to Shakespeare. Not only
TITUS and the HENRY VI trilogy, but three of the
" early " comedies—the SHREW, the ERRORS, and the
TWO GENTLEMEN—must be recognised as pre-Shakespearean work, revised by Shakespeare (a) only formally,
or (b) partially, or (c) considerably. To put the TWO
GENTLEMEN, as most of the chronologists do, nearly
alongside of the DREAM and before JOHN and I HENRY
IV, with no regard to *its* far higher percentage of double-
endings and *their* great superiority in verse style and
everything else save perhaps raw stage " effect," and
to assign all alike to Shakespeare, is to defy critical
science. The run of nine double-endings (including one
triple) in Act II, sc. iv, 100-108, is simply not of Shakespeare's writing.[2] To reckon such a phenomenon as
proving that he " led the way " in the use of the
double-ending is to follow a false light and to flout
right method.

VI

In a patient study of verse phenomena of all kinds,
perhaps, may be found one means towards a more

---

[1] This, of course, may be accounted for by the revision avowed on the title-
page of the 1598 quarto.
[2] The percentage for the whole scene is 25.6.

certain application of the style test. The diversity of
judgments on that side remains one of the most dis-
appointing aspects of the whole study. Not only do we
find trained scholars like Professor Parrott assigning
to Shakespeare diction and verse which to some of us
seem impossibly poor for him : we have good readers
who continue to see the style and diction of Shakespeare
in A Lover's Complaint ; we have Tennyson joining
in the ascription to him of the second Act of Edward
III ; and we find Swinburne, who could see and
strenuously assail the error of that judgment, assigning
to him Arden of Feversham, of which the general
verse movement is much further from Shakespeare than
is that of Act ii of Edward III. Such aberrations of
attribution look like failures in the primary human
function of distinguishing voices. But voices at a
distance do actually lose for us some of their distinc-
tions—especially if, as was the case with Swinburne, we
are swayed by an à priori hypothesis ; and it is only
by some resort to scientific analysis that we can hope
to make any approach to certainty about the far-away
cadences of Shakespeare's youth.

That the effort is urgently needed has been newly
borne in upon me by the pronouncement of Signor
Benedetto Croce that the speeches in Titus describing
its horrors are marked by " splendid " and " Shakespearean " eloquence.[1] When professional English
critics go a considerable length in the same direction,
it would be both idle and unfair to censure specially a
foreign critic who, unaware of the long predominance
of the contrary view in England, thus certifies as splendid what many of us find crude or even unbearable,
and ascribes to Shakespeare the technique of Peele and
Kyd. But it is necessary to insist that the æsthetic
in the name of which such a judgment is propounded
is so far vitally astray. That of Signor Croce is in the
main an æsthetic of ethico-philosophical literary content : as an æsthetic of artistic conception and execution it really does not rationally function. If for

---

[1] *Ariosto, Shakespeare and Corneille*, Eng. tr. 1921, p. 191.

most of us some of the rhetoric in which Croce finds
splendid Shakespearean eloquence is psychologically
and poetically a kind of imbecility, then Croce's æsthetic
can counter us only by pronouncing us æsthetically
ignorant on the poetic values we have been long wont
to study.   And we should be ready with a counter-
charge.   But instead of offering one I merely suggest
that the Italian critic has made an illicit leap from the
reasonable hypothesis that TITUS is a literary imitation
of an Italian tragedy of horrors to the position that it
would be " natural " (" What more natural ? " he
naïvely asks) for Shakespeare to do it.   In the first
place, Shakespeare did not, so far as we know, read
Italian ; while Kyd, Greene and Peele did.   In the
second place, he was quite another kind of artist than
these.   And even Professor Parrott, who alone among
living critics offers a reasoned judgment that at any
point countenances that of Croce, is quite convinced
that Shakespeare only revised in certain places an older
play.   Unfortunately we are compelled to impute to
Professor Parrott also a false æsthetic method, led up
to in turn by errors of data.   The present treatise thus
ends on æsthetic issues as did the earlier.

I would add that when I published the original
treatise in 1905 I had not seen or heard of the very
creditable youthful essay (1885) of Mr. Arthur Symons
on TITUS ANDRONICUS, lately reprinted in his STUDIES
IN ELIZABETHAN DRAMA (1920).   Though Mr. Symons
adhered to the Ravenscroft tradition of a " private
author," and made no attempt to trace contemporary
hands beyond noting the imitations of Marlowe, he had
in 1885 led the way to the extent of making some sound
discriminations of matter and manner, finding only
revision work by Shakespeare, with some possible
insertions.   But I should expect him now to concede
that the method of collation goes far to impugn even
some of his tentative ascriptions to Shakespeare, and
clears up the case as to Marlowe by representing him as
merely collaborating with Greene, Kyd and Peele, or
with the two former under a revision by the last.

Further, I would say an introductory word on an issue that is somewhat frequently raised—that of the risk of seeing too many hands in an Elizabethan play. A demur was made on this score by Dr. W. W. Greg in his very generous review of the first form of this book ; and an abstract dislike of ascribing a play to several hands seems to have had a share in causing the agitation of Mr. E. K. Chambers. The answer to all such general objections is (1) that the production of plays by as many as three or four collaborators is actually recorded in a number of instances by Henslowe, for the decade after the first publication of TITUS ; (2) that the practice is quite as likely to have been common among the Marlowe group on as large a scale— whether by primary co-operation or recast ; and (3) that every proposed assignment by me, right or wrong, is the result of an induction from " the facts themselves." Even an editor without an opinion is hardly entitled at once to accuse all previous critics of disregarding inductive method and to flout the first results of a scrupulous application of it.

In so far as such objections are the expression of à priori ideas, it may suffice to say that no such presupposition can well be firmer than the opinions I have reached by induction as to the actual error of unitary ascriptions made by some diligent students, notably Mr. Charles Crawford and Mr. Dugdale Sykes. Dr. Greg, at least, will, I think, grant that every assignment must be tested on its individual merits, in the light of all the evidence collated ; and readers in general, I trust, will so adjust themselves. None of us, in view of the records, has the right to assume in advance that any play is either from a single hand or from many. And the extent to which the most recent editors are newly led by bibliographical scrutiny to infer older forms behind the majority of the plays in the Folio is a hint to all students to beware of confidence in the mere semblance of proof supplied by the Folio itself.

As to the assertion of Mr. E. K. Chambers (p. 11). with regard to such variety of assignments in the first

form of this book, that " a literary equation comprising
five or six unknown quantities is likely to remain a
puzzle," it may suffice to point out the fallacy of the
analogy. The confident identification of an æsthetic
with a mathematical problem, of a concrete with an
ebstract, an inductive with a deductive, a perceptual
with a conceptual process of thought, is perhaps a
sufficient explanation of the propounder's failure
to carry his handling of the TITUS problem beyond
the stage of discomposure. It should be noted, however, that in his recently published compilation, THE
ELIZABETHAN STAGE (II, 130), Mr. Chambers puts the
view that TITUS ANDRONICUS is but a revision by
Shakespeare of the prior TITUS AND VESPASIAN, discussed below. It might perhaps be inferred that he
supposes himself to have reached that conclusion on
more unassailably scientific lines than those followed
by any of the rest of us who draw not only that but
the further inference that there are other hands than
Shakespeare's in the recast play. But it will be seen
on a moment's reflection that Mr. Chambers had no
critical right to say " by Shakespeare " until he had
given us the kind of proof he himself demanded as to
what are the evidential elements in style. And this he
has never done.

VII

In conclusion, it may be useful to students to take
note that not only does Mr. Chambers cancel his vetoes
by his practice, but his censures of the speculations,
as such, of other critics do not withhold him from
obtruding speculations without any of the support
which in their case he demands. In his introduction
(1907) to the COMEDY OF ERRORS, for instance (p. 9),
he writes (first italics ours) :—

    " It is a hazardous conjecture, and *therefore* has been made with
    much confidence, that a play performed at court by the choir-
    boys of St. Paul's on the 1st of January, 1577, under the title of
    The Historie of Error, represents an earlier composition, sub-

sequently worked up by Shakespeare. That is, I think, too much to hang on a similarity of name. ' Truth is one,' says Plato, ' but there are many kinds of error.' *Cuiusvis hominis est errare*, says the Latin grammar.[1] One recognises in *the breath-less guess* the spirit in which English literary history has not un-frequently been written."

Then, noting in the play the element of the jealousy of Adriana, and the inference drawn by " *the* commenta-tors " (as if it were general) from the Abbess's remarks on jealous women that Shakespeare was thinking of his own domestic experience, he reaches this view (p. 9) :—

" So much does the theme, *in its serious aspect*, turn upon jealousy, that when one finds the record of a play new at a date at which *The Comedy of Errors* may very well have been written, acted by a company with which Shakespeare almost certainly had other relations, and bearing the title of *The Jealous Comedy*, one is tempted to ask whether this and *The Comedy of Errors* are not one and the same: Here *again*, one cannot build *much* upon nothing but a name, and I am certainly not going to *insist* upon the identification."

What is meant by " insist " is not very clear. Mr. Chambers seems to imply that Malone and those who have followed him in his surmise that the HISTORIE OF ERROR was an early form of the COMEDY of ERRORS have " insisted " in a " breathless " fashion that he does not follow. They have, however, done no such thing. Malone, indeed, after citing[2] from his own Historical Account the record of the HISTORIE OF ERROR, concluded thus :—

" As the dramas acted by the singing boys of St. Paul's Cathe-dral were generally founded on classical stories, it may be *presumed* that this ancient piece was in a good measure founded on the comedy of Plautus, and *doubtless* thus the fable was transmitted to Shakespeare."

" Doubtless " is in its strict force a much stronger term than " presumed " ; but it is notoriously a term used by a multitude even of academic writers, English and

---

[1] It happens to have been Cicero ; and he added : *nullius nisi insipientis in errore perseverare*, which will be found to be relevant in the present case.

[2] Preliminary Remarks on the *Comedy of Errors*, Var. ed. 1821.

French, with the mere force of "highly probable".
When M. Loisy writes "*sans doute,*" as he does a hundred times, he does not really mean to pretend that
there can be no doubt on the subject. It is "doubtless " a bad habit ; but it is at least no more indefensible
than that affected by so many alumni of the more
important English universities, including Mr. Chambers,
of telling us that "*too* much importance *need* not be
attached " to certain data, which is rather the sillier
usage of the two. Malone used his term conventionally. The important thing is that his conjecture, so
widely assented to, was really what Mr. Chambers in
any other connection would term a plausible one. It
is reasonable not only on the ground Malone gives,
but on a ground which he was deterred from giving by
his heedless insistence on regarding the COMEDY as
entirely penned by Shakespeare as it stands. Critics
not hypnotised as he was by a special obstinacy could
see (as the latest editors now see) that the archaic
doggerel lines in the COMEDY tell of pre-Shakespearean
work and might very well be survivals from the HIS-
TORIE OF ERROR. But Mr. Chambers, for his part, has
made a conjecture that is not at all plausible ; and it
will be found that his sole ground for calling Malone's
conjecture " breathless," and for his explosive fling at
" the spirit in which English history has not infrequently been written," is the simple fact that Malone's
widely accepted conjecture runs athwart his.

As we have seen, he stresses the jealousy of Adriana
in the ERRORS as a reason for thinking that that may
have been originally entitled THE JEALOUS COMEDY.
In his large work on THE ELIZABETHAN STAGE, recently
published, he advances that conjecture three times
over[1]—in one place putting it as part of a narrative
of what he " can conceive " as being " somewhat "
" the order of events "—this while dismissing a conjecture of Fleay's in a footnote on the next page as " guess-
work." Now, Fleay happens to have put six times
over, in his LIFE OF SHAKESPEARE, a conjecture to the

[1] Work cited, ii, 123, 130, 201.

effect that THE JEALOUS COMEDY was the original of
THE MERRY WIVES OF WINDSOR ; and of that conjecture
Mr. Chambers takes absolutely no notice, either in his
magnum opus or in his introduction to the ERRORS.
Yet Fleay's conjecture is as justifiable as Mr. Cham-
bers's is unjustifiable.

The exact date of what appears to have been the first
production of THE JEALOUS COMEDY by Strange's men
is given by Fleay, but never by Mr. Chambers.   It was
5th January, 1592-3.   Now, on the view that this play
was the first form of THE MERRY WIVES, the date fits
perfectly with the episode of " Cosen Garmombles,"
which points to the actual visit of Count Mümpelgart to
Windsor in 1592—an incident which is reasonably held
by Dr. Greg and other critics to have bulked much more
largely in the first form of the MERRY WIVES than in
either of the forms in which it is preserved.   That episode, making fun of the use made by the Count of the
power indiscreetly given him to take post-horses anywhere at will, is plausibly held to have caused displeasure in official circles, and to have led to the withdrawal of the play.   On the other hand, unless we
refuse to draw the fair inference that ARDEN OF FEVER-
SHAM, entered on the Stationers' Register on 3rd April,
1592, echoes in one descriptive passage (II, i, 49 sq.) at
once a passage in the JEW OF MALTA (IV, iv) and one in
the ERRORS (V, i, 237-241) in which Antipholus of
Ephesus describes Pinch, we are bound to date the
ERRORS *before* ARDEN, and therefore *before* the historic
episode referred to as having been founded on in the
first form of the MERRY WIVES. On Fleay's hypothesis, the whole thing hangs together.   The JEALOUS
COMEDY embodied a comic episode which, giving
offence at Court, caused the withdrawal of the play.
In January, 1593, the story was a fresh sensation.
Years afterwards—perhaps, as the tradition broadly
goes, at the request of the Queen—the piece was
revived, naturally under a new title. On Mr. Chambers's hypothesis, no explanation is given for the pre-
Shakespearean aspects of the MERRY WIVES, which

he assigns[1] to the year 1600, with no suggestion of its
non-Shakespearean character ; and the ERRORS being
dated 1593, we are left to the tacit belief that the
description of Pinch in the ERRORS is a copy *by Shakespeare* from ARDEN.   That the ERRORS is in the main not
Shakespeare's work at all has, of course, never occurred
to Mr. Chambers, though its versification is in the mass
pronouncedly Marlovian.

But even if that issue be altogether waived, the guess
that the ERRORS was first entitled THE JEALOUS
COMEDY is a bad one on its merits.   For the play as it
stands, " The Comedy of Errors " is a good title, and
" The Jealous Comedy " would be a very bad one.
On Mr. Chambers's view, it was so reckoned by the
author, else why did he change it ?   But " The Jealous
Comedy " would have been a fit enough title for THE
MERRY WIVES, though the chance of its having given
official offence by making game of Count Mömpelgart
was a sufficient reason for changing its name on revival.
The COMEDY OF ERRORS turns all through on the
" errors " : the jealousy of Adriana is only an enhance-
ment of the imbroglio ; and in speaking of the play
as " at heart profoundly serious " Mr. Chambers does
but reveal the weakness of his case.

To draw from the play as a whole, as does Mr.
Chambers, the inference that Shakespeare, whatever
may have been his domestic experience, was " very
much convinced " that indiscreet obtrusion of jealousy
will not yield a cure, is a truly lame and impotent thesis
wherewith to back a hypothesis that has no other
backing—a really salient sample of " the spirit in which
English literary history has not infrequently been
written."   Here, as so often happens in our enquiries
in this field, we do but find a nugatory æsthetic criticism brought in to reinforce an unsound historical
criticism.   The discerning student, after such an excursion, will perhaps be adequately prepared to resist at
need the browbeating of the most breathful antiquaries,
even to the extent of holding that Shakespeare, in a

[1] Work cited, ii, 204.

given case, did not write a play that is assigned to him. The antiquaries are demonstrably fallible in their own special field, and are certainly no less so in fields in which they are less exercised.

What is most to be feared is that all save the more devoted students will demur to all this pother over such a problem. It is an old fashion to cry : " Hang the commentators : give me the text " ; and even one who recognises the ultimate utility of comment to the elucidation of the text may protest that a large volume on the authenticity of the worst of the plays is a rather portentous " approach " to the critical study of the whole. To such a protester I can but reply that the discussion has been forced on scrupulous students by loud attempts to vindicate the traditionary Canon where it cannot be rationally vindicated ; that a great many further problems are involved ; and that a thorough handling of one may prepare for the intelligent scrutiny of others. And if it be retorted that such labour is disproportionate to the fundamental importance of the issues, one can but confess that it is very hard to prove that any one interest in life is not over-rated by those whom it occupies. There be who hold that the one vital question is the ultimate structure of the atom—a problem that seems to me inevitably insoluble. On the other hand, there is a whole literature on Bridge. I can but plead that the problem of Shakespeare must be interesting to those who delight in him, and that it is worthy of being handled with patience.

PROLOGUE TO THE FIRST EDITION.
WITH ADDED NOTES.

It may be useful to preface the present treatise with a brief account of its evolution. Always unable to see that TITUS ANDRONICUS exhibited any of the characteristics of Shakespeare's work, I was long content to rest on the general consensus of English critics of the same way of thinking. Finding that attitude loudly challenged, however, I undertook, some years ago, to seek for grounds of a fully reasoned opinion, for or against. Beginning, with that aim, to re-read the Elizabethan drama, I ere long framed the provisional hypothesis that TITUS was the work of the " author " of LOCRINE, and that that writer was the author likewise of the SPANISH TRAGEDY. Finding subsequently that this theory had been put forward in the eighteenth century by so good a critic as Farmer, and endorsed by Ritson,[1] I naturally thought the better of it. When, however, I sought to reduce it to precision, I found it inadequate to the phenomena. The problem had been expanded, not solved.

On a wider survey, equally unaware that Mr. F. G. Fleay[2] and Mr. A. W. Verity[3] had suggested Peele[4] as the author of TITUS, I found plain proof of his large share in it, re-discovering in the process Mr. Verity's piece of evidence as well as those cited by Mr. Crawford in support of his contrary thesis. Still the ground

---

[1] Hartley Coleridge, apparently without knowledge of these predecessors, made the same suggestion as to Kyd. *Essays and Marginalia*, 1851, ii, 185.

[2] " It is . . . . clear from internal evidence that this play was mainly if not entirely produced by George Peele." Introd. to *Edward II*, ed. Collins, 1877, p. 14. I gathered from Fleay in 1905 that he had put this view also in the second edition (1878 ?) of his *Manual*, which I have not seen. Finding no support, he reverted to the Marlowe theory.

[3] In his ed. of *Titus* in the " Irving " Shakespeare.

[4] This suggestion, again, had been anticipated, in the late 'seventies, by Richard Grant White, who however thought the play was chiefly by Christopher Marlowe. *Studies in Shakespeare*, 1885, p. 5.

seemed not fully covered ; and Dr. Grosart's thesis of Greene's authorship, in his essay in the *Englische Studien*, while hopefully expanding the theory, did not adequately prove itself. I accordingly went afresh over the problem, with the result of finding more evidence for Greene's part in the play than Dr. Grosart had given in claiming for him the substantial authorship ; and finding also a certain measure of justification, if not of proof, for the Marlowe theory, which hitherto had never appealed to me. The result of the inquiry, therefore, whatever be its permanence, is a revised induction, in which all the known hypotheses are counterchecked.

Such an inquiry sets up in one a sense of his obligations to the succession of students who have gone before, albeit they either did not reach or did not establish what seems to be the just conclusion. But I must pay a special tribute to the works of Mr. Fleay, to whom, though I have ventured on several points to differ from him, I feel I am indebted for more help to the critical study of the Elizabethan drama in general, and of Shakespeare in particular, than I have had from any other writer. The fact that he has frankly recalled wherever he sees reason the opinions he set forth in the early stages of an original investigation, instead of fanatically leaving unredeemed error to be got rid of by posterity, in the fashion of some of his contemporaries, has been made a grievance against him by some who have made no such contribution as his to critical science. I can but hope that I may imitate his candour and courage if the course of investigation gives me cause. But for his wide and exact knowledge, the present inquiry would have been much more inexact than it is.

In addition, I have to acknowledge another debt of thanks to my friend Mr. Ernest Newman, who, going watchfully over part of the ground in sympathy with my thesis, detected some important evidence which I had overlooked.

1905.

CHAPTER I

THE CRITICAL SITUATION

Three generations ago, Charles Knight and J. P. Collier were the only English editors or critics who confidently maintained that the tragedy of TITUS ANDRONICUS is a genuine work of Shakespeare. From Lewis Theobald onwards, with an increasing disposition to retract even his concessions as to a " revision " by Shakespeare, the tendency of English editors and students, with the exception of Capell, had been to exclude the play confidently from Shakespeare's list. Johnson, ignoring Capell, wrote that all editors had rejected the play, and concurred, finding in it not even the touches of Shakespeare alleged by Theobald. Malone thought the question not worth arguing, though he actually marked 102 average lines as probably Shakespeare's. S. T. Coleridge, after making the comment : " Omitting TITUS ANDRONICUS as not genuine," wrote : " The metre is an argument against TITUS ANDRONICUS being Shakespeare's . . . . Yet I incline to think that both in this play and JERONYMO " [this was an idea of Lamb's] " Shakespeare wrote some passages."[1] But Crabb Robinson notes that in 1810 Coleridge and Lamb " agreed in this, that not a line of TITUS ANDRONICUS could have been written by Shakespeare."[2] Before them, E. H. Seymour pronounced that " this tragedy, originally printed without the name of its author, has no title to the place it holds among the works of Shakespeare, except what it may derive from Messrs. Hemings and Condell's having chosen to insert it in the folio " ; and he roundly disposes of that by declaring that,

[1] *Lectures and Notes on Shakespeare*, etc., Ashe's ed. pp. 304, 379.
[2] *Diary*, i, 309.

" studious of their own profit, ... their only care was to swell out the bulk of their volume."[1]

Hazlitt, after quoting Schlegel's loud affirmation of the genuineness of the play, which the German critic extended to LOCRINE, SIR JOHN OLDCASTLE, and the YORKSHIRE TRAGEDY, rejected it without reservation, deciding that the external evidence was over-ruled by the internal.[2] Hartley Coleridge chimed with his father. " Who," he asks, " was the author of TITUS ANDRONICUS ? Shakespeare it certainly was not ; yet it was no ordinary man. . . . . I think Thomas Kidd the most probable person. . . . . It is perhaps likely that Shakespeare had some hand in it after all."[3] Drake and Ingleby entirely rejected the piece. The vigilant Sidney Walker was " all but certain that Shakespeare did not write a word of the play, except (possibly) one or two passages."[4] Dyce concurred, warmly rejecting Cohn's dictum that the play " betrays numerous traces of Shakespeare's genius." Charles Bathurst is equally emphatic. " I beg," he writes, " to be allowed to reject the whole of this play. I wish I had never read it."[5] His reason is its absolute difference from all of Shakespeare's certain early work. Thus when Knight, fortifying himself with deliverances by Franz Horn and other Germans, undertook to reverse the standing verdict, he found little countenance. Students generally agreed with Hallam that "in criticism of all kinds, we must acquire a dogged habit of resisting testimony when *res ipsa per se vociferatur* to the contrary,"[6] and rested like him on their conviction that the play could not be the work of Shakespeare.

But when, in the discussions of the second Shakespeare Society, F. G. Fleay attempted, some fifty years ago, to re-establish the case against the play, he was

[1] *Remarks . . . . upon the Plays of Shakespeare*, 1805, ii, 423.
[2] *Characters of Shakespear's Plays* (1817), ed. 1869, p. 242.
[3] *Essays and Marginalia*, 1851, ii, 135-137.
[4] *Crit. Exam. of the Text of Shakespeare*, 1860, iii, 215.
[5] *Remarks on . . . . Shakespeare's Versification*, 1857, p. 11.
[6] *Introd. to Lit. of Europe*, ed. 1872, ii, 277, *note.*

met by some reiteration of Knight's arguments ; and
ever since, probably, there has been an English minor-
ity of Knight's opinion. They seem to have been
not so much convinced that the play had any merit,
or even obvious Shakespearean quality, as unable to
resist the " external evidence " ; and it is noteworthy
that they generally accept as Shakespeare's the three
HENRY VI plays, in the teeth alike of external and
internal evidence. In the revival of Shakespeare
studies after Coleridge, the antiquarian temper played
a large part, and men so disposed had a faith in documentary evidence which they did not give to anyone's judgment in æsthetics—a field in which they
themselves were as a rule little disciplined. Indeed the
æsthetics of the late Dr. Furnivall, who strenuously
ruled the New Shakspere Society, were ill-fitted to
train anyone in æsthetic discrimination.

Even before the establishment of that Society, re-
action had so far gained ground that Richard Grant
White, who then declared for the opinion that TITUS
" was written about 1587-1589 by Greene,[1] Marlowe,
and Shakespeare," and that Shakespeare revised it
as he did the Henry VI trilogy, reckoned in 1862 that
the consensus of Knight and Collier, who differed upon
so many other points, had swayed opinion in general
to a position " nearly if not quite the reverse of what
it was when Hallam wrote."[2] This seems to have been
quite a wrong estimate of English opinion in White's
day.[3] though it may have held for America, where
Dr. Verplanck in his edition (1847), following Knight,
had not only declared for the authenticity of the play
on the grounds of the external evidence, but founded

---

[1] For Greene, as above noted, White later substituted Peele, though he put
a " probably."

[2] Introd. to *Titus Andronicus*, in White's ed. of Shakespeare, ix, 335.

[3] Professor Ward, writing in 1875, noted that the negative view, supported
by Coleridge, Drake, Dyce, and Hallam, was held by " a virtually unanimous
chorus of recent English critics " (*Hist. of Eng. Dramat. Lit.*, ed. 1899, ii, 55).
Prof. Ward himself assigned several speeches in the play to Shakespeare.
Swinburne. (*Study of Shakespeare*, ed. 1918, pp. 31-32) treated as absurd the
ascription of the play to Shakespeare as author, but held that he had retouched
it. Browning " did not believe that Shakespeare wrote *Titus Andronicus* "
(*Life of Browning*, by W. H. Griffin and H. C. Minchin, 1910, p. 252).

confidently on the Imitation Theory, and, following Franz Horn, held that the faults of the play are " *precisely* such as a youthful aspirant, in an age of authorship (*sic*), would be most likely to exhibit."[1]   But it is true that a certain number of English Shakespeareans, including Halliwell-Phillips,[2] accepted Knight's view, being kept in countenance by a virtual unanimity of support from the critics of Germany, who have from the first, with few exceptions, taken that position.

The chief exception is Gervinus, who followed English lights, particularly that of Coleridge.   After carefully balancing internal against external evidence, and even weighing judicially the theory that the Master would naturally begin with an atrocity, he avowed himself " reassured " by the Ravenscroft tradition that " Shakespeare in TITUS had only worked over an older piece."[3]   The criticism of Gervinus was the most competent and philosophical thus far (1849) produced in Germany ; and he is still worth consulting ; but this ostensible reliance on a weak testimony naturally encouraged the opposite camp.   Ulrici was confident of Shakespeare's authorship, and contemptuous of " the often petty remarks of the early English critics, who were prejudiced by a false feeling of taste."[4]   Kreyssig does not even discuss the negative view beyond saying that the piece has " such indubitable traces of the Shakespearean genius that its genuineness would hardly be doubtful even without the express testimony of contemporaries. . . . . The

[1] Introd. to the play in ed. cited.

[2] The arguments of Halliwell-Phillipps, apart from his insistence on the testimony of Meres, are peculiarly unfortunate.   In *Titus*, he avers (*Outlines*, 8th ed., i, 115) " neither sternness nor profligacy is permitted to altogether (*sic*) extinguish the natural emotions, while at the same time, the unities of character are well sustained.   It is by *such tests as these*, not by counting its syllables or analyzing its peculiarities of style, that the authenticity of Shakespeare's earliest tragedy should be determined."   As if such a " test " did not let pass the whole work of Marlowe and Kyd.   The critic has never critically asked himself what a test is.

[3] *Shakespeare*, 4te Aufl. i, 135.   The English translation (i, 147-8) somewhat forces the sense with the word " acquiesce."

[4] *Shakespeare's Dramatic Art*, Eng. trans. 1876, i, 515, 520.

language not seldom reaches the beauty of the best
and most loved Shakespeare plays."[1]—a stupefying
proposition, unmatched on the English side. Hertzberg, in the introduction to his translation of the play,
in the revision of Ulrici's edition of the Schlegel-Tieck
translation issued by the Deutsche Shakespeare-
Gesellschaft (1877), makes a more careful attempt to
handle the problem, though he falls blindly into an
old trap when he writes that " Paynter mentions in
the Second Part of his PALACE OF PLEASURE (1567) the
story of Titus as a well known one, and notes specially
the cruelty of Tamora—see Malone and Delius."
There is no such passage in Painter, as several students
have found after much vain toil.[2] But Hertzberg's
better grounded reasonings lead to no sound critical
result. At the outset he grants that the negative
argument from the style and versification of TITUS is
important, and complains with justice that the negative critics had not developed it. He himself, however, carries his defence on this head no further than
asseverations in the manner of Ulrici and Kreyssig.
Of all the protests against the un-Shakespearean
character of the verse, the style, and the substance,
he disposes by the *petitio principii* (already made by
Franz Horn) that Shakespeare the beginner had to
reach mastery by setting-out in the fashion of his
contemporaries—a confident formulation of the Imitation Theory without any reflection on the kinds of
imitation involved. He sees a parallel case in Schiller's
ROBBERS, but never asks how in that case the style
test operates.

Such criticism is typical in nineteenth century

[1] *Vorlesungen über Shakespeare,* ii (1859) 158.

[2] Prof. Schröer, puzzled by this and other German statements, investigated
the matter with the help of Mr. Thomas Tyler, who explained that such a
statement was made by Steevens in the 1803 Variorum. (Prof. Herford has
noted the fact also in his introd. to *Titus* in the Eversley Shakespeare. But
in point of fact the note by Steevens is reprinted in the Variorum editions
of 1814 and 1821.) Though never openly challenged by Steevens's co-
commentators, the statement is quite false, and even open to suspicion of the
wilful fraud in which Steevens now and then indulged. Mr. Jacobs, the last
editor of Painter, knows of no such passage. See Schröer's *Ueber Titus
Andronicus,* 1891, p. 14.

Germany. Elze[1] finds Hertzberg " most convincing "
as to the decisiveness of the external evidence ; like
him he complains not unjustly that those English
critics who rely on the internal have not expounded it,
but makes no attempt to investigate on his own
account. The genial Dr. Timon[2] has no misgivings
whatever about the authorship, though he recognises
the poverty of the play, and sees plain imitation of
Marlowe. Setting out with a declaration of the
significance of style, he has no notion of discriminating
in detail between Shakespeare's and other men's.
Professor Creizenach learnedly follows the general
drift, finding that if Shakespeare worked over an
earlier piece he made it his own as completely as he did
with KING JOHN, LEAR, or HAMLET.[3] The play for him
calls to us " I am Shakespeare's."[4] Dr. Timon finds the
Moor a figure imaginable only in a bad dream ; Creizenach counts the presentment masterly ; and where
the other sees a strong Marlowe influence he finds only
that of Kyd.[5] Such a critic does well to shun æsthetic
tests ; and the Professor never thinks of applying
them.

It is only latterly that more discriminating judgments have asserted themselves in Germany. And
even now, Max J. Wolff[6] shews no misgiving about the
authorship, only partially dissenting from the judgment of Sarrazin that " only the son of a butcher
could have written such a tragedy".[7] It is obviously
unwarrantable to suggest lack of necessary familiarity
with Elizabethan English, or lack of feeling for Shakespearean verse and style, as explaining the German
critical attitude in general, when English critics are

[1] *William Shakespeare*, Eng. trans. 1901, pp. 348-9.
[2] *Shakespeare's Drama in seiner natürlichen Entwickelung dargestellt*, 1881,
pp. 470, 542.
[3] *Geschichte des neueren Dramas*, Bd. IV, I Theil, p. 641.
[4] *Id.* p. 645.
[5] *Id.* p. 643.
[6] *Shakespeare der Dichter und sein Werk*, 3te Aufl. 1913, i, 168, sq.
[7] Prof. L. Kellner of Vienna was one of the first Continental Shakespeareans
after Gervinus to accept the Ravenscroft tradition (*Shakespeare*, in Lothar's
" Dichter und Darsteller " series, 1900, p. 24) ; and he has shown himself
responsive to the sounder argument from internal evidence.

found latterly concurring, and this not under the German influence which swayed Knight. Professor Boas, who upheld the German view in his work on SHAKESPEARE AND HIS PREDECESSORS (1896), may have been so influenced ; but he had also the notable support of Halliwell-Phillipps ; and the late Professor Churton Collins, who affirmed it more confidently in his essay entitled " Shakespearean Paradoxes,"[1] confessed to having ignored German writings on his own· side. Other critics, including the late H. Bellyse Baildon, who edited the play in the " Arden " series, have with similar confidence maintained the Shakespearean authorship ; Dr. Edmund Gosse[2] incidentally avows the same opinion ; and though the majority, probably, of critical readers in this country remain unbelievers, it cannot be said that there is at present any clear prospect of agreement among students on the old footing.

This putting in doubt of a matter long ago commonly held to be settled, means a state of confusion in Shakespearean scholarship. Since the dissolution of what Dr. Furnivall called " the second Victorian school of Shakspereans," there has been till recently something like an arrest of all general progress towards a settlement of the outstanding disputes on the authorship of the plays. That school, typified by Spedding and Fleay, did settle, to the satisfaction of at least a number of students, the share of Fletcher in HENRY VIII and the share of Shakespeare in PERICLES, thus making important steps towards a critical edition of the Master. But beyond this it would be hard to show that anything has been achieved towards a further consensus. THE TAMING OF THE SHREW has not been satisfactorily disposed of, though its generally non-Shakespearean character is widely recognised. The authorship of the HENRY VI group, though probably most critics see in the trilogy little of Shakespeare, remains undecided ;

---

[1] In the *National Review*, Dec., 1902 ; reprinted in Prof. Collins's *Studies in Shakespeare*, 1904.
[2] *French Profiles*, 1905, p. 345.

and the traditionally-accepted works, as a whole, continue to be indiscriminately reprinted, and to be read by millions of people, whose taste is in multitudes of cases vitiated by the habit of reading as the work of a great artist that of inferior artificers. Now that a considerable number of professed students ascribe to Shakespeare a play once confidently excluded from some editions of his works, it becomes necessary to take up the whole problem afresh.

On the face of the matter, the solution is bound to be difficult—more difficult, indeed, for those who dispute the Shakespearean authorship than for those who affirm it. The former, as a rule, start from a strong impression of the extreme unlikeness of the diction and whole technique of the play to those of Shakespeare's unchallenged works. From the first line, this impression is for many as unequivocal as their revolt from the action ; and in youth, when conviction comes easily, zealous readers so impressed are apt to think it is as simple a matter to demonstrate what is or is not genuine in the plays as to see the immense inequalities which set up the sense of an alien presence. The reason for·this confidence is, broadly, that the strongest impression left by Shakespeare's style comes from its weightier and maturer forms, which are so utterly aloof from the prevailing manner of the disputed plays. It is only when we fully realise the comparative inferiority of the style in parts of the earlier plays which are not commonly disputed, that we perceive the manifold difficulty of proving with any scientific force the justice of our æsthetic impressions.

At that stage, some critics, with Delius, give up the problem as insoluble ;[1] and the fashion in which some others go about to impose their convictions by force of asseveration and disparagement is apt to bring recruits to the side of scepticism. The late Richard Grant

[1] Unfortunately they were kept in countenance by so good a scholar and critic as the late Dr. Ingleby, who roundly affirmed that " the author of *Titus Andronicus* it is now impossible to determine." (*Shakespeare : The Man and the Book*, 1877, Pt. i, p. 49.) For such peremptory affirmation there is no warrant. Dr. Ingleby had not contemplated the means of ascertainment.

White, for instance, rendered to the study of Shakespeare services for which many of us will always be grateful ; but his way of disposing of opposition to some of his ascriptions was not persuasive. Scientifically considered, the kind of problem involved is really very complex.

There is, however, ground for hope in the perception that thus far it has never been fully brought to exact tests, and that those critics who have pronounced for Shakespeare's authorship have, as a rule, least of all attempted such tests, though some have offered reasons for their view, with which we shall have to deal. It seems obvious that one of the first conditions of a critical appreciation is a comparison of TITUS ANDRONICUS with the work of all the other known English playwrights of Shakespeare's early years. Despite, however, some allusions by them to what has been said by critics on the other side as to non-Shakespearean hands in TITUS, neither Professor Collins nor Mr. Bellyse Baildon seems to have attempted independently any such comparison. Both disparaged or dismissed other men's theories without any such investigation as could alone entitle them to hold confident opinions of their own ; and Professor Saintsbury, as we have seen, adheres to their methods. Professor Schröer, who, writing in 1891, had less provocation to it, made much more of an attempt to look at the problem all round ;[1] but still did not come near compassing it. And all alike are so easy of assent to their view, making so little of the immense æsthetic difficulty felt by so many readers, putting so much weight on such inconclusive evidence, that the doubter is at least encouraged to think his own surmise may be valid.

The conviction of his opponents is certainly not in the ratio of their argumentation. Professor Collins, aware that the great majority of English critics for a hundred and fifty years had avowed either grave doubts or entire disbelief as to Shakespeare's authorship of TITUS, thought fit to impute to those who now think

[1] *Ueber Titus Andronicus*, von Dr. M. M. Arnold Schröer, Marburg, 1891.

with them " a spirit of paradox," in the popular and
perverted sense of that term, and to charge upon
opponents a species of wilful perversity.[1] It was his
declared opinion that certain successful questionings of
common literary fame, as in the case of works wrongly
attributed to Chaucer, have " unhappily " given " a
great impulse to the paradoxical ingenuity and sophistry on which illegitimate criticism relies " ; and he
spoke of the arguments against his view as " comprehensively illustrating the methods displayed by these
iconoclasts for the attainment of their paradoxical
purposes." When a professor of English literature
thus manipulates the literary record, it becomes necessary to explain at the outset that Theobald, Farmer,
Johnson, Steevens, Malone, Chalmers, the younger
Boswell, Coleridge, Hartley Coleridge, Hallam, Dyce,
Walker, and the rest, were in no way moved to their
conclusion by anyone else's success in disproving
current ascriptions, and that the " higher " criticism
of Chaucer's works was not in their day established.
The charge of " iconoclasm " in such a connection
reads somewhat like burlesque. Apparently, Professor
Collins would have charged with iconoclasm those
of us who do not believe that it was Shakespeare who,
in RICHARD III, made the ghost of Henry VI say to
Richard :—

> When I was mortal, my anointed body
> By thee was punchèd full of deadly holes.

Mr. Baildon, too, had a somewhat " high *priori* way "
of disposing of hostile views. He saw fit to describe
as " anti-Shakespeareans " those who do not think
TITUS to be Shakespeare's ; bracketed them with the
" Baconians " ; and passed judgment on all together
in this fashion :—

[1] Yet at the age of 32 (1880) he notes in his journal that Swinburne " agreed
with me when I thought that both Peele and Kyd may have had a hand in
Titus Andronicus." (*Life and Memoirs of J. Churton Collins,* 1912, p. 42.)
Eighteen years later, with no hint of his reasons for his change of view, he
writes to Sir Sidney Lee : " It seems to me that we really have no right at all
to question the authenticity of *Titus Andronicus*—it is the youthful Shakespeare to a T ; external and internal evidence seem to me conclusive." (*Id.* p.
146.)

" I have never seen it remarked, though the fact seems obvious enough, that the scepticism with regard to Shakespeare's authorship of the [sic] works at one time universally attributed to him, is part of that general sceptical movement or wave which has landed us first in the so-called ' Higher Criticism ' in matters of Religion, and finally in Agnosticism itself. The Baconian and the anti-Shakespearean, whether they know it or no, are merely particular cases of critical ' Agnosticism.' . . . All so-called scepticism has always been based on a kind of conceit, and is the work of persons with whom wisdom was born. Surely the world might by this time accept Kant's great proof of the futility of Pure Reason ! It is, at any rate, the use of an almost à priori form of reasoning which leads to the sceptical, or, if you like, ' higher critical ' views on the Bible, Shakespeare, or any other subject whatever. The position of the man who declines to believe that the Stratford Shakespeare wrote the works attributed to him is precisely the same as that of Hume on Miracles."[1]

It is not quite clear whether Mr. Baildon meant this impressive indictment to apply to all who dispute the Shakespearean authorship of TITUS as well as to the Baconians. So far as I am aware, not a single one of the former has ever held the Baconian position, which has no more in common with theirs than has Mahatmism with the system of Spencer. The Baconians are to a man blind supporters of the traditional canon. Doubtless Mr. Baildon's line of approach secured him some respectable suffrages, on the quality of which he might be congratulated ; but inasmuch as some other respectable persons are likely to be caused some painful perturbation by the hint that if they deny TITUS to be the work of Shakespeare, they will end in denying miracles with Hume, it is only humane to explain to them that Johnson and Hallam, Malone and the Coleridges, were really not Agnostics ; while, on the other hand, W. Watkiss Lloyd, who was very much of Mr. Baildon's opinion[2] as to TITUS, incurred much suspicion of heresy by his work on CHRISTIANITY IN THE CATACOMBS.

If Mr. Baildon did not mean his terrible theological

[1] Introduction to *Titus Andronicus* in " Arden " edition of Shakespeare (Methuen), 1904, pp. xx-xxi.
[2] See his *Critical Essays on the Plays of Shakespeare*, ed. 1875, p. 349 sq.

indictment to cover those who call TITUS non-Shakespearean, it is difficult to see why he raised the question ;
and if he did so intend it, his further and quasi-rational-
istic argumentation seems supererogatory. A study
of evidences in which Kant is cited at the outset to
discredit the process of rational proof, is apt to raise
even in orthodox circles more perplexities than it can
easily allay. Those of us charged by him à priori with
à priori proclivities can but leave it to the general jury
of the public to say whether the " sceptical " case,
either as now presented or in its earlier forms, is or is
not less respectful to inductive canons than that which
Mr. Baildon declared to be at once philosophically and
critically orthodox. To the pleasant charge of " conceit " it is perhaps unnecessary to reply.

Coming to the concrete issues, we have first to note
(1) that the chronological case as put by Professor
Churton Collins and the majority of the German critics
is irreconcilable with the external evidence ; (2) that
Professor Collins and Professor Boas fatally contradict
themselves ; (3) that some recent critics, who like them
affirm the Shakespearean authorship, take up a position
as to the date of the play which clashes violently with
theirs ; and (4) that Mr. Baildon is finally " in the air "
as to chronology, remaining undecided over the argument of Mr. Crawford, which brings the play down to
1594, and thus breaking company with Mr. Collins
and the Germans, but at the same time refusing to give
effect to evidence which, by his own admissions, would
tie him down to the latter date. Disturbed, despite all
their asseveration, by the crudity of the work, one
group date the play in Shakespeare's nonage. Another
group, staking all on the apparent purport of the records,
date it within a year of the DREAM. Yet another
group, cowed by the external evidence, which makes
Shakespeare *author* of the play, use that very evidence
to prove him a mere reviser of it. The affirmative
case, in short, is a chaos. That, on the other hand,
the negative case—the case against the ascription of
the play to Shakespeare—should in its earlier states

present a variety of hypotheses, was inevitable.   It is the writer's belief, however, that those hypotheses can now be reduced to unity by giving full effect to all the evidence which separately suggested them ; and by further enlarging the survey.

The inquiry involves two processes—the negative or destructive, and the constructive.   It is one thing to show reasons for not believing that the play is Shakespeare's : it is another thing to establish the real authorship ; and the second process must be carried at least some way before the results of the first can be regarded as broadly secure.   The following essay accordingly attempts both, setting forth a theory of the authorship in the light of all the evidence.   But the first step must be an examination of the affirmative position.

CHAPTER II

THE EXTERNAL EVIDENCE

§ I

The case for Shakespeare's authorship of TITUS has been most comprehensively put by Professor M. M. Arnold Schröer of Freiburg in his essay UEBER TITUS ANDRONICUS. In respect of painstaking it puts to shame the slight paper of Professor Churton Collins, who avows that he did not see fit to read it. Save, however, in so far as Dr. Schröer deals lengthily with the contrary arguments of Fleay, and greatly widens the scope of the æsthetic debate, he does not put the affirmative much otherwise than do Mr. Collins and Mr. Baildon, who both substantially repeat the pleas of Charles Knight ; so that, for the purpose of a condensed discussion, a study of their pleas may serve.

Professor Collins's position is that " if Shakespeare was not the author of TITUS ANDRONICUS, there is an end of circumstantial testimony in literary questions ; for the evidence external and internal is as conclusive as such evidence can possibly be." The word " circumstantial " appears to have been used at haphazard ; for no evidence so describable is cited save claims of coincidence of phrase and idea ; and what strictly circumstantial evidence there is tells the other way. Apart from alleged internal evidence, the whole case put is that (1) Meres ascribed TITUS to Shakespeare in his list in PALLADIS TAMIA in 1598 ;[1] and (2) that it is inserted in the first folio—items perfectly well known

---

[1] Large extracts from Meres's book are given in Part I of *Shakespeare Allusion Books*, issued by the New Shakespeare Society in 1874. Briefer but sufficient extracts are given by Mr. E. K. Chambers in *The Elizabethan Stage*, 1923, vol. I, and in many other compilations and Lives.

to all who deny Shakespeare's authorship. They are not " circumstantial" evidence ; they are testimonies, and, as already noted, they resolve themselves into one—the testimony of the theatre.

§ 2

It may be well, before going further, to remove from the field the false issue raised by some of the earlier doubters in respect of the pseudo-testimony of the playwright Edward Ravenscroft. That writer, who made an adaptation of TITUS, mentions in the preface to his published version (1687) a report made to him " by some anciently conversant with the stage," that TITUS was not originally written by Shakespeare, " but brought by a private writer to be acted, and he only gave some master-touches to one or two of the principal parts or characters." On the face of the case, such late and loose testimony in itself counts for nothing, and it was used by Malone merely as con-firming a disbelief which was already so strong as not to need fresh justification. Charles Knight, however, noted that in his original prologue to his play Ravens-croft had spoken of TITUS as really Shakespeare's ; and Mr. Baildon, following Knight, charged Malone with being " so disingenuous as to suppress this bit of evidence," and further found Ravenscroft and Malone together " convicted of a *suppressio veri* of the first magnitude." All this is but supererogatory strife, as is Professor Collins's similar denunciation of Ravens-croft.[1] Ten years had elapsed between the produc-tion and the printing of the play in question. Ravens-croft might very well have heard his tradition after the production ; and his citation of it in his published preface remains worth just as much and as little as it would have been if there were no prologue. But in reality it is valueless, save as testifying to a current doubt, in 1677, of Shakespeare's authorship of TITUS.

[1] *Studies in Shakespeare*, p. 106.

Mr. Baildon, constructing his transcendental case, followed Mr. Charles Crawford[1] without inquiry in the mistaken assertion that the sceptical view is "founded upon" the remark of Ravenscroft; and contended that if 'the anti-Shakespearean" rejects Ravenscroft, "he has no foothold for any anti-Shakespearean theory whatever."[2] I will not charge Mr. Baildon with a "*suppressio veri* of the first magnitude," preferring to suppose that when, as often happened, he omitted to deal with material evidence, he was either unaware or oblivious of its existence. He and Mr. Crawford (usually so vigilant in his search) had failed to pay proper attention to the documents. Shakespeare's authorship was disbelieved-in by Theobald and Johnson,[3] who both rejected Ravensc ft's tradition; and the series of critics who have respectively suggested one or another well-known contemporary dramatist as the real author of the play have naturally, as a rule, paid no heed to it, inasmuch as the legend of a "private author" does not harmonise with their theory, and is, further, too late to be of any evidential force. Dr. Grosart, who cited Ravenscroft in connection with his thesis that the play was "substantially" the work of Greene, has obviously worsened his case by assuming that Greene could be spoken of as a "private author." The *primary* ground for doubting whether Shakespeare had any hand in the play, let it be here said once for all, is simply the quality of the style, the verse, the workmanship and the matter from first to last. There are probably many who, like the present writer, never had the sensation of reading Shakespeare's verse in any complete speech throughout the play. The sifting and testing of that spontaneous impression of its spuriousness, however, is a task to be gone about with rather more circum-

[1] "All who doubt the genuineness of the tragedy accept without hesitation the tradition reported by Ravenscroft." C. Crawford, art. on "The Date and Authenticity of 'Titus Andronicus'" in the *Jahrbuch der deutschen Shakespeare Gesellschaft*, 1900, p. 110.
[2] Ed. cited, pp. xxii, lxxi.
[3] As is mentioned by Professor Collins, p. 106.

spection than was brought to the justification of his faith by Mr. Baildon ; and the next step is to deal with the external evidence before noted.

§ 3

Concerning the testimony of Meres, it was long ago pointed out[1] that his lists of plays, like some of his lists of poets, are very artifically drawn up in *sixes*, six tragedies being named to balance six comedies. A list so framed without documentary evidence is *prima facie* open to suspicion when the number is hard to make out (as it clearly was for Meres), whatever might be the good faith of the maker ; and in declaring that whoever refuses to accept the bare assertion of Meres " is deliberately giving himself over gagged and bound to the anti-Shakespeareans," Mr. Baildon[2] did but substitute vociferation for argument. Meres is not known to have had any personal acquaintance with Shakespeare before 1598, though he is very likely to have met him after the issue of PALLADIS TAMIA. Mr. Baildon's statement[3] that " Shakespeare read his MS. sonnets to him " is a pure fiction.[4] If Malone had made so explicitly such a baseless statement, we should have had a pretty string of epithets to his address from Mr. Baildon. It is quite true that, were there no strong counter-evidence, external or internal, the statement of Meres, repeating and coinciding with the claim of the theatre, would be practically decisive ; but, to say nothing at this point of the internal evidence, there are two items of external evidence against him, the weaker of which balances his as regards Shake-

[1] By Dr. R. B. Nicholson, in the *New Shakspere Society's Transactions* for 1874, Pt. I, p. 123.
[2] Ed. cited, p. xx.   [3] *Id.* p. xix.
[4] Mr. Baildon had credulously followed the reckless assertion of Schlegel (*Lectures on Dramatic Literature*, Eng. trans. Bohn ed. p. 442) that " Meres was personally acquainted with the poet, and so very intimately, that the latter read over to him his Sonnets before they were printed." Meres makes not the slightest pretence to personal acquaintance ; and in alluding to Shakespeare's " sugred Sonnets among his private friends " makes no claim to have seen any. Halliwell-Phillipps (*Outlines*, 8th ed. i, 293) strangely lends himself to delusion by calling Meres one of Shakespeare's " intimate friends".

speare's having written the TITUS of 1594, and one of
which is quite decisive against Mr. Baildon's case.

§ 4

The weaker of the two items in question is the fact
that, in the Quartos, TITUS is described as having been
played by the servants of the Earls of Derby, Pembroke, and Sussex ;[1] and that " Titus and Andronicus,"
as appears from Henslowe's Diary, was played in
January, 1593-4, by Sussex's men. Now, as Fleay
insists, " there is no vestige of evidence that Shakespeare ever wrote for any company but one."[2] This
company was at first known as that of Lord Strange,
who became Lord Derby in September, 1593, and died
in April, 1594 ; whereafter it entered the service of
the Lord Chamberlain (Hunsdon), whose official title
it bore thenceforth,[3] until it became known as the
King's. As it happens, Henslowe records the playing
of a " Tittus and Vespacia " (TITUS AND VESPASIAN)
many times by Lord Strange's men in 1592 ; but all
the evidence goes to show that this was an earlier
form of the play, and not that preserved as TITUS
ANDRONICUS. Seeing further that on the title-page
of the first quarto the companies concerned are named
in the order : (1) Derby's ; (2) Pembroke's ; (3)
Sussex's, the theory that best fits all the facts is that
TITUS AND VESPASIAN was the work of Kyd ; that
Shakespeare's company bought it as they did his
SPANISH TRAGEDY ; that TITUS ANDRONICUS was a
recast by another hand, or hands, made for the Pembroke company ; and that the Sussex men temporarily
acquired that. The quarto of 1600 adds the name of
the Chamberlain's men, a record of the fact that
Shakespeare's company acquired the revised play,

---

[1] In the First Quarto, 1594, this stands as " Essex," but as Dr. Greg notes,
that is unquestionably a misprint. There was no Essex Company in London
at that time. Mr. Chambers, in his *Elizabethan Stage*, gives the " Essex " as
" Sussex " (ii, 482.)

[2] *Life of Shakespeare*, p. 115.

[3] *Id.* pp. 21, 114-116. There has been much confusion on the point.

only after the Sussex men nad had it. Any addition
or recast would pretext Henslowe's account of the
play as " ne " in February, 1594.

Halliwell-Phillipps, however, taking it for granted
that Shakespeare wrote Titus Andronicus for
Sussex's company, in effect assumed that " he left
Lord Strange's men, who in 1593 enjoyed the highest
position of any then existing, and after having been a
member successively of two of the obscurest companies, returned to his former position within a few
months." This theory was by Fleay justifiably pronounced " utterly untenable."[1]   It would indeed never
have been framed save for the presupposition that
Shakespeare wrote or radically recast Titus. But it is
needed for the support of that opinion, and in the lack
of positive record as to Shakespeare's early life, Mr.
E. K. Chambers is in a position to say that " there is
really some basis "[2] for Halliwell-Phillipps's suggestion.

Professor Parrott, on the other hand, thinks that
in the autumn of 1593 Strange's men toured with a
Titus Andronicus which had belonged to Pembroke's
men, then in low water ; that this Titus, revised by
Shakespeare as it now stands, had been arranged by
him for his own company ; and that it was this play
that the Sussex men played early in 1594.[3] But no
explanation is offered of such a transference of a play
revised by Shakespeare from his company to another ;
and it is plainly more natural to suppose that the
Andronicus play, which had certainly been in the
possession of the Pembroke men, had been differentiated for them from the Titus and Vespasian previously played by Shakespeare's company.

This being as far as we can get on the basis of the
records, the question must be there left ; and the
presupposition as to Shakespeare's recast of Titus
and Vespasian into our Titus Andronicus, founded on
Meres and the Folio, must be dealt with on its merits.

[1] Fleay, *Life of Shakespeare*, p. 115. Cf. Halliwell-Phillipps, *Outlines*,
8th ed. i, 109 sq.
[2] *The Elizabethan Stage*, 1923, ii, 130.
[3] *Mod. Lang. Review*, Jan. 1919, p. 18.

§ 5

On the face of the case, the argument from Meres
is habitually overstrained. On no clear ground can
we say that a bare ascription by him counts for much
more than an ascription by a contemporary publisher.
As is well-known, the FIRST PART OF SIR JOHN OLD-
CASTLE, printed in 1600, has Shakespeare's name in
full on the title-page of the second impression ; THE
LONDON PRODIGAL, printed in 1605, was ascribed to
him on the title-page, and was included in the third
and fourth folios ; and A YORKSHIRE TRAGEDY is
ascribed to him on the title-page of the quarto of 1608.
On Mr. Baildon's principles we " deliver ourselves
gagged and bound to the anti-Shakespeareans " if we
decide that these plays are not Shakespeare's. Yet we
all do so decide. Why then are we to be gagged and
bound by Meres ?

Against this position, Dr. Greg argues that the testimony of Meres " was at least disinterested." But if,
as is obviously likely, Meres proceeds on the testimony
of the theatre company, the answer is that that testimony was emphatically *not* disinterested. A print
of the play, bearing no author's name, was in circulation, and over that, presumably, the company
had no control. The one way, then, in which the
company could affirm property in a piece which had
been in various hands was to claim it as Shakespeare's ;
and such a claim, in the then state of copyright, could
apparently be pretexted by the simple fact that at
one stage Shakespeare had revised the work.

How then, it may be asked, did Shakespeare come
to revise a play which at the date of its printing was
not the property of his company, though they came
in possession of it afterwards ? The first answer is
that the existing play may have been produced partly
in the interests of his company, which had for a time
played TITUS AND VESPASIAN, but had been in some
way deprived of it—how, we cannot tell. A com-

parison of our play with the older, as preserved in the
German version, raises the question, Why was it
recast ? As we shall see, all the main stage effects,
the characters, the types, the horrors, and most of the
" thrills," are in the old play, and it is likely to have
been as " attractive " as the compilation in the Folio.
The production of another version seems explicable
only on one of two grounds. Either the old play was
in prose—which is unlikely, as the author was probably
Kyd—and it was desired to give it the attraction of
verse, as had been done with the old RICHARD III,
the old HENRY V, and the old SHREW, or there was a
quarrel on foot with the possessors of TITUS AND
VESPASIAN, and a new version was desired to com-
pete with theirs. As to such a quarrel we can only
guess ; but if there were one, the companies would be
involved in it ; and it could quite conceivably happen
that Peele, Greene, and Marlowe were called upon to
rewrite the piece, and even that Kyd should take a
hand in the undertaking, contributing some fresh
matter. In that case, Shakespeare's company might
be sympathetic.

The second answer is that Shakespeare may have
revised the play expressly for publication. In 1594
there was entered on the stationers' books the tragedy
of LOCRINE, and in 1595 we have an edition of that
play " newly set foorth, overseene, and corrected
by W. S." As we shall see, LOCRINE is in all likelihood
a play planned or recast and partly written by Peele
in collaboration with Greene ; and that " W. S. " was
Shakespeare is the view finally reached by Fleay,
after he had for a time rejected it.[1] It is known from
Peele's own statement, in his letter of 1595-6 to Lord
Burleigh, that he was then suffering from a long illness,
and Fleay makes the reasonable surmise that Shakespeare supervised LOCRINE for publication by way of
helping a colleague in distress. The fact that Peele's
EDWARD I, as noted by Dyce, is one of the most care-

[1] *Biographical Chronicle of the English Drama*, ii, 321. Cf. his *Life of
Shakespeare*, 1886, pp. 24, 120, 291.

lessly printed of the old plays, goes to suggest that
such a supervision would be a real service.[1] If then
the thesis of the present essay—that Peele is the main
author or redactor of TITUS in its present form—should
be held to be established, there is no antecedent difficulty in supposing that Shakespeare similarly revised
TITUS.   And the fact that in 1594-5, when Peele was in
sore need of funds, there were printed his DAVID AND
BETHSABE and his BATTLE OF ALCAZAR, as well as
LOCRINE, is at least in harmony with the view that
TITUS, printed in 1594, was also his in part.

<h2 style="text-align:center">§ 6</h2>

In any case, whatever may have happened in that
connection, the fact that TITUS is accurately printed
without Shakespeare's name in the editions of 1594,
1600, and 1611 is a strong support to the negative case.
This grave difficulty Mr. Collins meets by citing the
facts that " his name was not on the title-pages of the
first quartos of RICHARD II, of the quartos of the
FIRST PART OF HENRY IV, or of HENRY VI (*sic*:
should be V), or of either of the first three quartos of
ROMEO AND JULIET."[2] Observe the questions implicated. It is only on the first of the quartos of
RICHARD II (1597), pirated by Simmes, that Shakespeare's name is lacking ; the second and later quartos
have it ; and the play has many traces of an earlier
hand.[3] The first quarto of ROMEO AND JULIET, again,
is spurious ; and in that play Shakespeare demonstrably worked over a draft by other men.   The 1600

---

[1] *Titus* is much more correctly printed than most plays of the period. But
one or two corruptions tell that the reviser was not the author. In Act II,
iii, 126, we have the line (dagger-marked in the Globe edition) :
        And with that painted hope braves your mightiness.
None of the proposed emendations has given satisfaction. I suggest that
painted is a misprint for *falsed*. The verb " to false " is used by both
Marlowe and Greene, and one of them is the probable writer of the passage.
Either Peele or Shakespeare, in reading the proofs, might fail to guess the
original.   As it is, we have a badly limping line.
[2] Work cited, p. 105.
[3] See *The Shakespeare Canon*, Part II, 1923, for a theory of the authorship.

quarto of HENRY V, and even those of 1602 and 1608,
which equally lack Shakespeare's name, are visibly
pirated, the text being extremely corrupt and imperfect ; and the absence of his name tends only to
support the view that it is not of his origination.[1] The
FIRST PART OF HENRY IV, again, is in the same case
with RICHARD II : the second quarto, by a second
printer, has Shakespeare's name. But in the case of
TITUS we have three careful prints, clearly authorised,
the first being evidently from the theatre copy, in
Shakespeare's lifetime, without his name ; though as
early as 1600 that name had so much selling-power
as to induce the ascription to him of published plays
that he certainly had not written. On the view that
he *wrote* TITUS, the absence of his name from the three
quartos is utterly inexplicable ; and the negative force
of such a fact countervails *pro tanto* the statement of
Meres.

§ 7

Yet further, the authority of the testimony of the
theatre, which is Meres's basis, is greatly impaired
by the fact that his list does *not* include any mention
of the HENRY VI plays, though these were certainly
in existence long before 1598,[2] and were ultimately
included as Shakespeare's in the Folio. Meres names,
" for tragedy," RICHARD II, RICHARD III, HENRY IV,
KING JOHN, TITUS, and ROMEO AND JULIET. But,
as we have noted, HENRY VI would better have suited
his case. The only reasonable inference is that in 1598,
with the CONTENTION and RICHARD DUKE OF YORK
circulating in print, the theatre management did not
venture to pretend that Shakespeare had written their
HENRY VI plays, or even 1 HENRY VI, which was not

---

[1] See *The Shakespeare Canon*, Part I.
[2] It is not certain, however, that Parts II and III at that time bore their
present titles. Meres's non-mention of any of the plays on the Wars of the
Roses, nonetheless, suggests that he did not ascribe to Shakespeare any share
in the old foundation plays, the *Contention* and the *True Tragedie of Richard
Duke of York.*

in print, but must have been known to many to be non-Shakespearean. Their *later* claim, then, was bad, and their testimony is thus suspect.

But if the HENRY VI plays were to be left out, Meres could not make out his list of six Shakespearean tragedies save by assigning to Shakespeare either TITUS or some other play he had not written ; and as TITUS was in some form the oldest play of all, and would be known to have been of various authorship and to have undergone frequent revision, any touch of correction known to have been given to it by Shakespeare would suffice to give the players the technical right to call it his, and Meres his needed sixth item. If, seeking a sixth tragedy to eke out his list, he asked the actors to name one, they could only point to TITUS, of which Shakespeare's revision gave them a stage copyright. As it happens, Meres has named all of Shakespeare's ascribed comedies that we can suppose to have been then in existence, with the exception of the TAMING OF THE SHREW, which is certainly an adaptation of an older work, and substantially non-Shakespearean at that. If, then, he were to make out his list of six tragedies, and it TITUS were not Shakespeare's, he was bound to make a wrong attribution—an easy thing in the then vague state of theory and practice as to dramatic authorship. The strongest countervailing argument is, of course, the fact that he made out his list of comedies mainly from theatrical report, LOVE'S LABOUR'S LOST being the only one in print ; and since he was informed as to that list, he is not lightly to be disregarded as to the other. But when we find the theatre ultimately assigning to Shakespeare all three of the HENRY VI plays, which Meres does not ascribe to him, his acceptance of the theatre list as to TITUS is seen to be but a citation of an authority which is certainly open to challenge. Thus, as against other external evidence (such as the absence of Shakespeare's name from the 1594, 1600, and 1611 quartos of TITUS), and strong internal evidence, his testimony falls.

Professor Henry Sidgwick put in a letter to J. A.

Symonds[1] the plausible argument for acceptance of Meres's testimony that " Shakespeare must have known of Meres's statement ; and the play is so bad that it is difficult to understand why he did not emphatically repudiate it if it was not substantially his." But how do we know that Shakespeare did *not* tell Meres, after the issue of the PALLADIS TAMIA, that the play was not of his writing ? There was no second issue of Meres's book ; and there was no journalistic means in that day by which an author could clear himself. We know from Heywood[2] that Shakespeare expressed due displeasure when he was credited with one of Heywood's poems ; but there is, for obvious reasons, no record of the protests he may be held to have made against the false ascriptions to him of other men's plays, to say nothing of the LOVER'S COMPLAINT. Professor Sidgwick's argument, then, falls. And when he goes on to express a doubt " whether the mere badness of the writing [in TITUS] ought to be made an argument at all " against Shakespeare's authorship, he immediately and dramatically answers himself. " Have you," he asks, " ever considered MACBETH ? I feel now *scarcely any doubt* that parts of it are not Shakespeare." That is to say, the relative badness of the writing in certain parts of MACBETH *is* an argument for the spuriousness of those parts. In TITUS, the " badness " is all-pervading.

§ 8

All the while, there is a conclusive rebuttal of the whole external case for Shakespeare's primary authorship of TITUS. Henslowe's diary gives " Titus and Ondronicus " as " ne " (=new or " with new matter ") on 23rd January, 1593-4 ; and as we now know with certainty from the recovered copy, TITUS ANDRONICUS was printed in 1594. It might seem safe to assume that Henslowe's play and that preserved are the

---

[1] *Henry Sidgwick : A Memoir*, by A. S. and E. M. S., 1906, p. 500,
[2] Letter appended to his *Apology for Actors*, 1612.

same ; but there is some puzzling evidence going to show that the publisher's rights in a printed play apparently called " Titus *and* Andronicus " (possibly a mistake for " Titus and Vespasian ") remained for long in different hands from those of the publishers of TITUS ANDRONICUS,[1] a book under the former title being entered on the Stationers' Register in 1602 by Millington, while the publisher of our TITUS in 1600 was Edward White, who republished it in 1611. The most likely explanation seems to be that there were two copies with some difference in structure ; and it is conceivable that scene ii of Act III, absent from all the existing quartos but given in the folio, had belonged to another edition of the piece.

On the general grounds Professor Baker, of Harvard, watchfully following up the investigation of Mr. H. De W. Fuller[2] as to the originals of the Dutch and German versions of TITUS current in the seventeenth century, agrees with Mr. Fuller that " two plays, TITTUS AND VESPACIA, the original of G. [the German version], and TITUS ANDRONICUS, the original of D. [the Dutch version], in the hands of the Chamberlain's company by perhaps late June, 1594, were made over by Shakespeare at some time after June, 1594[3] and before September 7th, 1598 [date of entry of Meres's book], into the play which stands under his name."[4]

§ 9

Here is a theorem which entirely negatives that of Shakespeare's having written his play at Stratford. The old play must be that alluded to with JERONIMO

---

[1] See Professor Baker's note on " *Tittus and Vespacia* and *Titus Andronicus* in Henslowe's Diary " in *Publications of the Modern Language Association of America*, 1901, vol. xvi, p. 75 ; and Mr. Arthur Symons as there cited.

[2] *Publications* cited, art. before Professor Baker's.

[3] This theory, of course, was framed before the discovery of the quarto of 1594, which is practically identical with the later quartos.

[4] Compare the details of the stage-history of the play given by Fleay in his *Life of Shakespeare* and *Biog. Chron.* The discovery of the 1594 edition limits the proposition to that year.

in the Introduction to Ben Jonson's BARTHOLOMEW FAIR, as being then twenty-five or thirty years old. That allusion, on the face of it, almost completely excludes the idea that Jonson held for Shakespeare's either of the plays in question, which he is treating as utterly antiquated. Such an estimate would be an enigma in face of his praise of Shakespeare in the folio. We can now be sure that he was talking of a play about as old as the SPANISH TRAGEDY, which probably appeared about 1585 or 1586.

It has not been noted by the experts that in Edward Hellowes' translation of THE FAMILIAR EPISTLES OF ANTONIE OF GUEVARA, published in 1584, the familiar story of Androcles and the lion is told of an *Andronicus*, whose lion pays him homage in a show before the Emperor Titus, who elicits from Andronicus the explanation. Here is a story of Titus *and* Andronicus which might conceivably have been dramatised, with a tame animal or a man in a lion's skin, as early as 1585. It is not a likely hypothesis ; but there is just a possibility that an old play with such a title may have preceded one of a more sophisticated kind, and that the title may have survived the animal-play, which could subsist only in a very primitive theatre.

Whatever may have been the peculiarities of " Titus *and* Andronicus," supposing a play so entitled to have existed, it is made clear by Mr. Fuller, despite his sudden conclusion as to Shakespeare's having written the existing play, that the latter is only a development on the older basis of Henslowe's TITUS AND VESPACIA[1] (played by Strange's men in 1591 and 1592), with the difference, among others, that Lucius in our preserved English play takes the place of an equally unhistorical Vespasian in the earlier, as preserved in

[1] Mr. Fuller seems at one point to doubt that the German version is made from *Titus and Vespasian*, citing Prof. Herford's surprising remark that the hypothesis is of " perilous frailty," since, as he puts it, " the mere title *Titus and Vespasian* would seem to indicate a play dealing with the two emperors." *This* inference is no ground for ascribing frailty to the inference that the old title did *not* introduce the two emperors. There *is* a Vespasian in the German play. Were there then *two* plays on Titus and Vespasian ?

the German version.   It is out of the question, then,
to suppose that Henslowe's " Titus *and* Andronicus,"
was anything more than a recast of the older play,
perhaps not identical with the later revision preserved
as Shakespeare's work, and it is far from certain that
Henslowe's title was anything more than one of his
many illiterate blunders.   But a conflict of copy-
rights seems the probable explanation of the fact that
not till 1623 is our play produced as Shakespeare's
work.   Had it really been Shakespeare's recast, it
would have been assigned to him on the quartos.

§ 10

That our TITUS is a recast of the old TITUS AND
VESPASIAN seems morally certain, despite the doubts of
so weighty an authority as Dr. W. W. Greg, who suggests[1] that the old German version, in which the son of
Titus is not Lucius but Vespasian, " is just the sort of
clumsy parody that an uneducated person might write
if he tried to reproduce a play after seeing it two or
three times."   The German TITUS is to be contemplated along with the old versions of HAMLET and
ROMEO AND JULIET dating broadly from the same
period.[2]   These are all inexplicable save as early
versions of the plays in the Shakespeare Folio, though
they are doubtless abridgments ; and indeed on no
other view could we understand their presence in the
repertory of a company of English actors travelling
abroad.   The fuller versions would be barred to them.
Professor A. W. Pollard and Mr. Dover Wilson have
pretty clearly established that curtailed quartos
usually or often stand for curtailed texts supplied to
travelling companies at home.   It is conceivable,
indeed, that the historical mystification set up by the
names Titus and Vespasian would give a ground for
changing the latter, apart from any further recasting ;

[1] See below, p. 83.
[2] All reproduced in Albert Cohn's *Shakespeare in Germany*, 1865.

but in point of fact the differences between the German play and ours all go to prove that the former was the earlier.

An outline of the plot will make this clear. In the first Act (there are eight, without scene divisions) Vespasian, son of Titus Andronicus, proposes to crown as emperor his father, with whom are the Queen of " Mohrenland " or Ethiopia[1] (Ætiopissa), her two sons and her attendant and paramour the Moor Morian, all four the captives of Titus. Vespasian declares the imperial throne vacant ; and there is present an un-named expectant or heir-apparent who resents and resists the proposal. Titus at once, as in our play, supports this heir, and places the crown on his head. The Emperor then solicits the hand of Titus' daughter Andronica, which is at once accorded him. Ætiopissa's group are then presented, and, the Emperor expressing a wish to have them, they are donated accordingly. There is no sacrifice. Exeunt all but Morian, who in a long soliloquy tells that he had already been the Queen's paramour in Mohrenland ; that she had poisoned the King on his account ; that he was the most famous warrior in the country, and known as " the Lightning and Thunder of the Moors' Country " ; and that when the Romans invaded " Ætiopia " he had hoped to destroy them. The irresistible Romans, however, had conquered, Titus in person unhorsing him, and taking him and the Queen and her two sons captive.

In Act II the emperor declares his passion for Ætiopissa, announcing that he has sent back Andronica to her father. Exeunt the pair, followed by Morian. The sons, Helicates and Saphonus, then avow to each other their passion for Andronica and proceed to fight, whereupon Morian intervenes as does Aaron in our play. They continue to attempt to fight till Morian persuades them that he will secure their joint wishes.

In Act III we have the hunting scene, very much as in our play. Andronica and her new husband, un-

---

[1] Called Ætiopia by Titus in the text.

named, are walking in the forest ; Ætiopissa, meeting them, makes an insolent remark, to which Andronica vigorously retorts, without, however, saying anything of the paramour as in our play, he not being present. The plot then goes on very much as in our play ; the Queen setting her sons to kill Andronica's husband and outrage her. There is one notable difference ; the whole sub-plot of the trapping and slaying of Quintus and Martius is lacking.[1] It is simply told that they have been imprisoned by the Emperor for insulting the Empress. But all the other main horrors are there—violation, mutilation, the trick by which Titus is led to cut off his hand, and the sending of his sons' heads. The trick on Titus is motived by the fear of his personal prowess. Andronica briefly reveals what has happened by the device of words traced with a staff in the sand, as in our play. Titus sends Vespasian (Lucius) to levy an army ; and it is as a result of the devastations then wrought that the Empress resorts to her device of bringing her sons to Titus to kill him. He butchers them as in our play, but not as there in his daughter's presence ; and it is by way of proposing a treaty of peace to the terrified emperor that he invites him and the empress to the Thyestean banquet. The episode of the Moor's black child, his killing of the midwife, and his capture and execution, occur as in our play, save that the execution is not delayed till the close. After the slayings at the banquet, Vespasian sadly accepts the throne.

Save at one point, it will be seen, the plot is rather more intelligible than that of our play. The empress having been queen of " Mohrenland," would presumably be a Moor also ; she is however described in the opening stage directions as " beautiful and white." But by this adjustment the part of the Moor in the piece is adequately motived, whereas by making Tamora Queen of the Goths it is not. Aaron in our play is " shot out of a gun." The rejection of Andronica, too, by the emperor, is a more natural episode,

[1] It appears in the Dutch version, which is clearly the later.

in the circumstances, than the abduction of Lavinia
by Bassianus, which is superfluous[1] in view of the fact
that the emperor has already been " courting Tamora
in dumb shew." The trick to make Titus maim himself, again, has in the German play a purpose, whereas
in ours it is a random atrocity ; and, finally, the planning of the banquet by Titus in the former is more
natural—if we can speak of nature in respect of such a
carnival of monstrosities—in the former play than
Tamora's planning of it in " Shakespeare." Our play
is in fact a highly elaborate complication of the other
action, already complicated enough ; and much of the
complication is otiose, the mock madness and the arrow
business of Titus no less so than the abduction of
Lavinia and Titus' slaying of his own son. It is such
a complication as tells of redaction ; and, as we shall
see at a later stage, the whole process is an application
of " academic " principles to tragedy.

§ 11

In the absence of any external evidence as to the
origination of TITUS AND VESPASIAN, we may suspect
that it is an adaptation from a lost Italian original.[2]
It is in Italy that the Renaissance drama of horrors

---

[1] Though the kinship of Bassianus furnishes a pretext for the execution of
Titus' sons.

[2] When I wrote this I was not aware that the proposition had been put by
Max J. Wolff (*Shakespeare*, i, 177) with regard to the existing form of the play.
In this connection, it may be well to guard against a mystification. In the
" Index of Plays " in Mr. E. K. Chambers's work on *The Elizabethan Stage*,
there is an italic entry :—" *Tito Andronico*, ii, 285 " ; but on the page referred to there is a reference only to the old German version of " Titus Andronicus." The entry seems to have been suggested by one in the Index to
the 1915 edition of Sir Sidney Lee's *Life of Shakespeare* : " *Tito Andronico*,
a German play," which refers to a note, p. 129, mentioning " A German play
called *Tito Andronico*." But this is an oversight. The German play is
entitled " Tragædia *von* Tito Andronico," which is simply a putting of the
Latin name in the dative after *von*, as was the German usage at that time.
It is only in this construction that the name so appears in the play. It is
always " Titus Andronicus " in the nominative and the vocative ; and in the
list of persons and the stage directions. " Tito Andronico " is not an Italian
form, but a Latin flection, just as in the passage " des Titi Andronici Tochter"
we have it in the genitive. The entry " Tito Andronico," then, should be
expunged from both indexes, and from Sir Sidney Lee's note.

takes its rise,[1] and it must surely be thence that the
contagion begins in England. The apparatus of mutilation and atrocity begins with Rucellai's ROSMUNDA
(pr. 1524) and takes new developments in the ORBECCHE
of Giraldo Cinzio (1541), whereafter it admittedly passed
all bounds, if any bounds were left.[2] The authors of
GISMOND OF SALERNE (1567 : recast as TANCRED
AND GISMUNDA by Wilmot, 1591) may or may not have
had an Italian play before them as well as Boccaccio ;[3]
but such a debauch of horrors as TITUS AND VESPASIAN
cannot well have been of native invention so early as
1585-90.[4] Greene, Kyd, and Peele all read Italian ;
and the two former were equally likely to adapt an
Italian original. Indeed the SPANISH TRAGEDY, for
which no " source " has yet been found.[5] has many
symptoms of Italian derivation, no less than of Senecan
influence. If Italian life was not very different then
from what it is now, there must have been an abundant
popular drama vieing with the more literary output
of the commemorated authors ; and a multitude of
plays must have passed away without literary record.
Tiraboschi declared as to those tragedies actually
published in the sixteenth century that he could make
" un lungo e nojoso catalogo " of works which are
nearly all beneath contempt.[6]

As regard the Italian influence on Tudor drama, it
has latterly been recognized that in comedy it is manifold ;[7] but in tragedy it has been little considered,
the Senecan influence having been often assumed to be
the sole impulse in the earlier stages. As Professor

[1] Étienne, *Hist. de la litt. ital.* pp. 255, 436-7; Hauvette, *Littérature italienne*, pp. 251-2.
[2] See the plot of the *Orbecche* outlined by Prof. Cunliffe, introd. to *Early English Classical Tragedies*, 1912, p. xxxiv. Cf. p. xxvi.
[3] Cunliffe, as cited, p. lxxxvii.
[4] It need hardly be observed here that the old ballad on *Titus* given in Percy's *Reliques* is founded on the play, not *vice versa* ; though the ballad of *The Lady and the Blackamoor* in the Roxburghe Ballads, which seems traceable to Bandello (Fuller, art. cited), may have given hints for Aaron.
[5] Schick, introd. to his ed. in " Temple " series, p. xxv.
[6] *Storia della poesia italiana* (ext. from the *Letteratura italiana*), cap. vi, pt. ii, § 55.
[7] Prof. R. W. Bond, *Early Plays from the Italian*, 1911, introd. essay. Cp. Cunliffe, as cited, p. xl.

Cunliffe observes,[1] the Elizabethan drama " affords to the young student a bewildering spectacle, and to the trained scholar a problem for endless study.   The systems of classification we adopt are mere pigeon-holes. . . . ." As the trained scholar, scarce at all times, is apt to have his hands too full of academic duties to permit of his undertaking expeditionary re-searches, it might be worth the while of any inquisi-tive student to make a search in Italian sixteenth century drama for the probable suorces of the SPANISH TRAGEDY and the first TITUS. It is even possible that the motives of human sacrifice and the astrological madness of Titus, added to the later play, had an Italian derivation. Symonds recognizes clearly that the early English tragedians " went to school with Seneca beneath the ferule of Italian ushers,"[2] but makes no detailed research ; and Burckhardt hardly glances at tragedy.

§ 12

But the question of *provenance* is here subsidiary, save in so far as there is involved the possibility that Greene or Kyd or Peele, or all three, may be the originators of the piece. Kyd is indeed by far the likeliest of the three to have framed the original TITUS AND VESPASIAN. Neither Greene nor Peele is much of a tragic plot-maker ; Kyd is so from the first.   But we must deal with the play as we find it in English ; and Peele, we shall find, is the outstanding author of the first Act as it now exists ; while Greene, Kyd, and Marlowe are in different degrees indicated later. If the mock-madness of Titus was not in the English original, it is to Kyd that we should naturally look à priori for its introduction in 1593. A recast about that date must have occurred, the metrical phenomena pointing clearly to a date after 1590 ; and all the

[1] As cited, p. lxvi.
[2] *Shakespeare's Predecessors in the English Drama*, ed. 1900, p. 175. Cp. pp. 173-4.

documentary facts here come into line.   On our hypothesis that the 1594 TITUS was revised for the press
by Shakespeare as was LOCRINE, double publishing
rights might be at most a matter of mere distinction
between a literary revision and the dramatic revision
which made TITUS AND ANDRONICUS "new" for
Henslowe in 1594. As Professor Baker remarks,
"Anyone who has carefully studied the DIARY [of
Henslowe] knows that the mysterious ' ne ' most often
means nothing more than an old play revised to make
it pass as a novelty."[1]   On the Professor's own showing, then, Shakespeare had at most merely revised a
recast.

And that this is the only form in which the maintainers of Shakespeare's authorship can claim to hold
their belief is made clear, finally, by Shakespeare's own
testimony. Mr. Baildon, who so lightly imputed
suppressio veri to a laborious scholar, virtually ignored
Shakespeare's prefatory description of his VENUS AND
ADONIS, published in 1593, as "the first heir of my
invention." This phrase has been ingeniously in-
terpreted to mean "first *acknowledged* offspring," *heir*
being taken to discriminate between acknowledged
and unacknowledged. But even if the context did
not, as it does, disown such an interpretation, we should
still be left noting that Shakespeare would not claim
any earlier work as completely his. With this declaration on record, and with the research of Mr.
Fuller and Professor Baker lying before him, Mr.
Baildon spoke of TITUS as written by Shakespeare
"between 1589 and 1593." And Mr. Collins, who
protested so loudly his respect for external evidence,
simply declined to let Shakespeare's own assertion
stand for anything.[2]

[1] Art. cited, p. 69.
[2] I am aware that at this point the traditionist school can claim the support not only of many conservative critics of standing, German and English,
but of so open-minded an inquirer as Fleay, who in his *Manual* put the writing
of *Venus and Adonis* as early as 1588.   I learned from Fleay in 1905, however, that he had latterly abandoned that chronology, which was framed by
him in accommodation to that prevailing before his time. He finally placed
the commencement of Shakespeare's *independent* dramatic authorship not

§ 13

The fashion in which that explicit and authoritative testimony has been overridden by a whole series of critics, German and English, who profess to stand or fall by " external " evidence, is instructive. Mr. Collins declares it to be " certain, as we know from Greene and Chettle, that he [Shakespeare] was writing plays before 1593." This is quite unwarranted. Neither Greene nor Chettle ever named Shakespeare as an *author* of plays. We are fully entitled to infer from the " Shake-scene " passage in Greene's GROATS-WORTH OF WIT that Shakespeare had had a hand *in* plays before 1593 ; but certainly not that he had written a whole one. On the latter head his own declaration is surely as weighty as the testimony of Meres. Seeking to override that declaration, Mr. Collins insists that " either VENUS AND ADONIS was written long before it was printed " (adding that he thinks it " highly probable that it was composed at Stratford before he came to London, as early perhaps as 1585 ") " or that for some reason he did not regard his early dramas as heirs of his invention." When we find Mr. Collins forgetfully avowing that VENUS AND ADONIS is plainly modelled on Lodge's SCILLA'S META-MORPHOSIS,[1] we may hold ourselves dispensed from discussing the former alternative. Lodge's poem was published only in 1589. Mr. Collins had not even taken the trouble to reconcile his assertions—and this in an essay in which he imputes to his gainsayers perversity, paradox, sophistry, and illegitimate criticism.

earlier than 1593, though he held that Shakespeare added the Talbot scenes to 1 *Henry VI* in 1592—a proposition upon which I remain unable to agree with him, though it is supported by Mr. E. K. Chambers with what may be termed " breathless " confidence. On the merits, see *The Shakespeare Canon*, Part II. Gervinus rejected the Talbot scenes as non-Shakespeare, though he held them to be by another hand than that which wrote the bulk of the play.

[1] Here Mr. Collins follows Sir Sidney Lee (*Life of Shakespeare*, 1st ed. p. 75), who follows Dr. Gosse (introd. to Lodge's works).

§ 14

Irrespective of the fatal admission as to the poem of Lodge, however, the proposition that VENUS AND ADONIS was written at Stratford-on-Avon[1] is a significant sample of the evidential methods of the traditional school. The structure of the passage should be noted. " I do not wish to indulge in conjecture," writes Professor Collins, " *but* it seems to me highly probable that it [the poem] was composed at Stratford before he came up to London, as early perhaps as 1585, *or* that *for some reason* he did not regard his early dramas as heirs of his invention. What is *certain* is, as we know from Greene and Chettle, that he was *writing plays* before 1593." It is thus put as equally highly probable that " for some reason " Shakespeare thought his poems were his inventions, while his original plays were not ; and that he had produced at Stratford an elaborate poem, carefully calculated for popularity, which he kept in manuscript through eight years of struggle for existence. Both propositions are improbable to the last degree. That Shakespeare wrote VENUS AND ADONIS before he came to London is a hypothesis which would never have been broached but for the need of saving the presupposition that he wrote plays as early as 1589. What should have induced him to withhold from the press for all those years so readily saleable a poem, when he was actually in need of whatever money he could come by ? The surmise will not bear investigation. When the " certain " turns out to be mere misconstruction, the " highly probable," naturally, is sheer fantasy on its merits, to say nothing of its being disallowed in advance by the propounder. And yet this illicit dating, by a critic professedly unwilling to indulge in conjecture, is concurred in by many of the German critics who stickle for the most literal acceptance of one part, and one

---

[1] This view seems to have been started by Coleridge. Collier's report, in Ashe's ed. of *Lectures and Notes on Shakespeare*, 1883, p. 9.

only, of the "external" evidence in regard to TITUS
ANDRONICUS.

§ 15

As for the alternative proposition, in which Mr.
Collins is supported by eminent critics (for instance,
Dr. Furnivall) who do not agree with him about TITUS,
it must here suffice to say that no one who professes to
stand by testimony has the right to put it.   Unless we
find *proof* that the poem was written some years before
publication, the plain force of Shakespeare's declaration is that before 1593, if he meddled in drama at all,
he was merely a collaborator with other men, or a
reviser or adapter of other men's plays.   By "invention" he cannot mean merely that he had not
invented his plots ; for in that sense he did not invent
the story of VENUS AND ADONIS : he must have meant
that he did not regard as originally or effectively *his*
any play in which he had thus far collaborated.   Mr.
Collins, however, like Elze[1] and other Germans, seemed
to hold that Shakespeare wrote or began TITUS at
Stratford ;[2] while Mr. Boas, after reasonably deciding
that Shakespeare in London "started with theatrical
hack-work, touching-up old plays and collaborating
with writers of established repute in stagecraft,"[3] and
that his first independent work was in comedy, proceeds to accept the view that TITUS was "written
by Shakespeare *immediately* after leaving Stratford."[4]
Thus, as might have been expected, we find flat

---

[1] *William Shakespeare*, Eng. trans., pp. 66, 96, 314, 348-9.
[2] "During or about the time he was engaged on *Venus and Adonis* and
The Rape of Lucrece" are Mr. Collins's words. (*Studies*, pp. 108-9.)
[3] *Shakespeare and his Predecessors*, 1896 ; p. 134.
[4] Compare pp. 137, 139. In similar fashion Prof. Quincy Adams (*Life of
Shakespeare*, 1923, p. 133) suggests that the *Comedy of Errors* "may well
have been the product of his days as a ' schoolmaster in the country.' " This
would make Shakespeare a writer of typically Marlowese blank verse before
Marlowe wrote *Tamburlaine*. See *The Shakespeare Canon*, Part II, for a
theory of Marlowe's authorship, upon a previous basis. Prof. Adams assigns
to Shakespeare the archaic doggerel which most editors are fain to deny to be
possibly his. *Titus*, however, Mr. Adams pronounces to be " mainly, if not
entirely, by George Peele."

self-contradiction in the positions of the critics who attempt to fix on Shakespeare the authorship of Titus in disregard of his own testimony.

§ 16

The case for the affirmative now falls back on its last line—the bare fact of the inclusion of Titus in the first folio. When, however, that position is analysed, it is found to give way as does the argument from Meres. Meres, it will be remembered, does *not* credit Shakespeare with the Henry VI plays, though under either that or older titles they had been much played by his company long before 1598 ; the folio includes them as Shakespeare's, even as it ascribes solely to him the Henry VIII, of which so much is visibly Fletcher's. The folio further omits Pericles, which had been printed with Shakespeare's name in 1609, and which, from internal evidence, we gather to be partly his, mainly not. Yet further, we know that the first copies of the folio even omitted the Troilus and Cressida, which is also composite, but in large part Shakespeare's recast of other men's work. The argument from the folio, then, conflicting with the argument from Meres, proves too much. We are driven to conclude that the action of the editors was in part determined by considerations of theatrical *property* in the plays they printed, and to infer that, when any play had become theirs and been merely revised by Shakespeare, they could best assert their right by printing it as his. That there was a feud between mere players and scholar-writers is[1] made clear by Greene's death-bed pamphlet and by the later dialogue in The Return from Parnassus (Part II), where a player boasts how " our fellow Shakespeare " gave a " purge " to Jonson of the writers' party. In

[1] Compare the verses of Thomas Brabine prefixed to Greene's *Menaphon*, in which the players are taunted with inability to produce such an effect as Greene there makes.

such a state of things the players were in the habit of claiming whatever they could as against the authors ; and to father on Shakespeare every piece in their repertory in which they had proprietary rights was for Heminge and Condell a way of maintaining their own interest.

This is the answer to Professor Parrott's claim that Heminge and Condell, by omitting PERICLES, SIR THOMAS MORE, and THE TWO NOBLE KINSMEN, in all of which Shakespeare shared, showed great scrupulosity about what they ascribed to him, and that we ought therefore to credit him with a *revision* of TITUS when we find it in the Folio.   The plea is unnecessary for the purpose of the revision theory, and it misses altogether the vital question of copyright.   There is nothing to show that the MORE play was ever played with Shakespeare's scene ;   it seems to have been officially " stayed " ;   and if the company had not proprietary rights in PERICLES and the KINSMEN they *could not* insert them in the Folio.   In short, Professor Parrott's proposition, reasonable in itself, that " if any men alive in 1623 knew what plays *Shakespeare had written*, they [Heminge and Condell] were the men,"[1] is not brought into argumentative relation with the thesis, for the Professor maintains that Shakespeare did not " write " TITUS.

Professor Collins's argument that, seeing TITUS was notoriously popular, " neither Meres nor Heminge and Condell would have been *likely* to assign it to Shakespeare " without solid ground, is thus a clear *non sequitur*.   If the play were the work of several hands, on an old basis, with Shakespeare for final corrector, its popularity was rather a reason why it should be mentioned by Meres, who was no very vigilant critic ; and further a reason why Heminge and Condell, whose company owned the stage rights, should put it in the folio, where most readers would expect to find it, after Meres's mention.   Hitherto it had always been published without Shakespeare's name, and it may have

[1] Essay cited, p. 21.

been that they had by special bargain acquired the publishing right.

The traditionist argument, then, has thus far broken down. The external evidence not only does not prove Shakespeare's authorship of TITUS : it presents an irreducible balance of matter irreconcilable with that view ; and to reach a conclusion we must come to the internal evidence.

POSTCRIPT TO CHAPTER II

THE STAGE HISTORY OF THE PLAY

Dr. W. W. Greg, our highest living authority on the history of the later Elizabethan stage and drama, has been kind enough to give me permission to use here the comprehensive note on TITUS ANDRONICUS in his invaluable edition of Henslowe's Diary. I cannot do better than reprint it verbatim, with a clause added by him in brackets.

37. TITUS ANDRONICUS.

    [8v–9. ' tit(t)us & ondronic(o)us ' ' andronicous.' Performed by Sussex' men, as a new play, 23 (24) Jan. 1593/4, and again 28 (29) Jan. and 6 Feb. Performed by the Admiral's and Chamberlain's men, 5 (7) and 12 (14) June 1594.]

Entered S. R. 6 Feb. 1594, and printed the same year as acted by Derby's (i. e. late Strange's), Pembroke's and Sussex' men. This edition, recently recovered, contains the same text as the previously known edition of 1600, on the title page of which the name of the Chamberlain's men is added to the other three. The history of the other plays in the Admiral's-Chamberlain s list suggests that Pembroke's men were the original owners. Two main problems are connected with this piece ; its relation to the Dutch and German versions, and its alleged Shakespearian authorship. The former of these has been discussed in an able and important article by H. De W. Fuller (Publications of the Modern Language Association of America, 1901, ix. p. 1). The German version (G) is preserved in the collection of 1620. The extant Dutch version by Vos (D²) was not printed till 1642, but was almost certainly preceded by an earlier one in the same language (D¹). There is also extant a programme (P) of a German version performed at Linz in 1699. This agrees in the main with D² and must represent either the original or a translation of D¹. Both G and D² differ considerably from the English play (E). Now with regard to G it must be remembered that the stage versions current among the English actors in Germany were undoubtedly much altered from their originals, and moreover G is just the sort of clumsy parody that an uneducated person might write if he tried to reproduce a play after seeing it two or three times. In the case of D², the close agreement with P shows that it must have reproduced D¹ very accurately in the matter of action but leaves room for almost any amount of alteration in the language. D¹, moreover, may have differed from the original as widely as G. I cannot therefore agree with Fuller when he finds a difficulty in supposing E to be the original of either G or D¹ taken independently. There are, however, obstacles in the way of supposing E to be the original of both G and D¹. In the first place there are a certain number of points found both in G and D² but not in E. Secondly there is the striking fact that while there is no incident of any importance in E which cannot be traced in either G or D², there are a number of important points common to E and either G only or D² only. These considerations lead Fuller to suppose that G and D¹ go back to different English versions, and that these versions formed the joint originals of E. The suggestion is undoubtedly ingenious, but the facts appear to me susceptible of a different explanation. The points in which G and D² agree against E may be due to alterations made by the English actors in their stage version. The fact that practically the whole of the action of E is found in either G or D² may be accounted for by supposing that the compiler of D¹, who probably based his version on a more complete performance than that which underlay G, was also familiar with G as printed in 1620 and deliberately omitted certain portions there preserved in order to avoid too close a similarity, while carefully retaining whatever had not been used in the earlier version. Thus I cannot regard the existence of one or more English versions of the play previous to the extant text as in any way established, though it is by no means inherently improbable (see also *Titus and Vespasian*, 21). I should add that I can see no reason to suppose that any distinction was intended between " titus & ondronicus ' and ' andronicus ' in the Diary, or between ' Tytus Andronicus ' and ' Titus and Andronicus ' in S.R.

The second problem of the play, that of authorship, has been frequently treated. The most thorough discussion is to be found in J. M. Robertson's book on the subject (1905), with which I am in general agreement. I need only say here that I fail to discover any clear internal evidence of Shakespeare having touched the play at all, though there are a few lines whose Shakespearian authorship I do not think impossible. Thus I cannot go so far as J. W. Craig, who told me, in the last talk I had with him before his death, that he thought that certain passages had actually come from Shakespeare's pen [a view also held by no less experienced a critic than W. Aldis Wright.][1] But I should like briefly to sketch out what I believe may have happened and leave others

---

[1] Addition by Mr. Greg on proof copy sent to me.

to take my theory for what it is worth. The outline of events would be as follows. In the Autumn of 1593 when the plague was raging in London, we know that Pembroke's men were in low water. Henslowe wrote to Alleyn on 28 Sept. to the effect that, being unable to meet the expenses of travel, they had returned to town and had been driven to pawn their wardrobe (MS, I. 14). They also parted with several of their plays which were printed the following year. Alleyn's answer is not preserved, but he most likely commissioned Henslowe to buy up such pieces as he thought worth while on behalf of Strange's men with whom he was then travelling. Some old Pembroke's plays, including *Titus*, are certainly found later in the hands of the Chamberlain's men. We might suppose that, pending Alleyn's return, Henslowe lent the piece to Sussex' men, but I do not think this was so for two reasons. One is that Henslowe did not as a rule mark as new plays which he lent to companies ; the other is that the mention of Derby's men proves that the piece must have been performed by the company with whom Alleyn was travelling between Sept. 1593 and Apr. 1594, and therefore almost certainly in the provinces.

It is probable then that Henslowe sent down the plays at once to their new purchasers. We must, therefore, suppose two copies, one in the possession first of Pembroke's and later of the Chamberlain's men, that performed by the latter company in June, and another which came into the possession of Sussex' men and was acted by them for the first time in Jan. ; and we may further suppose that the two versions differed even to the inclusion of wholly different scenes. Sussex' men performed the play for the last time on 6 Feb., and the same day the play, presumably handed over by them to the press, was entered in S.R. The company soon afterwards broke, and some of the members may not improbably have found their way onto the continent. Here we may suppose that they vamped up the stage version underlying the German and Dutch texts. Meanwhile the Chamberlain's men, following their practice in the case of the other Pembroke's plays, *Hamlet* and the *Taming of a Shrew*, caused *Titus* to be worked over by a young member of their company named William Shakespeare. Thus revised the piece achieved sufficient success to call for notice by Francis Meres in 1598, and thenceforth passed as one of the ' works ' of the favourite playwright-actor. This MS. perished in the fire at the Globe in 1613. Wishing to replace their prompt copy the King's men procured a copy of the printed edition (1611), a device to which they certainly resorted in other cases too. In this they made certain alterations in the stage directions, and in doing so noticed the absence of one scene at least (III, ii) which they were in the habit of acting and which had proved popular. This the actors were able to reconstruct from memory, and a manuscript insertion of some 85 lines was made in the quarto. Ten years later this doctored prompt copy was sent to press for the text of the collected folio.

To this careful and skilful theorem, from which I diverge to the extent of holding TITUS AND VESPASIAN to be clearly the basis of TITUS ANDRONICUS, I would only add the suggestion that it does not seem necessary to assume a continuous use of the old prompt-copy down to 1613. The printed texts being good, copies of them were likely to be used all along ; and the added scene may have been supplied at any time.[1] It cannot, I think, be Shakespeare's work. In method and diction, as we shall see, it rather strongly suggests Kyd, but also Peele, and may possibly have been Peele's last addition to the play. If, as I suppose, that was printed in 1594 for his pecuniary benefit, a commission to him to add a scene would be a likely way of helping him further in his distress.

[1] See above as to the possibility of its being in another early issue of the play.

CHAPTER III

SHAKESPEARE'S EARLIER WORK

Before we take up the argument from internal evidence, it is expedient to ascertain so far as may be the biographical facts as to Shakespeare's beginnings in play-writing. We have seen that he himself ostensibly disclaims any original or independent work before 1593. Not only, however, those who ascribe to him TITUS, but many critics who do not, insist upon crediting him with a whole series of original plays antedating VENUS AND ADONIS. The principles on which Dr. Furnivall,[1] summing up and pronouncing on the labours of his predecessors, dates no fewer than five Shakespearean plays before 1593, are somewhat startling to an awakened critical sense. LOVE'S LABOUR'S LOST is dated 1588-9 because (1) Dr. Furnivall has "no hesitation" in pronouncing it the earliest play in view of its abundance of rhyme, stanza forms, and word-play, and lack of plot and pathos ; and because (2) the COMEDY OF ERRORS is held to lie between 1589 and 1591 in respect of its allusion to France as "arm'd and reverted, making war against her heir." Yet that allusion, which in any case might be penned by a predecessor whom Shakespeare adapted, would hold equally good till 1594. Then, though in the DREAM there is an allusion to abnormal rains and floods, which would fit both the years 1594 and 1595, Dr. Furnivall "cannot let the possible allusion break through the other links of the play" (that is, his arbitrarily-selected "links of *likeness* and *difference*" in themes and character-types), and places it in 1590-1. Now, this is probably not far wrong as

[1] Introduction to the "Leopold" Shakespeare.

to the actual date of writing of the bulk of the COMEDY ;
but that decision will be found to involve a further
one, assigning its authorship to another hand.[1]   THE
TWO GENTLEMEN, in turn, is placed immediately after
the ERRORS, because it is æsthetically a " link-play "
to the " passion-group," which is made to begin with
ROMEO AND JULIET ; and *that* is dated 1591-3, on the
ground of the nurse's lines :—

> Come Lammas-eve at night shall she be fourteen . . .
> 'Tis since the earthquake now eleven years
> And she was wean'd . . . upon that day.

That is to say, we are to take it for granted that Shakespeare makes the life of Juliet in the play date from
the great earthquake of 1580, adjusting the nurse's
speech to the occasion, though the story of Romeo
and Juliet was notoriously an old one, and the verse
here suggests a pre-Shakespearean hand.   Dyce, who
called the inference of the date of the DREAM from the
floods of 1594 " ridiculous," might almost have said
as much here.   Shakespeare or another might in the
year 1591 have heard an English nurse use just such a
phrase, and might years afterwards reproduce it just
as he heard it.   Yet this is the sole specific ground—as
apart from the evidence of style, which certainly puts
it early among the tragedies—for dating ROMEO before
the year of its first publication, 1597.   For the rest,
Dr. Furnivall " inclines " to " put it before VENUS AND
ADONIS rather than after it," though, as regards
Shakespeare's recast of it, most people will hesitate
to do any such thing.

In calling attention to the insecurity of such chronology, I do not deny that there are æsthetic grounds
for Dr. Furnivall's general *order* ; nor do I maintain
that all the dates are wrong, though I think they very
well may be.   There is another way of reconciling
such dates with the avowal in the dedication to VENUS
AND ADONIS, which, being actually signed with Shakespeare's name, is an irreducible datum, whence all

[1] See *The Shakespeare Canon*, Part II.

chronology of his plays should start. Whether or not Dr. Furnivall and the rest are right in their previous dates, they are plainly wrong in not reckoning with that avowal. One and all, they are unduly reluctant to draw the proper conclusion from the obvious probability, put by Fleay and admitted by Professor Boas, that Shakespeare's playwriting in his earlier years was by way of collaboration in or adaptation of other men's work. And on no other assumption can their dates stand, down to 1593. If the plays in question are earlier than that year, they are not of Shakespeare's " invention."

The oddly worded proposition of Professor Collins, that it is " highly probable " that " for some reason " Shakespeare did not regard his plays as his inventions, need only be reduced to intelligible form in order to carry the day, to the discomfiture of his main thesis. Shakespeare for the best of reasons would not regard as heirs of his invention plays in which he merely modified other men's drafts or shared with others the task of revision or composition. Of such a nature, by general consent (Professor Collins dissenting), were the HENRY VI group. Why then should we refuse to believe that he had either collaborators or draftsmen for THE TWO GENTLEMEN, LOVE'S LABOUR'S LOST, the COMEDY OF ERRORS, and RICHARD II, even as he was refashioning other men's work in ROMEO AND JULIET and rewriting previous plays in KING JOHN and some later plays? Nothing that is said by Greene and Chettle is incompatible with this rational solution, which alone accords to Shakespeare's own precise avowal its natural interpretation. On the face of the case, it does not appear that Shakespeare had done more than take a share in the chronicle plays as late as 1592, the date of Greene's allusion to him in the preface to A GROATSWORTH OF WIT.[1]

[1] The allusion to writers born to the trade of *Noverint* in Nashe's epistle prefatory to Greene's *Menaphon* (1589) is most satisfactorily explained as a reference to Kyd. See Fleay, *Life of Shakespeare*, p. 100, followed in Schick's ed. of *The Spanish Tragedy*, in " Temple Dramatists " series, pref. pp. ix-xvi, and Professor Boas's pref. to his ed. of Kyd's *Works*, 1901.

This view, it should be explained, is not argued for in the hope of facilitating the true ascription of TITUS. On the contrary, it complicates the problem. If we could be sure of a whole play of Shakespeare's before 1594, we could much more easily decide as to what is and what is not in his early manner of blank-verse. When we grant, for instance, that there may be large survivals of other men's work in RICHARD II (as to some of us there appear to be),[1] we are further embarrassed as to our primary tests. And there remains the possibility that he lent a hand in some of the works planned and finished by other men. Several good critics, including Fleay and Professor Ward, have held that he had a share in EDWARD III—a problem to be discussed later.

On the other hand, the difficulty arising from the habit of collaboration affects the works assigned to the men who shared in some of those ascribed to Shakespeare. This has not been sufficiently recognised by the editors of Marlowe, Greene, Kyd, and Peele, who tend to credit those writers respectively with the whole of the plays reasonably assigned to them, merely noting the more obvious tamperings with those of Marlowe.[2] The resort to collaboration was finally unavoidable in the economic conditions of the Elizabethan theatre, inasmuch as plays were constantly being commissioned from playwrights whose initiative had been exhausted, and who had to produce a drama by a given date. By pooling their ideas, they facilitated their work. And to primary collaboration there has to be added the factor of revision ; for there are many proofs that plays were repeatedly eked out or recast by way of freshening their appeal to the public, or giving new opportunities to actors. Such a case of revision is seen in THE MASSACRE AT PARIS, ascribed to Marlowe. One of his latest and most

---

[1] See this problem developed in *The Shakespeare Canon*, Part II.

[2] Fleay, as usual, helped greatly in clearing up the case, pointing out how much of *Faustus* is not Marlowe's work. (Ch. on " Metrical Tests " in Ingleby's *Shakespeare : the Man and the Book*, Pt. ii, p. 70, and note in Prof. Ward's ed. of *Faustus*.)

competent editors[1] admits that only one part of the
play, the soliloquy of Guise, is up to Marlowe's higher
level ; but he has not suggested the most probable
solution—that that soliloquy is a surviving fragment
of Marlowe's TRAGEDY OF GUISE, preserved in a recast of the play by another hand or hands, in which
the main theme is no longer the fortunes of Guise, but
the general episode of the Massacre. And the variations of style in the later Acts of EDWARD II do not
appear to have suggested to Marlowe's editors that
there also there is cause to infer at points an alien
hand or hands, whether collaborating or revising.

All these considerations obviously increase the
difficulty of dealing with, say, the frequently advanced
theory that Marlowe is " the " author of TITUS. The
difficulty, however, must be faced. And whatever
opinions may be come to by students as to the authorship of any particular play, it may be claimed with
confidence that some of those who ascribe TITUS to
Shakespeare have by their own admissions counten-
anced the conclusion that his earliest works were
collaborations, and that accordingly TITUS, which they
represent as very early and yet homogeneous, cannot
as such be his. The most plausible part of Professor
Collins's essay, critically speaking, is that in which
he courageously affirms that Shakespeare's early work
is markedly imitative—" servile imitation " is his
repeated phrase,[2] which may bring upon himself, from
some, the charge of iconoclasm. The phrase,
" followed at first, with timid servility, the fashion,"
is indeed badly overcharged : youth is spontaneously
imitative, but, if it has genius, without timidity or
servility. But the very instinct of imitation would
naturally lead the beginner to take the ordinary
course of collaboration ; and for this Mr. Collins makes
no allowance.

---

[1] A. H. Bullen, Introd. to his ed. of Marlowe, 1885, i, p. xlvii.
[2] *Studies in Shakespeare*, pp. 104, 120.

CHAPTER IV

THE ALLEGED INTERNAL EVIDENCE

§ 1. ALLEGED SHAKESPEAREAN PARALLELS

Over the internal evidence for his claim, Professor Collins is as confident as over the external, declaring that a number of touches in the play " point *indisputably* to Shakespeare "—a pleasing way of quashing the contrary convictions of the great majority of English critics during a hundred and fifty years. By way of proof, he first draws comparisons between phrases in TITUS and phrases in the undisputed plays or poems of Shakespeare, going on, however, to cite phrases from the other disputed plays, and so to prove the doubtful by the doubtful.

(1) Like others, he sets out with the parallel passage about the mercifulness of the Gods (T.A., I, 116-7 ; M. OF V., IV, i, 195).[1] This was a current Ciceronian commonplace, and is to be found also in the play of EDWARD III (V, i, 41), which Mr. Collins has not proposed to ascribe to Shakespeare, and which is to be dated before 1593. Moreover, the wording in EDWARD III : " approach the nearest unto God," is verbally close to " drew near the nature of the Gods " in TITUS.

(2) Next, Mr. Collins claims to find an evidential parallel between this passage in TITUS (I, 144) :

The sacrificing *fire*
Whose smoke, like incense, doth *perfume* the *sky*

---

[1] This is presumably Professor Ward's ground for assigning the speech to Shakespeare (*Hist. Dram. Lit.*, ed. 1899, ii, 55). He offers, however, no definite grounds for thinking that it bears " the recognisable impress of Shakespeare's hand."

and this in CYMBELINE (V. v) :—

> Laud we the Gods ;
> And let our crooked smokes climb to their nostrils.[1]

Had he thought of comparing, as in such an inquiry is so obviously necessary, the play before him with the work of Shakespeare's early contemporaries, he might have found (*a*) in Peele's ARRAIGNMENT OF PARIS (Prologue) this much closer and more significant parallel :

> Flaming *fire*
> *Whose* thick and foggy *smoke*, piercing the *sky ;*

also, in the same author's BATTLE OF ALCAZAR (V, i, 183), the phrase " sacrifi*cing* fire,"[2] found nowhere in Shakespeare apart from TITUS ; again (*b*) in the same play (II, i, 32-3), the passage :

> Give and sacrifice her son
> Not with sweet *smoke* of *fire* and sweet *perfume,*

where all the ideas of the phrase in TITUS are further echoed, in specific context with the idea (here metaphorical) of the sacrifice of a son in his mother's presence ; and yet again (*c*) in the Prologue to the ARRAIGNMENT, always in reference to human sacrifice, the line :

> T'appease the anger of the angry heavens,

matching the line in TITUS (I, 126) :

> T'appease their groaning shadows that are gone.

As against such significant identities of phrase there is no force whatever in the previous loose comparison, or in that of the passage in TITUS (I, 150) beginning " Repose you here in rest " (quoted by Mr. Collins without the " in rest ") with the dirge in CYMBELINE and Macbeth's lines on Duncan.

---

[1] There are several reasons for supposing *Cymbeline* to be a late recast of an old play. Its titular theme marks it as belonging to the period of *Locrine* and *King Leir and his Three Daughters* ; and I have long suspected traces of Peele in it. But for the purpose of the present argument these surmises are waived, as is also the evidence for supposing Chapman or another to have had a hand in the recast.

[2] A phrase of Marlowe's also

(3) Next Professor Collins cites, as so many have done before, the lines (TITUS, II, i) :—

> She is a woman, therefore to be woo'd ;
> She is a woman, therefore to be won ;

of which variants occur in I HENRY VI (v, iii) and RICHARD III (I, iii), plays both held by other critics, on general grounds, to be wholly or partly non-Shakespearean. Had Mr. Collins paid due attention to previous literature on the authorship of TITUS, he would have known that this tag, which he in effect represents Shakespeare as having run to death, is shown by Dr. Grosart[1] to be primarily the property of Greene[2] who used it twice in early prose works, to wit in the PLANETOMACHIA (1585) and the PERIMEDES (1588), besides echoing it in many other passages[3]. That duplication, and the further identities of vocabulary between TITUS and the works of Greene, give Dr. Grosart a better ground for ascribing the play "substantially" to Greene than Mr. Collins can give for ascribing it to Shakespeare. They further add to the reasons for ascribing to Greene a share in the HENRY VI group, in which Mr. Collins notes (4) the double use of the term "blood-drinking," found also in TITUS. It does not appear to occur to him that the absence of the word from the undisputed plays of Shakespeare tells rather against than for his thesis. (5) Similarly, he does not realise that the allusion to

[1] Article, "Was Robert Greene substantially the author of ' Titus Andronicus ' ? " in *Englische Studien*, Bd. xxii, 1896. The point is noted by Dr. Ward in the 1899 edition of his *History*.

[2] Who, however, probably derived it from Lilly : " Ay, but she is wise ; yea, but she is a woman " (*Alexander and Campaspe*, ii, 2). Greene's phrase "caught on." Fairfax in his translation (1600) of Tasso's *Gerusalemme* (ii, 15) has the line

> For nature framed all women to be won.

This strains the original :

> Tu [Amor] per mille custodie entro al più casti
> Virginei alberghi il guardo altrui portasti.

[3] Readers who possess only Dyce's 1-vol. edition of Greene and Peele will find one such echo in the extract there given, p. 41, from *Pandosto*, and another, p. 97, col. 2, in *Orlando Furioso*. Compare further Greene's *Philomela* (Works, ed. Grosart, xi, 128) ; *Orphorion* (xii, 78) ; and *Never too Late* (viii, 88). The tag is constant in Greene.

gnats flying at the sun, doubled in TITUS and 3 HENRY
VI, and the allusion to the swiftness of swallows,
occurring twice in TITUS and once in RICHARD III,
but nowhere else in Shakespeare, should have given
him ground for suspicion rather than for confidence.
As we shall see, the latter item points pretty clearly
to Peele.

(6) Again, citing from TITUS (II, 2) the phrase, " The
morn is bright and grey," he affirms that " this is
Shakespeare's *favourite and constantly-repeated epithet*
for the morning and the morning sky, occurring in
Sonnet 132, in ROMEO AND JULIET, II, iii, and in
HENRY IV, I, iii " (should be 2 HENRY IV, ii, 3).   Thus
he offers only three citations—one of them wrong—to
prove a " constant repetition," though Shakespeare
refers to the morning more than a hundred and fifty
times in his other plays.   It is hardly necessary to
add that the epithet " grey " for the morning is common to a dozen previous and contemporary poets of
the Tudor period, *e.g.* :

" Star of the morrow gray."
(Skelton, *To Mistress Isabel Pennell*.)
" The morrow gray."   (Hawes, *The Pastime of Pleasure*,
Percy Soc. rep., of ed. 1555, cap. i, p.7.)
" The fayre morrowe gray."   (*Id*. cap. xxxvi, p. 189.)
" The morow gray."   (*Id*. cap. xxxix, p. 200.)
" The morrow gray."   (Sackville, Induction to *The Mirrour
for Magistrates*, st. 40.)
" As fair Aurora in her morning gray."
(Greene, Dyce's, one-vol. ed., p. 287.)
" How smug this gray-eyed morning seems to be."
(First line of *Englishman for my Money*, c. 1589.)

Had Mr. Collins found in TITUS the phrase " the
grey-eyed morn," and the line,

Shall make the morning haste her grey uprise,

he would doubtless have felt sure they were Shakespeare's.   They occur in DIDO, by Marlowe and Nashe,[1]

---

[1] Fleay, in his paper on *Queen Elizabeth, Croydon, and the Drama*, 1898, pp.
9-10, argues that the naming of Nashe on the title-page is a mystification.

and "the grey-eyed morning" appears again in SIR JOHN OLDCASTLE (IV, i), and in Nashe's SUMMER'S LAST WILL AND TESTAMENT (Works, ed. McKerrow, iii, 249). Not only the same epithet, but that which accompanies it, is found in Peele, in a singularly exact duplication of the rhythm and structure of the passage in TITUS. There we have :

> The hunt is up, the morn is *bright and grey ;*
> The fields are fragrant, and the woods are green.

In Peele's OLD WIVES TALE (350-1) we have :

> The day is clear, the welkin *bright and grey,*
> The lark is merry, and records her notes.

If there be any reasonable inference open, it is that Peele wrote both passages.

(7) For the rest, Mr. Collins cites from VENUS AND ADONIS a parallel to the phrase about blood on flowers in TITUS (II, ii), and the phrase " engine of her thoughts," also occurring in the play (III, i) ; and from Sonnet 128 the rather commonplace conceit (pronounced by him " exquisitely Shakespearean ") about the jacks kissing the player's hand, in comparison with

> Make the silken strings delight to kiss them
> (*Titus* II, iv).

It is an echo of Sidney :

> " Pamela having a while made the lute in his language show how glad it was to be touched by her fingers."
> *Arcadia*, B. ii, Ed. 1590, fol. 155 *verso*.

Of these parallels the first is discussed below. The second appears to be a tag of the Marlowe school. In I TAMBURLAINE (II, i, 14) the eyes are " instruments of sight," and again " *engines* of . . . . sight " (v. ii, 196). In the same fashion the voice becomes " the organ of my voice " (II, vii, 8). This, however, echoes Peele's " my hand, the organ of my heart " (ARR. OF PARIS, IV, i, 31 of b.v.) ; and as this again is echoed in

Griffin's "mine eyes, the agents of mine heart" (FIDESSA, 1596, son. vii), we are led to infer that such phrases were a common type of *cliché* in the period.[1]

(8) As to the passage in TITUS beginning,

> I am the sea : hark, how her winds do blow—
> She is the weeping *welkin*, I the earth,

which Mr. Collins declares to reproduce " exactly the note of Richard II's soliloquy in Pomfret Castle (v, v)," it may be left to the reader to say whether he can detect any resemblance whatever. Let him on the other hand compare the lines of Achitophel in Peele's DAVID AND BETHSABE (III, iv) :—

> Let all the *sighs* I *breathe* for this disgrace
> Hang on my hedges like eternal *mists*

with those cited by Mr. Collins, and with those others in TITUS (sc. cited) :—

> Or with our *sighs* we'll *breathe* the *welkin* dim
> And stain the sun with *fog*,

and say whether there is not here the same note, matter, and manner.

And let him further note these actual verbal coincidences :—

> When *heaven* doth *weep*, doth not the *earth o'erflow*.
> > (*Titus*, III, i, 222.)

> And for my death let *heaven* for ever *weep*.
> > (*D. and B.*, III, iv.)
> Then *weep*, you *heavens*, and all your clouds dissolve.
> > (*D. and B.*, III. i.)

> Then must my *sea* be movèd with her *sighs ;*
> Then must my *earth* with her continual tears
> Become a deluge *overflowed* and *drowned*.
> > (*Titus*, sc. cited.)

> *Drowned* with a *sea* that with our *sighs* should roar.
> > (*D. and B.*, III, i.)

---

[1] As Prof. Parrott notes in his paper on " Shakespeare's Revision of *Titus Andronicus*," the statement on this point in the first edition was left both erroneous and incomplete.

It is true that such parallels, if isolated, would not go far to prove identity of authorship. The figure " to drown with tears " was common, occurring frequently in both Shakespearean and non-Shakespearean plays ; and in the SPANISH TRAGEDY (II, v, 23) we have :

> To drown thee with an ocean of my tears.

But we have before us a whole series of echoes of words and figures from Peele ; and in the light of many more repetitions of the same kind they reinforce the case ; though we shall see, later, grounds for doubt as between traces of Peele and traces of Kyd.

(9) It is scarcely worth while to discuss further slight parallels such as " kill'st my heart " and " killed his heart " ; " thick-lipp'd " and " thick lips " ; " sad stories " ; " babbling gossip." Such phrases, when used only once in each of two plays, one of which is in dispute, have no *characteristic* quality : any two playwrights might make a character refer to " babbling gossip," or speak of a Moor or negro as " thick-lipped " ; and even " kill'st my heart !" has the air of an every-day phrase. If it be not so, however, it is not to Shakespeare that it points us. To begin with, we find it twice in Kyd's ARDEN OF FEVERSHAM, published in 1592—" thou hast killed my heart " ; and " it kills my heart " (I, i ; v, i : Bullen's ed. pp. 4, 85). In Peele's EDWARD I, sc. x and xxv, we have " slain my wretched heart " ; and " slays my heart with grief " ; in DAVID AND BETHSABE, " Thou wound'st thy kingly sovereign's heart " (sc. xiii) ; in THE MASSACRE AT PARIS, II, iii, " thou kill'st thy mother's heart " ; in EDWARD III, IV, iv, 58, " it kills his heart " ; in the FIRST PART OF THE CONTENTION OF YORK AND LAN-CASTER, published in 1584, " kill my woeful heart " (speech of Dame Eleanor in penance scene), and " my heart is killed with grief " (king to queen in Parliament scene) ; and in ALPHONSUS, EMPEROR OF GER-MANY (ascribed to Chapman, but certainly not by him) no fewer than four uses of the phrase : " Kills my heart " (I, i) ; " killed my heart " (II, iii) ; " al-

though my heart be slain " (IV, i) ; " kill his dastard
heart " (V, iv). It it should turn out that these thirteen instances are all from one hand, and that, apart
from TITUS, no contemporary playwright,[1] save
Shakespeare in HENRY V (II, i), uses the phrase over
his signature, we might indeed see reason to attach
weight to the expression ; but not in Mr. Collins's
sense. It would in that case appear to be one of the
mannerisms of another author much more likely than
Shakespeare to have written TITUS. Concerning
" babbling gossip," it seems hardly worth while to
inquire. Suffice it to note that Greene, in his play
ALPHONSUS, KING OF ARRAGON, has " babbling
tongue," in his story in PENELOPE'S WEB " babbling
poets " (Works, v, 158) ; and in his story TULLY'S
LOVE " babbling eloquence " (Works, vii, 155) ; besides
using " babbling " often.

(10-11) Mr. Collins further cites these parallels
between TITUS and Shakespearean plays :

> Marcus, *unknit that sorrow-wreathen knot*
> (Titus, III, ii) ;
> Sitting
> His arms *in this sad knot.*   (Tempest, I, ii).

> Two may keep counsel when the third's away.
> (Titus, IV, ii) ;
> Two may keep counsel putting one away.
> (Romeo and Juliet, II, iv).

Here again we are dealing with a common phrase and
a common proverb. The latter is found in Greene's
early prose work MAMILLIA (Works, ed. Grosart, iii,
30)—" Two might best keep counsel where one was
away " ; also in Lilly's MOTHER BOMBIE (ii, I) and
EUPHUES (Arber's rep. p. 67) ; and the former is
closely paralleled in Peele's phrase : " sadness with
wreathed arms " (D. AND B., sc. iv, 5), and again in

---

[1] But this is not the case. Heywood has " Kills my heart " twice at least
(*Edward IV*, 1600, Pearson's ed. of Works, i, pp. 83, 151) ; and Dekker has
" I would kill my soul," in *The Shoemaker's Holiday*, iv, 2.

his line " With folded arms and all amazèd heart "
(*Id.*, sc. iii, 77). Mr. Collins might as fitly have quoted
LOVE'S LABOUR'S LOST, where (IV, iii, 135) we have
" wreathèd arms," or THE TWO GENTLEMEN (II, i,
19)—" To wreathe your arms like a malecontent."
As it happens, there is good reason to regard both
ROMEO AND JULIET and the TWO GENTLEMEN as re-
dactions by Shakespeare of older plays;[1] but were
it not so, it would still be unwarrantable to argue his
authorship of TITUS from such a detail.

(12) And just as inconclusive is the parallel between
the TITUS lines :

> Upon whose leaves are drops of new-shed blood
> As fresh as morning's dew distill'd on flowers
>
> (II, iii, 199-200),

and the line in VENUS AND ADONIS (665) :

> Whose blood upon the fresh flowers being shed.

Here indeed there is an approach to identity of expression, the reference in one case being to fresh blood
on flowers, in the other to blood on fresh flowers. But
the idea is a dramatic and poetic commonplace. In
Greene's ALPHONSUS, KING OF ARRAGON (I, 84), we
have the passage—

> Where is the knight become
> Which made the blood besprinkle all the place ?[2]

and in one of the poems in his MOURNING GARMENT
(Dyce's Greene and Peele, p. 304) the metaphor :

> As if lilies were imbru'd
> With drops of blood to make the white
> Please the eye with more delight.

---

[1] As to the *Two Gentlemen*, see *The Shakespeare Canon*, Part II. In this
connection we may note Greene's
> But hanging down thy head as malcontent
in *Alphonsus King of Arragon* (I, i, Dyce's ed. p. 226b).
[2] This is perhaps echoed from Spenser (F.Q., III, v, 27) :—
> By tract of blood, which she had freshly seen
> To have besprinkled all the grassy greene.
The same idea occurs, however, in Ariosto.

Such parallels, in short, are non-significant apart from better evidence.

Apart from such obviously inconclusive cases, we shall find a number of characteristic because unusual uses of words, besides types of phrase and rhythm, common to TITUS and the undisputed works of Peele.

(1) As for the " sad stories," if there be any significant coincidence between

> I'll to thy closet and go read with thee
> *Sad stories* chanced in the times of old
> (Titus, III, ii)

and

> Let us *sit* upon the ground
> And tell *sad stories* of the death of kings
> (Richard II, III, ii),

what shall we make, again, of this in Peele ?

> Now, *sit* thee here, and tell a *heavy tale*,
> Sad in thy mood, and sober in thy cheer ?
> (Old Wives Tale, 182-3).

We are really led once more to the surmise that Peele was one of the draftsmen of RICHARD II. On the other hand, there is some significance in the parallel (2) between

> The *eagle* suffers little birds to sing . . .
> Knowing that with the shadow of his wings
> He can at pleasure stint their melody
> (Titus, IV, iv)

and

> A *falcon* towering in the skies
> Coucheth the fowl below with his wing's shade
> (Lucrece, 506-7).

But here again Dr. Grosart had cited a parallel passage from Greene's prose (Works, v, 72) :

> When the *eagle* fluttereth, doves take not their flight ;

to which may be added another from the prose romance MENAPHON (ed. Arber, p. 23 ; Works, ed. Grosart, vi, 36) : " birds make wing as the *eagle* flies " ;[1] another from the archaistic rhyming-play SIR CLYOMON AND SIR CLAMYDES :

> They fear as fowls that hovering fly from out the falcon's way
> (Dyce's ed. of Greene and Peele, p. 498) ;

and yet another from the old TRUE TRAGEDY OF RICHARD, DUKE OF YORK[2] :

> Neither the king nor him that loves him best,
> The *proudest bird* that holds up Lancaster,
> Dare stir a wing if Warwick shake his bells.

In Greene's prose work GREENE'S FAREWELL TO FOLLY, again (Works, xi, 269), we have :

> Dare the *proudest bird* bear wing against the *eagle* ?

This indeed is little more than a poetical commonplace ; and were it otherwise, the inference would necessarily be that the author of TITUS had echoed Greene or the old playwright, whose phrases date before 1592, whereas LUCRECE belongs to 1593-4.

(3) Similar imitation, again, must be imputed if we ascribe to Shakespeare the line in TITUS (II, iii, 46) :

> And wash their hands in Bassianus' blood,

on the strength of the line in CORIOLANUS (I, x, 27) :

> Wash my fierce hand in's heart

—where one would have expected Mr. Collins rather to cite from JULIUS CAESAR (III, i, 106) :—

> And let us *bathe* our *hands* in Cæsar's *blood*.

In the old play SELIMUS, warrantably ascribed by Dr. Grosart to Greene,[3] and in any case certainly to be dated before 1592, we have the line (2379) :

> Go, *wash* thy guilty hands in *luke-warm blood ;*

---

[1] Compare, in the same work, the poem on the Eagle and the Fly with the lines in *Titus.*

[2] Not to be confused with the older *True Tragedy of Richard the Third.*

[3] Six passages from *Selimus* are expressly ascribed to Greene by the compiler of *England's Parnassus* (1600). For a discussion of the authorship, see below, ch. viii.

and several others (1380, 1458, 1459, 2398) in similar
taste :

> And colour my strong hands with his gore-blood . . .
> Into his bowels thrust my angry hands . . .
> Your conquering hands in foemen's blood embay . . .

Yet again in LOCRINE (II, iv, 669) we have warriors
whose blades

> Were bathed in our enemies' *lukewarm blood.*

Seeing that Greene in his prose CARD OF FANCY (1584 ?)
has the phrase (Works, iv, 165) :

> Thou seekest to bathe thy hands in his guiltless blood,

the tag may be reasonably assigned to him, and it is
to the lines in SELIMUS and LOCRINE that the rhythm
of that in TITUS corresponds.   If Shakespeare's, then,
it is a mere echo ;[1] and, what is more, probably an
echo from the man who had jeered at him as " Johannes
factotum," " in his own conceit the only Shake-scene
in the country."

(4) The same conclusion is forced on us when we
follow up the parallel between the lines :

> Is the sun dimm'd that gnats do fly at it ?
>> (*Titus*, IV, iv, 82)

and

> And whither fly the gnats but to the sun ?
>> (3 *Henry VI*, II, vi, 9).

The latter line, with almost the whole of the speech
in which it occurs, is found in RICHARD DUKE OF YORK,
which was certainly in existence in or before 1592,
being quoted by Greene in his GROATSWORTH OF WIT ;
and if Shakespeare is to be credited with all that is
identical in that play and 3 HENRY VI, there must be
framed a new argument, in which " external evidence "
will go for little, while the FIRST PART OF THE CON-
TENTION must similarly be claimed for Shakespeare,

---

[1] So, obviously, it must be reckoned in *Julius Caesar*, if that is to be regarded as of Shakespeare's origination.   But the very line, and the speech in
which it occurs, are salient indications of the pre-Shakespearean character
of the original draft.   See *The Shakespeare Canon*, Part I.

on Knight's lines, with all its crudities on its head. As regards the line last cited from RICHARD DUKE OF YORK, Dyce would doubtless have argued that it was Marlowe's, on his principle that the best scenes are above the reach of both Greene and Peele. On that head it must here suffice to say that while there is reason to credit Marlowe with much matter in the HENRY VI plays and in RICHARD III, some of the evidence from phraseology and vocabulary in RICHARD DUKE OF YORK points to Greene ; and that allusions to gnats are common in Greene's works. Here once more then, if TITUS be ascribed to Shakespeare, the presumption must be that he is weakly copying a previous dramatist.

To this inference, in other cases, Mr. Collins could offer no objection, seeing that he declares Shakespeare to have " followed at first, with timid servility, the fashion," and pronounces TITUS to be " *full* of reminiscences of the plays on which it is founded, recalling particularly the SPANISH TRAGEDY, SELIMUS, and THE JEW OF MALTA." As we shall see, it is still more reminiscent of the works of Peele. Yet, immediately after these sweeping and indeed extravagant admissions, which really shatter his own case, Mr. Collins claims that " the moment " TITUS is compared with the dramas on which he holds it to have been modelled in " timid and servile imitation," " its immeasurable superiority to all of them becomes instantly apparent." Passing over the significant incoherence of the doctrine, let us check the evidence for the last-cited claim.

§ 2. ALLEGED SHAKESPEAREAN POETRY.

Before Professor Collins, as we have seen, there were Shakespearean critics who saw in TITUS poetry worthy of Shakespeare. Among these was Richard Grant White, who wrote :—

There are few readers of discrimination, I think, who would attribute such lines as the following to any other pen than his [Shakespeare's] :—

> In peace and honour rest you here, my sons ;
> Rome's readiest champions, repose you here in rest,
> Secure from worldly chances and mishaps !
> Here lurks no treason, here no envy swells,
> Here grow no damned grudges ; here are no storms,
> No noise, but silence and eternal sleep :
> In peace and honour rest you here, my sons !
>
> *Titus*, I, 150-156.[1]

We can but reply by challenging the " discrimination " which finds Shakespeare's hand in six repetitious and end-stopped lines of which two halt, without any sign of corruption save either the " readiest " or the " in rest," which last turns out to be a specialty of Peele's ; while the first and last lines are identical. Assigning to Shakespeare the phrase " Rome's readiest champions," White had also to accord to him the previous speech of the Captain, with its " Rome's best champion," thus assigning to Shakespeare a series of weak reiterations, and, as we shall see, a series of weak imitations of Peele's style, phrase, and cadence. Later, the student may be prepared to see in the speech above cited precisely *non*-Shakespearean matter. For the present, we return to Professor Collins.

In going about to prove further, from quality of style and substance, the " essentially " Shakespearean character of TITUS, Mr. Collins set out with a bold claim that " in Titus we have . . . *undoubtedly* an adumbration of Lear "—a claim which we may be content to leave undiscussed. The next argument runs :

> Could anyone doubt the touch of Shakespeare's hand in such a passage as this :—
>
>> I am not mad : I know thee well enough ;
>> Witness this wretched stump, these crimson lines ;
>> Witness these trenches made by grief and care ;
>> Witness the tiring day and heavy night ;
>> Witness all sorrow, that I know thee well.
>>
>> (*Titus*, v, ii.)

---

[1] White divides Act I into two scenes, making the second begin with the Captain's speech, l. 64.

Some of us, did we allow ourselves to proceed à priori, would be disposed to deny energetically that Shakespeare ever imagined such diffuse and infelicitous diction ; and we are sufficiently confirmed in doubt when we find in SELIMUS (177 sq.) the lines :

> Witness these handless arms :
> Witness these empty lodges of mine eyes !
> Witness the gods . . .
> Witness the sun whose golden-coloured beams
> Your eyes do see, but mine can ne'er behold ;
> Witness the earth that suckèd up my blood ;

and in LOCRINE (V, i) these :

> Witness the fall of Albioneus' crew,
> Witness the fall of Humber and his Huns.

Here, as usual, we find that the other plays are presumptively older than the existing TITUS. Another pair of such lines occurs in Marlowe's EDWARD II. (I, iv) :

> Witness the tears that Isabella sheds ;
> Witness the heart that, sighing for thee, breaks.

Yet another sample occurs in the FIRST PART OF THE CONTENTION :

> Witness my bleeding heart, I cannot stay to speak ;

and yet another in SOLIMAN AND PERSEDA, IV, i, 168. If we are to attempt any inference whatever, the balance of presumption is in favour of ascribing this type of line to Greene, since we find in a set of verses in his signed GROATSWORTH OF WIT the line :

> Witness my want, the murderer of my wit.

But the TITUS passage may just as well be Kyd's or Peele's.

Mr. Collins proceeds (a) to credit TITUS with an " admirably-proportioned, closely woven plot," in contrast with the " rambling, shambling, skimble-skamble of the SPANISH TRAGEDY," the plot of which Professor Boas in turn pronounces to be "well sustained,"[1] and Professor Schick to be "developed with remarkable artistic insight."[2] In truth the plot of TITUS is exactly of the type of that of the TRAGEDY, only heightened in point of horror—a chain of revenges in which the central personage partly feigns madness. As to the "unity" ascribed to the former, one can but say that such criticism ignores the facts. The plot of TITUS is certainly more elaborate than anything that precedes it in English drama—a feature in which it markedly differs, from Shakespeare's two earliest plays, the DREAM and the LABOUR—but a play more devoid of *moral* unity it would be hard to name. The first Act is spent in alienating our sympathies from Titus, who offers up as a human sacrifice one of the sons of Queen Tamora whom he has captured, and in a passion slays one of his own sons. The fourth and fifth Acts are occupied with claiming our sympathy for him ; and in the midst of the effort there is introduced a preposterous sub-plot, to enable him to bake the heads of the two sons of Tamora, whose throats he has cut, in a pie for their mother to eat. This is evidently part of the old play, as it figures in the German version, where Tamora is made to express her high appreciation of the pie. As we shall see, there is some reason to infer in the latter Acts the presence of a revising hand, which might well have been called in to struggle with the situation created by those which had gone before. But whether we ascribe the play to one hand or to four, its plot must be pronounced a moral imbecility.

Mr. Collins further presses his case (*b*) by arguing, (1) that Aaron in TITUS is a prototype of Richard III, Iago, and Edmund ; Chiron of Cloten ; and Tamora

---

[1] *Shakespeare and his Predecessors*, p. 65.

[2] Introduction to ed. in "Temple Dramatists" series, p. xxxvii. Similarly Professor Courthope judges that "Kyd, vulgar as he was, had a truer idea of the structure necessary for a drama than any of his immediate associates. His masterpiece has an intelligible and stirring plot." *History of English Poetry*, iv (1903), p. 17. Add that Kyd is the main author of *Arden of Feversham*, and his gift as a plot-framer is very well established.

of Margaret ; (2) that a number of passages in the play suggest scenes of nature which " must have been very familiar to a resident at Stratford-on-Avon " ; (3) that there are many references to Ovid's METAMOR-PHOSES, which had been read by Shakespeare for the VENUS and the LUCRECE ; (4) that in this play as in a number of the undisputed plays there are a number of legal allusions. Not one of these arguments has the slightest conclusive force. (1) The character of Aaron is admitted to resemble closely those of Marlowe's Barabas and Ithamore ; and is further duplicated in that of Eleazar in LUST'S DOMINION, which appears to proceed on a pre-Shakespearean play ; the Margaret of the HENRY VI. plays, also non-Shakespearean in inception, is only in the vaguest sense a parallel to the adulterous Tamora ; the figure of Richard III was handled by Marlowe and other dramatists before Shakespeare ; and the evil personalities of Iago and Edmund are a world removed from the bold daub in TITUS. (2) The allusions to natural scenes count no more in favour of Shakespeare's authorship than of any other :[1] Greene and Peele alike abound in such touches ; and there are rivers and meadows in other parts of England as at Stratford-on-Avon. (3) Greene and Peele and Marlowe and Kyd smack of the classics very much more than Shakespeare ever does in his acknow-ledged plays ; and nowhere in those plays do we find so many tags of Latin as in TITUS ; whereas the other playwrights have many such allusions and quotations. (4) As has been repeatedly shown, legal allusions abound in other dramatists of the period ; Peele's ARRAIGNMENT OF PARIS (1584) is full of them, and, as will be shown in detail in a subsequent section, they are to be found easily in other early plays.

Next (c) we are asked to contrast the " measured and dignified rhetoric of TITUS " with " the boisterous fanfaronade of the WORST parts of TAMBURLAINE ; its fine touches of nature and occasionally piercing

---

[1] See *infra*, ch. xii.

pathos with anything which had appeared on the English stage before " ; and Professor Collins cites, as being possible to none but Shakespeare, the following passages :

1. When will this fearful slumber have an end ?
2. Where life hath no more interest but to breathe !
3. O brother, speak with possibilities
   And do not break into these deep extremes ;
4. Blood and revenge are hammering in my head ;
5. No vast obscurity or misty vale ;
6.   We worldly men
   Have miserable, mad, mistaking eyes ;
7. This goodly summer with your winter mixt ;

and (8) the " noble " passage beginning :—

> King, be thy thoughts imperious like thy name.

Finally, quoting (9) from Act v, sc. iii, the speeches of Lucius and Marcus over Titus' body, beginning,

> O take this warm kiss on thy pale cold lips,

he demands :—" If anything more simply pathetic exists in dramatic poetry, where can it be found ? "

To this question we may at once answer : " In a dozen genuine plays of Shakespeare ; and in several of Kyd, Marlowe, Greene, Marston, Massinger, and Munday and Chettle, to name no others—postponing for the moment the demonstration of the essential weakness of the passage in question. First we have to note that the line, " When will this fearful slumber have an end ? " is closely paralleled by one in the pre-Shakespearean LEIR (sc. 16) :—

> When will this scene of madness have an end ?

which may fairly be surmised to be from the same hand —Kyd's. Still more certainly pre-Shakespearean is the " hammering " line, which has twice over been shown, by Professor Schröer and Dr. Grosart, to be but a slight variant of one used by Greene and Lodge in previous

plays.[1]   And, yet again, the line on summer and winter[2]
is closely paralleled in two lines in the SPANISH TRAGEDY
(III, xiii, 146-7) :—

> But suffer'd thy fair crimson-coloured spring
> With wither'd winter to be blasted thus.

The same idea, indeed, occurs twice again in the
TRAGEDY:—

> . . . In the harvest of my summer joys
> Death's winter nipped the blossoms of my bliss.
>
> (I, Induc.)
>
> My summer's day will turn to winter's night.
>
> (II, i, 34).

Only less close is the parallel between the second
of the group of lines above quoted by Mr. Collins and
one at the end of the SECOND PART OF TAMBURLAINE :—

> Leading a life that only strives to die.

[1] Hope and revenge sit hammering in my heart.
             Lodge, *Wounds of Civil War*, l, 1256.
For such as still have hammering in their heads
But only hope of honour and revenge.
             Greene, *Orlando Furioso*, l. 402.
The tag, with which we shall meet often in our quest, is further frequent in
Greene's prose.   For instances :—
Love, thus hammering in the head of Telegonus.
             Alcida : *Greene's Metamorphosis*, Works, ix, 41.
Hammering thus betwixt fear and hope, he built castles in the air.
             Philomela : *Works*, xi, 117.
He hammered in his head many means . . . .
             Menaphon, Arber's rep. p. 82, bottom.
It is probably derived, like so many other tags of Greene's and Lodge's, from
Lilly (*Euphues*, Arber's rep. p. 332 ; *Mother Bombie*, ii, 1).   But Lilly in turn
seems to derive it either from Surrey's
A hed where wisdom misteries did frame,
Whose hammers bet still in that lively brain
As on a stithe.   (*Tottel's Miscellany*, Arber's rep. p. 29),
or from Painter's *Palace of Pleasure* :
The Duchess, having a hammer working in her head, could not sleep.
             Tom. i, nov. 45. Haslewood's rep. i. 288.
It was, in short, a standing Tudor tag.

[2] This too was a standing tag.   Chapman has :—
I come in name of all the world
That now sustains dead winter in the spring
To have a graces from thy summer darted.
             Blind Beggar of Alexandria (1596) Shepherd's ed. p. 12.
Compare :—
Mix not my forward summer with sharp breath.
             (*The Play of Stucley*, l. 754).

But we have two more such passages[1] in EDWARD III :—

> Men that breathe a life
> Far worse than is the quiet sleep of Death.
>
> (IV, ii, 14-15).
>
> Since for to live is but to seek to die.
>
> (IV, iv, 158).

And hardly less close, yet again, is the resemblance between the lines in TITUS about " deep extremes " and these from Greene's GEORGE-A-GREENE :—

> I'll draw thee on with sharp and deep extremes . . .
> O deep extremes : my heart begins to break.

The term " extremes," it may be noted, occurs six times in the SPANISH TRAGEDY ; and Greene, further, has " deep extremes " in ORLANDO FURIOSO (ed. Dyce, p. 96) ; and " extremes " twice besides (p.110), and in the poem A MAIDEN'S DREAM (*id.* p. 279).

Mr. Collins took no account of these rebuttals of his thesis. Doubtless he would at a pinch have disposed of them by his formula of " timid and servile imitation " —the express negation of his whole argument from " Shakespearean " quality. By this alternation of contrary propositions he makes out Shakespeare alternately the most and the least original writer of his day. For the present, the thesis of imitation is hung up ; and originality is affirmed when we find ourselves, as it were, in Echo's cave. The argument now virtually proceeds on the assumption that no pre-Shakespearean

---

[1] This is in fact an old commonplace. In Gascoigne's *Jocasta* (1566) we have the lines (v, iii, *end*, and iv) :—
> Shall always die because thou canst not die,

and
> By fear of death maintain my dying life ;

and in Spencer's *Daphnaïda* (l. 435) :—
> That dying lives and living still does die.

In 1591 we have Daniel writing (*Delia*, xxi) :—
> If this be love, to live a living death,
> Lo, then love I and draw this weary breath ;

and Lodge in his *Rosalynde* (1592) has :—
> I live by that which makes me living die.
>
> (Rep. in Sh. Lib. ii, 46).

In the old play *Fidele and Fortunio : The Two Italian Gentlemen* (1584) again we have : " A living death," and " Your life is death " (Malone Soc. rep., 1909, ll. 252 and 917).

dramatist was capable of producing a sonorous, sententious, or nervous line. Now the fifth passage above cited is of a type often produced in the pre-Shakespearean drama. For instances :

> Within a hugy dale of lasting night
> > (*Spanish Tragedy*, III, 2).
> Through dreadful shades of ever-glooming night
> > (*Id.*, I, i, 56).
> The dreadful vast. The deepest vast.
> > (Lodge's *Wounds of Civil War*, ll. 221, 383).
> To bare and barren vales with floods made waste
> > (*David and Bethsabe*, sc. 3).
> Vast Grantland, compassed with the Frozen Sea
> > (2 *Tamb.*, I, i).
> > A canopy of clouds
> Whose massy darkness mazeth every sense.
> > Lines in Greene's story, *Perimedes the Blacksmith*, 1588.

Similarly the meagre measure of pathos in TITUS may be easily matched from the earlier SPANISH TRAGEDY :

> Ay, now I know thee, now thou nam'st thy son :
> Thou art the lively image of my grief :
> Within thy face my sorrows I may see.
> Thy eyes are gummed with tears, thy cheeks are wan,
> Thy forehead troubled, and thy mutt'ring lips
> Murmur sad words abruptly broken off ;
> By force of windy sighs thy spirit breathes,
> And all this sorrow riseth for thy son ; ·

and again :

> To wring more tears from Isabella's eyes
> Whose lights are dimmed with over-long laments.
> Heaven covereth him that hath no burial.

In a later section we shall see not merely analogies but parallels in the TRAGEDY to passages in TITUS ; but in the present connection we may note the eulogy unconsciously given by Mr. Baildon to one of its strokes, not hitherto selected for praise. In his introduction to his edition of TITUS he speaks of " splendid dramatic touches " in the treatment of the titular personage of that play, and affirms that " his sudden laughter, his

half hysterical ' Ha ! ha ! ha ! ' for swift and tremend-
ous effect can perhaps only be paralleled by the ' Knock-
ing in Macbeth ' for profound and startling dramatic
force." If it be so, Kyd was a great dramatist ; for
in one of the original scenes of the SPANISH TRAGEDY
(III, ii, end ; as well as in the additions to Act II, sc. v)
the student will find those three " Ha's " thrice over.
Further, in Mr. Fuller's careful investigation of the
Dutch and German versions of TITUS—an essay to which
Mr. Baildon refers with praise and acquiescence—it is
shown that the " Ha, ha " business occurred in the early
play which has been preserved in the Dutch.[1] The
Ha-ha school is thus pre-Shakespearean ; and it is to
be hoped that Mr. Baildon's liberal encomium will be
transferred to the proper quarter.

If his school are concerned to be impartial, they will
distribute his largess yet further. From LOCRINE,
structurally and æsthetically a very much worse play
than the TRAGEDY, may be cited lines (probably
Greene's) musical enough to recall Marlowe, and one
or two passages sententious enough to have passed
securely as the young Shakespeare's had they been
found in any of his earlier dramas. For instances :

> You gracious fairies which at eventide
> Your closets leave with heavenly beauty stored,
> And on your shoulders spread your golden locks
> >   (v, iv).

> Hard-hearted death, that, when the wretched call,
> Art furthest off, and seldom hear'st at all,
> But in the midst of fortune's good success
> Uncall'd for com'st and shear'st our life in twain
> >   (Ib.).

> Madam, where resolution leads the way,
> And courage follows with emboldened pace,
> Fortune can never use her tyranny :
> For valiantness is like unto a rock,
> That standeth in the waves of oceän ;
> Which though the billows beat on every side,
> Yet it remaineth still unmovable.
> >   (Id., ii, 1).

[1] Art. cited, p. 49.

> He is not worthy of the honeycomb
> That shuns the hive because the bees have stings.
> That likes me best that is not got with ease,
> Which thousand dangers do accompany
>
> <div align="right">(<i>Id.</i>, III, ii).</div>

The passage in TITUS which contains the lines :

> The birds chaunt melody on every bush ;
> The snake lies rollèd in the cheerful sun ;
> The green leaves quiver with the cooling wind,

is pronounced by Mr. Baildon " Shakespearean . . . in its extreme and rare poetic and rhythmic beauty." Had he found them in TITUS he would doubtless have said the same of a similarly monotonous group of lines in LOCRINE (II, i) :

> The airy hills enclosed with shady groves,
> The groves replenish'd with sweet chirping birds,
> The birds resounding heavenly melody ;

and of these in DAVID AND BETHSABE (SC. i) :

> The brims let be embraced with golden curls
> Of moss that sleeps with sound the waters make
> For joy to feed the fount with their recourse ;
> Let all the grass that beautifies her bower
> Bear manna every morn instead of dew.

And could he but have supposed it Shakespeare's he would doubtless have found superlatives for this passage in the SPANISH TRAGEDY, cited with moderate applause by Professor Schick :

> Our hour shall be, when Vesper 'gins to rise,
> That summons home distressful travellers :
> There none shall hear us but the harmless birds ;
> Haply the gentle nightingale
> Shall carol us asleep ere we be 'ware,
> And, singing with the prickle at her breast,
> Tell our delight and mirthful dalliance.

Certainly the better passages in LOCRINE are embedded in masses of rubbish ; but so are the presentable passages fished out of TITUS by those who seek to have it accepted as Shakespeare's. And it is in the recognition of the kindred quality of the rubbish in TITUS and in a number of the plays of the school to which it belongs that we shall find the clue to its authorship. It is in such inept attempts at pathos as this :

> Shall thy good uncle and thy brother Lucius,
> And thou and I, sit round about some fountain,
> Looking all downwards, to behold our cheeks,
> How they are stain'd, as meadows, yet not dry,
> With miry slime left on them by a flood ?
>
> (Titus, III, i),

that we see the average strength of the workmanship ; and it is only by consideration of the mass of the matter that we can reach any just conclusion. But our method must be more circumspect, our tests more scientific, than those we have been examining.

At this stage it is fitting to take note of the argument of Mr. H. D. Gray in his paper on " The Authorship of TITUS ANDRONICUS " in the Flügel Memorial Volume of 1916.[1] Mr. Gray's thesis is that Shakespeare is the author of the play, and that the many passages by other hands are to be regarded as the work of revisers. So early as 1593, he contends, Shakespeare would not have been allowed by his company to revise a work by such eminent playwrights as Peele, Greene, Marlowe, and Kyd ; whereas *they* might very well be called in to revise an early work of Shakespeare's. A priori, this is plausible enough, save for the *premier pas qui coûte*. When Shakespeare was too raw to revise the work of eminent contemporaries, he was too raw to undertake a whole tragedy ; and Greene's deathbed fling at him tells only of his meddling in the plays of the academics. But the whole thesis is otiose. The primary play on which Peele and Greene and Marlowe have worked is the old TITUS AND VESPASIAN, which no critic but Mr. Gray would now assign to Shakespeare. It must be dated within a year or two of the SPANISH TRAGEDY, when the undertaking of a tragedy by Shakespeare

---

[1] Published by the Leland-Stanford University.

would on Mr. Gray's own principles be out of the question. On that line the argument collapses. It is to the existing text, necessarily, that all the critics turn who argue for either authorship or a considerable revision by Shakespeare.

§ 3. ALLEGED SHAKESPEAREAN LEGAL ALLUSIONS

So much stress is laid by Professor Collins on his argument from the legal allusions in TITUS that it may be worth while to show in some detail how nugatory is his contention.   It runs :—

> " And lastly, we have in the diction one of Shakespeare's most striking characteristics.   All through his writings, but more particularly in the poems and earlier dramas, his fondness for legal phraseology and his profuse employment of it are so marked that its absence would be almost conclusive against the authenticity of a work attributed to him.   But *Titus Andronicus* will sustain this test.   Thus we have ' *affy* in thy uprightness ' (i, 1) ; ' true nobility *warrants* these words ' (i, 2) ; ' *Suum cuique* is our Roman justice ' (i, 2) ; ' the Prince in justice *seizeth* but his own ' (i, 2) ; ' rob my sweet sons of their *fee* ' (ii, 3) ; ' *purchase* us thy lasting friends ' (ii, 4) ; ' let me be their bail ' (ii, 4) ; ' the end upon them should be *executed* ' (ii, 4) ; ' do *execution on* my flesh and blood ' (iv, 2) ; ' do shameful *execution on* herself ' (v, 3) ; ' and make a mutual *closure* of our house ' (v, 3) ; ' the extent of legal (*sic*) justice ' (iv, 4) ; ' a *precedent* and lively *warrant* ' (v, 3) ; ' will *doom* her death ' (iv, 2).   Nor must we forget the masterly touch in the Fifth Act, which is peculiarly characteristic of Shakespeare—the fine irony which identifies Tamora and her two sons with revenge, rape, and murder just before retribution falls on them.[1]

I quote the entire paragraph lest any of the Professor's pleas should be evaded ; but I may be excused for dismissing the last sentence with the remark that if the habitual extolling of ineptitudes and commonplaces as " fine " and " Shakespearean " could settle the question, he and Mr. Baildon would have done so many times over.   That such darkening of critical counsel should be a part of the plea for Shakespeare's authorship

[1] *Studies in Shakespeare*, pp. 118-119.

of TITUS is an additional reason why we should seek to
clear up the issue.

The general thesis as to Shakespeare's legal knowledge or proclivities, maintained by Professor Collins
in a special essay, " Was Shakespeare a Lawyer ? " in
his volume of STUDIES IN SHAKESPEARE, was ex-
haustively dealt with five years before by Mr. Devecmon
in a treatise[1] to which the Professor makes no allusion.
As had been previously pointed out by Sir Sidney Lee,
" Legal terminology abounded in all plays and poems
of the period " ;[2] and Mr. Devecmon points out that
in Webster's THE DEVIL'S LAW CASE there are " more
legal expressions (some of them highly technical, and
all correctly used) than are to be found in any single one
of Shakespeare's works." Sir George G. Greenwood
has seen fit[3] to scout Mr. Devecmon's pronouncement
on the score that the " trial " in Webster's play is of a
very unprofessional sort—this while maintaining the
professional purity of the law in the plays of the author
of THE MERCHANT OF VENICE ! Those who are interested in the general problem may be referred to the
present writer's work on THE BACONIAN HERESY. In
the present connection it may suffice to add that in
Spenser's FAERIE QUEENE[4] we have a complete legal
setting of a case, as it were, in the Courts of Love,
running through four stanzas, full of technical legal
terminology; and that practically the whole Elizabethan
drama is coloured with legal phraseology, some playwrights, notably Jonson and Chapman, employing it
to a far greater extent than does Shakespeare. It is
more to our present purpose, however, to note that
legal allusions—especially in the extravagantly wide
sense in which Professor Collins interprets the term—
are equally abundant in the works of Shakespeare's

[1] " In re Shakespeare's ' Legal Acquirements,' " by William C. Devecmon.
Publications of the New York Shakespeare Society, No. 12. London, Kegan
Paul, 1899.
[2] Life of Shakespeare, p. 32, note.
[3] The Shakespeare Problem Re-Stated, 1908, p. 398.
[4] Bk. vi, c. vii, st. 34-37. The point was previously made by Sir Sidney
Lee in his essay on Spenser in Great Englishmen of the Sixteenth Century.

predecessors in drama.   In Peele's ARRAIGNMENT OF
PARIS (1584) we have the following :

> Aiders in her suit
> Do observance
> Sentence of a judge
> Bestow the bail and end the case
> By common doom
> A hard and doubtful case
> Answer his offence
> The court of Jove
> Plead his case (twice)
> At Juno's suit
> Join in suit
> Action is enter'd in the court of heaven
> With warranty
> To apprehend and find
> To answer his offence
> Answer his indictment
> To plead or answer by attorney
> Allow the man his advocate
> Arraigned of partiality (twice)
> Unguilty of the fact
> Sentence partial and unjust
> My tongue is void with process to maintain
> A daysman chosen by full consent
> Judged corruptly
> Sue to reverse my sentence by appeal
> Law and right
> Equity and law (twice)
> Doom with sentence of indifferency
> Quitted by heaven's laws
> In law and right
> Indifferent sentence
> Give it by voices, voices give the odds
> General doom
> Licensed according to our laws
> To conclude the cause ;

also the terms " doom "—judgment (eight times),
" bequeathed " (four times), " bail," " pledge," " fee,"
and " attaint."   In Peele's BATTLE OF ALCAZAR,
again, we have the following " legal " expressions :

> To invest his son in all
> Works affiance
> *Execute* Jove's justice
> Honour's fee

Pay satisfaction with thy blood
Sealed with blood
True succession of the crown
Intitle him true heir unto the crown ;

in his DAVID AND BETHSABE these :—

Execute the arrest of Jove's just doom
A cause to plead ;

and in his EDWARD I these :—

Return your *habeas corpus :* here's a *certiorari* for your
    procedendo
Heavenly ordinance decrees (twice)
The arrest of dreadful death
Death doth seize and summon all alike
Yearly fee
By doom of heavens it is decreed
Seized [in the legal sense] with honourable love
Seize desire
Invested in his rights
Lawful line of our succession
Make appeal
Submit to your award
Stand to our award
To *execute* on me
Benevolence (=gift)
The law shall take no vantage.

And in the SPANISH TRAGEDY of Kyd, who as one
" born to the trade of *Noverint* " had a right to be
legal, we have, in addition to the common " doom,"
the following phrases :

Valour's fee
Breach to common law
Laid my heart to gage
Place of execution
See this execution done
Compass no redress
The court is set
I had a suit with her
The law discharged
Hear my suit
Bankrupt of my bliss
An action of battery
An action of the case.

An *ejectione firmæ* by a lease
Plead your several actions, etc.
Here's my declaration
Here's my hand
Here's my lease
Cross my suit.
Sorrow and despair hath cited me.
To hear Horatio plead with Rhadamanth.

In Greene, yet again, to say nothing of the abundance
of legal diction in some of his stories, we have in one
short scene of ORLANDO FURIOSO the phrases : " put in
their pleas," " enter such a plea," " nonsuits your
evidence," " set a *supersedeas* of my wrath ; " while
elsewhere in the same play we have : " Pawning his
colours for thy warrantize," " to quittance all my ills,"
and " to quittance all my wrongs."   It seems unnecessary to carry further this particular issue.   *Solvuntur
tabulæ*.

CHAPTER V

REAL SHAKESPEAREAN PARALLELS

In the series of mostly nugatory parallels compiled by Prof. Churton Collins we have met, in addition to "tags," with some describable as real parallels, but also as mere variants of poetic commonplaces. To these, however, there fall to be added some which have been adduced by Professor Parrott as proving, not Shakespeare's authorship of the play, which the Professor confidently denies,[1] but Shakespeare's revision of it to the extent of inserting lines and passages, and even writing or re-writing a speech or two. This limited proposition it would not greatly concern us to dispute (seeing that it concedes our main case) were it not that the Professor in handling his case collides with tests which are essential to the whole investigation, and thus leaves the main problem ill-solved. For his limited proposition he has really adduced, with much that is unsound, better evidence than was collected by Professor Collins for his proposition that Shakespeare wrote the entire play. It is more than likely, therefore, that the traditionists will fasten on the new parallels as proving their case ; hence a necessity for re-stating the case against them, which Professor Parrott fully accepts, with the reservation only of the parallels he puts forward—one or two of them already advanced by the other side. It is therefore convenient to note them —produced as they are at a late stage in the debate— separately from those considered in the last chapter.

That Shakespeare in *some* fashion revised the play is, as aforesaid, conceded by all of us who deny his author-

---

[1] Though, using the word "authorship" as he does in a very elastic fashion, he seems at points to assert it.

ship.   When, therefore, Prof. Parrott puts the theory of
" *a more or less* thorough revision " as " a third possibility " in the dispute, and one accepted by the majority
of recent American students, he may possibly set up a
misconception.   There is here no third theory, unless
the " more " in the phrase " more or less " be understood to stand for something like rewriting.   Professor
Parrott's own express proposition is that the revision
was " superficial," which term will cover the estimates
of practically all the English critics who deny the
authorship, but admit presumptive intervention.   In
the present edition I have argued for a less superficial
revision than was suggested in the first, while still
failing, with Dr. Greg, to see Shakespearean quality in
any entire speech.   Professor Parrott goes further,
but no further, probably, than Garnett, Craig, Fleay,
Furnivall, Wright, Bradley, Ward, and others, would
have gone with him.   That is to say, they would have
assented to his general proposition, whether or not they
accepted his selections.   The critical service of Professor
Parrott consists in giving some definite grounds for
going so far as he does ; though, as we have seen, he
sets out from a false position as to the evolution of
double-endings, and, as we shall see, reaches some very
unsound conclusions.

§ 1

Accepting substantially the case put in my first
edition for Peele's authorship of the first Act, and
leaving to Greene, with slight hesitation, the first scene[1]
of the second, and to Peele the next, Professor Parrott
definitely claims the intervention of Shakespeare in the
third scene.   Proceeding on his fatally erroneous view
that Shakespeare at his outset began to lead the way
in the use of the double-ending, he finds the relatively
high percentage in this scene (11+) a sign of his presence,

---

[1] I had assigned to Peele the opening soliloquy of Aaron, and I should
ascribe to him ll. 112-135 of the dialogue.

and, finding two clear verbal parallels between the first speech of Tamora and two stanzas of the VENUS AND ADONIS, he in effect assigns either the whole of that speech, or the paralleled lines, to Shakespeare.   Here are the parallels :—

> And while the babbling echo mocks the hounds
> Replying shrilly to the well-tuned horns,
> As if a double hunt were heard at once . . .
> > *(Titus*, ii, iii, 17-19)

> Thus do they [the hounds] spend their mouths : Echo replies
> As if another chase were in the skies.
> > *(V. and A.*, 695-6)

> Whiles hounds and horns and sweet melodious birds
> Be unto us as is a nurse's song
> Of lullaby to bring her babe asleep.
> > *(Titus*, ll, 27-29)

> By this, far off, she hears some huntsman hollo ;
> A nurse's song ne'er pleased her babe so well.
> > *(V. and A.*, 973-4).

There can be no question as to the connection between the passages : each pair echoes the other.   And as this speech of Tamora seems quite homogeneous, it would seem to follow that if Shakespeare wrote the lines paralleled, he wrote the whole.

But did he do either ? I have already indicated the untenable character of Professor Parrott's postion as to Shakespeare's leading the way or forcing the pace with the double-ending.   He takes no note of the high percentage in Marlowe's version of Lucan, or of Marlowe's share in the percentages in the HENRY VI plays or in the CONTENTION originals, or of his probable share in RICHARD III, or of the percentage of 12 attained in the second Act of EDWARD III ; and, what is still more serious, he ignores altogether the discrepancy between the percentages he quotes from some of the early plays and that found in 1 HENRY IV (5.1%).   Neither does he note that in ARDEN OF FEVERSHAM, printed in 1592, Kyd has 12 double-endings in his first 100 lines ; and higher rates later ; or that in CORNELIA, published in 1595, Kyd, as translator, reaches 12 per cent. in the last Act, having actually twenty in the last 60 lines—a rate of 33 per cent.   In so far, then, as the Professor is led by his opinion on double-endings to assign the Tamora speech to Shakespeare, he is on false ground.   Either Marlowe or Kyd certainly, and Peele probably, could have produced the twelve double-endings in the first 100 lines of this scene in or before 1593, so far as that goes.   On the other hand, Shakespeare's figure in I HENRY IV being only 5.1 per cent., in JOHN only 6.3 per cent., and in the DREAM only 7.3 per cent., how are we to account for the 11 or 12 per cent. ascribed by the Professor to Shakespeare in this scene of TITUS, where the verse, admittedly earlier than any of these, is intellectually so much more primitive ?

Continuing to hold by the proofs that in 1593 Shakespeare certainly did *not* reach to anything like 12 per cent. of double-endings, I would next ask whether the verse of Tamora's speech is in the least like Shakespeare's early blank verse, say, in the first scene of the ERRORS (where the double-endings are only 2 per cent.), or in the LABOUR, or the DREAM, or JOHN ? The movement and the style are so different that I can here understand the inclination of some of the traditionists to put the play back to Shakespeare's nonage, and make it his very first attempt at blank verse.   That device is, of course, barred for all critical readers by the percentages of double-endings.   Are we then critically entitled to defy all other considerations and assign the speech before us to Shakespeare because of the undeniable parallels cited by Professor Parrott ?   I submit that we are not.   There are two obvious possibilities which the Professor has omitted to take into account— the possibility, first, that Peele, revising TITUS about the end of 1593, was diffusely echoing images which he had met with in Shakespeare's VENUS AND ADONIS, and alternatively that the young Shakespeare, writing VENUS AND ADONIS for the market in 1592-3 with that facility in which he seems to have distanced all his

contemporaries, echoed certain conceits which he had
heard at the theatre in or before that year, or read in
the MS. of a revision of the popular TITUS, to which
his attention would be specially called by the fact that
his own company had in 1592 played it, or a form
of it.

Let us put two correlative questions : (1) Which is the
likelier, that Shakespeare should use the same matter
both in a play and in a poem about the same time ; or
that the poem should echo or be echoed by someone
else's play ? (2) Which is the likelier, (*a*) that Shakespeare should handle the same poetical images loosely,
diffusely, flabbily in a play, and tersely in a diffuse poem,
or that either (*b*) he effected the terseness by recasting
someone else's diffuse diction, or (*c*) another dramatist
turned his terse figure into looser and feebler diction ?

As will be seen when we come to discuss the logic of
the problem, I do not deny that Shakespeare, like
most dramatists of his day, echoed himself at times ;
but I do argue that for him thus ineptly (one instance
being a very feeble parallel to the other) to duplicate
ordinary ideas in two pieces which he had in hand
about the same time is highly unlikely ; and that the
weak dilution of the diction in the Tamora speech as
compared with the lines in the poem is precisely the
kind of thing Shakespeare would not have done.
Professor Parrott speaks of the dramatic character of
the later parts of this scene : neither he nor anyone
else, I think, will suggest that there is anything dramatic in Tamora's vapid discourse. But let us take not
only the lines cited but those which precede them :—

> My lovely Aaron, wherefore art thou sad,
> When everything doth make a gleeful boast ?
> The birds chaunt melody on every bush ;
> The snake lies rollèd in the cheerful sun. ;
> The green leaves quiver with the cooling wind
> And make a chequered shadow on the ground.
> Under their sweet shade, Aaron, let us sit—

and compare them with this passage from Peele's
DAVID AND BETHSABE (Act I, sc. i) :—

Dav. Now comes my lover tripping like the roe,
And brings my longings tangled in her hair.
To 'joy her love I'll build a kingly bower,
Seated in hearing of a hundred streams
That for their homage to her sovereign joys
Shall, as the serpents fold into their nests
In oblique turnings, wind their nimble waves
About the circles of her curious walks,
And with their murmur summon easeful sleep
To lay his golden sceptre on her brows.

Is not this the verse movement, with the development of two run-on lines, but with the taste in imagery and the saccharine diction, of Tamora's speech? That Professor Parrott should recognise Peele's style in the first Act and not here, is to be understood only through the influence of the parallels he has noted. If he is right, Shakespeare has here humbly copied Peele's style, image, sentiment and cadence as Professor Collins, Mr. Crawford and others represent him to have copied Peele's tags and metaphors ; and if the traditionists ask why then he will not suppose Shakespeare to have copied Peele's style in the first Act, I do not see how he can meet them. It will really not avail to say that in the first Act there are not double-endings enough for the young Shakespeare. Remember the first scene of the COMEDY OF ERRORS, and the percentages of JOHN and 1 HENRY IV, the DREAM, and the LABOUR.

Even Peele's tags emerge later in the scene. Here we have " To 'joy [=enjoy] her love," as in DAVID AND BETHSABE : a little further on in TITUS we have

Let her 'joy her raven-coloured love.

" 'Joy " [=enjoy] is thus used by him many times ; and he uses " raven " to indicate black three times at least in his signed poems. If any of the longer speeches in this Act could plausibly be at first sight assigned to Shakespeare it would be Aaron's in reply to Tamora, on the score that the style of that is not like Peele. The vocabulary and phraseology partly point to

Greene, whose style, however, is not clearly suggested either.   It is one of the speeches that point to Marlowe by their comparative vigour ;   and as Aaron is the character that most suggests Marlowe's hand, we are tempted to declare for him here.   The speech, however (placed at the end of the scene with Tamora's, not where they now stand, at the beginning) seems to have been in the old play, as it is preserved (shortened) in the German version ;   and if the revision at this point was made about the end of 1593 it is not entirely Marlowe's as it stands.   But once more, the style is really not that of Shakespeare at any period ; and the same holds of the rest of the Act, though there appears to enter another hand than Peele's after Tamora's speech to her sons, which`Professor Parrott assigns to the old play.

Style apart, there is a further reason for incredulity as to Shakespeare's entrance here, save, it may be, in a line or a phrase, as was before suggested.[1]   The gross taunts cast by Bassianus and Lavinia at Tamora, which compose so ill with Lavinia's appeals after the murder, do not appear to have been in the old play, the altercation in the German version having no trace of them, though the relation of Tamora to the Moor is grossly enough obtruded afterwards.   Such taunts are easily accounted for as coming from Peele, whose academic method, as exhibited in DAVID, was to give a strong provocation or example for every deed of violence, without regard to the resultant cancelling of sympathy with every character in turn.   The result here is to make Bassianus and Lavinia alike crassly offensive ;   and to ascribe such a worsening of a situation both morally and æsthetically to Shakespeare seems unwarranted by anything we know even of his earliest work.   Professor Parrott pronounces the scolding match " dramatically appropriate," and " far livelier in movement than anything in Act I."   But, to say nothing of the liveliness of the abduction scene

---

[1] Above, p. 14-15.

in Act I, the " scolding match " seems to have been quite lively enough in the old play, where there is no indecency in Lavinia's language. And this gratuitous grossness is assuredly not Shakespearean ; while the scolding is easily matched in Peele's EDWARD I.

§ 2

After deciding that ll. 116-186 " *must* represent a fairly thorough re-writing by Shakespeare of the original," the Professor suggests a further touching-up at ll. 199-201 because of the parallel with the VENUS AND ADONIS passage about blood and flowers, before considered ;[1] to which he adds a second passage (ll. 1055-56) not noted by Professor Collins. The issue here is very much the same as over the other VENUS parallels above discussed. We have our choice of two possibilities besides that of Shakespeare having once more partly duplicated a passage in a play and in a poem about the same time ; and in this case the fact that a somewhat similar passage occurs in Greene, and an earlier one in Spenser, leaves it an open question whether, supposing another writer than Shakespeare to have done the lines in TITUS, that writer was copying or was copied by Shakespeare. Let us first note the bulk of the passage in TITUS, for the style :—

Enter AARON, *with* QUINTUS *and* MARTIUS.

Aar. Come on, my lords, the better foot before :
Straight will I bring you to the loathsome pit
Where I espied the panther fast asleep.
 Quint. My sight is very dull, whate'er it bodes.
 Mart. And mine, I promise you : were't not for shame,
Well could I leave our sport to sleep awhile.
                                             [*Falls into the pit.*
 Quint. What ! art thou fallen ?—What subtle hole is this
Whose mouth is covered with rude-growing briers,
Upon whose leaves are drops of new-shed blood,   200
As fresh as morning's dew distilled on flowers ?
A very fatal place it seems to me.
Speak, brother, hast thou hurt thee with the fall ?

---

[1] Above, p. 100.

Mart. O brother! with the dismall'st object hurt,
That ever eye with sight made heart lament.
   Aar. [*Aside.*] Now will I fetch the king to find them here,
That he thereby may give a likely guess
How these were they that made away his brother.

[*Exit.*

   Mart. Why dost not comfort me, and help me out
From this unhallowed and blood-stainèd hole?   210
   Quint. I am surprisèd with an uncouth fear;
A chilling sweat o'erruns my trembling joints:
My heart suspects more than mine eye can see.
   Mart. To prove thou hast a true-divining heart,
Aaron and thou look down into this den,
And see a fearful sight of blood and death.
   Quint. Aaron is gone; and my compassionate heart
Will not permit mine eyes once to behold
The thing whereat it trembles by surmise.
O! tell me how it is; for ne'er till now   220
Was I a child, to fear I know not what.

Compare now the passages in the VENUS:—

   Whose blood upon the fresh flowers being shed
   Doth make them droop with grief. (665-6).

No flower was nigh, no grass, herb, leaf, or weed,
But stole his blood, and seem'd with him to bleed. (1055-6).

Here, without any very notable poetic power, we have
two vividly worded conceits, in a diction quite above
the Elizabethan average for compactness. But who
will say that of the diction in the TITUS passage?
In comparison, it is flaccid and languid—though that
kind of realistic scene, first introduced by Kyd, was
possibly effective at the time on the stage; further,
the writing is essentially undramatic, a piece of laboured
and inappropriate description being thus elaborated
by Quintus just after his brother has fallen into the
pit. The lines:

   A very fatal place it seems to me.
   Speak, brother, hast thou hurt thee with thy fall?

are well within the compass of the average playwright
of the time; and only a weak or tired hand would have
put the last line where it stands, instead of at the
beginning. But the speech is all of a piece; and there

is no reason to suppose that the " fresh as morning dew distill'd on flowers " is an inserted patch.   If that is Shakespeare's, all is.   And is that credible ?   Professor Parrott virtually ignores the question, satisfied to have posited his parallels.   But this is surely not the right critical method.   He proposes to reach a a decision " by an unbiass'd consideration of ascertained facts and by the application of the proper tests."   But the style test is one of the most essential ; and here it negates the premature conclusion he has drawn from his parallels.

He goes on to suggest that the speech of Martius (ll. 226-236) has been " *touched* by Shakespeare : the Pyramus allusion is exactly in the manner of the famous passage at the beginning of the last Act of THE MERCHANT OF VENICE."   After this he finds " nothing of Shakespeare to the close of the scene." Again, let us note the passage in its context :—

> *Mart.*   Lord Bassianus lies embrewéd here,
> All on a heap, like to a slaughtered lamb,
> In this detested, dark, blood-drinking pit.
>   *Quint.*   If it be dark, how dost thou know 'tis he ?
>   *Mart.*   Upon his bloody finger he doth wear
> A precious ring that lightens all the hole,
> Which, like a taper in *some* monument,
> Doth shine upon the dead man's earthy cheeks,
> And shows the ragged entrails of this pit :
> So pale did shine the moon on Pyramus
> When he by night lay bathed in maiden blood.
> O brother, help me with thy fainting hand—
> If fear doth make thee faint as me it hath—
> Out of this fell devouring receptacle,
> As hateful as Cocytus' misty mouth.
>   *Quin.*   Reach me thy hand that I may help thee out,
> Or, wanting strength to do thee so much good,
> I may be plucked into the swallowing womb
> Of this deep pit, poor Bassianus' grave.
> I have no strength to pluck thee to the brink.
>   *Mart.*   Nor I no strength to climb without thy help.
>   *Quin.*   Thy hand once more, I will not loose again
> Till thou art here aloft, or I below :
> *Thou canst not come to me : I come to thee.*
>
>   [*Falls in.*

Here we have a scene in the *naif* realistic manner of
Kyd, as developed in ARDEN OF FEVERSHAM, " touched
up," I should guess, by Peele, if by anyone.   The plot-
work suggests Kyd all along : Professor Parrott gives
up the primitive business of Aaron's hiding of the bag
of gold at the outset of the scene as probably part of the
old play.   It may or may not be old : it is not indicated in the German version ; but it is far more
suggestive of Kyd than of Peele ; and it is in the key
of the later business of the pit dug for the sons of
Titus.   The feeble elaboration of the action, so quaintly
culminating in the last line ; the putting everything
into phrases, and the super-imposition of rhetoric
devoid of real fire, are all equally in the way of Kyd
and Peele ; and we may surmise a careful working-up
of a scene that had been found effectual on the stage.
But alike the action and the cheap rhetoric are alien
to the young Shakespeare, who never concerns himself
about style contraptions and has plenty of vigorous
rhetoric with the touch of passion in it for scenes of
tension.   I hesitate to express my sense of the difference between this and the unmatched felicity of the
" In such a night " scene in the MERCHANT, where
Jessica's

> *In such a night*
> Did Thisbe fearfully o'ertrip the dew,
> And saw the lion's shadow of himself,
> And ran dismay'd away,

is one of a series of musical chimes.   The proposition,
I take it, is that the two lines :—

> So pale did shine the moon on Pyramus
> When he by night lay bathed in maiden blood

are inserted by the young Shakespeare in the middle
of the speech, to eke out the picture of the lighting-up
of the pit by the precious stone in the ring.   They are
not bad lines, and might conceivably have been written
by the young Shakespeare.   But are they not part of

the speech as originally written ?   It is arguable, indeed, that the lines from Quintus's challenge :

> If it be dark, how dost thou know 'tis he ?

to the end of the description of Pyramus, may be an insertion, since the lines from " O brother " could follow naturally enough on

> In this detested, dark, blood-drinking pit.

But we have seen that Collins ascribed the " blood-drinking " figure also to Shakespeare because that epithet occurs twice in the HENRY VI plays. Will Professor Parrott follow him so far ?   And if not, why not ?

On the other hand, applying the " proper tests," we have to note that the idea of a precious stone serving as a lamp belongs to the apparatus of the pre-Shakespeareans :—

> A curious arch, of costly marble wrought,
> Hath Locrine framèd underneath the ground ;
> The walls whereof, garnished with diamonds,
> With opals, rubies, glistering emeralds,
> And interlaced with sun-bright carbuncles,
> Lighten the room with artificial day.
>> *Locrine*, IV, iii.
>
> Bearing the sun upon his armèd breast,
> That like a precious shining carbuncle,
> Or Phœbus' eye, in heaven itself reflects.
>> Peele, *Polyhymnia*.

In them too we find another of the formulas of this scene.   Compare :

> *Quin.* I am surprisèd with an uncouth fear ;
> A chilling sweat o'erruns *my trembling joints* ;
> My heart suspects more than mine eye can see.
>> *Titus*, I, iii, 211-13.
>
> *Bajazet.* Mustapha, if my mind deceive me not,
> Some strange misfortune is not far from me.
> I was not wont to tremble in this sort ;
> Methinks I feel a cold run through my bones.
>> *Selimus*, ll. 1248-51.

The same physiology is common in Kyd :—

> With this I woke and *trembled every joint.*
> > *Arden*, III, iii, 20.

> *My trembling joints* witness my inward fear.
> > *Id.*, III, i, 96.

And in Marlowe we have a line which very probably gave the cue to

> I am surprisèd with an uncouth fear.

In the first part of TAMBURLAINE (II, vii, 7) we have :

> An uncouth pain torments my grievèd soul.

The passage in TITUS is not Marlowe's ; but Kyd, Peele and Greene all imitated his phrases and echoed his epithets, and the diction here seems to be clearly Kyd's.   In the line following that cited we have " the organ of my voice," which we have seen to be echoed from Peele, and which, with Marlowe's " engines of my loathèd sight " (=eyes), may have given the cue to " engine of her thoughts." Whatever hand or hands may be credited with this patch-work of clichés, it is surely not Shakespeare's.

The bulk of the passage, then, would seem to be entirely in the taste of the Kyd-Peele-Greene school ; and only a very high confidence in the Shakespearean character of the Pyramus lines can justify the hypothesis that even that is an addition.   As the Professor avows (pp. 23-24), " it is manifestly absurd to go over the play and mark all that seems poetical as the work of Shakespeare. . . . *The ability to write pleasing verse was shared by Shakespeare with most of the playwrights of the day.*"

In his next ascription, the Professor, significantly observing that "the fourth scene contains three feminine endings," goes on :—

> " All these occur in the speech of Marcus, where Shakespeare's

hand is *plainly visible*. It contains two Shakespearean parallels :
cf. :—

> Sorrow concealèd, like an oven stopped,
> Doth burn the heart to cinders where it is,

with

> An oven that is stopp'd, or river stay'd,
> Burneth more hotly, swelleth with more rage :
> So of concealèd sorrows may be said . . .
>
> (V. and A., 331-3)

—a much closer parallel, by the way, than those which Robertson, p. 104, adduces from Greene— ; cf. also the conceit of the lute-strings kissing Lavinia's hands with the conceit in the *Sonnets* (cxxviii), where the jacks are said to *kiss the tender inward* of a lady's hand."

The Sonnet passage and that in TITUS, as we have seen, are alike echoes of Sidney ; though probably Shakespeare in the Sonnet was working up what he had heard in the play. The " Sorrow concealed " parallels will be found discussed below in connection with the general case for Greene's share in the play, and the reader may be left to judge whether the Greene parallels are less close than that from the VENUS. It could hardly be guessed from Prof. Parrott's pronouncement that Greene has quite a number of passages beginning with or including " Sorrows concealed," and several times combining the " oven " and " river " figures. This being so, it follows that if Shakespeare inserted the tag in TITUS he was copying a *habitual* twofold or threefold tag of Greene's, and this again *after* employing it in VENUS AND ADONIS.[1]   Again we must ask whether this was a likely proceeding for him ; and again we must put the style test, which Professor Parrott continues to ignore. So unlike Shakespeare's style at any period is the line :

> Doth burn the heart to *cinders where it is*,

that only his unfortunate presupposition about feminine endings, I think, could have led the Professor to ascribe it to him.

---

[1] Where, as we shall see, Shakespeare echoes Greene's habitual terms.

§ 3

For the Professor, further,

> " The classical allusions are quite in Shakespeare's *manner* : Philomel and Tereus appear in the RAPE OF LUCRECE (1593-4) ; and ll. 552-3 of that poem present a close parallel to ll. 48-51 of this scene. In the poem Lucrece pleads with her would-be ravisher, and
>
> His unhallow'd haste her words delays,
> And moody Pluto winks [=sleeps] while Orpheus plays.
>
> In the play Marcus says of Lavinia that if he had heard the harmony of her tongue he would have been charmed to sleep as *Cerberus at the Thracian poet's feet.* We have here something more convincing than mere verbal parallels—"

convincing, that is, as to Shakespeare's authorship of the whole detestable speech. The reader should here note, what Professor Parrott does not in effect do, that the long speech of Marcus is addressed to a newly violated and horribly mutilated woman, whose mere continuing to stand on her feet is a physical absurdity, and who is elaborately described to herself by the speaker as presenting an aspect of which the sheer horror sickens the imagination. Before this hideous vision he goes on spinning conceits which, heard as uttered in the actual scene, would make a bystander yearn to slay him. They represent the very extremity of dramatic unfitness ; and it is necessary in this regard to point to the fundamental fallacy of Professor Parrott's argument from the parallel between ll. 22-24 and those in LUCRECE (1734–8) :—

> from the purple fountain Brutus drew
> The murderous knife, and, as it left the place,
> Her blood, in poor revenge, held it in chase ;
> And bubbling from her breast, it doth divide
> In two slow rivers, that the crimsom tide
> Circles her body.

Here, certainly, as often happens in this poem, we have Elizabethan bad taste in that " in poor revenge." But the bad taste is merely æsthetic, consisting in the pursuit of the verbal conceit or image beyond the verge of

congruity.   In an age much given to *concetti*, these
artistic follies could pass muster anywhere, though we
find Ben Jonson deriding, even unjustly, some of those
of Daniel.   The affectation had not wholly died out
even in the days of Tennyson and Arnold ; and we must
regard it as a touch of the barbaric, cleaving to civiliza-
tion—the kind of æsthetic sin which Arnold proposed
to exorcise by the example of the Greeks.   But the
conceit in the LUCRECE makes us merely wince : that
in the play is fitted to make us stop our ears, with an
imprecation.

' The whole speech, in fact," argues Professor Parrott, " is a
sort of epitome (!) of LUCRECE, a poetizing and decorating, with
picturesque conceits, of the brutal fact of bodily outrage.   It
may (!) not suit the severer taste of our day, but it is *eminently
characteristic of the young Shakespeare.   So, too, is the movement
of the verse in this speech.*   It would be hard, perhaps impossible,
to find in the work of any of Shakespeare's predecessors such a
verse-period as ll. 16-21." (P. 30).

That is to say, there is inserted in a drama, as an ornate
description of an utterly horrible spectacle, a sort of
epitome of a long narrative poem.[1]

[1] Here is the whole speech, for the reader's convenience :

Enter MARCUS, *from hunting.*

   Marc. Who's this ?—my niece, that flies away so fast ?   11
Cousin, a word : where is your husband ?—
If I do dream, would all my wealth would wake me !
If I do wake, some planet strike me down,
That I may slumber in eternal sleep !—   15
Speak, gentle niece, what stern ungentle hands
Have lopped and hewed, and made thy body bare
Of her two branches, those sweet ornaments,
Whose circling shadows kings have sought to sleep in,
And might not gain so great a happiness   20
As have thy love ?   Why dost not speak to me ?—
Alas ! a crimson river of warm blood,
Like to a bubbling fountain stirred with wind,
Doth rise and fall between thy rosèd lips,
Coming and going with thy honey breath.   25
But, sure, some Tereus hath deflourèd thee,
And, lest thou shouldst detect him, cut thy tongue.
Ah ! now thou turn'st away thy face for shame ;
And, notwithstanding all this loss of blood,
As from a conduit with three issuing spouts,   30
Yet do thy cheeks look red as Titan's face

The fallacy here begins in the treatment of the two widely disparate æsthetic cases of a descriptive poem and a drama as if they were on exactly the same æsthetic footing.   In LUCRECE, as was remarked in the first edition of this book, Shakespeare has so elaborated the terrible tale as to make its psychic or spiritual aspect absolutely overlay the physical.   That figure of the trickling blood is touched-in where we look upon Lucretia self-slain : the long moral agony is done, and the tragic vision is one of mortal peace.   But the speech in TITUS is an intolerable expatiation on a living agony that would make men shriek to see.   " To see't mine eyes are blasted," cries Enobarbus at a spectacle of mere moral ignominy.   And we are asked to believe that it is " eminently characteristic " of the young Shakespeare *in drama* to revolt us with that simpering picture of the frightful face, the blood welling out " between thy *rosèd lips* " !   It seems sufficient here to meet one dogmatic assertion with another, and to say that such a violation of the most essential decencies of dramatic art is utterly alien to Shakespeare at any

> Blushing to be encountered with a cloud.
> Shall I speak for thee ? shall I say, 't is so ?
> O, that I knew thy heart ; and knew the beast,
> That I might rail at him to ease my mind !   35
> Sorrow concealèd, like an oven stopped,
> Doth burn the heart to cinders where it is.
> Fair Philomela, she but lost her tongue,
> And in a tedious sampler sewed her mind :
> But, lovely niece, that mean is cut from thee ;   40
> A craftier Tereus hast thou met withal,
> And he hath cut those pretty fingers off,
> That could have better sewed than Philomel.
> O ! had the monster seen those lily hands
> Tremble like aspen-leaves upon a lute,   45
> And make the silken strings delight to kiss them,
> He would not then have touched them for his life ;
> Or had he heard the heavenly harmony,
> Which that sweet tongue hath made,
> He would have dropp'd his knife and fell asleep   50
> As Cerberus at the Thracian poet's feet.
> Come, let us go and make thy father blind,
> For such a sight will blind a father's eye :
> One hour's storm will drown the fragrant meads ;
> What will whole months of tears thy father's eyes ?   55
> Do not draw back, for we will mourn for thee ;
> O, could our mourning ease thy misery !

period. When in LEAR he makes us shudder at the
horror of the blinding of Gloucester he absolutely
shrinks from any verbal equivalent, letting the horror
on the stage speak for itself. That in his rawest youth
he would have heaped that insufferable pile of pre-
ciosities on the hideous scene in TITUS, I at least am
quite unable to believe, counting it a vitally false
psychology that conceives the highest genius to emerge
from the grossest lack of artistic judgment.

Such a conception was long ago set forth in Germany.
Professor Parrott remarks (p. 16) that " German
scholars . . . have been somewhat inclined to scoff at
English prudery as the prime cause of the reluctance to
acknowledge " the authenticity of TITUS. Professor
Parrott is good enough to say that " the sneer is
undeserved." It is only the partial countenance lent
to the German æsthetes at points by such a critic that
withholds us from meeting the " sneer " with a strict
estimate of Teutonic taste in English poetry. After
the War, probably, German scholars will not be so much
disposed as formerly to see greatness in *Schrecklich-
keit.*

Further, the suggestion of Professor Parrott that the
movement of the verse in this speech is Shakespearean
is again an evasion of the style test. He found Shakespearean movement in the speech of Tamora, which is
thoroughly Peelean. If the movement here is that of
the young Shakespeare's verse, it is also that of the
verse of Greene, Lodge and Kyd ; and the only sound
conclusion would be that the young Shakespeare's
verse-movement was not differentiated from that of his
corrivals. But is that the case ? Let us take the first
scene in the COMEDY OF ERRORS, or the first in the
DREAM, or the first in LOVE'S LABOUR'S LOST. In the
first case we have three feminine endings in 156 lines ;
in the second, three (all in proper names) in the 170
blank lines down to the couplets ; and, in the third,
two feminine endings and five couplets in fifty lines.
But in the TITUS speech under notice, which is so inferior in *verve* of diction to all of these, we have three,

probably four, feminine endings in 46 lines.. The second line :—

> Cousin, a word, where is your husband ?

is imperfect, as is l. 49 :

> Which that sweet tongue hath made—

two flaws not likely to have been let pass by Shakespeare in his own work, corrected so carefully as this play is in general.   The second line was probably written :—

> Cousin, a word with you, where is your husband ?

If that were so, there would be a clear excess of double-endings for the young Shakespeare's serious work. But the vital tests are of course those of diction, style, and versification.   The young Shakespeare is diffuse as compared with the incomparable terseness of the mature Master ; but does he write of " stern[1] *ungentle* hands " committing hideous savageries ; or pen such ghastly inanities as :

> And, *notwithstanding all this loss of blood,*
> *As from a conduit with three issuing spouts,*
> Yet do *thy cheeks look red* as Titan's face,
> *Blushing to be encounter'd with a cloud.*
> Shall I speak for thee ? *Shall I say 'tis so ?*
> O that I knew thy heart, and knew the beast,
> That I might *rail at him, to ease my mind*

— ?   And is the end-stopped rhythm Shakespeare's at any age ?   Not to drag the issue further out, I submit that this bleating pathos is low in the scale for Greene or Kyd or Peele ; that Kyd improves on it in the SPANISH TRAGEDY ; and that the manner and the vein are the manner and vein of Kyd at his weakest, and of Peele in DAVID AND BETHSABE.   As we have seen and shall see further, the main run of the imagery is his.   The " sorrow concealed " passage, and the " cinders," point indeed to Greene ; and it is probable that the speech is a composite product of Kyd, Greene and Peele,

[1] " Stern " in Tudor days normally meant " cruel " or " fierce."

revised by the last, though it is difficult to think that three minds could miss seeing the egregious quality of the sentimentalism which makes the spectator expatiate elaborately and intolerably on *his own* disturbance in the face of the unspeakable thing before him.

As for verse-periods, it should suffice to refer the reader to those cited above, pp. 112-114 ; to twenty in Marlowe's signed works, in the TRUE TRAGEDIE of RICHARD DUKE OF YORK, and in the TROUBLESOME RAIGNE OF KING JOHN ; and to several in ARDEN OF FEVERSHAM (*e.g.* III, iii, v ; IV, i). It may not be amiss to add this from Peele (DAVID, III, iii, end) :—

> Friend him with deeds, and touch no hair of him—
> Not that fair hair with which the wanton winds
> Delight to play, and love to make it curl,
> Wherein the nightingales would build their nests,
> And make sweet bowers of every golden tress
> To sing their lover every night asleep.

§ 4

Here we have the vein of Marcus' speech, and the " ornaments." The movement is much the same, barring the double-endings ; and these could have been supplied in 1593 by either Kyd or Peele ; for even in DAVID, which is not a late work for Peele, though revised late, we get five in 40 lines (Act I, sc. ii)—seven if we reckon " tower " a dissyllable.

And while the metrical phenomena thus point to the pre-Shakespeareans, the classical allusions do so no less. It is true that the allusion to Pluto and Orpheus in the LUCRECE chimes in idea with that to " Cerberus at the Thracian poet's feet " in TITUS, though such a parallel might very well be set up by independent variants of a common tag. But once more we have the invariable contrast between terseness and point in the poem, where the allusion is fitting, and weak discursiveness in the play, where " the Thracian poet " is so inanely incongruous. If such a species of parallelism is " convincing " it is by reason of an inadequate critical method to start with. In this case the fair inference would be that Shakespeare had seen or heard the speech in TITUS, or such another, and transmuted the figure.

For the classical allusions in TITUS are emphatically in the taste of the pre-Shakespeareans. In LOCRINE (III, i), we have :

> O that I had the *Thracian Orpheus'* harp ;

and in the SPANISH TRADEDY (III, xiii, 115) :

> *The Thracian poet* thou shalt counterfeit.

Had Professor Parrott found " the Thracian poet " in LUCRECE, he would, I suspect, despite his statement, have been at least as sure that the phrase in TITUS was Shakespeare's. Why then, when it is found in the SPANISH TRAGEDY, should he not agree to assign it to Kyd, as to whose probable origination of the play he inclines to agree with me ? That kind of classical allusion abounds in Kyd, as in Peele, Greene, and Marlowe. For instances :—

> She, she herself, disguised in armour's mask,
> As Pallas was before proud Pergamas.
> > *S. T.*, I, iv, 19-20.
>
> My Bellimperia fall'n as Dido fell.
> > *Id.*, IV, v, 10.
>
> With love of me her thoughts are overgone
> More than was Phyllis with her Demophon.
> > *Soliman and Perseda*, III, ii, 40.
>
> [More][1] than Alexander sparèd warlike Thebes
> For Pindarus ; or than Augustus
> Spar'd[1] rich Alexandria for Arrius' sake
> > *Id.*, IV, ii, 56.
>
> Such fortune as the good Andromache
> Wish'd valiant Hector, wounded with the Greeks.
> > *Id.*, I, ii, 97.

When then we find in Kyd such another line as :—

> There, *pleasing Cerberus with honied speech*
> > (*S. T. Induc.*, l. 30.),

and note that in the other passage the task of the

---

[1] This word should probably stand at the end of the previous line.

Thracian poet was to charm " the triple-headed porter,"
we have simply no critical right to ascribe to Shakespeare the flaccid line under notice. The very test which
Professor Parrott puts as the weightiest rules out his
decision. While the verbal parallel between Kyd and
our play at this point is complete, the coincidence of
purport is also closer in Kyd's case than in that of the
line in LUCRECE.

Taking this double coincidence as decisive for at least
a part of the speech under notice, we are bound to consider the possibility that it is Kyd's as a whole, though
interpolated at points. And as a performance of Kyd's
it is quite intelligible, conforming as it does to his
peculiar psychosis, which in its way is scientifically as
interesting as that of the greater Marlowe. None of the
pre-Shakespeareans can imagine more vividly than
does Kyd at times ; but no one of equal occasional
power is more defective in imaginative co-ordination.
In ARDEN, his realism, in a key of prose, is almost as
notable as that of Shakespeare on the plane of poetry ;
but the co-ordinations are made by plot-mechanism,
not by imaginative fusion, and a series of æsthetic jolts
and jars is the consequence. When he writes verse,
the disjunction of his faculties is still more apparent.
In elegiac verse he is nearly always in falsetto, as if the
effort to produce poetry " switched-off " his sense of
reality, which functions on his prose side. Hence the
revolting incongruity between scene and comment
which we have been studying ; and which is so peculiarly un-Shakespearean.

It is hardly warrantable, again, to connect, as
Parrott does in a footnote, the " Titan's face, blushing "
of TITUS (sc. cited, ll. 31-32) with the " Titan . . . with
burning eye" in the VENUS (177-8). The poets of that
time, like their predecessors, were constantly alluding
to Titan.[1] Greene has " smiling Titan," and several

[1] One of the most memorable utterances of the Baconians is the pronouncement of Mr. Edwin Read (*Bacon and Shakespeare Parallelisms*, 1902, p. 284)
that " Both authors [Bacon and Shakespeare] call the sun by the *exceptional*
name of Titan." " Titan " was only a little less hackneyed than " Phoebus "
in pre-Shakespearean poetry, and in that of contemporary dramatists.

other mentions ; Peele has " Titan arm'd with fire,"
and " Titan . . . cloth'd in fiery-pointed beams " ; and
Kyd has :—

> Beyond the course of Titan's *burning* beams
> (*Sol. and Per.*, I, iv, 50),

besides the common " heaven's bright eye " (*id.* III,
i, 90), found (as is " Phoebus' eye ") in Peele (who has
" heaven's bright *eye burns*," D. AND B. I, i, 108) ;
in Greene, and in Kyd. And if the lamentable trope
of Titan's face " blushing to be encountered with a
cloud " is not Kyd's, it is assuredly not Shakespeare's.
I fancy it is Peele's.

§ 5

Coming to Act III, Professor Parrott, recognising
two hands in the first scene, challenges another comparative test when he says that " the new note begins
with the characteristically Shakespearean play on
words in ll. 89-91." They run in context (ll. 88-92)
thus :—

> *Marc.* O thus I found her, straying in the park,
> Seeking to hide herself as doth the deer
> That hath received some unrecuring wound.
> *Tit.* It was my deer, and he that wounded her
> Hath hit me more than had he killed me dead.

That a stale pun in a tragic speech should be reckoned
characteristically Shakespearean, in a theatre in which
everybody punned, seems hard measure for any sins
in that kind.   It would evidently be vain to suggest to
Professor Parrott that some of the bad puns in the
Shakespeare plays may be either actors' gags or survivals from adapted works ; and it is needless to
enlarge the debate at this point, seeing that the Professor proposes more or less confidently to assign to
Shakespeare these other items in TITUS speeches :—

1. ll. 12-22 (" touched up ")—because of the cognate passage in
Rich. II, III, ii, 146-7.

2. (" possibly ") l. 37 : *Therefore I tell my sorrows to the stones*, etc.
3. *Engine of her thoughts*, l. 82, which is duplicated in *V. and A.*, 367.
4. *Pleasing eloquence*, l. 83 ; because of similar endings of lines with " eloquence " in the *Two Gentlemen*, III, i, 83 ; *Dream*, v, i, 103 ; *Shrew*, II, i, 177 ; *R. and J.*, III, ii, 83.
5. Titus's figure of himself as *one upon a rock*, ll. 93-97.
6. " The weeping match proposed by Titus," ll. 122 sq., paralleled in *Richard II*, III, iii, 164 sq.
7. Titus's laments, l. 206 sq., 220 sq., because the " elaborate comparison between mortal grief and the wind-vexed sea finds a parallel even more elaborately worked out in *R. and J.*, III, v, 132 sq."
8. " The ugly figure of vomiting woes like a drunkard," l. 232, paralleled in *Lucrece*, l. 703.
9. " A possible insertion in the old work runs from l. 245 to l. 253, ending with the fine dramatic phrase :
   When will this fearful slumber have an end ? "
10. " The *starvèd snake* (l. 252) reappears in 2 *Hen. VI*, III, i, 343, a Shakespearean passage."

After this, concedes the Professor, " we have mainly the old-fashioned rant till the end of the scene." I have already given some reasons for regarding as part of the old-fashioned rant even what he certifies as Shakespearean ; and in omitting all reference to the parallel passages in Peele about pouring tears on the earth, weeping welkins, vexed seas, and so forth, the Professor, I fear, runs a risk of being charged with ignoring and suppressing important evidence against his opinion, though he seems to me entitled to praise for moderation in that he does not assign " a wilderness of tigers " to Shakespeare on the strength of the " wilderness of monkeys " in the MERCHANT OF VENICE. The trouble about his whole methods here, however, is that he is ready to see Shakespeare wherever there is a verbal parallel, and to exclude him where there is not, though the diction is much the same throughout. It is the " starvèd snake " that suggests to him an insertion including the lines :

Where life hath no more interest but to breathe,

and

When will this fearful slumber have an end ?—

already discussed. Concerning those lines, it must be left to the reader to say for himself whether they are not within the scope of any of the leading pre-Shakespeareans, who supply so many parallels to the first, and, as we shall see, one to the second. Concerning the " starvèd snake " there arises the new issue : How shall we determine the Shakespearean elements in the HENRY VI trilogy ? which problem, again, raises that other : How shall we prove that lines or phrases in RICHARD II and ROMEO AND JULIET, both demonstrably adaptations (there is some measure of consent as to ROMEO), and both probably shared in by Peele in their early forms, are not survivals from those forms ? I anticipate protest as to RICHARD II, and even ROMEO, though RICHARD was regarded as a recast by some critics even in the eighteenth century. But Professor Parrott grants, by implication, that Shakespeare's share in the HENRY VI plays was small ; and we may argue the point on that.

The long speech of York in 2 HENRY VI, III, i, is either a restoration or an expansion of that given in a curtailed form in the CONTENTION, where the " starvèd [=frozen] snake " passage does not appear. Is it then Shakespeare's ? If it be, he has within a year used " starvèd snake " in two different figures, this not long before using the HENRY VI figure without the " starvèd " but with the " sting the *heart* " in RICHARD II (III, ii, 131). The expanded speech of 51 blank lines in 2 HENRY VI has only four double-endings, which ill suits Professor Parrott's theory of Shakespeare's early practice, seeing that the style of the speech is so thoroughly Marlowesque. That it is by Marlowe would probably be the verdict of any student not committed to the theory of a close revision by Shakespeare ; and that the work is not Shakespeare's is surely proved by such lines as :

> Until the golden circuit on my head,
> Like to the glorious sun's *transparent* beams,
> Do calm the fury of this mad-bred flaw . . .
> And fought so long, till that his thighs with darts

> Were *almost* like the sharp-quilled porpentine ;
> And in the end being rescued I have seen
> Him caper upright like a wild Morisco . . ·

If there be any style-test at all, it is dead against the attribution of such verse and such diction to Shakespeare. On Professor Parrott's principles, it is to be feared, they are certified as his by the allusion to the porpentine, collated with HAMLET, I, v, 20 ; though how he can assign this speech to Shakespeare without giving him a great deal more in the HENRY VI plays, I cannot understand. The matter, then, must just be left to the suffrages of those who believe that Shakespeare *had* a style, and Marlowe another.

On the principle before posited, that duplications of phrase in TITUS and the VENUS, within a year, tell *against* the notion that Shakespeare penned both, we are led to reject as his the " engine of her thoughts " in the play ; and at the same time we dismiss the claim that Shakespeare wrote " blabb'd[1] them with such pleasing eloquence." The " saucy and audacious eloquence " of the DREAM and the " heavenly eloquence " of Romeo are of another mint.

Is the case then any better for the " one upon a rock " passage ? If we are to give any weight to the bare resemblance of lines ending upon the same word, as Professor Parrott does in respect of those ending on " eloquence," this is a Shakespearean line, for there are over a dozen in the Concordance ending in " rock " or " rocks " ; but he in turn should be led to suspect Shakespeare's hand in the already-cited passage of LOCRINE (II, i, 54) :

> For valiantness is like unto a rock
> That standeth in the waves of oceän ;
> Which though the billows beat on every side
> Yet it remaineth still unmovable—

to say nothing of Marlowe's

> I'll run to some rock
> And throw myself headlong into the sea
> (*Jew*, III, iv.)

[1] " Blab " is used as a poetic term in *The Troublesome Raigne of King John.*

and others en ling on the same word. In this case again we find the TITUS speech un-Shakespearean in respect of such diction as

> then fresh tears
> Stood on her cheeks, as doth the honey-dew
> Upon a gather'd lily *almost* wither'd.

And yet these are among the few lines of the play which Malone puts in inverted commas as probably Shakespeare's !

Again the image is partly an echo from the HENRY VI trilogy ; for in 3 H. VI, v, iv, 31, we have :

> Bestride the rock ; the tide will wash you off ;

and again we point to Marlowe as the probable author. If it be not his, but Shakespeare's, what are we to make of Meres's omission of all mention of these plays, in which, at this rate, there must be much more of Shakespeare than Professor Parrott finds in TITUS ?

This weighing of parallels as clues irrespectively of the contextual style may be concluded by noting the Professor's citation from ROMEO AND JULIET. There Capulet vehemently rates Juliet for counterfeiting " in one little body . . . a bark, a sea, a wind "—

> For still thy eyes, which I may call the sea,
> Do ebb and flow with tears ; the bark thy body is,
> Sailing in this salt flood ; the winds, thy sighs ;
> Who, raging with thy tears, and they with them,
> Without a sudden calm, will overset
> Thy tempest-tossèd body.

This may or may not be a redaction by Shakespeare of a previous author's work ; but the question need not here be raised. Between the styles of the two passages under consideration there is not the faintest resemblance. Capulet makes angry play with the *concetti* which were current coin in the poetry and drama of the day—figures used alike by Peele, Kyd, and Marlowe. If the passage is to implicate Shakespeare in TITUS in respect of the nature of the allusions, it equally implicates them ; the principle of discrimination, style, is ignored, in defiance of the critic's own professions. If there were any final validity in this mere collocation of *concetti*, the thesis ought to be changed from one of " superficial revision " by Shakespeare to one of his entire authorship ; for by this method he can be proved to have written the *whole* of TITUS, or, for that matter, of any other Elizabethan play. The obvious principles of style-comparison which deter Professor Parrott from assigning to him a Peelean speech (I, 70). where " mourning weeds " points to 3 HENRY VI (III, iii, 229 ; IV, i, 134), serve to veto the whole list of trifling analogies which we have been considering. As on the larger grounds, so on the smaller, the case breaks down. When all is said, however, it is but an attempt to trace steps in an admittedly " superficial revision " of a play not written by Shakespeare.

§ 6

The remainder of Professor Parrott's argument runs chiefly to inferences from analogy of phrase, on the lines of Professor Collins, and ascriptions made on the basis of his mistaken assumption as to Shakespeare's early use of double-endings. (I) He sticks to the parallel of " sorrow-wreathen knot " and " his arms in this sad knot "[1] ; and adds the line of Lucrece (1662) :—

> With sad set eyes and wretched arms across,

saying nothing of the closer parallels from Peele and Greene ; and actually stresses (2) " map of woe " (TITUS, III, i, 12)—a kind of phrase constantly used by the pre-Shakespeareans—because of " map of death " in LUCRECE (402). In the same connection, disregarding the parallel from Peele, he accepts as

[1] Above, p. 99.

Shakespearean (3) the counsel of Titus to Lavinia to make a hole against her heart, because it is " hardly more absurd " than Lucretia's lines, 135-8. Diction goes for nothing. And all this *because* in the scene in question, lacking from the quartos, the 11 per cent. of double-endings " suggest Shakespeare's hand "— the hand which years afterwards wrote 1 HENRY IV with only 5 per cent. For the same reason (4) " the episode of the *poor harmless fly* is too fancifully pathetic for any one but Shakespeare " ; and (5) the " read sad stories " parallel to RICHARD II, III, ii, 155-6, is taken as decisive, without a glance at the question whether the RICHARD II passage is a remnant of Peele, whose " sit . . . and tell a heavy tale " is in the very cadence. Nor does it ever occur to the Professor to wonder whether Shakespeare was likely to duplicate formulas exactly as did Peele and the rest, within the space of a year or two.

Applying his fallacious test wherever he can, the Professor decides that IV, i, cannot have any Shakespeare in it because there are only about $2\frac{1}{2}$ per cent. of double endings. Yet, just here, we find the diction keyed up to a higher pitch of concision than in the passages where the false clue has hitherto led him to look for Shakespeare. In the next scene he feels that he *must* find some Shakespeare because the double-endings rise to over $9\frac{1}{2}$ per cent., though he has " not been able to find *many* Shakespearean parallels in the scene," and cites none. Of (6) the " rest in her un-rest," which is a tag of Kyd's, he disposes by pointing to RICHARD III, IV, iv, 29 :

Rest thy unrest on England's lawful earth.

It does not occur to him to ask whether *that* line, with the next,

Unlawfully made drunk with innocents' blood

is really Shakespeare's. Then we have this summa-tion : " *If* Shakespeare borrowed the phrase [rest-unrest] once from Kyd, he may have done so again, and that he did not disdain to borrow from Kyd *is shown by the whole play of* HAMLET "—HAMLET, in which Shakespeare has left only so much of Kyd's diction standing as serves to corroborate the otherwise strong inference that the play was originally his.

(7) Led by the lure of the double-endings, the Professor looks for some Shakespearean diction, and finds it, with two double-endings to six lines, in Aaron's address to Demetrius and Chiron (ll. 116-121) :

> Why, there's the privilege your beauty bears :
> Fie, treacherous hue, that will betray with blushing
> The close enacts and counsels of the heart.
> Here's a young lad framed of another leer :
> Look how the black slave smiles upon the father,
> As who shall say, ' Old lad, I am thine own.'

It seems warrantable to say that in a scene with no other double-endings these lines would hardly have struck the Professor as Shakespearean. He sees no such quality in Aaron's previous rants, ll. 88-111, because there there is only one double-ending. But in the previous portion of the scene there are eleven double-endings to 80 complete lines, or over 13 per cent., and there the Professor finds no Shakespeare, unless it be the " rest-unrest " tag. What then is the value of the test ? Upon his theory, Shakespeare must have put the double-endings there !

In the passage quoted we have the noun plural " enacts," which occurs nowhere else in the plays or poems. If I found that noun in Greene I should be inclined to surmise that he wrote this as well as the rest of the scene, since half a dozen clues of trope and tag point to him, and the whole is somewhat in the manner of his previous work in the play, though not in his normal style. It is more likely to be Marlowe's. But whoever be the author, it is surely not Shakespeare. And the scene is of a piece. As for the double-endings, Greene reaches 12 per cent. in his part of EDWARD III ; and the reasonable inference is that he did revision work on TITUS near his end.

(8) It appears to be again the false clue of the double-endings that leads the Professor to find Shakespeare's hand in the speech of Marcus, III, iii, 70.   It is of a piece with what goes before, but, like the speech last cited from Aaron, it has two double-endings in six lines.   There is absolutely nothing else to recommend it.   One should be sorry to resist the Professor's plea (9) for Shakespeare's penning of the clown's " God forbid I should be so bold to press into heaven in my young days " ;   but when he further claims the malapropisms, which are of a piece with hundreds in the clown scenes of Greene and Peele, he loses hold.   The clown's phrase was probably a current jest.

(10) Scene iv of Act IV having about 8 per cent. of double-endings, Shakespeare is held to intervene at the outset because the opening lines form a " suggestive parallel " to 2 HENRY VI, IV, ix, 1-6.   The " Was ever seen " and " Was ever king " do suggest one hand ;   but I cannot assent to Professor Parrott's decision that the latter speech is by Shakespeare. Like the speech of Saturninus under notice, it is much more like Marlowe, to whom it has several verbal and phrasal clues, as well as a strong kinship of manner. When with such vocabulary clues (as ' an if,' ' disturbers of our peace,' ' buz,' ' scrolls ') we note such a formal echo as that between the TITUS line :

What's this but libelling against the senate ?

and one in EDWARD II (II, ii, 34) :

What call you this but private libelling
Against the Earl of Cornwall and my brother ?

there is fairly strong ground for surmising one hand. Even the slight echo between the TITUS phrase (l. 26) " the proud'st conspirator that lives " and that in the same scene of the other (l. 42) : " the proudest peer of Brittany," is in the general connection noteworthy.   And so again in the echo :—

Sweet scrolls to fly about the streets of Rome ;
Titus, l. 16.

> Libels are cast against thee in the street.
>
> *Edward II*, ii, iii.

> Give it me—I'll have it published in the streets.
>
> *Id.*, i, iv.

Scroll, as before noted, is a frequent word in Marlowe, albeit also with Greene. But a comparison of the manner, movement and key of the two scenes first compared, and of the analogy of the pacifying speeches of Tamora and Isabel, may go even further to suggest that Marlowe wrote the TITUS scene about the time he was working on EDWARD II. If it be not Marlowe's, it is the work of a very zealous imitator ; and those who are unable to conceive Shakespeare under that category might speculatively suggest that it could be part of the latest work of Greene on the play, since there are verbal clues to him also (' extent,' ' what an if,' ' proud'st conspirator.') The sole reason for assigning the scene to Shakespeare, as Professor Parrott admits, is its energy ; and that, surely, is a clue to Marlowe. In any case, the Professor will not say that the whole scene is Shakespeare's. " Here, as elsewhere, he is revising older work." In this connection he " neglects or suppresses " the fact that the passage on the eagle and the little birds which, with Professor Collins, he brackets with the LUCRECE passage on the falcon and the fowl, has closer parallels in Marlowe. Why cite one and ignore the others ? The hanging of the clown, be it noted, is in the taste of Greene (LOOKING-GLASS, second-last scene), and this episode comes between the speeches of Saturninus.

(11) The fatality of Professor Parrott's ' method ' is again exemplified over Act V, of which the first scene " shows the highest percentage [of double-endings] in the play, something over 20. Shakespeare *has evidently been at work here*, BUT *there is little characteristic poetry by which to identify his hand.*" It is the usual fatal dilemma. The high percentage points, when we have rightly traced the evolution of the

double-ending, to Marlowe ; and to Marlowe the speeches of Aaron are assignable both for style and for substance. But that too must go to Shakespeare, in fulfilment of a mistaken theory.

> (12) " In the next scene, v, ii, the percentage drops to about 6. This would indicate that Shakespeare had not greatly concerned himself with this scene, and, in fact, it belongs structurally to the old play with its preparation for the Thyestean banquet. It is written for the most part in flat low-toned blank verse, not unlike that of Peele in his less excited—one can hardly say inspired—moments."

This is quite satisfactory, despite the false premiss ; but Professor Parrott takes as a " sign " of Shakespeare's entrance the passage (53-57) beginning

> And when thy car is loaden with their heads,

where the " servile footman " becomes in HENRY V (IV, i, 289-93) the " lackey " who

> Doth rise and help Hyperion to his horse.

A parallel, a retouching, there certainly is ; but it consists in Shakespeare's transmutation (in a speech written, as I contend, years before 1599, with but two double-endings—apart from the three accidental cases of ' ceremony '—in fifty-five lines) of a passage in TITUS penned by Marlowe or Kyd. It was not Shakespeare who wrote " when thy car is loaden with their heads " ; any more than the concluding lines of the speech, which the Professor does not venture to assign to him, though the speech is quite homogeneous.

(13) After all the iteration of the thesis as to double-endings being the fundamental clue, yet further ascriptions are made to Shakespeare in this scene of low percentage. That of " miserable, mad mistaking eyes "—perhaps the most interesting of all the phrasal parallels—is discussed in a later section.[1] That of the

---

[1] In connection with the *Taming of the Shrew*.

" spring whom you have stain'd with mud " (l. 171) and the LUCRECE line (577) :

> Mud not the fountain that gave drink to thee,

is on all fours with the previously discussed parallels between TITUS and the VENUS. The poem echoes and transmutes the line in the play ; and to decide once more, as does Professor Parrott, that Shakespeare would use such a figure twice within a year, is to put him on a level, for resource, with Peele.

(14) At the close of Professor Parrott's essay, his double-ending clue is again racked :—

> " The last scene of the play shows a percentage rising to over 13." Yet " it cannot be original with Shakespeare, as it is connected structurally with the preceding ; but he seems to have revised it *rather thoroughly*. I *fancy* the colloquy between Saturnine and Titus just before the killing of Lavinia is his. The mistaken version of the story of Virginia implied in l. 38 is more likely to be Shakespeare's than Peele's, Greene's, or even Kyd's. The emphatic rhymed couplets, ll. 61-2 and 65-6, may also be his. But his hand is more plainly visible in the long speeches, beginning with l. 67, where Marcus and Lucius rehearse in turn the whole story of the play. The opening simile in the speech of Marcus finds a parallel in MIDSUMMER NIGHT'S DREAM, III, ii, 20-4."

Here, perhaps, the false theory of the double-endings may be seen to have committed suicide. There are eleven double-endings in the first 44 lines ; and therefore it is that, utterly un-Shakespearean as they are, Professor Parrott " fancies " they may be the work of the Master. They are among the most leaden in the play. The suggestion that Shakespeare was the likeliest person to distort the story of Virginia is a desperate expedient. When we find in the archaic ALPHONSUS EMPEROR OF GERMANY, admitted by Professor Parrott[1] to belong originally to the same period, the line :

> Then like Virginius, will I kill my child

---

[1] " I firmly believe , ... that the play was originally composed at the time when Marlowe, Greene, Kyd, and Peele dominated the stage." Introd. to *Alphonsus* in ed. of Chapman's Tragedies, 1910, p. 609.

—also in a scene (IV, iii) with a high percentage of double-endings (15+)—we are pointed to a general parallel of style, matter, and manner. Hedewick, like Lavinia, is there slain by her father as *having been* dishonoured, and he says he acts "like Virginius." Professor Parrott will certainly not suggest that the ALPHONSUS scene is by Shakespeare ; and I trust he will not argue that the academic group (Marlowe, Peele, Greene, and Kyd ?) who first put together the ALPHONSUS play were misled about the Virginia story by Shakespeare ! Marlowe assuredly wrote the first scene of ALPHONSUS, and he was dead when Shakespeare, on Professor Parrott's theory, "revised" TITUS. A mere perusal of that " Virginius " scene in ALPHONSUS might reveal to any open-minded reader that it is produced by the school who concocted TITUS, and that there is not a touch of Shakespeare in the scene-section of TITUS under notice.

(15) That Professor Parrott should be willing to assign to him such lines as 61-62, 65-66 :—

> Baked in that pie
> Whereof their mother daintily hath fed,
> Eating the flesh that she herself hath bred,

and

> Can the son's eye behold his father bleed ?
> There's meed for meed, death for a deadly deed,

is even at this stage of the debate surprising, there being at this point no lure of double-endings to mislead him. Such couplets were within the power of any of the old group.

(16) In the speeches of Marcus and Lucius which follow, the Professor claims Shakespeare's intervention first on the score of the parallel between

> By uproar sever'd, like a flight of fowl
> Scatter'd by winds and high tempestuous gusts

and

> As wild geese that the creeping fowler eye,
> Or russet-pated choughs, many in sort,
> Rising and cawing at the gun's report,
> *Sever* themselves, and madly sweep the sky.
> *Mid. N. Dream*, III, ii, 21-24.

Here, doubtless, there is a real echo ; and here as in every similar echo above discussed we find a clear and well-framed image in the lines of the young Shake-speare, as against a less clear and concise diction and imagery in the TITUS passage. There the scattered fowl become immediately " scattered corn " which is to be " knit *again* " into " one mutual sheaf." And our comment must be the same : this is not even the prentice Shakespeare's diction. The young poet in his play echoes and *transcends* the work of his pre-decessor. (17) Only the statistical pressure, on the other hand, could make the Professor hesitate to assign to Peele the lines about Troy and Sinon, ver-bally paralleled in his TALE OF TROY,[1] and incline to think that perhaps " Shakespeare was here copying a printed work of his esteemed[2] contemporary." Where the young Shakespeare echoes his predecessor, once more, he transcends him : here the echo is weaker than the weak original. It is Peele's own.

Only in two cases, I think, does Shakespeare in copy-ing a contemporary fail to excel him. The first is his repetition of two lines of Greene in the Sonnets, where he is in effect *quoting*, for a contemporary.[3] The other is his version of Marlowe's reiterated stroke (FAUSTUS, v, iii) :—

> Was this the face that launched a thousand ships
> And burnt the topless towers of Ilium

—" mighty " lines very hard to beat. Marlowe had begun (2 TAMB, II, iv) with :

> Helen, whose beauty summoned Greece to arms
> And drew a thousand ships to Tenedos ;

and after writing :

> Sweet Helen, make me immortal with a kiss,

---

[1] See next ch., section on " Traces of Peele."
[2] Esteemed, that is, by Nashe, who in his preface to Greene's *Menaphon* extols Peele by way of belittling Marlowe. Shakespeare could judge better.
[3] See below, discussion on *Edward III*.

in FAUSTUS, used the latter phrase again[1] in DIDO
(IV, iv). Where Marlowe had thus been charmed by his
own lines, Shakespeare was not unresponsive, but he
was content (TROILUS, II, ii, 83) with :

> Whose *price* hath launched *above* a thousand ships,
> And turned crowned kings to merchants—

a modest salute to the " dead shepherd " whom he
would not seem to emulate. But not thus could he
comport himself to Peele.

In the speech of Lucius, which follows, there are four
double-endings (Kyd's ?) in sequence :—

> Then noble auditory, be it known to you
> That cursed Chiron and Demetrius
> Were they that murderèd our emperor's brother ;
> And they it were that ravishèd our sister ;
> For their fell faults our brothers were beheaded ;
> Our father's tears despised, and basely cozen'd
> Of that true hand that fought Rome's quarrel out.

They ought to be Shakespeare's, on the Professor's
theory ; his hand is declared to be " more plainly
visible " in the speeches than in the couplets cited.
Are they then his ? Did he, in order to produce double-
endings, write more poorly than even the average of
the play ? Again and again, in an argument which
assumes that Shakespeare is traceable by superiorities,
we are thus in effect invited to credit him with inferiorities.

The fatality holds to the close of the Professor's
essay. When he decides (18) that the speech of Lucius
to his boy over the dead body of Titus " is in the same
vein of somewhat sentimental pathos that we have
already noted as Shakespeare's," some of us must needs
reply that *we* have not so noted it ; that there is no
such feeble pathos in the genuine plays, or in the poems ;
and that at no stage is Shakespeare to be supposed to

---

[1] It does not follow, of course, that *Dido* as a whole is later than *Faustus*.
There are several signs of additions.

have thought that he improved even TITUS ANDRONICUS
by such lines as :

> Come hither, boy ; come, come and learn of us
> To melt in showers . . .
> Shed yet some small drops from thy tender spring,
> *Because kind nature doth require it so :*
> *Friends should associate friends in grief and woe.*

And when (19) the Professor follows up that ascription
with the claim that " the last speech of Aaron and the
casting out of Tamora's body are *borrowed* from the
JEW OF MALTA, *which Shakespeare had used before to help
out his revision,*" we reply that, the previous proposition
as to borrowing from the JEW being wholly arbitrary,
this must be dismissed with it, as will be later shown.
(20) The casting out of Tamora's body is a bald repetition of the casting out of Estrild's body in LOCRINE ;
and the idea that Shakespeare could do no better
than outgo the platitude of Peele in such platitude as :

> Her life was beast-like, and devoid of pity ;
> And, being so shall have like want of pity,

must be regarded as one more instance of the ensnaring
effect of Professor Parrott's fatal misconception as to
the evolution of double-endings.   He ends by assigning
to Shakespeare, on that false assumption, two of the
deadest lines in the play.   It might well be that Shakespeare inserted something in the last scene by way of
elucidating the dénouement : it is impossible that he
should have inserted *that*.   And the clearing-up of the
story by speeches at the close, which the Professor
seems to indicate as a likely task for Shakespeare, is
entirely in the way of the pre-Shakespearean drama,
from the SPANISH TRAGEDY to ALPHONSUS OF GERMANY.

§ 7

When, finally, the Professor claims that his ascriptions are supported by Justice Madden's DIARY OF
MASTER SILENCE, because " with hardly an exception,

the passages which Madden cites as Shakespearean occur in scenes where I had already on other grounds detected his hand," we must again demur. In a later section it is pointed out that the express thesis of Justice Madden as to Shakespeare's lack of sympathy with bear-baiting tells *against* the ascription to him of the line (v, i, 102) :—

> As true a dog as ever fought at head.

But the bulk of Justice Madden's *à priori* argument on TITUS' only serves to illustrate the danger of that method. He actually takes the panther-and-hart hunt (I, 493) at Rome, in the first Act, as indicating Shakespeare's sport-loving vein because (1) Aaron " digresses to the falconer's art " in such a phrase as " mount her pitch," and (2) *in* the panther-and-hart-hunt scene there are allusions to striking a doe. If truth to fact be the mark of Shakespeare's treatment of sport, how came he to graft these allusions on the central absurdity? Would not the theory call for a substitution by him of something huntable for Peele's panther ? As it happens, Professor Parrott expressly rejects as Peelean the speech of Aaron in which Justice Madden sees Shakespeare because of the phrase " mount her pitch " ; and as to the rest of the scene the Professor goes no further than suggesting that if there be anything of Shakespeare it is " the *characteristically* Shakespearean reference to *poaching* [an assumption of legend as biography], and the *double entendre* in the phrase *hit it*," adding, " But I would not go to the stake even for this passage as authentically Shakespeare's." Where then is the concurrence between the Professor's results and those of Justice Madden which the former claims ?

Dr. Madden cites, apparently as bearing out his general thesis, the egregious speech of Marcus (II, ii, 20-22), so plainly Peele's work :

> I have dogs, my lord,
> Will rouse *the proudest panther in the chase*,
> And climb the *highest promontory* top.

---

¹ Work cited, 2nd ed. pp. 317-322.

Professor Parrott, having no double-endings here to
lead him astray, recognises that that is not a kind of
hunting conceivable by the youth from Warwickshire.
But where then is the concurrence of results ?   It
emerges only over the parallel from the VENUS about the
" chase in the skies."   But Professor Parrott did not
reach *that* ascription by his clue of double-endings,
which he declares to be the basis of his case.   He
founds on it simply as a clue of parallel, though, on his
own principle, there ought to be no Shakespeare in a
section so bare of double-endings.

In Tamora's reply to the insulting address of Bassianus, Justice Madden finds support for his general
thesis in the line :

> Should drive upon thy new-transformed limbs,

explaining that " drive " is " to this day a technical
term of the hunting language."   Does that then make
the passage Shakespeare's ?   Professor Parrott, as we
have seen, gets no clue here on his own theory, but pronounces the scene " dramatically appropriate," and
" lively."   Apparently he has accepted Justice Madden's clue in the absence of any of his own.   But this is
not a case of concurrent results from independent
methods ; it is a mere acceptance by one critic of the
arbitrary inference of another.

The Note on TITUS is really the weakest section in
Justice Madden's interesting and suggestive book.
With Professor Parrott and some people who have no
theories to grind, he finds something " Shakespearean "
in the trivial pun on " deer," as if Shakespeare were a
monopolist alike of bad puns and of animal names and
hunting terms.   Had he found in TITUS Marlowe's
lines on the hart and yelping hounds (EDWARD II, i, i)
he would have been practically bound to hold them
Shakespeare's ; and so with

> I have the jesses that will pull you down
> (*Id.* II, ii.)

or any other allusion to falconry in the drama of Shakespeare's contemporaries. By his method ARDEN must be Shakespeare's because of Arden's dream about the "toil pitched to overthrow the deer," III, iii, 7, and

> the longing water-dog
> That coucheth till the fowling piece be off,
> Then seizeth on the prey with eager mood.

By the same clue, EDWARD III must be Shakespeare's because of the lines (III, v, 46-47) :

> And dare a falcon when she's in her flight
> And ever after she'll be haggard-like.

To urge the few TITUS allusions to hunting, hounds, does, "images borrowed from country life," and poaching, and the pun on "deer," as amounting to a rebuttal of Hallam's *res ipsa per se vociferatur*, is only to arouse an indestructible doubt as to the value of the sport test in any play.

At the close of his Note on TITUS Dr. Madden asks : "If Shakespeare had no part in the composition, what induced the editors to print it as his ? The poorer the play, the less the temptation to foist it on the public as his." The answer to this argument has been given above. The ascription of the play to Shakespeare, in respect of his mere revision, was the only way for the players to preserve their copyright. On the other hand, the previous publishers, who had the strongest temptation to affix Shakespeare's name to the quartos in order to sell them, never did so. Justice Madden forgets, too, that a bad play can be very popular, and as such "valuable."

It remains to consider the suggestion made by Dr. Garnett, as noted in the introduction, with regard to parallels of phrase between the TITUS lines (v, iii, 76, 116) :—

> Do shameful execution on herself . . .
> But soft, methinks, I do digress too much,

and two in RICHARD II and HAMLET,

As to the very moderate claim which Dr. Garnett
makes for the entrance of the hand of Shakespeare, while
I admit the clear likelihood that he may have added
some touches, I find myself unable to see any truly
Shakespearean quality in the two lines cited. The first
occurs in a speech which not only contains a mosaic
of phrases from one of Peele's signed poems, but seems
to me Peelean from end to end, howbeit perhaps revised
and condensed by Shakespeare. I have re-examined
every line in the plays in which the word " execution "
occurs ; they number forty-five. The only passages
in which there is any near resemblance to that under
notice are these :—

Do execution on the watch.	1 *Henry VI*, III, ii, 35.
Is execution done on Cawdor ?	*Macbeth*, 1, iv, 1.
To do some fatal execution.	*Titus*, II, iii, 36.
Do execution on my flesh and blood.	*Id.* IV, ii, 84.

The first occurs in a play certainly non-Shakespearean
in the main if not entirely ; the third and fourth occur
in TITUS itself. If the line cited by Dr. Garnett be held
Shakespeare's, does it not follow that these are presumably his also ? If these be *not* his, why should we
suppose that to be his ? There remains to be considered the real parallel between the line cited from
TITUS and one in RICHARD II (II, i, 66) :—

> That England that was wont to conquer others
> Hath made a shameful conquest of itself.

Here the resemblance is indeed striking ; and several
primary surmises are open.
    1. Possibly the same hand originated both plays ; *or*,
    2. One imitates the other ; in which case it may be
that either
    (*a*) The RICHARD II line copies that in TITUS, the
earlier play, *or*
    (*b*) Shakespeare, revising TITUS for the press, either
made a first use of the tag which he was later to repeat
in RICHARD, or inserted a passage repeating what he
had already written there. Hesitating over such

hypotheses, we may revert to (1), in the form of the question,

3. Whether the lines in RICHARD may not be one of the remnants of non-Shakespearean matter in an earlier form of that play, the work, as I have claimed to show elsewhere, mainly of Marlowe, and perhaps in part of Peele ?

The problem is complicated by the fact that both passages are instances of a common trope, derived from Lucan or some other classic source. Marlowe in his version of Lucan's First Book has :—

> Wars worse than civil on Thessalian plains,
> And outrage strangling law, and people strong,
> We sing, whose conquering swords their own breasts lanced . . .
> Rome, if thou take delight in impious war,
> First conquer all the earth, then turn thy force
> Against thyself.

This, written some time before April, 1593, was not printed till 1600. But before Marlowe, and independently of him, the sentiment had dramatic currency. In the JOCASTA of Gascoigne and his friends (1566) occur the lines :—

> Seeing the town, seeing my flesh and blood,
> Against itself to levy threatening arms.   I, i, 8-9.

JOCASTA had no stage life, but in later plays privately or publicly staged we have the same sentiment, with iteration :—

> A Kingdom's hand hath gored a Kingdom's heart.
> T. Hughes, *Misfortunes of Arthur*, 1588, III, iii, 25.

Spenser in THE RUINES OF ROME (1591) has the line (st. 21) :—

> Her power itself against itself did arm.

In Lodge's WOUNDS OF CIVIL WAR, published in 1594, probably written before 1590, there are several lines of precisely similar purport (ll. 279, 292, 307-8, 328-9) :—

> What then are men that 'gainst themselves do war . . .
> . . . Thou dost raze and wound thy city Rome . . .
> For they that spread her glory through the world
> Are they that tear her proud triumphant plumes . . .
> Must they that reared her stately temples up
> Deface the sacred places of their gods ?

Again from an independent source, in Kyd's translation of Garnier's CORNÉLIE, published in 1595, we have :—

> [Rome] whose power
> Could never have been curb'd but by itself.
> > Act I, Sc. i.

> For thou that wont'st to tame and conquer all
> Art conquer'd now with an eternal fall.
> > Act III, S. ii, 10-11.

> Accursèd Rome, that arm'st against thyself . . .
> Thy children gainst thy children thou hast arm'd.
> O Rome, accursèd Rome, thou murd'rest us
> And massacrest thyself . . .

> Shall Rome, that hath so many overthrown,
> Now make herself a subject to her own ?
> > *Id.*, IV, i, 1, 4, 13-14, 161-2.

And in Jonson's CATILINE (1611) we have the passages :

> Why must Rome
> Be by itself now overcome ?
> > Act I, Sc. i, Chorus at end.

> Since they have sought to blot the name of Rome
> Out of the world, and raze this glorious empire
> With her own hands and arms turned on herself.
> > Act V, Sc. 6.

Evidently the sentiment was a widely current commonplace, and as such it can hardly be pronounced in any form signally Shakespearean. I at least feel in no way driven to ascribe either the TITUS or the RICHARD lines to Shakespeare, finding it easier to conceive Marlowe or

Peele doing both sets, or, at the worst, to credit Shakespeare with echoing another's TITUS lines in RICHARD
II.

On the other hand, the first inference—which will
naturally be drawn in the form " Both plays by Shakespeare," by the maintainers of the traditional view—is
in that form overborne by the argument of the following
treatise, to which I invite their critical attention. That
argument was accepted by Dr. Garnett, who drew the
inference numbered 2 (*b*). I have shown that it would
tend to carry us further, and plunge us again in the
morass of perplexity set up by taking TITUS ANDRONI-
CUS as a work of Shakespeare. The simplest way out
would be the acceptance of inference 2 (*a*). I confess
to finding that unacceptable for two main reasons.
Firstly, the closing lines of the speech of Gaunt in
RICHARD II represent a marked weakening of the previous diction, the last two in particular—

> Ah, would the scandal vanish with my life,
> How happy then were my ensuing death—

being singularly feeble and Peelean, though they *may*
be Marlowe's. Secondly, I have maintained—apart
altogether from this particular problem—that RICHARD
II is a recast by Shakespeare of a previous play of which
Marlowe was main author and Peele perhaps part
author. On that issue let the critical reader decide for
himself ; the particular issue does not really turn upon
it, unless on the view that Shakespeare was inveterately
given to echoing himself.

The second parallel, between Lucius's

> But soft ! methinks I do digress too much

and a passage in the ghost's speech in HAMLET :

> But soft ! methinks I scent the morning air :
> Brief let me be,

is again undoubtedly a real resemblance ; and as there
are very many lines in Shakespeare beginning " But

soft ! " that of Lucius might on that score be his, despite
its relative limpness.   We may leave it at that.   But
I would remind the reader that " But soft " is a very
common formula in the pre-Shakespearean drama. *E.g.*:

> This is the door ; *but soft, methinks 'tis shut.*
> *Arden of Feversham*, III, ii, 34.

It is finally noteworthy that we thus find " But soft,
methinks," in three speeches all reasonably attributable
to one hand—for the HAMLET line, which occurs in the
First Quarto, savours strongly of the old play, though
it comes just after an insertion by Shakespeare ; and
the speech of Lucius as a whole is far too poor to be his,
with its end-stopped lines.

CHAPTER VI

The Problem Inductively Considered

The alleged external and internal evidences for the Shakespearean authorship of Titus having thus alike collapsed on examination, it behoves us, not to give judgment by default, but to make an independent survey of the whole case in order to have a right to a final judgment. It remains thus far an open question whether the passages clearly paralleled in Shakespeare's poems are of his insertion in Titus, or are echoed by him thence ; and whether the passages clearly paralleled in some of his early plays are there penned by him, or are survivals of the diction of playwrights whose work he revised or adapted.

In forming our opinion it is well to face at the outset the final issue. By common consent Titus is the most horrible play in the whole Elizabethan drama. The young Burns and his less-gifted but worthy brother, it may be remembered, passionately refused to hear it read to them.[1] Besides a string of assassinations, it includes a human sacrifice ; the slaying of a son by his father ; a brutish rape committed by two princes with the consent of their mother ; the cutting-out of the tongue and lopping-off of the hands of the victim, who appears on the stage immediately with her violators ; and the cutting off, by a trick, of one hand of her father, the central character ; who in turn, having caused the violators to be bound and gagged, cuts their throats (their victim holding with her arms

---

[1] It may be that this youthful revolt from work ascribed to Shakespeare had something to do with Burns's lifelong lukewarmness on the plays, upon which Mr. Henley insists. Such a devotee of Byron as was Mr. Henley, however, should have noted that that poet too was an anti-Shakespearean. See Dr. James Kennedy's *Conversations on Religion with Lord Byron*, 1830, p. 156. William Morris is said also to have been an " anti."

the basin for their blood) ; whereafter their heads are baked by him and his daughter in pies, of which their guilty mother partakes. To complete the odious circle, the ravished heroine had beforehand found the other woman, the Empress of Rome, in the company of a Moor, and had commented on the situation in the language of the pot-house ; whence the manner of the revenge. If this play be the first work of Shakespeare, we are shut up to the conclusion that he who of all the dramatists of his age developed the most exquisite taste, began by exhibiting the very worst ; that he who most profoundly spiritualised tragedy began by brutalising it beyond the utmost measure of his competitors. Is it probable ?

And if, again, holding him to have merely revised the play for his company, we find embedded here and there in the piece passages which are undoubtedly paralleled in his poems and some of the early plays, and which are distinctly in the bad poetical taste of some of the school whose work he was revising, does it follow that he is to be held as having inserted these passages in TITUS and the early plays, because of the parallels in the poems ?   Is it likely that he *duplicated* passages, some of which are themselves duplicates of *clichés* in his predecessors ?

§ I. PRELIMINARY SCIENTIFIC TESTS

Certainly the *à priori* improbabilities must not determine the issue. Let us then, having seen how entirely inconclusive is the argument put forward for Shakespeare's authorship, first examine the whole drift of the internal evidence. As against the random tests applied by the traditionists, and the false test propounded by Professor Parrott, let us formulate all the real tests that the problem admits of, first putting a few necessary caveats.

    I. The presence even of one or two " superior " passages would not prove original authorship by the superior hand. That may have merely made additions, as Professor Parrott maintains.

2. By the virtual admission of the traditionists, bare resemblances of idea between a few passages in TITUS and passages even in undisputed Shakespearean plays and poems prove nothing. If Shakespeare is at times imitative in other plays, he may have echoed phrases from so popular a play as TITUS. But parallels between TITUS and other *disputed* plays are evidence rather against than for Shakespeare's authorship.

3. Those who argue that a few passages in the play are discernibly " Shakespearean," cannot go on to claim on that score that the whole play is so.

On the other hand, the authorship of any anonymous or disputed drama is not to be settled by mere occasional parallels of epigram or saw. Such parallels abound in Elizabethan literature, the tags of Lilly's EUPHUES, in particular, being current in all directions. We have to inquire how far a given writer is wont to echo others, and how far to echo himself. Greene, for instance, does both in an uncommon degree ; frequently repeating (as does Lodge) many of the saws of EUPHUES,[1] and as frequently formulas of his own. Kyd is a great copyist of Marlowe, and an echoer of himself. Peele, again, is notably given to repeating turns of expression of his own which have no epigrammatic quality. Marlowe comes under the same description, and is to be noted as copying Spenser in the printed TAMBURLAINE. Greene and Peele, again, were clearly much impressed by both Spenser and Marlowe, and imitate Marlowe's manner as well as adopt many of his terms. The sound clues to identification are, broadly speaking, first and foremost *versification* ; then frequent use of particular phrases, general or frequent notes of manner and mannerism, peculiarities of vocabulary, tics of style, and forms of phrase which are *not* noticeably epigrammatic in

---

[1] One phrase of Lilly's about the high soaring of the hobby hawk is repeated *ad nauseam* by Greene and Lodge.

character, though certain epigrammatic tags are much used by several writers.

As against the risks of error in ascription, obviously, we must apply the cardinal test of style wherever it can be brought to bear. It is unhappily much open to dispute, style being so often confused with substance, as in the case of a number of the inferences from parallels above discussed. But the student who is convinced that there is a Shakespearean style, even in the early plays, will never consent to let any apparent clues of phrase or vocabulary override the test of diction ; however doubtful he may sometimes be, in the early plays, whether he is reading a line of the young Shakespeare or one of a pre-Shakespearean, or a composite. To give up the style-test because of the lack of unanimity as to its application would be not merely to get out of touch with the most essential property of the matter we are analysing, but to open the way to wholly irrational speculation. That way Baconism lies. If we do not subordinate clues of word and phrase to the test of style, we may go about finding Shakespeare in a score of anonymous plays that, by that test, we know he never touched.

It is well, indeed, to recognise that in regard to a number of details we may never be able to reach anything like certainty, especially where, to begin with, we must recognise a high probability of revision of other men's work by Shakespeare. But where, on the other hand, we can find in early work assigned to him not merely coincidences of phrase and tag but in the same connection close parallels in style and cadence to the works of contemporaries concerning whom we know that they wrote more plays than have been published with their names ; and when further we find in the same plays much writing that is markedly below the level of most of his work that is unquestionably early, we have a clear critical right to suspect survivals of pre-Shakespearean work. In some cases, some of us can never believe we are reading Shakespeare in certain scenes, even if we cannot profess to show who did write them.   But where we can offer valid evidence, we are doing " legitimate " critical work in producing it.

It has been contended, on the other hand, by Professor Schröer[1] that " verbal coincidence between two poems speaks rather against than for identity of authorship." How far Professor Schröer really holds this opinion is left in much doubt when we find him arguing (p. 125) that Aaron's praise of blackness (IV, ii, 71, 99) :

> Is black so base a hue ?
> Coal black is better than another hue,

seems to be a favourite idea with Shakespeare (scheint . . von Shakspere mit Vorliebe behandelt zu sein) because we have in LOVE'S LABOUR'S LOST (V, i, 20, 41) the phrases :

> A light condition in a beauty dark . . .
> Beauteous as ink.

Certainly no worse argument from parallels was ever framed, seeing that the last citation flouts the plea of the first ; but if it stands for anything whatever it is a claim that the poet tended to revert to certain themes or phrases ; and the plea should be noted as showing to what extremities that view can be carried.

To some, on the other hand, the argument *against* all constructive inference from verbal coincidence may seem in itself worth acceptance, despite the framer's deviation from it. But while that opinion (which in any case conflicts flatly with the main arguments of Professor Collins and Professor Parrott) is intelligible as an à priori theory and is in some instances justified,[2] it is unintelligible to me that it can be held as a general principle after an inductive study of Elizabethan literature. Webster, who frequently

---

[1] *Ueber Titus Andronicus*, p. 73.
[2] As above in respect of duplications assumed to have been made *about the same time* by Shakespeare.

echoes Shakespeare and others,[1] also echoes himself
many times.[2]   Spenser thrice repeated one of his
most charming figures,[3] and several times varied the
picture of the " rosy red " " flashing " through a fair
face.[4] Jonson has several favourite phrases, as his
twice-used :

Safe from the wolf's black jaws and the dull ass's hoof,

and his thrice-used figure about life-threads spun from
the Fates' finest wool.[5] Marlowe repeats his image of
Helen's face launching a thousand ships (2 TAMB. II,
iv ; FAUSTUS, V, iii) and " make me immortal with a
kiss " (FAUSTUS, V, iii ; DIDO IV, iv). to say nothing
of a dozen of his less famous phrases and a score of his
tags. Chapman repeats many phrases of his own,[6]
alike in his plays and in his poems. Greene and Lodge,
who both copy Lilly brazenly and constantly, repeat
phrases and aphorisms in the same tale, sometimes
on the same page, in signed publications as to which
there arise no questions of mixed authorship. Peele's
reiterations, as distinct from the repetitive effects of
phrase noted below, occur throughout his signed
poems and plays, and so justify, when they concur
with a contemporary citation, the ascription to him of
the BATTLE OF ALCAZAR, which contains a number of
phrases used in his signed poems. This, in fact, was
the way of the age, as may be gathered from Latimer's
Sermons, Wiclif's tracts, and a hundred other common
books.[7] Clearly we must look out for echoes of one

[1] See the author's *Baconian Heresy*, p. 393 ; or Webster, Dyce's 1-vol. ed.,
notes on pp. 6, 13, 15, 21, 22, 31, 45, 67, 75, 78, 80, 82, 83, 88, 89, 91, 93, 96,
101, 109, 112, 162, 171, 174, 179, 250.
[2] *Id.*, notes on pp. 44, 61, 63, 66, 67, 74, 84, 109, 172, etc.
[3] See *The Baconian Heresy*, p. 392.
[4] See the author's *Elizabethan Literature*, p. 78.
[5] *Baconian Heresy*, p. 567.
[6] See Prof. Parrott's ed. of Chapman's Plays, notes, *passim*.
[7] The phenomenon is of course not confined to Elizabethan times. " Hazlitt
was a hardened reprinter, and those who know all his books get familiar with
passages which occur, word for word, in more even than two places " (Birrell,
William Hazlitt, p. 141). Carlyle is in the same case. As regards mere
phrases, the old habit still survives. In Professor A. D. White's *History of
the Warfare of Science with Theology* I find the phrase " German honesty "
repeated thrice, with no iterative purpose, in a few pages (ii, 255, 257, 259).
The fact that, as the context shows, there is nothing specially German in the
case, suggests the dominion of the " tag."

man by another, knowing that these certainly occur ; but that men in those days verbally echoed themselves many times over is also certain, and the fact is of prime importance in investigations of authorship. Shakespeare does undoubtedly repeat himself at times in turns of phrase in his undisputed works ; and it is this fact that best encourages the argument of Professor Collins from the parallels between TITUS and other " Shakespearean " plays, of which Professor Schröer's proposition takes no account.   We have seen, and shall see further, that far closer and more numerous parallels occur between TITUS and the signed works of Peele.   But in Shakespeare's accepted plays and poems we have such repetitions as these :—

> The glorious sun
> Stays in his course and plays the alchemist,
> Turning with splendour of his precious eye
> The meagre cloddy earth to glittering gold.
> > *King John*, III, i, 77-80.

> [The morning] kissing with golden face the meadows green
> Gilding pale streams with heavenly alchemy.
> > *Sonnet* 33.

> Turns into yellow gold his salt green streams,
> > *M. N. D.*, III, ii, 393.

> Or who is he so fond will be the tomb
> Of his self-love, to stop posterity.
> > *Sonnet* 3.

> What is thy body but a swallowing grave,
> Seeming to bury that posterity
> Which by the rights of time thou needs must have ?
> > *Venus and Adonis*, ll. 757-9.

There are many such echoes between the sonnets and the poems. We cannot argue, therefore, that the coincidences of phrase between TITUS and plays and poems which are either certainly Shakespeare's or partly his, yield arguments *against* his authorship of the questioned work, save on the express ground that the nearer they are in date the less likely are they to be both his, and that where the TITUS form is poor and the other superior, the latter alone is to be reckoned his. We can but scrutinise all echoes and parallels alike, and draw what inferences can be shown to be best justified.

Turning, then, to the concrete inquiry, we begin with vocabulary, and in that regard we have specially to consider :—

1.   Words found in TITUS and nowhere else in " Shakespeare."

2.   Words found there and in other disputed or composite plays inserted in the first folio, in which other hands are known or believed to have entered.

3.   Words used in TITUS and in Shakespearean plays or poems, but with a different sense or accentuation.

It will be seen on reflection that while the discovery of many words of any or all of these classes in the works of an early contemporary of Shakespeare would certainly not be conclusive as to the first man's authorship of the play, it would give on the one hand a fair ground for a hypothesis, to be otherwise tested, and on the other hand strong confirmation to other evidence pointing in the same direction.   The first test should be a search for the same words in other contemporaries ; and we shall find that this promptly checks a sweeping inference in the present inquiry.   But if such further discovery is reconcilable with a wider hypothesis in which the first is included, and which endures the remaining tests, we shall have reached an inference incomparably better founded than the slightly coloured pre-suppositions which we have hitherto examined.

In this connection it may be well to point out that the commonly-endorsed argument of Richard Simpson against any inference from " once-used words," on the score that every play contains such, is a statistical fallacy.   Simpson claimed[1] to negative all inferences from the occurrence of any word in one Shakespearean

---

[1] In the Transactions of the New Shakspere Society, 1874.   Dr. Elze (*William Shakespeare*, Eng. trans. p. 348, *note*) endorses this argument without discrimination, as does Professor Schröer, *Ueber Titus Andronicus*, p. 26.

play only. Taking all the words so indicated in Mrs. Cowden Clarke's concordance, and finding in every play a number of words peculiar to it, he concluded that nothing could be inferred from any case. But of the words so singled out many are French ; many are French or Welsh mis-pronunciations of English ; and many more are parts of verbs of which other parts appear often in other plays ; or adverbs or adjectives of which the correlatives are elsewhere used ; or compound nouns of which the elements are elsewhere common. Thus, *e.g.*, "abhorr'dst" appears in one play only, while "abhorred" is used in fifteen ; "abominably" occurs only in HAMLET, while "abominable" occurs more than a dozen times ; and "abbey-gate" figures as a once-used word, while "abbey-wall" occurs in three plays, "abbey" in three, and "gate" in many. To base an indiscriminate numerical argument on such instances is idle. The word "abbess" is used in only one play because in only one play does an abbess figure. But when general terms or idioms appear in only one play, or only in plays otherwise arraigned as in large part non-Shakespearean, they constitute an item in a reasonable presumption. As Simpson admits, words in this inquiry must be weighed as well as counted. And when we find in TITUS the forms "patient thyself" (fairly common in Elizabethan writers,[1] but not seen elsewhere in the alleged works of Shakespeare), and the verb "to passionate" (which is in similar case), we are so far supported in our surmise that the play is not his.

Many of the "once-used words," further, are proper names ; and here, clearly, there can be no general inference. But where proper names are introduced by way of random classical allusion, their recurrence may be ground for a certain presumption. Now, there are some fourteen or more classical proper names, allusively used in TITUS, which appear in no other play ascribed to Shakespeare, and one or two more which occur only

---

[1] It occurs in *Ferrex and Porrex* (iv, 2) which Peele frequently echoes. Kyd has it in *Arden*.

in disputed or admittedly composite plays. If all or nearly all of these are found in the works of one or two contemporaries, who are otherwise indicated by the evidence as sharers in the authorship of TITUS, the argument is still further strengthened. And if, finally, the great majority of the words special to TITUS among his reputed plays are found in the works of one or two contemporaries, the *prima facie* presumption that they are the authors is obviously strong.

§ 2. THE TRACES OF PEELE[1]

All instances, of course, are open to discussion on their merits ; and we can but submit them to criticism. To begin with, there occurs in TITUS the term " palliament," found in no other play ascribed to Shakespeare. Steevens observed that he had " not met with it elsewhere in any English writer, whether ancient or modern," and that it " must have originated from the mint of a scholar." Steevens, though very well-read, is sometimes far from accurate ; but this word is undoubtedly rare ; and when we find it in line 92 of Peele's poem, THE HONOUR OF THE GARTER, published in 1593, we have clear ground for examining the hypothesis—if it be otherwise supported—that Peele had a share in writing the play. When, yet further, we note that in TITUS the Roman palliament is described as " of *white* and *spotless* hue " ; and that in the HONOUR OF THE GARTER, further on (lines 314-315), the same garment is alluded to as

Weeds of *spotless white*
Like those that stood for Rome's great offices,

we are shut up to the conclusion that there is *some* connection between the two works.

At the outset we are met by the argument of Mr. Charles Crawford,[2] a learned and strenuous maintainer

---

[1] See chap. iv.
[2] Article on *The Date and Authenticity of " Titus Andronicus,"* in the *Jahrbuch der deutschen Shakespeare Gesellschaft*, 1900.

of the Shakespearean authorship of TITUS, that Shakespeare in the play has copied the expressions of Peele.
Here the play is at once brought down to the latter part
of the year 1593, and there is a complete schism between
the chronology of Mr. Crawford and that of Professor
Collins. Mr. Baildon, after comfortably dating the
play between 1589 and 1593, helplessly suggested that
both Peele and Shakespeare may have copied some
third poet. But Mr. Crawford, usually so vigilant, in
turn overlooks a series of objections to his conclusion
that Shakespeare wrote the play in 1593 ; and in
particular has failed to note a multitude of coincidences
between TITUS and others of Peele's works than the
HONOUR OF THE GARTER. When we collate these we
shall find that Mr. Crawford's solution is untenable.

To make the issue clearer, let us take another parallel
in which an uncommon term is used in TITUS and in a
Peele play, in a passage which is also a partial duplication. The noun " chase," meaning " park " or " game
preserve," occurs twice in TITUS and nowhere else in any
play ascribed to Shakespeare.[1] It also occurs four
times in Peele's early ARRAIGNMENT OF PARIS,[2] a line
of which we have already seen echoed in TITUS. Thrice,
again, in TITUS, but in no other play ascribed to
Shakespeare, we have reference to the panther ; and
this word also occurs twice in Peele.[3] In our play
(II, ii) we have the phrase :

> The *p*roudest *p*anther in the chase.

In the ARRAIGNMENT (I, i, 7) we find the line :

> The *f*airest, *f*attest *f*awn in all the chase.

The alliterations standing alone would count for nothing ; occurring in lines ending with the same uncommon
term, which thus form parallel pictures, they at once

---

[1] On the word " chase " in *Titus*, II, iii, 255, Mr. Baildon in his edition has
the note : " See the *Two Gentlemen*, I, ii, 116," which I cannot understand.
The word does not occur there, or, in this sense, anywhere else in Shakespeare.
[2] References below, § 2.
[3] References below, § 2.

infer either identity of source or imitation. Can we
then suppose that Shakespeare is here again weakly
imitating his predecessor ? When the very introduction of the panther as a beast of the chase is for him a
wild anomaly,[1] is not the rational inference simply
this, that Peele, who does name the panther twice in
signed poems—once as a beast for hunting—wrote the
passage before us ?

Another instance of unquestionable echoing will
further serve to test from both sides the theory that
in such coincidences there has been imitation of one
poet by another. In TITUS we have the lines :

> And *faster* bound to Aaron's charming *eyes*
> Than is *Prometheus tied to Caucasus,*

which point to two separate lines in Peele's EDWARD I
(sc. iv, 21 ; x, 201) :

> To *tie Prometheus' limbs to Caucasus* . . .
> *Fast* by those *looks* are all my fancies *tied*.[2]

In TITUS the two figures are combined in one eminently
grotesque trope. Are we then to suppose either (1)
that Shakespeare made this absurd combination immediately after reading EDWARD I (published in 1593),
or that Peele got his ideas yet again from hearing TITUS
played in the theatre, and frugally turned one stolen
trope to account by making two uses of it ? Are not
both inferences alike fantastic ? Is not the natural
explanation this, that Peele, writing the two plays
about the same time, used up his own rhetoric twice
over, one of his lines with " tie " in it recalling to him
the other ?

Such minutiæ of coincidence strictly count for much

---

[1] Cf. Professor Parrott, essay cited, p. 27.
[2] Echoes of Lilly :—" My thoughts are stitched to the stars " (*Endymion*,
I, i) and of Greene :—
> Fast-fancied to the keeper's bonny lass . . .
> And lock'd him in the brightness of her looks.
> > (*Friar Bacon and Friar Bungay*, Dyce, pp. 150-1)
—and various other passages. In *Locrine* (v, iv) we have :—
> As Tityus *bound* to houseless *Caucasus,*

more than identities of phrase which might be disposed
of as " tags." But echoes of tags swell the proof ;
and when we find in TITUS (I, 36) the phrase :

Laden with honour's spoils,

and in Peele's ECLOGUE GRATULATORY (st. 19) :

Laden with honour's spoil ;

and the further echo of " laurel boughs " in play and
poem (TITUS I, 74 : ECL. st. 21), we again infer not
imitation but repetition. And when we note that the
TITUS line (I, 75) :

To *resalute* his country with his *tears,*

occurring immediately after the echoed " laurel
boughs " and containing an uncommon word of Peele's,
" resalute " (HONOUR OF THE GARTER, 372), is paralleled by a line in EDWARD I :

With *tears of joy salutes* your sweet *return,*

we still more confidently infer repetition by one hand,
and not a complex of trifling plagiarisms.

Next let us take the naturally infrequent word
" zodiac," which occurs once in TITUS and only once
in all the other plays ascribed to Shakespeare. In
the latter case (M̶. FOR M., I, ii, 172) it is used very
loosely indeed in the line :

So long that nineteen zodiacs have gone round—

with the mere force of " a year." In the unquestionable works of Peele, on the other hand, not only
do we find the word used at least four times, and
that with exact meaning,[1] but one of the passages is

---

[1] *Honour of the Garter* : *Ad. Mæcen. Prolog.,* 9 ; *David and Bethsabe,* sc. i,
108-9 ; *Anglorium Feriæ,* 24 ; *Descensus Astrææ,* 4. Compare :
That admirable mathematic skill
Familiar with the stars and zodiac.
Honour of the Garter, Prol.
Titan mounted on the Lion's back.
Id., main poem, l. 29.

found almost to duplicate the line in TITUS.   That says of the sun that he

> *Gallops the zodiac* in his *glistering coach.*

In the ANGLORUM FERIÆ (1595) we have :

> *Gallops the zodiac* in his *fiery wain ;*

again in the DESCENSUS ASTRÆÆ (1591) we have :

> *Gallop the zodiac,* and end the year ;

and yet again in DAVID AND BETHSABE :

> Climbs
> The crooked zodiac with his *fiery sphere.*

Are we then to suppose that Peele, having heard in the theatre the first-cited of these lines, adapted it twice in separate poems and yet again in a play ? Is it not obviously more probable that he, who has four signed allusions to the zodiac, is the author of the fifth, and not Shakespeare, who (apart from TITUS) uses the term once only, and then inaccurately ? And when we note further that " glistering " is one of Peele's common epithets (occurring at least twelve times in his plays and poems), and that in the TALE OF TROY (461) he speaks of the sun's " glistering chariot,"[1] and in DAVID AND BETHSABE of the sun's " glistering robe," is not the probability much heightened ?

Again Mr. Crawford meets us with the claim that Shakespeare was simply copying Peele. Shakespeare, he writes, " copied Greene, Peele, and Marlowe in TITUS ANDRONICUS as well as in other pieces "[2]—a vigorous support to Professor Collins's formula of " timid and servile imitation."   On that view we are to suppose that Shakespeare, having once used Peele's favourite phrase about the zodiac—and this in what Mr. Crawford confidently asserts to have been " one of Shakespeare's favourite plays "[3]—nevertheless forgot afterwards what

---

[1] In the ed. of 1589 the passage reads simply, " the glorious sun his chariot." " Glistering " is a later change.

[2] Article cited, p. 112.   [3] *Id.,* p. 121.

the zodiac precisely was, and referred to it in MEASURE
FOR MEASURE as if it simply meant a year.   Doubtless
the traditionists will accept that as " highly probable."
But we have already seen that in TITUS there is a close
echo of two lines in Peele's OLD WIVES TALE, which
was presumably written before 1593, but was not
published till 1595.   Was Shakespeare then copying
lines he had heard (or, it may be, spoken) in the theatre ?
Either Mr. Crawford must add that to his list of cases
of plagiarism by the Master, or he must now decide
that Peele in the TALE was copying Shakespeare.
When, further, we find many close parallels to TITUS in
DAVID AND BETHSABE, which was registered for
publication in May, 1594, and probably published in
that year, we can take our choice of the same alterna-
tives.   In short, to gratify the determination of critics
who have pre-judged the cause, we are to credit the
young Shakespeare not only with a score of flagrant
plagiarisms, none of them worth his while, but, as we
shall see later, with a close imitation of the rhythms
and cadences of the least inspired of his three leading
competitors.   When we compare the " zodiac " passage
in TITUS with that in DAVID AND BETHSABE we find
" slavish imitation " indeed.   The latter runs :

> *As heaven's bright eye* burns most when most he climbs
> *The crooked zodiac with his fiery sphere,*
> *And shineth furthest from this earthly globe,*
> *So*, since thy beauty scorched my conquered soul, etc.
> (Act I, Sc. i.)

The other runs :

> *As when the golden sun* salutes the morn,
> And having gilt the ocean with his *beams,*
> *Gallops the zodiac in his glistering coach,*
> *And overlooks the highest-peering hills,*
> *So* Tamora.

And to both of these passages there is the further close
structural parallel, with special verbal coincidences, of
yet another passage[1] in DAVID AND BETHSABE,

---

[1] This is closely imitated from Spenser, *Faerie Queene*, Bk, I, c. v, st. 2,

As when the sun, attired in *glistering* robe
Comes dancing from his oriental gate,
And bridegroom-like hurls through the gloomy air
His radiant *beams* . . .
So looketh David King of Israel.[1]

(Act II, iii).

Here the imitation, alike of Spenser by Peele and of
Peele by himself, is beyond question : epithets, figures,
mode, period are all alike duplicated. What more
reasonable inference is open than that Peele, who
parodies himself in his signed play, has done it again in
an unsigned one ? On Mr. Crawford's theory, either
(1) Shakespeare must be held not only to have imitated
once more in one passage three of Peele's—one taken
from a printed poem, the other from a play perhaps not
then printed, and one of them itself an imitation from
Spenser—but to have artificially woven his borrowings
in a period elaborately and minutely imitated from the
Peele play ; or (2) Peele must be held to have revised
DAVID AND BETHSABE after 1594, and to have therein
imitated his imitator, working his favourite figure into
just such a period as the imitator has framed it in. Is
not common sense shut up to the conclusion that Peele
was repeating himself, here as in fifty other places ?

In view of such unquestionable parallelisms of style
in TITUS and the signed works of Peele, we are even
entitled to trace similar repetitions in some passages
where the resemblance is not pronounced enough to
leap to the eyes. In Peele's signed poem THE TALE
OF TROY, in which we shall find yet other clues to
TITUS, we have the exact phrase " wise Laertes' son "
(l.362), occurring in TITUS (1, 380). It is the more
likely that the TITUS lines (IV, i, 20) :

I have read that Hecuba of Troy
Ran mad through sorrow,

are from the hand that told how Hecuba,

Worn with sorrows, wexen fell and mad.

(*Tale*, l. 466.)

[1] Yet other " as " and " so " passages occur in *David and Bethsabe* ; *e.g.*,
one in the same scene as that last cited. This mode is common in Spenser.

In the same poem, again, there is a passage (400 sqq.) about Sinon's stratagem, in which occur the lines :

> While *subtle Grecians* lurk'd in Tenedos . . .
> And so *bewitched King Priam* and his court
> That now at last, to Troyans' *fatal* hurt . . .
> They 'greed to hoise this *engine* of mischance.

Compare these with the lines of Marcus in TITUS (v, iii, 84-86) :

> When *subtle Greeks* surprised *King Priam's* Troy.
> Tell us what Sinon hath *bewitch'd* our ears,
> Or who hath brought the *fatal engine* in.

In the first line quoted, as it happens, the words " subtle Grecians " form an emendation in the (posthumous) second edition of the TALE OF TROY, that of 1589 having " traytrous Greekes." Here once more, then, on Mr. Crawford's theory, Peele was echoing Shakespeare after Shakespeare had echoed him. In one case of single mimicry the theory of imitation might pass, for once in a way ; but before a long series of reciprocities it becomes futile. Why should Shakespeare so determinedly echo in one play, and in that only, one third-rate contemporary, who echoed him in return ?

As we shall see, such an obstinate presupposition is quashed once for all by a comparison of the versification of TITUS with that of either LOVE'S LABOUR'S LOST or the MIDSUMMER NIGHT'S DREAM, both reasonably to be assigned to Shakespeare's earlier years. The technique is vitally different. But even if this consideration were not before us, we might justly refuse to solve the problem of the manifold coincidences between TITUS and the work of contemporaries by arbitrarily assuming a long series of weak plagiarisms on Shakespeare's part, with an equally arbitrary resort to the contrary solution when the parallel passage occurs in a work printed after TITUS. It is arguable that Peele sometimes copied Shakespeare, or Shakespeare Peele ; but to argue that Shakespeare constantly aped Peele down to his most trifling peculiarities, and that on his part Peele freely parroted no less trifling peculiarities of Shakespeare, zealously copying his copyist, is to multiply difficulties instead of solving them.   If on the contrary we make the hypothesis that Peele had a main share in TITUS, all the difficulties disappear at once : the whole data come into harmony. The style test is satisfied all along the line.   Peele repeated *himself* in his avowed works as freely as either Marlowe or Greene.   The moment we apply the hypothesis that he is doing so in TITUS our problem begins to grow transparent.

This will appear anew when we take next one of the types of phrase picked out by Professor Collins from TITUS as particularly Shakespearean :

> As swift as swallow flies.
> Run like swallows o'er the plain.

The phrase is really so much of a mere tag that it cannot well identify anybody ; but let us treat it on the Professor's own principle.   Other allusions to the swiftness of swallows in the plays ascribed to Shakespeare occur in RICHARD III, one of the chronicle group in which, on general grounds, Peele has been supposed by several critics to have had a share, and in a jest of Falstaff's.   Here there is indeed no clear primary presumption against Shakespeare's origination of the phrase in TITUS.   But when again we find in Peele the two phrases :

> As swift as swallow flies   (*Ed. I*, Sc. IX) ;
> Swift as the swallow   (*Polyhymnia*, 169),

we are at least set inquiring as to dates.   POLYHYMNIA was published in 1590, and EDWARD I in 1593, after having been for some time acted.   TITUS was first published in 1594.   Are we here again to suppose that Peele was merely echoing another man's line which he had heard in the theatre ?   Such assumptions become increasingly inadmissible with each new test case.. If

Shakespeare's alleged work on TITUS was done in 1593, he was once more echoing a tag of Peele.

And still the cases multiply. The word "successful," for instance, might be supposed to be common enough,[1] yet it occurs only once in an undisputed Shakespearean play, the late WINTER'S TALE, while it is found twice in the disputed HENRY VI group, and twice in TITUS. Peele, on the other hand, uses it at least four times in the BATTLE OF ALCAZAR alone (I, i, 58 ; ii, 132, 135, v, i, 189) ; he also frequently has "success,"[2] and thrice "successless" (ARR. OF PARIS, I, ii, 21 ; FAREWELL, 240 ; ANGLOR. FERIÆ, 82) ; also "successively" (BATTLE) with the sense attached to "successive" in TITUS I, I. But the BATTLE OF ALCAZAR was not published till 1594. When then we find in this connection one more approach to a duplication of lines in the BATTLE and TITUS :

> Successful in thy [the ?] work thou undertakes
> > (*Battle*, I, ii, 135),

> Successful in the battles that he fights
> > (*Titus*, I, 66),

the presumption of his presence in the latter play becomes still stronger. We are here dealing not with a phrase that could readily pass current as a tag, but with a tic of style, a habit of repetition, seen running throughout Peele's whole work, and at the same time with a term at that date uncommon. When, indeed, we note such duplicated lines as :

> The venomous malice of my swelling heart
> > (*Titus*, v, iii) ;
> The fatal poison of my swelling heart
> > (*Battle*, II, iii, 3) ;

---

[1] The word "success," it should be remembered, originally meant only "sequence," or "succession" (Cp. *F. Q.*, II, x, 45) and normally had that force in Tudor times.   In Shakespeare's day it was only beginning to have its modern force ; and "successful" was a neologism. Marlowe uses it : "successful blasts" (*Jew*, I, i) in the sense of "sequent" = "following" winds, though also (*Ed. II*, IV, v—if the section be his) in the new sense.

[2] *E.g.*, "Fortunate success" : *D. and B.*, III, iv.   This occurs in Spenser (*F. Q.* B. VII, c. vii, st. 1) and often elsewhere.

> That woe is me to think upon thy woes
> > (*Titus*, III, i) ;
>
> Urias—woe is me to think hereon
> > (*David*, II, i),

we cannot draw the same conclusion, since the " swell-ing heart " tag points also to Marlowe.[1] *Such* tags were common property. But even such phrases as " The hollow prison of my flesh " (TITUS, III, ii) ; " The painful prison of my soul " (ED. I, Sc. 25) ; " The prison of my breast " (BATTLE. V, i), and " My soul . . . released from prison on this earth[2] " (*Id., ib.*) ; " their latest home "—the grave (TITUS, I, ii) and " their longest home " (BATTLE, I, 125) ; " Fortune's shot " (TITUS, II, i) and " envy's shot " (GARTER, 411)— though they *might* have currency as stage tags, may reasonably be reckoned with the stronger instances on the side of the inference that Peele had a main share in TITUS. So with the use of the peculiar phrase " sacrific*ing* fire ", found in TITUS (I, 144) and in the BATTLE (V, i, 183), but nowhere in Shakespeare. Every additional instance progressively strengthens the thesis. One line in TITUS (III, i, 15) :

> My son's *sweet blood* will make it shame and *blush*,

suggests the hand that wrote :

> With *blood* that *blusheth* for his conscience' guilt
> > (*D. and B.*, III, iii),

and

> And makes her fields *blush* with her children's *blood*
> > (*Id.* III, v),

---

[1] Compare the Marlovian line in I *H. VI*, III, i, 26 :
> From envious malice of thy swelling heart,

and yet another in the *First Part of the Contention*, sc. i :
> The big-swoln venom of thy hateful heart.

But the same tag is found in Kyd's *Arden of Feversham* (i, 326) :
> The rancorous venom of thy mis-swoll'n heart ;

and in that play there is no clear trace of Peele, though there are passages hinting at Greene, and some pointing strongly to Marlowe.

[2] This again is echoed in the *True Tragedy of Richard Duke of York* :
> Now my soul's palace is become a prison.
> Oh, would she break from compass of my breast.

no less than does the before-cited[1] passage in TITUS
about the sea being moved with sighs, and drowning
the earth, indicate the two passages in DAVID AND
BETHSABE about a plain

> Drowned with a sea that with our sighs should roar.

The duplication in the same passages of " weeping
heavens " and sighs that raise mists, tells to the same
effect.   And when we add these to the previously cited
lines :—

> The hunt is up ; the morn is bright and grey
> > (*Titus*, II, ii),
> The day is clear : the welkin bright and grey
> > (*Old Wives Tale*) ;
> Whose smoke, like incense, doth perfume the sky
> > (*Titus*, I, 145),
> Whose thick and foggy smoke, piercing the sky
> > (*Arr. of Paris*, 12),

and these :

> The imperial seat to virtue consecrate.
> > (*Titus*, I, i, 14) ;
> To villainy and vengeance consecrate,
> > (*Id.*, II, i, 121) ;
> To Virtue or to Vesta consecrate,
> > (*Polyhymnia*, 280) ;
> In deeds to fame and virtue consecrate.
> > (*Order of the Garter*, 384)[2]

—noting that in the first, third, and fourth parallels the
lines which follow in each case have the same cadence,
and that in the second there is reference in each context
to " sacrifice "—the inference is yet further reinforced.

[1] Above, p. 97.

[2] Compare :
> To whom those martial deeds were consecrate.
> > *Polyhymnia*.
> Consecrate to Saint George's chosen knights.
> > *Order of the Garter*.
> Consecrate purely to your noble name.
> > *Id. Epilogus*.

The fact that Marlowe has " vowed and consecrate " (*Ed. II*, III, ii) does not
affect the issue. Peele endlessly echoes Marlowe. But one of Marlowe's
phrases, "heaps of massy gold," is found before him in Peele (*Arr. of Paris*, II).

Given such a strong general case, our business is, as aforesaid, to apply to it all the tests that the problem admits of.   To be finally valid, our inference must be borne out by a general survey of Peele's vocabulary, style, versification, sentiment, and dramatic methods ; and the chronology, of course, must be corroborative. On the last head there is no trouble.   Peele was alive in 1595 ; and his first published work, THE ARRAIGNMENT OF PARIS, appeared in 1584.   This, probably a spontaneous production, shows no traces of collaboration ;   neither does his DAVID AND BETHSABE ;   and though there are some apparent interpolations in his EDWARD I, which he signed, and possibilities of collaboration or interpolation in his BATTLE OF ALCAZAR, a good deal of his collected work consists of his signed poems.   There is thus a considerable body of Peele's work as to the homogeneity of which we can be practically certain.   The BATTLE OF ALCAZAR, though anonymous, has been so generally accepted as his on the strong grounds put forward by Dyce, and is in the main so clearly in the manner of his EDWARD I and DAVID AND BETHSABE, that I shall here take his general authorship for granted.   Concerning SIR CLYOMON AND SIR CLAMYDES, which is ascribed to him on the strength of an inscription of his name on the old edition in a contemporary hand, his latest editor, Mr. Bullen, expresses[1] strong doubts as to its being Peele's, adding : " I suspect that it was written by *some such person as* Richard Edwards (author of DAMON AND PYTHIAS) when Peele was in his teens."   From this judgment I respectfully dissent.   Mr. Bullen had not taken into account the fact that one of the characters is named Sans-Foy, apparently in imitation of Spenser (F. Q. I, ii, 12).[2]   On that view, though the piece may be dated before the publication of the poem,[3] it cannot be carried back to the time of Edwards, who died in

---

[1] *The Works of George Peele*, 1888, Introd. p. xlii.

[2] The very first line of the play echoes Spenser (I, ix, 39) in the phrase " weary wandring wights " ;   and there are several other echoes, such as " Knights of the Silver Shield," " King or Keysar," etc.

[3] Cp. Dyce, p. 344.

1566.[1] I venture to say that the style and diction,
though archaistic, are not at all those of Edwards, the
metre and rhythm being far more nearly regular than
his ; and as the play has a large number of words and
phrases which appear to be favourites with Peele and
Greene respectively, I shall here treat it as a work by
Peele, probably revised or collaborated in by Greene.
The antique form of the verse—the old " fourteener "—
is no bar to such a conclusion. It was a form that had
long been popular ; it was actually adopted by Chapman for his translation of the ILIAD ; and a speech in
just such lines is inserted in Beaumont and Fletcher's
KNIGHT OF THE BURNING PESTLE. Peele introduces a
number of such lines in his EDWARD I, and has in his
ARRAIGNMENT OF PARIS not only a quantity of verse of
the same metre but a number of the very touches of
rustic dialect found in this play. Such an exercise in
verse was perfectly possible to both poets ; and it seems
to me visibly the performance not of men still in the
archaic period like Edwards, but of later scholars taking
to the archaic with half humorous, half heedless zest.[2]
While the rhythm is archaic, the general regularity of
it is not so. The lines in SIR CLYOMON are not only
much more nearly regular than those of Edwards :
they are more regular than those of the old comedy
FIDELE AND FORTUNIO : THE TWO ITALIAN GENTLE-
MEN, registered in 1584, which has the same line form.[3]
Some of the coincidences of SIR CLYOMON with Peele's
special vocabulary will appear in the next section ; and

---

[1] Since this was written, Professor Kittredge of Harvard University has
argued for the authorship of Thomas Preston, author of *Cambyses*. This
proceeds on a supposition of Fleay, who, though seeking other ascriptions,
found a parallel passage in that play, and proposed for *Sir Clyomon* a date
between 1570 and 1578. Continuing to hold that it exhibits the influence of
Spenser, I leave my general argument standing. Professor Kellner's argument (see Chambers, *Eliz. Stage*, iv, 6) that the piece cannot be Peele's unless
he wrote in a spirit of parody, consists with mine.

[2] If the play be not ascribed to the time of Greene and Peele it might much
more plausibly be assigned to the year of its publication, 1599, than to the
time of Edwards. The first cantos of Chapman's *Iliad*, in the same metre,
regularised, had appeared in 1598. But I prefer the earlier date. We shall
find Greene and Peele again associated in *Locrine*, where they revert to the
older Senecan tradition.

[3] Rep. by Malone Society, 1909.

the clues to Greene will be indicated in Chapter VII. Meantime we may note the frequent use in it of the words " sacred " and " sacrifice," as well as " hugy," " maugre," and " vital," all common to Peele and Greene ; the further occurrence of Peele's favourite words " policy " and " drift " ; of " engines " (twice), which he frequently employs ; of the form " gratulation," from his frequent verb " gratulate " ; and of such nouns as " propound," " expect," and " suspect," which are in his manner.   Such an uncommon word as " needly," found in his Tale of Troy (127) and thrice in Sir Clyomon, is a clue that cannot be neglected.[1]   Finally we may note the less significant " faltering tongue " as occurring in Sir Clyomon (ed. Dyce, p. 517) and in Edward I (sc. xxv).[2]

Beyond these assigned works, there is another mass of anonymous matter as to which we can be nearly certain that it is his ; but the proving of this is one of the more difficult parts of our inquiry ; and the proper procedure is to make clear first, in addition to the decisive duplications of phrase already noted, the significant identities of his vocabulary, as found in his actually signed and assigned works, with that of Titus. Such identities would certainly not of themselves establish his authorship, and it need hardly be said that each item is open to revision in so far as any word is to be found in other contemporary playwrights ; but collectively they form an important part of the cumulative proof.

§ 3. Peele's Vocabulary in " Titus "

The list of words and accentuations special to Titus in the Shakespeare Concordance, excluding common

---

[1] The passage in which this word occurs in *Romeo and Juliet* (III. ii, 117) is notably un-Shakespearean in style.   The word occurs also in Lodge's *Wounds of Civil War* (Malone Soc. rep. l. 1133).   But there is a measure of presumption in favour of Fleay's identification of Peele as one of the draftsmen (or adaptors from the old play) of *Romeo and Juliet*.

[2] This is likely to have been an echo from Spenser, *F. Q.* i, vii, 24.

flections of words otherwise used in other plays, is as follows :—

Alphabet	Gleeful	Self-blood
Anchorage	Grammar	Séquestered
Architect	Gratulate	Shive
" Aries "[1]		Solon[1]
	Honey-dew	Somewhither
Battle-axe	Hymenaeus	Spousal
Big-boned		Sprawl
Blowze	Libelling	Still (adj. =constant)
	Loaf	Sumptuously
Candidatus	Love-day	'Surance
Chase (=park)		
Cimmerian	Màintain	
Cocytus	Man-of-war	'Ticed (=enticed)
Codding	Meshed (in brewing)	To-fore
Compassion (vb.)	Metamorphoses	Triùmpher
Continence[2]		Tully[1]
Crevice	Over-shade	
		Unappeased
Devoid	Palliament	Uncurls
Devourer	Pantheon	Unrecuring
Dismallest	Panther (thrice)	Unrelenting
Dreary	Passionate	Unsearched
Drought	Patient (vb. imp.)	Uprightness
	Philomela[1]	
Egal (=equal)	Popish	Vaunter
Embrued[3]	Progne[1]	Venereal (=amorous)
Emperess	Prometheus[1]	Virginius
Enacts (noun pl.)		
Enceladus	Rapine	Weke
Execrable	Remunerate	Wind (vb. =to scent)
	Reproachful (twice)	Wreakful
Fere	Re-salute	Wreaks (noun)

There are also a number of compounds special to the play, as :

Counsel-keeping	Rude-growing	Gibbet-maker
New-shed	Shallow-hearted	Deadly-standing
New-transformed	Lurking-place	Sad-attending
Highest-peering	True-betrothed	White-lined
High-resolved	True-divining	Raven-coloured
Blood-drinking	Fatal-plotted	Sorrow-wreathen

[1] The use of such familiar classic names has of course no significance. They are here included merely to make the list complete.

[2] Shakespeare uses the form *continency*.

[3] Shakespeare twice has *imbrue*.

In addition to the foregoing we have to note a number of Latin words and quotations nowhere else occurring in a Shakespearean play, and further a number of words found in TITUS and, it may be, in other disputed and divided plays, but seldom or never in an undisputed and undivided play of Shakespeare's. The list of the latter is as follows :—

Aetna, once in *Titus*, once in *Merry Wives*.
Affy, once in *Titus*, once in *Taming of the Shrew*.
Basin, once in *Titus*, once in *Timon*, twice in the *Shrew*.
Bear-whelp, once in *Titus*, once in 3 *H. VI*.
Blood-drinking, once in *Titus*, once in 1 *H. VI*, once in 2 *H. VI*.
Braves (noun), once in *Titus*, once in the *Shrew*, once in *Troilus*, once in 1 *H. VI*.
Brinish, once in *Titus*, once in 3 *H. VI*, once in *Lucrece*.
Caucasus, once in *Titus*, once in *Richard II*.
Checkered, once in *Titus*, once in 2 *H. VI*.
Coffin (of a pasty), once in *Titus*, once in the *Shrew*.
Daunt, once in *Titus*, once in the *Shrew*, thrice in *H. VI* plays.
Daunted, once in *Lucrece*.
Effectless, once in *Titus*, once in *Pericles*.
Entreats = entreaties, once in *Titus*, once in *Richard III*.
Faggot, once in *Titus*, once in 1 *H. VI*.
Faint-hearted, once in *Titus*, once in 1 *H. VI*, once in 3 *H. VI*.
Guileful, once in *Titus*, once in 1 *H. VI*.
Irreligious, once in *Titus*, once in *Merry Wives*.
'Joy = enjoy,[1] once in *Titus*, once in 2 *H. VI*, once in *Richard II*.
Joyless, once in *Titus*, once in *Richard III*.
Meanwhile, thrice in *Titus*, once in *H. VIII*.
Miry, once in *Titus*, once in the *Shrew*.
Mourning weeds, once in *Titus*, twice in 3 *H. VI*.
Numb, once in *Titus*, once in 1 *H. VI*; "numb-cold" in *Richard III*.
Oratory, once in *Titus*, once in 1 *H. VI*, twice in *Richard III*.
Re-edify, once in *Titus*, once in *Richard III*.
Represent, once in *Titus*, twice in the *H. VI* plays.
Rolled, intrans., once in *Titus*, once in 2 *H. VI*
Ruinate, once in *Titus*, once in 3 *H. VI*.
Sapling, once in *Titus*, once in *Richard III*, once in *Pericles*.
Semiramis, twice in *Titus*, once in the *Shrew*.
Spleenful, once in *Titus*, once in 2 *H. VI*.
Styx, once in *Titus*, once in *Troilus*.
Sustenance, once in *Titus*, once in *Pericles*.
Tpyhon, once in *Titus*, once in *Troilus*.

[1] A different force from that of the verb joy = rejoice, which is more common.

Wall-eyed, once in *Titus*, once in *King John*.
Yelping, once in *Titus*, once in 1 *H. VI.*
Youngling, twice in *Titus*, once in the *Shrew*.

Of the first list the following occur in Peele :

Architect. *Desc. Astræœ*, 59 ; *Battle*, II, prol. 5 ; *David and Bethsabe*, sc. xv, 99 ; *Anglor. Feriœ*, 143.

Battle-axe. *Honour of the Garter*, 147 ; *Anglor. Feriœ*, 167 ; *Locrine*, I, i ; v, i.

Chase (= park). *Arr. of Paris*, I, i, 5, 122, 147, 189.

Cimmerian. *Edward I*, sc. xxv, 148.

Dreary. *D. and B.*, sc. i, 115.

Egal[1]. *Arr. of Paris*, IV, i, 281 ; v, i, 5.

Emperess. *Anglor. Feriœ*, 9.

Enceladus. *Garter*, 46.

Fere (pheere). *Arr. of Paris*, I, i, 20 ; IV, i, 282 ; v, 149. (Also five times elsewhere.)

Gratulate. *Arr. of Paris*, I, i (song) ; *Ed. I*, sc. v, end ; *Battle*, II, i, 20 ; *Desc. Astr.*, 12, 126 ; *Garter*, 372, 435.

Honey-dews. *D. and B.*, sc. iii, 163.

Men-of-war. *Ed. I*, l, 4 ; *Battle*, III, i, 55 (doubtful) ; v, i[2]

Patient (vb.). *Ed. I*, sc. i, 42.

Panther. *Tale of Troy*, 305 ; *Praise of Chastity*, 42.

Palliament. *Garter*, 92.

Prometheus.[3] *Arr. of Paris*, I, ii, 42 ; *Ed. I*, sc. iv, 21.

Philomela.[4] *Arr. of Paris*, I, ii, 37.

Reproachful. *Tale of Troy*, 198 ; *Locrine*, v, ii, IV ; *Jack Straw*.

Remunerate. *Ed. I.* sc. i, 139 ; xiv, 13 ; *Battle*, I, i, 24 ; II, i, 24.

Re-salute. *Honour of the Garter*, 372.

Séquestered. *D. and B.*, sc. xv, 259.

'ticed. *Edward I*, sc. vii, 85. ('ticing. *Tale of Troy*, l. 73 ; *Arr. of Paris*, III, i).

Triùmpher. *Battle*, III, iv, 24.

Wreak. *Battle*, I, i, near end ; II, prol., 21, 31 ; *D. and B.*, II, ii, 13, 102 ; *Jack Straw*, thrice.

Wreakful. *D. and B.*, II, iii, 50.

---

[1] This occurs in the first folio in *M. of V.*, III, iv, 13, but not in Q. i. In the folio it appears to be a misprint.

[2] Peele uses the phrase frequently for soldiers, so does Marlowe.

[3] Shakespeare twice has "Promethean" (*L. L. L.*, IV, iii, 304—duplicated in rewritten passage, 351, and *Othello*, v, ii, 12). Both passages partially echo Peele's phrase, " Prometheus' life-infusing fire " in *Anglorum Feriœ*, 180.

[4] Shakespeare twice has "Philomel" (*M. N. D.* and *Cymbeline*), which occurs four times in *Titus*.

Of the second list we find in Peele the following :

Ætna. *Garter*, 79 ; *Edward I*, sc. 6.
Affy. " Affiance " (= trust) in *Battle*, II, iii, 52.
Braves. *Ed. I*, sc. v, 61 ; sc. x, 210 ; sc. xiii, 69 ; *Farewell*, 19, 69.
Caucasus. *Ed. I*, sc. iv, 21.
Daunt. *Edward I*, sc. iv, 36 ; *Battle*, III, iv, 38 ; *Jack Straw*, III, l. 3 from end. (Daunted, *David*, IV, ii, near end ; *Jack Straw*, III, l. 9).
'joy. *D. and B.*, sc. i, 94 ; sc. iii, 19 ; *Id.* Chorus, 21 sc.[1] xv, 260 ; *Ed. I*, sc. xiii, 98 ; *Device of Pageant*, st. 8 ; *Speeches to Q. Eliz.*, Hermit's, l. 86.
Numb. *Old Wives Tales*, 364. Numb'd ; *Id.* 843 ; *Battle*, I, i, 21.
Miry. *D. and B.*, sc. xiii, 72.
Mourning weeds. *Battle*, I, ii, 20 ; *David*, sc. iii, 87 ; *Locrine*, V, I.
Meanwhile. *Arr. of Paris*, V, i, 123.
Styx. *Arr. of Paris*, thrice in one scene (v, i) ; *Battle*, v, i.
Youngling. *Ed. I*, sc. vi, 48 ; *Battle*, I, ii, 68.

When it is noted that a number of these words occur in the HENRY VI plays and the TAMING OF THE SHREW, in which so many critics have recognised the presence of other hands, and among them Peele's, the total force of the evidence is increased.

For the rest, " raven-coloured " is akin to Peele's " black[2] as the raven's-wing " (POLYHYMNIA, 105) and " like . . . to ravens' feathers " (ANGLORUM FERIÆ, 215-6 ; HONOUR OF THE GARTER, 25) ; " re-edified " (found in LOCRINE) to his " re-salute " and " re-obtain " (ED. I, sc. xiii, 52 ; BATTLE, I, i, 83 ; II, iv, 10) ; " vaunters " and " devourers " to his " forbearers " (ARR. OF PARIS, IV, i, 73) ; " love-day " to his " love-holidays " (ED. I, sc. vii, 97) ; " sorrowwreathen knot " (*i.e.*, folded arms) to " sadness with wreathed arms " (DAVID, sc. iv, 5 ; see also sc. iii, 77), and " popish " to his " popery " (FAREWELL, 36). The

---

[1] In all four instances in *David and Bethsabe* " joy " has the same application as in *Titus ;* and in one, as before noted, the phrase is " joy her love," duplicating " joy her raven-coloured love " in *Titus*.
[2] Peele also has " black as jet " (*Polyhymnia*, 83), which occurs in *Titus* (v, 2) and nowhere else in the Shakespeare concordance. But this is common enough, being found in Marlowe's and Greene's signed work, as well as in the *First Part of the Contention*.

phrase " weighed her anchorage," again, seems to be a
construction entirely in Peele's manner from the phrase
" weigh anchor " (also found in the FAREWELL, 51, and
the BATTLE, III, iii, 41, but not in any Shakespearean
play), somewhat as in LOCRINE (I, i) we have " Left unto
him for an inheritance "—a mere adaptation of the word
to fill the line.   So, too, we may surmise that the curious phrase, " our empress with her sacred wit " (TITUS,
II, i), which the commentators have taken to be a
Latinism, but which might as well be a Gallicism, suggested by *sacré*, is in all probability a mere case of line-
filling by Peele, seeing that the very phrase " sacred
wit " occurs in THE ARRAIGNMENT OF PARIS (IV, i, 285),
and " sacred " is one of his most overdone epithets,
So, again, " sharp revenge " is *prima facie* presumptively his ;   since among over a hundred and fifty
instances of " revenge " in the Shakespeare concordance the epithet " sharp " does not once occur save in
TITUS (I, 137), and the phrase is one of Peele's (DAVID,
sc. vii—II, i, 185 ; BATTLE, I, i, 88), though also found
in Greene and Kyd.   It is an inappropriate adjective.

As for the words beginning in " un," they are of a
type in which he abounds, as unpeople, unarm'd (vb.
trans.), unpartial, unclothed (vb. trans.), untwine,
unloosen, unpardoned, unvanquished, unhonourable,
unconstant, unbelieving, undeceivable ; and the term
" unrecuring " is a likely construction on his part from
" recure," which he has in common with Greene, Kyd,
Marlowe, Lodge, and others.   In EDWARD I, sc. xxv,
132, he has " recureless."   So, again, he abounds in
compound epithets, as :—Twenty-coloured, Britain-
sea, new-formed, new-ripe, true-succeeding, anchor-
hold, wide-commanding, bloody-crested, silver-shining,
angry-sounding, tragic-hued, fine-perfumed, well-
tempered, thrice-haughty, etc., etc.   Such noun-forms,
further, as " enact " and " entreat " are in the manner
of his nouns " exclaims," " imagine " and " encum-
ber " ; and to the contraction " 'surance " he has many
analogies, as :   " 'beisance," " 'nointed," " 'hests,"
" 'bash."

The majority of the terms in our lists being thus directly or by analogy traced to Peele, it might be argued that no difficulty arises from the absence of such chance formations as *rolled* (intrans.) ; *self-blood, guileful, gleeful ;* such terms as *alphabet, grammar, loaf,* and *sapling ;* and the vulgarisms ; or such classic names and words as Aries, Candidatus, Hymenæus, Typhon, Virginius, Progne. The latter sort of terms, we might argue, would come readily to Peele, who has such classical allusions by the hundred ; and he, like other men, would use a certain number of words once only. But we are finally debarred from such an imperfect solution, though Mr. Dugdale Sykes and Professor Quincy Adams appear to remain satisfied with it. We shall find reason to conclude, alike on grounds of style, vocabulary and phrase, that Peele had one or more associates, or predecessors, or revisers, alike in TITUS and in LOCRINE ; thus accounting for a number of the terms special to the latter play, and not otherwise traced to him in the former.

Meantime it should be noted that his large share in TITUS, yet with other hands, is to be further established by a general comparison of vocabularies, taking into account a number of words not special to TITUS in the Shakespearean plays, but specially common in Peele. There are certain words recurring in TITUS which are common in the HENRY VI group, but only once or seldom found in genuine works, and these again we find frequently in both Peele and Marlowe. For instances :

Ruthless, twice in *Titus ; Arr. of Paris*, prol. ; *David*, sc. vii, 18 ; xiii, 60 ; *Battle*, II, prol. i ; v, i, 94, 115.

Empery, thrice in *Titus ; Arr. of Paris*, v, i, 41 ; *Battle*, II, ii, 29 ; iv, 44 ; *Praise of Chastity*, 12.

Entrails, twice in *Titus ; Arr. of Paris*, IV, i, 114 ; *Battle*, II, iii, 5 ; *David*, sc. ix, 8.

Phoebe, once in *Titus ;* once in *L. L. L. ;* once in *M. N. D. ; Arr. of Paris*, nine times.

Coal-black, thrice in *Titus ; Garter*, 146 (also jet, black as jet, and ebon) ; *Polyhymnia*, 99 (also funeral black, etc.).

Consecrate (participle), thrice in *Titus ; Polyhymnia*, twice ; *Honour of the Garter*, thrice ; *David*, thrice.

"Consecrate," it will be remembered, is found in
TITUS in lines which obviously echo the Peele lines here
cited. But each of these words occurs in Marlowe, and
some of them frequently. So, too, the intransitive use
of the verb "dazzle," occurring in TITUS and in VENUS
AND ADONIS (1064), but nowhere else in Shakespeare,
is found in Peele (SPEECHES AT THEOBALD'S, ii, 34, ed.
Bullen)—also, however, in Kyd (S. & P. II, i, 244) and in
Greene (ALPHONSUS KING OF ARRAGON, l. 200, ed.
Grosart). Yet again, the common term "beautify,"
occurring in TITUS and in several plays in which
Shakespeare had fellow-workers, but expressly derided
by him in HAMLET, is common in Peele, who uses it at
least eight times—thrice in DAVID AND BETHSABE alone.
It is also frequent, however, in Greene and Marlowe,
as in most Elizabethan writers.

Finally, the specially frequent use in TITUS of a
word used in the other plays with only normal frequency
gives one more ground for inference. Such a use occurs
in the case of the noun desert (=deserving), which in
only two other composite plays (the TWO GENTLEMEN
and RICHARD III) is used as often as four times, but
occurs five times in the first Act of TITUS.[1] This, in
turn, is one of the tics of Peele, who uses the word eight
times in the ARRAIGNMENT OF PARIS alone, twice in the
last stanza of the PRAISE OF CHASTITY, and frequently
elsewhere. As the first Act of TITUS is notably Peelean
in respect of other clues, the general inference is here
freshly reinforced.

Further scrutiny would probably yield still further
evidence ; but the foregoing may suffice to establish,
as regards vocabulary and phrase, the pervasive
presence of Peele's hand in TITUS. We have next to
trace, by the primary test of vocabulary, the other hand
or hands not accounted for, leaving for later application
the tests of style, versification, mannerisms, matter,
and sentiment. The former task, however, can be best

---

[1] It should be noted that in the concordances of both Mrs. Clarke and Mr.
Bartlett the nouns dèsert and desèrt are not discriminated.

approached by collating TITUS with an earlier play several times hereinbefore cited—the old tragedy of LOCRINE.

§ 4. " TITUS " COMPARED WITH " LOCRINE."

Concerning LOCRINE, Richard Simpson mentions that it was " written, according to Sir George Buck, by Charles Tylney, who was executed for treason in September, 1586—with interpolations from Peele (pointed out by Dyce), and imitations from Greene, and perhaps from Marlowe."[1]   The first of these statements proceeds upon a statement by J. P. Collier to the effect that in an extant copy of the play there is a note " in the handwriting of Sir George Buck " assigning it to Tylney ; and as Collier's statement is otherwise unconfirmed,[2] it is open to the suspicion that so justly attaches to all of his discoveries of this kind.[3]   As Buck was licenser of plays in 1608, in succession to Edmund Tylney, whose deputy he had been,[4] the note, if genuine, would be weighty.   At the same time, it is quite clear that much of the play was written years after 1586[5] ; and there are correspondences between it and TITUS, as well as the works of Greene and Peele, which are of obvious importance.   Fleay has suggested[6] that for " by " Charles Tylney we should understand " concerning " him.   But it is difficult to see how the play can be regarded as written " concerning " Tylney.   It would be more plausible to surmise that it may have been written " for " him.   It is a pseudo-historical drama, based on the chronicle-legends made freshly current by John Higgins[7] in his section of the

---

[1] *Shakespeare Allusion Books*, Pt. i, p. xlvii.
[2] The note by W. C. Hazlitt to W. Hazlitt's *Characters of Shakespeare's Plays*, ed. 1869, p. 237, appears to proceed on Collier.
[3] Chambers, *The Elizabethan Stage*, iv, 27.
[4] Art. on Sir George Buc or Buck in *Dict. of Nat. Biog.*
[5] Cp. Cunliffe in the *Camb. Hist. of Eng. Lit.* v, 85, sq.
[6] *Biog. Chron. of the English Drama*, ii, 321.
[7] Cp. Fleay, *Biog. Chron.*, i, 18.

MIRROR FOR MAGISTRATES (1575), of which a second
edition appeared in 1578. Spenser outlines the story
in the FAERIE QUEENE (B. II, cc. ix, x). Pointing
at nobody in particular, the play is constructed on the
" revenge " model common to Peele and Kyd. On
the other hand, Fleay has argued from various allusions
—such as that to the " private amours " of Mary Queen
of Scots in the epilogue—that the play originally dates
from about 1586 ; but, even if this be accepted, we
shall see reason to regard it as having been shared in
by Greene a little later, inasmuch as it has imitations,
apparently by him, from Marlowe, whose TAMBURLAINE
can hardly be dated before 1587.

This is a somewhat more certain test of date than
the plagiarisms from Spenser's VISIONS OF THE WORLD'S
VANITIE and RUINES OF ROME, noted in LOCRINE by
Mr. Charles Crawford.[1] Those poems were published
only in 1591 ; but the common circulation of poems in
MS. in that period made it possible for the dramatist
to have read them years before ; and the fact that the
play, while largely copying those poems, shows no
certain trace of the FAERIE QUEENE, printed in 1590,
points, albeit only negatively, to its being written or
recast before the latter date. I say no certain traces,
because there are some apparent though slight clues.
LOCRINE (I, i, 88) has the phrase, " old Assaracus, mine
eame " ; and " eame " recurs (III, iv, 54). Now, in the
FAERIE QUEENE we have " old Assaracus " (II, ix, 56)
and " old Assarac's line " (II, x, 9) ; and shortly afterwards we come upon " Cassibalane, their eme " (II, x,
47). Higgins has neither " old Assaracus " nor " eame."
As the latter word is rare, and Greene often echoes words
of Spenser's, there is fair ground for supposing him to
have done so here. Spenser and Greene, of course,
might alike have echoed a chronicle or other source ;
but though writing by Greene after 1589 is the more
probable explanation, he, as well as Marlowe, might have

[1] *Collectanea*, First Ser., 1906, p. 47 sq. Mr. Crawford's theory of the
relation of *Locrine* to *Selimus*, and his ascription of the later play to
Marlowe, are discussed hereinafter.

seen the earlier cantos of the FAERIE QUEENE in MS.
The fact that Peele writes of

> Old Dardanus,
> And Ilus and Assaracus,

in the HONOUR OF THE GARTER (1593), is, however, also
to be noted.   On the other hand, certain plagiarisms,
two of which are in " Dumb Shows " prefixed to Acts
I and III of LOCRINE, are very likely to have been additions, made after 1591.   On the whole question of date
we can but say that the writing of the play and the
revision or revisions are to be placed between 1587 and,
say, 1594.   On examining the diction we shall see
reason to infer more than one hand.

   That the play has not been merely " interpolated
from Peele " with " imitations from Greene " can be
shown in various ways.   Let us first note the specific
Peele passages :

   1. In Act III, sc. ii, we have the lines :

> To arms, my lord, to honourable arms ;
> Take helm and targe in hand ;

which are echoes of these in Peele's FAREWELL (11, 23,
and 50). which appeared in 1589 :—

> Take helm and targe . . .
> Adieu.   To arms, to arms, to glorious arms . . .
> To arms, to arms, to honourable arms.[1]

On the fact that both in LOCRINE and in the BATTLE
OF ALCAZAR ghosts cry " *Vindicta !* " Dyce observes
that " such trifling coincidences afford us no ground
for supposing that Peele was concerned in the composition of that intolerably stilted and pedantic piece,"
LOCRINE.   But on the above-cited duplication of
phrase, which he himself notes, he offers no comment ;

---

[1] Similar echoes form confirmative clues to Peele's authorship of the *Battle*,
which is ascribed to him by quotation in *England's Parnassus*, but was published without any name.   It has, however, a dozen of his tics of style, and
many echoes of his signed phraseology.   Compare the pref. to the Malone
Soc. reprint.

and we must reject his general argument. Peele, surely, can be stilted, and is abundantly pedantic. Some of the pedantries of LOCRINE are among the clues to him. Thus the line (II, vi, 2) :

> Thund'ring alarums, and Rhamnusia's drum,

points to the "thund'ring drums" and "'larums" of Nemesis and "the thunder of Rhamnusia's drum" in the BATTLE OF ALCAZAR (I, i, 47 ; II, 15, 24), as well as to "thundering drum" and "Rhamnusia" in the ARRAIGNMENT OF PARIS (II, Juno's Show ; III, i) ; and in both plays we meet further with Alecto, Rhadamanth, Tisiphone, Erebus, Pluto, and Phlegethon. Mr. Tucker Brooke's argument[1] that the "excessive richness of mythological allusion" in LOCRINE is far greater than in any play of Peele's, and differently employed, ignores these facts.[2] Compare again the rant of Humber (LOC., III, vi) :

> Where may I find some desert wilderness
> Where I may breathe out curses as I would . . .
> Where may I find some hollow *uncouth* rock
> Where I may damn, condemn, and ban *my fill* . . .

with one in the BATTLE (V, i) :

> Where shall I find some unfrequented place,
> Some *uncouth* walk where I may curse *my fill* . . . ;

and the "revenge" lines in the rant of Corineus' ghost (LOC., V, iv) with those of Rubin Archis and Abdelmelec in the BATTLE (I, i). Yet again there is a somewhat close correspondence[3] between these lines of Estrild (LOC., II, i) :

> The plains, my lord, garnished with *Flora's* wealth
> And overspread with *parti-colour'd flowers* . . .
> The airy hills enclosed with shady *groves* . . .

---

[1] *The Shakespeare Apocrypha*, introd. p. xviii.
[2] Not only is the *Arraignment* as full of mythology as might be expected, but there are about forty mythological allusions in *Edward I*, and about as many in *The Battle of Alcazar*.
[3] Noted by Mr. A. F. Hopkinson in his *Essays on Shakespeare's Doubtful Plays*, 1900.

> Are equal to the groves of Thessaly,
> *Where* Phoebus with the learned ladies nine
> *Delight* themselves . . .
> The *silent* springs dance down with murmuring streams,

and some in the ARRAIGNMENT OF PARIS (I, i), where *Flora* speaks :

> These fields and *groves* and sweetest bowers
> Bestrew'd and deck'd with *parti-colour'd flowers,*
> Along the bubbling brooks and silver glide
> That at the bottom doth in *silence* slide . . .
> *Where* sacred Phoebe may *delight* to be.

And again we have the echoes of " parti-coloured " in the HONOUR OF THE GARTER (l. 72) and the " waves making soft music in their gentle *glide* " in ANGLORUM FERIAE (l. 5). Such echoes are substantially of the order of those we have above noted as between Peele's works and TITUS ; and Peele's ARRAIGNMENT (1584) antedates LOCRINE. Of course Tylney or another might in 1586 have echoed him ; but when we have seen how much he is given to echoing himself there is at least a presumption of that kind here ; and it becomes important to note how far the vocabulary of LOCRINE coincides with the non-Shakespearean terms in TITUS. That some of the same hands have been concerned in the two plays is made fairly clear by various phrases and speeches.

In the former there are preliminary allusions to wars against the " barbarous Gauls " ; in the latter it is the " barbarous Goths " ;[1] and, still in the first Act, we have the echo :

Remaineth nought, but to inter our brethren	(*T. A.*, i, 1) ;
It resteth now that we inter his bones	(*Locr.*, i, 2) ;

and " it resteth " is a common usage of Peele's, though

---

[1] It will be remembered that in *Titus and Vespasian* the country of the Queen and Aaron had been " Aethiopia" or " Moor-land." It was probably Peele who substituted Goths, at the cost of making the Andronici rely on the countrymen of the empress for troops to attack the empire. Again an Italian lead has been followed. As Wolff notes, the Goths had been introduced into Italian epic by Trissino, and put on the boards by Tasso in his *Torrismondo.*

not peculiar to him. Yet again, each play exhibits the peculiarity of names varied in form for metre's sake.[1] Thus " Saturnine" and " Saturninus," " Philomel " and " Philomela," " empress " and " emperess," in TITUS, are paralleled by " Locrine " and " Locrinus," " Estrild " and " Estrilda," " Gwendolen " and " Gwendolena," in LOCRINE. Finally, the two plays correspond so closely in the manner of their conclusion that were there no other evidence we should there be led to infer for them some community of origin. The closing speech of Lucius runs :

> Some loving friends convey the emperor hence,
> *And give him burial in his father's grave :*
> My father and Lavinia shall forthwith
> *Be closed in our household's monument.*
> As for that heinous tiger, Tamora,
> *No funeral rite, nor man in mourning weeds,*
> *No mournful bell shall ring her burial ;*
> But throw her forth to beasts and birds of prey :
> Her life was beast-like, and devoid of pity ;
> And being so shall have like want of pity.

In LOCRINE the victorious Guendolen made a similar arrangement :

> And as for Locrine, our deceased spouse
> Because he was the son of mighty Brute,
> To whom we owe our country, lives, and goods—
> *He shall be buried in a stately tomb,*
> *Close by his aged father Brutus' bones,*
> With such great pomp and great solemnity
> As well beseems so brave a prince as he.
> *Let Estrild lie without the shallow vaults,*
> *Without the honour due unto the dead,*
> Because she was the author of this war.

The hand in both speeches is probably that of Peele : the style is not Greene's, and the whole business compares closely with that of the final speech in THE BATTLE OF ALCAZAR. If the first-cited speech was written by Shakespeare he was a servile imitator indeed.

[1] Seen also in the *Two Gentlemen*—" Valentine " and " Valentinus."

And, whether it regard Peele or others of his school, there is so much imitation in TITUS of tricks of manner met with in LOCRINE and in Peele's plays that it becomes, to say the least, considerably simpler to assign TITUS to that school than to charge it upon Shakespeare. A general comparison of some of these characteristics may usefully precede the collation of vocabularies.

1. One of Peele's most obvious mannerisms is that of alliteration. A survival from Anglo-Saxon verse, it was indeed a vice of the whole pre-Shakespearean drama, setting-in with FERREX AND PORREX ; it is prominent in Spenser ; and it is equally flagrant in the prose of the Euphuistic school ; but Peele outgoes all competitors in the extravagance of his resort to it in all his dramas.   He has literally hundreds of lines such as this :

> Brandishing bright the blade of adamant   (*Ed. I*, sc. v).

Often it reaches burlesque, as in the rant of the Moor in the BATTLE (v, i) :

> Ye elements of whom consists this clay,
> This mass of flesh, this cursèd crazèd corpse,
> Destroy, dissolve, disturb, and dissipate . . . ;

in the lines :

> With men and ships, courage and cannon-shot . . .
> To finish fainting Dido's dying life . . . ;

and again in DAVID AND BETHSABE :

> Then let my presence with my sighs perfume
> The pleasant closet of my sovereign's soul.

Apart from burlesque effects, the practice is normal in DAVID :

> And shoot forth shafts as thick and dangerous
> As was the hail that Moses mixed with fire
> And threw with fury round about the fields,
> Devouring Pharaoh's friends and Egypt's fruits   (sc. ii).

Thou and thy sister, soft and sacred Air ;
Goddess of Life, and governess of health (sc. i).

And makes their weapons wound the senseless winds
(sc. ii).

And suffered sin to smite his father's bones . . .
Gives us the hook that hales our souls to hell . . .
Which with a rusty weapon I will wound,
And make them passage to my panting heart . . .
On whose sweet beauty I bestow my blood . . .
So merely consecrate to her content . . .
And views the passage with such piercing eyes
That none can 'scape to cheer my pining cheeks,
But all is thought too little for her love. (sc. iii).

And fill the face of every flower with dew . . .
Droop, drown, and drench in Hebron's fearful streams
(sc. v.)

Of this sort of thing there is an infinity in LOCRINE :

And fill'd his furious heart with fretting ire . . .
Passèd the greedy gulf of oceän . . .
My sinews shrink, my numbèd senses fail . . .
A grateful gift given by a gracious king . . .
Where murmuring rivers slide with silent streams . . .
A savage captain of a savage crew . . .
The cursèd captain of that damnèd crew . . .

2. Another of Peele's tics (common to Kyd, Greene
and Peele) in his signed work is that of reiteration,
whether by way of (a) groups of lines beginning with
one word, or (b) of repetition of words and phrases. In
this fashion also he is apt to be absurd :

But follow to the gates of death and hell,
Pale death and hell, to entertain his soul
(*Battle*, I, ii, 122-3).

Thus Europe, rich and mighty in her kings,
Hath feared brave England, dreadful in her kings
(*Ed. I*, sc. i).

Yet were their lives valued at thousand worlds
They cannot 'scape th'arrest of dreadful death,
Death that doth seize and summon all alike (*ib*).

O fortune cruel, cruel and unkind,
Unkind in that we cannot find our sister,
Our sister, hapless in her cruel chance
>   (*Old Wives Tale*, 141-3).

So thoroughly did the habit possess him that it entered into his later non-dramatic verse :

And be that day England's high holiday,
And holidays and high days be they all,
High holidays, days, minutes, months, and hours,
That multiply the number of her years ;
Years that for us beget this golden age,
Wherein we live in safety under her,
Wherein she reigns in honour over us
>   (*Anglorum Feriæ*, ll, 46-52).

To slip remembrance of those careful days,
Days full of danger, happy days withal,
Days of her preservation and defence ;
Behold the happiest day, the holiday
That young and old and all don celebrate,
The day of joy, the day of jollity,
The best of all the days that we have seen
>   (*Id.*, ll, 67-73).

In his signed plays, the mannerism is seen everywhere.   For instances :

What warlike nation, trained in feats of arms,
What barbarous people, stubborn, or untam'd,
What climate under the meridian signs   (*Ed. I*, sc. i).

Welcome, sweet queen, my fellow-traveller,
Welcome, sweet Nell, my fellow-mate in arms   (*Id., ib.*).

Follow the man that means to make you great ;
Follow Fluellen, rightful Prince of Wales   (*Id.*, sc. ii).

Thy sin, thy shame, the sorrow of thy soul :
Sin, shame, and sorrow swarm about thy soul
>   (*D. and B.*, sc. iv).

Traitor to heaven, traitor to David's throne,
Traitor to Absalon and Israel   (*Id.*, sc. iii).

And in the morning sound the voice of war,
The voice of bloody and unkindly war   (*Id.*, sc. x).

But Absalon, the beauty of my bones,
Fair Absalon, the counterfeit of love,
Sweet Absalon, the image of content   (*Id.*, sc. xv).

Of these devices, again, we have countless examples in LOCRINE :

Brutus, that was a glory to us all ;
Brutus, that was a terror to our foes . . .

We'll either rent the bowels of the earth,
Searching the bowels of the brutish earth . . .

If all my care, if all my grievous wounds,
If all my diligence were well employed . . .

Where'er Aurora, handmaid of the sun,
Where'er the sun bright guardian of the day,
Where'er the joyful day with cheerful light.
Where'er the light illuminates the world . . .

Thus in the morning of my victories,
Thus in the prime of my felicity . . .

So perish they that are our enemies !
So perish they that love not Humber's weal.

The Hun shall die, had he ten thousand lives :
And would to God he had ten thousand lives.

This sword shall reave his master of his life,
That oft has saved his master's doubtful life.

For now revenge shall ease my lingering grief,
And now revenge shall glut my longing soul.

In TITUS, though that is a distinctly less archaistic play than LOCRINE, the alliterations start with the first line :

Noble patricians, patrons of my right . . .
Romans, friends, followers, favourers of my right . . .
Princes, that strive by factions and by friends . . .

So begin the first three speeches. Of the scores of instances which follow, a handful may suffice :

> Safe out of fortune's shot, and sits aloft
> Secure . . .
> Clear up, fair queen, that cloudy countenance,
> Though chance of war hath wrought this change of cheer . . .
> Therefore, great lords, be, as your titles witness,
> Imperious, and impatient of your wrongs . . .
> Full well I wot the ground of all this grudge . . .
> Woe to her chance, and damn'd her loathed choice . . .
> That woe is me to think upon their woes . . .
> For peace, for love, for league, and good to Rome . . .
> O, handle not the theme, to talk of hands . . .
>   With revengeful war
> Take wreak on Rome . . .
> The story of that baleful burning night
> When subtle Greeks surprized King Priam's Troy . . .

It is the same with the trick of iteration. In TITUS we have many instances, as :

> These, that survive, let Rome reward with love ;
> These, that I bring unto their latest home   (I, ii).[1]

> In peace and honour rest you here, my sons !   (twice)
> In peace and honour live Lord Titus long   (*Id., ib.*).

> To wait upon this new-made emperess.
> To wait, said I ? to wanton with this queen,
> This goddess, this Semiramis, this nymph,
> This siren, that will charm Rome's Saturnine   (II, i).

> For all my blood in Rome's great quarrel shed ;
> For all the frosty nights that I have watched   (III, i).

> Perchance she weeps because they killed her husband ;
> Perchance because she knows them innocent   (*Id., ib.*).

> Then must my sea be moved with her sighs ;
> Then must my earth with her continual tears
> Become a deluge   (*Id., ib.*).

> Coal-black is better than another hue,
> In that it scorns to bear another hue   (IV, ii).

---

[1] Latterly Act I is usually treated as a single scene.

> As if we should forget we had no hands
> If Marcus did not name the word of hands.   (III, ii, 33).

The usage, in short, pervades the whole play. We have to note, however, that alliteration and reiteration and pleonasm in the blank-verse drama all date from FERREX AND PORREX. Witness the following :

> For you, for yours, and for our native land . . .
> For kings, for kingdoms, and for common weals . . .
> When fatal death shall end my mortal life . . .
> To serve, to aid, and to defend your grace . . .
> Your age in quiet shall the longer last :
> Your lasting age shall be their longer stay . . .
> Ruthful remembrance is yet raw in mind . . .
>
> What princes slain before their fatal hour !
> What waste of towns and people in the land !
> What treasures heaped on murders and on spoils !

And these mannerisms, be it further noted, abound in Kyd's SPANISH TRAGEDY no less than in the works of Peele and Greene.

It might accordingly be argued that the problematic Tylney, writing in 1586, copied the old tragedy as Kyd and Peele and Greene did. The same tics and tricks, again, are met with in Robert Wilmot's TANCRED AND GISMUNDA, originally written in rhyme in 1568, and published " newly reviv'd, and polished according to the decorum of those days," in 1592. There we find such groups of lines as these :

> Yet in this wound I see mine own true love,
> And in this wound thy magnanimity,
> And in this wound I see thy constancy ;
>
> No love of parents to their child[e]ren ;
> No love of princes to their subjects true ;
> No love of ladies to their dearest love ;

and such lines as :

> What hope of hap may cheer my hapless chance . . .
> My lord, my love, my life, my liking, gone . . .
> Curst be the stars, and vanish may they curst
> (Act I, sc, iii).

But as Wilmot apparently had not imitated FERREX AND PORREX in his original play, the presumption is that in 1592 he either sedulously imitated Peele and Kyd and Greene, or got one of them to dress up his play for him. And as we cannot well be sure that an amateur, writing in 1586, would write in blank verse at all, the clear balance of presumption goes towards the view that LOCRINE is in part written or revised by Peele. The epilogue, girding at Mary Queen of Scots and glorifying Elizabeth, is very likely to be his, as he apotheosises Elizabeth in almost every one of his plays and poems, and vilifies a Queen of Spanish race in EDWARD I.

Peele's hand, however, covers only part of the ground. Even the frequent mention of " Troyno-vant " (= New Troy = London) is not certainly made by him, though it is one of his favourite allusions. Greene uses the word frequently also ; and it occurs several times in Higgins. There are further many peculiarities of vocabulary not to be matched in any of Peele's signed plays ; and in looking for the source of these we find good cause to assign them to Greene. In LOCRINE there occur : (a) three times the term " captivate " (= take captive), which is also found in Greene's prose and poetry (Dyce, p. 315), but not in Peele, though it is in the SPANISH TRAGEDY ; (b) the rare word " agnominated," not found in Peele, but occurring in Greene's prose ; (c) the unusual word " occision " (= slaughter), not to be met with in Peele's known works, but found in SELIMUS,[1] which is reasonably assigned by Dr. Grosart to Greene[2] ; (d) " transfreting," which occurs in SELIMUS (72) but not in Peele ; (e) " pittering," which is in the same case ; and (f) " anthropophagi," which also is in the same case, and is found in Greene's prose, as well as in ORLANDO FURIOSO ; while (g) the epithet " arm-

[1] Line 2476 of Malone Soc. rep. ; 2485 of " Temple " ed. It is misprinted " occasion " in the latter reprint, but correctly in Dr. Grosart's ed. of Greene's Works. The word is both Latin and Italian (occisione) and Greene knew Italian.
[2] See the discussion below, ch. viii.

strong," occurring in SELIMUS and three times in LOCRINE, is nowhere found in Peele's signed works, and is shown by Dr. Grosart to occur in Greene's prose (MENAPHON : Works, vi, 83) in a duplicate of one of the phrases of LOCRINE—" the arm-strong darling of the doubled night." Similarly (*h*) the verb " to cut," in the sense of crossing the sea or making a journey, found in ORLANDO FURIOSO, also in the MOURNING GARMENT (xi, 132-3), in LOCRINE (II, i, 8), and several times in Greene's prose, and (*i*) " cor'sive," found in LOCRINE and SELIMUS, and often in Greene's prose, are absent from Peele's works.[1] To Greene, too, we must allot the word " roseal " (Loc. iv, i, v, i end) which occurs in JAMES II (v, 3), and which in LOCRINE is repeated in thoroughly Greenean phrases about white-and-rose cheeks and " entangling " looks. Yet another phrase, " cursed charms," found in LOCRINE (II, v), appears to be a specialty of Greene's, who has it thrice in ALPHONSUS (ed. Dyce, pp. 225, 235, 244). Further, some of the rants about " Puriphlegethon " in LOCRINE are also without close parallel in Peele, and read very like semi-burlesques of Marlowe, as do portions of Greene's ascribed play ALPHONSUS KING OF ARRAGON. As regards Kyd, again, it is not here possible to detect any similarities of diction, though he uses the old tricks of iteration and alliteration as do the others.

Passing from vocabulary to phrase, we find a number of echoes and duplications in LOCRINE and SELIMUS.[2]

The image of true magnanimity	(*Sel.*, 1472).
Locrine, the map of magnanimity	(*Locr.*, v, iv).
Thou hast not Fortune tièd in a chain	(*Sel.*, 2420).
Leads Fortune tièd in a chain of gold	(*Locr.*, II, i, 15).
Crack my lance upon his burgonet	(*Locr.*, II, i, 84).

[1] " Cor'sive " is one of a number of words apparently taken by Greene from Lilly, whose *Euphues* he echoes so often in his prose. It is of course older than Lilly, but not common before him. It occurs also in the *Faerie Queene*, but, as above noted, *Locrine* in its first draft antedates that poem.

[2] The multitude of resemblances between the two plays has been repeatedly noted. See Mr. Tucker Brooke's introduction to *The Shakespeare Apocrypha*, 1908, p. xviii.

> Engrave our prowess on their burgonets   (*Sel.*, 2430).
> The Trojan s glory flies with golden wings   (*Locr.*, I, i).
> Mounteth to highest heaven with golden wings   (*Sel.*, 2031).

The two last lines are among the Spenserian echoes found in the two plays, Spenser having the line :—

> But Fame with golden wings aloft doth fly.
> *Ruines of Rome*, l. 421.

But each of the other phrases, as it happens, is a tag found in Greene's signed works. (1) As we shall see, the " map " formula occurs there many times ; (2) in the FAREWELL TO FOLLY (Works, ix, 256) we find : " He thought Fortune had been tied to his thoughts in a string " ; and in ALPHONSUS KING OF ARRAGON : " I clap up Fortune in a cage of gold " (Act IV, near end)[1] ; and (3) the " burgonet " tag, we shall see later, is also used by him. Still more precise is the duplication in LOCRINE of a line in Orpheus' song in the ORPHARION :

> Unkind, she wrong'd her first and truest fere.
> (Dyce, p. 316.)
> Unkind, thou wrong'st thy first and truest fere.
> (*Loc.* v, iv.)

It is of course impossible to say which line was the first written ; but on either view Greene's share in the play need not be put later than 1589 (the date of ORPHARION), which would consist with its general primitiveness. And there are other clues of the kind. In a blank-verse interlude in Greene's signed story PERIMEDES THE BLACKSMITH (1588), occurs the line :

> And rent the bowels of the middle earth.

Compare it with these in LOCRINE :

> We'll either rent the bowels of the earth . . .   (I, i, 78).
> Renteth the bowels of the fruitful fields . . .   (IV, i, 20).
> And rent thy bowels with my bloody hands   (IV, ii, near end).

[1] Marlowe has :—
> I hold the fates bound fast in iron chains.
> (I *Tamb.* I, ii).
Greene affects " Fortune " and " gold."

Compare again the lines of LOCRINE (II, i, 1-4) which parody Watson's HECATOMPATHIA :

> At length the snail doth climb the highest tops
> Ascending up the stately castle walls ;
> At length the water with continual drops
> Doth penetrate the hardest marble stone,

with these (Dyce, p. 318) from a song in Greene's signed tale ARBASTO, which dates from 1584 :—

> In time we see the silver drops
> The craggy stones make soft ;
> The slowest snail in time we see
> Doth creep and climb aloft ;

and note further the phrase in MENAPHON (Arber's rep. p. 39), which dates 1589 :—" Affection is like the snail, which stealeth to the top of the lance by minutes." In that story, again, we have the phrase " Hard-hearted death " (Arber's rep. p. 62), which occurs in LOCRINE (v, 4). The echoes are mostly slight, and never tell us anything as to priority ; but they all point to Greene.

Again, five lines of rant, partly echoed from Spenser and from TAMBURLAINE,[1] in LOCRINE II, v, are duplicated in SELIMUS with only three slight verbal differences[2] :

> As when Briareus arm'd with an hundred hands
> Flung forth an hundred mountains at great Jove ;
> And when the monstrous giant Monychus
> Hurl'd Mount Olympus at great Mars's targe
> And shot huge cedars at Minerva's shield ;

and two lines of another rant in each play (SEL., 1801-2 ; LOC. III, vi) are similarly duplicated :

> And utter curses to the concave sky
> Which may infect the region of the air.
>   airy regions.

---

[1] *Ruines of Rome*, st. 10, 11, 12, 16 ; 1 *Tamb*, v. 1, 512-3 ; 2 *Tamb*. IV, i, 132-3.

[2] In *Locrine* we have " shot " where *Selimus* has (" darted." In both plays the word " dart " or (" darteth ") has previously occurred, and the presumptio₁ arises that in *Locrine* there has been a revision. But the matter is of little importance to the argument. The original source of the passage is Spenser.

" Concave," we may note, occurs twice in two successive speeches in FRIAR BACON, sc. viii, also in LOCRINE, v, 2. It is probably an echo from Marlowe,— 2 TAMB., III, ii and iv ; FAUSTUS, III, Chorus.

As it happens, the speech in LOCRINE is one to which we have already found a parallel from a rant in Peele and we are thus reminded that the collaborators may at times have echoed each other. In another rant in LOCRINE, however (II, v), the line :

> I'll pass the Alps to watery Meröe,

echoes ORLANDO FURIOSO (ed. Dyce, p. 104) :

> I'll pass the Alps and up to Meroe
> . . . that watery lakish hill ;

and as in the LOCRINE speech we have the uncommon word " chequered," otherwise traceable to Greene, and not found in Peele, the passage as a whole must be provisionally assigned to the former. So, too, with the rare[1] word " Venerean " (= amorous) found in LOCRINE, v, i. Greene in his prose has twice the word " Venerie," also formed from " Venus," and Peele has neither. The TITUS word " Venereal " is therefore tentatively assignable to Greene, not Peele. Nor can there be much doubt that the phrase " a confused chaos of mishaps " (LOC. v, iv) is Greene's, seeing that he has " a chaos of confused mishaps " in his PERIMEDES, 1588 (Works, vii, 25) ; " a chaos of confused precepts " in Part II of the TRITAMERON OF LOVE (Works, iii, 143) ; again " a confused chaos of her [fancy's] follies," in TULLY'S LOVE, 1589 (vii, 166) ; " a confused chaos of sorrowful and disquieted passions " ; and " a restless chaos of confused passions " in PENELOPE'S WEB (v, 177-178) ; " a confused chaos of contrary conceits " in the CARD OF FANCY (iv, 18) ; and yet again " confused chaos " in the FAREWELL TO FOLLY ; also in the Epistle Dedicatory to NEVER TOO LATE (viii, 6 ; ix, 306).

---

[1] It occurs in Chettle's *Kind Harte's Dream*. Sh. Allusion Books, i, 64.

Again, the phrase " lukewarm blood,"[1] occurring twice in LOCRINE (II, iii, 4 ; v, iv) and once in SELIMUS (2379), may be Greene's, as it occurs in the Alleyn MS. of ORLANDO FURIOSO (Dyce, p. 107), and " luke-warm " is frequently and gratuitously used in his prose—*e.g.*, " luke-warm drops " (= tears) in ALCIDA (Works, ix, 22) and in MENAPHON (Arber's ed. p. 32)—though Peele also uses the word " luke-warm " frequently. Finally there are in both plays scenes of a starving man, with comic relief, in exactly the same manner.

Having thus seen good reason to divide LOCRINE substantially between Greene and Peele, giving perhaps most of it to the former, we may with some approach to confidence assign between them, as follows, the non-Shakespearean words in TITUS which are also found in the former play :

First List.

Cocytus. *Loc.* III, vi ; IV, iv. Probably Greene's, as it occurs in *Orlando Furioso.*

Devoid. *Loc.* I, i, 16. Probably Greene's, as it occurs frequently in his prose (*e.g.*, at least five times in the *Card of Fancy ;* Works, ed. Grosart, iv, 21, 25, 135, 143, 171) and never in Peele. (It occurs four times in the old *King Leir.*)

Re-edify. *Loc.* II, iii (song). Greene's ?[2]

Remunerate. *Loc.* II, iii. Probably Peele's, as he has the word frequently.

Reproachful. *Loc.* v, ii, iv. Once in Peele ; often in Greene.

Venerean. *Loc.* v, i. Probably Greene's, as we have seen.

Second List.

Faint-hearted. " Faint-heart " in *Loc.* II, i, 3 ; III, i ; v, iv. Probably Greene's. The word, however, is frequent in Marlowe, and is found in Kyd.

Numb'd. *Loc.* I, i. Probably Greene's, though Peele also uses the word, as does Marlowe.

[1] Another echo from Marlowe.
[2] The word occurs in Spenser (*F. Q.* Bk. II, c. x, st. 46), in Marlowe, and several times in Nashe ; but it had been made current in England by the dying words of Henry V ; and it is found in Robinson's trans. of More's *Utopia* (1551). It is in fact a fairly common Tudor word.

Chequered. *Loc.* II, v. Probably Greene's. See his *Quip for an Upstart Courtier* (Works, xi, 214) ; also the poem *Eurymachus in Laudem Mirimidae*, Radagon's Sonnet, and Francesco's Roundelay—all in *Never too Late* (Dyce, pp. 298, 301).

Semiramis. *Loc.* II, i. Probably Greene's there ; it is common in his prose, his plays, and his poems.

Braves. *Loc.* v, iii. Common to Peele and Greene.

Youngling. *Loc.* v, iv. Ditto.

There are thus some clues from vocabulary in the single play of LOCRINE to Greene's work in TITUS ; and it becomes necessary to collate his signed and otherwise assigned work for further evidence.

§ 5. GREENE AND KYD IN " TITUS "

Seeking to trace further Greene's hand in TITUS, we are at once faced by Dr. Grosart's claim that the play is " substantially " his[1]—an advance upon Grant White's assignment of it to Shakespeare, Greene, and Marlowe. For this thesis the evidence is at first sight fairly strong. Not only is Greene shown to be probably the introducer of the tags about " a woman, therefore to be won," and " hammering in my head " : a list of over twenty significant words, special to TITUS in the Shakespearean concordance, is made out from his works, with SELIMUS included. This, of course, will not serve to make out Dr. Grosart's claim, though he refused to contemplate a rival theory. Mr. A. W. Verity had produced, in his introduction to TITUS in the " Henry Irving " Shakespeare, one of the noteworthy parallels from Peele above presented ; and Dr. Grosart, without giving the quotation, dismissed it in a fashion which probably dissuaded some of his readers from examining it for themselves. It is true that, as he says, the *idea* in the " zodiac " line in TITUS is a poetic commonplace—a similar figure is frequent in Greene—but he of all men should have noted that the question is not here of ideas but of words and phrases. In his turn

[1] Art. " Was Robert Greene substantially the author of ' Titus Andronicus ' ? " in *Englische Studien*, Bd. xxii, 1896.

Dr. Grosart received still more violent treatment from Mr. Baildon, who wrote of his list of words :

> "If this list were correct it would amount to very little that out of so many hundreds and thousands of words used by those two writers *twenty-five should be common to Greene and 'Titus Andronicus.'* . . . But the list is very inaccurate ; it is on the verge of being disingenuous. Certainly no less than one-half of the words consist either (1) of words like 'architect,' 'alphabet,' etc., which, having practically no synonyms, must be used by any writer if he wishes to express a certain idea ; (2) of proper names like Enceladus, Hymenæus, Progne, and Philomela, which were doubtless (!) familiar to both writers, and in two out of the four the difference is merely in form, as Shakespeare has *Hymen* and *Philomel* frequently ; (3) of words which *do* occur elsewhere in Shakespeare, as 'continence,' 'dandle,' 'dazzle,' 'gad,' 'headless,' and 'extent' ; (4) of words which *do not* occur in Greene, as the form 'bear-whelp,' 'devourers,' 'passionate' (the verb), and 'venereal.' Deducting these words, fifteen in all, we get the grand total of *ten words common to Greene and 'Titus Andronicus'* ! This surely speaks for itself as to the forced feebleness of this argument."

Mr. Baildon has here fallen twice into a bad blunder in the act of charging disingenuousness on Dr. Grosart. The phrase italicised completely mis-states the issue. The words in common between Greene and TITUS are to be counted by hundreds, since the play draws on the normal English vocabulary. The list which Mr. Baildon so summarily reduces to ten is made up of words found in Greene which occur *only in* TITUS ANDRONICUS *among the plays ascribed to Shakespeare*— an entirely different thing. The total number of words thus special to TITUS, excluding compounds, is only some eighty odd, and twenty-five would be about thirty per cent.

As for Mr. Baildon's objections to Dr. Grosart's list, they are partly erroneous and partly inconclusive. Dr. Grosart committed the easily-made mistakes of putting "dazzle" and "dandle" in his list of words special to TITUS in Shakespeare, whereas "dazzle" as an intransitive verb occurs in VENUS AND ADONIS, and "dandle" should be in the list of words occurring in TITUS and in a disputed play (2 HENRY VI). But "dandle" thus remains a valid clue ; and even " dazzle " is not void of significance. Concerning " headless " Dr. Grosart had probably meant to note that only in TITUS in the Shakespeare concordance is this word used metaphorically : elsewhere it is used literally. As to " alphabet " and " architect " Mr. Baildon's argument breaks down, for both terms are used in TITUS figuratively, not literally ; and he is obviously wrong in saying that they have no synonyms. Practically speaking they have several,[1] " architect " being used *metaphorically*. He might indeed have argued thus concerning " Aries " ; but Dr. Grosart does not cite that word, though it occurs in Greene's poem put in the mouth of the palmer in NEVER TOO LATE (which has stanzas to all the zodiacal signs), and several times in his prose. With regard to the mythological proper names " *doubtless* familiar to both writers " Mr. Baildon at once begs the question and ignores the elenchus ; for what he calls " doubtless " is the thing doubted : and part of the argument from vocabulary is that a man is to be traced by his mannerisms. Mr. Baildon has thus failed to overthrow Dr. Grosart's thesis.

The warranted criticism of that thesis is that it ignores the concurrent claims of other writers, as will appear when we study Dr. Grosart's word-lists. The first, justly corrected, runs :—

Alphabet	*Enceladus*	*Panther*
Architect[2]	Entreats[3] (noun)	*Philomela*
Battle-axe	*Fere*	Progne
Big-boned	Hymenæus	*Re-salute*
Continence	*Love-day*	To-fore
Dandle	Metamorphoses[4]	Venereal
Dazzle (vb. intrans.)	Over-shade	

Of words occurring in TITUS and other disputed plays,

[1] Greene elsewhere (Lamilia's Song, in the *Groatsworth of Wit*) has " A.B.C."
[2] I have italicised the words seen already to occur in Peele.
[3] Dr. Grosart refers to a passage in which Greene uses the verb, not the noun. But the noun occurs in the verses at the end of his *Groatsworth of Wit* (*New Sh. Soc. Allusion Books*, i, 1874, p. 32, line 28).
[4] This, as before remarked, being the title of a familiar book, has no evidential force.

but not common in Shakespeare, Dr. Grosart further finds the following more or less common in Greene :—

Affy	Complot	Insinuate (=wheedle)
Braves	*Empery*	*Maugre*[1]
Checkered	*Gratulate*	

To these may be added :

Sumptuously,[2] twice in *Pandosto* (near end), again in *Card of Fancy* (end) ; in *Farewell to Folly* (Works, xi, 318) ; in *Euphues his Censure* (vi, 164), and in *Orpharion* (xii, 15).

Meanwhile, twice in *Looking Glass for London* (ll. 1136, 1759.)[3]
Execrable (*id*. l. 787).

Guileful, occurring in Francesco's sonnet in *Never Too Late* (Dyce's Greene and Peele, p. 299), and in the Hexametrae Rosamundae in *The Mourning Garment* (*id*. p. 306).

Mistletoe (spelt *missenden*) in *Never Too Late* (Works, viii, 174) ;
Sustenance (*Looking-Glass*, ed. Dyce, p. 138) ; and
Shipwreck, which is frequent in Greene's prose, and is probably his in *Sir Clyomon* (Dyce, p. 511, twice).

Nor is this all. Dr. Grosart has overlooked two clear parallels of phrase between TITUS and Greene's prose works, as to which there can be little doubt of his authorship. In TITUS (II, i, 85) we have :

> More water floweth by the mill
> Than wots the miller of.

In Greene's NEVER TOO LATE (Works, viii, 81-82) we find :

> Much runs by the mill that the miller never knows of ;

and again in PHILOMELA (Works, xi, 141) :

> They may let much water slip by the mill that the miller knoweth not of.

---

[1] I have put aside " vild " and some others, as common Elizabethan terms. Dr. Grosart further cites the *adjective* " passionate " as a parallel to the verb-form ; and claims to find " bear-whelp " in Greene where there is only a reference to bears *and* their whelps, such as occurs also in Peele. To " Venereal " he gives no reference, citing only " Venerie " ; " extent " he includes by oversight ; and he has one or two other mistakes. But " Venereal " as we have seen, points to " Venerean " in *Locrine*, which is apparently from Greene.

[2] This is a normal flection of " sumptuous " ; but even that word is found only in the *Henry VI* plays in " Shakespeare."

[3] It should be noted that Grosart's line numberings include the stage directions.

Equally evident is the source of the Titus lines :—

> *Sorrow concealèd*, like an *oven stopped*,
> Doth burn the heart to *cinders* where it is.

Shakespeare, it is true, has in Venus and Adonis, as we have seen, the lines (331-4) :

> An oven that is stopped, or river stay'd,
> Burneth more hotly, swelleth with more rage ;
> So of *concealed sorrow* may be said :
> Free vent of words love's fire doth assuage ;

and, as we have seen, not only Professor Collins but Professor Parrott claims that the crude phrasing in Titus is from the same hand. Clearly there is a connection ; but that summary decision will not bear scrutiny. As I pointed out in the former edition, the sorrow-and-oven tag is very frequent in Greene ; and a collation of a number of the instances will reveal that the passage in the Venus is certainly an echo *from* him. I would now add that the parallel passage in The Two Gentlemen, which has not been cited by either critic in this connection, is a ground, not for endorsing the ascription of the Titus passage to Shakespeare, but for assigning to Greene both the comedy and the tragedy passages. The former runs (II, vii, 26) :—

> *Luc.*   I do not seek to quench your love's hot fire,
> But qualify the fire's extreme rage,
> Lest it should burn above the bounds of reason.
> *Jul.*   The more thou *damm'st* it up, the more it burns.
> The current that with gentle murmur glides,
> Thou know'st, being *stopp'd*, impatiently doth rage ;
> But when his fair course is not hinderèd,
> He makes sweet music with the enamelled stones, etc.

Already in Act I, sc. ii, l. 30, we have had the same tag in brief :—

> Fire that is closest kept burns most of all.

Upon Professor Parrott's principles, these further echoes of the Titus line are also Shakespearean ;

Shakespeare being thus credited with *four* spontaneous uses of one common trope, all about the same year ; and a trope, too, which had been many times used in closely similar wording by Greene.

In GREENE'S VISION we have the parallel :

> *Sorrows concealed* are the most sour ; and the griefs smothered, if they burst not out, will make the *heart to break* (Works, xii, 211) ;

in TULLY'S LOVE :

> The *oven*, the closer it is *dammed up*, the greater the heat . . . *conceal* not sorrows lest thou overcharge (Works, vii, 144) ;

in NEVER TOO LATE :

> The *oven damped up* hath the greatest heat. Fire suppressed is most forcible ; the *streames stopt* either break through or overflow, and *sorrows concealed*, as they are most passionate so they are most peremptory (Works, viii, 84) ;

and again in the same tale :

> Heat suppressed is the more violent : the *stream stopt* makes the greater deluge ; and *passions concealed* procure the deeper sorrows. (p. 103.)

Then in ORPHARION we have :

> by *staying the stream* maketh the flood flow more fiercely ; to repress the fire is to increase the flame ; and to *conceal* love is to smother smoke in the nosethril, which will either out or else stifleth (Works, xii, 34) ;

and in the CARD OF FANCY :

> By covert *concealing* of inward *sorrow*, the flame so furiously fired within her. . . (Works, iv, 94).
> *Concealing* his *grief* so covertly, which so much the more furiously flamed within him. (*Id.* p. 151.)

The idea occurs yet again, with a phrase about " concealing sorrow," in the last-cited piece (p. 100). We are dealing, then, with a habitual tag of Greene's.

It may be, of course, that Shakespeare has " touched up " the passage in the TWO GENTLEMEN, which I take to be clearly of Greene's origination as it stands, and of which the diction and versification remain clearly inferior to those of the DREAM. But on any view the oven-and-river trope is Greene's both in the comedy and in the tragedy, the fundamental diction remaining non-Shakespearean. Shakespeare, we must infer, did but once echo, in the VENUS, with a conciseness of diction not found in the comedy, and with a grace of touch not shown in the tragedy, a tag with which he had become familiar on the stage. To hold him the author of all three passages would be to reckon him as weakly repetitious a writer as Greene, who in his prose outgoes all writers of his time in psittacism.

Professor Parrott puzzles me by pronouncing (p. 29) that the VENUS passage makes with that in TITUS " a much closer parallel than those which Robertson adduces from Greene." It is true that in the former edition I gave only the first three of the eight above cited, and the third only in part ; but even these, surely, show that Greene is the original for both, whether or not he penned the TITUS lines. The third and fourth parallels show him combining the sorrow-oven trope with that of the stopped stream ; and the first, sixth, and seventh point to " burn the heart to cinders." True, the general idea about suppressed sorrow being the sorest occurs, like so many of Greene's saws, in Spenser :—

> He oft finds med'cine who his grief imparts;
> But double grief afflicts *concealing* hearts,
> As raging flames who striveth to suppress.
>
> *F.Q.* B.II, c. I, st. 34 ;

and the " oven " figure comes, like so many more, from EUPHUES :—

> The oven *dammed* up, baketh soonest.   (Arber's rep., p. 63).

But it is clear that Shakespeare got his VENUS tropes directly from Greene—unless, indeed, they reached him, as they well might, by way of verbal quotation in a world so much given to tags. Seeing, however, that

Greene's usual direction of his oven trope is (as in the Two GENTLEMEN) to the destructive result of the 'damming," and that in the VENUS there is put the other alternative—the relief of love's fire by utterance ; while in the TITUS passage the formula ends with the Greenean point, the balance of correspondence is heavily on that side. Greene supplies all the applications made in the play and in the poem ; while the latter does not closely parallel the play. But what is most decisive is the crudity of the phrasing in TITUS— the " burn the heart *to cinders where it is.*" The entire speech, as we have seen, seems to be a mosaic ; and either Peele or Kyd may have borrowed Greene's hardworked metaphor. It is, however, especially likely to be from his own pen seeing that " cinders " is one more of his metaphors-of-all-work, occurring a score of times throughout his prose pieces.[1] To bring it into "poetry" was hardly likely to be Shakespeare's feat.

That Greene himself supplied the diction in TITUS is the natural inference, seeing that his hand so often enters ; and the same presumption arises in the case of the line :

And wash their hands in Bassianus' blood.

And when in the same scene we note how the lines (144-5) :—

The milk thou suck'dst from her did turn to marble :
Even at thy teat thou hadst thy tyranny,

with this phrase in Greene's ORPHARION (Works, xii, 29) :—

Hast thou forgot that which thou sucke[d]st out of thy nurse's teat ?[2]

we are strengthened in our inference from the changed style that his hand enters in this section.

[1] Thrice in *Menaphon* (Arber's rep. pp. 26, 82, 90) ; in the *Card of Fancy* (Works, iv, 17) ; *Tully's Love* (vii, 151) ; *Mourning Garment* (ix, 199) ; *Philomela* (xi, 190) ; *Vision* (xii, 215) ; *Orpharion* (xii, 12), etc. The last-cited phrase runs : " Troy consumed to cinders."
[2] We have this again in *Romeo and Juliet*, I, iii, 68. Cp. *Hamlet*, v, ii, 195. But the style in *Titus*, at least, is quite pre-Shakespearean.

Yet again, as we have seen, he has the proverb about two keeping counsel while the third is away ; and in his works we find the phrases " vain suppose " (PENE-LOPE'S WEB : Works, v, 203) and " mourning weeds " (A MAIDEN'S DREAM, ed. Dyce, p. 281 ; ORL. FUR. *id.* p. 108 ; HEXAM. ROSAMUNDÆ, *id.* p. 306), which occur in TITUS, but not in any other play ascribed to Shake-speare, though the noun " suppose " occurs in TROILUS. Such single parallels, of course, prove nothing by them-selves ; but they serve to corroborate a case founded on significant and reiterated parallels.

As regards simple coincidences of vocabulary, the argument is not so clear. It is obviously impossible to determine by the mere word-test the authorship of passages in TITUS which point to the vocabulary alike of Greene and Peele ; and a study of the relations of the two writers raises further difficulties. Four lines of the OLD WIVES TALE, with slight variations, are found in Greene's ORLANDO FURIOSO ; the phrase " sweet content " in the TALE (186) savours of Greene, who uses it so many times, though Peele also employs it in his signed work ; and its Sacripant suggests the same hand as drew the Sacripant of ORLANDO FURIOSO. Yet again, the play of SELIMUS contains, as we saw, one rant partly identical (ll. 1800 sq.) with one in the BATTLE OF ALCAZAR (V, i) as well as with one in LOCRINE (III, vi) ; and so many of the favourite words of Peele's vocabulary that we are compelled to inquire whether the hands of the two can be distinguished. It is in SELIMUS that Dr. Grosart finds a number of the TITUS-words in his list given above ; and to that list may be added the following :—triùmpher, and the scansion " màintain," both in SELIMUS (the latter also in FRIAR BACON and in GEORGE-A-GREENE, ed. Dyce, pp. 175, 259) ; and " Sibyl," occurring in ALCIDA : GREENE'S METAMORPHOSIS, published in 1588 (Works, IX, 57), as well as elsewhere in Greene's works.

And there are still further complications. The word ' cor'sive,' found in LOCRINE and SELIMUS (and only in 1 and 2 H. VI of the " Shakespearean " plays), is found

in the SPANISH TRAGEDY (I, ii, 143), where also occur
'complot' (twice) and 'misconster,' which in SELIMUS
Dr. Grosart assigns to Greene; 'hugy,' found in
LOCRINE and SELIMUS and several times in Peele;
'ding,' found in Peele (BATTLE) and in SELIMUS; 'captivate,' found several times in LOCRINE; 'fear'
(=frighten), occurring in LOCRINE and SELIMUS and in
the BATTLE (v, i, 253); 'sapling,' 'ruthless,' 'successive' ('successive line,' noticeably comparing with
'successive title') and 'cleanly' (=secretly or adroitly),
found in TITUS; 'closely,' credited in SELIMUS to
Greene (who has both 'closely' and 'cleanly' often
in his prose); 'adamant,' also ascribed to Greene by
Dr. Grosart, but common in Peele; and so on. Yet
again, in the TRAGEDY (I, iii, 59; III, xiii, 29), occur the
lines :—

> Then rest we here awhile in our unrest . . .
> Thus therefore will I rest me in unrest;

echoed twice in TITUS (II, iii; IV, ii) :

> And so repose, sweet gold, for their unrest . . .
> But let her rest in her unrest awhile;

and again in LOCRINE (V, iv) :

> Their uncontented corps were yet content;

and yet again twice in the TRAGEDY itself (III, xiii, 30;
xvi, 22) :

> Dissembling quiet in unquietness . . .
> For in unquiet quietness is feigned.

It is clearly impossible to draw any secure inference
from such a list of cases. Spenser, if no other, had
given the lead to such primitive exercises in word play.[1]
In the absence of proof to the contrary, we are bound
provisionally to credit the four instances of the word-
play in the TRAGEDY to Kyd, who is the only writer
to whom we have any contemporary reference as

---

[1] *E.g. F. Q.* B. i. c. xi, st. 35.

having had a hand in the first form of it ; though such a catching kind of tag might easily be echoed by other writers.

On the other hand, a Kyd element in our play is not only suggested by some of the phraseology, but likely as a matter of dramatic history.   If we suppose TITUS in its first form to have been, as above suggested, an adaptation from an Italian play, Kyd is, as aforesaid, the likeliest playwright to have made it.   No other pre-Shakespearean can be shown to have ever elaborated a plot of so much complexity, and of such regular progression.   Its horrors are carefully marshalled, as in the TRAGEDY ; and though an Italian play might supply all that, we do not find Peele or Greene elsewhere attempting any such construction.   And supposing Peele to have wrought over a Kyd original (Greene entering either with him or in earlier collaboration with Kyd), traces of Kyd might be expected to remain in the vocabulary and the phraseology.   In that case, though Peele's re-writing would alter much of the declamatory matter, we might expect to find traces of Kyd both there and in the more business-like parts of the action ; and as a matter of fact we do find strong suggestions of his stage work in the primitive gold-hiding episode at the beginning of II, iii ; in the pit scene ; in the supererogatory scene III, ii, lacking in the quartos ; in portions of IV, iii, especially the business of the arrows ; and in the masquerade and murder business in V, ii. All these have something of the manner and method of the later Acts of the TRAGEDY ; and the mock madness of Titus often recalls that of Hieronimo.   But, further, we have seen a notable double-trace of Kyd's phraseology in one of the highly elaborated speeches.   It is therefore desirable to bring together the apparent echoes of phrase in the two plays.   Besides the " rest-unrest " lines we have :

> To drown thee with an ocean of my tears.   *S. T.*, II, v, 23.
> Rain showers of grief upon your rose-like cheeks
> And dew yourselves with springtides of your tears.
> > *Cornelia*, v, 419-20.

O gush out, tears, fountains and floods of tears ;
Blow, sighs, and raise an everlasting storm.   *S. T.*, II, v, 43-44.
And make a brine-pit with our bitter tears.   *T. A.*, III, i, 129.
When heaven doth weep, doth not the earth o'erflow ?
If the winds blow, doth not the sea wax mad ? . . .
I am the sea, hark, how her *sighs* do *blow !* . . .
Then must my earth, with her continual tears
Become a deluge, overflow'd and drown'd.   *T.A.*, III, i, 222-230.

On whom I doted more than all the world
Because she loved me more than all the world.   *S. T.*, II, vi, 5-6.
I care not, I, knew she and all the world
I love Lavinia more than all the world.[1]   *T. A.*, II, i, 71-2.

But with the bitt'rest tortures and extremes
That may be yet invented for thine end.   *S. T.*, III, i, 100-1.
We will devise th' extremest kind of death
That ever was invented for a wretch.   *Id.*, IV, iv, 211-12.
More let them bide, until we have devised
Some never-heard-of torturing pain for them.
                                   T. A., II, iii, 285.

Compare :—

To find and to repay the man with death,
With death delayed and tortures never used.
                          Massacre at Paris, I, v, 4-5.

O that that damnèd villain were alive again
That we might torture him with some new-found death.
                                   Id. v, iv, near end.

What bull of Phalaris, what strange device,
Shall we invent to take away thy life ?
                 Alphonsus Emperor of Germany, v, iv, 460-1.

Solicit Pluto, gentle Proserpine . . .   *S. T.*, III, xvi, 2.

Beat at the windows of the highest heavens.
Soliciting for justice and revenge.   *Id.*, III, vii, 14-15.

Hieronimo, 'tis time for thee to trudge :
Down by the lake that flows with purple gore
Standeth a fiery tower : there sits a judge
Upon a seat of steel and molten brass . . .   *Id.*, III, xii, 6-9.

Compare :—
     Because he loves me more than all the world.
                                   Edward II, I, iv.

Away, I'll rip the bowels of the earth
And ferry over to th' Elysian plains . . .
I'll make a *pickaxe* of my poniard . . . *Id. ib.*, 70-75.

I'll down to hell and in this passion
Knock at the dismal gates of Pluto's court,
Getting by force, as once Alcides did,
A troop of furies and tormenting hags
To torture Don Lorenzo and the rest. *Id.*, III, xiii, 108-12.

And art thou come, Horatio, from the depth,
To ask for justice in this upper earth ? *Id. ib.*, 131-2.

'Tis you must dig, with *mattock* and with *spade*,
And pierce the inmost centre of the earth :
Then when you come to Pluto's region,
I pray you, deliver him this petition ;
Tell him it is for justice and for aid
And that it comes from old Andronicus . . .
　　　　　　　　　　Pluto sends you word,
If you will have Revenge from hell, you shall :
Marry, for Justice, she is so employed,
He thinks, with Jove in heaven, or somewhere else,
So that perforce you must needs stay a time. . . .
I'll dive into the burning lake below
And pull her out of Acheron by the heels. . . .
And sith there is no justice in earth or hell,
We will *solicit* heaven, and move the gods. *T. A.*, IV, iii.

Talk not of chords, but let us now begone
For with a cord Horatio was slain. *S. T.*, III, xiii, *end*.

O, handle not the theme, to talk of hands. . . . *T. A.*, III, ii, 29.

　　　　　What accursed hand
Hath made thee handless in thy father's sight ?
　　　　　　　　Id., III, i, 66-67.

The slight verbal coincidence in the use of the word
solicit may perhaps appear more significant when we
note in TITUS the line (IV, iii, 60) :

There's not a God left *unsolicited*,

and the other frequent uses of the word in the
SPANISH TRAGEDY :—

> Solicits me for notice of his death (III, ii, 15) ;
> Yet is my mood soliciting their souls (III, xvi, 18) ;
> And all the saints do sit soliciting (IV, i, 32) ;
> Her had this bashaw long solicited (IV, i, 117) ;
> See where his ghost solicits (IV, ii, 24) ;
> Tyrant, desist soliciting vain suits (IV, iv, 58) ;
> Soliciting remembrance of my vow (IV, iv, 126).

We have the word again in SOLIMAN AND PERSEDA :

> But still solicit God for Soliman (IV, i, 201) ;

and thrice in ARDEN OF FEVERSHAM (I, 329, 431 ; II,
i, 124).
Again, such a line as :

> That woe is me to think upon thy woes (*T. A.*, III, i, 240),

though paralleled also in Peele, is very much in the
manner of the lines on hands and cords above cited ;
and when we find ALPHONSUS EMPEROR OF GERMANY
(V, i, 483) the line :

> Whose hearts are bruised to think upon those woes

there again emerges a surmise of Kyd's presence. As
we shall see in examining that play, the choice of
author at that point probably lies between him and
Peele ; but in the series of passages above given in
which Titus declaims of justice and revenge there can
be no question of Peele's hand. His versification is
usually smooth. Kyd's, sometimes smooth, is often
irregular ; and the irregularities here are as like him
as they are unlike Shakespeare.

It is not to be disputed that a number of these
parallels are compatible with simple imitation ; and
the TRAGEDY is often echoed, seriously and otherwise,
by Kyd's contemporaries. Greene, for instance, seems
to have written this :—

> I conjure thee, by Pluto's loathsome lake,
> By stinking Styx, and filthy Phlegethon
>   To come with speed. . . .

> Go, get thee hence to Pluto's lake again,
> And there inquire of the Destinies
> How Amurath shall speed in these his wars.
> > *Alphonsus King of Arragon*, III (Dyce, p. 235 *b*).

The punning on " handle . . . handless . . . hands,"
and " chord, cord," too, was likely enough to be
common. But the series of flights in the TRAGEDY
about going to Pluto's court and seeking justice
alternately there and in heaven are so iteratively akin
to those in TITUS that they constitute, with the other
parallels and echoes, a strong ground for ascription to
Kyd, especially seeing that the arrows scene is not
for its diction and versification in general assignable
to any of the other three hands under observation
Greene's verse, like Peele's, is normally smooth and
regular : this is not. When we find, further, in the
TRAGEDY (III, vi, 23) the line :

> Come, come, come on ; when shall we to this gear ?

and in TITUS (arrows scene, l. 52) :

> Come, to this gear,

the minor identity of phrase counts for a good deal
So with the frequent special use of the verb " martyr "
in TITUS :—

> Hark, wretches, how I mean to martyr you (v, ii, 181).
> Who hath martyr'd thee ?   (III, i, 81).
> I can interpret all her martyr'd signs (III, ii, 36).

Compare :

> Why bendst thou thus thy mind to martyr me ?
> > (*S. T.*, III, ix, 6).

In all three of the TITUS passages there are other clues
that seem to indicate Kyd, though the speeches, as
already noted, appear to be composite. And though
" sapling " is a very slight word-clue, it may be cited
as also pointing to Kyd.

If we suppose him to be first draftsman, we should

expect to find traces of him in passages wrought over by Peele, as well as in scenes not so rewritten ; and we might surmise his work in the pit scene (III, iii—or iv), which is not fitly assignable to either Peele or Greene ; and of which the whole circumstantial progression is so much more in his way than in theirs. But as this scene is absent from the German version, it remains uncertain whether it was there merely suppressed, as unduly delaying the action, or whether it is a later addition : in which latter case, however, it might still be Kyd's.

A similar problem arises in regard to scene ii of Act III, omitted from all the Quartos, and first found in the Folio. This circumstance, as we have seen, has encouraged the notion that the scene was added by Shakespeare after the issue of the first Quarto in 1594. That it cannot be Shakespeare's, has been argued above. That it is an addition seems likely enough, its elaboration of superfluous detail being in the spirit and manner of the additions to the TRAGEDY. But it is quite possible, on the other hand, that such elaboration took place before 1594, as it apparently did in the harangue of Marcus to the mutilated Lavinia. There are touches strongly recalling both Kyd and Peele in the fly-killing scene. Marlowe is as unthinkable here as Shakespeare, but there is a hint of Greene. The warranted inference, then, would seem to be that Kyd really contributed the groundwork of the scene, including the fly-killing, to the original play ; and that Peele and Greene worked over it—unless, as above suggested, Kyd himself had a hand in revising his own piece—a thing likely enough.

A final ground for such a view is given by his translation of CORNELIA, which, though it gives little help to us in diagnosing his blank-verse style, yields clues of phraseology. In one or two places it suggests that phrases which we have been inclined to assign to Peele *might* be Kyd's—*e.g.*, the line (II, 207),

With folded arms I sadly sit and weep,

which compares with Peele's " sadness with wreathèd arms " and " with folded arms and all amazed soul," above noted in connection with " sorrow-wreathen knot " in TITUS ; and again the line (second from end) :

When my soul earth's prison shall forgo,

which compares with several Peelean phrases above cited in parallel to the TITUS line (III, ii, 10) :—

Beats in this hollow prison of my flesh.

The ' prison ' and ' sorrow-wreathen-knot ' passages in TITUS both occur in the scene under notice ; so that we may have been tentatively crediting Peele with phrases of Kyd's coining or echoing. Leaving the matter thus doubtful as between Kyd and Peele, we can but note that the egregious lines in which Titus urges Lavinia to get a knife in her teeth to make a hole in her breast for her tears recall Thamar's lines :—

my bloody side
Which with a rusty weapon I will wound
To make a passage to my panting heart (D. and B., I, iii) ;

and that in the same tragedy Peele uses in an " elevated " passage (III, ii) the unimpressive verb " to thump," which also is tragically employed here (l. 11).

For the sake of completeness of survey, it may be worth while to consider whether a play so added to after its author's death as we know the TRAGEDY to have been may not have been eked out by other hands before it was first printed. Without making any confident suggestion we may note, in addition to those above cited, several parallels between the TRAGEDY and Greene's work which raise the question whether he had not some hand in that play. His share, if any, can be but little ; and I put the point tentatively, seeing no clear case. In the former edition I noted that one of the lines of the Induction :

For there in prime and pride of *all* my years,

is echoed by one in Greene's ALPHONSUS KING OF ARRAGON (ed. Dyce, p, 240),

> Here in the prime and spring of *all* their youth.

But this is a kind of phrase found also in Peele :—

> In pride of youth, when I was young and fair.
> > *Edward I*, sc. 23 (Dyce, p. 412).

In the former edition I also cited the use in the TRAGEDY of words affected by Greene, such as *passport, martialist, corsive, entreats, captivate, complot*; his phrase " my sorrows' map," the use of the " summer and winter " tag thrice in the TRAGEDY and at least twice in his prose ; and the use in the play and in his PHILOMELA (Works, xi, 137), in nearly the same words, of the tag about the nightingale singing with the prickle at her breast. But that tag occurs also in Dekker's song in the SHOEMAKER'S HOLIDAY (III, v) ; and the items of vocabulary noted cannot constitute more than a bare ground for surmising that Greene may have revised the TRAGEDY. In view of the large number of its scenes and the ramifications of its plot, such revision might be suspected even if we did not know that the practice was usual, and that Jonson was actually paid for making such additions to this very play. I suggest, however, that Greene really may have had a share in SOLIMAN AND PERSEDA, which has the following more-or-less uncommon words, otherwise connected with Greene :

Aby. v, iii, 46. Found in *Selimus* (2267).

Captivate. IV, i, 20, 21. Noted in *Locrine*, etc.

Dazzle (vb. intrans.). II, i, 244. Found in *Menaphon* (ed. Arber, p. 60) and *Alphonsus*, I, i (Dyce, p. 227).

Entreats (Intreats). IV, i, 28, 165. See above, p. 219.

Faint-hearted. III, ii, 33. See above, p. 215.

Guileful. II, i, 125, 154. See above, p. 219.

Lavolto (dance). I, iv, 31. Found in *Friar Bacon* (ed. Dyce, p. 165), in *Menaphon* (p. 23) and in Francesco's Roundelay in *Never Too Late* (Dyce, p. 298).

Surquedry. II, ii, 64. Common to Greene and Peele.[1]

[1] Very common in Spenser.

On the whole, there is better warrant for crediting
some of these to Greene than for assigning them to
Kyd ; and we shall see other grounds for inferring
Greene's presence in SOLIMAN.

There is some slight reason, however, to infer Peele's
hand there also ; and yet further in SELIMUS. Greene's
large share in SELIMUS, as it happens, is proved *prima
facie* by Dr. Grosart first from the fact that six passages[1]
in it are assigned to Greene in ENGLAND'S PARNASSUS
(1600), and secondly, from a number of uncommon
terms used there and in his signed works (*e.g.*, polypus,
echinus, overslip, negromancy, nutrimented),[2] and
might almost be summarily adjudged on a reading of
the stanza parts of the play ; which, further, are
thoroughly congruous with what is avowed by Greene
on his death-bed as to his having paraded irreligious
opinions, and of the best of which the quality is, for
the most part, as much above the level of Peele and
Kyd as the matter is alien to their way of thinking.
The only contemporary who seems likely to have written
them is Marlowe ; Lodge, suggested by Fleay, is quite
unlikely ; and it would be arbitrary to suppose
Marlowe, the special champion of blank verse, to have
written a large part of a play in stanzas, whereas
Greene protested against confining drama to blank
verse, and used the stanza form in his late JAMES IV.

But I do not see how, on the principles on which
Greene is to be assigned a predominant share in
SELIMUS, and a large part in LOCRINE and TITUS, he
can be confidently credited with the whole of the first-
named play. Some of its blank verse [ll. 990-1012 ;
1260-1340 ; 1439-1456 ; 2111-2181] is as like the work

---

[1] Professor Collins in his edition of Greene—either independently or with
the help of Mr. Crawford —traced all six passages, where Dr. Grosart had
noted only two.

[2] Some other words put on a par with these by Dr. Grosart—as, forged,
harbinger, and the verb " to enterprise "—are to be found in Peele and Kyd.
Harbinger, indeed, is common ; though it happens that the special metaphor
in which it occurs in *Selimus* is found in Greene's prose. " Gratulate " is
cited by Dr. Grosart only from *Orlando Furioso* in Greene's works. It occurs
also in *James IV* and *Selimus*. In Peele it is also common. And " forged "
= invented, common in Lilly, is found twice in the *Spanish Tragedy*. It is,
however, unquestionably a favourite word of Greene's.

of Peele as the rhymed parts are otherwise ; and we are
the more moved to assign a possible though small
share to Peele when we note such a line as :

> Sprung from the loins of mighty Ottoman
>
> (*Sel.* 1523)

and compare it with

> Sprung from the loins of great Cadwallader,

found in EDWARD I (sc. ii, 4), which Peele signed.
Even a single signature or a claim on a title-page, it is
true, does not, in an Elizabethan play, negate collaboration ; and some scenes in EDWARD I are visibly
additions. In Greene's ALPHONSUS, too (I, i, 23), we
find the line :

> Sprung from the loins of the immortal gods.

Greene then (though the clue is very slight) may have
had a hand in EDWARD I and the BATTLE as he had in
LOCRINE and TITUS ; as, on the other hand, he may
have echoed Peele in SELIMUS and ALPHONSUS. But
such a formula may safely be classed as a standing
tag, and it need not sway us. We have tracked Peele
in LOCRINE and TITUS by tests drawn from his poems
as well as his plays ; and when we find in SELIMUS not
only lines in his manner but several tags which he
specially affected, we are so far bound by the balance
of evidence to admit his possible intervention ; though,
on the other hand, some of the LOCRINE-words in
TITUS are more probably Greene's than Peele's. Such
a tag as :—

> The poor remainder of Andronici,
> > *Titus*, v, iii, 131 ;
> The poor remainder of my Alemshae,
> > *Selimus*, l. 1289 ;
> The poor remainder of the royal fleet,
> > *Edward I*, i, 5 ;
> The poor remainder of those that fled from Fess,
> > *Battle of Alcazar*, iii, ii,

raises a typical issue. The speech in TITUS remains hard to assign because of the special use of " closure." The same hand may have done all three ; but it is not easy to identify. Verse assignable to Greene on the strength of verbal and phraseological clues is sometimes very like Peele's, though Greene's blank-verse is often vivacious and Peele's is seldom so. Thinness of quality is normal in both. But in this case Peele's line and that in TITUS are alike natural, and the other is an inappropriate echo ; whence Peele seems the true claimant.

Then there is the question, to be fully discussed later, of the possible share of Marlowe in SELIMUS. Putting aside for the moment the echoes of audacious thought in the rhymed portions of the first Act, which recall his power, but which are so unlikely to be his in respect of their being written in stanzas, we may note his manner in the blank-verse lines 531-573 ; 661-694. Such lines as :—

> Here the Polonian he comes hurtling in,
> Under the conduct of some foreign prince ;
>
> Thinks he to stop my mouth with gold or pearl
> Or rusty jades fet from Barbaria ?
>
> Were his light steeds as swift as Pegasus
> And trod the airy pavement with their heels ;

and

> Upon my sword's sharp point standeth pale Death,
> Ready to rive in two thy caitiff breast,

are either by him or by a determined imitator. We can but say that nearly all the latter part of the play is poor enough for Greene at his poorest, as in ALPHONSUS OF ARRAGON, and inconceivably poor for Marlowe.

As many of our instances suggest, the share of Greene in TITUS will fall to be finally established by another order of test, in addition to and in control of that of vocabulary, which is merely the primary clue, and that of phrase and tag, which are much more imitable than style. In the present connection, however, in addition to parallels of words, we have to consider one or two further parallels of phrase not noted by Dr. Grosart. A good deal of discussion has taken place on the line in TITUS (III, i, 170) : —

> Writing destruction on the enemy's castle,

some arguing that "castle" should read "casque," others explaining that "castle" was a name for a form of casque. That both explanations are astray is suggested by a comparison of the line with a passage in Greene's ORLANDO FURIOSO (ll. 392-3, ed. Grosart) :

> On this *castle*-wall
> I'll *write* my resolution with my blood.

The idea is once more echoed in his PHILOMELA (Works, xi, 187) in the phrase "paint revenge upon the gates of Venice."

Again, the line in TITUS (II, i, 48) :

> Full well I wot, the ground of all this grudge

—though the opening phrase is common enough[1]—is possibly by Greene, to whom we shall see reasons for assigning more of the same scene, and who has in ALPHONSUS OF ARRAGON (ed. Dyce, pp. 230, 231, 233, 234, 243, 244) at least six lines beginning "For well I wot," besides one in a poem (Dyce, p. 302), and two ending with "full well I wot" in the LOOKING-GLASS FOR LONDON (ed. Dyce, p. 135, 144). Yet again, the crude lines (TITUS, III, ii, 37, 38) :

> She says she drinks no other drink but tears,
> Brewed with her sorrow, mesh'd upon her cheeks,

occurring in a speech in which we find his word "alphabet," might have been penned by Greene at the primitive stage of his art in which he wrote

> the salt-brine tears
> *Distilling down* poor Fausta's withered cheeks.
> *Alphonsus*, Act v (Dyce, p. 245).

[1] E.g., Peele, *Order of the Garter*, l. 159. See also *Ed. I*, sc. iii, 13, pp. 355, 412.

This again suggests that Greene may have written the
lines in SIR CLYOMON AND SIR CLAMYDES (Dyce, p.
520) :—

> My eyes from *down-distilling* tears, when thus alone I am,
> Resistance make, but must they not through ceaseless sorrows
>   frame
> A river of *distillèd* drops, for to *bedew* my face ?

—where the " for to " is almost a mark of his early
work.   But these are at best only arguable possibilities.
The scene in TITUS last cited is not in Greene's manner ;
and the " distilling " figure is very common.   In the
old CAMBYSES, which dates from 1569 (Hazlitt- Dodsley,
iv, 97), we have

> *Bedews* my cheek with *stillèd* tears ;

which suggests that the tag was long hackneyed.[1]
On the other hand, a parody by Greene is the probable
explanation of similarity of conceit in the four lines
which begin the second Act of LOCRINE (above, p. 213)
and four of the six lines from the HECATOMPATHIA of
Watson, the friend of Peele, which are embodied in
the TRAGEDY (II, i, 3-6, 9-10) :—

> In time the savage bull sustains the yoke,
> In time all haggard hawks will stoop to lure,
> In time small wedges cleave the hardest oak,
> In time the flint is pierced with softest shower . . .
> No, she is wilder, and more hard withal,
> Than beast, or bird, or tree, or stony wall.

At all events, the former lines are much more in Greene's
manner than in Peele's ; and Greene had already used
the same figures in his works.[2]

---

[1] Thus we have the " distilled " figure in Shakespeare (*R. and J.*, v, iii, 15) ;
in Marlowe's *Edward II* (second last line) ; and in Peele (*D. and B.*, l. 3 ;
Edward I, Dyce, p. 413).   The figure is very old, and surprisingly common.
See it in the Coventry Mysteries, Sh. Soc. ed. p. 28.   Tudor poets, including
Spenser, use it continually.

[2] See *Menaphon* (ed. Arber, p. 39) where the " snail " figure actually
occurs ; and the second song in *Arbasto* (quoted above, p. 213).

§ 6. MARLOWE IN " TITUS "

We have next to examine the theory, first mentioned
by Reed and repeated by the younger Boswell in the
Variorum Shakespeare (1821), that Marlowe is the
author of TITUS. It was acquiesced in for a time, as
above mentioned, by Fleay ; and has been held by Mr.
A. H. Bullen, one of Marlowe's most accomplished
editors ; also, for a time, by Dr. Garnett. No one, I
think, has offered any detailed evidence in its support ;
but after our inductive investigation has yielded us
proof of the presence in the play of Kyd, Peele, and
Greene, it is found to present also a strong presumption
for the presence of Marlowe.

On applying the primary test of vocabulary, we at
once find some justification for the Marlowe theory.
In the FIRST PART OF TAMBURLAINE we find at least ten
of the words special to TITUS in the Shakespearean
vocabulary, or found elsewhere only in a composite
play :—

Coal-black (thrice)	Emperess (five times)	Styx (twice)
Cocytus (v, 2)		
Cimmerian (iii, 2)	Progne (iv, 4)	'Tice
Dreary (v, 2)	Rapine (I, 2 ; ii, 2)	Typhon (iii, 3)

In Part II we have six more :—

Aetna	Daunt (thrice)	Faggots
Brinish (twice)	Joy =enjoy (thrice)	Re-edified ;

with repetitions of coal-black, Cimmerian, Styx. In
FAUSTUS we have :—

Execrable (ii, i)	Scroll (twice)

and in the JEW repetitions of *scroll* and *Cocytus ;* while
in EDWARD II we find eight more :—

Architect (iv, 5)	Libelling (ii, 2)	Sustenance (twice)
Caucasus (v, 5)	Numbed (v, 5)	Yelping (i, 1)
Braves (twice)		Youngling (v, 2)

In the MASSACRE AT PARIS come :—

| Popish (twice) | Irreligious (iii, 4) | Ruinate (iii, 4) |

And in DIDO :—

| Men-of-war (i, 1) | Spousal rites (v, 2) | 'Ticed |
| Prometheus (iii, 4) | Sprawling (ii, 1) | 'Ticing |

In HERO AND LEANDER, again, we have :—

| Affied[1] (ii, 26) | Numbing (ii, 246) | Oratory (ii, 226) |

making in all a list of some thirty-six TITUS-words, as against the same number for Peele.   It is impossible for us to evade the *prima facie* presumption thus set up ;   and though many of the words just noted are freely used by Peele and Greene, we shall find in TITUS a number of passages which savour distinctly more of Marlowe than of either Greene or Peele.   To begin with, the long scene which constitutes the first Act has suggestions of Marlowe from the point at which Bassi-anus seizes Lavinia.   The quarrelling here is much more life-like and less wordy, setting up a kind of tension which Peele rarely, if ever, attains ;   and there are some verbal clues which point only to Marlowe, though there are also some to Peele, and partial resumptions of his manner.   For instance, the lines :—

> *Tit.*   O monstrous !   What *reproachful* words are these ?
> *Sat.*   But go thy ways ;   go, give *that changing piece*
> To him that flourished for her with his sword :
> A valiant son-in-law thou shalt enjoy,
> One fit to bandy with thy lawless sons,
> To ruffle in the commonwealth of Rome,

are substantially Peelean, and expressly indicate the line (198) :

> Touched with the rape of this *reproachful piece*

in the TALE OF TROY, ed. 1604, and " *that changing*

---

[1] Also in trans. of *Ovid's Elegies*, III, vi 31.   Other repetitions occur in the translation of Lucan.

piece " in the edition of 1589 (Dyce, p. 555a, 11th note).
So that, though " bandy with " is an expression of Marlowe's (EDWARD II, I, i, 132), the passage as a whole
may fairly be assigned to Peele. And though the
phrase " spousal rites " (l. 337) seems to occur only in
Marlowe (DIDO, V, ii, 52) among the pre-Shakespeareans,
Peele has " spousals " (TALE OF TROY, l. 246), and the
passage continues to be in his manner. The line :

> Now climbeth Tamora Olympus' top

which opens Act II, is one of the grounds on which the
play has been assigned to Marlowe, since he has :

> Did mount him up to scale Olympus' top

in FAUSTUS (III, Chor., l. 3) ; but scrutiny will show
that Aaron's speech here has a dozen clues to Peele,
that the verse is his, and that the phrase from Marlowe
is only one of his many echoes. Aaron's reply to
Tamora in sc. iii is, as before observed, more Marlowesque ; and if Aaron be Marlowe's creation he may have
contributed this to the original play. The movement
and the diction are not Peele's ; but they may be
Greene's, and to him the verbal clues point.

Traces of Marlowe appear in Act IV, scene iv, where
the verse-movement is far more nervous than that of
Peele, and is also unlike Greene's ; and as we have
already noted, we may fitly assign to him the bulk of
the scene, with a reservation of something for Greene.
Marlowe, too, appears by far the most likely author of
the speeches of the second Goth, Lucius, and Aaron in
Act V, scene i, where we have the same nervous versification. The lines of Aaron (98-120 ; 124-144 ; 147-
150) flaunting his villainies and expressing his hate, form
a signally close parallel to those of Barabas and Ithamore in Act II, scene ii, of the JEW, and the last speech
of Barabas at the close of Act V. Sad stuff it is, for
Marlowe : the hack-poet out-Heroding Herod in the
raw portraiture of burlesque villains. But only he
could have done it, unless we are to surmise an imitator
who would copy him without stint.

Some of the details in the speeches referred to are in effect duplicated in the two plays. Aaron's account of his exploits in the way of setting dead men's bodies upright at their friend's doors tells of an actual episode in the JEW (IV, ii) ; and his lines :

> And on their skins, as on the bark of trees,
> Have with my knife carvèd in Roman letters,
> " Let not your sorrow die, though I am dead,"

are thus adumbrated in the other play :

> And now and then one hung himself for grief,
> Pinning upon his breast a long great scroll,
> How I with interest tormented him.

Aaron's self-portraiture Professor Saintsbury would have us regard as " genuinely Shakespearean " ; Professor Parrott acquiescing. The TITUS passages may well be efforts to outgo the others ; but to assume that Shakespeare committed such abject parodies is to put him below any known copyist of his age. Such a challenge alone might serve to shake once for all the conventional acceptance of his authorship of TITUS. It is conceivable that Greene, who imitated Marlowe in phrase and theme, might copy him in some such fashion ; but after striving to associate Greene with the portraiture of Aaron, I feel compelled to avow that the verse movement and the diction in the later Aaron scenes are not his.

Professor Parrott, on the other hand, assures us that he has no misgiving about ascribing the speech to Shakespeare :—

" In the catalogue of crimes which the Moor recites with devilish glee (ll. 124-144) he appears to revert to the old inhuman villain. But, paradoxical as it may seem, I hold this speech to be by Shakespeare. It is a patent imitation of the rhapsody of Barabas (*Jew of Malta*, II, iii [—should be ii]), and was *probably* inserted by Shakespeare to provide Alleyn as Aaron with a tirade of the sort he had delivered with effect as Barabas. Shakespeare would not have hesitated for a moment at such an imitation of his great forerunner, if he thought he could thereby render his hasty revision of *Titus* more effective on the stage. Possibly l. 102 with its reference to bear-baiting might be noted as a sign-manual of Shakespeare."[1]

Professor Parrott claims that he has for the first time applied a right method to the problem of TITUS. He has here, however, posited a judgment which conforms to no intelligible method, and which cancels in large part the method he has been applying. When he finds in TITUS parallels of image and idea to passages in the VENUS and the LUCRECE, applying no guarding test of style, he confidently decides that Shakespeare was thus duplicating himself within, it might be, a month or two. When he finds in TITUS what he confesses to be " a patent imitation " of a rhapsody in Marlowe, he forthwith decides that Shakespeare "would not have hesitated for a moment at such an imitation." By what method is such an inference reached ? And why, drawing it in this case, does not the critic draw it in the case of what he admits to be plain duplications of Peele ?

By Professor Parrott's "method," Shakespeare can be made out to have written anything ever printed as his. Matter in the style of Marlowe, Greene, or Peele, is salvable at will on a thesis of "imitation " ; and it is impossible to show why anything should ever be ruled out ; for the style test, though founded on from time to time by the Professor when he blenches at some of the matter, is by him thus explicitly discarded at pleasure, and implicitly often. The only explanation of his course here appears to be the fatal lead given by his false datum that Shakespeare first multiplied the double-ending. The " scene shows," he writes, " the highest percentage in the play, something over 20. Shakespeare has *evidently* been at work here, *but* there is *little characteristic poetry* by which to identify his hand." Again and again the Professor thus collides with his own postulate. But here he is determined to salve it somehow, and we get the solution of deliberate imitation of Marlowe.

[1] Essay cited, p. 54.

Now, if Shakespeare by way of specially imitating Marlowe reaches the highest percentage of double-endings in the play, it would follow that Marlowe was *known to him as resorting to such abundant use of that form ;* and the primary assumption is thus unwittingly cancelled by its framer. As a matter of fact, *there is not one double-ending* in the Barabas speech in the JEW : Marlowe does not in that play reach any high percentage ; and if Shakespeare here suddenly resorted to a high percentage he was doing it gratuitously, as regards " imitation." But such an assumption is as utterly arbitrary as the contrary ascription of the speech to Marlowe is natural. Only the false assumption as to Shakespeare's being the leading innovator could have suggested it. The reasonable inference, upon any consistent or intelligible " method," is that Marlowe wrote the speech in TITUS about the end of his life, when, as Greene's tirade implies, he was working for Shakespeare's company. He had gone on increasing his percentage in the CONTENTION and the DUKE OF YORK, and, on the present writer's view, in RICHARD III, where the high percentages are utterly irreconcilable with Shakespeare's authorship at the early date to which the play must be assigned. On any reasonable application of metrical tests, the high percentages in TITUS are to be assigned to Marlowe. To assign them to Shakespeare is to defy the facts, on a demonstrably false assumption.

To found, finally, on the allusion to bear-baiting as " possibly " a " sign-manual " of Shakespeare, is again to run a theory to death in defiance of the evidence. Justice Madden argues[1] that Shakespeare always makes fools, knaves, and his villains interested in bear-baiting, his own strong preference being for the nobler forms of sport. But even if that interesting theory be sound, it cannot carry the corollary that every speech in " Shakespeare " in which a villain speaks of bear-baiting is therefore of his penning. For that matter, Octavius, who in JULIUS CÆSAR (IV, i, 48) makes such a

---

[1] *Diary of Master Silence*, ed. 1907, pp. 188-9.

reference, is not presented as either a knave or a fool, still less as a villain ; and still less so is Gloucester, who makes the same reference in LEAR (III, vii, 54). Olivia in TWELFTH NIGHT (III, i, 129) uses the image as describing a cruelty ; but that is another matter. It is idle, further, to assign to Shakespeare passages in the HENRY VI plays on the sole ground that Richard there uses such imagery. The line, " as true a dog as ever fought at head," is as natural for Marlowe in the speech in TITUS as it could be for Shakespeare. It is in fact an encomium on the bear-baiting dog, which Shakespeare in all the cited allusions does not give ; and Justice Madden's own theory justifies us in denying it to Shakespeare.

Consistent method, then, leads us to the Marlowe assignment, in the absence of any clue to an imitator (such as Heywood) who early developed a high percentage of double-endings. To assume that Shakespeare, reaching only 6 per cent. in JOHN and 5 in I HENRY IV, leapt to 20 at an earlier period in one scene in a wilful imitation of a Marlowe speech which had *none*, is to defy every judicial principle. Our vocabulary clues, certainly, must be finally governed by tests of style and substance ; but so must the arbitrary hypotheses which are pitted against them. Thus far we have found TITUS non-Shakespearean by all tests, while we have found a multitude of clues of word, phrase, and manner, to contemporaries who are obviously eligible as authors or adaptors of TITUS matter. And as sound critical method is but vigilant common-sense, " method " is so far against Professor Parrott.

And before we can even take as certain the results thus far reached from a scrutiny of vocabularies, we shall have to inquire how far we can rely on Marlowe's complete authorship of the plays assigned to him. In raising that issue we shall be applying the tests by which the authorship of TITUS is finally to be adjudged.

§ 7. Lodge's Vocabulary in " Titus "

Our search for clues would not be complete if we ignored Lodge, who collaborated with Greene in the LOOKING-GLASS FOR LONDON. Fleay, who knew that ground well, ascribed to him also a share in MUCEDORUS, the WARNING FOR FAIRE WOMEN, the old KING LEIR, SELIMUS, THE TROUBLESOME RAIGNE OF KING JOHN, and A 'LARUM FOR LONDON. Leaving these five plays for subsequent examination, we have to consider here his signed work. As regards simple vocabulary, we find there the TITUS-words " gratulate," " wreak," " dazzle " (vb. intrans.), " entreats, " " Ætna, " " devoid," " guileful," and the form " 'joy "=enjoy. On this it is impossible to base any argument, the first three words being common to the others, and " 'joy " specially frequent in Peele ; but a further problem arises over the frequent use in Lodge's ostensible work of the " hammering " tag, above assigned to Greene. Not only has he in THE WOUNDS OF CIVIL WAR the line cited above (p. 110), he has several repetitions :

> But, senators, I hammer in my head
> With every thought of honour some revenge.
>
> Malone Soc. rep., ll 563-4.

" Hammer " has here been amended by Mr. W. C. Hazlitt[1] to " harbour," which, in view of the parallel passages, is unwarranted ; though in the line (459) :

> A rash revenging hammer in thy brain

he has some excuse for substituting " humour." And yet again we have the line (1979) :—

> Whose heart doth hammer nought but mutinies.

It is reasonable, however, to infer that Lodge was here imitating Greene, who in ORLANDO FURIOSO has two lines (above, p. 110) very like the first two cited ; and

---

[1] In his edition of Dodsley's Old Plays (vii, 124).

who has phrases about "hammering in the head" at least five times in his prose. On any view, it is impossible to assume Lodge's presence in TITUS on the strength of this phrase, seeing that ORLANDO appears to be an older tragedy than his. There is a distinct suggestion of Peele, further, in the whole passage containing the formerly cited line from the WOUNDS, which raises questions of interpolation :—

> My countrymen and favourites[1] of Rome,
> This melancholy desert where we meet
> Resembleth well young Marius' restless thoughts.
> Here dreadful silence, solitary caves,
> No chirping birds with solace singing sweetly,
> Are harbour'd for delight ; but from the oak,
> Leafless and sapless through decaying age,
> The screech-owl chants her fatal-boding lays ;
> *Within my breast, care, danger, sorrow dwell ;*
> *Hope and revenge sit hammering in my heart ;*
> The baleful babes of angry Nemesis
> Disperse their furious fires upon my soul.
>   (*Wounds of Civil War*, Act III, near end : Hazlitt-
>   Dodsley, vii, 149 : Malone Soc. rep., ll. 1247-58).

The occurrence of the phrase " dart these furious flames upon my soul " in a Lodge speech in the LOOKING-GLASS FOR LONDON (Dyce, p. 132b) is the main reason for assigning these lines to Lodge despite their Peelean character. It will be observed that in the passage in TITUS the context has a close structural resemblance to the lines above italicised :

> Vengeance is in my heart, death in my hand,
> *Blood and revenge are hammering in my head.*

It is to be remembered that the WOUNDS, though doubtless written before 1590, was not published until 1594, when, as we have seen reason to infer, Peele was revising LOCRINE and DAVID for the press, and when he actually issued the BATTLE OF ALCAZAR. Though, however, we shall find some special reasons for sur-

---

[1] In this play "favourites" repeatedly seems to carry the sense of "favourers."

mising that Peele may have revised Lodge's text, it is impossible to pass beyond a surmise on that score ; and as regards the " hammering in the head " tag we are driven to suppose that it is Greene who uses it in TITUS as in ORLANDO, seeing that in the former play there are so many other verbal clues to Greene, and that Peele never uses the phrase in his signed work.   Yet, when we examine the plays attributed to Lodge by Fleay, we shall find some further clues which point to the possibility of his having contributed slightly to TITUS ; and the question must for the present be left open.

CHAPTER VII

PEELE'S UNSIGNED[1] WORK

§1. FLEAY'S ASCRIPTIONS

The evidence we have already seen of the composite authorship of pre-Shakespearean plays is an incentive to a search for the handiwork of the more productive men in other than their assigned plays. A composite work was, in the nature of the case, likely to go unfathered, being the property of the theatre, which would not divide publishing profits (if there were any) among a number of collaborators ; and of these in turn none could claim the authorship. Peele must often have been so placed. " It may be regarded as indisputable," says Professor Ward, " that he wrote many plays now lost."[2] But among the unsigned or disputed plays of his period that are preserved, cannot his hand be further traced ? I think it can. As it happens, four plays have been independently assigned to him by Fleay on grounds quite apart from the present inquiry—ALPHONSUS EMPEROR OF GERMANY, JACK STRAW (1593), THE WISDOM OF DOCTOR DODYPOLL (printed 1600), and WILY BEGUILED (printed 1606). Of these, DOCTOR DODYPOLL is the most difficult to assign. If the opening scenes are Peele's, it must be about the last thing he did, for there are five double-endings to 26 blankverse lines in the first scene ; eleven to 47 in the second (22 per cent.), and five to 22 in the third. It has one line :

> I'll seek me out some unfrequented place
> (Act III, Bullen's *Old Plays*, III, p. 123)

---

[1] I use this term to cover also "unassigned" work. The BATTLE of ALCAZAR is not assigned to him on the title-page, though admittedly his.
[2] *Eng. Dramat. Lit.* ed. 1899, i, 374.

which echoes his

> Where shall I find some unfrequented place,
> *(Battle*, v, i) ;

but that is a very slight basis for an attribution of authorship of the entire play. The excessively intricate and artificial plot suggests a variety of hands. It is true that the play contains the song : "What thing is love ? " doubly certified to be Peele's ; but we know from Drummond that it occurred in his masque, THE HUNTING OF CUPID ; and the duplication of a song is more likely to be done by someone else than by the author. On general grounds, for once, I am unable to concur with Fleay, beyond agreeing that the piece was probably written about 1590. For the rest, the piece throws no appreciable light on the authorship of TITUS.

The ascription to Peele of WILY BEGUILED raises many difficulties. Fleay pronounced the piece " possibly a University play," adding that it " has all the appearance of a play written for a London audience, and adapted for a University performance " ; and Dr. Greg (pref. to Malone Soc rep.) thinks that " the suggestion may be hazarded that the play was in its origin at least a Cambridge piece of the circle of PARNASSUS." One or other of these suggestions may very well be right ; the play has the general quality of the Parnassus pieces. But the " humorous George " of the prologue, held by Fleay to refer to Peele as author, is a very poor clue. The prologue is late, and echoes HAMLET (" swifter than meditation ") as well as the Marston-Jonson wrangle : why should the Juggler address its writer as Peele, who had been dead for years ? It is true that the play has slight echoes of Peele (" sunshine day " twice, for instance, and " all amort ") ; but, as Fleay notes, it has also a clue to Greene in the name Wily, which appears in GEORGE-A-GREENE. If, as Fleay confidently held, the original date of the play is 1596-7, the assignment to Peele is almost cancelled. The play as a whole suggests neither him nor Greene ; and the echoes of both are reasonably ascribable to young play-haunters penning it for a University audience. The prologue seems to me more likely to be Marston's than to be Jonson's, as Fleay argued ; but Jonson's it might be.

JACK STRAW, on the other hand, is certainly in part Peele's. Its rustic doggerel and prose may be his or anybody's ; but its blank verse, also a poor thing, is his very own ; its theme, loyalty, is his common burden ; and its vocabulary frequently points to him. Its " sandy plains " (Hazlitt-Dodsley, v. 395), as Fleay notes, is one of his supererogatory phrases (ED. I, sc. xiii, 61 ; BATTLE, V, i, 217 ; ANGLOR. FERIÆ, 29 : " sandy bottom " in D. and B., III) ; its " true-succeeding prince " (pp. 384, 399) occurs thrice in the BATTLE OF ALCAZAR ; it repeats several times his noun " wreak " ; it has his " unhonourable " (p, 412 : BATTLE, II, ii, 24), and his frequent " execute " = effect ; and its " sacrifice of thanks " (p. 408) is a note on which he harps. Finally, it gives two clues to TITUS.   The closing line :

> Where we'll repose *and rest* ourselves all night,

taken with one in EDWARD I (sc. iii, 6) :

> Now then let us repose *and rest* us here,

suggests that the phrase in TITUS (I, i, 151) " repose you here *in rest*," sometimes treated as corrupt, is no tautology, but Peele's deliberate diction. It is in fact an unskilful echo of Sackville :

> In woe and plaint reposèd was her rest.
> Introduction to the *Mirror for Magistrates*, 1563, st. 12.
> (As " repose " primarily means " place " or " lay down," there is strictly no tautology).

And when we note in JACK STRAW the lines (Act IV, p. 408) :

> Sith mercy in a prince resembleth right
> The *gladsome sunshine* in a winter's *day*,

we have a fresh reason for crediting him with the " mercy " lines in TITUS, of which the third runs :

> Sweet mercy is nobility's true badge.

" Gladsome " is one of his favourite words, though it is also found in Greene. Compare :

> Began the *gladsome summer day* to shine
> (Polyhymnia, l. 7),
> And *gladsome summer* in her shady robes
> (D. and B., I, ii, 159),
> Her *gladsome* birthday   (*Anglorum Feriæ*),

and

> This *gladsome day* wherein your honours spring.
> (Desc. Astrææ, near end).

It may be further interesting to note that in JACK STRAW is found the line (Act I, p. 384) :

> The multitude, a beast of many heads,

which occurs also in THE TROUBLESOME RAIGNE OF KING JOHN (Pt. II, sc. iii). In that play, Peele is to be traced by such words as " popelings " (five times) and " popery " (twice) ; and of the three TITUS-words found in it—" languor," " execrable," and " remunerate " (" Tully " is non-significant)—the third at least points to him, while the two others go to complete our list.

The problem thus raised in regard to the RAIGNE, however, is a complicated one ; and it may usefully be postponed to a consideration of another important ascription, to which Fleay has lent support.

§ 2. " ALPHONSUS EMPEROR OF GERMANY "

Concerning this play, which is traditionally assigned to Chapman and included with his works, Fleay writes :—

> " The external evidence is certainly in favour of Peele's authorship of this play. It was published as Chapman's in 1654 by Moseley, who attributed authorship in a most reckless way.

See my *Life of Shakespeare*, pp. 358-360. On the other hand, Wood and Winstanley, ' misled by former catalogues,' says *Biog. Dram.*, attribute it to Peele. Surely the former catalogues are a better authority than Moseley. The play is palpably an old one, dating c. 1590. It was revived May 5th, 1636, at Blackfriars ' for the Queen and the Prince Elector.' Chapman died in 1634, and therefore had nothing to do with the revival. This is a revenge-play, and would seem to be the ' *Richard Conqueror* ' alluded to in the *Taming of the Shrew*, Ind., which has given the commentators so much trouble : cf. v, i, ' If we be conquerors or conquered.' As it was in 1636 a King's men's play (chosen for performance before the Prince Elector on account of the Teutonic part in it), it probably was originally produced by the Lord Strange's men for presentation before some Ambassador from Deutschland."[1]

Professor Ward, without pronouncing on the attribution to Peele, decides that

> " Beyond all doubt the tragedy as we possess it exhibits very marked differences from the dramatic works which are unquestionably Chapman's . . . If . . . it is supposed to be his workmanship, it cannot be anything but a juvenile tragedy which he afterwards laid aside . . . It is as a whole in no respect worthy of his genius, and in truth but an indifferent piece of literary work."[2]

As usual, there is dispute. Dr. Karl Elze, who has edited the play, writes :

> " In our opinion the tragedy of Alphonsus was one of the latest works of its author, and in all probability was not written before 1622, if not later. It could not possibly have been written before 1620 if, *as I strongly suspect*, the poet owed part of his acquaintance with German politics to the English translation of the Golden Bull, which appeared in 1619."[3]

In attributing the play to Chapman's old age, Dr. Elze is following an article in the RETROSPECTIVE REVIEW, iv, 337. But the arguments in support are significantly strained. The play is admittedly written in large part in the style of the earlier drama ; and Dr. Elze is reduced to arguing that " the archaic dis-

---

[1] *Biog. Chron. of the Eng. Drama*, ii, 156.
[2] *Hist. of Eng. Dram. Lit.*, ii, 427-9.
[3] Ed. cited, 1867, pp. 35-36.

solution of the final *ion* and of similar terminations
in the end (sometimes even in the body) of the line
is intentionally and almost religiously observed."
This argument—which Elze supports by the plea that
a reversion to archaic diction is common in elderly
writers—is in point of fact quite unnecessary for the
critic's purpose.   The dissolution of *ion*, " sometimes
even in the body of the line," is really common in
Chapman's signed tragedies, which all lie between 1600
and his death.   Take these examples from BYRON'S
CONSPIRACY, published in 1608 :—

Within the powers of our instruction.	(I, i)
Leave me then to my own projection.	(*ib.*)
And made him chief in the commission.	(*ib.*)
What place is this ? What air, what region ?	(I, ii)
And strive to grow out of privation.	(*ib.*)
Is reckoned now amongst privations.	(*ib.*)
And absolute decessions of nature.	(*ib.*)
No true power doth admit privation.	(*ib.*)
So shall these terms and impositions . . .	(*ib.*)
Their human noblesse shamed : the mansions . . .	(*ib.*)
Were he but taken in affection.	(*ib.*)
With all state's highest observations.	(*ib.*)

Here we have twelve examples in one Act, nine of them
in one scene.   And they continue, both in the middle
and at the end of lines :—

Temptation to treason is no treason.	(II, i)
As she came quitted to confession.	(*ib.*)

Examples occur in his late tragedy, THE ADMIRAL OF
FRANCE :

And she seals all perfection. My lord. . .	(I, i)
And endless in our circumventions.	(*ib.*)
All justice tastes but affectation. . .	(*ib.*)
Is sure, and subtile to confusion.	(I, ii)
Though in the act and prosecution . . .	(*ib.*)
There's something more in's composition.	(*ib.*)

First and last, Chapman uses the form freely.   The
real question is, whether his style, his vocabulary, his
phrase, his matter, or his methods, can be traced in
ALPHONSUS, EMPEROR OF GERMANY.

In the first edition of this work, I denied that the play was at all in Chapman's manner ; and Elze, who amazingly affirmed that it was " written throughout in *Chapman's well-known manner,*"[1] had offered no shadow of evidence for his assertion. He further claimed that " no critic has doubted its authenticity." If this were true at the time of writing, it could only be because the critics had not yet taken up the problem ; but, if so, how came Elze to argue so anxiously for the authenticity ? His only further plea, indeed, was that " the frequent display of classical learning seems more indicative of an old than of a younger poet."[2] As every student will remember, the balance of fact is the other way. Greene, Peele, and Marlowe all abound in classical allusions and quotations from the first ; and Greene's late GEORGE-A-GREENE and JAMES IV are unclassical, as is Peele's DAVID. Shakespeare has fewer classical tags in his maturity than in youth. Ben Jonson is pedantic all along ; but his classical tragedies are not among his late works.

While, however, Elze's case is thus strangely bad, I am willing to re-open it in view of Chapman's apparent share in some of the Shakespeare comedies, which suggests a possibility, not before suspected, that he may have *collaborated* in other early plays before his own tragic style was formed. A study of his BLIND BEGGAR reveals a verse style wholly imitative of the pre-Shakespeareans. Could Chapman, then, at *that* stage, have had a hand in such a play as ALPHONSUS OF GERMANY ? An absolutely negative answer is given by Professor Parrott, the highly-qualified editor of the standard edition of Chapman's plays. To Elze's assertion that it is written throughout in Chapman's manner he gives " a complete and peremptory denial," adding : " nor are there any detached scenes or isolated passages which in any way recall his manner."[3] Professors Koeppel, Schelling, Herford, and Boas are either

[1] *Id.* p. 33.
[2] *Id.* p. 37.
[3] Ed. of Chapman's Tragedies, 1910, p. 684.

strongly or substantially of the same view. " In
ALPHONSUS," says Professor Parrott, " I have not been
able to find a single parallel to a passage in one of
Chapman's undisputed works." Seeing then that self-
repetition is about as common in Chapman as in any
of his contemporaries ; and that even in his early and
imitative work in the BLIND BEGGAR we find nothing
at all reminiscent of ALPHONSUS, the old attribution
to Chapman may be definitely abandoned as the mere
device of a publisher long after Chapman's death.

Having rejected the Chapman claim, I proceeded,
in my previous edition, to argue that " the play,
prima facie, is as likely to be Peele's as it is unlikely to
be Chapman's. Chapman's, indeed, it cannot be ;
and it can be shown to be almost certainly, in large
part, Peele's." To this claim, however, Professor
Parrott demurs, on grounds so far good that I am
moved to modify it. Granting that the strong anti-
Spanish animus of the story in itself supports the
view of Peele's authorship as strongly as it repels the
attribution to Chapman, who never shows any anti-
Catholic animus, Professor Parrott contends (1) that
" the dialogue is, for the most part, livelier and more
realistic " than any in Peele's signed work ; and (2)
that the plot is far more elaborately and skilfully
constructed (barring one or two absurdities) than any
of his. Peele has, I should say, less sense of plot and
structure than any playwright of his day." If the
first proposition be restricted to Peele's tragedies it
will, I think, hold good ; and the second is so far
weighty as to justify a denial to Peele of the origination
of the play.

I am now inclined, indeed, to surmise for it, as for
TITUS, an Italian ancestry in respect alike of its
horrors and its intricacies of plot. The opening scene,
after frequent reconsideration, I am compelled to
assign to Marlowe ; and Marlowe seems very unlikely
to have schemed the whole construction. Tentatively,
we might surmise a plot-construction (whether or not
on an Italian basis) by Kyd, with Peele, Greene and

Marlowe for collaborators or revisers, as in TITUS ;
and a collation of the title of this play with that of
Greene's ALPHONSUS KING OF ARRAGON strongly
suggests that this was the earlier, and that Greene's
very theme for his swiftly scribbled play was suggested
by it. On this hypothesis, the " Emperor " piece
originally dates as far back as 1589.

However that may be, Peele's share in it is, I think,
more clearly demonstrable than Professor Parrott is
disposed to admit. He grants distinct echoes of Peele
in Act III, scene i ; and admits that "such repetitions
as are noted in v, i, 182-3 and v, i, 192-6 are, to say the
least, akin to Peele's manner," adding : " It is worth
noting that these phrases and these echoes occur close
together in ALPHONSUS, possibly indicating old sections
of the play left untouched by a later reviser."[1]   That
is to say, Peele's hand is to be traced in III, i, where the
admitted echoes occur, and in v, i. The Professor's
final judgment, however, is that " the *most* that we can
grant Peele is, I think, to *admit* the *possibility* that he,
perhaps in collaboration with another author, composed an old play on this subject, which has been
subjected to so thorough a revision as to leave only
a few traces of his hand." Why, after his own
admissions, the Professor should not put " high
probability " of Peele's presence in place of bare
" possibility," I cannot divine. But even this, after
all, is granting a good deal. A late revision there
doubtless was ; but if we can still find numerous traces
of Peele, it need not here concern us. I readily assent
to the Professor's view (developing a suggestion of
Professor Ward's) that the German dialogue in the play
was contributed by the accomplished German Rudolf
Weckherlin (who married an Englishwoman, settled in
England before 1624, and served for over sixteen years
as an English secretary of state), for a court performance before the Elector Palatine in 1636—under-
standing the Professor to mean that Weckherlin put
into German what had been previously, in the main,

[1] *Id.* p. 689.

English dialogue. I see no adequate ground for inferring that either Weckherlin or anyone else substantially revised the play; but some rewriting of scenes, I think, has taken place—for instance in scene ii. Certainly none of the English dramatists, so far as we know, could have written the German parts; but if we are to suppose them original interpolations we must almost suppose the whole sub-plot as to Edward and Hedewick to have been such an interpolation. And seeing that Professor Parrott admits the general archaism of the style throughout, and can only suggest that " the reviser may have preferred, quite properly, to retain the old style,"[1] we are entitled, I think, to put that thesis aside as not admitting of substantiation, and, finally, as not affecting the issue.

On the other hand, there has come to the support of my original claim—overstated, as I now think—for Peele, a reinforcement in the shape of a series of papers in NOTES AND QUERIES (Dec. 9, 16, and 23, 1916) by Mr. H. Dugdale Sykes on " Peele's Authorship of 'Alphonsus, Emperor of Germany.'" Mr. Sykes has made a very thorough collation of the diction of ALPHONSUS with that of Peele in general, for which all students owe him thanks, whether or not they agree with his conclusions. Finding in ALPHONSUS not only a number of significant tricks of Peelean phrase not noted by me, but a number of passages marked by his verse-movement and structure of phrase, Mr. Sykes comes to the conclusion that the play is wholly his; and in particular he brings against my denial to Peele of the opening scene a really notable piece of evidence to prove that " it is, on the contrary, this very scene that most plainly bears his stamp."[2] We thus reach the interesting development that whereas I have been led to retrench my original position, Mr. Sykes claims to prove that even that position was under-stated.

To permit of a well-considered judgment I will

[1] *Id.* p. 692.
[2] *Notes and Queries*, Dec. 23, 1916, p. 505.

accordingly recapitulate the case for Peele's general authorship as I originally put it ; then reproduce the powerful case put by Mr. Sykes ; and finally indicate my reasons for adhering to the restricted position even in view of the important evidence which he has adduced. All will agree, I think, that Peele is *in* the play, and however suffrages may go as to his sole authorship, there will, I think, be further general agreement as to the early date of the work.

First, as to Peele's vocabulary, I gave the following list of words as primary clues. Professor Parrott, apparently supposing me to regard them as conclusive proofs, justly denied to them any such weight ; while Mr. Sykes no less justly holds that the list " raises a strong presumption of Peele's authorship."

Até (III, near end. Often in *Locrine* ; *Arr. of Paris*, 1, i).
Doom (II, ii ; v, i. Often in *Arr. of Paris*).
Emperess (twelve times in *Alphonsus*. *Anglor. Feriæ*, 9).
Gratulate (II, ii, I. See above, p. 193).
Hugy (IV, ii, II. Thrice in Peele).
Manly (IV, iii. Six times in Peele).
Massacre (IV, i ; v, iv. Often in *The Battle*).
Policy (five times in *Alphonsus* ; many times in Peele).
Progeny (v, iv. Thrice in the *Battle*).
Sacred (ten times in *Alphonsus* ; at least thirty times in Peele).[1]
Sacrifice (v, ii, iv. *Arr. of Paris*, prol. 13 ; *Edward I*, p. 390;)
Anglor. Feriæ ; *Battle*, I, l. 24 ; II, i, 32 ; *Tale of Troy*, 251, near end).
Solemnized (five times in *Alphonsus* ; *Ed. I*, sc. I, 194 ; *Garter*, 165).
Successively (I, ii, 5 ; *Battle*, I, i, 73).
Suspect (noun ; four times in *Alphonsus* ; thrice in *Edward I*).
Triùmph and Triùmphing (III, i ; v, i, iv. See above, p. 193).
Underbear, (IV, i, near end ; *Garter*, prol. 26 ; *Anglor. Feriæ*. 202).
Wreak (noun, v, iii. See above, p. 193).
Zodiac (IV, ii, 3. See above, p. 179).
[To this list Mr. Sykes adds the verb *scour* (v, i, 346) which is used by Peele in *Edward I*, sc. II, and in the *Tale of Troy*, l. 255. But it is also used thrice by Kyd in his version of Garnier's *Cornélie*, and at least thrice by Greene.]

---

[1] Nearly as common, however, in Dekker, who uses it twelve times in *Old Fortunatus* alone.

I further noted parallels of phrase :—

(*a*) ALPHONSUS EMPEROR OF GERMANY has some
" tag " phrases found in Peele's accepted plays :

Bloody banquet, v, i, 37.	*Battle*, IV, l. 6.
Vital blood, v, i, 39.	*D. and B.*, sc. ii, 45 ; sc. iii, 14.

(*b*) It also exhibits the mannerisms with which we
have become familiar, though, being in respect of its
metrical peculiarities a later work, it runs considerably
less to alliteration than do LOCRINE, DAVID AND
BETHSABE, and the BATTLE OF ALCAZAR :

Till then I'll pine with thoughts of dire revenge,
And live in hell until I take revenge   (I, ii, *end*).

Thou must imagine nothing but revenge ;
And if my computation fails me not,
Ere long I shall be thoroughly revenged   (IV, ii, *end*).

My father's yelling ghost cries for revenge,
His blood within my veins boils for revenge,
O give me leave, Cæsar, to take revenge.   (v, iv).

This shameful guilt and our unguiltiness   (v, ii).

In the same style we have a group of five lines beginning
with " How " (*ib.*).

(*c*) Without making anything of the iteration of the
phrase " Kill'st my heart," which we have seen so
often used by Peele elsewhere, we may note that the
line :

And fill'd thy beating veins with stealing joy   (II, i)

is an echo of one in the ARRAIGNMENT OF PARIS (II,
i, 176) :

To ravish all thy beating veins with joy.

(*d*) In the last instance not only the expression but
the application is the same.

Taking the presence of Peele to be thus " tentatively
established," I added a number of parallels as constituting " plain traces of one hand—or, let us say, of
the same hands "—in ALPHONSUS and TITUS :—

1. In ALPHONSUS, Alexander, accepting the emperor's counsel as to his revenge, says :

> I do subscribe unto your sound advice   (II, ii).

In TITUS (IV, ii, 130) Demetrius says to Aaron :

> Advise thee, Aaron, what is to be done,
> And we will all subscribe to thy advice.

2. A few lines earlier in TITUS occurs the epithet " shallow-hearted '"—not found in any Shakespearean work.[1] In ALPHONSUS (I, i, 7) we have " shallow-brained."

3. In TITUS we have the compound " counsel-keeping." In ALPHONSUS we have " counsel-keepers " and " counsel-breaking " (I, i, 151, 186—prose not counted). In 2 HENRY IV we find " counsel-keeper "; but that is the sole instance in the Shakespeare concordance.

4. In TITUS we have " map of woe " (III, ii, 12), and in ALPHONSUS " map of misery," and both phrases are applied to women in distress.

5. In TITUS (V, iii) there are two allusions to the slaying of his daughter by Virginius ; and to this classical reference we have thus far found no parallel in Greene, Marlowe, or Peele. But in ALPHONSUS (IV, iii, 60) we have the same allusion :

> Then, like Virginius, will I kill my child ;

and the action is in both cases suited to the phrase.

6. Another parallel occurs in ALPHONSUS to some of the lines of Aaron's avowal of his crimes in TITUS (V, i). The general situations are equivalent ; and where Aaron speaks of

> Complots of mischief, treason, villainies,

Alexander has the lines (V, 390) :

> All plots and complots of his (Alphonsus'] villany . . .
> Of every mischief that hath troubled you.

[1] " Shallow-rooted " occurs in 2 H. VI—another significant detail.

In the light of these signs of kinship we can see
significance in the slighter echo in the phrases about
the "faltering" tongue hesitating to tell a story of
guilt in ALPHONSUS (same scene) and in EDWARD I
(sc. xxv) ; and of the occurrence in ALPHONSUS of
TITUS-words such as *gratulate, wreak, emperess, zodiac,
entrails,* etc.

I then suggested that as in TITUS, there are in
ALPHONSUS other hands than Peele's. The opening
scene cannot be Peele's (here Professor Parrott agrees);
and I inclined (wrongly, as I now see) to assign it to
Greene, writing in his Marlowesque manner, as in
FRIAR BACON. And there are other items, both of
phrase and vocabulary, which point towards Greene or
Lodge or Kyd.[1]

(1) Our old friend "hammering in the head" is
here too :

> Unprincely thoughts do hammer in thy head   (IV, iii).

(2) The line :

> Hath from my knife's point suck'd his deadly bane   (III, i)

recalls one in SOLIMAN AND PERSEDA (I, iii, 32), which,
suggesting as it does the "point envenom'd" of
HAMLET, is one of the reasons for surmising Kyd's part
authorship of the foundation play as well as of the
line in SOLIMAN :

> His weapon's point empoisoned for my bane.

(3) In ALPHONSUS we find three times the word
"complots," which we have seen to be common to
Kyd (that is, in THE SPANISH TRAGEDY) and Greene,
but is not found in Peele's signed plays or poems.

(4) "Map" appears to be a specialty of Greene's
—copied at times by Lodge, but also used by Marlowe.

(5) The word "ambodexter"[2] (II, ii, 51) appears to

---

[1] Thus "counsel-keeper" in the opening scene points to the author of the
speech in *Titus* mentioning a "counsel-keeping cave." In *Edward III* again,
II, ii, 56, ; IV, vii, 13) we have "counsel-bearer" and "counsel-giver."
[2] The name of the "Vice" in the old play *Cambyses* (1569).

be Greene's, occurring as it does in his prose (A Quip
for an Upstart Courtier ; Works, xi, 252), and
again in Sir Clyomon and Sir Clamydes, in a section
otherwise ascribable to him.

" These details," I concluded, " point, albeit not very
insistently, to the probable factor of collaboration,
without affecting the inference that Peele did a good
deal if not the bulk of the work," adding that the
cumulative effect of the parallels to Titus, as of those
to Peele's signed works, could be countervailed only
by similar parallels, in similar numbers, in plays by
other writers.

No such parallels have been produced ; but Mr.
Dugdale Sykes, as aforesaid, has strengthened the
case for Peele, though to my thinking he overstates it.
To begin with, he notices tics of phrase such as these :—

1. Now speak, and speak to purpose, *in the cause.*
> *Alphonsus,* 1, i, 89.
We do admire your *wisdoms in the cause.*   *Id.* 11.
Then may I speak my conscience *in the cause.*
> *Battle of Alcazar,* 11, ii, 22.
Your *wisdoms* would be silent *in that cause.*
> *Edward I,* sc. xxv, 61.

[Add :—
And if you will but justice *in the cause.*
Arraignment of Paris, iv, i.   Dyce's Greene and Peele, p. 366*b.*
To speak uprightly in *this doubted cause.*   *Id.* p. 367*b.*]

As Mr. Sykes, with some justice (save in terms)
claims, " such trifling peculiarities of style are often
quite as useful in determining a question of authorship
as striking parallelisms in phrase such as " that given
above, about " beating veins." " So obvious a
resemblance," he observes, " is as consistent with a
supposition of plagiarism as with identity of authorship." That I take to be substantially true.   It is the
more surprising that, putting this caveat, Mr. Sykes
refuses to recognise the possibility of plagiarism of
Marlowe by Peele in the passage of David which
corresponds to one in the first scene of Alphonsus.
The " determining " principle surely must be, not, as

he suggests, the use of mere tags like " in the cause " (which are not " peculiarities of style ") but corres-pondency or compatibility of style in the larger sense— diction, manner, degree of pregnancy, concision and force, cadence, point, movement. Tags and tics of phrase really cannot " determine " a question of authorship. The style test, where it is clearly and strongly applicable, is final ; and no single clue of tag or phrase can overrule it. But the tag clue is itself precarious, even as such, and Mr. Sykes uses it too trustfully. The phrase " in the cause " is not peculiar to Peele : at least it occurs in the MASSACRE AT PARIS (II, vi) ; and though it *may* there be Peele's, this is not certain. In any case, the *style* of the opening scene of ALPHONSUS excludes Peele, and points con-clusively to Marlowe.

The difficulty about relying on mere tags even as clues emerges again when Mr. Sykes notes (2) three uses in ALPHONSUS of Peele's " kills my heart," and the further variant of " slain," As above pointed out, that tag occurs in ARDEN, assigned by Mr. Sykes (rightly in the main, though too absolutely) to Kyd, to say nothing of its being found thrice in Heywood. (3) As to " vital blood," Mr. Sykes points out that in Peele's DAVID there are phrases about " sucking " blood, and that " suck the vital blood " is the phrase in ALPHONSUS. That, doubtless, strengthens the clue, as clue. But (4) his single clue :

> Brave Earl, *wonder* of princely patience   (*Alphonsus*, II, 1, 20)
> Courageous King, the wonder of my thoughts
> (*Battle of Alcazar*, II, iv, 93),

though suggestive, especially in respect of the parallelism of " brave earl " and " courageous king," is indecisive, as we find in FAUSTUS (IV, i, 1) :

> *Wonder of* men, renowned magician.

Nevertheless, the scene in ALPHONSUS may be Peele's : the style test does not exclude him ; and there are only four double-endings to the 49 lines.

Then we have (5) the further parallels :—

> Therefore the better to *dive into the depths*
> Of this most devilish murderous complot.
> > *Alphonsus* II, iii, 139-40.

> Nor shall it me become
> To *dive into the depths* of his device
> > *Anglorum Feriæ*, ll, 275-6.

[As the ANGLORUM FERIÆ was written late in 1595, the possibility must be recognised that Peele was there echoing another man's phrase.]

6. Hath from my knife's point *sucked his deadly bane.*
> > *Alphonsus,* III, i, 359.

> The wanton baits that made me *suck my bane.*
> > *Edward I,* xxv, 112.

[Noted also by Professor Parrott.   Compare, however, Kyd's " *point* empoisoned *for my bane,*" noted above.]

7. With just *effusion of their guilty bloods.*   *Alphonsus,* v, i, 26.
   T'avoid *th' effusion of our guilty blood.*   *Edward I.,* v, 156.
8. *This damnèd deed.*   *Alphonsus,* v, 351 ; *Edward I,* xxv, 130.

[This is a weak clue.   Kyd has " damned deed " (S.T., III, iv, 34) and often uses the adjective.   And it is frequent in the WARNING FOR FAIRE WOMEN.]
9. More significant than the last is the structural parallel of—

> Which burning eats, and eating burns my heart.
> > *Alphonsus,* IV, ii, 21.

> We come to fight, and fighting vow to die. *Battle,* IV, ii, 8.

10. *Bear with* my interrupted speeches, lords ;
    Tears stop my voice.   *Alphonsus,* I, ii, 62-3.

> *Bear with* your mother, whose abundant love
> With *tears* of joy salutes your sweet return. *Edward I,* i, 50-51.

> *Grief stops my voice.*   *Alphonsus,* IV, ii, 116.

> Shame and remorse doth *stop my course of speech.*
> > *Edward I*, xxv, 56.

> Suddenly a griping at my heart
> Forbids my tongue his wonted *course of speech.*
> > *Alphonsus*, III, i, 440-1.

[As we shall see hereinafter, these parallels are weakened by another found in Marlowe.]

11. And *I, poor I*, am comforted in nothing.   *Alphonsus*, I, ii, 243.

> Then had not *I, poor I*, been unhappy.
> > *Arraignment of Paris*, III, i.

At this point Mr. Sykes turns to Peele's unsigned work. Rightly he accepts Fleay's assignment of JACK STRAW to Peele ; but over-adventurously he avows the conviction that Peele was also " sole author " of THE TROUBLESOME RAIGNE OF KING JOHN (printed 1591), a position which I venture to pronounce untenable. It is reached by a leap from verbal and phrasal clues, unchecked by counter-clues or by the style-test. Mr. Sykes always wants to find a play homogeneous ; but scores of Elizabethan plays are demonstrably heterogeneous even by external evidence, and the RAIGNE can by internal tests be shown to be in that category. To this issue we shall return. That Peele is *in* the play is quite clear ; and Mr. Sykes very warrantably traces him by an " I, poor I " in the Second Part. The speech in which it occurs is a close parallel in the style, sentiment, and trick of phrase to that in which the tic occurs in ALPHONSUS OF GERMANY :—

> 12. Dead, ay me, *dead*, ay me, my life is *dead*,
> Strangely this night bereft of life and sense ;
> And I, poor I, am comforted in nothing,
> But that the Emperor laments with me.
> > *Alphonsus*, I, ii, near end.

> *Grief* upon *grief*, yet none so great a *grief*
> To end this life, and thereby rid my grief.
> Was ever any so infortunate,
> The right idea of a cursèd man,
> As *I, poor I*, a triumph of despite.
> > *Troublesome Raigne*, Part II.
> > Hazlitt's Sh. Lib. vol. iv, pp. 308-9.   (Act IV, sc. i.)

[It is indeed difficult to deny these speeches, especially the second, to Peele, even apart from the " I, poor I " clue in the ARRAIGNMENT. The " right idea " is also a Peele touch ; and the whole flaccid diction is in his manner. But I would at this stage point out that the immediately preceding speech in the RAIGNE has not these characteristics, and is on grounds of diction and phrase much more plausibly to be assigned to Lodge ; while in the ALPHONSUS scene, the matter preceding and following is not Peelean.]

13. Loudly exclaiming in their *half-dead* ears.
Alphonsus, v, i, 33.

Fall *half-dead* among thine enemies.   *Id. ib.*, 263.

To men *half-dead* who lie killed in conceit.
Jack Straw ; Hazlitt-Dodsley, v, p. 208.
And twit with cowardice a man *half-dead.*
1 *Henry VI*, iii, ii, 55.

[An item in the assignment of Peele's share in the last-cited play.]

14.   Conspiring all your deaths,
I mean your deaths, that are not dead already.
Alphonsus, iii, (near end).
But ah, the sweet remembrance of that night,
That night, *I mean*, of sweetness and of stealth.   *Id.* iv,

                  So good a gentleman
As is that knight, Sir John Morton, *I mean.*
Jack Straw ; Hazlitt-Dodsley, v, p. 389.

I mean against your manor of Greenwich town.   *Id.* p. 392.

Excepting mainly those his foremost men,
I mean the priest and him they call Wat Tyler.   *Id.* p. 410.

[It is noteworthy that Mr. H. C. Hart, who in his editions of HENRY VI has endorsed the ascription of JACK STRAW to Peele, pronounces this phrase " a weak unpoetical trick of Peele's." Mr. Sykes accordingly has ground for assigning to Peele the ALPHONSUS passage last cited, and this : —

> She is content to be at your command,
> Command, *I mean*, of virtuous chaste intents.

As he further notes, the tic occurs twice in TITUS : —

> Their heads, *I mean*   (III, i, 203).
> *I mean*, she is brought to bed   (IV, i, 62).

But here, it will be observed, the phrase is not merely expletive in either case, but proper to the matter ; and probably neither of the ALPHONSUS speeches is Peele's work.   In this connection it may be interesting to note that the phrase occurs twice in ROMEO AND JULIET, I, i, 4 ; I, iv, 44.   But neither there is it merely pleonastic ; and it is thus invalid as a clue to the supposed draftsmanship of Peele in that play. When further we note the " I mean " tic four times in Greene's ALPHONSUS OF ARRAGON, with " I do mean " twice and " I did mean " over and above (ed. Dyce, pp. 228, 232, 235-6-7) ; also in Kyd (S. AND P. IV, ii, 20) ; and at least seven times in Marlowe (ed. Cunningham, p. 100, 102, 125, 145, 148, 161, 165), we have further reason to qualify the inference drawn by Mr. Sykes.]

15. Short tale to make.   *Alphonsus*, V, 455.
    Short tale to make.   *Tale of Troy*, l. 474.

[Mr. Sykes notes the same idiom twice in the RAIGNE, always, as here, at the beginning of a line.   But the clue is weak at best, the phrase being common.[1]   It occurs, also at the beginning of a line, in 3 HENRY VI, II, i, 120, where it reproduces a speech from RICHARD DUKE OF YORK.   That might be held to be Peele's, but the contextual scenes have a number of clues to Kyd ; and when we find the phrase again in HAMLET (II, ii, 146), even though it is not in the First Quarto, the possibility presents itself that it was a Kyd tag also.

---

[1] See it in *Sir John Oldcastle*, IV, i, in a line ending with " I mean."

But, again, it occurs in Greene's GROATSWORTH OF
WIT, and *he* is not confidently to be excluded as a
sharer here. It must accordingly be discounted in all
cases ; and in the RAIGNE passages cited, the style is
not Peele's.]

16. There is rather more point in the next item :—

> For good thou hast an *heir indubitate*.   *Alphonsus*, IV, iii, 55.

> If first-born son be *heir indubitate*.   *Raigne*, Part I, Sh. Lib.

[The first-cited passage is probably Peele's, the
second probably not. The phrase occurs also in the
old LEIR :—

> That God had lent you an heir indubitate.   (I, i, 42).

This scene, as it happens, includes a line :

> The world of me, I of the world am weary   (24),

which nearly duplicates this :

> The world hath wearied me, and I have wearied it,

occurring in the scene in Act IV of the RAIGNE from
which Mr. Sykes has cited the " I, poor I " tic and
" Short tale to make." Clearly there is some connection between the two pieces ; but we cannot infer one
hand in all the phrases under notice. As Mr. Sykes
has avowed, such phrases often stand for simple
plagiarism ; or, we may add, find common currency
as proverbs or tags. Though the speech in LEIR has
a common mark of Peele—" the prison of your life "—
and may be his, " heir indubitate " must be regarded as a widely current phrase. The word " indubitate " occurs frequently in Hall's Chronicle, and
always with application to a king or prince.]

17. But *private cause* must yield to *public good*
>   *Alphonsus*, I, ii, 126.
> Let *private sorrow* yield to *public fame*   *Id*. V, 503.

> But *private cause* must *common cause* obey   *Tale of Troy*, l. 219.

I hope, my lord, this message so will prove
That *public hate* will turn to *private love.*
Jack Straw, as cited, p. 392.

Here we have a better piece of evidence, though the
common antithesis of " private " and " public "
occurs, with a difference, twice in LUCRECE, and once
in PERICLES ; also in THE JEW, I, ii, 99.   And Mr.
Sykes produces yet other interesting items when he
turns for parallels to LOCRINE and SELIMUS, which he
accepts as involving both Greene and Peele.   There
is no great weight perhaps in the item :

> *To arms*, great Duke of Saxony, *to arms*
> *Alphonsus*, IV, iii, near end,

which he collates with the before-noted parallels
between LOCRINE and the BATTLE ; but there may be
some in the " helm and targe " of the same Act (IV, i,
20), which also points to LOCRINE and the FAREWELL
TO NORRIS AND DRAKE.   But much more remarkable
is the parallel, previously noted by Professor Parrott,
between a passage in ALPHONSUS and one in SELIMUS :

> The fox is subtle, but he wanteth *force,*
> The lion strong, but scorneth policy ;
> *I'll imitate Lysander in this point,*
> *And where the lion's hide is thin and scant*
> *I'll firmly patch it with the fox's fell.*
> Let it suffice I can be both in one.
> *Alphonsus*, I, i, 103-8.
>   Nothing is more doubtful to a prince
> Than to be scrupulous and religious.
> *I like Lysander's counsel passing well ;*
> *If that I cannot speed with lion's force,*
> *To clothe my complots in a fox's skin.*
> . . . .
> And one of them shall still maintain my cause
> Or fox's skin, or lion's rending paws.
> *Selimus*, ll, 1731-5, 1742-3.

Mr. Sykes comments that " This repetition is of so
significant a kind that it can only be explained on the
supposition that one of these plays is indebted to the

other, or that Peele was concerned in both." Certainly one echoes the other ; and it may be that one hand penned both passages ; but the hand was surely not Peele's. Mr. Sykes once more unduly ignores the test of style, which is so often cardinal. The parallel raises in a most interesting way the problem, to be discussed in a later chapter, as to the authorship of SELIMUS. The passage from that play is either by Marlowe or by Greene closely copying Marlowe. I suggest the latter solution, and add the proposition that the passage in ALPHONSUS is the original, and by Marlowe. Peele has no signed verse like either.

There, as aforesaid, I am at issue with Mr. Sykes, who strikingly parallels another passage from the first scene of ALPHONSUS with one from DAVID AND BETHSABE[1] :—

> I, not unruffled in simplicity . . .
> Haste to the augur of my happiness
> To *lay the ground* of my ensuing wars.
> He learns his wisdom, *not by flight of birds,*
> *By prying into sacrificed beasts,*
> By hares that cross the way, by howling wolves,
> By gazing on the starry element,
> Or vain imaginary calculations ;
> *But from a settled wisdom in itself*
> Which teacheth to be void of passion.
>   *Alphonsus,* I, i, 34-44.
>   Thou power
> That now art framing of the future world,
> Know'st all to come, not by the course of heaven,
> By frail conjectures of inferior signs,
> By monstrous floods, *by flights and flocks of birds,*
> *By bowels of a sacrificed beast,*
> Or by the figures of some hidden art ;
> *But by a true and natural presage,*
> *Laying the ground* and perfect architect
> Of all our actions now before thine eyes.
>   *David and Bethsabe,* sc. xv.

Here once more, assuredly, there is copying either of a poet by himself or of one by another. Once more we

---

[1] I have dealt with this matter in the *Shakespeare Canon,* Part II ; but for the convenience of the reader I here quote the passages in full.

find ourselves visibly among the Marlowe group.
But, as Mr. Sykes put it in the previous case, one
author may borrow from another. As he previously
avowed, such close correspondences between passages
which are not at all hackneyed may stand for simple
plagiarism. Rejecting my view that ALPHONSUS shows
traces of other hands than Peele's, he remarks[1] that
" there are doubtless one or two words and phrases
somewhat suggestive of Greene or Marlowe, *but then
Peele was an imitative writer.*" Quite so ; and when
I reconsider the opening scene of ALPHONSUS, which
is written with a vigour and directness and freedom of
style so Marlowesque, I am compelled to conclude that
here we have the great innovator, and that the passage
in DAVID is an imitation of this.

Support may be sought for Mr. Sykes's view on the
score that in some metrical aspects ALPHONSUS is a
later play than DAVID. But this takes us back at
once to the question of authorship. In the first scene
of the former play, which I ascribe to Marlowe, the
percentage of double-endings is nearly 10 ; in the
second scene, where we seem to hear Peele at the close,
it is 20. No fewer than 8 occur in the concluding
section of forty lines, a percentage of 20. Now, the
highest percentage in any whole Act of DAVID is that
of the first, which is under 7. If Peele wrote
ALPHONSUS it would be, for him, very late work in this
respect. But it is all a question of the hand. Marlowe had reached higher percentages than those ; and
the data thus point once more to him. On both
counts, then, we must consistently dispute Peele's
authorship of the first scene in ALPHONSUS, and maintain the opinion that in DAVID he has imitated that
scene in the passage under notice. Neither can we
assign to him the bulk of the second scene, which also
is largely Marlovian.

And this view will, I think, be found to square with
the other literary phenomena. It is clear that DAVID
was revised by Peele with unusual care. It is far

[1] As cited, p. 505.

more carefully written—falsetto as it is—than either the BATTLE or EDWARD I ;[1] and it will be found that the concluding scene in which David speaks the lines under notice is one of pure rhetoric down to the entrance of the Messenger. The dialogue among Bethsabe, David, Nathan and Solomon contributes absolutely nothing to the action : it is wholly didactic and undramatic, illustrating Professor Parrott's criticism that Peele is rather a poet (albeit no great one) than a dramatist. Of course it may fairly be replied that, collaborating in a vigorous melodrama, a play of high-piled action, he might very well lend himself to the conditions and write serious dialogue with some such businesslike effect as he could certainly compass in comedy. And this may be said of his work in TITUS. But to say this is to say that in TITUS and ALPHONSUS he was working in a frame not of his own making. If either play as a whole could have been *invented* by Peele he must have been metamorphosed indeed from what he was when he penned his signed plays.

That he carefully embellished DAVID for publication ; and that David's speech in disparagement of heathen augury, partly copied from that of Alphonsus, is part of such embellishment, seems to me the true inference from all the data. Alphonsus' speech is spontaneously fitting, in Marlowe's way ; the excursus of David is absolutely incongruous. Devoutly to tell the Hebrew Deity that *he* knows the future not by astrology, *or* floods, *or* pagan auguries of any kind, *or* by magic art, " but by a true and *natural* presage," is a procedure so grotesque in the circumstances that the hypothesis of a highly artificial literary adaptation is really necessary to explain it.

As to Mr. Sykes's opinion that the play presents only " one or two words and phrases somewhat suggestive of Greene and Marlowe," I would say, first,

---

[1] Here, however, it should be noted that both of these texts are visibly mutilated. See Dr. W. W. Greg's *Two Elizabethan Stage Abridgments*, 1923, as to the *Battle*.

that Marlowe is not a poet of one style, like Peele ; that his manner changes markedly as between TAMBURLAINE and his later work ; that there is again a difference as between his historical plays and THE JEW and FAUSTUS ; that HERO AND LEANDER yet again is a new departure ; and that while he repeats a number of his own favourite phrases in different plays he is not permanently given as was Peele to small and weak mannerisms of style. Though there are a number of verbal and phrasal clues which point to him, the best evidence of his presence is furnished by (1) the verse movement,[1] (2) the theme and the characterization, and (3) the action, of the opening scene. My original hesitation about ascribing it to him arose out of the opinion that certain parts of TITUS to which it gives clues of vocabulary were the work of Greene, who so notably follows Marlowe's various leads, copying the TAMBURLAINE manner, poorly and palely enough, in ALPHONSUS OF ARRAGON, and the freer manner of the JEW and FAUSTUS in FRIAR BACON and JAMES IV, besides approximating to Marlowe in the chronicle plays in which they collaborated

But while a whole series of clues makes fairly certain the presence of Greene in the Demetrius and Chiron section of Act II, scene i, of TITUS, I am finally much less certain of his authorship of the Tamora and Aaron section of scene iii than of Peele's absolute authorship of the Aaron speech at the opening of scene i. In the Tamora-Aaron episode there are several verbal and phrasal clues to Marlowe as well as to Greene. Finally then, the apparent Greene clues in the opening scene of ALPHONSUS OF GERMANY are negligible as against the weight of the very strong general presumption for Marlowe that is set up by the whole style, character and content. He who will compare it with the prologue to the JEW, the Guise speeches in the MASSACRE

---

[1] When Mr. Sykes undertakes to show (p. 504) that the versification is " indistinguishable from " Peele's in general he gives some good illustrative examples. But the *rhythm* of the opening scene is of a markedly different kind, and this he does not recognise.

and the general presentment of Barabas, will, I think, realise that it is a thoroughly Marlovian piece of work. As against such characteristic and structural identities, apparent verbal clues are to be discounted as matters of imitation, all the dramatists of the group being apt to dip into each other's special vocabulary. Still, there are a number of special verbal and phrasal clues which point to Marlowe in ALPHONSUS OF GERMANY. They may be thus enumerated :—

1. *Jacob's staff*, III, i, 87.

> I've a Jacob's staff
> Shall take the elevation of the pole.

Professor Parrott notes the expression in Webster, Nashe, and Overbury; " but nowhere with the implied [technical] meaning it has here." That meaning is found in Marlowe :

> And with the Jacob's staff measure the height
> And distance of the castle from the trench.   2 *Tamb.* III, iii.

2. We'll be *with ensigns spread* before the walls.[1]

> *Alphonsus*, III, i, 286

Their ensigns spread   III, i, 459.

We marchèd to the walls *with colours spread*.   *Id.* IV, i, 35.

When wert thou in the field *with banners spread ?*

> *Edward II*, II, ii,

3. We must with cunning level at the heart,
Which pierced and *perished*, all the body dies.

> *Alphonsus*, II, ii, 241.

So shall not England's vine be *perishèd*.   *Edward II*, v, i.

4. Quenchless, IV, ii, 4.   This word occurs at least six times in Marlowe.

5. Scroll.   Thrice in *Alphonsus* ; thrice in Marlowe.   (Also in Greene's prose).

6. To compass and *begirt him* in his *fort*.   *Alphonsus*.

What care I though the Earls *begirt us* round.

> *Edward II*, II, ii.

---

[1] Peele, it is true, has in the *Battle of Alcazar*, IV, i, the line :
Approach the field *with warlike ensigns spread* ;
but here again the diction is dilute, and suggests imitation.

Marlowe has also " girt *with* siege " and " girting *with* siege " ; while Greene has " begirt it," " begirt *with* siege," and " *girt* his *fort* " (ORLANDO FURIOSO, Dyce's Greene and Peele, p. 93 *b*).

7. Underprops.   Occurs in Marlowe, *Dido*, i, i.

8. Merit =reward :   IV, i, 48.   Cf. *The Shakespeare Canon*, Part II, pp. 61, 99.

9. Portcullis : Act III, third line from end.   Used by Marlowe, *Jew.*

Such instances illustrate at once the community of vocabulary and phraseology among the Marlowe group and the difficulty of assigning unsigned passages on such clues without controlling tests.   In the previous edition I spoke of Peele as echoing Marlowe's line :

Brave horses bred on the white Tartarian hills,   i *Tamb.*, III, iii,

in this of ALPHONSUS (IV, ii, 7) :

Water from forth the cold Tartarian hills.

But now, seeing that in the same speech we have Marlowe's " quenchless " and " scroll," I am moved to ask doubtfully whether here Marlowe is not weakly echoing himself.   I still suspect a Peelean imitation (" from forth " is a Peele tic as well as a Marlowe one) and it is in the next speech of ·Alphonsus that Mr. Sykes notes the line :

Which burning eats, and eating burns my heart,

as constructed on a weak Peelean model.   But if Mr. Sykes holds to that assignment, what does he make on his principles of the " cold Tartarian hills " ?   It seems a reasonable compromise to avow that while this scene-section may be Peele's, it may possibly not be ;   and that the line last cited may be a bad stroke of Marlowe's which Peele elsewhere copied.   It is noteworthy that in the first 65 lines of this scene there are eleven double-endings, or 17 per cent.—a rate never nearly approached in Peele's signed work, but attained in Marlowe's translation from Lucan, and exceeded in the first hundred lines of that piece. It would be rash to say that Peele cannot have done the scene; but no less rash to affirm confidently that he did.

Another difficulty arises in regard to the line:

> Forbids my tongue his wonted course of speech   (III, 441),

which Mr. Sykes justifiably cites as a Peelism. But the immediately preceding line:—

> Though suddenly a griping at my heart—

points to one in the MASSACRE AT PARIS (II, iii, 10):—

> A griping pain hath seized me at the heart;

and in EDWARD II (I, iv) we have:

> Anger and wrathful fury *stops my speech*.

In a later section I show cause for thinking that there are bits of Peele in the MASSACRE, and even in EDWARD II; but the last-cited line is Marlowe's; and the question as to whether or not Peele is diluting him in the "Tartarian" passage in ALPHONSUS remains dubious.

I incline to sum up, roughly, that the opening scene is wholly Marlowe's; that the line:

> They ward, they watch, they cast, and they conspire,

cited by Mr. Sykes as Peelean, is really Marlowe's, being notably more powerful than the parallel line from Peele, even as the whole scene is far above Peele's known level; that the bulk of scene ii is also Marlowe's, though Peele enters at the close, and probably in the first scene of Act II. The second is partly nondescript, perhaps through the revision of 1636, though here and there suggesting Greene; but the long dialogue between Alphonsus and Alexander seems to me substantially Marlowe's. In Act III, the "Jacob's staff" passage seems distinctly Marlovian, as is the dialogue in which we find "begirt his fort" and "ensigns spread" (ll. 270, 286). And either Peele wrote the following scene between Alphonsus and Alexander, or else Marlowe here (as sometimes elsewhere) echoed a line of Peele (III, i, 337). On that view the "griping at my heart" and the next line (440-1) are Marlowe's, with the rest of the dialogue.

In Act IV, scene i, we have the Peelean "helm and targe," but the diction of the scene is quite above Peele's general level of energy, and the "with colours spread" and the "perished hair" hint of Marlowe. In scene ii we have the "cold Tartarian hills," and other Marlowesque touches, in a scene which may yet be Peele's (the great difficulty being the double-endings) ; and to him seems assignable the concluding speech of Alexander, with its "I mean" and its closing iterations. But the third scene does not at all indicate him. The first line, with its "map of misery," had originally suggested to me Greene, but what follows is not in Greene's manner. Marlowe, as it happens, has "map of weatherbeaten woe" in Dido (I, i, 158). The concluding section may be Peele's ; and to him I am disposed to assign the bulk of Act V, which has a number of verbal and phraseological clues to him, and little trace of Marlowe. But there are several passages which appear to me to be Kyd's ; and these will fall to be considered in a later chapter. They raise the general question of his probable share in the plot, and of the possible re-writing in Alphonsus of an original (or translated) play of his, as seems to have happened in the case of Titus.

§3. "The Troublesome Raigne of King John"

The most important claims made for Peele as a dramatist are unquestionably the ascriptions to him by Mr. Dugdale Sykes of the entire authorship of the old KING JOHN and the old KING LEIR. Save for a possible stand over the once-admired DAVID AND BETHSABE, it will be admitted that these plays are in general power superior to all of Peele's signed dramatic work ; and it is the more necessary to test the claim closely. If it is to stand, it will go some little way to carry with it Mr. Sykes's claim[1] that the RAIGNE "reveals Peele as the pioneer of our national historical drama, as the progenitor of Marlowe's EDWARD II and the still more famous chronicle-plays of Shakespeare. The TROUBLESOME RAIGNE, if it is not the first real chronicle-history, is, as Professor Schelling says, 'the earliest vital representation of historical events on the English stage.'" This makes nothing of the old RICHARD THE THIRD ; and takes for granted that there was no HENRY V save the primary FAMOUS VICTORIES (dismissed by Mr. Sykes as insignificant) as early as 1591. But it further takes for granted— unless " vital representation " is to carry some special force—that neither the FIRST PART OF THE CONTENTION nor RICHARD DUKE OF YORK existed in 1591 ; and this is not a warranted assumption. If the proposition is simply to mean that the RAIGNE gives a kind of " vital representation of historical events " which is not yielded by the CONTENTION, or RICHARD DUKE OF YORK, it is difficult to realise the issue. As history, the plays are pretty much on a par ; and " vital representation " is far to seek in any of them.

Still, it may be granted that the TROUBLESOME RAIGNE OF KING JOHN stands out notably among the first chronicle plays in blank verse. It will be the more remarkable if it should turn out to be as a whole the work of Peele, who does not otherwise rise above the rank of a minor contributor to the series of those plays. The claim, in fact, presents Peele as having done his best work first, declining thereafter to a poorer level. If that were the fact, he would present a marked exception to the upward evolution seen in

[1] *Sidelights*, p. 124.

the work alike of Marlowe, Greene, Kyd, and Shake-spear.

Mr. Sykes's general claim is, as before noted, sup-ported by some sound clues of vocabulary and phraseology. The great difficulty over his theorem is that he dwells upon these alone, and takes no account of a number of phenomena which tell of the presence of other hands as well as Peele's. Granting at once the tentative value of his verbal clues to tic-words of Peele's, such as *flatly*,[1] *hitherward, dare say*; and of the clues of cadence, formula and phrase which he notes in Queen Elinor's opening speech, with its "stole of dismal hue" echoed from the ARRAIGNMENT (III, i); as well as of a dozen echoes of phrase between ALPHONSUS, the RAIGNE, and Peele's signed work, we are always faced by aspects of the play which these do not cover. Before the appearance of Mr. Sykes's book I had written of the RAIGNE :— ' Here and there the style distinctly suggests Peele by its forcible-feeble diction, notably in the scene which seems to begin Act III,[2] beginning :—

> This is the day, the long desired day.

Such lines as :

> Pardon my rashness, and forgive the zeal
> That carries me in fury to a deed
> *Of high desert, of honour, and of arms,*

and the still more pleonastic four which follow, are like nobody but Peele ; and he may very well have written the irregular rhyming scene of Philip and the friars, which seems to constitute Act IV of Part I. His, too, might be the scene beginning :

> Pandulph, as gave his Holiness in charge,

where we have the spelling " Lewes " as against the " Lewis " of Part I.'

---

[1] Though that is used by Marlowe, Greene, and Kyd.
[2] There are no divisions of act or scene in the old text.

Then there are the stronger scenes and invective speeches which by their general vigour have always set up a surmise of the presence of Marlowe. On this issue there has been much debate. Malone ascribed to Marlowe the whole play ; Dyce the concluding portion only. Mr. Bullen on the contrary declares that " Earless and unabashed must be the critic who would charge Marlowe with any complicity in THE TROUBLESOME RAIGNE OF KING JOHN," to the indignation of Fleay, who held Marlowe to be " the chief plotter,"[1] with Lodge, Peele, and Greene as collaborators. And Mr. Ivor B. John, while pronouncing that " the character of the play as a whole does not encourage belief in Marlowe's authorship," is of opinion that " no one but an admirer or a pupil of Marlowe's could have produced Falconbridge's soliloquy,"[2]

> What wind of honour blows this fury forth ?

in Part I.

I am disposed to go further, and say that Marlowe did write it. It is in his middle manner, the freely vigorous manner of the JEW, FAUSTUS, and the MASSACRE ; and it has specific Marlowe marks. Compare :—

> The whistling leaves upon the trembling trees
> Whistle in consort I am Richard's son

(where the " whistling " is probably a misprint, suggested by the " whistle ") with

> The rattling of the winds
> With whisking of these leaves.   *Dido*, ii, end.

In " fumes of majesty," again, we have an uncommon use of the first word, which compares with

> And plant our pleasant suburbs with her [Egypt's] fumes
> *Dido*, v, i, 15.

[1] *Biog. Chron.*, ii, 53.
[2] Iutrod. to " Arden " ed. of *King John*, p. xi.

Throughout the scene we have the Marlowe touch.
The line :

> This gross attaint so tilteth in my thoughts

points to one of his tic-words :—

> Even as the windy exhalations,
> Fighting for passage, tilt within the earth
>
> > 1 *Tamb.*, I, ii.
>
> Auster and Aquilon . . .
> > tilt about the watery heavens
> >
> > > *Id.*, III, ii.
>
> Trotting the ring and tilting at a glove
> > 2 *Tamb.*, I, iii.
>
> As every tide tilts 'twixt their oaken sides.
> > *Dido* I, i.

—to which we may add the two literal uses in EDWARD
II ; and much of the subsequent diction has a vigour
that does not belong to the rest of the Marlowe school.
The second Act, too,[1] begins with a Marlowesque
energy of style ; and though the " braine that hammers
shifts " suggests either Greene or Lodge, the soliloquy
of Falconbridge beginning :

> What words are these : how do my sinews shake ?

has Marlowe's ring in a marked degree.   The line :

> This heart that choler keeps a consistory

points to several uses of " consistory " in FAUSTUS ;
and the " sinews shake " is from TAMBURLAINE.   But
in the third Act,[2] apart from the speeches of Falconbridge, the Marlowe quality appears to vanish ; though
it perhaps returns in Act V, in Arthur's speech to
Hubert, beginning " Ah, monstrous damned man " ;
and Part II appears to be divided among Lodge,
Greene, and Peele.'
  Mr. Sykes has notably strengthened the case for
Peele by the clues before mentioned, and others ; but

---

[1] Taking this to begin with King Philip's speech, rep. p. 237.
[2] Taking that to begin with King John's speech, p. 252.

he has noted neither the Marlowe clues nor those which,
as will be shown in another section, point to Lodge ;
and, neglecting these, he has in effect failed to apply
to the play throughout the test of style. A number
of speeches, after those of Philip, are in a markedly
non-Peelean style, notably that of King Philip (II, i)
beginning :

> Now 'gin we broach the title of thy claim,

and the others of that scene.

In the next scene, the Bastard's speech beginning :

> And art thou gone ? misfortune haunt thy steps !

is assigned by Mr. Sykes to Peele apparently because
of the opening phrase, which recurs ; but that phrase
is not otherwise assignable to Peele, and this speech is
not in his manner. If it is not Marlowe's, it is
probably by Lodge. The style throughout is non-
Peelean, though, as aforesaid, he seems to begin the
scene (III, i) which follows. On the other hand the
recurring word *flatly*, which Mr. Sykes takes to be a
clue to Peele, is used by Marlowe (ED. II, III, ii) and
by Greene (Lamilia's song in the GROATSWORTH OF
WIT) ; also by Kyd (SP. TRAGEDY, III, xiv, 22) ; and is
indeed common. In the next scene, again (III, i), the
Bastard's speech, which, with the action, is the whole
of the scene, is not in Peele's style, though he seems
to enter in the next. In the Bastard's speech, too,
we have the scansion " trìumpht," whereas, as Mr.
Sykes notes, Peele is given to " triùmph," which
recurs in III, iv. But again in III, v, we return to the
former style, suggestive of Marlowe or Lodge, though
Act IV, dealing with the friars and nuns, is doubtless
Peele's.

Among the word clues in the non Peelean scenes
are the four uses of the word " orisons " (Sh-Lib. rep.
pp. 260, 270, 273, 300), which is not found in Peele,
but occurs in Marlowe (EDWARD III, IV, iv, 78 ; JEW,
, ii, near end) ; in Greene's ALPHONSUS (I, i) ; twice

in FRIAR BACON (Dyce, pp. 162*b*, 178*b*) ; in Lodge's
prose ; and often in Greene's prose. Yet again, the
expletive " Trust me," which Mr. Sykes assigns to
Peele, occurs in FRIAR BACON (Dyce, p. 177*a*) ; thrice
in ORLANDO (*Id.* 91*a*, 93*b*, 99*a*), and in Kyd's ARDEN
(IV, iii, 28), as well as in Lodge's ROSALYNDE (Sh. Lib.
rep. p. 78)—one of the many warnings of the risk of
building confidently on such clues of phrase. " Trust
me " is an every-day expletive, like " I warrant you,"
not a mannerism of a single author. Seeking to
follow up the more hopeful clue of " orisons," let us
note the style of one of the speeches (Pt. I, v, ii) containing the word :—

> *John.*   Why so, now sorts it, Philip, as it should.
> This small intrusion into abbey trunks
> Will make the popelings excommunicate,
> Curse, ban, and breathe out damned orisons,
> As thick as hailstones 'fore the kings approach :
> But yet as harmless and without effect
> As is the echo of a cannon's crack
> Discharg'd against the battlements of heaven.
> But what news else befel thee, Philip ?

This is not at all clearly the style of Peele ; neither
is that of the speech which follows :—

> *Bast.*   Strange news, my lord ; within your territories
> Near Pomfret is a prophet new sprung up,
> Whose divination volleys wonders forth.
> To him the commons throng with country gifts ;
> He sets a date unto the beldame's death
> Prescribes how long the virgin's state shall last,
> Distinguisheth the moving of the heavens,
> Gives limits unto holy nuptial rites,
> Foretelleth famine, aboundeth plentie forth :
> Of fate, of fortune, life and death, he chats,
> With such assurance, scruples put apart,
> As if he knew the certain dooms of heaven
> Or kept a register of all the destinies.

The occurrence of five double-endings in fifteen
lines, so early as 1591, suggests first Marlowe ; and,
as the style is very like him, to him we must assign
them pending some better claim than Peele's. But

in the same scene, in John's speech after his corona-
tion, with the same style, we have a " for to " which
militates against the ascription, since that locution
occurs in Marlowe only in what appear to be interpolated speeches[1] ; and unless we can be sure enough
of the style to ascribe the speech to him in spite of
that counter-clue, we must choose between Greene
and Lodge. Now, in the later speech of John in the
same scene beginning " False dreamer," we have two
tags of Greene's, " vain suppose " and " cut off the
cause, and then the effect will die."[2] And though,
apart from his tags, Greene is relatively a difficult
author to trace in unsigned work, having a variety of
styles of which only one is highly mannered, he is so
frequently to be traced by tags in this play that he
cannot safely be excluded as a probable sharer. And,
sharing as he did with Peele in the York-Lancaster
chronicle plays, he is likely enough to have shared in
this. The difficulty is to distinguish with certainty
between him and Lodge, as imitators of Marlowe ;
and, again, to make sure how much of the more
vigorous and clearly non-Peelean versification in the
play is really Marlowe's, as so much seems to be, Mr.
Bullen notwithstanding. These problems will be
further dealt with in later sections ; but enough has
been said to indicate the force of the rebuttal by the
style test of Mr. Sykes's claim that Peele wrote the
whole play.

Too many of his phrasal clues, as we have seen,
are indecisive. In addition to those above given may
be noted that of " brazen gates," which is common to
Marlowe (" brazen gates ") ; Greene (" brazen doors "

---

[1] See *The Shakespeare Canon*, Part I, p. 24.
[2] Compare :

> *Ablata causa, tollitur effectus* :
> Lacy, the cause that Margaret cannot love . . . .
> Take him away, and then th' effects will fail.
> *Friar Bacon* (Dyce, p. 1656).
> The cause efficiat of their woes.   *Id.* p. 175 b.

Greene has the tag many times. It recurs in the old *King Leir*, sc. 10, where
it sets up a problem, also in *Soliman*.

and " gates of brass ") ; and Kyd (" brazen gates,"
S.T. III, vii, 9). Equally invalid is the clue of the
phrase " trust me," which, assigned by Mr. Sykes as
a specialty to Peele, is common to Marlowe, Greene,
and Kyd :—

> So, trust me, Franklin, when I did awake . . .
> *Arden*, III, iii, 28.
> For, trust me, daughter, like of whom thou please.
> *Orlando*, sc. i (Dyce, p. 91*a*).
> But, trust me, princes, I have girt his fort.   *Id.* p. 93*b*.
>
> Trust me, Orgalio, Theseus in his rage . . .   *Id.* p. 99*a*.
>
> And trust me, Orlando, Angelica . . .   *Id.* p. 107*a*.
>
> Trust me, by truth of knighthood, that the king . . .
> *Friar Bacon* (Dyce, p. 177*a*
> Trust me, to give, it is a witty thing.
> *Marlowe*, tr. of *Ovid's Elegies*, VIII.
> On then, but trust me, 'tis a misery
> To see a man in such affliction.   *Jew of Malta*, I, ii.

In view of so many instances, it is idle to found on the
phrase as a clue to Peele.

Thus even if, as Mr. Sykes claims, words and phrases
and certain mannerisms recurred " not merely in
particular scenes, but throughout the work," the fact
would not, as he argues, " preclude any supposition of
mixed authorship." But they do *not* thus constantly
recur : some of them occur in only two or three scenes ;
some only in one. In one case he adds to his single
instance (in this play) of Peele's " mounting mind "
the passage :

> My brother's mind is base and too too dull
> *To mount* where Philip lodgeth his affects.

But " mounting mind " is a tag as old as Gascoigne ;
and what most craves attention in those lines is the
" too too," of which no instance is given from Peele's
signed work, whereas it is thrice used by Marlowe[1]

---

[1] *Dido*, v, i and ii ; *Hero and Leander*, i, 395.

and at least six times by Greene,[1] who also frequently uses the noun "affects." In the RAIGNE "too too" occurs thrice.[2] Who used it there? The style of the context in each case is unlike that of Peele. In the first passage, it points to Marlowe: in the second, if not to him, to Greene or Lodge.

§ 4. THE OLD "KING LEIR"

The danger of seeking a single author for an anonymous old play is again illustrated in Mr. Sykes's claim[3] "that Peele is the sole or main author of THE TRUE CHRONICLE HISTORY OF KING LEIR AND HIS THREE DAUGHTERS, entered in the Stationers' Register, May, 1594, and played by Sussex' men and the Queen's men in that year. In the first edition of this work it was noted that there is considerable evidence from vocabulary of Peele's presence in the play,[4] assigned by Fleay[5] to Lodge and Kyd. I pointed out, however, that Fleay's dating of the play in 1588 is irreconcilable with the multitude of double-endings,[6] which brings it at least down to 1591; and I pointed to a number of apparent clues to Greene. These Mr. Sykes rejects as invalid, pronouncing for Peele's authorship "substantially, if not wholly," and saying nothing of Fleay's claim for Lodge and Kyd, which I admitted to be tenable to the extent of their having had "a hand" in it.

After being led to various hypotheses on the history of this play, including one of a revision by Peele for publication, I offer one that would embody Fleay's

---

[1] *Locrine*, near end ((l. 2154); *Selimus*, l. 2365; *Friar Bacon*, sc. 5 (Dyce, p. 161 b); *James IV*, v, iii, near end; *Alphonsus of Arragon*, iv, ii (Dyce, p. 241 a); Fable of Aesop in *Groatsworth of Wit* (*id*. p. 311 b).

[2] Sh. Lib. rep. pp. 235, 277.

[3] *Sidelights*, p. 126, sq.

[4] Mr. Sykes says (p. 127) I "admitted" this. I think I was the first to assert it.

[5] *Biog. Chron*. ii, 51-52.

[6] Sc. i (deducting rhymed lines) 9.5 per cent.; Sc. ii, 10 per cent.; sc. iii, 10; sc. iv, 13; sc. v-vi, 20; sc. vii, 20. The progression is noteworthy.

notion of an early play, for which he no doubt had grounds. It may be that LEIR is a recast of an early play somewhat like LOCRINE. It approximates to that in theme—a pseudo-historical one from legendary history—yet differs so widely in treatment that the two plays may be said to represent opposite extremes of technique. LOCRINE is all stilted rant, with a little incongruous comic relief. LEIR is more realistic, as regards rhetoric, than any of the chronicle plays. Ragan and Gonorill are at the outset shrews of comedy, and though Ragan plots her father's murder she and her sister are not the terrible things of Shakespeare's tragedy, who must perish. LEIR is in fact a chronicle-comedy; and as comedy it belongs to the nineties, not to the eighties. Mumford and the King of France are modern comedy figures imposed on a legend play.

Various items indicate its primary consanguinity with LOCRINE. " Brittany " for Britain,[1] in the earlier acts, is one. One of its tic-words is " perfit " (perfect), which occurs eight times in the first four acts, beginning with l. 12 :

A perfit patterne of a vertuous life.

In LOCRINE (I, i) we begin with :

A perfect pattern of all chivalry ;

and the " perfect pattern " formula recurs twice (IV, i ; V, 14). " Bewray your secrecy " (LEIR, I, i, 90) recalls

Have I bewray'd thy arcane secrecy ?

in the other play (V, iv). " Regiment " = kingdom occurs in both. The broad difference between the plays is that LOCRINE is wholly archaic-romantic, never emerging from poetic rant and bombast and heroics unless it be to fall into buffoonery, whereas

[1] So also in Marlowe.

LEIR is realistic alike in the serious and in the comic vein. It testifies to the discovery that the old vein was worked out as regarded popular appreciation.

Now this may be a result of a re-shaping by Kyd of an early chronicle-play by Greene and Peele. Kyd can be seen to have been a main, if not *the* main factor in imposing realism both of tone and topic on the academic blank-verse play, in which Marlowe begins with TAMBURLAINE, and Greene and Peele jointly with LOCRINE. The spirit of realism emerges even in the SPANISH TRAGEDY ; realism of comedy is imposed on SOLIMAN AND PERSEDA ; and though the old rhetoric at times recurs in ARDEN, the topic, the action and the character-drawing there represent the establishment of realistic methods. In detail, the realism is often halting and incongruous, expressing a bias ill-reduced to art ; but the bias is compulsive. It is under the influence of this bias that LEIR, as we have it, is con-structed ; and if, as we are led to infer, TITUS is broadly a recast by Peele and Marlowe and Greene of an early Kyd play, it is possible that LEIR may be a recast by Kyd of an early play of the other school. Such a hypothesis would account for the phenomena of the many traces of Greene and Peele in a play which, as it stands, is not in the manner of either, and is probably to be dated after Greene's death.

Mr. Sykes has unquestionably strengthened the claim for Peele's presence by a number of verbal and phrasal clues ; but again he treats as special to Peele certain tics of phrase which were common to his colleagues. Citing three separate lines of LEIR begin-ning " O how," he writes that " these exclamatory lines beginning with ' how ' or ' O how ' are, I believe, peculiar to Peele—at least I do not find them in Mar-lowe, Kyd, or Greene " ; and notes a " how " line from EDWARD I, an " O how " line from ALPHONSUS OF GERMANY, and another from 1 HENRY VI (III, i, 106) as pretty certainly traceable to Peele. Now, whereas he has found *no* " O how " line in Peele's signed work, that form is fairly frequent in all three

of the contemporaries in whom he has failed to find
it. Marlowe has :—

> O how a crown becomes Æneas' head.   *Dido,* IV, iv.

> O how these irksome labours now delight.   *Id.* III, iii.

> O how this sight doth delight my soul.   *Faustus,* II, ii.

Kyd has :—

> O how she'll chafe when she hears of this.
>   *Arden,* III, vi, near end ;
> Oh, how cunningly she can dissemble.   *Id.* v, i, 190—

—also " for how " and " ah how " lines (III, v, 69, 147).
Greene has :—

> O how my mother's mourning moveth me.
>   *Looking Glass* (Dyce, p. 130*b*).
> O how I fainted when I wanted thee.   (*Id.* p. 136*b*).

> O how he talks as if he should not die !   *James IV,* II, i.

> O God ! how I am ravished in your worth.
>   *Id.* I, near end.

Yet further, we find two instances in Greene's
SELIMUS (ll. 1030, 1064)[1] ; and yet again in JAMES
IV we find the simple " How " form which Mr. Sykes
reckons to be in point :—

> How little shape much substance may include.
>   *Id.* III, near end.

And in Greene as in Kyd we find an " Ah, how " line.
That gambit, then, would seem to be closed. And
others of Mr. Sykes's clues equally fail ; for instance,
the use of " good fellows " to indicate bad fellows,
which he assigns only to Peele, occurs in ARDEN (II,
i, 26, Temple ed.). Other clues of manner, such as
the antithesis : " certain cause of this uncertain ill,"
and the clues of tautology and alliteration, in such

---

[1] It is arguable, indeed, that *these* are penned by Peele, as the scene section contains two of his tags.

phrases as "To make of mortal foes immortal friends," equally indicate Kyd, abounding as they do in all his plays; while the Biblical allusions are similarly suggestive of Lodge, as represented in the LOOKING GLASS FOR LONDON. The matter then must be more narrowly scanned.

An outstanding feature in the old LEIR is the large number of uses of the infinitive form "for to"—a mode specially affected by Greene, who has it no fewer than 71 times in ALPHONSUS OF ARRAGON. No one else approaches him in the strength of this proclivity. Peele has used the form some dozen times in all his signed work, having six instances in EDWARD I; but Kyd has eight in ARDEN; and Lodge (a great imitator of Greene) has fourteen in his WOUNDS OF CIVIL WAR; so that either of these, to say nothing of Greene, is a more likely source than Peele on that aspect of the case. But the play divides largely into scenes with many "for to's" and scenes with none, or few. Thus the first three have eight instances; the next three none. The first three scenes, further, have the lower percentages of double-endings: the figures rising, as above noted, from 9 or 10 to 20 for the fifth, sixth and seventh together. In the second three, we have one or two of the apparent Peele clues noted by Mr. Sykes, as "it resteth" and "what resteth?"; but, to say nothing of style and of the fact that "it resteth" occurs twice in ARDEN, it is very difficult to accept as Peele's, even about 1594, so high a percentage of double-endings. In one speech of Leir's in sc. vi, we have five in thirteen lines. And when we find there the tag about

> the princely eagle
> That kills her young ones, if they do but dazzle
> Upon the radiant splendour of the sun,

and note also in SOLIMAN AND PERSEDA (III, i, 85) the lines:

> As air-bred eagles, if they once perceive
> That any of their brood but close their sight
> When they should gaze against the glorious sun,

> They straightway seize upon him with their tallents [talons],
> That on the earth it may untimely die
> For looking but askew at heaven's bright eye,

we are faced by the alternative inferences (*a*) that one writer has copied another, or (*b*) that Kyd is the author of both passages—if we can be sure that he penned the lines in SOLIMAN. But the clue leads us further. In 3 HENRY VI (II, i, 91) we have :

> Nay, if thou be that princely eagle's bird,
> Show thy descent by gazing 'gainst the sun.

This comes entire from RICHARD DUKE OF YORK, scene iv, where there are apparent verbal and phrasal clues to both Peele and Kyd. We can but say that the balance of presumption as to the lines in LEIR is against Peele and in favour of Kyd. A little earlier in the DUKE OF YORK scene we have : " the piteous spectacle That e'er mine eyes beheld," where " piteous" is clearly an error for " piteous't," and we shall find that that awkward superlative (altered in 3 HENRY VI to " saddest ") is in the manner of Kyd. When then we weigh the item of the numerous double-endings, which we find in keeping with Kyd's practice in both ARDEN and SOLIMAN, it is to him that the balance inclines.

Leaving to later sections the further assignments of his share and those of Greene and Lodge, who are indicated by various clues, we may for the present pronounce that Fleay's assignments appear to be valid as regards a large part of the play ; while recognising that Peele and Greene had a share in it. Mr. Sykes, as in the case of the RAIGNE, has claimed too much. The play as a whole has an orderliness and elaboration of plot that belong to Kyd and not to Peele ; and there are too many styles unlike Peele's to admit of his being credited with even the bulk of it. Among the clues suggested by Mr. Sykes we may note, in scene 25 (V, i), the line :

> And melt as butter doth against the sun,

which recalls " a dish of butter in a sunny day," in
EDWARD I (Dyce, p 383b) ; but the style of the scene
is not Peele's, though that of the next clearly is ; and
one of the phrases in Ragan's speech, " an agony of
doubt," points to " an agony of spirit " in ARDEN (IV,
iv, 33). *That* scene-section is noteworthy as having
been apparently introduced on the " academic "
principle of exhibiting the prospective victim as himself guilty of a wrong which mitigates our sympathy
with him. Peele certainly worked on that principle ;
but so did Kyd, and in the scene-section in ARDEN
I can find no style-clue to Peele. The hand appears
to be that which has penned the bulk of the play—a
hand deliberately eschewing " filed points," and,
indeed, little gifted for fine blank verse. Further, the
one outstanding phrasal clue, the line :

<blockquote>It is the railingest knave in Christendom,</blockquote>

seems to point to SOLIMAN AND PERSEDA (I, iii, 211) ;
and the balance of evidence is in favour of assigning
both the ARDEN scene-section and sc. 25 of LEIR to
Kyd. Both appear to have been after-thought insertions, by a careful planner, which Kyd was, and
Peele was not.

§ 5. " THE SPANISH TRAGEDY " AND " SOLIMAN AND PERSEDA "

Semblances of Peele's style occur, on the other hand,
in the SPANISH TRAGEDY and SOLIMAN AND PERSEDA ;
and he is not unlikely to have collaborated in or
retouched these plays. But in the case of styles at once
so little individual and so near akin it seems impossible
to identify different hands in passages of a conventional
kind, such as the allusions to sighs and tears in the
TRAGEDY (II, V, 43, 44) and in DAVID AND BETHSABE
(above, p. 97). Such rhetoric was a common copper

currency for the minor playwrights. In SOLIMAN the cues are rather clearer, notably the line (I, ii, 56) :

> The Moor upon his hot barbarian horse,

which echoes one in the BATTLE OF ALCAZAR (V, i, 239) :

> He [the Moor] mounteth on a hot barbarian horse ;

and further the lines :

> To be enrolled in the brass-leaved book
> Of never-wasting perpetuity,

which occur at the beginning of sc. iii. of Act I. They are preceded by these :

> Brave knights of Christendom and Turkish both,
> Assembled here in thirsty honour's cause,

which have a quite Peelean ring ; and shortly (l. 13) we have the scansion " countery " :—

> Graced by thy country, but ten times more.

which occurs in the BATTLE OF ALCAZAR (II, iv) :

> And bravest blood of all our country,

but not, so far as I remember, in the SPANISH TRAGEDY. The parade of this scene, up to the advent of Basilisco, is quite in Peele's spirit ; but the main clue remains the " book " trope, which recalls his " Remembrance' golden register," kept for " time's eternity " (ANGLOR. FERIÆ, 12-13) ; his register of Fame

> Written in leaves and characters of gold
> (*Garter*, 407-8) ;

his golden " book " of Fame[1] (*id.*, 173, 183, 274-9) ; and his lines (BATTLE, III, iv) :

> Renown'd and chronicled in books of fame,
> In books of fame and characters of brass,
> Of brass, nay, beaten gold.

---

[1] Echoed, like so many of his words and phrases, from Spenser, *F.Q.*, I, x, 59.

It is one of his recurring formulas : *e.g.*, the lines :

> Consecrate to eternal memory,

and

> And Fame shall register her princely deeds,

in the DEVICE OF THE PAGEANT BORNE BEFORE WOL-
STAN DIXIE. In EDWARD I (Dyce, p, 384 *b*.) we have
" Book of *time* " and " characters of *blood*." Again
in the PRAISE OF CHASTITY we have the line :

> Enrol his name in books of memory ;

and in the DESCENSUS ASTRÆÆ :

> Enrolled in register of eternal fame.

The two lines cited from SOLIMAN, however, are nearly
duplicated in the old LEIR (I, i, 69-70) :

> To be enrolled in chronicles of fame
> By never-dying perpetuity,

in a scene which is more like Kyd than Peele, so that
it is impossible to assign to the latter the SOLIMAN
passage with confidence. We are in the land of tags,
and in LEIR this tag, having no substantive fitness in
its place, looks like a mere quotation.

§ 6. THE ALTERED PLAYS OF MARLOWE

We have now to consider, in connection with Peele,
the generally admitted presence of other hands in the
plays published as Marlowe's. Professor Ward has
given the opinion, assented to by Mr. Verity, that
EDWARD II is the sole " unadulterated expression " of
Marlowe's art.[1] It is therefore with diffidence that I
advance certain reasons for surmising adulteration even
in that play. But the very fact that so much of Marlowe's work, as preserved, is composite, gives at least a

---

[1] Verity, Temple ed. of *Edward* II, introd. p. vi, *note*.

ground for claiming a hearing for the view that his
EDWARD II is also to some extent composite. It has
been justly held by many critics that he collaborated
with Greene and Peele in the HENRY VI plays : may
not Peele then have shared in some of those credited to
Marlowe, or partly recast them after his death ? Manipulation is generally recognized in FAUSTUS and the
MASSACRE ; but we may see cause to go further.
Several critics have pointed to the transformation
effected in the characters of the Queen and Mortimer in
EDWARD II, a transformation certainly justified by
history, but one apparently not contemplated by Marlowe at the outset. Now, this change is wholly in the
spirit of Peele, who in his HONOUR OF THE GARTER
(219 sq.) has the lines :

> And Mortimer, a gentle trusty lord,
> More loyal than that cruel Mortimer
> That plotted Edward's death at Killingsworth :
> Edward the Second, father to this king,
> Whose tragic cry even now methinks I hear,
> When graceless wretches murder'd him by night.

The motive was, of course, the obtrusion of loyal sentiment as regards the crown at a time when the succession
was felt to be doubtful. In the same way, the apparent
transformation of Marlowe's TRAGEDY OF GUISE into a
play whose main theme is the Massacre of St. Bartholomew and the wickedness of Papists, is quite in Peele's
spirit. If then we find in EDWARD II and the MASSACRE
verse that is notably in Peele's manner and not in Marlowe's, we have some ground for surmising his intervention. And such verse we do find.

In EDWARD II (III, iii), to begin with, there is a line
that duplicates one in EDWARD I (SC. v) :

> It is but temporal thou canst inflict.

Here it may be argued that Peele is the copyist; though
Fleay, seeking on general grounds to date the two plays,
puts EDWARD I slightly earlier than the other. It is
certainly not to be disputed that Peele often copied

Marlowe, as he copied Du Bartas and Spenser.   Even
if there be dispute on the point above discussed as to
whether he echoes in DAVID a Marlowe passage from
ALPHONSUS, there are other passages in DAVID where he
certainly echoes Marlowe.   The line in the prologue :—

> The golden wires of his ravishing harp,

echoes

> With ravishing sound of his melodious harp
> > (*Faustus*, II, i) ;

and

> Within the entrails of a jetty cloud
> > (*David*, II, ii),

comes from

> Wrapt in the bowels of a freezing cloud
> > I *Tamb.* iv, 2,

and

> Into the entrails of yon labouring cloud
> > *Faustus*, v, 4.

In such echoes he abounds ; and here there can be no
question as to which came first.   In his TALE OF TROY,
again, we find him copying FERREX AND PORREX.
There we have the lines :

> The noble prince, pierced with the sudden sound,
> Out of his wretched slumber hastily start.

Peele (TALE, 430-2) has :

> Th' unhappy Priam, mazed with frights and fears,
> Out of his wretched slumber hastily start.

Less explicitly, his lines about sacrificial smoke ascend-
ing the sky[1] are reminiscences of :

> To send the sacred smoke to Heaven's throne,

in the old play (I, i).

[1] Above, pp. 92-3.

But, to say nothing of the religious sentiment in the line before cited from EDWARD I and EDWARD II, we have to look to the quality of the verse in the latter play before we decide that words in it which belong to Peele's vocabulary had really been used by Marlowe. Mr. Verity, in his edition of EDWARD II, has pointed to a notable duplication of a line of Peele, where he is not the copyist but the originator. In the ARRAIGNMENT OF PARIS, III, i, 115, we have the line :

> For Paris' fault, y-pierced th' impartial skies ;[1]

and in the JEW, III, ii, end, a feeble speech in which that is embodied :—

> Then take them up, and let them be interred
> Within *one sacred monument* of stone ;
> Upon which altar I will offer up
> My daily sacrifice of sighs and tears,
> And with my prayers *pierce impartial heavens*,
> Till they [reveal] the causers of our smarts,
> Which forced their hands divide united hearts :
> Come Katherine, our losses equal are ;
> Then of true grief let us take equal share.

But why assume copying on the part of Marlowe ? There is nothing of Marlowe here. The stage at which he could have thought fit to borrow the words italicised is not to be imagined ; but that is not all. The whole of the dialogue between the Governor and Mathias's mother, here concluded, is non-Marlowe ; and only the exigencies of the moral law can move us to charge it even upon Peele, who seems to have been given such dramatic odd-jobs for the very reason that he had no faculty for handling them. It will be observed that

---

[1] In the *Speeches to Queen Elizabeth at Theobald's*, again, we have :
> when my devotion 'gan
> To pierce the heavens ;
and in *David and Bethsabe* (III, iii) :—
> hear his voice
> That never yet *pierced piteous heaven* in vain.
Pierce is a tic-word of Peele's. It occurs five times in the first scene of *David*.

besides eking out his patch from his early work he
vaguely echoes his wind-up of TITUS:

> My father and Lavinia shall forthwith
> Be closed in *one household monument.*

Inept as the episode is, it seems more likely to be a late
addition by Peele than an item of original collaboration ;
and the same view would hold good of the line, " It is
but temporal," in EDWARD II, if it be taken as Peele's.
The same inference, again, is set up by the duplication
of another line in the two plays, noted by Mr. Verity :—

> Hence, feigned weeds ! unfeigned is my grief ;
> > *Edward I* : Dyce, p, 413.

> Hence, feigned weeds ! unfeigned are my woes ;
> > *Edward II*, IV, vi, 96.

In this case the portion of the scene after Rice's " Away
with them ! " has an aspect of elaboration, whether or
not it is from that point wholly Peele's. But Peele's
entrance in the JEW seems certain ; and the fact that
such an intervention could happen is a sufficient
ground for examining watchfully the stylistic features
of EDWARD II.

That play lies in the path of several investigations
into the Shakespeare canon. The TITUS-words in it,
as before noted, are : Tully, libelling, architect, sustenance (twice), and the doubtful " numbed." Taken
alone, they form a very narrow basis for an opinion ;
and the result is very doubtful. " Tully " (a negligible
item) and " libelling " occur in the first and second
Acts, where there is small sign of descent from Marlowe
to Peele, though the lines (II, iv) :

> Whose pining heart her inward sighs have blasted,
> And body with continual mourning wasted,

are bad enough for the latter ; and " foreslow " is
one of his words (BATTLE, IV, ii, 40). In the third Act

of EDWARD II his hand seems clearly to enter at the lines

> Long live my sovereign, the noble Edward,
> In peace triumphant, fortunate in wars ;

and though the passage in which occurs the line so much in his manner,

> Are to your highness vowed and consecrate, [1]

is above his average, there are further touches of his iterative habit.   In the fourth Act he seems to have a share.   There (sc. iii) we have the Marlowe line :

> Gallop apace, bright Phœbus, through the sky,

which gives a type for his three lines (before cited[2]) beginning with " gallop " and conveying a similar idea ; and further sets up the surmise that the " gallop apace " speech in ROMEO AND JULIET may have been of his drafting.   In EDWARD II, iii, iv, we have his word " architect " in a passage stamped with his manner, sentiment, and mannerism, his tic-word " successful " occurring in it twice :

> *Successful* battle gives the God of Kings
> To them that fight in right, and fear his wrath.
> Since then *successfully* we have *prevailed*
> Thanked be heaven's great *architect* and you . . .
> Deal you, my lords, in this, my loving lords,
> As to your wisdom fittest seems in all.

Such diffuseness, flatness and tautology, couched in such a completely Peelean movement, cannot be Marlowe's.   In this scene and the next, also, we have two uses of the noun " suspect," found several times in Peele's signed plays.   As to the fifth Act, in which " sustenance " occurs twice, it is hard to come to any conclusion.   And a special puzzle arises over the lines :

> Immortal powers that know the painful cares
> That wait upon my poor distressed soul,
> O level all[3] your looks upon those daring men.

---

[1] See above, page 187.   [2] Above, p. 180.   [3] Cunningham omits " all."

" Distressed soul," though echoed by Peele in DAVID
AND BETHSABE (II, iii), comes from FAUSTUS (V, iii) ;
but the limping third line raises an inquiry. Lodge
imitates Marlowe so often that when we find in the
WOUNDS any echo of the greater poet we at once assign
priority to Marlowe. Such is the natural first procedure in regard to the lines (WOUNDS, ll. 1814-17 :
Act III) :

> Immortal powers that know the painful cares
> That wait upon my poor distressed heart,
> O bend your brows and level all your looks
> Of dreadful awe upon these daring men.

But is Lodge here really the imitator ? The " all "
in the EDWARD II version spoils the scansion, whereas
in Lodge the metre is correct ; and we are almost forced
to infer that the passage in Marlowe's play, as it stands,
is the imitation. The dates of both plays being
unascertained, this is possible.[1] But there is another
possibility. The line which follows in EDWARD II :

> That wrong their liege and sovereign, England's king,

is much more suggestive of Peele than of Marlowe ; and
I hazard the hypothesis that Peele may have inserted it,
borrowing from Lodge's play (published in 1594) so
literally as to lame a line by retaining an unnecessary
word.

There remains the possibility that Lodge did the
revision of EDWARD II, and simply echoed himself
straightforwardly ; but I do not see how such a hypothesis can be made out as against the case for insertion
by Peele. One is led to infer a general pot-boiling
activity by Peele about 1594, the year of issue of the
BATTLE OF ALCAZAR and of the old LEIR, and of the
entry of LOCRINE on the Stationers' Register ; and it
may be that he supervised in this way not only Lodge's
WOUNDS and Marlowe's EDWARD II, but even, perhaps,
an edition of the JEW OF MALTA, though it did not then

---

[1] Fleay dates Lodge's play 1587, and *Edward II* 1590.

get to press as did EDWARD II and DIDO.   As above
suggested, he may have so revised LEIR.

In the play of DIDO, the work of Marlowe ostensibly
finished by Nashe, there is, as was to be expected, no
clear trace of any other hand.[1]   But in the MASSACRE
AT PARIS, as already noted, the case is otherwise ;   and
here, as in EDWARD II, there arises the question of
Peele's intervention.   His hand is suggested in the first
lines :

> Prince of Navarre, my honourable Lord,
> Prince Condé, and my good Lord Admiral.

Again and again the impression is renewed at the
beginnings of scenes ;   in the first scene we have an echo
of one of his phrases, already noted :

> To stop the malice of his envious heart ;

and much of the rest of the play has the weak ring of
the thin coinage of Peele :

> Methinks the gloves have a very strong perfume,
> The scent whereof doth make my head to ache.

> My noble son, and princely Duke of Guise,
> Now have we got the fatal straggling deer
> Within the compass of a deadly toil.

> How fares it with my Lord High Admiral ?
> Hath he been hurt with villains in the street!

> My lords of Poland, I must needs confess,
> The offer of your Prince Elector's far
> Beyond the reach of my deserts ;
> For Poland is, as I have been informed,
> A martial people worthy such a king
> As hath sufficient counsel in himself
> To lighten doubts, and frustrate subtle foes

---

[1] Mr. Verity, while finding EDWARD II "unadulterated," is of opinion that
in DIDO, Marlowe's share "can seldom be traced with certainty."   I should
say there is very little Nashe in DIDO ; and that Marlowe is in general easily
recognisable there.   Nashe seems to have merely revised the play—elimi-
nating double-endings, which he himself eschewed.

—and so on, *ad libitum*. The idea of " kill'st my
heart," certified for pathos by Professor Collins because
it occurs in TITUS, is here imbedded in a death scene as
devoid of pathos as any in the Elizabethan drama.
The dying King Charles says :

> Oh ! hold me up, my sight begins to fail,
> My sinews shrink, my brain turns upside down,
> My heart doth break : I faint and die.   [*Dies.*

The Queen Mother then expresses herself as follows :

> What, art thou dead, sweet son ?   Speak to thy
>   mother !
> Oh no, his soul is fled from out his breast,
> And he nor hears nor sees us what we do !
> My lords, what resteth now for to¹ be done ?
> But that we presently despatch ambassadors
> To Poland, to call Henry back again,
> To wear his brother's crown and dignity ?

There is unanimity in pronouncing the MASSACRE Marlowe's worst play. The surprising thing is that such
writing as this should ever have passed as Marlowe's.
It is excessively bad even for Peele ; if it be really his,
it is Peele at his worst : the hack-writer at the end even
of his rhetoric.   And it is in this scene that we have an
allusion to " the popish power," repeated in the phrase
" popish prelates " at the end of the play, and echoed
in " papal monarch " in Act II, sc. vi, and " popery "
and " papal " in the closing scene. In view of the
constantly effusive Protestantism of Peele—who speaks
of " popery " in the FAREWELL—there need be little
hesitation in assigning the word to him, with the reservation that such stuff might have been written by men
of smaller literary qualifications than his. His, too,
is the use of " irreligious " in Act III, sc. iv. Mr.
Baildon has bestowed one of his free-handed panegyrics
on the line

> O cruel, irreligious piety !

¹ This form, before referred to, occurs four times in Peele's *Arraignment*
and six times in *Edward I*, though not in *David and Bethsabe*.

in TITUS. The phrase is simply the converse of Peele's
other phrase, " religious piety " (FAREWELL, 26) ; as
the " irreligious Moor " and " misbelieving Moor " in
TITUS are only variants of the " unbelieving Moor " in
the BATTLE OF ALCAZAR (I, i, 32).[1]

The lines on " popery " in the FAREWELL run as
follows :

> Even to the gulf that leads to lofty Rome ;
> There to deface the pride of *Antichrist,*
> And pull his *paper walls* and popery down—
> A famous enterprise for England's strength,
> To steel your sword on Avarice' *triple crown.*

But here we are moved to suspect imitation of these
in the MASSACRE (III, v) :

> Which if I do, the papal monarch goes
> To wrack, and th' *Antichristian*[2] kingdom falls.
> These bloody hands shall tear his *triple crown,*
> And fire accursèd Rome about his ears ;
> I'll fire his *crazèd buildings* and enforce
> The papal towers to kiss the lowly earth, etc. ;

which are so much more energetic, and to ascribe to
Peele's revision the introduction of a partly identical
passage in EDWARD II (I, iv), where it is a ludicrous
anachronism :

> Proud Rome ! that hatches such imperial grooms,
> With these thy superstitious taper-lights,
>
> Wherewith thy *Antichristian* churches blaze,
> *I'll fire thy crazed buildings and enforce*
> *The papal towers to kiss the lowly ground* !

But here, again, there can be no certainty.

---

[1] Though Greene and Lodge have " irreligious zeal " in the *Looking-Glass
for London.*
[2] Greene has the line
> He hated Antichrist and all his trash
in *A Maiden's Dream* (ed. Dyce, p. 281) ; and he uses the word frequently
also in *The Spanish Masquerado* ; and " Romish Antichrist " occurs in the
third line from the end of the *Looking-Glass for London,* in which he collaborated with Lodge.

§ 7. " EDWARD III "

There remains one more pre-Shakespearean play for scrutiny. Seeing that Peele wrote the bulk of EDWARD I, and apparently had a finger in EDWARD II, may he not have had a share in EDWARD III ? Here we take up one of the most important of our problems. Peele, it is quite certain, did not and could not write the bulk of EDWARD III : the parts in which the Countess of Salisbury appears are beyond him in every respect, and are utterly alien to his manner. Swinburne's asseveration that the writer of Act II is a " docile and capable pupil " of Peele[1] is one of the most astonishing of the commitments made by critics on the play. The sample he cites is utterly unlike Peele in diction, cadence, and movement. By a number of the most prominent critics indeed the episode is assigned to Shakespeare. Professor Ward pronounces EDWARD III " a play in which I cannot help thinking that Shakespeare had a hand " ;[2] Collier, Ulrici, and others assigned it wholly to him ; while Fleay, more cautiously assigns to him only the episode of the Countess :

> In my opinion, only the love story, Act I, Sc. ii, Act II, is his. Mr. Tennyson tells me, however, that he can trace the master's hand throughout the play at intervals. . . . Unlike Shakespeare's undoubted historical plays in containing a love story and involving the principal personage in unhistorical adventures. In these and other respects it is like Peele's *Edward I* ; but the flow of metre is not like Peele's. Did Shakespeare finish and correct this play as he did *Richard III* ? The metre is like that of this play as corrected. Or is it by Lodge ?[3]

In his later works, Fleay, while maintaining his ascription of the Countess episode to Shakespeare, thus developes his theory of the play :

> The Shakespearean part of this play, I, iii, II, i, ii, . . . which contains lines from the then unpublished *Sonnets*, II, i, 10, 450,

---

[1] *Study of Shakespeare*, 1918 rep. p. 243.
[2] *Hist. of Eng. Dram. Lit.*, ed. 1899, i, 401.
[3] *Shakespeare Manual*, 1876, p. 27.

and an allusion to the recently published *Lucrece*, ii, ii, 194, was clearly acted in 1594, after May 9th, when *Lucrece* was entered on S.R. *Edward III* was entered December 1st, 1595. This love-story part is from Painter's *Palace of Pleasure*. The original play is by Marlowe, and was acted in 1590, and is thus alluded to in Greene's *Never too Late*, c. December in that year : " Why, Roscius, art thou proud with Æsop's crow, being prankt with the glory of others' feathers ? Of thyself thou canst say nothing ; and if the cobbler hath taught thee to say *Ave Cæsar*, disdain not thy tutor because thou pratest in a king's chamber." *Ave Cæsar* occurs in i, i, 164 ; but not in any other play of this date have I been able to find it. There are many similarities between the Marlowe part of this play and *Henry VI*.[1]

It is with the greatest diffidence that I ever reject an attribution of Fleay's ; but in this case, while agreeing with him that Marlowe wrought in the HENRY VI plays and drafted RICHARD III, and had an original and large share in EDWARD III,[2] I remain wholly unable to assent to the opinion of Fleay and Ward and Tennyson that the strongest part of the play was written by Shakespeare, which I take to arise out of recognition of kinship between the style and that of the TWO GENTLEMEN—a play which I contend cannot have been drafted by Shakespeare.

To upset the decision of such judges would be a bold undertaking ; and I do not lightly venture upon it, though, as Mr. Moore Smith has noted in his valuable edition, there are some names of weight on the contrary side. The parts of the play assigned to Shakespeare by Fleay are so far worthy of him, in comparison with his other early work, that if there had been much of such matter in TITUS the critical debate might not thus far have arisen. But I venture to submit some considerations which do not appear to have been present to the minds of the eminent critics who have maintained Shakespeare's authorship, of whom Tennyson is, on such a question, not the least authoritative. That much of the play, and in particular the Countess

---

[1] *Life of Shakespeare*, p. 282. Same positions in *Biog. Chron.*, ii, 62.

[2] On this point, as before mentioned, I have come round to Fleay's view. My original dissent arose in the bias to a single assignment, which is one of the snares of the inexperienced investigator.

episode, was written or recast by Greene can be shown, I think, with something like certainty.

In the meantime I would note that the apparent traces of Peele's hand in EDWARD III are slight. Mr. Tucker-Brooke " would like to see this fine though very imperfect play recognised as the crown and conclusion of the work of George Peele, a poet who has perhaps received scant justice, but who in the fire and melody of his poetry rises high above all but the two greatest of his contemporaries. DAVID AND BETHSABE is only just inferior in its best parts to EDWARD III, and the two works bear a very marked resemblance in all essential particulars. . . . . Both are characterized by nearly total abstinence from the mythological jargon of Greene, by the peculiar liquid beauty of Peele's best poetry, and *by a verse movement which is almost identical.*"[1] Mr. Tucker-Brooke is a discerning critic on the psychic side ; but his technical estimates sometimes appear to be made without analysis ; and in this case he seems to have followed too trustingly the lead of Swinburne. He may be defied to produce from Peele any body of verse which resembles that of Act II of EDWARD III as does that of Greene's JAMES IV. Peele's verse is certainly " liquid " in the sense of being highly diluted and thus smoothly fluent ; but dilution is not the mark of the verse of either the first or the second act of EDWARD II, or indeed of the bulk of the rest of the play. There we have comparatively varied pausation, colour, point, epigram, vigour of epithet, albeit no supreme distinction in those kinds. Swinburne, rightly denying that any of it is Shakespeare's, unduly belittles it, though he finds one phrase worthy of Marlowe ; but he is as alive to the manifold difference of the technique from Shakespeare's as he is blind to a

---

[1] Introd. to *The Shakespeare Apocrypha*, p. xxiii. Prof. J. Quincy Adams (*Life of Shakespeare*, 1923, p. 163) agrees that " the author may be George Peele." It is hard to understand how experienced students can give such assents, when not the slightest attempt has been made to justify the attribution, whether by parallels of style, of phrase, or of theme. To ascribe this play to a single hand, and that hand Peele's, is an avowal of inadequate investigation.

greater difference in ARDEN. The diffuseness of the
Countess scene is the *excited* and vivid diffuseness of
Greene at his best, not the vapid diffuseness which is
almost invariable with Peele.

As has been already noted, the argument from the
absence of mythology in EDWARD III is erroneous.
Peele naturally puts little heathen mythology in
DAVID—though even there he mentions Jove—but in
EDWARD I he has a multitude of mythological and
other classical allusions, while in Greene's JAMES IV
there are hardly any[1]—fewer, indeed, than in EDWARD
III, where we have :—Ave Caesar ; Caesar, flint-heart
Scythian, Achilles' spear, Hero and Leander, Helles-
pont, Sestos, Lucrece, Catiline, Agamemnon, Troy,
Xerxes, and Nemesis—all in the first half. Mr. H. C.
Hart, who had closely studied Peele's text, expressed
himself in his introduction to I HENRY VI[2] as inclined
to assign EDWARD III " to Shakespeare and Peele,"
but gives only the reason that it has five [really six]
cases of the laudatory form " thrice " (" thrice-
gracious " etc.), which is so common in Peele, and is
found in Marlowe, but not in Greene's signed or
assigned plays. This overlooks the fact that the
" thrice " form occurs in Greene's prose.[3] Its non-
appearance in his plays certainly sets up an arguable
point ; though an exactly equivalent argument would
substitute Greene for Peele in respect of the several
uses of " bonny." The sufficient answer, however,
is that, as it happens, four or these " thrice's " occur
in passages wholly out of Peele's style and reach ;
and if we are to stress the clue we must on grounds
of style turn to Marlowe, as regards the first 76 lines
of scene ii of Act II, to begin with. And though
Swinburne pronounced that in the first scene of the
first Act " the impotent imitation of Marlowe is piti-
fully patent,"[4] we shall do well to withhold our assent,

---

[1] The allusions to Saturn and Venus are astrological, not mythological.
[2] Arden ed, p. xxxv.
[3] For instance, in Tne *Planetomachia* (1585), Works, v, 17, 39.
[4] *Study of Shakespeare*, rep. p. 237.

especially when the oracle proceeds to concede that " possibly there may also be an imitation of the still imitative style of Shakespeare," yielding " a study after the manner of Marlowe, not at second hand, but at third . . . . obviously too flat and feeble to show a touch of either godlike hand." If no quasi-"touch " of either be visible, where then is the imitation ?

Marlowese, unlike Swinburnese, is subject to variation. The manner of the opening scene of EDWARD III is not that of TAMBURLAINE ; and it is not the lyric manner of the opening of EDWARD II ; but the verse-movement is not fundamentally different even from that ; and alike in versification and diction it is perfectly akin to that of the bulk of EDWARD II. This poet makes his lines in just that fashion, and with the same bounding fluency of end-stopped metre ; and so far is the style of the opening of the play from being flat or feeble in comparison with the other that we may reasonably say Swinburne would have given it the liberal praise he accords to the bulk of Elizabethan drama had he not been prepossessed by the task of denying the presence of Shakespeare in the piece. Seeking unnecessarily to disparage it in general to that end, he has missed recognition of its style elements. Approaching from any other angle, he would have cried : " *Aut Christophorus Marlowe, aut Diabolus.*"

That Marlowe planned, opened, and largely wrote the play will be shown when we come to deal with his unassigned work ; and that, probably on a basis laid by Marlowe, Greene largely rewrote the second Act is a contention to be developed in the next chapter. At the present point it is sufficient to endorse Fleay's opinion that the differences between the Countess episode and the rest of the play, alike in point of rhyme and of double-endings " are far too great to allow the play to have been all written by one author at one period " ;[1] and to add that while Peele probably did contribute a little, he has no part whatever in the

---

[1] *Manual*, p. 303.

Act which Swinburne so strangely declared to show discipleship in his regard.

The first point at which his presence might at all plausibly be suspected is the speech of the Mariner to King John in III, i. Mr. Sykes, who finds " marching hitherward " a finger-print of his, might here cite I, ii, 49,

To fetch in booty, marching hitherward.

But though the first line occurs in a quite Peelean passage, marked by his weak diction, Marlowe has " ploughed the deep " in DIDO (I, i, near end) ; the King's speeches are not all in Peele's style ; and the second speech of the Mariner in the same scene is so evidently Kyd's (or yet another's) that the first, which contains the " plough " line, must be held to lie between him and Marlowe. There is much more likelihood of the hand of Peele in scene V, in the concluding section in which Prince Edward " enters in triumph." That has his dilute diction and his flaccid verse movement ; and his word " wistly " is in a line that might be his ; though it occurs previously (II, ii, 90) in a speech not at all like him.

Again in IV, ii, in the final section in which Lord Percy announces the defeat of David and Copland's refusal to surrender his prisoner, the manner seems to be his, and we have his tic, " the sandy shore." But the King's reply to the French Captain, which follows, is again quite unlike Peele. Nor can I find any clear trace of him again until the section of V, ii, in which Copland brings in his prisoner. That seems to be the sum of his contribution. If the assertors of his authorship desire assent to any larger assignment, let them tell where and how they find his handiwork.

CHAPTER VIII

GREENE'S UNSIGNED WORK

Of Greene, even more certainly than of Peele, it may be said that he " wrote [and wrote *in*] many plays now lost " ; and we may confidently add : " in some which are preserved but not now assigned to him." In his REPENTANCE OF ROBERT GREENE he speaks of playwriting as having been for years his " continual exercise."[1] In his GROATSWORTH OF WIT, again, written in 1592, the year of his death he protests to his fellowcraftsmen Marlowe, Peele, and Nashe (or Lodge) : " Unto none of you, like me, sought those burrs [the players] to cleave " ; and Nashe describes him as " chief agent for the company " (of Queen's players), " for he writ more than four other."[2] Yet there have been editorially ascribed to him only seven plays : ALPHONSUS KING OF ARRAGON, ORLANDO FURIOSO, FRIAR BACON AND FRIAR BUNGAY, JAMES IV, A LOOKING-GLASS FOR LONDON (with Lodge), GEORGE-A-GREENE, and SELIMUS—the last being only in our own generation ascribed to him by Dr. Grosart. By many critics, however, he has been reasonably credited with a share in the HENRY VI group by way of a share in the two older plays adapted in parts II and III ; and in the preceding chapters we have seen reason to ascribe to him parts of several anonymous plays. As he died in 1592, while Peele lived till 1596 or 1597, the latter might on the whole have equalled his output ; but it seems clear that up to 1592 Greene's was much the more abundant. Our problem is to trace some of it. His probable share in LOCRINE we have already noted ; and

[1] Cited by Dyce, ed. of Greene and Peele, p. 25.
[2] Nashe's *Strange Newes*, etc., 1592, Sig. C. 2, 3, cited by Dyce, p. 85, note. McKerrow's ed of Nashe's Works, i, 271.

his presence in SIR CLYOMON AND SIR CLAMYDES might be surmised, though of course not proved, from a number of words and phrases otherwise associated with him, all occurring in four successive scenes : " ambodexter "[1] (see above, p. 262) ; " King or Keysar "[2] (four times in ALPHONSUS OF ARRAGON, once in PERIMEDES : Works, VII, 28) ; " faint-hearted " (above, p. 215) ; " Venery " (above, p. 214) ; " vital breath " (song in MENAPHON : " You restless cares ") ; " put in ure " (*infra*) ; and " princox " (LOCRINE, II, iv, IV, ii ; MENAPHON, ed. Arber, p. 84 ; and QUIP FOR AN UPSTART COURTIER : Works, XI, 225). But we shall find much fuller traces of him in other plays.

§ 1. SELIMUS

His authorship of SELIMUS has been strongly oppugned by Mr. Charles Crawford, whose valuable services to Elizabethan scholarship, including his careful notation of the borrowing from Spenser in LOCRINE and SELIMUS, entitle his judgment on such a point to the most careful attention. Mr. Crawford, proceeding on his own researches, assigns LOCRINE to Greene,[3] but insists that SELIMUS cannot be from the same pen, and ascribes it to Marlowe.[4] Mr. Tucker Brooke[5] endorses the ascription of LOCRINE to Greene, without seeking to meet the arguments for Peele's collaboration ; and contemptuously rejects the claim that Marlowe wrote SELIMUS, without attempting to meet Mr. Crawford's argument, which is really entitled to consideration. It may be summarised as follows :—

a. Though LOCRINE copies whole passages from Spenser's VISIONS OF THE WORLD'S VANITIE and

---

[1] Scenes iv, v, vi, vii, Dyce's ed. pp. 498-503.

[2] Possibly echoed from Spenser, who has it at least six times—twice in the first three cantos of F. Q. (1590), once in *Tears of the Muses* (1591). But it was an old tag : see it in Sackville's Introduction to the *Mirror for Magistrates*, st. 76 ; *Complaint of Buckingham*, st. 23, 108, 111.

[3] *Collectanea*, First Series, 1906, p. 53.

[4] Id. pp. 47, 59, 90.

[5] *The Shakespeare Apocrypha*, 1908, pp. xvii-xx.

RUINES OF ROME (from Bellay), both published in 1591, it contains no borrowings from the FAERIE QUEENE (1590), save in a few passages where LOCRINE borrows from SELIMUS, whereas SELIMUS is full of them. " If the two plays were by one writer, we should catch glimpses of Spenser's great poem in both : the absence of such material in LOCRINE renders the theory of a common authorship a psychological impossibility."[1]

b. Several passages in SELIMUS are closely copied in LOCRINE. "No author in dramas repeats *himself* in this slavish manner, nor would he imitate a whole scene of one of his plays as LOCRINE, IV, ii, imitates ll. 1874 to 1990 of SELIMUS."[2]

c. "There is nothing in SELIMUS to suggest Greene ; and, as a matter of fact, its atheism, its bold advocacy of the doctrines of Machiavelli, its style, and its phrasing, are totally dissimilar from anything that can be found in that author's known work."[3] " Greene was not a proselytizing atheist who vented his opinions in all companies, nor was he a follower of Machiavelli. Indeed he had such an aversion to Marlowe's opinions that he went out of his way to make the fact publicly known. In the GROATSWORTH OF WIT Greene admonishes Marlowe to abandon atheism and to guide his life and his thoughts by other and better precepts than those of ' pestilent Machivilian policie.' "[4]

d. The ascription of six[5] passages of SELIMUS to Greene in ENGLAND'S PARNASSUS has no decisive evidential value, as the latter work admittedly makes several mistakes of ascription. For instance, it assigns to Greene three passages of Spenser.[6]

This is the gist of Mr. Crawford's case, and I regret that here, as in regard to the authorship of TITUS, I am

[1] *Id*. p. 66, cp. p. 59.
[2] *Id*. pp. 58-59.
[3] *Id*. p. 67.
[4] *Id*. pp. 85-86.
[5] Dr. Grosart, as aforesaid, traced only two of the quotations in *England's Parnassus* to *Selimus*. The other four are noted by Professor Collins, and by Mr. Crawford in his valuable edition of the *Parnassus*, for which all students are his debtors.
[6] *Id*. pp. 67-68.

unable to assent to his reasoning, though I grant that
Marlowe may conceivably have written some passages
in SELIMUS.

a. To begin with, Mr Crawford takes for granted
that for LOCRINE and SELIMUS there is in each case only
one author, whereas we have seen in the former play
fairly clear evidence of two hands. Secondly, he
overlooks the obvious possibilities (1) that the same
man might have written LOCRINE before reading the
FAERIE QUEENE, and SELIMUS after reading it ; and
(2) that he or another might further have touched up
LOCRINE at a later date. As we have seen, the first-
named play has on independent grounds been dated
about 1586. It is true that Spenser's VISIONS and
RUINES OF ROME, from which the play as it stands
undoubtedly borrows passages, were not printed till
1591 ; but even if we were to assume—which, however,
we are not at all bound to do—that the plagiarisms
belonged to the first draft, we are not thereby shut up
to so late a date. The poems in question have been
independently dated about 1580.

> " During Spenser's sojourn in the society of the Sidneys and
> the Dudleys . . . we hear of other works written by Spenser,
> ready to be given to the light. The works thus heard of are
> *Dreams, Legends, Court of Cupid, The English Poet, The Dying
> Pelican, Stemmata Dudleiana, Slumber, Nine English Comedies,
> The Epithalamium Thamesis,* and the *Faerie Queen* commenced.
> Of these works the *Dreams* and *Slumber* probably are one and the
> same, and perhaps identical with the *Visions* published in 1591,
> which were, in fact, as we have seen, but a revised form of the
> pieces published in the *Theatre of Voluptuous Worldlings* ; per-
> haps the *Legends, Court of Cupid,* and *Epithalamium Thamesis*
> were subsequently incorporated in the *Faerie Queen* ; the *Stem-
> mata Dudleiana, Nine English Comedies, Dying Pelican,* are
> altogether lost, unless some parts of the first survive in the *Ruines
> of Time.* The *Faerie Queene* had been begun."[1]

And since not only the RUINES OF ROME but the
earlier Cantos of the FAERIE QUEENE had, on Mr.
Crawford's own view, been seen by Marlowe before the

---

[1] Prof. J. W. Hales, memoir of Spenser in Globe ed. of Works, pp. xxvi-vii.

writing of TAMBURLAINE,[1] he cannot reject the possibility that MS. copies of the VISIONS and RUINES may
have been seen by Greene (to say nothing here of Peele)
when *he* (on our hypothesis) added to or collaborated on
LOCRINE about 1587 or later. He was one of the men
likely to read the FAERIE QUEENE as soon as might be.
If then he wrote or collaborated in LOCRINE, and that
play shows no such conning of the poem as is evidenced
in SELIMUS, we are so far but confirmed in our view
that it antedates the poem, and that SELIMUS is a later
work, though LOCRINE may have been revised by Peele
or another for publication, in which case passages of
SELIMUS might have been adapted to and inserted in
the earlier play. (See, however, the case of possible
echoing noted above, p. 270.)

b. To Mr. Crawford's argument that no dramatist
repeats *himself* as SELIMUS is " copied in LOCRINE," the
answer is (1) that we find very many instances of self-
repetition among the Elizabethan dramatists ; (2) that
Mr. Crawford himself claims to identify the work of
Marlowe and Kyd in many instances *by* self-repetition ;
and (3) that the post-dating of LOCRINE begs the question. Suppose it to be the earlier ; then Marlowe, who
on Mr. Crawford's view wrote SELIMUS, is on the same
view copying Greene or another second-rate dramatist.
As we have seen, there is evidence of another hand than
either Greene's or Marlowe's in LOCRINE. But all the
while Mr. Crawford is ascribing to Marlowe,[2] in respect
of duplications between his plays, just such habitual
self-repetition as he declares to be impossible in respect
of an echo between SELIMUS and LOCRINE.

c. There are so many " things in SELIMUS to suggest
Greene " that Dr. Grosart built a confident case on
them ; and Fleay, even in flouting Grosart, avowed
that " the most cursory reading shows that Greene
had a hand in SELIMUS," adding only : " his worst
enemy would not, I think, assert that he wrote the
whole of this wretched production."[3] In point of fact

---

[1] It is more probable that the lines were added when the play was printed.
[2] As cited, pp. 90-97. [3] *Biog. Chron.* ii, 315.

there is hardly a scene of the play without one or more clues of diction which point to Greene and not to Marlowe. There are literally scores of such clues. Mr. Crawford himself admits that the play has thirteen instances of the tic " for to," and that the locution " occurs but rarely in Marlowe's other work, but is extremely common in Spenser, whom the author of the play imitates throughout." Quite so ; but of this particular imitation there is no trace in Marlowe's signed plays, apart from the apparently redacted first scene of TAMBURLAINE and the certainly redacted MASSACRE AT PARIS, where it occurs five times ; whereas Greene, after using " for to " only four times in ORLANDO FURIOSO, runs it at least seventy times in ALPHONSUS KING OF ARRAGON.[1]   Greene was, in fact, as much influenced by Spenser as was Marlowe.   Among the tic-words and phrases in Greene's vocabulary, some of which we have noted at various points in our inquiry, the following, all found in the SHEPHERD'S CALENDAR and the early cantos of the FAERIE QUEENE, may more or less plausibly be traced to Spenser :—

Stowre	Passport	Embrued
King or Keysar	Younglings	Geason
Sumptuous	Lightfoot	Gore-blood
Gorgeous	Jouissance	Eme (*Locrine*)
Recure	Assot	Surquedry
Lovely	For to	Bonny
Misconstrue	Well I wot	Bonny lass

Mr. Crawford notes many more Spenserian terms in SELIMUS, but some in his list are not, I think, fairly to be so specified ; and on the other hand the certain works of Greene can be made to yield an equally large crop. So that Mr. Crawford's main ground for denying Greene a hand in SELIMUS remains the fact that that play draws often on the FAERIE QUEENE while LOCRINE does not—

[1] Fleay makes *Alphonsus* the earlier play on the score of its allusion to its author's previous handling of " the praise of love, and Cupid's peerless power," and of " Cupid's games."   Fleay takes these phrases as pointing to Greene's early prose tales.   But both might refer either to *Orlando* or to other plays now lost.

a circumstance easily and naturally accounted for by
the obvious hypothesis that LOCRINE is the earlier
play.

The argument as to Greene's opinions is no less
invalid. As we have noted, Greene on his death-bed
actually avows and deplores having paraded irreligious
opinions. His words are explicit : " Wonder not . . .
that Greene, who hath said with thee, like the fool in
his heart, there is no God, should now give glory unto
his greatness : for . . . his hand lies heavy upon me.
. . . Look unto me, by him [Machiavelli ?] persuaded
to that liberty, and thou shalt find it an infernal
bondage. . . . Do not delight, as I have done, in
irreligious oaths."[1] As regards his dramatic work,
the Ateukin speeches in JAMES IV are on all fours with
the declamations of Selimus and Acomat.

d. Doubtless all ascriptions in ENGLAND'S PARNASSUS
are singly open to suspicion ; but, as the one contemporary record, it must be allowed primary weight ; and
its harmony with so much internal evidence counts for
a great deal. Six several quotations, all ascribed to
Greene, exclude the surmise of such accidental errors
of ascription as Mr. Crawford shows to have arisen in
the anthology from the cutting up of sheets of extracts
with *idem* for the same author. Allot evidently held
SELIMUS to be Greene's.

Still, we are not thus far called upon to reject absolutely the argument for Marlowe. Mr. Crawford
undoubtedly brings forward many striking parallels
between SELIMUS on the one hand and TAMBURLAINE,
THE JEW OF MALTA, DIDO, EDWARD II, and THE
MASSACRE AT PARIS on the other. He is well entitled
to express surprise that many of these parallels were
wholly overlooked by Dr. Grosart and those of us who
accepted the ascription of the play to Greene ; though
it is no less surprising that, in making out such a case,
he should argue that no dramatist would repeat himself
as LOCRINE " repeats " SELIMUS. It is precisely as
self-repetitions, once more, that his own Marlowe

---

[1] Greene's *Groatsworth of Wit.* N. S. S. ed. pp. 29-31.

parallels tell in support of his claim that SELIMUS is Marlowe's. The alternative inference to which we seem to be led, here as in so many other cases, is that of joint handiwork. Either Greene echoed Marlowe in SELIMUS to a quite uncommon extent, or Marlowe had a hand in the play, if we decide that one or other author wrote the play. But on the other hand we cannot override the abundant evidence for Greene's pervading presence in it, save by surmising an outsider who was steeped in Greene. Mr. Crawford seems to ignore that, as Grosart ignored the other set of data. If we assign to Marlowe the Marlowesque portions, we have to note how, after one of these (234-444, ed. Temp. Clas.), in the speech of Bajazet on the Egyptian crocodile, copying Spenser (F. Q., I, v, 18) and recalling that in LOCRINE (Dumb Show, III)—which again, as Mr. Crawford notes, closely copies Spenser (VISIONS OF THE WORLD'S VANITIE, st. vi)—we have Greene's " echinæis." And if Greene could so closely copy Spenser in LOCRINE, he might well echo Marlowe in SELIMUS. The argument from the superior force and concision of some of the verse in SELIMUS will not suffice in itself to establish Marlowe's presence ; for Greene's own verse in JAMES IV is remarkably superior in those qualities to most of ORLANDO and most of ALPHONSUS ; and there is further a great deal of very poor stuff in SELIMUS and some good in LOCRINE. The bulk of SELIMUS is no better than ALPHONSUS OF ARRAGON, Greene's poorest play. On a balance, we cannot deny all weight to the argument for Marlowe's touch in SELIMUS, though we cannot assent to Mr. Crawford's thesis that it is Marlowe's first play, and a forecast to TAMBURLAINE. The large amount of matter in stanza form in SELIMUS is much less naturally to be assigned to him than to Greene, who expressly protested against the reducing of dramatic " scholarism " to blank verse.

It has perhaps not been generally observed, though Swinburne[1] noted it, that the mass of rhymed matter constituting Act I of SELIMUS is in stanzas, beginning

[1] *A Study of Shakespeare*, rep, 1918, p. 30.

at line 3 with a stanza of six lines (*ababcc*), followed by
a series in eight (*abababcc*), which is interrupted by two
shorter staves (*abab, ababb*) and again goes on till blank
verse begins at l. 147. Again, at a new scene (l. 232),
there begins a series of seven-line stanzas (*ababbcc*) of
the form (rhyme-royal) made familiar by Daniel's
ROSAMOND and Shakespeare's LUCRECE. This, with
some deviations into sextets and an irregular quintet,
with a run of blank verse, goes on till nearly the end of
the Act. Another batch of stanzas in five, six, seven
and eight lines occurs in Act II (l. 745 onwards) continuing to l. 852, whereafter stanzas disappear. Apparently the poet had tired of his effort.

Now, it is not decisive for Greene's authorship that
he wrote much in all of these stanza forms in his signed
works, and that he has eight six-line stanzas in LOCRINE
(IV, i) and two in JAMES IV (IV, iv, i ; v, i) ; but the
fact counts for a good deal.[1] The seven-line stanza
is that of his MAIDEN'S DREAM (1591) ; the eight-line
that of " The Palmer's Verses " in his NEVER TOO LATE
(1590) ; and he has a score of poems in the six-line
stanza. Of the very small handful of stanza-verse
left us by Marlowe, on the other hand, the only sample
at all corresponding to any of these is the doubtful
fragment of eight-line stanzas cited in ENGLAND'S
PARNASSUS, beginning :

I walk'd along a stream for pureness rare ;

which is an extremely slender ground for attributing
to Marlowe, as does Mr. Crawford, the stanza-work in
SELIMUS. Greene's previous practice, on the other

---

[1] The mode is as old as *Ferrex and Porrex*, where the rhymed choruses run
mainly to the six-line stanza, *ababcc*. Whetstone's *Promos and Cassandra*,
dated 1578, begins with quatrains (see also III, i) and has a six-line stanza
(III, ii) ; and in *Fidele and Fortunio : The Two Italian Gentlemen* (1584) there
are many such stanzas. In the *Spanish Tragedy* (III, xii) after two quatrains
and an imperfectly rhymed stanza of seven lines, there are six lines which
would make a stanza if at the end of line 14 we had instead of " straight " the
word " anon." It was at first probably so written. Lodge, a diligent imitator
of Greene, has eight six-line stanzas in his *Wounds of Civil War* (ll. 1199-1228,
2318-2349, 2347-2352), besides quatrains. Greene was simply reverting to
an old usage, which is followed in *Tancred and Gismunda* in 1592.

hand, and his definite and vehement protest against a limitation of dramatic poetry to blank verse,[1] are entirely in keeping with his production of a mosaic of blank and stanza verse. The more laborious form, it is true, is soon abandoned ; but that too is in Greene's way ; as it was the way of his immediate predecessors. Some of the octaves, besides, are so thin in diction as to make it no tribute to Marlowe to assign them to him, while others, besides being thoroughly in Greene's manner, have plain clues to his vocabulary and tags. This, as already remarked, does not prove that the stanzas are his, since an outsider bent on that form for dramatic purposes could echo him at will. But, though some of the stanza work carries little suggestion of his versification in general, the following might very well be his :—

> First shall the sun rise from the occident,
>   And leave the steeds benighted in the East ;
> First shall the sea become the continent ;
>   Ere we forsake our sovereign's behest.
> We fought not for you 'gainst the Persians' tent,
>   Breaking our lances on his sturdy crest ;
> We fought not for you 'gainst the Christian host,
> To become traitors after all our cost.

This is surely not the voice of Marlowe ; while " occident," a word not found in his signed works, occurs in Greene ;[2] and the sixth line is a variant of a common Greene tag.[3]

And there are other grounds for rejecting Mr. Crawford's conclusion.

(1) He strangely takes[4] TAMBURLAINE to be the fulfilment of the promise at the close of SELIMUS :

> Next shall you see *him* with triumphant sword
> Dividing kingdoms into equal shares,
> And give them to his warlike followers.

---

[1] Pref. to *Perimedes the Blacksmith* (1588), cited by Dyce, p. 35.
[2] *Orlando Furioso*, ed. Dyce, p. 103.
[3] See next section, p. 330.
[4] Vol. cited, pp. 82, 83.

How could the deeds of Tamburlaine figure as deeds
of Selimus ? Is not the natural inference this, that
the two references to " Tamburlaine " in SELIMUS
point to Marlowe's *play*, and that SELIMUS is the work
of a theme-imitator who meant to frame, in a different
technique, a second part as Marlowe had already done
for TAMBURLAINE ? The actual title of the 1594 quarto
is : " The First part of the tragical reigne of Selimus,"
etc., and at the close of ALPHONSUS OF ARRAGON we
have the same (apparently unfulfilled) promise of a
sequel as is made at the end of SELIMUS. And is not
the mention in SELIMUS (ll. 1749-52) of the previous
Bajazet " whom the Tartarians lockèd in a cage " an
obvious reference to the cage scene in I TAMBURLAINE,
I, 2, and the line :

> Keeping in iron cages emperors,

in Part II, I, iii (iv), (l. 2816 of play) ? Was *Marlowe*
likely to call Tamburlaine " the Scythian thief," *first*
in SELIMUS and again in his own TAMBURLAINE ? The
dating of SELIMUS after LOCRINE, and after TAMBUR-
LAINE, FAUSTUS and THE JEW, really solves the confusion which Mr. Crawford's theory creates.

(2) That Greene, while freely copying the RUINES OF
ROME in the text of LOCRINE, should there ignore the
FAERIE QUEENE if it had then appeared, is so unlikely
a thing that we have no right to suppose it without
strong reason. By Mr. Crawford's own (questionable)
account, Marlowe and Greene " were friends and
inseparables."[1] Would Greene then be likely to remain
in total ignorance of the FAERIE QUEENE after Marlowe
had read and admired it ?

(3) The whole question of the copying of Spenser,
indeed, calls for a more exact investigation. If we
provisionally suppose the Até speeches after the " Dumb
Shows " of LOCRINE to be, as they well may,[2] late

---

[1] Vol. cited, p. 68. This is an overstatement, however. Cp. Simpson in
N. S. S. Shakespeare Allusion-Books, p. xlv.
[2] The closing speech, by Até, actually dates itself 1595-6, the year of printing ; but here, of course, the " eight " may have been an alteration to fit the
date of issue. The speech is quite in Peele's style.

additions made by Peele for the printed play, we are
left, as regards Spenser imitations, to (*a*) the three lines
about the cedar (I, i, 17-19) from the VISIONS OF THE
WORLD'S VANITIE ; (*b*) the lines about Orpheus and
Amphion (III, i, 5-12) from the RUINES OF ROME
(st. 25) ; and (*c*) the " thunderbolts of war " passages
(II, v) from the RUINES, which occur also in SELIMUS
(418-20 ; 2431-38). These poems of Spenser were
published, as above noted, in 1591. Could they have
been seen by Greene earlier ? They may or may not.
It is a noteworthy fact that the three lines about the
cedar in the first scene are totally irrelevant to their
context, and cry aloud to be detached. In the fifth
scene of Act II, again, Humber, after flying pursued by
Albanact, is introduced to declaim the " thunderbolt "
passage in terrified acknowledgment of Albanact's
prowess. On his exit, Albanact re-enters and passes
on again in pursuit, only to re-enter anew, himself
defeated. The intermediate speech of Humber, so
ill-suited to the action, could very well be a later patch.
And even the Spenserian passage about Orpheus and
Amphion in Act III, sc. i, is perfectly detachable,
though manipulated (torn to tatters, as Mr. Crawford
complains) into some congruity with the context.

If, then, all three passages *could*, like the Até speeches,
be late additions, we are the more free to date the play
years before 1591, and before SELIMUS. But if on the
other hand SELIMUS is to be put just before TAMBUR-
LAINE, we have to account for imitations not only of
the poems above named but of the FAERIE QUEENE
before 1587, whereas Abraham Fraunce's citation of a
few lines from Book II in 1588 is the earliest indication
Mr. Crawford can offer of the MS. currency of any part
of that poem. Inasmuch as SELIMUS echoes Spenser
more than does TAMBURLAINE, Mr. Crawford boldly
reasons that the latter is the later work, the young
poet growing less imitative as he grew older.[1] Is it not
much more economical, once more, to date SELIMUS
later ? Even in the case of TAMBURLAINE there was

[1] Vol. cited, p. 84.

time to work up the stage version, both by Spenserian imitations and otherwise, between the first production in 1587 and the printing in 1590 ; and we are really not entitled to assume that the Spenser passages in either part were in the first acting-copy. Any one who closely examines the Spenserian passage in TAMBUR-LAINE'S speech at the end of Act IV of Part II will grant, I think, that it has every appearance of being an after-insertion, not part of the original composition. And the same may be argued of the speech at the end of scene ii (i in Dyce) of the same Act. But if SELIMUS out-goes TAMBURLAINE in the amount of its Spenser-echoes, much more have we reason to date its produc-tion later.

(4) If this be done, Mr. Crawford's main reason for ascribing the play to Marlowe disappears ; and the more plausible view that it is substantially a work of Greene, partly imitative of Marlowe, holds the field, in virtue of the citations in PARNASSUS. If it be still objected that no dramatist imitates himself as Greene on this view does in copying his own work in LOCRINE, the answer is fairly clear. Firstly, the " thunderbolt " passage in LOCRINE is probably a late addition to that play, made by another hand. *Peele*, be it remembered, echoes Spenser in his DAVID AND BETHSABE, probably printed in 1594 ; and if we recognise *his* share in LOCRINE we are led to the surmise that it was he who interpolated the Spenserian passages in that play before its publication. In reality the Até speeches are much more in his style than in Greene's. But Greene, in any case, was really not the man to scruple about eking out one play from another. It is much more likely that he wrote the twin comic-scenes in the two plays than that Marlowe wrote any such feeble scene at all. In the ORLANDO FURIOSO (*circa* 1588) occurs the phrase " well-nutrimented " (ed. Dyce, p. 93, *a*) which is duplicated in SELIMUS (l. 1979). Such self-repetition was for Greene normal : the mere penning of the phrase by Marlowe would be an incongruity. The comic scenes in JAMES IV are very much on a par

with those in LOCRINE and SELIMUS : TAMBURLAINE has no such " relief " scenes at all: though comic scenes were played by the actors, the publishers avowedly discarded them.[1]

(5) And still it may be that Marlowe contributed passages to SELIMUS. " Friends and inseparables " they hardly were ; but they would be doubly likely to have a hand in each other's plays at a time when collaboration was the common practice of playwrights. It may be—though I prefer to look to Kyd—that the redacted first scene in TAMBURLAINE, with its two " for-to's " and its bad opening lines, represents a manipulation by Greene[2] for the purpose of breaking up a too slow and heavily rhetorical beginning ; and there are other scenes in both parts, with far-from-mighty lines, which suggest alien hands. As we have seen, such hands seem to intervene in the MASSACRE AT PARIS and even in EDWARD II ; and the same holds of FAUSTUS and the JEW OF MALTA. Contrarily, the greater poet, who certainly collaborated with Peele and Greene in the HENRY VI plays, may have lent his stronger hand to Greene in SELIMUS ; though imitation by the less original Greene can perfectly well account even for a number of Marlowese passages. The warranted conclusion is simply that the play is one in which Greene (or an imitator of Greene) either very frequently echoed Marlowe or collaborated with him. But that Greene has a main hand in the piece is reasonably arguable ; and there is no good warrant for the assumption that any of it is beyond his powers. Rather we might say that the verse is not of his best. Indeed if we lay stress on the intellectual vigour of some of the stanza verse, we collide with the claim for it as early work by Marlowe ; because it is in one or two respects

---

[1] Dyce indeed thought (introd. to 1-vol. ed. of Marlowe, p. xxii) that Marlowe wrote those scenes ; but this seems unlikely. In that case the publisher would hardly have dropped them. And what are we to make of Marlowe's thrust at " such conceits as clownage keeps in pay " ?

[2] In *Selimus* the opening is an extremely long and undramatic speech. Kyd from the first is relatively crisp in his openings. But there remains the possibility that *Selimus* was planned by an outsider, ambitious of writing poetry for the stage.

more mature, though certainly not more poetical, than
anything in TAMBURLAINE. On the other hand most
of the work is slight and hasty enough to have been done
by Greene in his most heedless mood. Hence the conflict of verdicts. But between the disparaging estimate
of Fleay and the eulogies of Dr. Grosart and Mr.
Crawford we may rank the bulk of the play as easily
possible for the uneven Greene about 1590, when
TAMBURLAINE had passed its first vogue. Even in
LOCRINE there are lyrical lines that Marlowe *might*
have written, and that are superior to most of SELIMUS.
There is in fact only one considerable section of SELIMUS
that can reasonably suggest the superior power of
Marlowe, to wit, the long speech (in stanzas) of Selimus
on his first appearance (ll. 235-385), with its bold parade
of " irreligion " ; and in that speech we twice find
Greene's " for to." The blank-verse speech of Selimus
which constitutes scene 4 (ll. 534-573) might also conceivably be Marlowe's ; but in the next scene we have
two " for-to's " in the first fourteen lines, and Greene's
" polipus " in the nineteenth. Thereafter, though
there are Marlowesque tones in the short blank-verse
scenes up to the entrance of Acomat, there is little
suggestion of Marlowe's strength, though the presence
of Peele might be surmised in scene 10, which appears
to end Act II. In the remaining three Acts Marlowe
is not plausibly to be indicated ; and the conclusion so
far appears to hold good that the play is one of Greene's
planning as well as substantially of his execution.

When, however, Professor F. G. Hubbard, in his
studious paper on " LOCRINE and SELIMUS,"[1] independently reaching, as against Mr. Crawford, the sound conclusion that LOCRINE preceded SELIMUS, yet declines
to decide as to the authorship of either play, he is not
to be met with any confident claim. The compiler of
PARNASSUS may have been misled as Meres was misled.
SELIMUS may be the work of an amateur, ambitious
to write a play more or less in stanza form, prone to
season his verse with familiar lines from Greene and

[1] Rep. from *Shakespeare Studies*, Wisconsin University, 1916.

Marlowe, and ready to copy comic matter without scruple. Still, as we know of no such quotatious outsider, and as we know Greene to be given to self-repetition, it is reasonable to say, first, that probably the same hand penned the comic scenes in LOCRINE and SELIMUS, and further that one of the hands at work in the first play had a constructive share in the second.

§ 2. " EDWARD III "

A dislike of Greene's character is natural to the students of the Elizabethan drama, for though he never wrote in his signed plays anything so base as Peele's wretched calumny on Queen Elinor in EDWARD I, his self-portrayed vices, his enviousness and faithlessness, set up a repulsion to him as a man.[1] By his own confession, he was a forsworn liar and the companion of thieves. He was indeed something of an English Villon —a *very* English Villon, with a passion for preaching. With his character, however, we have strictly nothing to do in this inquiry ; and a caveat on that head is a proper preamble to an investigation which turns upon his poetic and dramatic faculty

Fleay, in his vigilant scrutiny of EDWARD III, notes in the vocabulary of the supreme episode " expressions such as *hugy vastures, muster men, via, imperator, encouch,* which are either of frequent occurrence in Shakespeare, or have the true ring of his coinage in them." On the other hand he cites the following, found in other parts of the play, as non-Shakespearean :

Bonny (thrice). Found in 1 *H. VI,* and 3 *H. VI* (*Bonnier* in III, i).
Patronage (vb. infin.), III, iii. Found twice in 1 *H. VI.*
Hòrizon. V, i.
Ave Cæsar. I, i.
Whinyard. I, ii.

[1] Professor Raleigh writes (*The English Novel,* 2nd ed. p. 60) : " It is easy to condemn the man, impossible not to love him." Such love may come at first sight : it can hardly survive a detailed study.

Bayard. III, i.
Plate (= silver). I, ii . IV, iv.[1]
Nemesis. III, i, 120.
Martialist. III, iii.
Solitariness. III, ii.
Quadrant. V, i.
Ure. I, i.
Battle-'ray. III, iii ; IV, iii ('*rayed* in a clearly non-Shakespearean part of the *Taming of the Shrew*).
Burgonet. IV, iv, 83. Thrice in 2 *H. VI*. Once in *Antony and Cleopatra*, but in no other Shakespearean play.
Expulsed. III, ii. Found in 1 *H. VI*, III, iii, 25.
Quittance (vb. infin.). Found in 1 *H. VI*.

" Cataline," he adds, " in the TRUE TRAGEDY OF RICHARD DUKE OF YORK, has been replaced by Machiavel in 3 HENRY VI, but remains undethroned in Act III, sc. i, of our play."[2]

Now, " hugy " is found in no Shakespearean play, and is common to Greene, Marlowe, Peele, and Kyd, all of whom had seen it frequently in FERREX AND PORREX ; " vasture " is equally absent from the Shakespearean concordance ; so is " encouch " ; whereas we have " the deepest vast " and " the dreadful vast " in Lodge's WOUNDS OF CIVIL WAR (I, i, 221 ; II, i, 9) ; and in SOLIMAN AND PERSEDA, in the line (III, vi, 4)

Nay, that was love, for I couched myself,

the metre needs " encouched." " Via " is certainly frequent in Shakespeare ; but we find it also in RICHARD DUKE OF YORK ; and, though we have " muster men " in both RICHARD II and RICHARD III, that locution is ordinary enough. It is common in Greene, who in his death-bed letter to his wife writes : " All my wrongs muster themselves about me "—a fairly " Shakespearean " expression. Again he has " mustering his men " in EUPHUES HIS CENSURE TO PHILAUTUS (Works, VII, vi, 213) ; and " muster " in MENAPHON (p. 68).

[1] This, however, is really frequent in the Shakespeare Concordance.
[2] *Shakespeare Manual*, pp. 305-6.

Peele, again, has "muster all the men" in DAVID (III, ii) ;
and Marlowe has " musters men " in his translation from
Lucan (l. 396) ; also in 2 TAMBURLAINE (I, i). It seems
summary, finally, to credit ' imperator ' to Shakespeare
on the strength of its one appearance in LOVE'S
LABOUR'S LOST.

Turning by way of primary test to the list of non-
Shakespearean words, we find that *every one of them*
points to Greene.[1]   As thus :

Bonny.   *Perimedes*, twice (vii, 83, 92) ; *George-a-Greene*, twice,
I, i, and ii ; *James VI*, I, iii (twice) ; IV, near end ; *Friar Bacon
and Friar Bungay*, four times (ed. Dyce, pp. 153, 160, 163, 174) ;
also in Doron's jig in *Menaphon* ; in one of the sonnets in *Perimedes* twice ; and in the Hexametra Alexis in *The Mourning
Garment* (ed, Dyce, pp. 287, 293, 305).   Fourteen times in all.

Bonnier.   *Friar Bacon*, l. 49.

To patronage.   Five times in Greene's prose : *Francesco's
Fortunes*, Ep. Ded. ; *Euphues his Censure*, Ep. Ded, and text ;
The Royal Exchange : To the Citizens of London ; *Alcida* :
Greene's Metamorphosis, Ep. Ded. (Works, ed. Grosart, vi, 151,
236 ; vii, 226 ; ix, 6, 117).

Hòrizon.   *Orlando Furioso*, l. 20.

Whinyard.   *James IV*, Induction, thrice.

Bayard.   *Euphues his Censure* (Works, vi, 209, 264) ; *Mamillia*,
Ep. Ded, (ii, 6) ; *Greene's Vision* (xii, 212) ; *Orpharion*, Ep. Ded.

Nemesis.   Thrice in *Orlando Furioso*.

Solitariness.[2]   *Groatsworth of Wit*, Ed. *New Sh. Soc.*, p. 17,
l. 5 ; *Card of Fancy* (Works, iv, 42, 97) ; *Mamillia*, ii, 21, 43 ;
Alcida (ix, 40, 67).

Martialist.[3]   Four times in Greene's prose (*Euphues his
Censure*, 1587, Ep. Ded. to Philautus—Works, Grosart's ed., vi,
152, and p. 201 ; *Greene's Farewell to Folly*, 1591—Works, ix,

---

[1] In his valuable edition of the play, Mr. Moore Smith demurs somewhat to
inferences from such facts, remarking that though in *Henry V* there are many
words not used elsewhere by Shakespeare, " no one on that account would
doubt the genuineness of that play." I have dealt with that problem elsewhere. In the present connection, meantime, I would repeat the stipulation
that the tracing of words to a particular author is only a primary clue. Some
in Fleay's list may not be really Greene's in this play, being also found in
Marlowe.

[2] Echoed perhaps from Sidney, who works it hard (*Arcadia*, B. II, last poem),
or from *Euphues* (Arber's ed. pp. 117, 118). In North's Plutarch (*Coriolanus*,
in Skeat's *Shakespeare's Plutarch*, p. 15) it is told that wilfulness in a governor
is " that which Plato called ' solitariness.' " This may have given the word
its vogue. Greene has " solitarily " in the *Card of Fancy* (p. 45), and in the
Tritameron of Love (Works, iii, 55).

[3] Also a word of Lilly's—*The Woman in the Moon*, II, i.

247, 249). (Also twice in the induction to the *Spanish Tragedy*, ll. 46, 61).

Quadrant. *Menaphon* : Nashe's Epistle " To the Gentlèmen Students " (Works, vi, 14).

Expuls*ive*. *Perimedes* : Works, v, 20. (Expulse. *Spanish Tragedy*, III, ii, 107. It is a common Tudor word ; but " expulsed " in *Edward III* may be from another hand).

To Quittance.[1] *Greene's Vision* (xii, 246) ; *Philomela* (xi, 117) ; *Orlando Furioso*, twice (ed. Dyce, pp. 95, 108). Quittanced. *Life and Death of Ned Browne* ; and *Repentance of Robert Greene* (Works, xi, 34 ; xii, 179).

Battle 'ray. *James IV*, v, vi ; *Alphonsus of Arragon*, IV, near end (Dyce's ed. p. 242, col. 1).[2]

Ure. *Alphonsus*, Induction : Speech of Venus ; also Act III (Dyce, p. 236).[3]

Plate. *Groatsworth*, ed. cited, p. 9, l. 1 : *Friar Bacon*, ed. Dyce, p. 165, col. 2, l. 2 ; *Menaphon*, ed. Arber, p. 33 ; *Never too Late* (cited by Dyce, p. 6).

As to *Ave Cæsar*, Mr. Fleay has noted[4] that the phrase occurs in Greene's NEVER TOO LATE ; and he infers that a reference is there meant to this play. But why should it be so ? The point of the remark cited lies in the Æsopism about the crow figuring at court, not in any literal suggestion as to an actor saying " Ave Cæsar " in a play. As a matter of fact, a phrase about " crying ' Ave ' to his majesty " while " aiming Cæsar's death " occurs in Greene's own ORLANDO FURIOSO[5] (Dyce, p. 94), which is certainly to be dated before 1590 ; and the sentence " Cæsar's crow durst never cry *Ave*, but when she was perked on the capitol " is found in the Epistle Dedicatory to PANDOSTO, published 1588.[6] Are we not rather forced to infer, then, that it was one of Greene's recurring tags, and that, with all the other non-Shakespearean modes above noted as coming from

---

[1] Found in Marlowe only as a substantive (five times). Greene has also the form " to acquittance " (*Never too Late* : Works, viii, 16), found in *Richard III*, III, vii, 233.

[2] Also, be it noted, in Marlowe, trans. of Ovid's Elegies, I, i, 15.

[3] Also in Marlowe, *Jew*, II, ii (Cunningham unwarrantably printed " use ").

[4] Above, p. 306.

[5] This is noted by Fleay in *Biog. Chron.* i, 263 ; but is forgotten by him in the passage before cited, *Life of Shakespeare*, p. 282, and in *Biog. Chron.*, ii, 62 (Above, p. 306).

[6] This also is overlooked by Fleay.

him, it points *pro tanto* to his presence in this play ?
And again, seeing that the reference to Lucrece is in the
phrase " the vain endeavour of so many pens," are we
entitled to think that it must refer to Shakespeare's
poem in particular ?   Is it likely, further, that Shakespeare would gratuitously introduce such an allusion to
his own poem ?[1]   And are we not bound to date the
play before 1593 ?[2]

Burgonet, again, seems to be a term of Greene's :

> My spear and shield
> Resounding on their *crests* and *sturdy helms*
> Topt high with plumes, like Mars his burgonet
> > (*Orlando Furioso*, ll. 30-32).
> *Breaking our lances* on his *sturdy crest*
> > (*Selimus*, 144).
> Engrave our prowess on their burgonets
> > (*Id.*, 2430).
> And *crack my lance* upon his burgonet
> > (*Locrine*, ll, ii).

As each of these passages expresses the same idea, the
passage in EDWARD III (IV, iv, 82-83) :—

> My tongue is made of steel, and it shall beg
> My mercy on his coward burgonet—

is likely to be from the same mint as the others ;[3] and
as the tag is not to be found in Peele's signed works we
are led tentatively to ascribe it to Greene both in
LOCRINE and SELIMUS. Without going into the question of the authorship of the FIRST PART OF THE CON-
TENTION, we may note in passing that this is one of the
clues to Greene's hand in that play, since in a single

[1] Mr. Moore Smith rightly characterises as " strange " the argument of
Warnke and Proescholdt that " no author would speak *so slightingly* of his
own work." But is it likely that Shakespeare would in a play allude to his
own poem at all ?
[2] There is only one double-ending in the first 130 lines ; only five in the first
scene of 163 blank-verse lines=3 per cent ; and only twelve in the 120 blank
lines of scene ii=10 per cent. Twelve per cent is reached in II, i, and
II, ii. In Act V there is only one in 243 lines, This is early work. Query,
1590 ?
[3] Yet again in *Alcida, Greene's Metamorphosis*, Ep. Ded., we have "' registered his valour on the helm of his enemy " (Works, ix, 5) ; and in *Orlando*
" register upon his helm " (Dyce, p. 91).

scene (as in 2 HENRY VI, v, i) we have " burgonet "
thrice ; one of the lines running :

> And that I'll write upon thy burgonet.

If the inference be not otherwise upset, it would follow
that the equivalent passages in 2 HENRY VI are his,
though the word " burgonet," used as a metaphor,
occurs in CORIOLANUS. And so with the words
" bonny " and " bonniest " in the same plays though
Shakespeare has " bonny " elsewhere.[1] In Greene they
are common.

But even in the second Act of EDWARD III, claimed
as Shakespeare's, there are yet other words and names
found in no other play ascribed to him. The following
are probably not all :

> Chess. i, 50. Besiege (noun). i, 416 (412).[2]
> Delineate. ii, 91 (88).
> Flankers. i, 189 (105).
> Foragement. i, 400 (396). (Forage in *V. and A.*)
> Inwired (or Envir'd). i, 418 (414).
> Judith. i, 171 (169).
> Leprous. i, 424 (420). (" Leperous " in *Hamlet*.)
> Love-lays. i, 98 (97).
> Sarah. i, 258 (254).
> Sots (vb.). i, 81.

Further we have " ventages " (ii, 70), found only in
HAMLET, and there with a different force ; " satirical,"
also found only in HAMLET ; " star-chamber " (ii, 169),
here used metaphorically, applied literally in the MERRY
WIVES, and nowhere else occurring in Shakespeare ;
" heart-blood," found in RICHARD II, and thrice in the
HENRY VI group, but not elsewhere ; " conventicle,"

---

[1] In no case, however, does the word seem to be his. In *Much Ado* and
Hamlet it occurs in old songs ; in the *Shrew* it is taken over from the old play ;
in 2 *H. VI* it is in the same case ; and in *R. III* the passage is plainly non-
Shakespearean. As for " bonny " in *As You Like It* (ii, iii, 8), surprisingly
retained in the Globe ed., it is surely a misprint for " bony."

[2] The numbering of the lines differs in the editions of Delius (Leop. Sh.)
and Mr. Moore Smith. I here give both.

found only in 2 HENRY VI ; "wistly," found only in
RICHARD II ; "intellectual soul," found only in the
COMEDY OF ERRORS ; "endamagement," found only in
KING JOHN ; and "cynic," found only in JULIUS
CÆSAR, where it is used with its stricter application,
not as here in a metaphor. And in other Acts we
naturally have a number of words either seldom or
never found in the Shakespeare concordance, as :—
"Impall "=impale=encircle (III, iii, 180), found only
in 3 HENRY VI in this sense ; "sapless" (III, iii, 217),
found only in 1 HENRY VI (twice) ; "meatamor-
phosed " (IV, v, 39) occurring only in the TWO GENTLE-
MEN (twice) ; "rebate " (I, i, 40), found only in MEAS-
URE FOR MEASURE ; "texted " (IV, iv, 130), occurring
nowhere in Shakespeare ; "faceless " (I, ii, 78), also
non-Shakespearean. Here again we have clues to
Greene :

Chess. *Perimedes* (Works, vi, 71) ; *Philomela* (xi, 154) ;
Groatsworth of Wit (Sh. Soc. rep. pp. 20, 21—thrice).
Conventicle. *Never too Late* (Works, viii, 61). Also in the
Troublesome Raigne, in a scene which has Greene's word " deaths-
man," found in *Menaphon*, the *Groatsworth*, and *Tully's Love*,
and twice in *Alcida* (Works, vi, 143 ; vii, 145 ; ix, 110, 112 ; xii,
145).
Cynic. *Tully's Love* (Works, vii, 172). *Menaphon* (ed. Arber,
p. 49). Cynical, *id.* p. 48 ; *Farewell to Folly* (Works, ix, 279).
Endamage. *Euphues his Censure to Philautus* (Works, vi, 221).
Endamaged. *Philomela* (Works, xi, 150). *Selimus*, 1378.
Forageth. *James IV*, v, i. Forage. *Id.* v, 4. Forraged.
Menaphon, p. 57. (Foragement occurs in Peele, *B. of A.*, II, iii).
Impall. Impales (same force), Sonnet from Ariosto in *Pen-
elope's Web*; Barmenissa's Song, *ib.* ; *Verses in Alcida* ; Dyce's
ed. pp. 317, 319.
Inwired (or Envir'd). This seems to be the true reading of the
word printed as " invironed " in *Euphues his Censure to Philautus*
(Works, vi, 220), which as it stands is unintelligible.
Love-lays. *James IV*, I, ii.
Rebate. *Orlando Furioso*, twice ; ed. Dyce, pp. 90, 110 ;
Looking Glass, id. p. 117 ; *Menaphon*, p. 72.
Sapless. *Menaphon*, Melicertus' Madrigal, p. 54.
Satirical. *Menaphon*, ed. Arber, p. 25 ; *Greene's Vision*
(Works, xii, 215, 223) ; *Euphues his Censure* (Works, vi, 169) ;
Second Part of Tritameron (iii, 117) ; *Never too Late*, viii, 23 ;
Farewell to Folly, ix, 294.

Sotteth (the senses). *Penelope's Web* (Works, v, 156).

Sotted. *Planetomachia* (Works, v, 58) ; *Mamillia* (ii, 32) ;
Tritameron of Love, iii, 73, 78, 79, 89) ; *Debate between Folly and
Love* (iv, 210) ; *Pandosto* (Sh. Lib. rep. p. 37).

Let us take further three words, *intricate*,[1] *invectives*,
and *stratagem*, which invite special examination as used
in EDWARD III. The first occurs only once in a
Shakespeare play :

> What an intricate impeach is this !
> > *Comedy of Errors*, v, i, 269.

The second also occurs only once, in an admittedly
doubtful play :

> Breathe out invectives 'gainst the officers.
> > 3 *Henry VI*, I, iv, 43.

Stratagem, again, occurs fifteen times in the Shakespeare
concordance, but nearly always in its normal modern
force. In EDWARD III it has the special Tudor
meaning[2] of a mere act of war or violence ; and this
sense, which in the Shakespeare concordance occurs
only once quite definitely—in a non-Shakespearean
piece—

> What stratagems, how fell, how butcherly
> > 3 *Henry VI*, II, v, 89—

is the normal force of the word in Greene, who also uses
frequently the words *invective* and *intricate* :

Invective(s). *Greene's Vision*, twice (Works, xii, 213, 219,
234) ; *Tully's Love* (vii, 172) ; *Philomela* (xi, 145) ; *Planetomachia* (v, 7) ; and " invective verse " in Verses against Courtezans
in the *Groatsworth of Wit*.

Intricate.   " Such an intricate danger ;" : *Orpharion* (xii, 35) ;
The knot of gordian at the shrine of Jove
Was never half so hard or intricate.
> > *Orlando Furioso* (Dyce, p. 95a).

---

[1] This is probably *not* a Greene word in *Edward III*, though he uses it
elsewhere.

[2] Occurring several times in Marlowe.

Stratagem. " Cursed stratagem "=act of outrage : *Perimedes*
(vii, 48) ; " So shalt thou glut the ruthless destinies with a most
baleful stratagem " (*Id*. p. 26) ; " The poor inhabitants thought
Mars had been sent to fill the country with stratagems " :
Orpharion (xii, 45) ; " Now I see the beginning of your wars, and
the pretended (= intended) end of your stratagems " : *Menaphon*,
Arber's rep. p. 82 ; " To close up the comedy with a tragical
stratagem he slew himself " ; *Pandosto*, rep. in Sh. Lib. Pt. I,
vol. iv, p. 83 ; " Performing strange and ruthless stratagems " :
Orlando Furioso (Dyce, p. 106b).

Here we have the loose use of the word seen in EDWARD
III :

> Receive this lance into thy manly hand ;
> Use it in fashion of a brazen pen
> To draw forth bloody stratagems in France.
>
> III, iii, 194-96.
>
> Thyself art bruised and bit with many broils ;
> And stratagems forepast with iron pens
> Are texted in thine honourable face.
>
> IV, iv, 127-29.

Take yet again the special use of the word " reverent "
in our play (II, i, 9) :

> Anon, with reverent fear when she grew pale.

Such uses of the word in Shakespeare are wholly confined to the HENRY VI group, so largely consisting of
other men's work.   In Greene they are common :

> Reject him not so rigorously that regardeth you with such
> reverence.   *Orpharion* : Works, xii, 39.

> Giovanni who with a reverent love favoured the countess.
>   *Philomela* : xi, 120.
> Saluted him reverently.   *Id*. p. 161.

> Whose age contained a multitude of reverent advertisements.
>   *Greene's Mourning Garment* : ix, 185.
> She rose up and reverently saluted him.
>   *Pandosto* : rep. in Sh. Lib. I, iv, 62.

Other words, such as " passionate " (=amorous) and
" orisons," are used in EDWARD III in a special sense,

which again may point to Greene. In his main plays, Shakespeare uses the latter word literally :[1] in HENRY V, in 3 HENRY VI, in EDWARD III, and in Greene constantly, it has a merely metaphorical force. " Passionate," again, is one of Greene's very commonest words, nearly always used with the force " in love," as in this play. And though " squadrons " is not un-Shakespearean, it is worth noting that Edward's lines (II, i185-6) :

> Lodwick, thou knowst not how to draw a battle ;
> These wings, these flankers, and these squadrons
> Argue in thee defective discipline,

chime with a passage in Greene (ORPHARION : Works, xii, 45) about a leader " politique in placing the squadrons of his men," and another in his FAREWELL TO FOLLY (ix, 24), where we have the phrase : " how cunningly they ordered their squadrons." On the other hand, the passage savours of Tamburlaine's counsels of war to his sons, and thus again suggests a Marlowe substratum.

Yet again, the Marlowe word " topless," found only in TROILUS in the Shakespeare plays, and there in a moral sense, occurs in EDWARD III (IV, v, 114) and in a Greene scene in the LOOKING GLASS FOR LONDON (i, 16), in both cases in the sense of physically lofty. " Mickle," " passions," and " misconster," all occurring within twenty-five lines (v, i, end), are all habitual words of Greene's.

If we look next to the tags, we are led to the same attribution. In II, i, 390-1, for instance, we have the passage :

> The poets write that great Achilles' spear
> Could heal the wound it made.

The same trope is found in 2 HENRY VI, v, i, 100, taken from the CONTENTION :

> Like to Achilles' spear,
> Is able with the change to kill or cure,

[1] E.g., Hamlet, III, i, 89.

but nowhere in the whole range of the genuine Shake-speare, who, indeed, never names Achilles save once in LOVE'S LABOUR'S LOST, and as a character in TROILUS AND CRESSIDA.   But the same formula is found in Greene's ORLANDO FURIOSO (ed. Dyce, p. 95, col. 1) :

> As those that with Achilles' lance were wounded
> Fetched help at self-same [? deadly-] pointed spear ;

and it is common in his prose ; for instance :

> " Pierced with Achilles' lance must be healed with his spear "
>   *Orpharion*, ad init.—Works,xii, 9 ;
> " Wounded with Achilles' lance . . . must be healed with his truncheon "   *Philomela*, Works, xi, 141 ;
> " Achilles' lance that did wound and heal "
>   (*Tully's Love*, Works, vii, 109) ;
> " Achilles' sword to cut and recure "
>   (*Never too Late*, viii. 223).

Equally typical of him is the passage (II, 1, 286-9) :

> O that I were a honey-gathering bee,
> To bear the comb of virtue from his flower ;
> And not a poison-sucking envious spider,
> To turn the vice I take to deadly venom.[1]

The figure of the spider sucking poison from the most precious flowers occurs in his REPENTANCE (Works, xii, 180) ; and when we find it in SOLIMAN (II, i, 130) we have a fresh reason for querying his presence there. A variant occurs in GREENE'S VISION (Works, xii, 202) :

> The serpent is then therefore an odious creature, for that he sucketh poison from the odoriferous flowers, from whence the painful bee gathers her sweet honey.

Again, the line (ii, 74) :

> For poets term the wanton warrior blind

has reference to the " blind Bayard " referred to in the

---

[1] This again is a tag from *Euphues* (rep. p. 107).

four passages of Greene above cited, and in the parallel
line in the third Act (i, 58) :

> Then Bayard-like, blind overweening Ned . . . ;

while the passage (i, 122-3) :

> Ah, what a world of descant makes my soul
> Upon this voluntary ground of love,

is a reproduction of an idea very common in Greene's
prose. In Shakespeare we find " descant " twice as
verb, and twice as noun ; but (save one instance in
LUCRECE) all occur in plays not drafted by him—
RICHARD III and the TWO GENTLEMEN OF VERONA.
The phrase in the latter play gives the word the exact
musical application so common in Greene :

> Singling out the simplest plainsong, that your descant might
> seem the more refined.   *Orpharion* : Works, xii, 72.
> A humorous descant of their prattle.   *Menaphon*, ed. Arber,
> p. 55 ; Works, vi, 88.
> Ran so merry a descant on the pride of scholars.   *Farewell to
> Folly* ; Works, ix, 252.
> Playing most cunningly upon a lute certain lessons of curious
> descant.   *Philomela* ; Works, xi, 174-5.
> What is the reason you diversely descant of the fruition of love ?
> *Id.* p. 126.
> You run descant upon this word.   *Penelope's Web* ; Works,
> v, 197.
> You keep me for a plainsong whereupon to descant.   *Trita-
> meron of Love* ; Works, iii, 58.
> Peratio at the first sight began thus to descant.   *Second Part
> of Tritameron* ; *Id.* p. 168.
> You men . . . have your shifts of descant, to make sundry
> points upon one plain song.   *Id.* p. 122.
> Can so cunningly run a point of descant that, be the plain
> song never so simple, thou canst quaver to please both parts.
> *Mamillia* ; Works, ii, 226.
> Upon poor Lentulus' plain song they all began to descant.
> *Tully's Love* ; Works, vii, 156.

If demur be made to the proposition that the TWO
GENTLEMEN is not of Shakespeare's drafting, I will but
refer to the reasons given by me elsewhere[1] for such a

[1] The *Shakespeare Canon*, Part II.

conclusion, and add that the opening scene develops a discussion that fills a page of GREENE'S MOURNING GARMENT, where occur the phrase :

> Travel, father, is the mother of experience.
>
> (Works, ix, 133),

and other saws to the same effect.   Thus the " descant " formula points still to Greene.

Another tag occurring in EDWARD III (III, iii, 112), at first sight seems to point to a similar conclusion :

> Before the sickle's thrust into the corn.

In SELIMUS (l. 497) we have :

> And thrust my sickle where the corn is reaped ;

in SOLIMAN AND PERSEDA (IV, i, 223) :

> That thrust his sickle in my harvest corn ;

and again in the SPANISH TRAGEDY (II, vi) :

> The sickle comes not till the corn be ripe.

Now, we have repeatedly seen reason to question whether Greene had not a hand in SOLIMAN AND PERSEDA ;   and there is a temptation to solve the problem summarily by referring to him the phrase under notice.   But there is a piece of evidence which in some measure challenges that solution.

§ 3. "ARDEN OF FEVERSHAM"

One of the notable Elizabethan tragedies which preceded TITUS is ARDEN OF FEVERSHAM (1592), assigned by Fleay to Kyd.   I have nowhere been more impressed by the value of his ascriptions.[1]   ARDEN sets out with a versification which is certainly not Greene's,

---

[1] Since this was written, Mr. Charles Crawford, who had reached the same view independently, has published a convincing demonstration of Kyd's authorship of the play (*Collectanea*, First Series, 1906, p. 101, sq.).   But he does not note Greene's insertions, though he rightly pronounces *Arden* and *Soliman and Perseda* to be alike recasts.   (*Id.* p. 102).   Mr. Drydale Sykes, more recently, after reaching the same view independently, has effectively borne out Mr. Crawford's attribution of *Arden* to Kyd.   The rejection of Fleay's attribution by Professor Boas is thus overborne.

and is as certainly not Peele's ; and in the first Act we
find in it an accentuation never met with in their verse—
" jealous " pronounced as a tri-syllable. There can
be no mistake about the intention. At first the word
is spelt " jelyouse " ; afterwards it goes " jelious " ;
and, though in one instance it may be read in two
syllables, in four others it has clearly three.[1] Now
though this pronunciation is found in some plays in or
after 1592, notably in RICHARD III, in a quite un-
Shakespearean passage[2] (I, i, 92) :

> Well strucκ in years, fair, and not jealous,

it never occurs in earlier plays, so far as I remember,
save in the SPANISH TRAGEDY in the line (II, ii, 56) :

> Ay, danger mixed with jealous despite.

The spelling, indeed, is " jealous " in the 1594 quarto,
followed by Professor Boas in his edition of Kyd's
works ; but in the prose tract THE MURDER OF JOHN
BREWEN (1592), assigned to Kyd by a note in contemporary handwriting, we have the common spelling
" ielious."[3]

[1] Act I. Bullen's ed. 1887, pp. 3, 7, 10, 17, 18 (I, ll. 48, 134, 213, 380, 415).

[2] Suggesting the presence of Kyd in *Richard III*—a hypothesis which
might clear up several difficulties as to the composite authorship of that play.
An alternative hypothesis is that the hand may be that of Heywood, who in
the First Part of *Edward IV* (1600) (if that play be really his) has both the
spelling and the scanning " jealious " (Pearson's Heywood, i, p. 132). " The
gelyous comodey " figures as " ne " in Henslowe's Diary on 5th January,
1592 (3). " Jealous " as a trisyllable is found in Heywood's *Fair Em.*, l. 1330.

[3] Ed. of Professor Boas, p. 291, l. 26. It may be noted that the spelling
" jealious " is common in the period even where the word is certainly a dissyllable. Mr. Aldis Wright (*Richard III*, Clar. Press Ser. p. 124) observes
that ' jealious " is the uniform spelling of the word in *Othello* in the first folio
" even where the metre does not require it." The metre *never* requires it
there or in any unquestionable verse of Shakespeare. Fleay's assertion to
the contrary as regards *Othello* will not stand. The trisyllabic spelling was
simply one of the innumerable Elizabethan variants. It is found in the 1593
ed. of Peele's *Edward I*, sc. 1, where the scansion rejects it. It is also found
several times in Lilly's *The Woman in the Moone* as reprinted in Fairholt's
ed. from the quarto of 1597 (ed. cited of Works, ii, 168, 183, 184) ; but in the
two instances in which the word occurs in verse (pp. 168, 182) it scans perfectly as a dissyllable, and in the second of these it happens to be spelt
" jealous." In Greene's prose the word is spelt in many ways. In *Philomela*
alone (Works, xi, 137, 143, 156, 169, 172, 182, 183, 197) I find seven different
spellings: ielous, gelous, iellous, iealous, ielouse, ieliousҽ, and ielious (twice).
As the word never scans with three syllables in his verse, we may take it that
the last two spellings at least are the printer's.

Now, in the first quarto of HAMLET, after the " Enter
Horatio and the Queen " (iv, 7) we have a speech by
Horatio, not reproduced in Q2, in which occurs the
line :—

> For murderous minds are always jealous

—the tri-syllabic scansion. Evidently this speech is
wholly Kyd's. Here then we have a very clear though
a slender clue, justifying, so far as it goes, Fleay's
ascription. But after Mr. Crawford's and Mr. Sykes's
demonstrations, no further support is needed : the
play is primarily Kyd's.

In ARDEN, we have the line (III, i, p. 45) :

> What dismal outcry calls me from my rest ?

closely echoing that in the TRAGEDY (II, V, I) :

> What outcries pluck me from my naked bed ?

Nowhere, I think, does that formula occur in Greene ;
and to Kyd, accordingly, we seem bound to ascribe
prima facie not only that but the tag we have just been
considering, which occurs thus in ARDEN (IV, i, p. 69) :

> Why should he thrust his sickle in our corn ?

So far as I remember, the formula never occurs in
Greene's prose, where he repeats so many proverbs
and catch-words. If then we find it (1) in no signed
work of his, but only in SELIMUS,[1] and there with a
difference of turn and application which consists with
a separate authorship ; (2) in the TRAGEDY ; and (3)
in SOLIMAN AND PERSEDA, which on any view is only
in small part Greene's, and which is so closely associated
with the TRAGEDY, the fair inference is that in three if
not in all four cases it is Kyd's. Of course the phrase
is proverbial, and might be used by anybody ; and
such a phrase Greene may have adopted in several

---

[1] In a rhyming passage, which certainly appears to be Greene's,

plays without introducing it in his prose ; but though
that is possible, the first presumption is against that
conclusion. And we shall see other grounds for
recognising Kyd's presence in EDWARD III.

The matter, however, cannot rest there. As Mr.
Crawford shows, we have decisive ground for ascribing
to Kyd a main share in SOLIMAN AND PERSEDA ; and
ARDEN we may confidently assign to him as original
and main author. In ARDEN, as in SOLIMAN, there are
several words and phrases which suggest the special
vocabulary of Peele. The old tag " kills my heart,"
as before noted, occurs twice in the former play ; and
we find in it also the words " 'ticing," " fore-slowed,"
" 'joy "=enjoy, " bedesman " (found in his signed
SPEECHES AT THEOBALD'S, i, 83 ; in EDWARD I, i, 130,
and in the sonnet " His golden locks time hath to silver
turned ") ; " long home " (the metre calling for
" longest home ") ; " complices " (found in the MASSA-
CRE AT PARIS) ; and the form " patient yourself."
But such phrases do not carry us far ; and on the other
hand we shall find, when we come to discuss the play in
connection with Kyd, reasons for recognising the
presence of Marlowe. In the present connection we
have to note what seem to be marked traces of Greene.
Of passages which suggest both writers we may note
that in Act III, sc. ii, l. 91 (Temple ed.) where Black
Will, who had formerly spoken in realistic prose, now
suddenly speaks in blank verse of Alice Arden, of whom
he has hitherto heard nothing in the dialogue. The
balance of presumption from style points here to Marlowe ; and it might seem to do so in the speech of
Michael at the close of the Act were it not for a " for
to " which strongly hints of Greene.

But in Act III, sc. 5, there are stronger grounds for
suspecting the intervention of Greene. In previous
scenes we have had flights of poetic blank verse which,
like that of Black Will just mentioned, deflect the play
partly from the realistic aim professed in the epilogue ; and in these deviations there is strong suggestion
of other hands than Kyd's. Here (III, v) we have a

scene beginning clearly enough in Kyd's own hand, in a
blank verse that has his pedestrian quality, despite
poetic touches. But after Mosbie's soliloquy the
workmanship changes, and we come to a versification
more rapid, nervous and impassioned and at the same
time more precisely iambic than Kyd's. And though
this is one of the stronger scenes of the play, and the
assignment of it to another hand somewhat weakens
Kyd's credit for the whole, I cannot evade the impression that the workmanship is Greene's.

Simple vocabulary clues must be followed with
caution, here as elsewhere. Such a clue seems to point
to Greene in the pseudo-Marlowesque lines :

> Such deep pathaires, like to a cannon's burst
> Discharged against a ruinated wall.

The unexampled word *pathaires* has been explained by
Professor Gollancz[1] as " some special form of *petarre=
petard*." But why "*deep* petard" ? The word is, I think,
simply a misprint of Greene's word *pathemas* (=violent
emotions) in NEVER TOO LATE (Works, viii, 103) :

> Finding myself full of *Pathemas*, as stung to the quick . . .

I know no other instance of this term, which is not
noted in the New English Dictionary, though there are
nineteenth-century examples of " pathematic " and
" pathematically " ; but it is an intelligible formation
from the Greek, and it makes a perfectly good reading
for the passage in ARDEN. Such a word, of course,
may have been borrowed from Greene by Kyd : the
speech containing it is in versification, indeed, rather
more like Kyd than Greene. But as the scene goes
on we get the Greene movement more and more ; and
Alice's long speech of revulsion is markedly Greenean
alike in verse and in phrase. Such an impression,
coupled with that of the occasional presence of Marlowe
in the same play, prepares us to find those three associated elsewhere.

[1] Cited in Mr. Bayne's (Temple) ed. of *Arden*, note *in loc.*

§ 4. EDWARD III *(Continued)*

Returning to EDWARD III, we find grounds of a stronger kind for connecting the Countess episode with Greene. More notable and more cumulatively significant than coincidences of tags, are these virtual duplications, in this play, of ideas from signed work of Greene's :—

> There is no summer but in her cheerful looks.
> > *Ed. III*, II, i, 42.
>
> And makes perpetual summer where she is.
> > *Menaphon*, p. 63.
>
> She comforts all the world as doth the sun . . .
> When she is set, the gladsome day is done.
> > Verses in *Pandosto*.

Even so common a phrase as " fair and wise," which was proverbial, and which occurs twice in JAMES IV, becomes more significant when thus used :—

As wise as fair.	*Ed. III*, I, ii, 162.
As wise as beautiful.	*Menaphon*, p. 46.

And there is more than a proverbial quality in the following :—

> The greater man, the greater is the thing,
> Be it good or bad, that he shall undertake.
> > *Ed. III*, II, i, 434-5.
>
> Sin in kings is sin, we see,
> And greater sin 'cause great of 'gree ;
> *Magis peccatum*, this I read,
> If he be high that does the deed.
> > Ode in *Philomela*, 1592.
>
> When she would talk of peace, methinks, her tongue
> Commanded war to prison.
> > *Ed. III*, i, 36.
>
> And when she sings, all music else be still.
> > Verses in *Pandosto*, 1589 (Dyce, p. 294*a*).
> > > Her crystal eyes
> Wherein triumphant sat both peace and wars,
> From out whose arches such sweet favour flies
> As might reclaim Mars in his highest rage,
> At beauty's charge, his fury to assuage.
> > Canzone in *Never too Late* (1590).

Comparisons of beauty's eyes to sun and stars are too
common in poetry to permit of any more than a corroborative inference in such a case as this ; but the
following resemblances are notable :

> Now in the sun alone it doth not lie
> With light to take light from a mortal eye ;
> For here two day-stars, that mine eyes would see
> More than the sun, steals mine own light from me.
>> *Edward III*, I, ii, 131-35.

> And those that gaze on him to find out thee
> Will lose their eyesight, looking in the sun.
>> *Id.* II.

> And thus I mused until I darked mine eye,
> Finding the sun too glorious for my sight.
>> Canzone in *Never too Late.*

> Shut are the day-bright eyes that made me see.
>> *Looking-Glass for London* (Dyce, p. 174).

> Their eyes that have gazed with the Philosopher against too
> bright a sun, and such are blind.
>> *Orpharion* : Works, x[i]i, 19.

> I . . . have dazzled mine eyes and fired my heart with desire.
>> *Philomela* : Works, xi, 139.

> Whereas my nymph, impatient of the night,
>> Bade bright Astræus with his train give place,
>> Whiles she led forth the day with her fair face,
> And lent each star a more than Delian light.
>> Melicertus' verses in *Menaphon.*

> Her eyes, fair eyes, like to the purest lights
> That animate the sun or cheer the day.
>> *Id.* Menaphon's Eclogue.

> Fired with gazing at such glimmering stars
> As, stealing light from Phoebus' brightest rays,
> Sparkle and set a flame within my breast.
>> Madrigal in *Perimedes.*

> Starry eyes, whereat my sight
> Did eclipse with much delight.
>> Francesco's Ode in *Never too Late.*

> Her eyes were stars.
>> *Id.* Eurymachus' Fancy.

But there is a still more significant piece of evidence.
Lodwick's line, rejected by Edward (II, i, 141) :

> *More chaste* and fair than is the queen *of shades,*

is a close echo of Greene's

> *More chaste* than Vesta, goddess of *the maids*
>> Verses in *Alcida* (Dyce, 319*b*) ;

and, what is finally decisive, the next rejected line
(*id.* 168-9) :

> More bold in *constancy* than Judith was,

is a figure-parallel to the next in Greene's poem, last
cited :—

> Of greater *faith* than fair Lucretia.

It is hardly possible to doubt that we are reading from
the same poet. If it be not so, either the author of
ALCIDA is consciously echoing the lines in the play,
which at Greene's death had not been printed, or the
playwright is (*a*) slavishly echoing Greene or (*b*) girding
at Greene by calling his lines bad. And as the other
poet could only be Marlowe, both of the latter alterna-
tives may be ruled out. That the same poet should
vary his lines is obviously likely. Lodwick clearly
could not talk of Lucretia for a king apparently inclined
to play Tarquin ; and to drag in Judith is just the
device that he might be supposed to resort to. It is
the poem that is the original : in the play, the poet uses
his old matter with a necessary difference, even as he
puts the Moon-Goddess for Vesta in the previous line,
and yet keeps in rhyme with the old one. And as
ALCIDA dates 1588, there can be no surmise of copying
there, for no one would date the play—or at all events
the second Act as it stands—so early.

It seems impossible to discount all these parallels.
Common as such ideas are, they are evidently a special
" line " of Greene's. No other poet of the period,
perhaps, has so rung the changes on a few sets of
metaphors. And the natural inference is strengthened
when we find in his prose a hardly less abundant crop
of another flower of rhetoric that is prominent in
EDWARD III. In the opening scene of Act II, the theme
of Lodwick's soliloquy is the changing of colour of both
king and countess. It is one of Greene's tics[1] :—

---

[1] Though Marlowe too has :
His colour went and came. *Hero and Leander*, ii, 214.

No sooner did he spy her but he changed colour as a man in a doubtful extasy.   *Never too Late* : Works, iii, 48-9.
Changing colour, he could scarce stand on his legs.
Penelope's Web : v, 218.
The change of his [Lentulus'] colour brewrayed his new entertained passions ; which noted by Terentia, half angry at love's folly she discovered her choler with such a blush . . .
Tully's Love : vii, 116.

The blushes of his heroines are constantly recorded,[1] his usual colour-term being " vermilion," as : " tempering the porphyry (!) of her face with a vermilion blush." (TULLY'S LOVE, p. 115). That epithet he uses at least a dozen times. In the description by the secretary in EDWARD III we have " scarlet " and " oriental red " ; but they are pretty evidently laid on by the same brush :—

His cheeks put on their *scarlet ornaments*.
Ed. III, ii, i, 10.
Her *oriental red*.   *Id.* l. 11.
The *orient ornaments* of her [the Marigold's] beauty.
Menaphon, p. 59.
Tullie . . . stood amated at beauty's *ornaments*.[2]
Groatsworth of Wit, N. S. S. rep. p. 15.
Her mantle was *vermilion red*.
Philadora's Ode in *The Mourning Garment*.
Dye her crystal cheeks with a *vermilion red*.
Pandosto, Sh. Lib. rep. p. 57.
Her cassock was of *scarlet red*.
The Mourning Garment, Description of
Shepherd and Wife.
Her coat was of *scarlet red*.
The Shepherd's Ode, in *Ciceronis Amor*.
As if her cheeks, by some enchanted power
Attracted had the *cherry* blood from his.
Ed. III, ii, i, 7-8.
Face rose-hued, *cherry* red.
Hexametra Alexis, in the *Mourning Garment*.
Ruby lips, *cherry* cheeks.   Ode in *Never too Late*.
Thy cheeks, like *cherries*.
Infida's song in *Never too Late*.

---

[1] Cp. *Friar Bacon*, Dyce's Greene and Peele, pp. 155a, 157b.
[2] The word occurs in some such sense in *Titus* (ii, iv, 18) where also the cue may be to Greene.

Compare again :

> No further off than her conspiring *eye*
> Which shoots infected *poison* in my *heart.*
>> *Ed. III*, I, ii, 128-9.

> Love is hatched in their [women's] eye ;
> Thence it steppeth to the *heart* ;
> There it *poisoneth* every part.
>> Isabel's Ode in *Never too Late.*

> Compar'st thou her to the pale queen of night ? . . .
> What is she, when the sun lifts up her head,
> But like a fading taper dim and dead ?
>> *Ed. III*, II, i, 123-24-5.

> *Pale-coloured* Phoebe's borrowing of her light.
>> Orpheus' song in *Orpharion.*

He could compare her beauty to no worse show than the glister of the moon in a silent night and a clear sky.
>> *Philomela* : Works, xi, 173.

> Better than beautiful, thou must begin.
> Devise for fair a fairer word than fair ;[1]
> And every ornament that thou wouldst praise
> Fly it a pitch above the soar of praise.
>> *Ed. III*, II, i, 84-87.

Whatever may deserve the name of fair have I seen before ; beauty have I beheld in his highest orb ; but never set eye on immortality before this hour.   *Menaphon*, Arber's rep. p. 60.

> Fixing my thoughts, and with my thoughts mine eye,
> Upon the·sun, the fairest of all fair ;
> "What thing made God so fair as this," quoth I.
>> Canzone in *Never too Late.*

> Forced to confess before that I had done,
> Her beauty far more brighter than the sun.   *Id.*

And again :

> Writing of her eyes,
> I'll say that like a glass they catch the sun,
> And thence the hot *reflection* doth rebound
> Against my breast, and burns my heart within.
>> *Ed. III*, II, i, 117-19.

[1] This of course recalls the line
> Fair is too foul an epithet for thee,
in I *Tamburlaine*, v, ii, and may be made a ground for ascribing the drafting of this section to Marlowe. And draft it he probably did. But here the expression is *weakened*, which is what we expect from Greene imitating Marlowe ; and the *idea* occurs in Greene elsewhere :—
> Tush, Lacy, she is beauty's overmatch.
>> *Friar Bacon*, sc. i.
> Those eyes, fair eyes, too fair to be described.
>> Melicertus' Eclogue, in *Menaphon.*
And see the other passages above quoted.

> Seeing her eyes to dazzle with the *reflex* of his beauty, and her cheeks tinted with a blush of disgrace by too much gazing on his face, etc.
>
> *Menaphon*, Arber's rep. p. 60.

Such frequent recurrences of idea and trope must be admitted to reinforce the inference from identities of " tag," to our list of which we may now add these :—

1. In the first scene of EDWARD III occurs the line (47) :

> But now doth mount with golden wings of fame,

which echoes two, imitating Spenser, above cited (p. 97) from LOCRINE and SELIMUS. This, however, is a kind of line that might have been written by Marlowe.

2. The tag about the nightingale with the prickle at its breast, above noted as occurring in Greene's prose and in the SPANISH TRAGEDY, is worked up in this play (I, i, 109-111) :—

> Fervent desire that sits against my heart,
> Is far more thorny-pricking than this blade,
> That, with the nightingale, I shall be scarred[1]

3. The uncommon phrase " pacify yourself " (v, i, 1) squares with " pacify your grace " in JAMES IV (Dyce, p. 192, *a*).

4. In Act I, i, 129, we have the expression " begirt with siege " applied to a castle ; and again in Act III, v, 107 :

> And there begirt that haven-town with siege.

This is a common formula of Greene's :

> Melicertes begirt the castle with such a siege . . .
> *Menaphon*, Arber's rep. p. 81.

In ORLANDO FURIOSO (Dyce, p. 93*b*) we have " girt his fort " ; and in ALPHONSUS KING OF ARRAGON (Dyce, p. 228*a*) the line :

> For to begirt it [Naples] with his bands about.

---

[1] Mr. Moore-Smith reads " scar'd ". *Scarred* is clearly the *meaning*.

Here, again, however, there is a possible prior source in Marlowe :

> Who means to girt Natolia's walls with siege.
>
> <div align="right">2 <i>Tamb.</i>, III, v, 7.</div>

5. The expression '" To buckle for a kingdom's sovereignty " (III, i, 126) is also a note of Greene :—

> Long and desire to buckle with the foe
>
> <div align="right"><i>Alphonsus</i>, p. 242<i>a</i> ;</div>
>
> That dares at weapons buckle with thy son,
>
> <div align="right"><i>Friar Bacon</i>, p. 175<i>b</i> ;</div>

though this too is Marlovian, and the style of the context points definitely to Marlowe.
6. In the line (III, iii, 30) :

> And set our foot upon thy tender mould,

though it refers to France, the last word probably means not " earth " but " body " ; and the figure is one of Greene's :—

> And I, in touching of her milk-white mould.[1]
>
> <div align="right"><i>James IV</i>, IV, v, near end.</div>

Yet the line in EDWARD III, here also, is probably Marlowe's.

7. The line (IV, ii, 33) :

> The lion scorns to touch the yielding prey,

echoes one in JAMES IV (v, iii, 24) :

> The king of beasts, that harms not yielding ones,[2]

and a sentence in PANDOSTO (Sh. Lib. 1, iv, 60) :—

> The lion never preyeth on the mouse, nor falcons stoop not to dead stales.

---

[1] Cp. " fair unhappy mould " in verses in *Alcida* (Dyce, p. 318*b*).
[2] A standing aphorism :—
> The fierce lyon will hurt no yelden things.
>
> <div align="right">Wyatt, <i>To his Lady cr[.]el over her yelden I o[.]er.</i></div>

See also *The Baço ian Heresy*, pp. 441-3.

and the application of both recurs in JAMES IV in the same scene :

> I, eagle-like, disdain these little fowls,
> And look on none but those that dare resist ;

while in the first and last citations the speaker is the King of England.

8. The phrase " patterns of despair and woe " (IV, ii, 12) in the scene of EDWARD III last cited, like the equivalent phrases formed on " map " and " platform," occurs in Greene's prose (Works, viii, 41).

9. The phrase cited below (p. 354) about decking an ape in tissue points to one in the Epistle Dedicatory to the TRITAMERON OF LOVE (Works, iii, 48) :

> The Persians caused their apes always to mask in cloth of gold, to cover their deformity.

§ 5. SOLIMAN AND PERSEDA

Of these nine instances the first, as it happens, takes us back again to SOLIMAN AND PERSEDA ; and it may be well here to group the main data for the surmise that Greene had a hand in that play.

1. " Golden wings " occurs twice (II, ii, 38 ; iii, 13).

2. The tag of the spider sucking poison from flowers occurs also (II, i, 130) :

> As in the spider good things turn to poison.

3. As before noted, the tag about choosing the least of two evils occurs here and in Greene's prose.

4. The line (IV, ii, 7),

> And where a man lives well, that is his country.

is nearly duplicated in Greene's MOURNING GARMENT (xi, 132), in the phrase : " Tully said, every country is a wise man's native home."

5. The not very common use of " dazzle " as an intransitive verb, above noted in Greene, occurs here (II, i, 244).

6. The line, IV, i, 50,

And tears suppressed will but increase my sorrow,

is a variant of a tag which we have seen to be a favourite with Greene.

7. The word " passions," occurring several times in this play, is found hundreds of times in Greene.

These parallels, however, though of some cumulative force when taken with the previously noted clues from vocabulary, are singly slight. Not so are the following.

8. As regards structure, not only is the situation of Soliman's love for Perseda (as we shall see) of a type constantly recurring in Greene's tales, and in his JAMES IV and FRIAR BACON : the violent veerings of Soliman, and his absolute recoil from a pledged course, are peculiarly characteristic of Greene. They are also partly paralleled in EDWARD III.

9. Soliman's description of Perseda's charms (IV, i, 67 sq.) might almost be said to be stamped with Greene's sign manual, so signally does it correspond with a dozen other descriptions of female beauty scattered through his works. Let it be compared with the following passages, cited from Dyce's edition—the Description of Silvestro's Lady, from the TRITAMERON OF LOVE (p. 285) ; Doron's Description of Samela, from MENA-PHON (p. 287) ; Menaphon's Eclogue (p. 289) ; Meli-certus' Eclogue (p. 290) ; Francesco's Ode, from NEVER TOO LATE (p. 296) ; the Canzone (p. 297) and Francesco's Roundelay (p. 298), from the same tale ; the Hexametra Alexis, from the MOURNING GARMENT (p. 305) ; the description of the Lady Mæsia and the lines translated from Guazzo (both p. 309) in the FAREWELL TO FOLLY ; the Shepherd's Ode (p. 313) from TULLY'S LOVE ; and finally Orlando's description of Angelica in ORLANDO FURIOSO (p. 102)—and it will hardly be disputed that the passage in question is

peculiarly in Greene's taste and manner. Until equally numerous and significant parallels from other authors be pointed out, the presumption of Greene's presence in Soliman stands provisionally justified. It may be added that this play too has a line of a type we have seen reason to ascribe to him :

> Witness the heavens of my unfeigned love,

and that the allusion to Sara in Edward III echoes one in the closing speech of Kate in the old Taming of a Shrew—a play in which there are several apparent traces of Greene, though the speech in question is difficult to assign.[1] Finally, Greene twice in his prose mentions the story of Erastus and Perseda (Card of Fancy and Mamillia : Works, ii, 61 ; iv, 53), and was evidently interested in it.

§ 6. Edward III (*Continued*)

Returning yet again to Edward III, and seeking to make a final decision, let us take up the difficult task of applying the higher tests. We may begin by considering some good examples of the style and substance of the second Act, for instance (1) those lines of the Countess :

> That love you offer me, you cannot give ;
> For Cæsar owes that tribute to his queen :
> That love you beg of me I cannot give ;
> For Sarah owes that duty to her lord.
> He that doth clip or counterfeit your stamp
> Shall die, my lord ; and will your sacred self
> Commit high treason against the King of Heaven,
> To stamp his image in forbidden metal,
> Forgetting your allegiance, and your oath ?
> In violating marriage' sacred law

---

[1] I have set forth in *The Shakespeare Canon*, Part II, pp. 135-143, the reasons for regarding this play as Marlowe's in respect of the blank-verse portions—a view reached through versification tests and style-test after other hypotheses had been tried. But the final speech of Kate does not suggest Marlowe either in style or in substance.

You break a greater honour than yourself.
To be a king, is of a younger house
Than to be married , your progenitor,
Sole-reigning Adam on the universe, .
By God was honour'd for a married man,
But not by him anointed for a king :

(2) those lines of her father, Warwick :

> *The poets write that great Achilles' spear*
> *Could heal the wound it made* ; the moral is,
> What mighty men misdo, they can amend.
> *The lion* doth become his bloody jaws
> And grace his foragement *by being mild*
> *When vassal fear lies trembling at his feet.*
> The king will in his glory hide thy shame ;
> And those that gaze on him to find out thee
> *Will lose their eyesight, looking in the sun.*
> What can one drop of poison harm the sea,
> Whose hugy vastures can digest the ill,
> And make it lose his operation ?

(3) those lines of the Countess's reply :

> No marvel, then, though the branches be infected
> When poison hath encompassed the root :
> No marvel though the leprous infant die,
> When the stern dam envenometh the dug.
> Why, then, give sin a passport to offend
> And youth the dangerous rein of liberty :
> Blot out the strict forbidding of the law ;
> And cancel every canon that prescribes
> A shame for shame, or penance for offence :

(4) those of Warwick's reply :

> Why, now thou speak'st as I would have thee speak,
> And mark how I unsay my words again.
> An honourable grave is more esteem'd
> Than the polluted closet of a king ;
> *The greater man, the greater is the thing,*
> *Be it good or bad, that he shall undertake.*
> An unreputed *mote, flying in the sun,*
> Presents a greater substance than it is :
> The freshest summer's day doth sooner taint
> The loathed carrion that it seems to kiss.
> Deep are the blows made with a mighty axe :

That sin doth ten times aggravate itself,
That is committed in a holy place :
An evil deed, done by authority,
Is sin, and subornation ; *deck an ape*
In tissue, and the beauty of the robe
Adds but the greater scorn unto the beast.[1]
A spacious field of reasons could I urge,
Between his glory, daughter, and thy shame :
That poison shows worst in a golden cup ;
Dark night seems darker by the lightning flash ;
Lilies that fester, smell far worse than weeds ;
And every glory that inclines to sin,
The shame is treble by the opposite.
So leave I, with my blessing in thy bosom ;
Which then convert to a most heavy curse,
When thou convert'st from honour's golden name
To the black faction of bed-blotting shame !

Here, on the one hand, we have to reckon (1) with the
marked iambic movement, rapid yet monotonous,
which is specially characteristic[2] of Greene's later
blank-verse, and (2) with the notable correspondences
between the italicised lines and passages above or
below cited from Greene's signed work ; and on the
other hand with the important facts (*a*) that the line
" Lilies that fester " occurs in Shakespeare's sonnet 94,
even as (*b*) " scarlet ornaments " (II, i, 10) occurs in
sonnet 142 ; and (*c*) that the phrase about the sun
kissing carrion is echoed in HAMLET. Though those
who insist on Shakespeare's habitual imitation of
Greene and Peele can argue nothing from such circumstances, they must be reckoned, on the principles
followed in this investigation, a ground of *prima facie*
presumption that he may have had a share in EDWARD
III. But the primary presumption must undergo
further tests.

The passages above cited are perhaps not the most
poetic parts of the Act, but they give a good idea of
its style and intellectual substance. Now, if we turn

---

[1] The lines italicised thus far have all been paralleled in the extracts from
Greene.
[2] See *The Shakespeare Canon*, Part II, pp. 14, 22-23. The iambic quality
is not so marked in the earlier plays as in *James IV*.

to the third and fourth Acts, which Fleay assigns to
another hand, we find, not indeed the same style
throughout, but speeches pretty much on a level with
those above cited, at least as to manner, rhythm, and
sententiousness.   For instance, the speech of the
second Frenchman in Act III, sc. ii :

> Ay, so the grasshopper doth spend the time
> In mirthful jollity 'till winter come ;
> And then too late he would redeem his time
> When frozen cold hath nipped his careless head.
> He, that no sooner will provide a cloak,
> Than when he sees it doth begin to rain,
> May, peradventure, for his negligence,
> Be throughly wash'd when he suspects it not.
> We, that have charge, and such a train as this,
> Must look in time to look for them and us,
> Lest when we would, we cannot be relieved ;

and the speech of Audley to the Prince in Act IV, sc. v :

> To die is all as common as to live ;
> We do pursue and hunt the time to die ;
> First bud we, then we blow, and after, seed ;
> Then, presently, we fall ; and, as a shade
> Follows the body, so we follow death.
> If then we hunt for death, why do we fear it ?
> If we [do] fear it, why do we follow it ?
> If we do fear, with fear we do but aid
> The thing we fear to seize on us the sooner ;
> If we fear not, then no resolved proffer
> Can overthrow the limit of our fate :
> For whether ripe or rotten, drop we shall,
> As we do draw the lottery of our doom.

Here we have the same repetitious brevity, the
same accumulation of sententious dicta, the same nervous yet monotonously iambic versification as in the
second Act.   It would be unwarrantable to say that
Marlowe *could not* have written thus ; but nowhere in
his known work does he ever do so.   If the same poetic
height be not maintained it is partly because the level
of the action falls from that of a highly individualised
situation to the ordinary drum-and-trumpet purport

of a chronicle-drama.   And there are other passages in
the fourth and fifth Acts which equally justify Tennyson's verdict that the hand which wrote the second
wrought in other parts of the play.   But for that
matter the hand of Marlowe, which penned the first
Act and probably drafted the second, is largely present
in the third and fourth Acts ; and the frequent vigour
of the writing is sufficient to make it intelligible that
some critics should ascribe the play as a whole to
Shakespeare.

Even if, however, we assign to a " superior " hand
more than the 'episode of the Countess of Salisbury, we
have still to settle whose the hand was.   Is there not,
let us ask, substantially the same touch and movement
here :

> Did we not taste the bitterness of war,
> How could we know the sweet effects of peace ?
> Did we not feel the nipping winter's frosts,
> How should we know the sweetness of the spring ?
> Should all things still remain in one estate ?
> Should not in greatest arts some scarres be found ?
> Were all upright and changed, what world were this ?
> A chaos, made of quiet, yet no world,
> Because the parts thereof did still accord ;
> This matter craves a variance, not a speech.
>
> Did each man know there were a storm at hand,
> Who would not clothe him well, to shun the wet ?
>
> The higher the tree the sooner is his fall.
>
> That tree is fertile which ne'er wanteth fruit ;
> That year is rare that ne'er feels winter's storms.
> What, do you think that if the tree do bend,
> It follows therefore that it needs must break ?
>
> A wresting power that makes a nose of wax
> Of grounded law ; a damned and subtle drift
> In all estates to climb by others' loss ;
> An eager thirst of wealth, forgetting truth :
> Might I ascend unto the highest states,
> And by descent discover every crime,
> My friends, I should lament, and you would grieve
> To see the hapless ruins of this realm.

These passages are all from Greene—the first two and the last from JAMES IV ; the others from the induction to ALPHONSUS OF ARRAGON. They indicate a quality in his work which we miss if we merely run through ORLANDO FURIOSO, taking it as typical. Greene developed in his few years of dramatic work as rapidly if not so powerfully as Marlowe ; he is truly " both as a dramatist and a novelist a man of many styles."[1] Already in the hastily scribbled ALPHONSUS we see his turn for sententious, Euphuistic sayings in nervous verse—a development of the same Euphuistic vein so constant in his prose, from MAMILLIA onwards ; and in JAMES IV we find him striking a psychological note never sounded by Peele or even by Marlowe in his signed work. In that play, too, and yet again in GEORGE-A-GREENE, we have a handling of the very problem dealt with in EDWARD III, the virtuous lady (a wife in GEORGE-A-GREENE ; an unmarried woman in JAMES IV) resisting the advances of the King ; and the appeal made by the character of Countess Ida in JAMES IV is doubled with that of the figure of Queen Dorothea, who is forgiving love personified, as Ida and the other Countess stand for sheer chastity. It has been very justly surmised[2] that in Queen Dorothea, Greene meant to picture his own wronged wife, Dorothea, on whose forgiveness he relied on his death-bed ; and critics who pay him small tribute are at one with those who prize him more highly in admitting that he was " the first of our playwrights to feel and express the charm of maiden modesty upon the public stage."[3] It is the old story : the blackguard poet had in him a seed of genius, which the stress of life at last ripened for a brief flowering.

[1] Professor Ward, *Hist. Eng. Dram. Lit.* i, 393.

[2] So Professor Brown and Professor Storojenko (Grosart's ed. of Greene, I, p. xxxix) ; Professor Courthope, *Hist. of Eng. Poetry*, ii, 396 ; and Fleay, *Biog. Chron.*

[3] J. A. Symonds, *Shakespeare's Predecessors*, 1884, p. 360. To the same effect Professor Ward, *Hist. of Eng. Dram, Lit.*, i, 218 ; Dr. Grosart, introd. to his ed. of Greene's Works, Huth Library, vol. i, p. xli ; and Professor Courthope, *Hist. of Eng. Poetry*, ii, 396. Professor Courthope remarks that Greene created " the prototype of Viola and Imogen."

This is indeed denied by some who in effect place him high ; for instance, Professor Courthope, who writes that Peele's " vast intellectual superiority to Greene " is seen when we compare DAVID AND BETH-SABE with the LOOKING-GLASS FOR LONDON. I am fain to regard this judgment as framed without due consideration of such a play as JAMES IV. The LOOKING-GLASS, though vigorous enough in its prose scenes (some of which appear to be Lodge's), is a moral chaos, a bad composite, doubling the defects of both Greene and Lodge, and as a serious whole worthless from every point of view. Its comic scenes are better than the poetic. But DAVID AND BETHSABE, though a coherent and careful piece of work, is finally worthless in another way. From first to last it is mere unctuous, intoned rhetoric ; and the ascription to it of " tenderness and poetic beauty " by Dyce must be pronounced a symptom of an obsolete conception of poetry. Greene's ORLANDO and ALPHONSUS consist for the most part of rhetoric of an even cheaper sort ; the product of a vagabond scribbler who took nothing seriously ; but in his later FRIAR BACON and GEORGE-A-GREENE he does succeed in what Peele (apart from his comic scenes, which are vigorous) never attains-to save once, and that faintly, in his slight OLD WIVES TALE. He succeeds, that is, in reproducing at times the vibration of living voices ; and in JAMES IV, working on an extravagant motive in an ill-balanced plot, he so wakes it as to arrest once for all the ear of every attentive reader.

The extravagance and the want of balance belong to his unhappy character : in every one of his tales we have the same effects of heedless invention, the same lack of moral sanity, the same strange perversity of action.[1] It is as if the boundless fluency which is his

[1] It is this that makes him the likeliest first draughtsman of *The Two Gentlemen of Verona*, *All's Well that Ends well*, and *Much Ado about Nothing*, in all of which we are invited to pardon the unpardonable, as so often in Greene's tales, and in his own life. And if there was, as I surmise, an intermediate play between Wheatstone's *Promos and Cassandra* and Shakespeare's *Measure for Measure*, it is not unlikely to have been drafted by Greene, for the same reason. But a certain falseness of drawing, a falsetto tone, a moral incoherence, mark in a less degree the romances of Lilly and Lodge. *Euphues* is fundamentally odious, despite the championship of Kingsley.

outstanding characteristic were let play at haphazard,
unruled by moral judgment or sense of fitness.   Yet,
though at a long interval of gift and in a much narrower
world, the congenital fluency of Greene evolved into a
faculty for a flight of intensive utterance, somewhat
as that of the poet of VENUS AND ADONIS deepened into
the incomparable power that pulses through his great
tragedies.   Through the darkened and degraded life
of the debauched hack there gleamed fitfully a vision
or memory of noble womanhood, which at last kindles
into the figure of Dorothea, a forecast of Imogen, one
of Shakespeare's women born out of due time.   It was
only in his dramatic poetry that he thus at last found
himself ; the women of his stories are at best Euphuistic
talking-machines of the egregious brood of Lilly, reciting
volubly through conventional masks.   Lodge in his
ROSALYNDE comes nearer to making real women than
does the other in his prose romances : it was the stage,
which he would fain have abjured, that put upon
Greene the stress needed to transform his lay figures
of the chaste woman and the wronged wife into human
beings, whom we can remember as we do those of flesh
and blood.   He thus typifies in his person the æsthetic
evolution through which the drama, under the pressures
alike of actors and of audiences, moved towards
naturalness at once in action and diction, and at length
forced a similar movement on the novel,[1] so long given
up to didactic tedium and puerile improbability.

   It is this measure of success in his signed work that
entitles us to pronounce Greene capable of writing
or re-writing even the best scenes of EDWARD III, where
the motives are so near akin to those employed in JAMES
IV.   A comparison of the dialogue between King
James and Countess Ida with that of Act II of EDWARD
III will further show the affinity between Greene's
work and what has been assigned to Shakespeare in the
play in question.   On the lower and duller plane,
further, of his prose romances, which have neither moral

---

[1] It was near the end of his life that Greene wrote his realistic stories of
vice and roguery, so much more arresting than his romances.

nor artistic merit of any high kind, though they exhibit him as the most facile of all the Euphuists, we find the situation recurring again and again, as in the Tale of Cosimo in the FAREWELL TO FOLLY, and in the Second Part of NEVER TOO LATE, where the virtuous Semiramis and Isabel respectively meet their lawless suitors—one a king, the other a magistrate—with appeals and arguments entirely in the vein of those of Ida and the Countess. In Greene's early MIRROR OF MODESTY, Susanna answers the Elders in the same style. And King Ninus, in the Tale of Cosimo, employs his secretary in his suit (with a difference) as does the king in EDWARD III. Yet again, the situation set up in FRIAR BACON AND FRIAR BUNGAY by Prince Edward's love for the rustic maiden Margaret, who has fallen in love with his deputy, Earl Lacy, is closely akin to that created in the play before us. In the former, Prince Edward finally addresses himself :

> So in *subduing* fancy's passion
> *Conquering* thyself, thou gett'st the richest spoil ;

in the latter the king asks himself :

> Shall I not
> *Master* this little mansion of myself ? . . . .
> I go to *conquer* kings ; and shall I then
> *Subdue* myself, and be my enemy's friend ?

and yet again in the fifth Act (i, 50 sq.), he proclaims :

> It shall be known that we
> As well can *master* our *affections*
> As *conquer* other by the dint of sword.

So, in JAMES IV (ii, 1), Ida says :

> The world may shame to him account
> To be a king of men and worldly pelf,
> Yet hath no power to rule and guide himself.

This idea, again, comes up frequently in Greene's prose, as in the FAREWELL TO FOLLY, where we have the remark (Works, ix, 299) that

> "Alexander made a *conquest* of his thoughts"

in a similar situation ; twice over in the ANATOMIE OF FORTUNE (1584) :—

> How dost thou think to *subdue France* which canst not rule thine own *affections* ?
> Art thou able to quell a kingdom which canst not quell thine own mind ?
> *Subdue* thy affections ; be *master* of thy mind
> (Works, iii, 193, 194) ;

again in the CARD OF FANCY (1587) :—

> Whc as yet hath not *subdued* the youthful conceits of fancy, nor made a *conquest* of his will by wit ;

again in the ORPHARION, where Marcion soliloquizes :

> Thou camst from Sicilia to be victor, and here thou art arrived and art vanquished [by love] ; *Affections* are harder to be suppressed than enemies to *subdue* ; (Works, xii, 87),

in the customary situation of unlawful and rejected love ; again, in a non-criminal situation, in PANDOSTO :

> *Subdue* then thy *affections* and cease to love her whom thou couldst not love unless blinded with too much love
> (Rep. in Sh. Lib. Pt. i, vol. iv, p. 55) ;

and yet again in TULLY'S LOVE (1589) :

> Intreats him to bridle *affection*, and to *make a conquest* of himself ; (Works, vii, 215).

We may argue, if we will, that Shakespeare could have copied this much-reiterated formula as he copied other current phrases ; but the reasonable literary inference is that the writer who employed it so often in his tales, and twice in signed plays, has penned it yet another time in EDWARD III. And in this connection, once more, in a speech of Soliman in SOLIMAN AND PERSEDA (IV, i, 144-6) :

> My word is passed, and I recall my passions.
> What should he do with crown and empery
> That cannot govern private fond *affections* ?

we see reason to ask whether Greene had not a hand in that play.

It is in any case clear that the situation of the virtuous woman, unlawfully solicited by a powerful lover, was constantly recurring to Greene's mind as a literary theme. Again and again he rings the changes on the situation dealt with in EDWARD III. The handling in that play is indeed by far the best ; but such a consummation, occurring near the close of his life, is quite in keeping with the development we have noted in his whole work. It is simply the best of many attempts. First, in the MIRROR OF MODESTY, he elaborates the story of Susanna and the Elders. In the ORPHARION, Marcion woos Argentina, queen of the defeated Philomenes, very much as Edward does the Countess; and she too saves herself by a stratagem. In the same fashion the Burgomaster seeks to seduce Isabel in NEVER TOO LATE. In other tales there arises the device of the intermediary, used also in JAMES IV. In PHILOMELA, the suspicious husband urges his friend to make love to his wife, and the friend employs the arguments of the Burgomaster ; in the tale of Cosimo, the king attempts to make the husband, Mænon, persuade the wife to yield to his purpose, and, setting no bounds to his passion, slays him when he refuses ; in EDWARD III, the king orders the father, Warwick, to command his daughter to yield ; and Warwick, revolting from the order, goes through the form of obeying it. In JAMES IV, the villain Ateukin fans James's passion and seeks to secure his end for him. Here again the dialogue has some of the nervous and incisive quality met with in the second Act of EDWARD III, with the same monotony of verse :

> *Ateukin.*—These lets are but as *motes against the sun*
> Yet not so great ; like dust before the wind
> Yet not so light. Tut, *pacify your grace* :
> You have the sword and sceptre in your hand ;
> You are a king, the state depends on you ;
> Your will is law. Say that the case were mine,
> Were she my sister whom your highness loves,

She should consent, for that our lives, our goods,
Depend on you : and if your queen repine,
Although my nature cannot brook of blood,
And scholars grieve to hear of murtherous deeds—
But if the lamb should *let* the lion's way
By my advice the lamb should lose her life.

Here the use of the noun " lets," very rare in Shakespeare, points back to EDWARD III, where it occurs several times ; and " motes against the sun " closely echoes the " mote flying in the sun " in that play. " Pacify your Grace " recalls the " pacify yourself " in the first line of Act v of EDWARD III, though that is a weak clue. And again, in the dialogue between Dorothea and Douglas, we have a quality of style and substance which would probably have passed unchallenged as " Shakespearean " had it been found in an early Shakespearean play ; though the monotony of the iambic movement should have barred the assumption :

Dorothea.—Ah, father, are you so estranged from love,
From due allegiance to your prince and land,
To leave your king when most he needs your help ?
The thrifty husbandmen are never wont,
That see their lands unfruitful, to forsake them ;
But when the mould is barren and unapt,
They toil, they plough, and make the fallow fat :
The pilot in the dangerous seas is known :
In calmer waves the silly sailor strives [? serves].
Are you not members, lords of commonweal,
And can your head, your dear anointed king,
Default, ye lords, except yourselves do fail ?
Oh stay your steps, return and counsel him.

Douglas.—Men seek not moss upon a rolling stone,
Or water from the sieve, or fire from ice,
Or comfort from a reckless monarch's hands.
Madam, he sets us light that serv'd in court,
In place of credit, in his father's days.
If we but enter presence of his grace,
Our payment is a frown, a scoff, a frump ;
Whilst flattering Gnatho pranks it by his side,
Soothing the careless king in his misdeeds ;
And if your grace consider your estate
His life should urge you too, if all be true . . .

Dorothea.—. . . . Should we disdain our vines because they sprout
Before their time ? or young men if they strain
Beyond their reach ?   No, vines that bloom and spread
Do promise fruits, and young men that are wild
In age grow wise.

Some of Ida's lines, though probably written earlier
and in a less inspired mood, might form part of a speech
of the Countess ; for instance :

O, how he talks, as if he should not die !
As if that God in justice once could wink
Upon that fault I am ashamed to think !

Some of her dialogue with Eustace, again, may compare
with the rhymed lines at the end of the first Act of
EDWARD III :

Ida.—Good sir, look on : how like you this compact ?

Eust.—Methinks in this I see true love in act :
The woodbines with their leaves do sweetly spread ;
The roses blushing prank them in their red ;
No flower but boasts the beauties of the spring ;
This bird hath life indeed, if it could sing.

And parts of her dialogue with her mother (II, i) would
have passed very well with the rest of the rhymed
dialogue, had they been found there :

Might you have wealth and fortune's richest store ?

Ida.—Yet would I, might I choose, be honest-poor ;
For she that sits at fortune's feet a-low
Is sure she shall not taste a further woe,
But those that prank on top of Fortune's ball
Still fear a change, and, fearing, catch a fall . . .
Madam, by right this world I may compare
Unto my work, wherein with heedful care
The heavenly workman plants with curious hand,
As I with needle draw each thing on land,
Even as he list ; some men, like to the rose
Are fashion'd fresh ; some in their stalks do close,
And, born, do sudden die ; some are but weeds,
And yet from them a secret good proceeds ;

I with my needle, if I please, may blot
The fairest rose within my cambric plot ;
God with a beck can change each worldly thing,
The poor to rich, the beggar to the king,
What then hath man wherein he well may boast,
Since by a beck he lives, a lour is lost ?

If it be still impossible for some, after reading such work of Greene's later years, to be quite sure that the second Act of EDWARD III is *not* the young Shakespeare's, they must admit that, if it be his, Shakespeare was learning to speak with Greene's voice, cadence, and thought. Apart from this issue, it has been said, not untruly, though not with complete truth, by the writer who first did critical justice to the lesser dramatist's faculty, that " In style Greene is father of Shakespeare."[1] But Shakespeare's style is really not at any stage the style of Greene ; and much of the ground for connecting them is probably a matter of survivals of Greene in the early comedies, as in THE TWO GENTLEMEN. On the other hand, there are many inferiorities even in the second Act of EDWARD III which distinctly recall Greene, and do not at all suggest Shakespeare. Let us take for instance, in EDWARD III, one of two groups of repetitive lines, and compare it with a group in JAMES IV, one in FRIAR BACON, and one in the early LOCRINE. The first runs :

And let me have her liken'd to the sun ;
Say, she hath thrice more splendour than the sun,
That her perfection emulates the sun,
That she breeds sweets as plenteous as the sun,
That she doth thaw cold winter like the sun,
That she doth cheer fresh summer like the sun,
That she doth dazzle gazers like the sun,
And, in this application to the sun,
Bid her be free and general as the sun.

[1] Professor J. M. Brown, art. " An Early Rival of Shakespeare " in the *New Zealand Magazine*, No. 6, April 1877, p. 101, quoted by Grosart, as cited. It may be worth noting that Greene's influence is also very apparent in Dekker's early play, *The Shoemaker's Holiday*, which imitates his diction, his rhythms, and his choice of theme. The introduction of working-folk tells of *George-a-Greene*.

That in JAMES IV is as follows .—

> What, murder of my queen ?
> Yet to enjoy my love what [? who] is my queen ?
> O, but my vow and promise to my queen !
> Ay, but my hope to gain a fairer queen !

That in FRIAR BACON (Dyce, p. 173) runs :—

> But now the braves of Bacon have an end ;
> Europe's conceit of Bacon hath an end ;
> His seven years' practice sorteth to an end ;
> And villain, sith my glory hath an end,
> I will appoint thee to some fatal end.

That in LOCRINE (v, ii) is as follows :

> For Locrine hath forsaken Guendolen ;
> Behold the heavens do wail for Guendolen,
> The shining sun doth blush for Guendolen,
> The liquid air doth weep for Guendolen,
> The very ground doth groan for Guendolen,
> Ay, they are milder than the Britain king,
> For he rejecteth luckless Guendolen.

Effects of this kind Shakespeare reserves for a humorous situation in comedy,[1] where they had their contemporary effect from their amusing contrast with heroics in the same mould ; never once does he employ them in a quite serious scene. A group of them in the TWO GENTLEMEN[2] points to another hand. They belong to the school of his predecessors ; and the presumption here once more is that in EDWARD III, Act II, we are reading Greene. I recall no such speech in Marlowe. As for the parallels in the Sonnets, they must on this view be regarded as real echoes by the young Shakespeare of lines current on the stage ; and when we find in Greene's prose the phrases :

> "Let lilies wither on the stalk . . . fair but unsavoury"
> *Tully's Love :* Works, vii, 165,

---

[1] *Merchant of Venice*, v, 193-7.
[2] Act II, sc. vi, 1-3. This kind of thing, once more, goes to indentify Greene as the draftsman of *The Two Gentlemen*.

and

"Like the violets in America, which in summer yield an
odoriferous smell and in winter a most pestilent savour "
(*Card of Fancy* ; Works, iv, 26) ;

and again in his verse the lines :

> The fairest flower, nipt with the winter's frost,
> In show seems worser than the basest weed
> (Verses in *Alcida* : Dyce, p. 319, col. 2),

there is no difficulty about assigning the line on lilies
and weeds to him.

Professor Quincy Adams[1] inclines to take it for
granted, nevertheless, that the line in the play is
borrowed from the sonnet. " It seems likely," he
writes, " that this unknown writer was familiar with
Shakespeare's cycle in a manuscript copy ; and we are
informed in 1598 that such a manuscript copy was well
known among the poet's friends." We really are not :
Meres merely specifies " sonnets among his private
friends " ; but even if they were then collected in one
manuscript it would not prove that there was a " cycle,"
reaching to Sonnets 94 and 142, in 1593. If, however,
there is any validity in all the fore-cited mass of
parallels from Greene, he had wrought the crowning
revision of the play in or before 1592, when the " cycle "
was probably not begun.[2] But even apart from dates,

---

[1] *Life of Shakespeare*, p. 164.

[2] Professor Adams (p. 164, *note*) seems to argue for an early dating of the
whole body of the Sonnets, objecting to the view that Sonnet 107 refers to
the death of Elizabeth. " It is not at all clear," he writes, " that the allusion
is to the death of the Queen (neither ' endure ' nor ' eclipse ' seems appropriate) rather than to *some actual eclipse of the moon*." He then proceeds to
cite from Mrs. Stopes a letter of 1595 in which a court personage is referred
to as the moon. This is a curious way of supporting the view that the Sonnet
alludes to an actual eclipse. In point of fact " mortal moon " is as appropriate
a designation for Elizabeth, the " Cynthia " of her poets, as it would be
absurd for the actual moon. " Hath her eclipse endured " is a perfectly
likely figure for the death of the Queen. To those who, with Dowden and
Mr. Thomas Tyler, argue that the moon in the sonnet is understood to come
out as bright as before, it seems necessary to point out that Elizabeth was
regarded as an immortal soul like other believers in the Christian religion.
The idea would be that, eclipsed as a mortal, she went to heaven to a future
life.

the balance of literary inference is heavily against the assumption that the play borrows from the sonnets. Mr. Moore Smith, in his introduction,[1] justly assents to Mr. Tyler's remark that in Sonnet 94 the " Lilies " line " is forced, as though to bring in a rhyme to the second ; " and adds his own opinion that " in the 142nd Sonnet the phrase ' scarlet ornaments ' is far less natural than in its place in EDWARD III." It must be a determined traditionism that contests the verdict in either case ; and when it is noted that the line :

> Lilies are fair in show but foul in smell

occurs in Lodge's ROSALYNDE,[2] published in 1592, the attempt to date the play after the sonnet may be regarded as desperate. In view of the industry expended in applying the Imitation Theory to so many instances in which the phrases and styles of other writers are reproduced in the Shakespeare plays, the reluctance to see in the Sonnets two echoes of EDWARD III is a little anomalous. It seems a simple matter to recognise that the young poet was interested in the play, which was acquired by his company in 1594.

§ 7. THE VERSIFICATION OF " EDWARD III "

It may be expedient at this point to note, with special reference to the Countess scenes in EDWARD III, the bearing of that versification test which has so often been incidentally mentioned in our survey, and which will be applied to TITUS in a later chapter. If indeed there had been any general resort to that test in the past, it might have made unnecessary the foregoing discussion of vocabulary and phraseology. But though Dyce remarked of Greene that " his blank-verse is so

---

[1] *Edward III*, Temple ed. pref. p. xix.
[2] Sh. Lib. rep. p. 18. This, it will be observed, is a less close parallel, apart from the word " lilies," than the two cited from Greene. But Greene, who would certainly read *Rosalynde*, might have taken thence the special application of his trope to lilies.

monotonous as to pall upon the ear,"[1] neither he nor
any other prominent critic has sought to reduce such
impressions to exactitude for use as clues to authorship.
For that matter, little had been done in the last century
even with the tests we have been considering. But
when these have been followed up, it may be that the
approach from the side of versification will avail in some
degree to dissipate that presupposition as to Shakespeare's presence in EDWARD III which has so· far
occupied us, and which seems to be in large part
independent of any study of phraseology. There is
reason to think, in fact, that it proceeds upon an
unanalysed reminiscence of the *versification* of one
disputable Shakespeare play in particular.

It is quite evident that there is *some* common ground
in men's impressions of the Shakespeare plays and in
those set up by the Countess scenes in EDWARD III.
Not only do we have Tennyson chiming with such
virtuosi as Ward and Fleay ; not only do we have
Mr. William Archer declaring that without any previous
knowledge of the play he instantly and confidently
recognised in those scenes, on a mere hearing, the very
tones of Shakespeare ;[2] but we find Swinburne, even in
the process of contemptuously repelling the ascription
of any part of the play to Shakespeare, conceding
repeatedly that there are real resemblances between
lines or passages, both rhymed and unrhymed, and the
early work of Shakespeare. He grudgingly admits, in
fact, that there is a general resemblance of style ;
though he is constantly seeking to disparage the work
in EDWARD III even where he has to concede to it some
merit. In the face of all this, there is clearly something
to explain.

Swinburne, of course, never explains it, save in his
usual way of dialectic, by tumid rhetoric about the
facility with which " poeticules " can imitate masters.
Few critics with so much zest of appreciation and
palate for qualities have so often darkened counsel by

[1] Account of Greene in 1-vol. ed. of Greene and Peele, p. 34.
[2] *The Theatrical World of 1897*, 1898, p. 231.

sheer surrender to afflatus where there is needed a
patient and vigilant psychological analysis. Swinburne obliviously takes it for granted that the author
of the Countess scenes is *following* Shakespeare, though
he has more than once inconsequently noted archaisms
in the text which point to the pre-Shakespeareans.   In
the extremity of his *parti pris*, he actually alleges that
the line on festering lilies is ill-placed in the play and
well-placed in the sonnet, when every judicial reader
will confess, with Mr. Tyler and Mr. Moore Smith, that
it is the other way about.   If only the poet had
bethought him to try the hypothesis that Shakespeare
might echo in his Sonnets a line or two from a play that
had interested him, he might have seen his way to a
solution that would establish itself on a better basis than
declamation.

The great defect in his handling of all such problems,
however, is that he never analyses his impressions of
versification.   Always he relies on his unanalysed
impression, and catches either at mere points of phrase
or at further impressions of *dramatic* quality to decide
what ought to be a question of verse-manner.   Thus
we shall find him ascribing ARDEN OF FEVERSHAM to
Shakespeare on the score of an impression of dramatic
power and originality, in entire disregard of the vital
question of versification.   Mr. Archer, rightly applying
that test to ARDEN, besides stressing the difference in
psychology, justly decides[1] that Shakespeare had
nothing to do with it.   On the other hand, sensing in
EDWARD III those vaguely remembered similarities
of manner which swayed the judgments of Tennyson
and the rest, and which are unwillingly admitted by
Swinburne, he forthwith decides that " Shakespeare
it must be " ; and comes instantly to the conclusion
that if such clues as the " lilies " line are not to settle
the matter " we must abandon all arguments based upon
style."[2]

The infirmity of all such reasoning comes freshly into

---

[1] Vol. cited, pp. 234-5,
[2] *Id*. p. 232,

view when we proceed to the necessary business of noting the versification. What Swinburne must have felt, but could not pause to ascertain, is that much of the versification of the Countess scenes accords closely with that of THE TWO GENTLEMEN OF VERONA. There, and almost there only, in the early plays, do we find the, so to speak, vivacious monotony of line-ended iambics which so strongly marks the verse of the Countess scenes, rhymed and unrhymed. The line-ended stamp, indeed, is upon much else of the early work—notably in the COMEDY OF ERRORS and RICHARD II ; but there the iambic movement is not the same. And the proof at once of the non-Shakespearean craftsmanship of the EDWARD III work, and of its real composite authorship, lies in the combination of the line-ended norm with the marked iambic proclivity which pervades the verse of Greene, rhymed and unrhymed.

Let the reader of Swinburne's Appendix, and of the sixth section of the present chapter, note attentively the formation of the great majority of the lines quoted. He will find an almost invariable ending of the clause with the line, and even where, as occasionally happens, the clause runs beyond the line, a still marked line-ending of the rhythm. And, with equal regularity, he will find the verse movement in general rigidly iambic. And now the issue may be put in a nutshell : Does the young Shakespeare ever write, habitually and helplessly, in this line-ended and monotonously iambic fashion ?

The answer is : If he wrote the TWO GENTLEMEN, Yes ! But if we form our judgment of him from the DREAM, from the opening scene of the ERRORS, and from LOVE'S LABOUR'S LOST, it must be emphatically No ! Between the verse-manner of nine-tenths of the GENTLEMEN and that of the DREAM, there is a difference that cannot well be exaggerated, a difference so great that, if the plays had not been assigned by the publishers to the same hand, no vigilant critic, with an ear for verse, would have thought of so assigning them. The difference is as that between the gait of different men, different animals, the flight of different birds. To bring the matter to a strictly symbolic shape, the verse-manners may be baldly reduced to these cadence-forms :—

    a. Ĭ gō tŏ gēt thĕ gōld Ĭ pūt ăwāy,
        Ănd lāy ĭt sāfelў ūnder lōck ănd kēy,
        Fŏr lífe ĭs nāught wĭthōut thĕ prēcĭŏus mētăl.
(Movement of most lines in the *Gentlemen* and the Countess
                        scenes.—Greenean.)
    b. Wĭth thĕ lōng swīng ŏf thĭs făcīlĭtў.
(This and those following are among the movements found
many times over in the *Dream* and the *Labour*.—Shakespearean.)
    c. Cōme tŏ thĕ ārtĭstrў ŏf s̄yllăblĕs,
    d. Tŏmōrrŏw | nĕar thĕ mĭddlĕ būrnĭng nōon.
    e. Ĭn vērse thăt līngĕrs tŏ thĕ līstĕnĭng ēar.
    f. Nēvĕr ăn īnstănt dŏes thĕ rhȳthm cēase.
    g. Mūsĭc ănd mēanĭng jōinĭng ĭn thĕ sēnse.
    h. Cōme tŏ thĕ vītăl qūestiŏn : strīke thĕ nōte.
    i. Āftĕr thĕ dāy, bĕ sūre, āll wĭll bĕ wēll.
    j. Tŏ thĕ pōōr mēasŭre ŏf ă shākĕn strīng.
    k. Thĕ gōōd mān nēvĕr ŏn thĕ bād rĕlīes.
    l. Ĭn lēndĭng gōōd thīngs fŏr thĕ gāin ŏf bād.
    m. Ōnlў thĕ gōōd hēart ĭs̄ thĕ mōnĭtŏr.
    n. Ĭn thĕ fūll scōpe ŏf mēdĭōcrĭtў.
    o. Thĕ slōw dāy sīnks, thĕ nīght ĭs fāllĭng fāst.

We might go on thus for many lines. The verse rhythm of even the young Shakespeare, in work which all admit to be his, varies to the utmost possibility of the line ; and, in addition, the sense frequently runs beyond the line, as here :

> Now, fair Hippolyta, our nuptial hour
> Draws on apace : four happy days bring in
> Another moon ; but, O, methinks how slow
> This old moon wanes.
>   (First lines of *Dream.*)

Of such free running-on of the sense there is no instance in the Countess scenes : the line is almost always a separate whole ; and it goes mainly to one quick iambic tune, which possesses the brain of the author—or one of the authors—so that he never diverges save, as it were, by accident. Finding the same tune through nine-tenths of the TWO GENTLEMEN, we may well surmise that he who wrote that wrote the bulk of the Countess scenes. But unless we are to commit ourselves to the irrational belief that Shakespeare at the same period wrote alternately as a man possessed by one monotonous verse tune and as a born master of rhythm, achieving without effort the widest variety ever yet attained, we must conclude that he wrote neither the TWO GENTLEMEN nor the Countess scenes.

Any one can test the matter for himself. I have set against the mechanical trip of the Greenean iambic, which pervades the Countess scenes, fourteen samples all framed from a handful of some two dozen lines, mostly taken in sets from the DREAM and the LABOUR. It would be easy to produce as many more differing samples from these plays. I have purposely given, instead of actual Shakespearean lines, sets of words that only in rhythm equate with actual lines, so that there may be no risk of deflecting judgment by force of poetic values. Let the reader now go for himself to the text, and carefully scan the first ten lines of Titania's speech, beginning:

These are the forgeries of jealousy;

and he will find that no two lines have the same pulsation. We have in succession ten different variants from the iambic norm. The balance of presumption against identity of hand in the endlessly varied and in the nearly unvarying movement is obviously overwhelming; and when to that conclusion is added the fact that the actual diction and ideation of Greene are to be traced at fifty points alike in the GENTLEMEN and the anonymous play, the case is tolerably complete. Swinburne's heedless solution of an unknown author is to be dismissed as an unnecessary evasion of the problem; and Mr. Archer's argument from identities of phrase is far outweighed by the much larger mass of parallels which identify Greene. In fact, the two echoes from the play in the Sonnets are enough in themselves to prove that what has happened is not repetition but quotation.

Let it be added, however, that inasmuch as there *are* distinct differences of verse-movement in the Countess scenes, it is to be inferred that there are differences of hand. The iambic tune occurs in about 75 per cent of the lines : in the opening speech of Act II there are but three trochaic first feet in the 24 lines ; and we sometimes have the sheer iambic run for ten or a dozen or more lines together, *e.g.*, II, i, 16-33, 354-366. Nor does it follow that where that absolute monotony is departed from, the hand is different. Such a run of repetitive lines as that of 155-163, though they begin on trochees, yields only a new monotony, and may very well be from the same hand that penned the repetitive run of lines 16 to 33. The chance of beginning five lines with " that " tells of no gain of variety in rhythm. On the other hand, however, there are not only clues of phrase and style to Marlowe, suggesting the inference that, as planner of the play, he may have drafted this scene, but variations of the iambic rhythm in his direction—variations which strengthen the tune, but leave it end-stopped. *That* feature is all-pervading : not once in the whole Act does there occur such a prehensile movement as meets us in the second speech of the COMEDY OF ERRORS, surely one of the very earliest samples of Shakespeare's blank-verse, since it occurs in a fairly long scene almost devoid of double-endings. There, at his outset, we have the endless variation of rhythm to which Marlowe and Greene at their best only make an approach.

Greene, it is true, is not invariable in his iambic monotony in his signed work. In JAMES IV, where he approximates to the energy he attains in his part of EDWARD III, there are deviations, chiefly in first feet, from the iambic tune. But the mere relief of trochaic beginnings does not alter the iambic movement of the whole ; and when we find in the Countess scenes an appreciable number of lines in which the iambic norm is radically changed within the line by a more vigorous rhythm, arising out of a more powerful diction, we must in loyal induction confess the probability that Marlowe's draft is the source.

As to Mr. Archer's rash verdict that " if this be not Shakespeare's work, all I can say is that some nameless poet has out-Shakespeared Shakespeare "—a verdict to which, I surmise, he would not now stand without reservation—it may suffice to say that while there is assuredly no transcending of Shakespeare here, the combination of Marlowe and Greene at their best might well make a strong poetic and dramatic impression ; while Mr. Moore Smith's conclusion that the work is " at least in Shakespeare's manner " is to be met by the whole argument against Shakespeare's authorship of the Two GENTLEMEN. If that holds good, there is no " Shakespeare manner " in EDWARD III.

§ 8. SUMMARY

As the case now stands, we are entitled, I think, to say that the evidence for Greene's presence in EDWARD III is overwhelming, as regards the portion of the play which Fleay assigns to Shakespeare. Marlowe is to be recognised as opening and planning the whole, since his hand is to be seen in the third and fourth Acts as well as in the first. Kyd enters in certain scenes ; and Peele, as aforesaid, on a small scale. But Greene, as we have seen, has the salient share. Mr. Moore-Smith, in the preface to his very careful edition (1897), observes that " Anyone who reads Lodge after EDWARD III will, of course, finds points of resemblance ; he will find them, though perhaps fewer of them, if he reads Greene." The latter part of this judgment will perhaps not now be persisted in. The number of parallels to Greene, as we have seen, is very great : to Lodge, there are only a few ;[1] one of which we have just noted in connection with the line on " Lilies that fester." Mr. Moore Smith cites only one : " milk-

---

[1] The matter is further discussed in the next chapter.

white pledge of wisdom " [=hair] in the WOUNDS of CIVIL WAR (l. 37) suggesting " milk-white messengers of time " in EDWARD III (IV, iv, 125). But " milk-white " is a common epithet of the Marlowe school, and is frequent in Greene :—

> The milk-white path
> That leads unto the senate-house of Mars.
> > *Orlando Furioso*, Dyce, p. 102*b*.
> Her face silvered like that milk-white shape
> That Jove came dancing in to Semele.
> > *Id*. p. 104.
> And I, in touching of her milk-white mould.
> > *James IV*, IV, v, near end.
> The milk-white galaxia of her brow.
> > Francesco's Roundelay, in *Never Too Late*.

And Marlowe, besides using " milk-white " many times, has

> Their hair as white as milk and soft as down.
> > 2 *Tamb*. i, 3.

Now, Lodge in the WOUNDS expressly copies Marlowe (I TAMB., i, 2) in the lines (207-8) :

> And know these hairs that dangle down my face,
> In brightness like the silver Rodope ;

and as Lodge unquestionably imitated Greene a hundred times, the balance of presumption is in favour of ascribing the " milk-white " figure in EDWARD III to Greene or Marlowe, and reckoning Lodge's use an echo. Taking the Countess episode as it stands to be one of Greene's latest pieces of dramatic work, we are bound to date the original play earlier ; and it is difficult to assent to Fleay's dating of the WOUNDS as early as 1587. Even if, however, we assume that Lodge's play had the priority, we should rather infer that Greene in this instance had imitated Lodge than assign our play, with its mass of Greenean details, to the latter. Lodge, it is true, recurs to " milk-white hair " in the WOUNDS (l. 443), but he also recurs to " silver " ; and there is no good warrant for ascribing to him originality in one case more than in the other. The term " milk-white " for hair, in any case, is old, and presumably common. " His head was white as milk " occurs in Tarleton's TALE OF THE TWO LOVERS OF PISA.[1] And Peele more than once writes of " the milk-white way."

It may be worth while to note, in this connection, that the parallels of phrase and vocabulary between EDWARD III and some of the plays of Heywood must be set down to imitations by the last-named author. They include " the iron pen of Fate " (LOVE'S MISTRESS : Pearson's Heywood, v, 129 : *cf.* E.III, III, iv, 128) ; " text upon thy breast " (IRON AGE : Pearson, III, 321 : *cf.* E.III, last cit. 129) ; " barricadoed " (GOLDEN AGE ; P.III, 58 : *cf.* " barricadoe's open front " E.III, v, i, 134) ; and his frequent " rarieties " also suggests the influence of this play. And though these echoes do not all point to Greene's work, it is substantially to that work that the main impression made by the play is due. If, as is here argued, the Countess episode as it stands is Greene's recast of a Marlowe draft, it is quite the best thing he ever did ; and when we come to metrical tests we find that its versification, in respect of double-endings, marks it as belonging to his last years, probably to 1591-2.

[1] In *Newes out of Purgatorie*, 1590. Rep. in Sh. Lib. Ft. I, vol. iii, p. 62.

CHAPTER IX

The Unsigned Work of Marlowe, Kyd, and Lodge

In the foregoing chapters we have seen reason to concur in ascriptions to Marlowe of larger or smaller shares in plays which do not bear his name ; and in The Canon of Shakespeare I have claimed his origination for more of the Folio plays than most readers will be at all willing to give up to him. Leaving those controverted issues out of the present survey, I will merely remind the reader that if the Comedy of Errors be dated, as is fitting, in 1591 and still assigned wholly to Shakespeare, it makes him at that date multiply double-endings up to percentages immensely in excess of any attained in his unchallenged plays till years later, and, further, makes him copy Marlowe's versification as it were hypnotically in a play where he preludes with a scene absolutely in his own early verse manner, with only 2 per cent. of double-endings.

The " orthodox " choice, then, lies between that staggering conception and the no less staggering proposition of Simpson, adopted by Professor Quincy Adams, that the young poet wrote the Errors at Stratford, before coming to London. On the one hand we have the Imitation Theory in almost its crudest form (the crudest being that which represents the young Master as impartially and industriously imitating four different styles in Titus) : on the other the no less indigestible proposition that he independently invented Marlowe's versification before Marlowe. In face of these prodigies of æsthetic speculation, it will perhaps be found a comparatively plausible course to accept at least tentatively the view that Marlowe is the main if not the sole author of the verse-portions of the old TAMING OF A SHREW, and to contemplate the possibility of his having a hand in yet other plays outside the Folio ; whereafter the reconsideration of the Canon may be gone about in a more illuminated atmosphere.

§ 1. EDWARD III

One of the plays held to be largely assignable to Marlowe, as we have seen, is EDWARD III, which in the first edition of this work was mistakenly denied him. A longer and closer study of Marlowe leads to the conviction that he is the primary author ; and there can at least be no à priori objection to the view that he would be about as readily interested in the figure of Edward III as in that of his luckless father. The presumption is, indeed, that he would handle the hero-King first, and the failing King afterwards, when he awoke to the dramatic possibilities of such presentments.

As against Swinburne's vociferous dismissal of the thesis of Marlowe's presence in Act I of our play, above considered, it may suffice to point (*a*) to the verse-movement, which is indistinguishable from that of the bulk of EDWARD II, with which it is properly to be compared ; and (*b*) to the diction. That has from the outset the forthright vigour which marks Marlowe off from his lesser contemporaries, as well as the dramatic note which he reached after TAMBURLAINE. At the tenth line we come upon one of his simpler devices of exposition :

K. Ed.—But was thy mother sister unto those ?
Art.—She was, my lord . . . .

With which compare :

Kent.— . . . But hath thy potion wrought so happily ?
Y. Mor.—It hath, my lord . . . ;
Edward II, IV, i, 13.
Bar.—The ships are safe, thou sayest, and richly fraught ?
Merch.—They are.
Jew of Malta, I, i.

We are thus at once prepared to note the small as well as the large correspondencies in technique in HENRY V, which, whether or not we recognise it as of Marlowe's origination, is beyond question the " twin " play of EDWARD III. The student may fitly ask himself whether Marlowe or Shakespeare was the likelier to put in the first scene of the former play (I, i, 93) :—

> *Cant.*— . . . Is it four o'clock ?
> *Ely.*—It is.

In a word, the preliminary exposition of HENRY V, if it be of Shakespeare's original composition, is a " slavish " imitation of that of EDWARD III.

Marlowe's hand is further to be traced in the opening of our play by (*a*) such a phrase as " the fragrant garden of her womb," which points to and ante-dates RICHARD III, IV, iv, 223-4—if we can be sure that Marlowe penned that ; and (*b*) " brittle sand," which parallels " brittle glass " in RICHARD III, IV, ii, 62 ; (*c*) " my *tongue* thus *lavish* in report "—where the noun and adjective form a common Marlowism ; (*d*) " golden wings of fame " ; and (*e*) the line :—

> Even to the bottom of thy master's throat—

another Marlowism, echoed repeatedly in RICHARD II[1].

Later in the play, we can emend a line by referring back to Marlowe. It reads (III, v, 58) :

> The dismal charge of trumpets loud retreat.

Mr. Moore Smith in his edition asks, " Is the word a mistake for *clang* or *clangour* ? And, further, is *loud* for *sound* . . . ? " The first word is obviously a mistake for *clange*, which we find in Marlowe (I TAMB., IV, i, I, ed. Tucker-Brooke) and the second emendation proposed is clearly right, so that we get the line :

> The dismal clange of trumpets sound retreat.

---

[1] Refs. in *The Shakespeare Canon*, Part II, pp. 54, 55, 60.

Other Marlowe clues are " airy fowl " (IV, iii, 77) and
" airy floor of heaven " (IV, v, 33), recalling " airy
wheels " [of Hebe] (DIDO, I, i) and " airy creatures "
(*Id*. iv, ii) ; " hushed and still " (IV, v, 3, suggesting
" whist and still " in HERO AND LEANDER, i, 346) ; and
" ragged heaps of stones " (V, i, 204), pointing to
" ragged stony walls " (EDWARD II, III, iii). But much
more significant is such an echo as :—

> By land, with Xerxes we compare of strength,
> Whose soldiers drank up rivers in their thirst.
> > *Edward III*, VII, i, 57 ;
> The host of Xerxes, which by fame is said
> To have drank the mighty Parthian Araris.
> > I *Tamb.*, II, iii.[1]

To call such passages " impotent imitations " is as idle
as to set down to imitation the abundant Marlowese
verse in the old SHREW, where the actual repetitions
from Marlowe plays are only items in a mass of equally
Marlovian matter. The lines last cited from EDWARD
III are as exactly in Marlowe's style and versification
as the thought is that of the lines from TAMBURLAINE.
But perhaps the most decisive parallel is one which
occurs in the portion of the play which we have assigned
to Greene as reviser. The passage (II, ii, 114-117) :

> The sin is more to hack and hew poor men
> Than to embrace in an unlawful bed
> The register of all rarieties[2]
> Since leathern Adam till this youngest hour,

points definitely back to THE JEW (I, ii) :—

> Why, I esteem the injury far less
> To take the lives of miserable men
> Than be the causes of their misery.

[1] Compare :
> Think them in number yet sufficient
> To drink the river Nile or Euphrates.
> > 2 *Tamb.* III, i.

[2] Mr. Moore Smith is certainly right in restoring this reading. The word
occurs at least thrice in Heywood, as well as in the *Tempest* (II, i, 58, 60—
Folio) where the spelling *rarieties* ought to be retained. The word was pronounced as a quadrisyllable.

This is not a duplication of thought : it is, however, an unmistakable duplication of voice and manner. And here again it is idle to suggest imitation, for the EDWARD passage is better than the other. It is extremely improbable that Greene (to say nothing of Peele, who is impossible) could improve on Marlowe at such a point ; and we must take this passage, with some others, as definitely proving that Greene's revision proceeded on an original scene by Marlowe, which Greene has greatly expanded.

The interesting question arises, whether Marlowe began the rhyming at the end of Act I of our play. I have elsewhere claimed that he wrote the Talbot scenes in I HENRY VI ; and if we could find him in the rhymed work here it would complete the cancelment of Swinburne's mistaken inference that by his allusion to the " jigging vein of rhyming mother wits " in the prologue to TAMBURLAINE he banned the rhymed couplet. But, as we have seen, though " ragged walls " (I, ii, 157) here suggests Marlowe, the earlier rhymed lines seem to point definitely to Greene ; and Marlowe's readiness to use rhyme in drama can be sufficiently inferred from his work in the old KING JOHN, as well as from the internal evidence pointing to him in the TALBOT scenes.

It is in blank-verse lines in Act II that he is to be confidently traced ; and it is difficult to deny him the lines (II, i, 36-37) :

> When she would talk of peace, methinks her tongue
> Commanded war to prison,

when we recall these from I TAMBURLAINE (V, ii) :—

> Whose looks might make the angry god of war
> To break his sword and mildly treat of peace ;

—though here we have clues to Greene also.

Another problem arises over Fleay's suggestion, in his MANUAL, that Lodge may have had a share in EDWARD III. It is not repeated in his later books ; but inasmuch

as there is apparently a hand (or hands) in EDWARD
III which is neither Marlowe's nor Greene's, nor yet
Peele's, it is worth considering. The hand in question
is to be seen in the speech of the fourth Frenchman in
Act III, scene ii, beginning :—

> Fly, countrymen and citizens of France !
> Sweet-flowering peace, the root of happy life
> Is quite abandoned and expulsed the land ;

and again in King John's speech in Act IV, scene V,
beginning :—

> A sudden darkness hath defaced the sky,
> The winds are crept into their caves for fear,
> The leaves move not, the world is hush'd and still.

The verse-movement has a staidness and gravity somewhat alien to Marlowe, and unlike the brisk iambics of
Greene : at its best it has more kinship with the early
versification of Shakespeare, though it lacks his poetry,
being simply careful rhetoric, which at times collapses,
as here :—

> The form whereof, even now myself beheld,
> Upon this fair mountain, whence I came.
> For so far off as I directed mine eyes
> I might perceive five cities all on fire.

And the collapse is not like Lodge, whose weak point
is rather stiffness than lameness.
    The clue, I think, is to be found in the second speech
of the Mariner in Act III, scene i, introduced by the
French King's question :—

> My heart misgives :—say, mirror of pale death,
> To whom belongs the honour of this day ?
> Relate, I pray thee, if thy breath will serve,
> The sad discourse of this discomfiture—

where we seem to have the same careful movement.
Now, the Mariner's speech, which follows, is either
Kyd's or an astonishingly close parody of him. Let
the reader compare the description of a battle on land

in the Spanish Tragedy (I, ii, 22-84), and he will see
that this account of a sea-fight is a planned companion
piece to that ; written in exactly the same style and
metrical manner, and practically duplicating two lines.
In the Tragedy we have :—

> Here falls a body sunder'd from his head,[1]
> There legs and arms lie bleeding on the grass :

In Edward III we have (III, ii, 165-6) :—

> Here flew a head dissever'd from the trunk,
> There mangled arms and legs were toss'd aloft.

The two lines which follow :

> As when a whirlwind takes the summer dust
> And scatters it in middle of the air,

imitate two in Tamburlaine's account of the effect of
cannon-shot (2 Tamb. III, ii) :—

> Whose shatter'd limbs, being tossed as high as heaven,
> Hang in the air as thick as sunny motes ;

and " dissever'd " is one of Marlowe's words.   But the
careful Kyd—if it be he—is using his own early material
at the same time : it is hardly conceivable that anyone
else should have produced such an actual copy of his
constrained style and matter as is constituted by the
whole speech.   The naval-battle-picture in Edward
III, like the land-battle-picture in the Tragedy, is
devoid of double-endings ; and in the narrative of
devastation in the next scene there is only one.   In
the Mariner's first speech also (ll. 62-78) there is only
one, and here too the style is identical with that of the
second.   As the manner and movement are exactly

---

[1] Cp. *Cornelia*, v, 257, where we have :—
> Here one new-wounded helps another dying :
> Here lay an arm, and there a leg lay shivered ;
> Here, etc.

This would seem to have given the cue.   Compare ll. 250-251 :—
> Dismembered bodies drowning in their blood,
> And wretched heaps lie mourning of their maymes.

the same, we seem bound to assign them all to Kyd
before 1590, noting that " expulse," which, though a
fairly common Tudor word, is not found in Marlowe
or Peele or Greene, and only in 1 HENRY VI in " Shakespeare," occurs in the TRAGEDY, as before noted.
And as " bonnier " occurs in the Mariner's second
speech we have here traced to Kyd two word-clues
which seemed to point to Greene, who has " expulsive."
The style-test has corrected that of vocabulary.

It may be that other speeches than those cited in
EDWARD III are also by Kyd. King John's lines
(III, i, 79-84), with the spider image, may as well be
Kyd's as Greene's ; the iterative speeches in Act III,
scene iii, in which the King, Derby, Audley, and
Artois bestow the items of knighthood on the prince
might be either Kyd's or Peele's ; and the prince's
speech in Act III, scene v, beginning :—

> First having done my duty, as beseem'd,

might similarly be disputed as between them. But
when these assignments are tentatively made, and
Peele is credited with the Copland episode, there is no
room left for Lodge. The rest of the play must be
divided between Marlowe and Greene.

§ 2. " LEIR "

Seeing that Lodge in 1589 professed to renounce
the stage, though such a declaration is not to be taken
as proof of his having done so,[1] we are at least not led
to look for any such quantity of unsigned work by him
as may be inferred in the cases of Peele and Greene.
But there is no antecedent presumption against his
collaborating in other plays as he did with Greene in
the LOOKING-GLASS FOR LONDON ; and Fleay's ascrip-

---

[1] Fleay (*Biog. Chron.* ii, 45). Lodge's later declaration of repentance for
his literary sins (1596) would seem to have been final; but it may be inferred to
imply that he had lapsed after 1589. See the summary of this document of
renunciation in the papers of the old Shakespeare Society, 1845, vol. ii, p. 156.

tions to him of shares in the old KING LEIR, the
TROUBLESOME RAIGNE OF KING JOHN, and (more
doubtfully) the 'LARUM FOR LONDON and the WARNING
FOR FAIR WOMEN, deserve to be carefully weighed in
connection with TITUS and EDWARD III.

As we have seen, LEIR has seven of the non-Shakespearean words in TITUS, and most of them point, as it
happens, to Peele ; but it also has two tags noted by
Fleay as occurring in the WOUNDS OF CIVIL WAR :
" cooling card " and " razor of Palermo " ; as well as
some we have seen to be possibly Greene's. But
" cooling card " also occurs in 1 HENRY VI (v, iii, 83),
in a scene which the tag " She is a woman," etc., invites
us to ascribe to Greene ; and in any case such a phrase
as " cooling card " could well be common slang to the
two men, who would both find it in Lilly.[1]

In point of fact, it occurs in Greene's prose work at
least six times ; and it is found in the old RICHARD THE
THIRD, which precedes RICHARD DUKE OF YORK.
In the cited scene in 1 HENRY VI, again, we have
" gorgeous beauty," which points to Greene, who uses
" gorgeous " constantly, and applies it at least a dozen
times to the beauty of women.[2] Yet again we have
" captivate," which is one of his common terms. On
the other hand, Lodge, who so often echoes Greene's
words and phrases in his prose, uses " gorgeous "
several times in his prose ROSALYNDE,[3] with the same
application. " Captivate " is common ; and the fact
that *both* the card and razor tags occur in both the
RAIGNE and LEIR as well as in the WOUNDS sets up a
natural if slight presumption of his presence in both of
the former cases. The main counter-consideration as
to LEIR is, as before noted, the large number of " for
to's " (over forty), which occur in similar profusion

---

[1] ' A Cooling Card for Philautus " in *Euphues, the Anatomy of Wit*; and
Euphues and his England (Arber's ed., pp. 106, 313).
[2] *Card of Fancy, Mamillia, Tully's Love, Orpharion, Never too Late*, and the
Anatomie of Fortune—Works ii, 188 ; iii, 190 ; iv, 84 ; vii, 106, 144 ; viii,
221 ; xii, 29 ; see also *Menaphon*, ed. Arber, p. 31 ; *Alphonsus*, iii, ed. Dyce,
p. 236 ; poems from *Never too Late, Id.* pp. 297, 301 ; and *Friar Bacon*, i, i.
[3] Rep. in Hazlitt's Sh. Lib. pp. 26, 131.

only in Greene's ALPHONSUS OF ARRAGON. The hypothesis of an original LEIR in which Greene and Peele
collaborated with Lodge, and which Kyd recast, may
be the solution. That there are a number of arresting
clues to Kyd we have already seen in discussing Mr.
Sykes's attribution of the play as a whole to Peele ;
and the fullest analysis will be found to strengthen the
Kyd theory. On a general view the bulk of the play
is ascribable to Kyd on the score (1) of the general
naïveté and naturalness of the diction, as distinct from
the weakly orotund manner of Peele in verse ; (2) the
orderly planning and complication of the action
throughout, despite frequent crudity of device and
detail ; and (3) the frequent parallelism both in action
and in phrase to those of Kyd's ascertained plays,
including his draft of HAMLET. The opening lines :

> Thus to our grief the obsequies performed
> Of our (too late) deceased and dearest Queen . . .

by their style, suggest that draft, having a distinct
resemblance in cadence and purport to those of Claudius
beginning :

> Though yet of Hamlet our dear brother's death
> The memory be green, and that it us befitted . . .

and there is a still closer parallel to HAMLET'S

> Now might I do it pat, now he is praying,

in the line (sc. 19) :

> Now could I stab them bravely, while they sleep ;

though neither passage is preserved in the first quarto
of that play, with its many lacunæ. And there are
various verbal clues to the SPANISH TRAGEDY.
" Extremes," which appears there six times, comes
thrice here ; and " import " (vb.), which is a favourite
of Kyd's, appears some half-a-dozen times. The
" murderer " business, further, smacks strongly of

his ARDEN ; and as he there uses "for to" at least
eight times,[1] though never in the TRAGEDY, he may have
come to employ that form latterly as freely as he did
the double-ending. And the phrasal clues to him,
as we have seen, are numerous. Further instances
obtrude themselves. The line in scene 31 (V, vii) :—

> And add fresh vigour to my willing limbs

points to

> Pouring fresh sorrow on his weary limbs

in ARDEN (III, i, 53) ; which in turn involves :

> And add fresh courage to my fainting limbs

in SOLIMAN (I, ii, 52). "Thy fainting limbs" recurs
in LEIR in scene 13. The LEIR line is not a quotation :
it is a variant of the writer's formula ; and it is difficult
to see on what grounds it can be denied to Kyd by
Mr. Sykes, on his own principles. Again, as he notes,
urge is a tic-word of Kyd's. In the SPANISH TRAGEDY
(IV, iv, 152) we have :

> Urge no more words :

and in LEIR (sc. 6).

> Urge this no more,

which is a closer resemblance than any other cited by
him in Kyd's uses of that term. Another of his own
clues to Kyd (as regards ARDEN) is the rather dubious
one of the "indiscriminate use of the possessive case."
Greatly doubting whether this is a mark so special to
Kyd as he declares it to be, I would point to these
instances of the usage in LEIR : "winter's frost," "a
pastor's care," "a child's part," "a loving daughter's
part," "holy Palmer's guise," "Hymen's sacred

---

[1] One of the uses, indeed, occurs in a speech (end of Act II) which has the
appearance of being the work of Greene. But the others seem to belong to
the hand that penned the bulk of the play.

bonds," " Nature's sacred law," " cause of nature's power," " heaven's hate, earth's scorn," " wormwood's bitter stalk," " half my kingdom's gift," " flatterers' persuasion." If the more poetic forms of the possessive trope are not much in evidence, it is because the whole rhetorical tone of the play is lower than that of any other ascribed to Kyd, save ARDEN as regards its realistic parts.

Yet again, Mr. Sykes accepts as a clue to Kyd's authorship of ARDEN the echo there of

> The bragin'st knave in Christendom

from SOLIMAN (I, iii, 211) in the ARDEN line (IV, iv, 54) :

> The railing'st knave in Christendom.

On Mr. Sykes's own principle that the tic of mannerism is a stronger clue than the sheer duplication of phrase, he seems bound to recognise as a clue to Kyd

> The gainful'st trade in Christendom

in LEIR (sc. 15, end). Similar superlatives in LEIR are " the parlousest old man " (sc. 19) and " the perjured'st man " (sc. 24) ; and in both cases the style of the context suggests Kyd. As against tics of manner like these, a mere proverbial phrase like " sink or swim," which Mr. Sykes takes as a clue to Peele, is doubtful evidence, though the ascription in this case may be right. It is not a specialty of Peele's, and, used twice by Marlowe (JEW I, ii ; DIDO IV, iii), might be used by any imitator. Of greater value as a clue, again, is that between " tie my tongue from speaking " and " ties silence to their tongues " in LEIR (scenes 4 and 6) and " tied to silence " in SOLIMAN (III, i, 65). " Try this gear " (sc. 19, p. 352) is a weaker clue, but such as it is, it points to Kyd, who has " this gear " many times, and thrice in one page of the TRAGEDY. Clues to Peele there certainly are; and, as we have seen, there are so many clues of vocabulary and tag to

Greene that a probable share in an early form of the play cannot reasonably be denied to him ; but the general argument for Kyd, resting alike on tags, style, action, and structure, is much stronger ; and the view that he is the final reviser of a previous play seems to meet the case.

We have now, however, to consider the claim for the participation of Lodge. In LEIR we have not only the " cooling card " and " razor of Palermo " clues, beforementioned, upon which Fleay seems to have laid a stress to which he was not entitled by his own principles, but such a parallel as this :—

> Have I not seen the depth of sorrow once,
> And then again have kissed the Queen of Chance
> > (*Wounds*, ll. 2077-78).
> How may I blame the fickle Queen of Chance
> That maketh me a pattern of her power ?
> > (*Leir*, Sh. Lib. rep. pp. 324-5)—

—an echo not only of phrase but of cadence. These references to Chance in the WOUNDS recur in other terms. It seems probable, indeed, that " Queen of Change," near the end of Act II (l. 804) is a misprint for " Queen of Chance," as the reference is to *Fortuna*. But we have also these :—

> The wayward lady of this wicked world
> That leads in luckless triumph wretched men
> > II, iii, ll. 705-6 ;

> The blindfold mistress of incertain chance
> > II, i, l. 2 ;

and they may be held to point to the lines :

> Or made a forfeit of my fame to chance,

and

> Methinks it differs from a warlike mind
> To lower it for a check or two of chance.
> > *Raigne*, pp. 237, 260.

And " Queen of Chance " in LEIR occurs in the same speech as " labyrinth of love," which is a tic phrase

with both Lodge and Greene. Further attempts to
fix Lodge's share in LEIR bring us to scene 13 (II, vii),
consisting of Cordella's speech beginning :—

> I have been over-negligent to-day
> In going to the temple of my God.

It has at least five vocabulary clues to Greene—
(" devoid," " sweet content," " mirrors of his time,"
" commonweal," and " nutriment ")—but Mr. Sykes
denies that it is at all in Greene's style, though its
cadences are those of

> In pure devotion, praying to my God

and

> And doted more on him than on my God

in FRIAR BACON (sc. 13 and 14). One would guess that
if the scene be not Greene's it is by Lodge, whose hand
it seems to be that puts " my God " six times in the
mouth of Jonas in one page (Dyce, 144) of the LOOKING-
GLASS. But the speech of Cordella closes with this
couplet :

> I will go to church, and pray unto my Saviour
> That ere I die I may obtain his favour ;

and when we note in the previous scene the line :

> This do, thou win'st my favour for ever,

we are forced to infer that *favour* is in both cases meant
to be pronounced *faviour*. For this aberration I know
no parallel in Greene or in Lodge ; and though Marlowe rhymes " favour " with " behaviour " in his
translation of Ovid's AMORES[1], his hand does not enter
in this play. On the other hand, Kyd's deliberate
scansion of *treas-i-ure* in the TRAGEDY (I, iii, 35) :—

> And with my treasure my people's blood ;

[1] Lib. II, eleg. iv, 3-4. This seems to have been a matter of allowed pronunciation, as Congreve has the same rhyme in the prologue to his *Way of
the World*.

and his similar scansion of "pleasure" in SOLIMAN (IV, i, 74), as well as his frequent *jeal-i-ous*, would seem to indicate him as the offender here. And in ARDEN (V, V, 10) we have : "meditate upon my Saviour Christ." A clear clue to Lodge, however, seems to be given in the phrase "proud pert peat," applied by Gonorill to Cordella (sc. 2). "Pretty peat" occurs both in Lodge's ROSALYNDE (Sh. Lib. rep. p. 142) and in what appears to be a Lodge scene in the LOOKING-GLASS (Dyce, p. 124), and is not found in Kyd.

Our examination of this play, finally, throws some little fresh light on TITUS. The TITUS line (III, i, 253) :—

> When will this fearful slumber have an end ?

as before noted, is from the same mint as

> When will this scene of madness have an end ?

in LEIR (sc. 16) ; and the LEIR line (sc. 19) :

> And yet for fear my feeble joints do quake

is an equally plain pointer to the TITUS line (II, iii, 212) :

> A chilling sweat o'er-runs my trembling limbs,

and the ARDEN lines (III, i, 96 ; III, iii, 20) :

> My trembling joints witness my inward fear.
> With this I woke and trembled every joint.

The notion that Shakespeare in 1593 was capping in this fashion lines so freely current in the theatre will perhaps at this stage be dismissed by most readers.

§ 3. "A 'LARUM FOR LONDON"

In the 'LARUM FOR LONDON we find a few more vocabulary clues. It has three of the once-used words in TITUS : *crevice, blowse,* and *guileful ;* .the first two not yet traced elsewhere ; the third occurring

twice in one of Greene's poems. Further it has " map
of sad destruction " ; Peele's " successful " ; Greene's
" foreslow " ; and several words and phrases found
in EDWARD III, which, however, taken in connection
with the prevailing diction, the sentiment, and the
structure, point not to Peele or Greene, but to Marlowe.
The play was entered for publication in 1600, and
is otherwise undatable ; but the siege of Antwerp,
with which it deals, was in 1576 ; and as there are
only some 140 double-endings to the whole play,
as against some 210 in LEIR—a much longer play,
however—it may have been written, so far as that
test goes, before 1594. While some have seen fit to
pronounce it a work of collaboration between Marlowe
and Shakespeare, the balance of opinion has gone
with Dyce, who reckoned it too poor even for Marlowe.
But the case has not been argued. Dyce, justly
distrusting Collier's citation of lines " written in an
early hand " on his copy of the play, assigning it to
Marlowe, pronounces that throughout the play
certainly " no traces of his genius are discernible."
I would suggest that there are " traces " of it in the
lines on Antwerp (74-76) :—

> Oh, she is amorous as the wanton air,
> And must be courted : from her nostrils comes
> A breath as sweet as the Arabian spice.

But that is not all. For Dyce, " genius " was apt to
mean the production of highly rhetorical poetry.
But there is a playwright in Marlowe as well as the
poet ; and the marked difference in manner and
method between TAMBURLAINE and EDWARD II, to
say nothing of the line-for-line translation of Lucan's
first Book, tell of an artistic transformation which
might go further. I confess to having failed at first to
recognise Marlowe in the opening scene of EDWARD
III, as Dyce failed to find him in the 'LARUM : renewed scrutiny discloses him in both, in his lowered
key. Those who, with Swinburne, cannot associate
Marlowe with anything approaching to flatness in

style should scrutinise EDWARD II, where he so often
eschews all rhetoric and descends to a nearly pedestrian
level by way of securing a kind of dramatic realism
that is incomparable with his " heroic " vein.   For
instance, Pembroke's speech in Act II, sc. v :—

> My lord Mortimer and you, my lords, each one,
> To gratify the king's request therein,
> Touching the sending of this Gaveston,
> Because his majesty so earnestly
> Desires to see the man before his death,
> I will upon mine honour undertake
> To carry him, and bring him back again ;
> Provided this, that you my lord of Arundel
> Will join with me.

A further development on this plane of naturalism
would give us work like that of the 'LARUM.   And if
we ask, what *could* have been made dramatically of
the siege of Antwerp by Marlowe's later methods,
we shall perhaps see reason to pause before pronouncing that he did not try to put the subject on
the stage.   In FAUSTUS, it will be remembered, he
makes an allusion (I, i, 124) to the fiery Keel at
Antwerp's bridge, which tells of a special interest in
it ; and in the opening scene of EDWARD II we have
a quite supererogatory introduction of a topic which
in the 'LARUM is capital :—

> Gav.— . . . And what art thou ?
> 3 Man.—A soldier, that hath served against the Scot.
> Gav.—Why, there are hospitals for such as you ;
>   I have no war ; and therefore, sir, begone.
> 3 Man.—Farewell, and perish by a soldier's hand,
>   That wouldst reward them with an hospital.

Here is the theme of Stump, the main lesson of the
'LARUM FOR LONDON.   Compare the lines :—

> He shall at least, when he hath lost his limb,
> Be sent for harbour to a spittle-house
>   ('*Larum*, ll. 603-4),

and those which follow.   That the play is throughout

realistic, and that it lacks the kind of central figure usually sought by Marlowe for his plays, is not to be disputed : but in this case there was simply no central figure available apart from the Spanish leaders ; and the presentment of Alva and Sancto Danila is distinctly in Marlowe's vein. The one contemporary who compares with him in the delineation of ruthless savagery is Lodge, who in the WOUNDS of CIVIL WAR so clearly shows Marlowe's influence ; and it is between Marlowe and Lodge, we shall find, that we shall be led to assign the play if we follow the internal evidence.

Fleay assigned it wholly to Lodge, but gave no reasons, though he never made an assignment without a reason. But while the versification of the latter part of the play seems to me to be clearly Lodge's, the style of the first Act appears to be no less clearly Marlowe's. The clues of vocabulary point to him a score of times. " Swilling epicures " (l. 21) applied to the " Dutch " of Antwerp, points to

> those ever-bibbing Epicures,
> Those frothy Dutchmen, puff'd with double beer,
> That drink and swill in every place they come,

in one of the most Marlowesque passages of EDWARD III (III, i, 25-27) ; and " swilling " recurs (l. 177), in the same application. As we have in the Jew (V, iv) the line :

> Go swill in bowls of sack and muscadine,

we may plausibly ascribe all to Marlowe. In the first Act of the 'LARUM, again, occur the following words and phrases which are either common terms specially frequent with him or uncommon terms and scansions used by him once or oftener :—

> *Expedition* (= furtherance or hastening), *effeminate, dalliance, commanders, tread a measure, scroll, ent-e-rance, strike terror, ordnance, linkstock* (= lintstock), *centaurs, reverberate* (ptcple.), *empty air.*

And in line 4 of Act II we have his common *conduct* (=convoy).

But there is not a clean cleavage, though at the close we find pure Lodge. Marlowe-words occur from time to time after the appearance of stiff and formal verse in Lodge's manner : *e.g.—quenchless, entrails, artire, tottered* (=*tattered*), *sweet fruition, antic, severed* (limbs), *dissevering*. But Lodge's imitativeness might account for some of these, as " tottered " recurs in the epilogue, which in style seems to be his, while the prologue, beginning :

> Round through the compass of this *earthly ball*—
> The *massy substance hanging in the sky*—·

seems to be from Marlowe, with whom " massy " was a tic-word[1] :—

Hang massy chains of gold.	1 *Tamb.* I, ii.
For he is gross and like the *massy earth.*	*Id.* II, vii.
As when the *massy substance of the earth.*	
Quivers about the axle-tree of heaven.	1 *Tamb.* I, i.
And clothed in costly cloth of massy gold.	*Id.* IV, iii.
Within the *massy entrails of the earth.*	*Faustus,* I, i.
Oärs of massy ivory.	*Dido,* III, i.

On the other hand " Iberian " (last scene, l. 23 from end) is a word of Lodge's (WOUNDS, l. 1544) ; and it appears to be his hand that we meet here in the 'LARUM :—

> Behold the silver cognisance of age,
> Soiled with dissolving drops of sorrow's rage
> > (Ed. Simpson, p. 62.   Malone Soc. rep. l. 1035),

where the forced diction suggests an attempt by Lodge to repeat a favourite allusion :—

> Upon whose reverend head
> The milk-white pledge of wisdom sweetly spreads.
> > *Wounds,* ll. 36-37.
> These silver hairs that hang upon my face.
> > *Id.* l. 132.
> Each milk-white hair amid this mincing beard.
> > *Id.* l. 443.

It is found, however, in Peele's early *Arraignment of Paris*, and in Greene.

> These hairs that dangle down my face
> In brightness like the silver Rodope.
>
> *Id.* ll. 207-8.

—the last case being a specific copying of Marlowe
(1 TAMB. I, ii). Earlier in the same scene, however,
we have the lines :

> Thou hast a daughter whom till we enjoy,
> All pity that proceeds from us sits here
> Upon the sharp point of my scimitar,

which are so much like Marlowe that it seems idle to
decide for one or the other. But the later use of " cog-
nisance " (l. 1572) seems to be distinctly Lodge's.

The General Editor of the Malone Society's reprints
has noted that, seeing the play was given by the Lord
Chamberlain's men, and that there is no trace of such
a piece in their repertory while they were associated
with Henslowe, that is, up to the summer of 1594, it is
presumably to be dated between that year and the
spring of 1600, when it was published. The solution
seems to be that it was either written in collaboration
by Marlowe and Lodge, and withheld, or left unfinished
by Marlowe in 1593, and finished by Lodge later.
The alternative thesis of Simpson, that the play is by
Marston, seems untenable, though Marston may have
had a hand in the piece.

Simpson's main grounds are that a number of the
words and phrases in the play savour of Marston's
" ruffianly style," instancing :—

> " the world's corrupt enormities," " swilling epicures," " bouz-
> ing Bacchanalian centaurs," " frothy Rhenish fats," " bestial
> gormandize," the coarse use of the verb " prostitute," " belch-
> ing puffs that fly from your full paunches," Death's " wild friscoes
> in the streets," " this butter-box," " the tallow-cake, the ram-
> mish fat," " this dunghill of thy carrion flesh," " Hence, tumbril,"
> " like Leviathan, his clumsy limbs walk not, but tumble," " her
> streets lie thwackt with slaughtered carcasses."

All this is doubtless broadly Marstonian, but Marston

had no monopoly of such phraseology.   In the old TRUE
TRAGEDIE OF RICHARD III we have :

> How was the Thames thwackt with ruffians.

We have seen that " swilling Epicures " points to
Marlowe in EDWARD III, where also we have " frothy
Dutchmen, puff'd with double beer," " belly-god," and
other " boist'rous boasting " terms.   Surely Marlowe
was equal to most of them !¹   Lodge was less given to
the vernacular, but he writes of " heaps of slaughtered
souls " (WOUNDS, l. 225).

It is true that " blowze " is a word of Marston's
(WHAT YOU WILL, III, i) ; but that is a frail ground
as against the marked dissimilarity of the play in the
mass to his work.   The strong simplicity of the first Act
is wholly unlike him ; and if we attach weight to such a
clue as " blowse " to the extent of bringing him into
the 'LARUM, we shall have to bring him into TITUS, to
which we must now return.

The words " blowse " and " crevice " both occur
there in speeches of Aaron, the second in the fifth Act ;
and here there is a resemblance in the lines in the two
plays :—

> I pry'd me through the crevice of a wall   (*Titus*) ;
> They'll hide them in the crevice of their walls
> ('*Larum*).

Further, the line in TITUS nearly duplicates one in the
additions to the SPANISH TRAGEDY (III, sc. xii A), not
printed till 1602 :

> I pry through every crevice of each wall.

Such a line, of course, might be an echo by the writer
from a play he had seen or read ; but if the additions to
the TRAGEDY published in 1602 were all Ben Jonson's,
as is commonly supposed, the difficulty of that solution
is great.   Fleay, however, was satisfied that they are
not.²   From the revised edition of Henslowe's Diary

¹ Cp. *The Jew of Malta*, IV, v.
² *Biog. Chron.* ii, 30.

we know that the TRAGEDY was re-produced in 1597 as " ne "—that is, as freshened-up ; and the scene-section in question may have been inserted then or earlier. It may then have been the work of Lodge ; or it may have been the work of another, say Marston. But while Lodge might have made an addition to TITUS in 1593, Marston could not have done so, having taken his B.A. degree only in that year. On the other hand, Marston was likely enough to echo a current play ; as he imitates Shakespeare in style hardly less than Lodge does Greene in phrase. But there is Lodge's own vehement renunciation of poetry in 1596 to be considered. If that is to be trusted, he could have worked on the TRAGEDY only at an earlier date.

It is probable that the " crevice " line was the ground for Charles Lamb's suggestion that the author of the additions to the TRAGEDY had a hand in TITUS, and such a ground can hardly carry us. Some of the additions are quite above the TITUS level of psychology. On the other hand the " crevice " line in TITUS occurs in one of those speeches of Aaron in Act v, scene i, of which one is so close a parallel to those of Barabas and Ithamore in scene ii of the second Act of the JEW. Of course, Lodge or another may have deliberately parodied the matter and manner of those avowals ; but if so, it was a sustained parody not easily to be parallelled. The lines :

> Yet for I know thou art religious,
> And hast a thing within thee, called conscience,
> With twenty popish tricks and ceremonies. . .
> An idiot holds his bauble for a god,

echo the prologue to the JEW, the speech of Guise in the MASSACRE, and the line :—

> Thee as a holy idiot doth she scorn

in HERO AND LEANDER (1, 303) ; while " conscience " points to three closely similar uses of the word by Marlowe (2 TAMB. IV, i ; JEW, I, i ; MASSACRE, I, iv) ; and the anachronism of " popish " is on a par with that of the " ruined monastery " of the Elizabethan world. In any case, " blowse " and " crevice " both occur in characteristic speeches of Aaron, and are ostensibly from the same hand ; and when we find both in the 'LARUM, which seems assignable to Marlowe and Lodge, and where as in TITUS " blowse " is the epithet for a nursemaid,[1] we have an inducement to ascribe them to one hand in both plays. I confess to finding the speeches in the 'LARUM in which they occur (ed. Simpson, pp. 38, 55 : Malone Soc. rep. ll. 59, 765) distinctly in the manner of Marlowe and not at all in that of Lodge, even as are the speeches containing the words in TITUS.

On the general question, I lean to the view that Marlowe worked on the 'LARUM near the end of his life. The versification is, for him, mature, and often careful. The number of run-on lines (*e.g.*, the dialogue of Egmont, Stump, and the others (ll. 555-626) is notable, as is the careful phrasing ; but both of those features are marked in his rendering of Lucan, where also we find the free resort to double-endings found in parts of the 'LARUM. But indeed they are to be found in Marlowe's portions of TITUS, where he is working on a lower literary plane. And if the best verse in the 'LARUM be not his, it cannot well be Lodge's any more than Marston's. Another claimant must be found.

4. " THE TROUBLESOME RAIGNE OF KING JOHN "

It will perhaps be useful to clear up as far as may be the question of Lodge's surmised authorship of or share in the TROUBLESOME RAIGNE OF KING JOHN and the old LEIR. Beginning inductively on the vocabulary, we find traces both of Marlowe and Greene. In the RAIGNE, the frequent " sinews shake " (Sh. Lib. rep. pp. 241, 253, 284) points primarily to Marlowe (2 TAMB.

---

[1] At least I so read the passage, though some take the word to refer to the babe.

II, ii, 9, etc.), as does the frequent use of " peasant "
as a term of abuse (pp. 241, 245, 275, 278 : Cf. DIDO,
III, iii, 21, and IV, iv ; MASSACRE, III, ii ; FAUSTUS,
IV, ii, iii ; 2 TAMB. IV, ii ; EDWARD II, I, ii, iv, etc.),
though this also is found in Greene, Lodge, and Kyd.
Similarly the line (p. 260) :

> Her passions stop the organ of her voice

recalls :

> And death arrests the organ of my voice.
>
> 1 *Tamb*. II, vii, 8,

though we have noted a variant of this in Peele (above
p. 266) and in a Peelean passage of ALPHONSUS OF
GERMANY. " Superficies " (pp. 253, 270, 276) is also
a Marlowe word (2 TAMB. I, iii, iii, iv) ; as is the thrice-
repeated " orisons " (pp. 260, 270, 273 ; JEW, I, ii,
near end ; EDWARD III, IV, iv, 78)

Among the possible clues to Greene are the then
unusual term " Aenigma " (pp. 228, 295), which occurs
frequently in his prose, and " cònventicle " with the
accent on the first syllable, as in EDWARD III, III, i, 63.
But these verbal clues do not carry us far, and we are
always checked by the verse movement and the general
style, which though they at times strongly suggest
Marlowe, do not often hint of Greene, but at times
do recall Lodge. Fleay's attribution of the play to
the latter was probably motived by the " cooling
card " phrase (Sh. Lib. rep. p. 306) and the " hammer "
tag (p. 241) ; and since Greene is the only rival claimant
for these, and his style is not in evidence, the assignment to Lodge so far holds good. But there are some
rather stronger grounds for the attribution. One of
the recurring words in the WOUNDS is " instìnct " :—

> And *some divine instìnct* so presseth me (l. 1031) ;
> Cornelia, man hath power by some instìnct (l. 2561) ;

and this occurs notably often in the RAIGNE (pp. 295,
299, 306) :

> A strong instìnct hath framed this cònventicle . . .
> By *some divine instìnct* laid arms aside . . .
> The other on a natural instìnct . . .

Then we have his substantive " resist " :

> Only the heart impugnes with faint resist.
> *Raigne*, p. 315.

Other clues are " ingràte " and " heartless "=faint-hearted :

> That will accuse or say I am ingràte.
> *Wounds*, l. 2386.
> Thou lent'st them me, I will not be ingràte.
> *Raigne*, p. 271.
> Ah ! be not so ingràte to dig your mother's grave.
> p. 306.
> So farewell heartless soldiers and untrue.
> *Wounds*, l. 361 (cp. 346).
> Like heartless men attainted all with fear. l. 832.
> Fond heartless men, what folly have I seen. l. 1157.
> So heartless fled our warmen from the field.
> *Raigne*, p. 308.

There are more of these indecisive clues ;[1] but in addition there is one of considerable force. In Part II, in the second scene of Act I, occurs the line :

> Unto the moonsted circle of th' antipodes,

which is unintelligible, the word *moonsted* being otherwise unknown. But in the second sonnet of Lodge's PHILLIS we have the phrase :

> The northern noon-stead,

which evidently supplies the right reading here. I do not remember to have met the word in any other dramatist, though it occurs in Drayton's poetry ;[2] and such a coincidence is highly suggestive of identity of authorship. After this, other clues of less significance singly, become better worth noting. It may be well, however, to keep in view the possibility of Drayton's being concerned in the play.

---

[1] " Ingràte " occurs also in Peele.
[2] *Baro's Wars*, i, 47: *The Moon Calf* (Poems, 1627, p. 162).

§ 5. " ARDEN OF FEVERSHAM "

Taking Fleay's attribution of " Arden " to Kyd as established[1] by the investigations of Mr. Crawford and Mr. Sykes, we have still to note that Kyd's hand does not cover the whole ground. Reason has been shown for surmising the collaboration of Greene, and there remains ground for inferring the intervention of Marlowe. Inasmuch as Kyd has certainly echoed Marlowe at times in the play, it is natural to set down to imitation all passages in which students can recognise a " Marlowe influence." But it is necessary to guard against an undue extension of such inferences. If we are to set down to imitation the Aaron speech in TITUS which admittedly parallels so closely a speech of Barabas in THE JEW, there is no way left of discriminating between imitation and actual authorship in any composite play. And while it is true that Marlowe's coadjutors did tend to imitate him to an extent of which we refuse to believe Shakespeare imitative, we are really not entitled by any available evidence to regard them as capable of long passages which could pass for good Marlowe matter.

We can, for instance, regard as merely Marlowesque the lines of Arden which open Act IV :—

> See how the hours, the gardant of heaven's gate,
> Have by their toil removed the darksome clouds,
> That Sol may well discern the trampled path
> Wherein he went to guide his golden car ;
> The season fits ; come, Franklin, let's away.

But I feel with Mr. E. H. C. Oliphant, who has done so much original and discriminative work in Elizabethan and Jacobean drama, that it is not warrantable to describe as mere imitation by Kyd such a distinctly

---

[1] Sarrazin's doubts (*Thomas Kyd und sein Kreis*, p. 73) were put even with recognition of a number of echoes of the *Tragedy* in *Arden*; but the later accumulation of detail by the English investigators has probably convinced the German scholar.

Marlovian speech as that of Shakebag which opens
the second scene of Act III :—

> Black night hath hid the pleasures of the day,
> And sheeting darkness overhangs the earth,
> And with the black fold of her cloudy robe
> Obscures us from the eyesight of the world,
> In which sweet silence such as we triumph.
> The lazy minutes linger on their time,
> As loth to give one audit to the hour,
> Till in the watch our purpose be complete
> And Arden sent to everlasting night.

This is surely the stride and the diction of Marlowe,
both firmer and more fluent than Kyd's.

But the conception, the shaping, and the general
conduct of the piece remain Kyd's. On a retrospect,
it is at once instructive and astonishing to note in
regard to Arden how many critics have ascribed to
Shakespeare a play in which not a single speech has
the rhythmic characteristics of his verse. In total
disregard of that vital test, a whole series, English
and German, have reasoned that the psychological
originality and dramatic force of the play could be
ascribed to him alone. Swinburne, who claimed, and
might be supposed, to be quick to diagnose poetic
quality of all things, showed himself thus temporarily
style-blind and rhythm-deaf in the very act of charging
his antagonists with being able to " hear only with
their fingers."[1]   In total disregard alike of the verse
quality and of the immense differences of diction, he
declared it " not pardonable merely or permissible,
but simply logical and reasonable, to set down this
poem, *a young man's work on the face of it,* as the possible work of no man's youthful hand but Shakespeare's."[2]   As Mr. Bullen justly insisted, a young
man's work is precisely what Arden is not.[3]   And,
powerful and original as the play is, its psychology
does not any more than its style attain to the delicacy

[1] *Study of Shakespeare,* p. 3.
[2] *Id.* p. 141.
[3] Mr. Archer here coincides.

of that of even the early work of Shakespeare. The judgment which pronounces it the work of an unknown and entirely independent author is intelligible as proceeding on an inexact knowledge of Kyd and Marlowe : that which finds in it either the verse or the diction, the planning or the psychology of the young Shakespeare, is intelligible only as proceeding from a general impression of power to an illicit inference in disregard of all the considerations which should check the induction.

The assumption that no contemporary could attain to the degree of dramatic force seen in the play before us is quite unwarranted. The progress made by Kyd between the SPANISH TRAGEDY and ARDEN within a period of some five years (ARDEN must be dated before 1592) is indeed remarkable. But no less so was the progress made by Greene between his ALPHONSUS and JAMES IV, by Marlowe between TAMBURLAINE and EDWARD II, and by Shakespeare between his early work and HAMLET. In those free lists men's thews strengthened and their minds ripened swiftly up to the limits of their congenital power.

Our actual assignments must proceed upon specific tests. The essential tests of authorship in regard to anonymous or otherwise disputable plays, after notation of methods of construction, are those of the diction and the quality of the verse. Only the habit of reading as Shakespeare's the non-Shakespearean verse of TITUS and the ERRORS and the HENRY VI plays could have blinded so many English critics to the profound differences of pulsation and movement between Kyd's lines and those even of LOVE'S LABOUR'S LOST. They are as different in texture and flexure as is a hempen from a silken rope ; and this flagrant fact cancels all Swinburne's convulsive panegyric. To describe as a " great poet " an artist whose most ambitious verse (supposing the Marlowe and Greene passages to be assigned to the main author) is but vigorous rhetoric on established lines, and whose average verse is homespun, is to confuse dramatic with poetic criticism.

For those, however, who cannot see this, there remain
the tests of vocabulary and phraseology; and these,
as applied by Mr. Crawford and Mr. Sykes, may serve
to satisfy anyone who is not determined to rely on
an unquantified and unanalysed standard of " power "
vaguely applied to an æsthetic work.

§ 6. " A WARNING FOR FAIRE WOMEN "

As regards A WARNING FOR FAIRE WOMEN, which
Fleay thought might be a late work of Lodge's, but
which Mr. Sykes more warrantably ascribes to Kyd,
there is little to be said in direct connection with TITUS.
It is, however, well worth examining as a probable
work of Kyd, a companion piece, in fact, to his ARDEN.
The case for his authorship is strong, though, as we
shall see, there are difficulties. Its method is emphatically his ; careful planning and studied realism being
carried even further here than in ARDEN ; though
here as there there remain jarring strokes of incongruity. The dumb shows also savour of his workshop.
And, though not printed, so far as we know, before
1599, it could quite conceivably have been written
soon after ARDEN, its percentages of double-endings
being much the same, and its mostly toneless verse
closely akin to much of the other play. It represents
in fact a more determined realism than that of ARDEN.
Here the pulse of poetry is seldom felt, the didactic
purpose is persistently obtruded, and still the dramatic
suspense is preserved throughout, the delays and
frustrations being schemed with the same calculating
care as is revealed in ARDEN and the TRAGEDY. This
particular device of frustrations, as employed in ARDEN,
seems special to Kyd, and the crudity of the plannings
of the murder in both plays is curiously alike.
Swinburne, vigorously repugning Richard Simpson's
foolish suggestion that the play might be Shakespeare's,
strenuously sought[1] to differentiate it from ARDEN,

---

[1] *Study of Shakespeare*, as cited, p. 129 sq.

which he so heedlessly assigned to Shakespeare. The
WARNING, he insisted, is prosaic realism ; ARDEN is
poetic art. This is but the exaggeration of a difference
of degree into a difference of kind. Kyd, after such a
marked incursion into realism as ARDEN, might very
well decide to go further. Even in the WARNING there
are such flights into the poetic as :

> Yonder she sits to light this obscure street,
> Like a bright diamond worn in some dark place ;
> Or like the moon, in a black winter's night,
> To comfort wandering travellers in their way
>
> Act I, sc. ii (ll. 308-311),

and the " Shakespearean " passages to be afterwards
noted. The gist of Swinburne's case is that the guilty
women in the two plays are differently conceived, which
could very well happen in one man's work. Anne
Sanders is less vivid than Alice Arden : her fall is so
sudden as to be unintelligible ; but she is at points very
well drawn ; and in ARDEN too there are flat inconsistencies.

The outstanding difference is that in ARDEN the
woman is already given up to her passion when the play
begins, and continues in it, with one or two angry
revulsions, till the end, when she is conventionally
transformed by ill-explained penitence ; whereas Anne
Sanders is at the outset ostensibly impregnable ; and
the only attempt to explain her transformation is left
undeveloped. The play is thus vitally faulty ; but
there are vital flaws in ARDEN also ; and Swinburne's
undertaking to prove the two plays the work of
different men is a mere stroke of àpriorism, resorted
to for the unnecessary rebuttal of the suggested
ascription to Shakespeare. Could he have realised
that ARDEN was Kyd's, such a divergence from the
SPANISH TRAGEDY would have prepared him for such a
slight divergence from ARDEN as is represented by the
WARNING ; while the identities of method—in
particular the frustrative delays—might have had for
him an illuminative significance.

Apart from the strong marks of kinship in method and realism, there are phrasal clues to Kyd :—

> Tremble every joint. II, 476. See above.
> Agony of soule. II, 522. See above.
> My other self. II, 1392.
> My second self. *Sp. Tr.* II, iv, 9,

and the frequent " damnèd " (damnèd deed, train' murther, drifts, feast, house) points to three such phrase[s] in the TRAGEDY. The use of " circumstance," too (ii, 275), points to the old play (III, ii, 48). In respect of double-endings, the WARNING approximates to ARDEN. The Induction has 12 per cent. ; the first scene 5.5 ; the second 4.5 ; the third 13.8 ; the fourth 21. We might surmise a play begun, held over for a time, and then carried to completion.

As the story of the murder of Sanders by Browne, recorded in 1573, had been retold in 1591,[1] Kyd may have met with it either before or after producing ARDEN, and been led by its obvious adaptability to handle it. Only in the Induction, which savours rather strongly of Marston,[2] is there any clear sign of another hand ; the play is homogeneous : and the Dumb Shows seem to belong to the period and the technique of Kyd.

Its main interest for Shakespeare students, however, lies in its surprising echoes of MACBETH. Compare :

> Neither time
> Nor place consorted to my mind.
> > *Warning*, I, 446.

> Nor time nor place
> Did then adhere.
> > *Macbeth*, I, vii, 51.

> Oh, sable night, sit on the eye of heaven
> That it discern not this black deed of darkness . . .
> Be thou my *coverture*, thick ugly night
> > *Warning*, II, 98-9, 102.

---

[1] Simpson's *School of Shakespeare*, i, 239.
[2] Though the description (l. 81) of History as " domineering " on the stage seems to belong to the period of chronicle plays. The " brawling sheep-skin " echoes *Edward III*, II, ii, 50.

> Come, thick night
> And pall thee in the dunnest smoke of hell
> That my keen knife see not the wound it makes
> Nor heaven peep through the *blanket* of the dark.
>
> *Macbeth*, I, v, 51-54.

> Ten wounds at least, and deadly ev'ry wound.
>
> *Warning*, II, 774.
> With twenty trenched gashes on his head
> The least a death to nature.　*Macbeth*, III, iii, 27-28.

> Let blood be paid with blood in any man.
>
> *Warning*, II, 817.
> It will have blood ; they say, blood will have blood.
>
> *Macbeth*, III iv, 122.

In view of these resemblances, significance attaches also to " the fatal entrance " (II, 2), where, as in the speech already cited in MACBETH, we must scan " enterance "—which scansion again is required in the SPANISH TRAGEDY, III, i, 61. Yet further, what might singly have seemed a mere chance coincidence, the echo of Lady Macbeth's " Give me the daggers " in the SOLIMAN line (v, iii, 52) :

> What, dared thou not ? give me the dagger then !

—also uttered by a woman—raises further question as to a possibility of Kyd's hand having been at work in a pre-Shakespearean MACBETH. In the speech of " Tragedy " in which we have " fatal enterance " in the WARNING we have also this :—

> The ugly screech-owl, and the night raven
> With flaggy wings and hideous *croaking* noise
> Do beat the casements of this *fatal* house—

which again savours of the speech of Lady Macbeth. It has been suggested that the lines (Induc. 43-44) :

> How some damn'd tyrant to obtain a crown
> Stabs, hangs, impoisons, smothers, cutteth throats !

refer to MACBETH ; but they fit rather better RICHARD III, which had probably been finished by Marlowe as

early as 1592. In any case, they could refer to the old
TRUE TRAGEDIE OF RICHARD THIRD, and can hardly
be pressed into the service of a hypothesis of a pre-
Shakespearean MACBETH.

Still, the echoes noted, taken with the equally
noticeable echoes in the EARL OF HUNTINGTON plays
by Munday and Chettle, make it practically certain that
there was a MACBETH before 1599 : was there one then
in the early nineties when the WARNING was probably
penned ? That may seem so unlikely as to cancel the
assumption of so early a date for the WARNING ; and
the further occurrence of an echo of JULIUS CÆSAR in
our play may seem to point decisively to 1599 for its
origination :—

> I gave him fifteen wounds,
> Which now be fifteen mouths that do accuse me :
> In every wound there is a bloody tongue.
> > *Warning*, II, 1041.

> See how their wounds do gape unto the skies,
> Calling for vengeance.   *Id.* II, 525.

> Over thy wounds now do I prophesy,
> Which, like dumb mouths, do ope their ruby lips,
> To beg the voice and utterance of my tongue.
> > *Julius Caesar*, III, i, 259-261.

> Show you sweet Cæsar's wounds, poor poor dumb mouths,
> And bid them speak for me.
> > *Id.* III, ii, 229-30.

For the existence of a pre-Shakespearean JULIUS
CÆSAR, however, there is a strong case ;[1] and long ago
Fleay was satisfied of the existence of a MACBETH
before 1596.[2] The difficulty, however, of accepting
at once a pre-Shakespearean MACBETH and a pre-
Shakespearean CÆSAR, containing matter preserved in
the familiar play, will probably be held by many to
bar an early date for the WARNING, and therefore to
exclude Kyd's authorship. Seeing that a hypothesis
of insertions made in 1599 in a Kyd play would be but a
weak compromise, the matter must be left open for

---

[1] See *The Shakespeare Canon*, 1922, Sec. ii.
[2] *Life*, p. 28.

further light, with the reminder that both as to CÆSAR and MACBETH there is irreducible evidence to be faced.

In any case, Fleay's unconfident suggestion of Lodge as author of the WARNING may be dismissed. It was probably motived by the occurrence (1, 705) of the much-reiterated " hammer in the head," common to Lodge and Greene. For the rest, it has the TITUS-words : " complot," " 'ticing," " Cimmerian," and " unrest "—words and phrases already accounted for through Kyd, Marlowe, Greene and Peele. In the second Act (ll. 881-2) occurs the archaic phrasing :

> Thus lawless actions and prodigious crimes
> *Drink* not alone the *blood* of them they hate ;

and on the same page we note " immanity "=in-humanity, a word found in 1 HENRY VI (v, i, 13), in a scene more in the style of Lodge or of Kyd than in that of either Greene or Peele. MUCEDORUS, again—a worse piece than the LOOKING-GLASS—gives us no clues to TITUS ; and if Lodge had a hand in the first as in the second, which yields us so little, the circumstance tells against the hypothesis of his collaboration in TITUS.

§ 7. OTHER LODGE CLUES

There are, however, a few slight clues which do, so far as they count, point to him ; and they have now to be noted. (1) In our lists of TITUS-words there has not been included " closure," which occurs in RICHARD III, also (in the phrase " closure of my breast ") in VENUS, and in one of the sonnets. But, as it happens, the word is used in TITUS with a quite different force, in the line (v, iii, 134) :

> And make a mutual closure of our house.

In RICHARD III it has the customary force of " en-closure." In SOLIMAN AND PERSEDA (II, i, 92) we have the participle :

> And I must die by closure of my wound,

where the force seems to be " closing up."

By Lodge, and by him only among the playwrights, so far as I remember, the word is used as in TITUS— " closure of the evening."[1]   But as this occurs in Spenser (F.Q. III, iii, 27), it counts for little, Greene and Marlowe and Peele being as likely to have followed that lead.

(2) In Lodge's WOUNDS OF CIVIL WAR, again, occurs the line :

> Content to live, yet living still to die,

which comes as close as the parallel before cited from Marlowe to the TITUS-line :

> Where life hath no more interest but to breathe,

and that last cited from LEIR.   This kind of line seems to have been a standing mode among the group.

3. The TITUS-line (IV, iv, 82),

> Is the sun dimmed that gnats do fly at it ?

is slightly echoed in Lodge's phrase (equally proverbial), " A moth (=mote) is soonest spied in the sun " (EUPHUES' SHADOW, rep. p. 15 : Works, vol. ii).

4. The TITUS-line (IV, iv, 81) :

> King, be thy *thoughts imperious* like thy name

compares with

> The mighty *thoughts* of his *imperious* mind

in the WOUNDS (III, i : Malone Soc. rep. l. 976).

Further resemblances I have not noted ; and these are just sufficient to set up a faint suggestion, which cannot carry us beyond surmise, though enough to induce us to admit Lodge's possible intervention in TITUS, but rather in the Aaron scenes of the fifth Act than in the " hammering " passage to which the reiterated phrase in the WOUNDS would *prima facie*

---

[1] *Forbonius and Prisceria*, p. 64 of rep. in Dr. Gosse's ed. of Works, vol. i.

point. To the bulk of the versification of TITUS, indeed, there is no resemblance in that of the WOUNDS ; but it is to be remembered that Lodge, like his compeers, could make progress in his technique ; and in an interval of five years might exhibit great changes.

Apart from TITUS, it remains to note some further verbal clues which, *pro tanto*, support Fleay's suggestion that Lodge may have had a hand in EDWARD III.

1. Lodge has in his prose[1] the tag about the bee gathering honey and the spider poison.

2. He more than once uses the word " solitariness."[2]

3. It should be added that he too has a number of descriptions of female beauty (*e.g.*, poem in FORBONIUS AND PRISCERIA, pp. 70-76 ; and the last poem in the SCILLAES METAMORPHOSIS collection), somewhat in the manner of that above ascribed to Greene in SOLIMAN AND PERSEDA. If there is anything certain about Lodge's work, however, it is that he imitates Greene no less than he does Lilly—their common model. A word or mode occurring in all three, then, bears no inference.

We may discuss in connection with Lodge, finally, one of the most interesting of the special problems arising in TITUS. One of Fleay's hypotheses that has not yet been made good is that as to Lodge having shared in THE TAMING OF THE SHREW. His metrical reasons for the proposition were not good, and have commonly been rejected ; but the open-minded student will keep it in view. In the SHREW the phrases " mistaking eyes " and " mad mistaking " (IV, v, 45-49) clearly echo " miserable, mad mistaking eyes," in TITUS (V, ii, 66)—one of the expressions which strike some readers as Shakespearean. But if that be so, then the others may be ; and Fleay actually held

---

[1] *Reply to Gosson's School of Abuse*, p. 35 of rep. in Gosse's ed. of Works, vol. i.

[2] *Forbonius and Prisceria*, as cited, p. 67 ; *Life of Robert of Normandy*, p. 8 of rep. in Works, vol. ii.

Kate's speech in the SHREW to be from the Master's hand.   Here again, then, he is conceived as weakly repeating *himself,* reiterating in comedy a phrase he had used rather effectively in tragedy.   Demurring to that conception, we might ask whether, if Lodge really had a hand in the SHREW, it might not be he who thus reiterated himself.

But the SHREW scene has 21 per cent. of double-endings ; and while the versification is clearly pre-Shakespearean, we have no warrant to ascribe such a percentage to Lodge.   The style, in fact, is Marlowe's in all respects ; and though the *cliché :*

> Such war of white and red within her cheeks

is one used a score of times by Greene,[1] we must not let one *cliché* put us in the mood of Kate, who professes

> That everything I look on seemeth green.

This versification, with its varying vigour, is not his, though at an earlier stage of study I had thought it might be.   Having assigned the blank verse parts of the old TAMING OF A SHREW to Marlowe, I am not at all led à priori to suppose him to have recast it as THE SHREW ; but the internal evidence at this point is all in that direction.   And as the scene section in TITUS is also markedly Marlowese in diction, I cannot, *pro tanto,* evade the induction that the iteration of " mad mistaking " and " mistaking eyes " is his.[2]   There is yet another clue-connection between TITUS and *The* SHREW which leads to a similar conclusion.   Only in those two plays in the Folio (SHREW IV, iii, 82 ; TITUS, v, ii, 189) do we find the word " coffin " (" custard-coffin " in the SHREW) used in the culinary sense ; and as it occurs in TITUS in the same scene with

---

[1] Cp. *Friar Bacon,* in Dyce's G. and P., p. 154.   The figure abounds in his prose ; but, to take only the poems, see Dyce's ed. pp. 285, 289, 290, 294, 296, 297, 298, 302, 305, 313.

[2] Though " mlstaking " occurs as an adjective in *Arden* (IV, i, 27).

" mad mistaking eyes " the presumption of a single hand is very strong. And the final choice, I think, must be Marlowe,[1] and not Lodge, though as regards the " coffin " clue there may be a case for Kyd.

[1] The small number of double-endings in the *Titus* passages points to the conclusion that Marlowe's revision work in *The Shrew* is later than this portion, at least, of his *Titus*-work. Among the minor Marlowe-clues are the four successive lines (188-191) beginning with " and " (see *The Shakespeare Canon*, Part II, p. 140) and the " Inhuman traitors " (Cp. *Edward II*, v, i, *Henry V*, ii, ii, 95, cited in Part I of *Canon*, p. 25).

CHAPTER X

THE TESTS OF VERSIFICATION AND DICTION

The presumption thus far established is that Peele, to whom we have found in TITUS the larger number of clues both of vocabulary and phrase, wrote or rewrote the bulk of the play ; that Greene, to whom there are fewer but still many clues of the same kind, collaborated with him or revised his work ; that Marlowe had also a considerable share, notably in developing the part of Aaron ; that Lodge may possibly have added something ; and that Kyd is indicated alike by substance and diction in certain scenes, besides being the likeliest framer (or adaptor from the Italian) of the original plot. To reach any more precise assignment we must apply the tests of (*a*) metre, (*b*) versification, (*c*) diction and mannerism, and (*d*) plot and action.

§ 1. METRE

By the first of these tests, it is seen to be once for all æsthetically impossible that TITUS as it stands can be one of the early works of Shakespeare. Every close student of the Elizabethan drama has noted in it a certain technical progression in the matter of " double-endings " of blank-verse lines. Retrospectively, the evolution can be seen to have been inevitable ; but the steps are none the less interesting. The original model of English dramatic blank verse, as cast by Sackville and Norton, is a simple substitute for the normal rhymed line, each verse being a clause, as was in general necessary to secure the effect of the rhyme. The primary result is a rhythmic monotony as great as that of rhyme, without the charm of consonance.

Sackville and Norton had not the artistic gift of Surrey,
in whose hands epic blank verse has a quality of grace
and strength not recovered for generations.[1]   Thus
though in their monumental Senecan drama of FERREX
AND PORREX (1561) they have dozens of run-on lines,
the verse is so metronomically framed that they avail
nothing for elasticity, and seem rather miscarriages
than intentional alleviations.   It was doubtless by
way of a compensating relief to felt monotony that
they reverted so freely to the early English device of
alliteration, in which they were followed by the popular
playwrights of the next age.   Even in their drama
there are occasional double-endings :

> And that most cruel hand the wretched weapon
> (IV, ii).
> No, no : then parliament should have been holden
> (V, ii).
> With fire and sword thy native folk shall perish
> (V, ii).

as well as speech-endings on short lines. But these
accidents are not improved upon ; and when Marlowe
came on the scene the double-ending had still only an
accidental footing. The early date of THE SPANISH
TRAGEDY, for instance, might almost be established
from its paucity of double endings, were external and
other internal evidence lacking. It has not in all
twenty lines which can be read as having the feminine
ending ; and of these three may be alexandrines ; four
end with " heaven," which may at choice be taken as
a monosyllable ; one ends with " spirit," which is
frequently so scanned ; and two more, ending with
" thickest " and " fairest," coming together, suggest a
wish to rhyme. Thus there are not ten certain instances.
Accordingly, the author of that play, which is otherwise tentatively dated on external grounds 1585-6, is
apparently entitled to the distinction so often awarded
to Marlowe,[2] of having written the first blank-verse

---

[1] In the original edition I did less than justice to Surrey's rhythmic faculty.
[2] So J. A. Symonds, *Blank Verse*, 1895, pp. 20-21 ; Professor Boas, *Shakespeare and his Predecessors*, p. 38; T. Seccombe and J. W. Allen, *The Age of
Shakespeare*, 1903, ii, 33.

drama for the popular stage. Nor is it fully warrantable to say, as do so many critics, that the credit of creating blank verse as an effective dramatic instrument belongs solely to Marlowe.[1] As regards mere verse movement, poetry and force of diction apart, Marlowe in his plays makes no new departure save the freer use of the double ending, and this he does not so develop in his accepted plays as to effect any vital improvement in rhythm. His greatest advance in sheer variety of rhythm is made in his line-for-line translation of the first book of Lucan, where the composition and movement are inevitably cramped by the line-for-line limitation : in his early dramas his verse remains structurally akin to that of the TRAGEDY and LOCRINE, greatly surpassing them indeed by its bounding energy and continuity of flow, no less than by its poetry and its force of phrase, but still remaining in the main a succession of end-stopped lines. The tone or key indeed alters : from the as-it-were chanted verse of TAMBURLAINE we come to spoken verse ; but the rhythm is not radically changed, though the total vitality is greatly heightened. At times he makes a line run on ; but so does the TRAGEDY ; and more frequently so does FERREX AND PORREX. In the last-named play, for instance, we have such lines as the following (IV, ii) :

> But what of these we will resolve to do
> Shall yet remain unknown.   Thou in the mean
> Shall from our royal presence banished be
> Until our princely pleasure further shall
> To thee be showed.   Depart, therefore, our sight,
> Accursed child

—where there emerges not only the run-on line but the varied pause. In this case the impelling force would almost seem to be the poet's indigence. Kyd, who certainly did not lack fluency, rarely carries his clause

---

[1] So A. W. Verity, *The Influence of Christopher Marlowe on Shakespeare's Earlier Style*, 1886, p. 92 ; and A. H. Bullen, who writes : " The rest of Shakespeare's predecessors are shadows ; Marlowe alone lives." Introd. to ed. of Marlowe, 1885, vol. i, pp. ix-x.

beyond his line ; and when he does it is without any change in the rhythm, as :

> To knit a sure inextricable band
> Of kingly love and everlasting league
>
> (III, xii, 44-45).

There is a much more marked advance towards variety of pause in Thomas Hughes's MISFORTUNES OF ARTHUR (1587), where we have such lines as these :

> All Britain rings of wars ; no town nor field
> But swarms with armed troops ; the mustering trains
> Stop up the streets ; no less a tumult's raised
> Than when Hengistus fell, and Horsa fierce,
> With treacherous truce did overrun the realm.
> Each corner threateneth death : both far and near
> Is Arthur vexed.

Marlowe in his assigned dramas does not formally get so far, his advance in dramatic verse after TAMBURLAINE consisting mainly in freedom and concision and intension of phrase, as in EDWARD II :

> The haughty Dane commands the narrow seas,
> While in the harbour ride thy ships unrigged . . .
> Libels are cast against thee in the street,
> Ballads and rhymes made of thy overthrow . . .
> When wert thou in the field with banners spread ?
> But once ; and then thy soldiers marched like players,
> With garish robes, not armour : and thyself,
> Bedaubed with gold, rode laughing at the rest [? head],
> Nodding and shaking of thy spangled crest
> Where women's favours hung like labels down.

His occasional run-on lines in his early work are but chance expedients, not improved upon, as :

> Stir not, Zenocrate, until thou see
> Me march victoriously with all my men
>
> (1 *Tamb.*, III, iii).

In his commonly-assigned work, it is in his translation of the first book of Lucan that he first developes variety of pause, besides resorting freely to the double ending.

Apart then from his obvious poetic superiority, and his substitution of natural action, whether epic or dramatic, for the conventional plots of his predecessors, he is hardly entitled to the praise above cited, at least from writers who credit him only with his signed plays; though when we assign to him the Roses scene in 1 HENRY VI, and argue from his visible work in RICHARD DUKE OF YORK to his authorship of RICHARD III, the case for him becomes stronger. His advance is, broadly speaking, as that of a swift runner over pedestrians. The effect is memorable; but he is still far from creating the true or final dramatic blank verse; though we see him within his six crowded years making a marked approach to it. This is the more noteworthy in view of the fact that in his unfinished HERO AND LEANDER he at a stroke raised the heroic couplet to a pitch of flexibility that after him was lost, and was hardly recovered till the nineteenth century. It would seem as if his faculty in verse were essentially metric rather than rhythmic in the sense in which Shakespeare is rhythmic: that is to stay, his power rested on the stay of metre; whereas Shakespeare's greatness emerges in rhythm.

Greene, again, contributes nothing to the rhythmic evolution, excelling as he does only in a certain occasicnal plangency. Only in some of the most vivid passages in EDWARD II does Marlowe reach the rapid vibration, the pulse of sheer feeling outgoing rhetoric that we find repeatedly in Greene's JAMES IV and in his share of EDWARD III; and it is from Greene and Marlowe that Shakespeare takes his flight into the higher air in the early comedies, where he first tries the potentialities of the medium. Marlowe's contribution, with all its signal energy of phrase and poetic splendour, is only a stage in the evolution: in him the old pedestrian movement, with its occasional rapidities, has become that of the bounding runner: in Shakespeare,. following and transcending Marlowe and Greene, there is a vital transmutation: the movement has become winged. After him there is no advance among the dramatists. He alone—with his occasionally successful imitators Marston and Middleton—so manages the double-ending and the varied pause as to set up a continuous flow of living rhythm. Jonson, who used the double-ending freely from the first, and at times, as in SEJANUS, so handles the varied pause as perhaps to compare momentarily with Shakespeare, never attained to fluidity for long together. He was capable of series of seven consecutive double-endings[1]—a kind of fault rarely if ever committed by Shakespeare after HAMLET.[2] Fletcher and Massinger, starting from the faulty model of Jonson despite of Beaumont, who so visibly prefers that of Shakespeare,[3] by mere unbroken recurrence of double-endings reduce their verse chronically to a worse because a more marked monotony than that of the school before Marlowe. Milton instinctively rejects their manner, and, having little need of the double-ending for his epic purpose, finds his triumph in long-drawn variation of stress and pause and flow.

Marlowe's principal contribution, then, is the definite introduction of the double-ending.[4] So late as 1590 the Countess of Pembroke in her translation (printed 1592) of Garnier's ANTOINE has only one or two double-endings. But Marlowe, as we have seen, had in some of his additions to his early plays reached percentages which are not found in the genuine work of Shakespeare till long after Marlowe's death; and Kyd and even Greene had followed his lead before 1592.[5]

---

[1] E.g., The Magnetic Lady, II, i.
[2] As in the first four lines of the " To be " soliloquy.
[3] See a very good criticism of the rhythms of Beaumont and Fletcher in the old introduction by George Darley, a critic of uncommon delicacy for his time; and compare Fleay's Manual, Mr. G. C. Macaulay's Francis Beaumont (1883), and Professor C. M. Gayley's Francis Beaumont, Dramatist (1914), as to the division of their work.
[4] See the previous discussion (pp. 27 sq., 122 sq.) as to Professor Parrott's error in assigning the innovation to Shakespeare.
[5] It may be well to warn the student as to the risks of variation in counts of double-endings. The differences, for instance, between Fleay's first and second counts of the Shakespeare plays, and between even his second counts and König's, are apt to be disconcerting, but are quite easily explicable. In a number of cases it is disputable whether a line-ending is strictly to be reckoned " double." The words " heaven," " power," " tower," " hour," " prayer," etc., are often to be read within a line as monosyllables, often as

The innovation, once made, was irresistible. Peele and Greene at their outset seem to make the double-ending only by accident, or—in Greene's case—by way of accommodating a recurrent proper name ;[1] and Lodge does as much at the outset of THE WOUNDS OF CIVIL WAR. It has been suggested by Collier[2] that Lodge seems anxious to shun the trochaic ending, actually curtailing such words as " resistance " and " repentance " to avoid the effect :

> And will you fly these shadows of resist . . .
> Their valour, Tuditanus, and resist . . .
> A wrathful man not wasted with repent . . .

But such formations of nouns from the infinitive of a verb are common in the rhymed verse of the time ; and " repent," for instance, is frequently so used by Greene even in his prose ; as are " suspect " and other forms by Peele in his verse. " Suspect " and other words of the kind are in fact found in early Tudor prose. And as Lodge has the noun " resist " in his prose (THE DIVELL CONJURED, 1st par.), as well as " impeach " for impeachment, Collier's inference falls to the ground. In point of fact, though Lodge goes so far in the WOUNDS as to write :

> What means this peasant by his great rejoice[3]?

he has some ten double-endings such as :

> But I have haste, and therefore will reward you,

disyllables. It is therefore disputable whether or when they are to be counted as double at line-ends. Again, a line may at times read either as a full alexandrine or as a pentameter, with a trisyllabic ending which can easily be scanned as a double-ending. Fleay seems to have begun by minimising the double-endings. Shröer and König, rightly I think, count trisyllabic endings as doubles. A further element of variation is set up by the question whether certain lines are to be reckoned as verse or as prose, or as lines at all. It matters little how we count, provided we are consistent all round ; and even some inconsistency will not seriously affect the value of the test. (König's counts are tabulated in Mr. Morton Luce's *Handbook to Shakespeare's Works*).

[1] As with ' Angelica " in *Orlando Furioso*.
[2] *Hist. of Eng. Dram. Poetry*, ed. 1879, iii, 39-40.
[3] This noun also occurs in his rhymed verse—Eclogue in *Rosalynde*, as cited, p. 46.

and some ten more in lines ending with proper names.
There are at least twenty double-endings in the play.
The just inference seems to be that he was not wilfully
resisting the double-ending, but was writing in or before
1590, when it had not been fully adopted by Greene,
Kyd, and Peele. Any such positive reluctance on
Lodge's part would be the more remarkable seeing that
in his rhymed verse he has freely and even exuberantly
used the double-ending, which was obtruded on the
English poets of his day by the verse-models alike of
Italy, Spain, and France, and had been much employed
by Sidney, who even resorts to rhymed treble-endings.
Lodge's rhymed poem Scillaes Metamorphosis, or
the History of Glaucus and Silla (1589), has scores
of rhymed double-endings ; in the sonnets which compose his Phillis (1593) there are many ; An Ode has
nothing else ; The Complaint of Elster has a number ;
and they recur in A Fig for Momus (1595).

Peele and Greene, in turn, avail themselves gradually
of the new facilities opened up to them by Marlowe.
Peele, we know, preceded Marlowe in his use of blank
verse ; while Greene, even after employing it, protested
against its encroachments. But though Peele was the
readier to acknowledge Marlowe's greatness, Greene
also soon learned to imitate him ; and as regards the
double-ending Peele and he developed concurrently.
Peele in the first act of his David and Bethsabe has
nearly 7 per cent. of double-endings to blank-verse
lines ; and in the first act of his Battle of Alcazar
nearly 6 per cent. In Alphonsus Emperor of Germany, as we saw, the proportion has greatly risen.
Greene latterly developed more rapidly in this as in
other directions. As against the seven double-endings
in Locrine there are some forty-six in Selimus, and
this in only some 1,680 lines of blank verse. Whoever
were the authors, the play is by this test put later than
Locrine. If George-a-Greene be Greene's last play,
as it is held to be by Storojenko and Grosart, it cannot
be his last piece of dramatic work. Having many
corrupt lines, it is difficult to count ; but I make out 74

double-endings to 1029 blank-verse lines, or over 7 per cent.   If, however, the second Act of EDWARD III be his, as above suggested, we must put that later still, for it has 75 double-endings in 625 blank-verse lines, or 12 per cent., as against only 5 per cent. in the first Act, less than 2 per cent. in the third, 7 per cent. in the fourth, and only 1 per cent. in the fifth.   The second Act, therefore, if Greene's, represents either a revision by him at high-pressure or a new section in an old play. Of course this addition may have had two stages—a draft by Marlowe and a recast by Greene.

And even this, it may be, is not the furthest development of Greene as regards mere double-endings, though it must be reckoned his high-water mark as to style and dramatic power.   If, as has been argued above and elsewhere, he is the main author of THE TWO GENTLE-MEN OF VERONA, he had there, about the end of his life, reached a total percentage of 18.   But Marlowe remains to the last the chief agent in this metrical variation.   One of the problems of Shakespeare-study which cannot be solved without resort to metrical tests is that of the authorship of the FIRST PART OF HENRY VI.   Critics who assign nothing else of that to Shake-speare (as Fleay), ascribe to him the Talbot scenes and that of the rose-plucking in the Temple Garden (II, iv). For our present purpose we may restrict ourselves to the latter.   It has no fewer than 34 double-endings to 126 lines of blank verse ; or nearly 27 per cent.   If then it be Shakespeare's, it must be placed, metrically, in his third period—the period of HAMLET and OTHELLO —for only then does he reach any such percentage of double-endings in his unchallengeable work.   On the other hand, the verse is rhythmically quite inferior even to that of his second period, being wholly end-stopped, unvaried, and wanting in Shakespearean concision. Let it be compared with, say, the speech of Young Clifford in the scene of 2 HENRY VI (v, ii) in which he finds his father's body, and it will be realized that the rhythm and diction of that, which come from the Shakespeare of 1595-6, are quite incompatible with the undeveloped technique of the Roses scene, which yet must in respect of its double-endings be put after 1600 if it is to be counted Shakespeare's.

The Clifford speech, which is a substitution (down to " stony ") for old matter, would perhaps have been rhythmically impossible for him in 1592 : the manner and the primary rhythm of the Roses scene would have been impossible for him at the period at which he multiplied double-endings above 20 per cent. The Clifford speech is very much in the manner of that of Northumberland in 2 HENRY IV, i, i, 136-160. The latter has no double-ending, and the former has only one, counting by complete lines ; but it has four mid-line pauses on trochees and one short line so ending, and the total effect is one of a variety of pause and rhythm of which the Roses scene has no trace, and even the second Act of EDWARD III only a trace. Now, neither in dramatic content nor in vigour of diction does the Roses scene suggest Greene. The rhythmic movement, though not of Marlowe's best, is much more like Marlowe than Greene ; and the only word-clue pointing to the latter is " blood-drinking," which he may have taken from Marlowe as he did other resonant terms. On the whole, it is much more likely that Marlowe, whose verse movement was always more sinewy than that of his companions, and who virtually introduced the double-ending, should first have reached so free a use of it, than that Greene should in this one scene have not only reached so high a percentage, but developed an energy of phrase worthy of Marlowe. The first hundred lines of Marlowe's translation of Lucan's first book yield 26 double-endings—nearly the proportion found here ; and nowhere in any confidently assignable work of Greene's have we so high a proportion. What is clear is that the scene is late even for Marlowe : if it be not assignable to him as a late reviser or expander, we must look to some such hand as Heywood's.

As to manner and diction, I invite a comparison of

eight lines of the Roses scene with eleven from an undoubtedly Marlowese scene in EDWARD II :—

> Between two hawks, which flies the higher pitch ;
> Between two dogs, which hath the deeper mouth ;
> Between two blades, which bears the better temper ;
> Between two horses, which doth bear him best ;
> Between two girls, which hath the merriest eye ;
> I have perhaps some shallow spirit of judgment ;
> But in these nice sharp quillets of the law
> Good faith, I am no wiser than a daw.
>
> 1 *H. VI*, ii, 4.

> 'Tis not a black coat and a little band
> A velvet-caped cloak, faced before with serge,
> And smelling to a nosegay all the day,
> Or holding of a napkin in your hand,
> Or saying a long grace at a table's end,
> Or making low legs to a nobleman,
> Or looking downwards with your eyelids close,
> And saying, " Truly, an't may please your honour,"
> Can get you any favour with great men :
> You must be proud, bold, pleasant, resolute,
> And now and then stab, as occasion serves.
>
> *Ed. II*, ii, 1.

The movement and the method are noticeably similar ; and though the second last line is slightly echoed in MACBETH (IV, i, 79), that does not affect the presumption towards a Marlowese element in the seven uses of " resolute " in the HENRY VI group and RICHARD III. But the metrical facts are in this connection the more important ; and the progression of Marlowe's verse should be kept carefully in view.

A similar progression as to technique was made, as we have seen, by Greene's other contemporaries. Kyd, who in the SPANISH TRAGEDY has so few double-endings about 1586, is found using them freely in ARDEN, in SOLIMAN, and in his translation of Garnier's CORNÉLIE, published in 1594. Thus each of the likely collaborators in TITUS had before 1594 approximated to the practice seen in the later portions of it in the matter of verse-endings, while Shakespeare in his homogeneous work

had not.[1]   In König's tables, LOVE'S LABOUR'S LOST
has only 7.7 per cent. of double-endings ; the DREAM
only 7.3 ; ROMEO AND JULIET only 8.2 ; KING JOHN
only 6.3 ; I HENRY IV only 5.1 ; and even RICHARD
II only 11 per cent. ; though the quality of the verse in
that play is often much higher than that of the verse
in TITUS.

It remains to examine from the side of the metrical
test the old assumption that Shakespeare wrote whole
plays, whether or not TITUS, before 1593.   The zealous
students who more than a generation ago did so much
to determine the sequence of the plays were withheld
by that pre-supposition from reaching a coherent
chronology, and left on the very face of the case a
series of unsolved anomalies.   Dr. Furnival, for
instance, printed in parallel columns[2] a passage from the
COMEDY OF ERRORS and one from HENRY VIII to show,
among other things, that the early Shakespeare had
next to no double-endings, while the late Shakespeare
had many.   But while the first scene of the COMEDY
has only three double-endings to 152 lines of blank
verse, or 2 per cent., the second scene has 24 to 103
lines of blank verse, or 23 per cent.[3]   The difficulty is
not merely left unsolved, it is not even recognised.
Equally ignored is the problem set up by the fact that
in the TWO GENTLEMEN OF VERONA, sometimes dated
about 1589, we have a high proportion of double-endings—in one scene 18 per cent. ; in another 20[4], in
another 25—while in the verse part of the first scene of
ROMEO AND JULIET (usually dated about 1595) there
is only one double-ending to over 100 lines of blank
verse ; and not one in Juliet's " Gallop apace " soliloquy
of 33 lines, or in Mercutio's " Queen Mab " speech of
42.   And in the brilliant, if premature, MANUAL of

[1] Professor Schröer's industrious handling of the question in his *Ueber Titus
Andronicus* seems to me to miss final relevance through his never facing the
fact of the evolution all round.   In any case his argument, being directed
solely against Fleay's statement of the Marlowe hypothesis, does not obstruct
mine.

[2] Introd. to the " Leopold " Shakespeare, pp. xix, xx.

[3] König's figure for the whole play is 16.6.

[4] König's figure for the whole play is 18.4.

Fleay, which went so far towards establishing scientific principles in Shakespeare criticism, the same pre-supposition led to the positing of a number of dates which that acute critic afterwards saw to be untenable,[1] but which still pass current. Thus he agreed with Malone in bracketing the DREAM and the ERRORS as being written in 1592, though he counted in the former play only 59 double-endings,[2] and in the second 178.[3] [These figures would mean percentages of 6.7 and 15.4 respectively. König's percentages are 7.3 and 16.6.] He was consistent in so far as he put LOVE'S LABOUR'S LOST, with only 26 double-endings,[4] in 1591; but ROMEO AND JULIET, in which he counted 118 double-endings among 2174 lines of blank verse—5 per cent.[5]— he placed in 1596 (describing it, however, as a revision of Peele), four years later than the COMEDY, in which his first figures worked out at nearly 12 per cent. Such results force us once more to the inference, either (1) that in the earlier plays Shakespeare was collaborating or adapting, and that in the COMEDY the work of another hand or hands predominates; or (2) that he greatly re-wrote that play in later life—a conclusion not easily to be accepted.

The dating of TITUS in 1589, again, as is done by Delius and several of the critics before cited, is still

---

[1] In his paper on " Metrical Tests " in Dr. Ingleby's *Shakespeare: the Man and the Book*, 1877 (Pt. II, pp. 62-63) Fleay rejected as fallacious the notion that percentage of double-endings progresses with the time order of production, though he affirms such a progression in percentages of blank to rhyme. Other metrical characteristics he then held to be ' for the most part suddenly adopted or resigned." I surmise, however, that this view was dependent on the acceptance of former chronology, and falls with that. If not, I must demur to it as a virtual surrender of his own principles. The choice of rhyme as against blank verse is a matter of considered volition; and in this respect an author might well vary. But his technique in blank verse is a matter of his whole artistic evolution, and is the last thing to be classed as arbitrary.

[2] Revised metrical table appended to paper on " Metrical Tests " in Dr. Ingleby's *Shakespeare: the Man and the Book*, Part II. The *Manual* counts only 29 double-endings in the *Dream*.

[3] In the *Manual*, the number was put at 137.

[4] Nine in the *Manual*. The higher figure means 4.5 per cent. König gets 7.7.

[5] This percentage is doubled in the revised table. I find some 160 double-endings in *Romeo and Juliet*—nearly 8 per cent. König gets 8.2.

more irreconcilable with the metrical phenomena. If we count the double-endings in the play on Professor Schröer's principle of noting alike treble-endings and dissyllables which might or might not be slurred, they amount in all to 203,[1] or nearly 9 per cent. [König, 8.6] : as against 6.7 per cent. of double-endings to blank verse lines in LOVE'S LABOUR'S LOST,[2] and 6 per cent. in the DREAM.[3] In the fifth act of TITUS, further, there are 68 double-endings to 575 blank verse lines, or nearly 12 per cent. The rhyme test, for what it is worth, is equally hostile. TITUS has only 144 rhymed lines to 2,338 blank ; while the two comedies have respectively 1082 of rhyme (excluding songs) to 579 blank, and 869 rhyme to 878 blank ; and even ROMEO AND JULIET has 486 rhyme to 2111 blank.

By the double-ending test, further, TITUS in its present form is seen to be late for any of the writers to whom we have been led to ascribe it. It not only cannot be an early work of Shakespeare's : it is in parts late for Greene ; rather late for Kyd ; and late for Peele. Even Marlowe's part is not early work for him : it is later than THE JEW. If the first Act of ALPHONSUS OF GERMANY were wholly Peele's—which, however, it is not—it would inferribly be his latest play, as it has 69 double-endings in 461 lines of blank verse, or nearly 15 per cent.—a higher rate than we find in any signed play of Greene's, or even in the second Act of EDWARD III. There is the more reason to infer the hand of Marlowe.

If, further, the " superior " portion of EDWARD III be dated 1594, as it is by Fleay (it was published in 1596 as having been " sundry times played "), it can

---

[1] As illustrating the inexactness of the earlier commentators on such points, it may be noted that Steevens spoke of *Titus* as being non-Shakespearean in that it had neither double-endings nor plays upon words. It has an abundance of both.

[2] Fleay counts 617 blank lines (revised table. The earlier has 579) ; Professor Schröer 553 ; König 579. I count 38 double-endings.

[3] Fleay counts 729 blank lines. I count 46 or 48 double-endings (two are doubtful) and 760 blank lines. König somehow gets 878, yet, after reckoning the prose and the rhyme, leaves 201 lines unaccounted for! The differences do not greatly affect the percentages.

be brought within the scheme of Shakespeare's metrical evolution only, as we saw, by dating LOVE'S LABOUR'S LOST 1591 and the MIDSUMMER NIGHT'S DREAM 1592, whereas Fleay latterly dated them 1593 and 1595. The arrangement, besides, would still break down in regard to KING JOHN, in which Fleay at first counted only 2 per cent. of double-endings ;[1] and also in regard to 1 HENRY IV, in which he found less than 4 per cent[2] The psychology of the best part of EDWARD III, again, is distinctly superior to that of RICHARD III (dated 1594 by Fleay and also by Delius), of which the opening scene is in some respects the crudest presentment of character in all the plays ascribed to Shakespeare. Inasmuch as RICHARD III has over four times as many double-endings as KING JOHN, which must be dated between 1593 and 1596, the rational inference is that one or other can be only partially Shakespeare's work— the opinion spontaneously formed by some of us as regards much of RICHARD III, on the first critical reading. That Marlowe had a main hand in RICHARD III, and that the double-endings are mainly his, is thus highly probable, even apart from the weighty evidence of style and phrase.

In fine, TITUS ANDRONICUS cannot with any critical regard to its metrical phenomena be assigned to Shakespeare. Its higher percentages of double-endings, intelligible as coming from Marlowe, or Greene, or Kyd, are inexplicable as coming from him before 1596 ; while its other characteristics are inconceivable as coming from him as late as 1593. If there were any satisfying evidence of other kinds that the play is his work, we might indeed set aside as an enigma such a singular deviation from the otherwise recognisable order of his artistic development ; but when all the other internal evidence, and a clear balance of the external, point wholly away from him, the confirmation afforded by the metrical test to the negative view is strong indeed.

[1] In the *Manual*. By some oversight, he omits the play from his second count. König gives 6.3.
[2] About 6 per cent. in the revised table.

§ 2. RHYTHM.

We have now to apply the test of rhythm, or versification in general. To a critical ear, the complete rhythmical duplication presented by the two pairs of lines :

> The hunt is up, the morn is bright and grey ;
> The fields are fragrant, and the woods are green
> > (*Titus*, I, ii, 1-2) ;

> The day is clear, the welkin bright and grey ;
> The lark is merry, and records her notes
> > (*Old Wives Tale*, 350-1),

is as real as the parallel in the phrasing of the first line. A blank-verse line, of course, permits of no great number of permutations in rhythm[1] ; but absolute coincidence of rhythm for lines together, when it occurs, reasonably raises question of possible identity of authorship ; and a poet's normal type of rhythm is for all attentive readers as significant of his identity as is his diction.

Let us illustrate. Blank verse, apart from pause-variation, admits of certain general differences of flow in respect of tendency to trochaic, spondaic, and iambic beginnings. A few samples will make the point clear :

> To be or not to be, that is the question . . .

> What's Hecuba to him or he to Hecuba ? . . .

> Led by a delicate and tender prince . . .

> Courage, ye mighty men of Israel . . .

> Mourn, Bethsabe, bewail thy foolishness . . .

> O proud revolt of a presumptuous man . . .

> Proud lust, the bloodiest traitor to our souls . . .

---

[1] This has been disputed, but rather on mathematical than on artistic grounds. The number of combinations *capable of easy scansion* is much smaller than the theoretic total.

The last four lines are from Peele's DAVID AND
BETHSABE, and they represent his prevailing fashions
of opening a blank-verse speech. In the first Act
of that play he has 109 speeches in blank verse, of
which 31 begin with trochees (as " courage ") ;
32 with iambs (as " To be ") ; and 46 with spondees
(as " Proud lust ").

This is not the bias of the young Shakespeare. In
the first Act of LOVE's LABOUR's LOST there are 32
speeches in blank verse, of which 19 begin with iambs ;
and in the second Act, of 45 blank-verse speeches 24 so
begin. Of markedly spondaic beginnings he has hardly
any. In the first scene of the DREAM, from l. 20 to the
end (ll. 1-19 being put aside as probably a re-writing),
we have 46 speeches, of which 25 begin with iambs, 16
with trochees, and only 5 with spondees. In the first
Act of TITUS, again, there are 111 blank-verse speeches ;
and of these 37 begin with trochees, 33 with spondees,
and 41 with iambs—a fairly close approximation to
the trochaic and spondaic distribution of DAVID AND
BETHSABE. Of the trochaic beginnings, many are
intended, as it were, to have a spondaic effect, as
"noble," " Romans," "Princes," "Marcus," "Brother "
" Father." We are thus led tentatively to assign to
Peele, in TITUS, on grounds of rhythm alone, the speech
beginning :

Hail, Rome, victorious in thy mourning weeds.

That, it will be seen, has almost exactly the rhythm
of a score of Peele's, such as :

Brave sons, the worthy champions of our God

in EDWARD I (sc. i, 48) ; and we find in the latter
speech the line :

With tears of joy salutes your sweet return,

which so closely approaches to a line in the speech
in TITUS :

To resalute his country with his tears ;

and yet again, in the BATTLE (I, i), the lines,

> All hail, Argard Zareo, and ye Moors,
> Salute the frontiers of your native home

—the same verse-movement, and the same thought.

If now we turn to the total rhythmic aspect of the opening scene of TITUS, we find a set of predominant characters markedly different from those of the earliest blank-verse in the Folio which we can recognise as Shakespeare's—that, namely, of the opening scene of the COMEDY OF ERRORS, which so strikingly differentiates from the second scene. Visibly the former is in the main the work of Shakespeare at an early stage, " trying his hand," so to speak. *For him*, much of the verse is relatively monotonous, lacking in his later diversity of movement, formal, we might even say stiff. And yet it is a world apart from the far more monotonous and incomparably feebler movement of the opening scene of TITUS. There, every line is end-stopped in rhythm even when there is no punctuation pause : we have a series of lines, hardly any " periodic " composition. True, it is not of the most primitive order of metre, not mechanically iambic : there are spondaic and trochaic as well as iambic openings : it is the work of a man who has written plenty of verse of a sort, and makes his line easily enough. But it is always a process of line-making, the progression of one who in thought composes line by line whether or not he carries the grammatical structure beyond the measure :[1]

> Noble patricians, patrons of my right,
> Defend the justice of my cause with arms . . .
> I am his first-born son that was the last
> That wore the imperial diadem of Rome . . .
> If ever Bassianus, Caesar's son,
> Were gracious in the eye of royal Rome,
> Keep then this passage to the Capitol,
> And suffer not dishonour to approach
> The imperial seat to virtue consecrate.

[1] This is not at all special to old drama : it is the mark of the average practitioner in the subsequent centuries, alike in drama and in poem.

This is the normal movement, a succession of easily penned decasyllabics, avoiding rigidity within the line by pedal variation, but always stressing the last syllable, never attaining to any supra-linear rhythm ; the work of one never " lifted from his feet " by any surge of inspiration, therefore always commonplace alike in his thought, his phrase, and his tune. He is an essentially commonplace poet, trained to letters and quite percipient of rhythmic possibilities within the line-limit, a not ungraceful cart-horse, who knows neither wings nor fire, though sheer familiarity with literature gives him command of the shifts of conventional rhetoric. We can almost divine his nervous structure : he has in him nothing electric : his ardencies, when he has any, will be those of the appetites and the normal " cultural " impulses of creed and patriotism : never can he transfigure human experience into " something rich and strange " by way of hyperæsthesis and the magic of great speech or great rhythm.

Turn we now to the primary Shakespearean verse of the opening scene of the ERRORS. The key, so to speak, is that of TITUS : the dramatic plane is much the same : the Duke is speaking publicly in his hall, with gravity and emphasis, as were Saturnine and Bassianus in the tragedy. And yet how different is the pulsation of the verse, the vibration of the tense diction !

> Merchant of Syracusa, plead no more ; . . .
> The enmity and discord which of late
> Sprung from the rancorous outrage of your duke
> To merchants, our well-dealing countrymen,
> Who, wanting guilders to redeem their lives,
> Have seal'd his rigorous statutes with their bloods,
> Excludes all pity from our threatening looks.

What has become of the line-limit ? At one flight, after the firm, strong stroke of the opening line, and the next line, we are in a prehensile construction of six lines, all in poised rhythm but continuously interfluent. The versification here is as different as the diction, which is as variously colorate as the other was conventional, as close as that is lax. We are in presence of an utterly different nervous system—as different, roughly speaking, as is the stag's from the cow's. Yet the two hands are working in the same media, the blank-verse of the early 'nineties, the common fund of Elizabethan vocabulary, the norms of Elizabethan poetics. The greater work is not exempt from conventional fault, from regulation rhetoric :

> Excludes all pity from our *threatening* looks

is not a good line : it rings even of " line-making " and the hackneyed sonorities of the stage. We are clearly not listening, yet, to a ripe Master. But we are just as clearly not listening to the flaccid line-lengths of the fat-voiced, short-winded vocalist who opens TITUS, who must draw breath after every verse, and cannot dream of a long construction. We have listened to two profoundly different performers, two disparate instruments, two *timbres*—to a man of talent and a man of genius.

Over such a challenge the traditionist will probably revert to his theorem of stages : the first performance, he will say, is that of the " aspirant " finding his way by aping the old hands ; the second that of the performer who has found his footing, or his wings. But the cheap sophistry of the Imitation Theory will not avail the rhythm-deaf traditionist here. The COMEDY will not let itself be dated after 1594 : if we are loyal to all the data we must place it in 1591, before ARDEN. Mr. E. K. Chambers will not put it later than the beginning of 1593. Most chronologists put it in 1592, though the high rate of double-endings tells that the bulk of it *cannot* at that date be Shakespeare's. The opening scene, in this respect, is quite alien to the second. It might indeed be argued that the opening of the Duke's speech, with its prehensile sentence of six lines, is a later re-writing. But even if we waive that passage as late—which we are not all entitled to do, seeing that the very small number of double-endings *throughout the scene* testifies to an early date, and that in the DREAM and in JOHN we have the same mark of long-breathed construction—the rest of the scene still reveals the winged beginner : it is in the main as marked by the supra-linear movement as TITUS is by the linear. The young Shakespeare, in short, is from his very start writing his own verse, singing with his own voice, *before* the 1593 recast of TITUS which stands for us in the Folio. The Imitation Theory thus collapses here as everywhere else.

If we turn to the other parts of TITUS, where we have the voices of Greene and Kyd and Marlowe, the differentiation is no less obvious, though these are much more akin to each other. For these, with all the differences of movement within the line, are line-steppers also. The best poetry in TAMBURLAINE[1], free-flowing as it is, is still linear, without involution, the work of a far more powerful poet and rhetorician than Peele or Greene, but *not* the interfluent *cantabile* verse which marks the advent of Shakespeare.

In TITUS, where we have some of Marlowe's latest work, the line often runs over, as in the speech of Saturnine beginning scene iv of Act IV :

> Why, lords, what wrongs are these ?   Was ever seen
> An emperor in Rome thus overborne,
> Troubled, confronted thus, and for the extent
> Of egal justice, used in such contempt ?
> My lords, you know, as know the mightful gods,
> However these disturbers of our peace
> Buzz in the people's ears, there nought hath pass'd,
> But even with law, against the wilful sons
> Of old Andronicus.   And what an if
> His sorrows have so overwhelmed his wits . . .

This is vigorous verse, suggesting a capacity in Marlowe for yet further advance in dramatic power.   But it is not Shakespearean verse or diction.   The progression is still fundamentally linear ;   the music, so to say, still of the wind instrument of brass, never " the vast

---

[1] The well-known speech of Tamburlaine in Part I, v, ii.

curve of the gradual violin." And so with the rapid movement of the dialogue in the Demetrius—Chiron—Aaron scene-section in II, i, which partly suggests Greene. Neither here nor in the Kyd passages do we have the evolving and involving rhythmic construction that Shakespeare produces from the first. We have it in one of his insertions in RICHARD III, (III, vii, 117) which cannot be much later, and might be earlier than TITUS :—

> The supreme seat, the throne majestical,
> The scepter'd office of your ancestors,
> Your state of fortune and your due of birth,
> The lineal glory of your royal house,
> To the corruption of a blemished stock :
> Whilst in the mildness of your sleepy thoughts,
> Which here we waken to our country's good,
> This noble isle doth want her proper limbs . . .

Here, in work that is visibly early for Shakespeare, being partly line-marked, we have an unbroken period of ten lines, which is followed by one of seven lines, in a diction " delicately pompous," as distinct from the loud force and thrasonical stress of Marlowe, and the commonplace mouthing of Peele, as is the long reach of the period. And yet the writer of this accomplished verse is held, on the Imitation Theory, to have at the same time slavishly imitated the diction of Marlowe at the outset and through the bulk of the play, multiplying double-endings to percentages even above those of the Roses scene in I HENRY VI and the translation of Lucan.

So long as these organic differences in versification are not recognised as evidencing differences of voice, the student of Shakespeare is missing a vital aspect of his problem. Professor Schröer, seeking to keep TITUS in the Canon, argues that " in spite of many deserving labours on the verse of Shakespeare and his contemporaries, we have yet not progressed so far in our knowledge that we can confidently build on the results."[1]

---

[1] *Ueber Titus Andronicus*, p. 31.

He is thinking of simple metrics or metronomics, being naturally indisposed to take account of such rhythmic phenomena as weak-endings and speech-endings within the line. Further, his assumption that Marlowe had *always* a low percentage of double-endings makes it impossible for him to apply that test without fallacy. But what makes his whole handling of " manner of versification " irrelevant and nugatory is just his failure to realise that Shakespeare has from the beginning a verse-movement of his own, which is utterly different from that of his corrivals.

The real connoisseurs of verse movement, as Walker and Bathurst, saw this spontaneously ; though some of those who rejected TITUS, as Malone, had little sense of verse-quality. Unfortunately, the percipients never analysed their perceptions ; they were in fact hampered for that by their acceptance of the bulk of the Canon ; and they have thus far had only the assents of those equally percipient. Whether or no many of the others can be instructed to see what is not obvious to them ; whether or not we can count on such a culture at the " more important universities " as shall ensure that at least Professors of English Literature shall not be style-blind, is not to be foreseen. The Board of Trade has automatic tests for colour-blindness ; but style-tests are not automatic, inasmuch as they involve both versification and diction. At best we can indicate principles of diagnosis, as thus :—

1. Shakespeare's verse is first and last in the main long-breathed, the thought reaching out beyond the line, so that even when the clauses keep to the line-measure, there is a " periodic " control. He proceeds by flights, not by steps, overseeing his ground. This verse is " winged."

2. It has, therefore, a spontaneous tendency to elude the line limit even in punctuation, carrying on the clause and varying the pausation.

3. As compared with contemporaries who at times can do this, as Marlowe in his later work, Shakespeare writes *cantabile*, where Marlowe never transcends save

for a line or two the linear breathing : the Marlovian
clauses are hardly ever involute, or the syntax prehensile :   phrase is added to phrase as beads are strung,
without organic composition.

4.   Let us take instances.   Marlowe at his best has
an easy energy, suggesting a succession of bounds, as
here :

> Sweet lord and king, your speech preventeth mine.
> Yet have I words left to express my joy :
> The shepherd nipt with biting winter's rage
> Frolics not more to see the painted spring
> Than I do to behold your majesty.
>
> *Edward II*, ii, ii.

This is a variant of a speech in 2 TAMBURLANE (i, iii)
beginning :

> Your presence, loving friends and fellow-kings,
> Makes me to surfeit in conceiving joy ;

and ending :

> It could not more delight me than your sight.

When then in RICHARD II (i, iii, 88) we find this, and
draw comparisons :—

> Never did captive with a freer heart
> *Cast off* his chains of bondage and embrace
> His golden uncontroll'd enfranchisement,
> *More* than my dancing soul doth celebrate
> This feast of battle with mine adversary,

the traditionists hurriedly recite the Imitation Creed
and explain that Shakespeare is still learning to write
from Marlowe.   But in this very play, in a speech
which is probably a rewriting of Marlowe, we have the
winged *cantabile* movement (iii, ii, 160-170) beginning :

> Within the hollow crown
> That rounds the mortal temples of a king

—a manifold period of eleven lines of silvery song such
as Marlowe never wrote.   And this, too, is certainly

early work, the play being placed by most of the chronologists in 1593, while the construction of this speech is only partially involute. We are asked, then, to believe that " the beginner " who *could* write thus yet folded his wings and coarsened his voice to frame in the same play the raucous vituperation of the Marlowese scolding-matches and the careless and unashamed linear imitation of a Marlowe allocution which we have been comparing above with its Marlowe variants. The stumbling-block in this inquiry is always the assumption that Shakespeare *must* have written everything in the Folio—except the things which even the traditionists are fain to dismiss as not possibly his. But if the student will be faithful to the " star-ypointing " testimony of the true Shakespearean work *in* the early composite and other plays, he will not be coerced out of his critical senses by the phantom authority of a Canon which is but a compilation of the theatre, presenting composite plays as wholly of Shakespeare's penning. In the MIDSUMMER NIGHT'S DREAM, if he listen well, he will catch the true voice of which we have been noting snatches.

5.   In sum, a style which from the first is *sui generis*, masterly even in its tentatives, is not sanely to be conceived as being, at any period, habitually cast off by its possessor in order to expatiate in the styles and manners not only of Marlowe, but of Peele, Greene and Kyd.

6.   With regard. finally, to the use of the double-ending, which for Marlowe soon became a necessary relief to the monotony of the decasyllabic line, and was embraced by the other linear performers for the same reason, under his example, the simple fact that Shakespeare's manifold verse did *not* so need the relief[1] enforces the recognition that in the early plays high

---

[1] When he does develope the double-ending he still differentiates from all rivals in his preservation of the prehensile movement. Writers like Fletcher fall to a line-ended monotony of double-endings which is worse than that of the primitives. Yet such a poet as Meredith found in such Fletcherian passages in *Henry VIII* some of the finest speeches in " Shakespeare." The rhythmic sense is often imperfectly developed even in poets.

percentages of double-endings are of other men's making. In TITUS, when double-endings multiply, as in the speeches of Aaron in v, i, they are to be assigned to Marlowe no less on the strength of the high percentage (18 for the whole scene) than on that of the phrasing, the sentiment, and the absolute matching of the matter in ll. 98-144 to that in the JEW of MALTA, II, ii. The percentage here is high above those of JOHN and I HENRY IV, both to be dated later. To Shakespeare the double-ending came gradually, as a minor form of freedom added to an ever-growing mastery which from the first had been emancipate from other men's congenital limitations. When we find in 2 HENRY IV a sudden and large rise in the percentage over that of I HENRY IV, there is cause for surmise as to a substratum of alien matter, merely recast—a surmise strengthened by such incompatibilities as the sudden widowing of Mrs. Quickly, and the no less sudden appearance of the page and Pistol in Falstaff's retinue, while the action of the plays is continuous. To ignore such phenomena is to shirk problems.

And this disregard of significant phenomena can be shown to be a fruitful source of error in contingent inquiries. One of the definite gains latterly made for Shakespearean scholarship is the demonstration that the central insurrection scene in SIR THOMAS MORE, long ago recognised, by many students, as Shakespeare's work, is actually penned by Shakespeare's hand, in the composite manuscript preserved in the British Museum. This conclusion, made probable by the facsimiles in the Malone Society's reprint of the play in 1911, was soundly reached, on expert grounds, by Sir E. M. Thompson in his work on SHAKESPEARE'S HANDWRITING in 1916. The recent issue of the volume in the " Shakespeare Problems " series of Messrs. A. W. Pollard and J. Dover Wilson[1] has made the matter more widely known, certain journalists announcing as " new " the discovery of the MS and the opinion that the central scene is Shakespeare's work.

[1] *Shakespeare's Hand in the Play of Sir Thomas More*, 1923.

Next to the identification of the handwriting, the most important section of the volume is that by Mr. R. W. Chambers on " The Expression of Ideas . . . in the Three Pages and in Shakespeare," tracing identities of phrase and political thought in MORE and CORIOLANUS and TROILUS, down to the verbal duplication of the phrase " Would feed on one another " in the two former plays,[1] and " And last eat up himself " in TROILUS.[2] But even this otherwise excellent paper, which with true insight corrects all the heedless dicta of hasty readers as to Shakespeare's hatred of " the mob," quotes from (HENRY VI and RICHARD II) as Shakespeare's, verse which alike in diction and in rhythm refuses to be affiliated to the passages quoted from the other plays. And in the whole volume there is, I think, no suggestion that the MORE matter is recognisably Shakespeare's in sheer style.

Yet there must be many who, like the present writer, never had a moment's doubt of Shakespeare's authorship of the MORE scene from the moment of first perusal. One's instant conviction was that no other man of the time could so write. Every feature of the work tells of him ; the versification, with its tense and effortless continuities and its sudden breaks, is without match save in the genuine plays and in the Shakespeare parts of the TWO NOBLE KINSMEN.

Equally clear is it that this particular sample belongs not to the early but to the middle period, where force is become of joint status with melody. Yet Mr. A. W. Pollard had dated the play 1593-4 ; whereas the mere number of the double-endings, far outgoing the percentages of JOHN and I HENRY IV, should have made that view impossible. Mr. E. H. C. Oliphant, on other grounds, had with great verisimilitude dated the play 1598-9 ; and Mr. Pollard candidly avows that, one of his external clues having broken down, he cannot stand to the earlier date. The resort to and reliance on slight external clues when the internal

[1] *Coriolanus*, I, i, 192 ; *More*, Add. II, l. 210.
[2] I, iii, 124.

evidence is dead against their supposed bearing, is the standing source of error. There ought never to have been any claim for the early date. Dyce, who suggested 1590, and Simpson, who proposed 1586-7, had simply never asked themselves who was to produce so many double-endings at that period, or whether Shakespeare's style was then matured. Consider the lines :—

> Grant them removed, and grant that this your noise
> Hath chid down all the majesty of England ;
> Imagine that you see the wretched strangers,
> Their babies at their backs, with their poor luggage
> Plodding to th' ports and coasts for transportation ;
> And that you sit as kings in your desires,
> Authority quite silenced by your brawls,
> And you in ruff of your opinions clothed :
> What had you got ? I'll tell you ; you had taught
> How insolence and strong hand should prevail ;
> How order should be quelled ; and by this pattern
> Not one of you should live an aged man !
> For other ruffians, as their fancies wrought,
> With self-same hand, self reasons and self right,
> Would shark on you, and men, like ravenous fishes,
> Would feed on one another.

It is as clear that these are not of 1593-4 as that they are Shakespeare's. The whole is indeed but a re-writing of one section of a scene in a composite play. Yet it has the unfailing compactness of his diction no less than the unique rhythm of his verse. But the verse has now undergone the tempering of manifold experiment ; the diction is more " pressed," more masculine, more truly dramatic ; the cluster of four double-endings is not an early touch ; and when we find in ll. 130-156 thirteen double-endings (all but 50 per cent.), we ought to admit instantly that this is not work of the period of the DREAM or the opening scene of the ERRORS.

None the less consummately perverse is the thesis of Professor Schücking,[1] that the play as a whole is an imitation *of* Shakespeare, made about 1604-5.

---

[1] Cited by Mr. R. W. Chambers in vol. above named, p. 144.

The Professor calls it " The Pseudo-Shakespearean ' Sir Thomas Moore,' " apparently implying that it had been treated as a Shakespeare *play*. On traditionist lines, indeed, that would have been the regulation procedure ; and had the play been put in the Folio we should have had it claimed as wholly his because a piece of it perceptibly is. But as it is not in the Folio,[1] no prominent critic has so far fallen from sanity. Professor Schücking, however, for his part, has reached a no less preposterous position. To his judgment, it was possible for an average craftsman in 1604-5 at once to reproduce alike the thought and the style, the diction and the rhythm, the essential cast of Shakespeare's versification, and, thus singularly gifted, still to prefer to do the rest of the piece on the ordinary plane of immemorable handicraft. Such a masterpiece of confusion in criticism tells of an academic world where the differentia of great and small art in verse have never been glimpsed.[2]

§ 3. DICTION

The test of diction is perhaps harder to apply than that of rhythm, being apt to be interfered with by clues of vocabulary and phrase, which may run athwart the more general test. Two writers may affect the same words and the same tags, and yet differ considerably in their diction as a whole. What distinguishes Shakespeare from all, and Marlowe from his lesser contemporaries, is degree of originality, force and pregnancy of phrase. Only a few times, over TITUS, can we say with any cordiality, " that is good enough for the young Shakespeare." The difficulty is to distinguish at times between the other manners, vocabulary being often equivocal. For instance, we find thrice in Peele[3] the phrase " mourning weeds," which is found twice in TITUS, and twice

---

[1] Having never been played, it seems to have fallen out of sight.

[2] Will Professor Schücking oblige us with an imitation of Catullus ? He might find the attempt educative.

[3] *Battle*, I, ii, 20 ; *David*, sc. iii, 87 ; *Locrine*, v, i.

in 3 HENRY VI, but in no other play ascribed to Shakespeare. Here, the test of mere vocabulary is controlled by others. The phrase in question is common to Peele, Greene,[1] and Marlowe ;[2] but in this case we *pro tanto* prove it Peele's by the higher tests. The TITUS speech further contains the word Styx, found in no Shakespearean play save in a non-Shakespearean scene in TROILUS AND CRESSIDA, but common in Peele ; another confirmation. This also is repeatedly found in Kyd, Marlowe and Greene ; but the general test excludes them here also.

The previous speech again, contains the markedly Peelish line :

> Successful in the battles that he fights,

followed by the line :

> With honour and with fortune is returned ;

which recalls :

> With truth, with honour, and with high success
> (*D. and B.*, I, iii, 186) ;

and seeing that the opening scene has the line :

> The imperial seat, to virtue consecrate,

the second clause of which we have found to be a Peelean formula, though derived from Marlowe, and that the whole Act down to line 275 has substantially the same rhythmic movement, we are entitled to ascribe to him the bulk thus far. Certainty, of course, we cannot have as to whether he is here a draftsman or a reconstructor. We can but note that at line 276, spoken by Bassianus, the versification quickens ; and we have a cut-and-thrust dialogue which is not like him, either in rhythm or in diction. Again, after the exit of all but Titus, the re-entry of

[1] See *Orlando Furioso*, I, 1421, ed. Grosart ; and *A Maiden's Dream*, 304.
[2] 2 *Tamb*. I, i, 44.

his brother and sons leads to a supererogatory scene
of dispute over the burial of the slain Mutius ; and
here some of the clues of vocabulary point to Greene,
though the mode of the dialogue suggests Marlowe,
to whom also there is a word clue. We have also
seen some reason to ascribe to Marlowe the preceding
speech of Saturninus. The words " sumptuously re-
edified " are both non-Shakespearean ; " re-edified "
being found only in a non-Shakespearean scene in
RICHARD III, and the other word in no genuine play.
As Greene has the phrase " " sumptuously entomb'd "
at the end of PANDOSTO, and " sumptuously solemnized " at the end of the CARD OF FANCY, and uses
the adverb repeatedly, and again has " sumptuous
tomb " in ALCIDA (Works, ix, 116), and " sumptuous
sepulchre " in the TRITAMERON OF LOVE (iii, 53), and
the ANATOMIE OF FORTUNE (*id*, p. 176), and " sumptuous " twice again in the CARD OF FANCY (iv, 25),
there is a presumption that it is his here ; though the
speech in which it occurs is in a rhythm that might be
Peele's, as is the dialogue in RICHARD III, where there
occurs the term " re-edified "—found, as above noted,
in LOCRINE. But Marlowe too has " re-edified," and
the rapid dialogue which follows is more like him
than Greene.

Towards the close of the Act, again, we have one
or two slight verbal clues to Greene—as, the phrase
" vain suppose," the noun " entreats "[1] (twice), and
" love-day." They all occur in the closing part of
the scene, in which Tamora persuades Saturninus to
dissemble—an action hardly likely to have been conceived by the dramatist who had just before made her
plead in vain to Titus for the life of her son sacrificed
in her presence. Indeed the gross incoherence of the
whole scene, morally considered, forces the inference
that there has been a reconstruction. Greene's early
blank verse, too, approximates so far to Peele's that
the lack of marked difference in the rhythm is no
argument against his intervention here. As to the

---

[1] Also found, as before noted, in *The Spanish Tragedy*.

earlier part of the Act, however, save for possible revision, there seems no reason to ascribe it to anyone but Peele, to whom point the clues alike of phrase, vocabulary, and rhythm. Since, too, it includes the unique word " palliament," found in a signed poem of Peele's, we may fairly conclude that even the unusual word " accited "[1] is here from his pen, though we do not find it elsewhere in his works, but twice (once as a malapropism) in 2 HENRY IV.

It is further to be noted, however, that in the entire first Act of 495 lines there are only 19 double-endings, or less than 4 per cent. It is thus probable that this part of the play is of older date than the fourth and fifth Acts as they now stand, since, although they have much that is in Peele's manner, they contain a far larger proportion of double-endings. And some signs of a change of versification appear early in the second Act. The opening speech, which contains the before-noted line :

> Gallops the zodiac in his glistering coach,

is absolutely in Peele's diction and rhythm ; and, as we saw, contains a further Peelean parallel in the phrase " Prometheus tied to Caucasus " which is echoed in EDWARD I (sc. iv, 21) : " To tie Prometheus' limbs to Caucasus " ; while the lines :

> Safe out of fortune's *shot*, and sits aloft,
> Secure of thunder's crack, or lightning's flash :
> Advanced above pale *envy's* threatening *reach*,

anticipate or echo the rhythm and diction of the line :

> Out of Oblivion's *reach* or *Envy's shot*

in the HONOUR OF THE GARTER (411).[2]

---

[1] Found in Wyatt : " Afore that Queen I caused to be accited." *Complaint upon Love.* See *The Baconian Heresy*, p. 279.

[2] In the *Battle*, ii, i, end, we have the line :
> In *spite* of fortune's *spite* or enemies' threats,
which is probably a misprint for ' fortune's *shot*,"

But in the next scene there is a different movement, in the speeches of Demetrius and Chiron, in one of which occurs the passage we have referred to Greene, " She is a woman," etc.   The lines which follow :

> What, man ! more water glideth by the mill
> Than wots the miller of ; and easy it is
> Of a cut loaf to steal a shive, we know,

are in the Greenean metre and not in Peele's *tempo* or diction ; and as the proverb of the water and the mill actually occurs twice in Greene's prose,[1] and both are said to be Scotch, the use of the second also is consistent with the knowledge of Scotch dialect shown by Greene in parts of JAMES IV. Peele's manner, however, is resumed in the next long speech of Aaron, which, beginning with " For shame, be friends," *after the youths have already been persuaded by him to cease quarrelling*, indicates that there has been an interpolation. Yet again, the speech of Aaron in hiding the gold smacks more of Kyd than of Peele ; and the reply of Aaron to Tamora, in which occurs the " hammering " tag of Greene, is certainly more in Greene's style than in Peele's. And here again there is some concurrent evidence. In EDWARD III (II, ii, 56 ; IV, vii, 13) occur the compounds " counsel-bearer " and " counsel-giver." The scenes are partly in Marlowe's and partly in Greene's manner, not in Peele's ; whence we are led to surmise that the similar compounds in ALPHONSUS OF GERMANY may be Marlowe's or Greene's, and also the " counsel-keeping " in this scene in TITUS. In the latter case, Greene is the more likely. The word " Venereal " in the same passage, again, is presumptively Greene's in LOCRINE, in the form " Venerean " ; as also the word " check-ered," which belongs to his signed plays and poems.

The Peele manner recurs in the scene with Bassianus and Lavinia, of which the moral stupidity, further, seems to make it almost impossible for Greene, who

---

[1] See above, p. 219.

tends to be perverse rather than stupid; and in
Tamora's account of the "barren detested vale" and
"dismal yew," with its allusions to the "nightly
owl or fatal raven," there are noteworthy echoes of
similar passages in DAVID AND BETHSABE and the
BATTLE OF ALCAZAR :

> To bare and *barren vales* with floods made waste
> (*D. and B.*, sc. iii, 81) ;
>
> Night-ravens and owls to rend my bloody side
> (*ib.*, 88) ;
>
> Night-ravens and owls shall ring his fatal knell
> (sc. xiii, 98).
>
> Deadly *yew* or *dismal cypress* tree   (*Battle*, I, ii, end).

In all four of the passages in question the psychological
process consists in associating a painful state of mind,
or a contemned person, with repulsive surroundings—
an idea seen again in those of Peele's rants in which a
defeated personage demands some "uncouth vale"
or other appropriate spot to curse in. "Mistletoe,"
it is true, suggests Greene's "missenden"; but that
slight clue is over-ruled by the much more significant
parallels above cited. The hand seems to be on the
whole Peele's down to the slaying of Bassianus, whereafter the dialogue is much more suggestive of Marlowe, with hints of Shakespeare's revising hand. In
the pit scene I find no clear clues of any kind to Peele;
and that episode, with the introductory one of Aaron's
depositing the bag of gold in scene iii, I assign to Kyd,
for the reasons given above. In the first section of
the fifth scene, there are only the "an if's" to suggest
Greene; and in the speech of Marcus, a little beyond, the
Greenism about "sorrow concealèd." And the verse
movement is so little like Greene that one suspects a
re-writing of a speech of his by Peele. This is a possibility to be always kept in view.

Act III, again, begins entirely in Peele's manner;
and the action of Titus in throwing himself on the

ground and professing to water it with his tears is
noticeably similar to that of the king in DAVID AND
BETHSABE. The rhythms and the actions are also
closely similar :

> *Season this heavy soil with showers of tears,*
> And fill the face of every flower with dew.
> Weep, Israel, for David's soul dissolves,
> Lading the fountains of his drowned eyes,
> *And pours her substance on the senseless earth*
>
> (*D. and B.*, sc. viii).

> For these, these, tribunes, in the dust I write
> My heart's deep languor and my soul's sad tears.
> *Let my tears stanch the earth's dry appetite* ;
> My sons' sweet blood will make it shame and blush
>
> (*Titus*, III, i, 12-15).

And the last line, further, as before noted, with its
blood and *blush*, points to two in DAVID. It is true
that the one dramatic use we have noted of the word
" languor " occurs in the TROUBLESOME RAIGNE OF
KING JOHN (Pt. I, sc. of Hubert and Arthur). The
passage seems above the level of Peele, and suggests
Marlowe ; but the passage in TITUS, on the other hand,
is entirely beneath Marlowe. In all likelihood it is by
Peele, making a single use of an unusual word.[1]

With the entrance of Aaron, however, there super-
venes another style. Whether it be Greene's or
another's it is hard to say ; it is to Greene that we
are pointed by the clues of vocabulary and phrase, in
the line " Writing destruction on the enemy's castle,"
and those on " deep extremes." But if it be he, he is
putting on the manner of Marlowe in the lines :

> Did ever raven sing so like a lark
> That gives sweet tidings of the sun's uprise ?

Titus's speech beginning :

> If there were reason for these miseries,

---

[1] It should be noted that " languor " had at that period a much greater
force than at present. Thus in the *Raigne* the phrase runs: " And of the
languor tell him thou art dead." Compare Spenser, *Faerie Queen*, B. III,
c. ii, st. 52 ; c. xii, st. 16 ; Bk. IV, c. xiii, motto and st. 20. It had then this
force in French—*e.g.*, Rabelais.

savours again of Peele in rhythm and diction. The
" wat'ry eyes," it may be noted, occurs in LOCRINE
(v, iv) ; in MENAPHON (ed. Arber, p. 91),[1] and in
EDWARD III (v, 153) ; and " watery " is one of Greene's
common epithets. But it occurs also in Peele (BATTLE
I, i, 52) ; and though it cannot be said that there is
any certainty as to the diction of these scenes, it
points broadly to him. Some of it, however, could
conceivably be Kyd's.

A fresh problem arises with the second scene of
Act III, which is lacking in the quartos of 1594, 1600
and 1611, but found in the first folio.[2] Here, in
Titus's second speech, there is a return to the more
nervous versification which suggests Greene ; but the
manner here is not his, being rather strongly suggestive
of Kyd, while there are phraseological clues to Peele.
As the scene in no way advances the action, it is
possible that it existed in the early manuscript, and
was dropped by the actors ; but that would not be a
conclusive reason for its omission in the print. Certainly it cannot have been written by Shakespeare
after 1600. As we have seen, the phrase " sorrow-
wreathen knot," suggesting the " arms in this sad
knot " of the TEMPEST, has been pronounced Shakespearean ; but we have found it paralleled in Peele's
" Sadness with wreathèd arms," and in a line of Kyd's
translation of Garnier's CORNÉLIE. The archaic verb
" to passionate," too, found nowhere else in Shakespeare, and probably copied from the FAERIE QUEENE,[3]
is distinctly in Peele's taste ; and the " hollow prison
of my flesh " we have seen to be one of his formulas,
though that also is found in the CORNELIA. But the
" map of woe " is a Euphuistic tag of Greene's and

[1] This phrase, like so many others, occurs in Lilly's *Euphues* (ed. Arber, pp.
36, 101) ; but it is found also in Sidney's *Arcadia* (B. II, third sentence) and
in the *Faerie Queene*, Bk. I, c. ix, st. 15 ; III, v, 34, etc. It seems to have had
a fascination for the Elizabethans. One finds it everywhere.
[2] No reprint of the 1594 quarto, so far as I am aware, has yet been published ;
but as Mr. Ljunggren has stated in the *Athenæum* that ' the text is substantially the same as that of the quarto 1600," there is presumably no
difference at this point.
[3] B. I, c. xii, st. 16—published in 1590.

Kyd's as well as Lodge's ; and though the lines of advice to Lavinia to make a hole against her heart that she may drown it with her tears is an imbecility very much in Peele's taste,[1] other clues of phraseology in the speech point to Greene. Again, however, there suggests itself the possible intervention of Kyd. The pseudo-pathetic passage about " hands," containing the line :

> O handle not the theme, to talk of hands,

recalls that in the SPANISH TRAGEDY (III, xiii) ending :

> Talk not of chords, but let us now be gone,
> For with a cord Horatio was slain ;

and the (possibly corrupt) line in EDWARD II (v, 5) :

> Forgive my thought for having such a thought.

These feeble devices may have been thought worth imitating by several writers, but there is a monotony about them that suggests a single hand. The last word-clue in the scene is the use of the intransitive verb " to dazzle," common to Shakespeare, Greene, Lodge, and Peele. It cannot be said that the scene is notably in Peele's manner ; but the poverty and crudity of the pathos is more suggestive of his or Kyd's hand than of Greene's.

The fourth Act, like all the others, appears to be opened by Peele. The flaccid movement is his, and the

> I have read that Hecuba of Troy
> Ran mad through sorrow,

points directly to his TALE OF TROY, as we have seen. Only in Titus' speech (i, 95) beginning " 'Tis sure enough " do we seem to revert to the more rapid movement of Greene ; and here comes the clue of the " gad of steel." And though in scene ii the

> But let her rest in her unrest awhile

---

[1] See Thamar's lament in *David*, sc. 3, already cited.

echoes the SPANISH TRAGEDY, the quick verse movement is unlike Kyd, and may be either Greene's or another's. And as the same movement continues in the scene of the nurse and the infant, in which Aaron's character developes, we are led both by style and matter to surmise the hand of Marlowe. Even at the close of the scene, where we have Peele's " swift as swallow flies," the movement and the diction are rather Marlowe's than his. It may be that Peele in revising inserted the first three lines of the closing speech; the " come on, you thick-lipped slave," points to Marlowe in point of diction.

The third scene, again, reverts to a more nervous and dramatic manner, but not that which we have associated with Greene. It has not his usual movement, though it has some word clues to him. Thus we have his word " big-bon'd "—found also, however, in SOLIMAN AND PERSEDA (I, ii, 59). In the same play we find the phrase " Take her and use her at thy pleasure " (IV, i, 74), which echoes Tamora's mandate to her sons in TITUS (II, iii, 166)—a speech which we have surmised to be Peele's. In SOLIMAN, however, the scansion of " pleasure " as a trisyllable points to Kyd, since we have " pleasure " so scanned twice in the TRAGEDY (I, iii, 35, 36) ; and, as we have already seen, Kyd there and elsewhere scans " jealous " in three syllables. As above noted, further, Titus' speeches, with their references to Pluto, and the whole business of the arrows, are distinctly suggestive of the manner and method of Kyd. As a whole, the scene has a composite air, lines 27-34 being apparently interpolated by Peele ; while 42-52, with their echo from ALPHONSUS OF ARRAGON, (Dyce, p. 235), point to Greene.

The clown scene again points to Peele and Greene. Professor Collins has confidently claimed for Shakespeare the clown's answer to Titus : " Alas, sir, I know not Jupiter : I never drank with him in all my life." Had he turned to LOCRINE he would have found in one of the clown scenes of that play a slight

variant of the same visibly venerable jest : " O alas,
sir, you are deceived ; I am not Mercury, I am
Strumbo," and in SELIMUS the same kind of retort is
put in the mouth of Bullithrumble (l. 1949). If
Shakespeare saw fit to steal such witticisms, he was a
humble imitator indeed.

Thus far the line which in respect of poetic content
most strongly suggests Marlowe is the one before
noted :

> Where life hath no more interest but to breathe ;

and to that we have seen parallels in EDWARD III as
well as in Lodge. Still it suffices to raise yet again
the question of his presence. We are not indeed
entitled to suppose that he could not write poorly at
a pinch. Seeking, however, for distinct clues, we can
but say that the scene section in which this line occurs
(III, i, 234-300) has something of his energy ; and that
the line

> Now let hot Ætna cool in Sicily

is in his manner ; though we have found " Ætna "
also in Peele, and in the SPANISH TRAGEDY ; and it is
a common allusion of Greene's. The hideous device,
in the same scene, of making Lavinia carry her father's
hand in her teeth, suggests nobody in particular ;
but since in SELIMUS (l. 1437) we have Aga carrying
his own lopped hands in his breast, Greene cannot
here be excluded. It is in the fourth scene of the
fourth Act that we meet with versification in Marlowe's
latest dramatic manner ; and here we note the word
" libelling," which occurs in one of his scenes in
EDWARD II. But in Tamora's speech beginning :

> King, be thy thoughts imperious like thy name,

we seem to return to the sententious manner of Greene,[1]
who appears also to be indicated by the lines about the

---

[1] Lodge's line, above cited, may have been an echo of this ; but the primary presumption is the other way, regard being had to chronology. Perhaps Lodge echoed another play of Greene's.

eagle and gnats—both common subjects of allusion
in his plays and prose-writings (*e.g.*, SELIMUS, ll. 2477,
2541).

In the fifth Act, again, we revert obviously to the
epic and undramatic manner of Peele, which, however,
is intruded upon at the entrance of Aaron, whose
speeches we have seen much reason to ascribe to Marlowe.   On that view it is to him and not to Peele that
we must assign the "ruinous monastery" and the
absurd allusion to "popish tricks and ceremonies."
Mr. Baildon, commenting on the "ruinous monastery," writes :

> Another anachronism ; but Shakespeare is persistently careless
> on such points.   But as we do not know in the least the date of
> the play's historic action, the anachronism may be the other way
> on in making Titus and the other Romans still pagans.

Our dry investigation is relieved by such a stroke of
conscientious apologetic.   Since the period of a non-
historical play is to be determined, if at all, from its
action, the effect of the plea, if any, is to suggest that
in the Christian period the Romans may have practised
human sacrifice *ad manes*—a somewhat gratuitous
enormity from so avowed an enemy of agnosticism.
Over the subsequent allusion to "popish tricks" Mr.
Baildon again sighs :

> Another anachronism for which Shakespeare must be held
> responsible ; for, *however little or much he wrote of this play, he
> stood godfather, if not father*, to it, and could have easily removed
> these flaws, some of which may have been actors' *gag* to raise a
> smile or draw a cheer from the audience.

This is a somewhat pathetic collapse for an introduction of 76 pages which, after somewhat stronger
affirmations, ends with an expression of belief that
TITUS is "essentially and substantially the work"
of Shakespeare.   It is perhaps of no great importance
to relieve the "persistently careless" Master of the
charge of anachronism ; but as we are apt to suppose
him exceptionally lax in such matters, it may be worth

while to note that not only does Peele, the Master of
Arts, introduce panthers and popery and Protestantism
at Rome in the period of the pagan empire, and again
set up Protestantism in the reign of Edward II ; but
the no less academic Lodge in his WOUNDS OF CIVIL
WAR makes " Pedro, a Frenchman," speak broken
English in the period of Marius and Sylla—that is, if
Lodge be the author of the scene.   The authors of
EDWARD III, too, make artillery a standing feature
of the fighting ; as Marlowe does in TAMBURLAINE.
And Marlowe himself translates Lucan's *exiguum
asylum* by " one poor church."   In any case, the
allusion before us is probably not actors' gag : it is
apparently the wilful writing of Marlowe.   Peele, who
is quite capable of the anachronism, would hardly
have used " popish tricks " as a heathen's fling at a
normal moral standard :   the stroke is in the
" irreligious " vein of Marlowe's villains in general ;
and the rough vigour of the speech is not Peelean.
The poet, too, who put " poor church " in his rendering of Lucan, might very well posit the " ruinous
monastery " here.

If, however, Marlowe's be the hand in the speeches
of Aaron, it disappears at the close in the second scene,
which is substantially in the style of Peele, though not
without suggestion of Kyd.   In this scene the double-
endings are few—only 12 in 205 lines, or 6 per cent.,
whereas in the previous scene there are 32 in 165 lines,
or nearly 20 per cent.   On the whole, there is a presumption of revision and retouching throughout the
Act ;   and though Peele is frequently recognisable,
and notably at the close, the work is certainly not
homogeneous.

CHAPTER XI

The Tests of Plot, Structure, and Substance

It is when we apply the final tests of plot and structure that Marlowe is most clearly acquitted of any constructive share in Titus, while Peele, Kyd, and Greene are more or less certainly implicated. The play is, broadly, an artificial composition on the Italian lines of the Spanish Tragedy, with a superfœtation of crimes and horrors, involving a chain of revenges, on the lines of the Tragedy, Selimus, Locrine and David and Bethsabe. The whole sequence is the conception of men academically or classically trained, proceeding as it does on the Aristotelian maxim, received by them through Seneca, by way of Italy, that the spectacle of a good man suffering without cause is unnatural. On this view every destined victim has to begin as a wronger or slayer in order to qualify for penalty or assassination; and the presence of such motives in the history of David seems to have recommended it to Peele for dramatic purposes. David betrays Urias, whereupon Amnon violates Thamar, Absalon kills Amnon, and Joab Absalon ; as in Locrine hero after hero in turn is slain and avenged, their ghosts and the figure of Até playing leading parts. Revenge is the keynote of the Spanish Tragedy ; and in Arden the playwright is at special pains to exhibit the victim as having himself been guilty of cruelty to others, his dead body being cast on a field unjustly held by him. So in Selimus the villain-hero makes war on his father, who nevertheless, on his submission, makes him his heir ; whereupon another son, Acomat, makes war on both ; while Selim in turn poisons Bajazet, strangles his brother Corcut, and conquers and kills Acomat. It is to be presumed that the fall of Selim was reserved for the promised second part : even Greene, who in his tales and plays so often lets the scoundrels go unpunished, could hardly have contemplated the final success of his fiendish conqueror. Marlowe, going deeper than the Senecan formula, generally brings his sinners to the dust. The sanity of Shakespeare refused to develope the conception ; but it was passed on to him in ROMEO, JOHN, and RICHARD II ; and in the second and third parts of HENRY VI the alternate murders by Lancastrians and Yorkists tell of the same academic formula. It is on this principle that there is committed, in the first Act of TITUS, the gross moral blunder of making Titus sacrifice the son of Tamora in cold blood—a deed which entirely disqualifies him for sympathy when he suffers in turn. Yet it appears to result from the investigation of Mr. De W. Fuller[1] that the sacrifice is an addition to the older play—so blinded was the reviser by his theory of dramatic construction. The sacrifice is the special contribution of Peele : the traditionists would make it Shakespeare's. Even Lavinia, before being mutilated, duly earns the hate of Tamora by a speech of which the hard immodesty excludes any sympathetic conception of her character, though a German Professor[2] contrives to frame of her a pleasing abstraction, and Mr. Baildon did his best to bear him out.[3]

And as the æsthetic theory of these early tragedies is the same, they hold in common their æsthetic machinery. Their fundamental moral motive is vengeance ; the word " revenge " pervades the dialogue to the point of burlesque ; and the action is often moved to its end by a personification of Até or Revenge ; or by the ghost of a victim, or by both. And both devices, again, are borrowed from Seneca. In Shake-

---

[1] Art. cited, p. 52.

[2] Professor Schröer, *Ueber Titus Andronicus*, p. 86.

[3] See Mr. Baildon's Introduction, where he challenges Mr. Arthur Symons to say what Lavinia as a modest woman *ought* to have said to Tamora.   In a note on II, iii, 74, he suggests that Mr. Symons, in pronouncing (like every critic before him) Lavinia's speech to be in execrable taste, must have been thinking of the speech of Bassianus. The reader need but glance over the scene to be enabled to make the fitting comment.

speare's HAMLET, which certainly proceeds upon an older play (in all likelihood by Kyd),[1] we see the apparatus which best appeals even to the modern spectator— the Ghost of the victim urging on his avenger, who employs certain devices to convict or slay the criminal, or to do both ; and in HAMLET we see still preserved the idea of a double revenge, the chief avenger himself incurring the vengeance of another. Ghosts being freely employed in the SPANISH TRAGEDY, LOCRINE, and the old HAMLET, it may have been thought expedient in TITUS to do without them ; but the further plan of pretended madness on the part of the avenger, which occurs in the TRAGEDY and in the old HAMLET, figures also in TITUS. In both the TRAGEDY and TITUS, again, Revenge is personified—a reason for surmising the collaboration of Kyd. Finally, the device of a play-scene—a development from the more primitive " dumb-show " as we have it in LOCRINE, which also occurs in the TRAGEDY, and figured in the old HAMLET—is abandoned in TITUS in favour of an absurd masquerade of the guilty persons.

There has also taken place a progression in atrocity. LOCRINE has no attempt to transcend the simple effects of slaughter, extreme hunger, and suicide ; it tells only of native inspiration. In the " Italianate " SPANISH TRAGEDY, the effect of the chain of assassinations had been heightened by Jeronimo's feat of biting off his own tongue. SELIMUS, a slightly more intellectual performance than LOCRINE, later than that[2] and following on TAMBURLAINE, but still an early play, has no artifice of plot, but adds to the horrors of Kyd those of the tearing-out of eyes and cutting-off of hands, as DAVID AND BETHSABE adds that of a violation. TANCRED AND GISMUNDA, a play of Italian inspiration, as revised in 1592, has a scene in which the heroine kisses the pierced heart of her husband, sent her in a cup by her father. And whereas, in the fragment preserved of the first

[1] Cp. Fleay, *Biog. Chron.* ii, 32-33 ; Sarrazin, *Thomas Kyd und sein Kreis,* 1892, p. 94 sq. This view is now generally accepted. [It is set forth in the author's " *Problem of Hamlet,*" 1919 ; and " *Hamlet* " *Once More,* 1923].

[2] See above, p. 317 sq.

version, Tancred at the close says he will enter the tomb and pierce his heart, in the revised play he tears out his own eyes. The horrible had come into fashion.[1]

TITUS, in turn, combines the horrors of all its predecessors, outgoing Jeronimo's burlesque achievement by making Lavinia's violators cut out her tongue as well as lop off her hands ; adding a sickening scene of throat-cutting and a Thyestean banquet ; making Titus slay his wronged daughter ; and flavouring the whole action with the open grossness of the amour of Aaron and Tamora. The complication tells of a process of evolution. Professor Baker is probably quite right in his conclusion that " Even as far back as 1585 the story of Titus had been staged,"[2] though the phrase of Ben Jonson in BARTHOLOMEW FAIR, making TITUS and JERONIMO 25 or 30 years old in 1614, is a somewhat insecure basis for certainty. Mr. H. De W. Fuller, after his minute study of the old German and Dutch forms of TITUS AND VESPASIAN and TITUS ANDRONICUS, comes, as we have seen, to the conclusion that they were founded on two different versions of the story. This may well be so : the two versions would just be the earlier and the later of our theory ; but in avowing that he believes " Shakespeare to be the author of practically every line of the play we possess, and that it belongs to the year 1594,"[3] Mr. Fuller proceeds in disregard of the whole æsthetic phenomena. To say nothing of the manifold proofs that it is not Shakespeare's, the play as it stands is not all of one structure ; and Mr. Fuller has in effect shown that its plot underwent a complication.

As regards plot and substance, Peele would seem to be specially indicated by the sexual element, which is prominent in his DAVID AND BETHSABE and EDWARD I ;

[1] There is some cause to suspect that the scene of Bajazet's burlesque suicide in 1 *Tamburlaine*, v, ii, is an addition to the first draft, by another hand.
[2] Note after Mr. De W. Fuller's paper on " The Sources of ' Titus Andronicus ' " in *Publications of the Modern Language Association of America*, vol. xvi, pt. i, 1901, p. 76.
[3] Paper cited, p. 76.

and of which there is little savour in Kyd, who eschews grossness even in ARDEN OF FAVERSHAM, though not in SOLIMAN. But the complication and artifice of the whole suggests Kyd (considered as main author of SOLIMAN and THE SPANISH TRAGEDY) much more strongly than either Peele or Greene, neither of whom has separately shown any notion of plot elaboration apart from ALPHONSUS OF GERMANY, where the plot savours so much of Kyd ; or than Marlowe, whose plot remains relatively incomplex even in THE JEW. The woodenness of the figure of Lavinia, too, seems impossible to the mature Greene, and suggests the draftsman of that of Bellimperia in the SPANISH TRAGEDY. If it be Kyd's, the work was early for him ; as his Alice, and even Perseda, are much more alive than the heroine of the TRAGEDY. To assign to him the Andronica of the German play, and to Peele the re-writing in Act I, squares with all the data. In any case, the plot gives us still farther reason to look to Peele and Kyd when we compare it with that of ALPHONSUS OF GERMANY, which we have seen, by other tests, to be in part Peele's. The central motive of that play is notably in his taste ; his animus—whether religious or commercial—against everything Spanish and Catholic being there exhibited still more elaborately than in his base treatment of the Queen in EDWARD I. Like DAVID and TITUS, ALPHONSUS OF GERMANY includes a violation (in this case by fraud) ; and the sexual motive is freely played upon. To the horrors of previous plays it adds that of the dashing out of an infant's brains by its grandfather, who, likening himself, as does Titus, to Virginius, slays likewise its mother, his daughter, and further suggests TITUS by recommending its putative father, who is starving, to eat the body.

No less significant is the duplication in ALPHONSUS of one of the crudest plot-expedients in TITUS. Even Mr. Baildon is moved to protest by the absurdity of the forged letter given by Tamora to Saturninus in Act II, sc. iii. It seems to mean, writes Mr. Baildon,

PLOT, STRUCTURE, AND SUBSTANCE

that if the writer fails to meet Bassianus and kill him himself, the receiver of the writ is to kill Bassianus and bury him in the said pit. Anything clumsier than such a letter between conspirators, naming the person plotted against twice in full, cannot be conceived. Fancy an anarchist writing to another and designating his victim as the " Empress of Austria" or the " Czar of Russia " ! I cannot help thinking that in this scene we have, more than in almost any other part of the play, *relics of an older and cruder version of the story.*

That is to say, Shakespeare preserved an extremely primitive absurdity, on which any intelligent novice might have improved. The guess is not warranted by dramatic history. No earlier play presents such a device; and in this scene-section there are six double-endings in 47 lines, a rate of over 12 per cent. What is more, a closely similar device, only, if possible, more grossly absurd, occurs in ALPHONSUS OF GERMANY, where the villain announces :

> By letters which I'll *strew within the wood*
> I'll undermine the boors to murder him.

This episode too is in a scene where double-endings abound ; and, like the other, would belong to Peele's closing period if it were his. It is certainly not a stroke which Kyd's admirers need care to claim for him ; but though Peele in the OLD WIVES TALE shows a certain tendency to plot-complication, we are led by such machinery to think of Kyd, seeing that in the old HAMLET there seems to have been a resort to a " plotted scroll," retained or adapted in the play as left us by Shakespeare. It might be worth while to inquire whether the " strewed letters " expedient came from Italy ; but that seems unlikely.

And all this seems alien to Marlowe, whose own development is so notably independent, and so rapid as between TAMBURLAINE (1587) and THE JEW (1588). If we should consider only the former we might say, with Professor Schröer, that Marlowe's genius was epic, not dramatic.[1]   Dramatic power of a new kind, however

---

[1] *Ueber Titus Andronicus,* p. 95.

untrained, THE JEW surely discloses ; and the essential originality of the man is seen in his disregard, in both plays alike, of the methods of his predecessors. THE JEW is already in a higher æsthetic world than LOCRINE and the SPANISH TRAGEDY ; and the style alters in sympathy with the change of theme. But this very originality, seen also in FAUSTUS, and yet again in EDWARD II and DIDO, excludes the possibility of such a complete surrender to other men's worse and weaker modes as would have happened had Marlowe planned TITUS. On that view, we should have to regard him as not merely writing a long and elaborate play without a single " mighty line," but lapsing into the feeblest devices and the most vacuous mannerisms of Peele, and combining them with the primitive revenge-mongering of Peele and Kyd. Mr. Bullen once backed the suggestion that Marlowe wrote TITUS by citing the speech beginning " Now climbeth Tamora Olympus' top," which actually contains a duplicate of a Peele line.[1] But Mr. Bullen, it may be remarked, had not at the time of his putting that opinion edited Peele's works, in which there is so much pseudo-Marlowese. Doubtless Marlowe in his outset echoed at times the phraseology of the men then in possession of the boards ; but he took his own way.

What he seems to have had in common with them all is the tendency to rant, though it is not certain that the close resemblances of this kind in the plays of the period are not partly the result of adaptations by actors. But revenge and rant went naturally together ; and it is to the pre-Shakespeareans, not to Shakespeare, that we must attribute such an effect as this[2] in TITUS (IV, iii) :

> Pluto sends you word,
> If you will have Revenge from hell, you shall :
> Marry for Justice, she is so employ'd

[1] He was misled by the fact that the line cited echoes one in *Faustus* (III, chorus 3) :— " Did mount him up to scale Olympus' top."

[2] Compare *Tancred and Gismunda*, Act IV, sc. i, where " Before this Act Megæra riseth out of hell, with the other furies, Alecto and Tysiphone dancing an hellish round." This play was printed in 1592, and may have given hints for *Titus*.

He thinks, with Jove, in heaven, or somewhere else . . .
I'll dive into the burning lake below,
And pull her [Justice] out of Acheron by the heels.

Compare it with the following :

Though on this earth justice will not be found
I'll down to hell, and in this passion,
Knock at the dismal gate of Pluto's court,
Getting by force, as once Alcides did,
A troop of furies and tormenting hags . . .

S. T., III, xiii.

I'll pass the Alps to wat'ry Meroë . . .
I'll overturn the mountain Caucasus . . .
I'll pull the fickle wheel from out her hands,
And tie herself in everlasting bands.   Locr., ii, 6.

I'll pass the Alps and up to Meroë . . .
And pull the harp out of the minstrel's hands,
And pawn it unto lovely Proserpine.

Orlando Furioso, ed. Dyce, p. 104.

I hold the fates bound fast in iron chains
And with my hand turn fortune's wheel about.

1 Tamb., I, ii.

And again compare these :—

I tell you, younglings, not Enceladus,
With all the threatening band of Typhon's brood,
Nor great Alcides, nor the god of war,
Shall seize the prey out of his father's hands.

Titus, IV, ii.

Not aged Priam, king of stately Troy,
Grand emperor of barbarous Asia,
When he beheld his noble-minded son
Slain traitorously by all the myrmidons,
Lamented more than I for Albanact.

Locr., III, ii.

As has been already remarked, the play further
belongs to the same school in point of its Latin
tags, Seneca quotations, and classical allusions.
Peele, Greene, Marlowe, and Kyd, alike abound
in these ; and it is probably due to its being preserved only in a late and revised edition that we
find no quotations in ALPHONSUS OF GERMANY in

addition to its classical allusions, which include Até, Athamas, Aristotle, Apollo, Achilles, Menetiades, Laocoon, Lysander, Patroclus, Phalaris, Plato, Cancer, Scorpion (reminiscent of the constellations in TITUS and Peele's frequent " zodiac "), Virginius, and Æneas's pilot.   But there are special reasons for ascribing to Peele certain classical allusions in TITUS.   The traditionists have not succeeded in turning the point of two annotations by Theobald and Steevens, to the effect (1) that the allusion in TITUS (I, 137-8) to Hecuba's " sharp revenge " upon the " Thracian tyrant " " in his tent " (a clear error of the press for " her tent," as Theobald suggested), is to be traced only to the HECUBA of Euripides, which had not been translated in Shakespeare's time ; and (2) that the subsequent allusion to the burial of Ajax points only to the AJAX of Sophocles, also untranslated in Shakespeare's day.

With regard to the first, Mr. Baildon boldly alleges that the story of Hecuba's revenge on Polymnestor " is told in Virgil's ÆNEID, where Shakespeare could read it for himself, or in Phaer's translation."   There is no such passage in the ÆNEID :   Virgil tells nothing of Polymnestor's death, The story is briefly told in Ovid's METAMORPHOSES (xiii, 549-564) ;   but that version does not fully yield the allusion.   Steevens, in his perverse way, sought to upset Theobald's reference to Euripides on grounds which would equally have upset his own to Sophocles ; and referring to the METAMORPHOSES, argues that " The writer of the play, whoever he was, might have been misled by the passage in Ovid, ' vadit *ad artificem*,' and therefore took it for granted that she found him in *his tent*."   How anyone should infer " his tent " from " ad artificem " is hard to divine.   It would have been a little more plausible to cite the phrase " colloquiumque petit."   But, in point of fact, Ovid expressly says :   " Credidit Odrysius . . . . *in secreta venit*," which excludes the inference of " *his* tent " without specifying hers ; while in Euripides the tent is expressly mentioned twice (ἀποστῆναι δόμων, 980 ; ἀλλ ἔρπ᾽ ἐς οἴκους, 1019), and the apprehensive entrance of Polymnestor is the outstanding feature of the scene. The writer of TITUS, then, had that scene in view ; and that Peele knew his Euripides is not a mere inference from his status as M.A. : it is proved by the Latin verses addressed to him by Dr. Gager, testifying to his having translated one of the two IPHIGENIAS of Euripides into English verse.[1]

The traditionists will fall back, perhaps, on the thesis that Shakespeare read the Greek tragedies in the original—a thesis maintained by Professor Collins with a confidence that is in the inverse ratio of his evidence. Mr. Baildon, for his part, got over the reference to the funeral of Ajax by the plea that " Many of us know something of books we have never read from the talk of others," which is a mere evasion of the problem set up by the peculiarly specific character of the allusion in (TITUS (I, i, 379-81) :

> The Greeks upon advice did bury Ajax
> That slew himself ; and wise Laertes' son
> Did graciously plead for his funerals.

This is not the kind of " general acquaintance " that men get with the contents of books they have not read : it is the express pedantry of a scholar. For the rest, Peele alludes specifically and lengthily to the quarrel and suicide of Ajax in the TALE OF TROY(349-375), where he uses the very words " wise Laertes' son " (l. 362), and where he also mentions the murder of Polydore by Polymnestor (393-399) ; and that he had read Sophocles as well as Euripides might be taken for granted even if we did not possess his lines to his friend Watson, who had published a Latin translation of the ANTIGONE, there referred to, in 1581. It was in all likelihood from the HECUBA

---

[1] MS. .Brit. Mus. printed by Dyce and by Bullen in their introductions to Peele.

that Peele drew the unhappy idea of the human sacrifice *ad manes fratrum* in TITUS.

It is unnecessary for our purpose to go into the origin of the scene of the arrows, which has been dubiously traced to Byzantine sources.[1]   If the play is derived from an Italian original, the scene of the arrows may come thence.   Suffice it that such an episode also points to Kyd or to any of the academic group rather than to Shakespeare.   As regards the story of Philomela and Progne, he might, as Professor Schröer points out,[2] find it in George Gascoigne's COMPLAINT OF PHILOMENE (1562-1576), where, indeed, there are some slight verbal parallels to TITUS ;[3]   but so well-known a myth is not a ground for raising the question of classical knowledge.   What is obviously non-Shakespearean is the classicism of the passages above discussed and of the Senecan and other quotations.   The astonishing assertion of Professor Schröer[4] that these are peculiarly Shakespearean (*so echt shakspereisch wie nur irgend etwas*) is justified solely by references to the SHREW, which is not only based on a previous play, but is almost wholly un-Shakespearean as it stands ; to 3 HENRY VI, which Shakespeare merely worked over ; to TIMON, which is his only in part ; to LOVE'S LABOUR'S LOST, where the classical matter clearly points to a second hand ; to the bare mention of Ovid's captivity in AS YOU LIKE IT ; and to the passage on " the poet's eye in a fine frenzy rolling " in the DREAM, which is gravely cited as an echo of the *amabilis insania* of Horace, who in Shakespeare's day was not translated in print.   Finally, it is suggested that the initials W. S. on a copy of the METAMORPHOSES in the Bodleian,

---

[1] As to these see Professor Schöer's *Ueber Titus Andronicus*, p. 19 sq. and refs.

[2] *Id.*, p. 27, *note*.

[3] One of these is the common use of " fact " as = deed or crime.   But this is common in Greene, and is found in many other writers.   It is a normal Elizabethan word.   " Bloody fact " occurs in *Ferrex and Porrex*.   Greene has " bloody fact " " heinous fact," " devilish fact," " filthy fact," etc. Fact = *act* occurs thrice in Peele's *David and Bethsabe*; and four times in the early *True Tragedie of Richard III*.

[4] *Id.*, p. 31.

somehow connected with the Hall family, prove Shakespeare to have been a reader of the "classics." Such pleas need no answer. The pedantries of TITUS are as alien to the spirit and method of Shakespeare's real work as are its atrocities and moral stupidities.

But indeed the case constructed by Professor Schröer is substantially irrelevant to the proofs before cited of the non-Shakespearean character of most of the play under examination. He argues learnedly and elaborately to explain away "parallels" of no importance, such as the use of "capitol" in Peele's EDWARD I ; a detail devoid of significance, seeing that the word appears many times in Lodge's WOUNDS OF CIVIL WAR and in Kyd's CORNELIA and SOLIMAN. He seems indeed to have seen every sort of parallel except those which do decisively prove Peele's and Greene's and Marlowe's and Kyd's presence in the play. It is those parallels, and the perpetual presence of non-Shakespearean styles, that must be faced by conservative criticism if it would maintain a semblance of scientific justification for the continued ascription of TITUS to Shakespeare.

When the thesis of his authorship is thus negatived by such a mass of internal evidence, and a counter theory is seen to consist with such a multitude of details, it seems unnecessary to argue at any length on the abstract "æsthetic" problem. It is enough to say that those who could not believe in the Shakespearean authorship of such a play as TITUS are abundantly justified. In the foregoing inquiry no argument whatever has been drawn from the glaring unlikelihood of the theory that the greatest of dramatists began by writing the most detestable of plays. It was necessary to meet with irreversible evidence those who could maintain such a hypothesis. But it may now be urged, as against those who find psychological solutions for the inconceivable, that æsthetic is after all a specialisation of trained common-sense. We have been in effect asked by the traditionists to believe that Shakespeare, whom we find laughing genially at the " Ercles vein " of Peele and Marlowe and Kyd as early as I HENRY IV, had only a year or two before been performing at their most *banal* level, imitating their weakest mannerisms, employing their cheapest devices, and outdoing their grossest barbarities. We may now put aside without misgiving so grotesque a " paradox." Youth, as we have said, is spontaneously imitative ; but youth of genius imitates what it admires ; and its admiration must needs be not less but more discriminative than that of the uninspired.[1]

Shakespeare in 1593—when, according to the critics who latterly justify the traditional view by investigation, he must have written TITUS ANDRONICUS—was in his thirtieth year : as old, that is, as was Marlowe when his work was done ; and within a few years of writing the MERCHANT OF VENICE. We are to suppose him writing at that point the most brutal tragedy of the era. Simple common-sense would endorse Fleay's summary decision that " the introduction of rape as a subject for the stage would be sufficient to disprove Shakespeare's author-ship."[2] Mr. Baildon's reply is memorable :

A more ridiculous and fatuous remark it would be impossible to find in the annals of criticism. DID MR. FLEAY FORGET that about the time this play must have been written Shakespeare had it in his mind, AS WE SEE FROM THE PLAY ITSELF, to devote his utmost *poetic* powers—which he then regarded with infinitely greater reverence than he did his *dramatic* powers—to writing the *Rape of Lucrece* ? If Shakespeare thought this subject fit for a poem, which was to gain him the favour of the highest in the land, HE COULD HAVE NO POSSIBLE SCRUPLE AGAINST TREAT-ING SUCH A SUBJECT DRAMATICALLY.[3]

The italics are Mr. Baildon's, the small capitals

[1] Signor Benedetto Croce has astonished some of us by asking (in *Ariosto, Shakespeare e Corneille*, Eng. trans. 1920, p. 191): " What more natural " than that the young Shakespeare should write such a play as *Titus* by way of a literary imitation ? *This* æsthetic seems to have originated in Germany. (See below, p. 418). But if Signor Croce will go into the technical problem he will probably see reason to withdraw his assent to it.

[2] *Life of Shakespeare*, p. 280.

[3] Introd. to ed. cited, p. xxvii.

the present critic's.   It may be left to the reader
to find countervailing epithets for so perfect a
specimen of the argument in a circle, presented by
way of convicting a ripe student of unparalleled
fatuity. Fleay had not Mr. Baildon's faculty of
forgetting the main facts of his case ; and his argument
plainly turned on the very fact so idly trumpeted.   In
the RAPE OF LUCRECE, as in VENUS AND ADONIS,
Shakespeare has treated at great length an action
which would have been ABSOLUTELY IMPOSSIBLE on
the stage. Even Thomas Heywood, who went far
into lubricity in his GOLDEN AGE, could not have
ventured on this.   Mr. Baildon goes on to allude to the
" very revolting " theme of VENUS AND ADONIS : and
his argument commits him to the proposition that
Shakespeare " could have no possible scruple " against
putting on the stage the action of that poem.   In the
struggle with æsthetic obscurantism we are finally
forced to dwell on the fact, " gross as a mountain, open,
palpable," that *he could not* have done so in any theatre
in Europe.

The method of Shakespeare in LUCRECE is at the
other psychological extreme from that of the play.   He
has written at astonishing length of one atrocious act,
with the effect of making its psychic or spiritual aspect
absolutely overlay the physical.   Even in the other
poem, the amount of psychic commentary and
poetic discourse is so great as to overlay the action.
And on the strength of these poems we are told that
he was the very man to flaunt on the stage, to the
utmost verge of endurable brutality, the kind of
physical atrocity which, even for his readers, he
had put in the background of a long-drawn psychological excursus.   On Mr. Baildon's principles, any
poet who should treat in his poetry of the subject
of cannibalism would feel free to put on the
stage a cannibal banquet.   The authors of TITUS
have gone as far in *that* direction as they dared.   Byron,
according to Mr. Baildon, could have " no possible
scruple " about going further.   Mr. Baildon's æsthetics

compel to silence those who do not care to borrow his epithets.

Yet even this is not the limit of the criticism which insists upon ascribing TITUS to Shakespeare. Mr. Baildon once gets so far as to avow that the line,

> Brewed with her sorrow, mesh'd upon her cheeks,

is "a very clumsy and offensive conceit from the operation of brewing"; and over another nauseous passage he is slightly apologetic. But concerning the throat-cutting, at which the maimed Lavinia holds the basin (a species of horror which only Zola has ventured to handle in a realistic novel), while he reluctantly admits its "gruesomeness," he alleges—by implication—that in this as in other plays,

> Shakespeare soared above the "Tragedy of Blood" school, not by excising the horrors from his plots, but by treating them in so noble and elevated a manner that we forget the physical horrors in the awe and pity with which his marvellous handling of his themes inspires us.

This of one of the most grossly horrible scenes of bestial revenge in all drama. And even this is transcended by the critic when, in his introduction,[1] he thus disposes of the hideous scene in which Tamora eats of a dish in which her sons' heads have been baked by Titus and Lavinia :

> Is it then so unjust, *is it even so gratuitously horrible*, to make this woman . . . eat the flesh and blood of her own offspring ? For the woman, indeed, who was the moral murderer of her two sons, in encouraging them to commit the vilest of crimes, and who was in intention an infanticide, *could there be any more appropriate horror of punishment* ?

If we could have had Mr. Baildon as licenser of plays, with his notions of "making the punishment fit the crime," we might have seen some sensational æsthetic developments. "Something with boiling oil in

---

[1] As cited, p. lxii.

it " would probably have been frequent. Comment is superfluous. His argument, like the abominable play which he glorifies, attains the effect of burlesque.

Otherwise inadequate is the more guarded yet self-confuting plea by which Professor Boas seeks to meet the æsthetic dilemma. Having accepted the German verdict on the " external evidence," he proceeds to find that

> A breeze from the *Warwickshire glades* blows fresh at times through the reeking atmosphere, and amidst the festering corruption of a *decadent society* we have glimpses of nature that make us less forlorn. The constant allusions, however, to animals and birds in " Titus Andronicus," as in other of the early plays and poems, are due *not only* to Shakespeare's familiarity with the country but to the influence of *Euphuism, one of whose most notable features is the persistent use of illustrations from the natural world.*[1]

That is to say, the hand of Shakespeare is to be traced inasmuch as he writes like many other people. As Professor Boas had thus disposed of his own case, it is hardly necessary to add that every species of " illustration from the natural world " in the play is common to the school of Greene, Peele, Marlowe, and Kyd. One of the animals thrice mentioned is the panther, never found in a Shakespearean play, but here made to be hunted in the neighbourhood of Rome, even as Lodge introduced the lion into the forest of Arden. Like every other animal alluded to, he belongs to the menagerie of Greene and Peele, who speak of lions, tigers, boars, bears, whelps, wolves, dogs, eagles, birds, falcons, serpents, as well as flowers, times without number. It is needless to add a comment on the æsthetic which finds in zoological allusions, avowed to be partly derived from Euphuism, a ground for compliment to the society of Elizabethan Warwickshire, while ascribing to the Warwickshire youth of the theory the deliberate invention of the chain of utterly unhistorical horrors which forms the story of TITUS.

[1] *Shakespeare and his Predecessors*, p. 139.

Even Professor Herford, one of the ablest and best equipped of our English professors of native literature, offers in part a similar, though tentative, support to the traditionist view, remarking that the bookish allusions to the play are " tempered with many touches caught from the open-air life of nature such as nowhere fail in the young Shakespeare. A woodland brake— a ' pleasant chase '—is the scene of the most tragic deed in the whole play."[1]   In point of fact there is *much more* of " open-air " suggestion in this play than in any of the genuine *tragic* work of the young Shakespeare, which does *not* abound in such touches ; and these suggestions are entirely in the spirit of Peele and Greene, whose works, tragic and non-tragic alike, are full of them.   Peele's ARRAIGNMENT OF PARIS is a pastoral ; his BATTLE OF ALCAZAR and DAVID AND BETHSABE contain elaborate imagery from nature ; and his SIR CLYOMON has a dozen open-air and forest scenes, as in the Forest of Marvels and the Isle of Strange Marshes.   Greene's ORLANDO FURIOSO treats of clouded moons, private walks, shady lawns, and " thickest-shadowed groves " ; the plot turns on the engraving of the names of Medor and Angelica on the bark of trees ; there is a song which in two lines names groves, rocks, woods, watery springs, cedar, cypress, laurel, and pine ; the mad Orlando speaks of " woods, trees, leaves " ; Angelica disguises herself as a shepherdess, and " wanders about in woods and ways unknown."   FRIAR BACON AND FRIAR BUNGAY involves a rustic romance, in which the heroine is first pictured " among the cream-bowls," and half the talk is of country life ; GEORGE-A-GREENE is a village drama, wherein men fight about the putting of horses into corn ; in JAMES IV, Queen Dorothea, wounded in the woods, is there healed of her wound.   Even in the SPANISH TRAGEDY, the lover is slain in a pleasant bower.

But it is needless to multiply instances.   There is something wrong with a critical method which thus

[1] Introd. to the " Eversley " ed. of *Titus Andronicus*, p. 292.

employs æsthetics, not as a scientific means of discovering truth, but as a mere source of tropes to eke out a proposition irreconcilable with any fundamental æsthetic. All æsthetic inference is indeed hard of reduction to logical fixity ; but in the present inquiry, it is submitted, the incurable incongruities are associated with the thesis combated.

It may be useful, in conclusion, to meet one possible claim for Shakespeare's authorship of TITUS—a claim, namely, on the score of its " dramatic effectiveness." As played of late at the " Old Vic," it is found to " go very well." And when we point out the weighty reasons for regarding RICHARD II and RICHARD III as plays really composed by Marlowe and only touched at points by Shakespeare, we are met in some quarters by confident assurances that if only we had " the dramatic sense " we should see that the hand that constructed EDWARD II could not have constructed the RICHARD plays, which act so much better. The assumption seems to be that Marlowe, setting out with TAMBURLAINE, proved himself fundamentally defective in the dramatic sense ; and that inasmuch as RICHARD III in particular is very effective on the stage, it must be the work of one with higher dramatic faculty.

Those who reason thus make no attempt to meet the argument from internal evidence. They do at times argue that if Shakespeare let such plays as RICHARD III be ascribed to him while they were really of Marlowe's origination, he was guilty of fraud. They do not, however, attempt to meet the argument that if Shakespeare wrote RICHARD II and RICHARD III he was stealing Marlowe's thunder in a very ignominious fashion. The rule in these discussions is for defenders of the Canon to evade all the points which fatally tell against them and to fasten solely on a point which they think sets up a difficulty for the critics of the Canon. Naturally they never ask how Shakespeare could have hindered Meres from printing his list when the theatre, for commercial reasons, called the play his, or whether he had any knowledge in advance of what Meres was going to say.

But that issue cannot be allowed to block the other, which must be tried on its merits. And the answer to the claim of " effectiveness on the stage " is that that is precisely the ground on which Shakespeare was *not* likely to excel Marlowe *at the outset*. This is not an à priori argument. Apriorism would suggest that the young actor would as such be at once a better playwright than the academic ; whereas his stage experience, with his innate faculty, only made him alive to the need for a more natural *utterance* than Marlowe's. Our argument founds on the fact that the two early plays in which Shakespeare's hand is certainly either wholly or largely present—the DREAM and the LABOUR—are *not* effective on the stage. Perhaps the claimants to " the dramatic sense " will have the prudence to admit this. One thoughtful critic, Mr. Thomas Donovan, has gone so far as to argue[1] that the DREAM is probably the " displeasing play " which is apologised for in the epilogue to 2 HENRY IV—an interesting and plausible suggestion which raises the question of an early date for the latter drama. And the LABOUR has admittedly the marks rather of a " private " than of a " public " play.

Marlowe, on the other hand, is obviously likely to have made great progress in " the dramatic sense " in his six crowded years. FAUSTUS and THE JEW are much more interesting than TAMBURLAINE ; and ALPHONSUS OF GERMANY, where Marlowe is clearly revealed in the opening scene, would be in its day about as effective as TITUS if its political elements did not interfere with its run. Our play, in fact, was effective on the stage precisely because it was the outcome of the joint efforts of four " old hands," who must have learned something of stage needs if they were capable of learning anything. If, as we contend, Marlowe added the Roses scene and the Talbot scenes

[1] Pamphlet on *The True Text of Shakespeare and his Fellow Playwrights*, 1923, pp. 15-17.

to the primary form of 1 HENRY VI, he was there exhibiting just his eye for stage effect. And it is only after years of practical training that Shakespeare adds such efficiency to his mastery of the higher elements of dramatic and poetic art,—right feeling, vision for character, and command of perfect utterance in admirably rhythmic verse. To the practical mastery he attains, not by any equally innate faculty for stage effect, but by the simple successive handling of other men's plays which he revised, of course, by help of his own experience as an actor.

Nay, to the end his higher faculty was apt to function in disregard of the other. While TITUS made, and in a way still makes, an effective acting play for any audience that can or will stand it, TROILUS AND CRESSIDA does not ; though it contains as much fine poetry as TITUS holds of bad. TROILUS, a composite work as it stands, is " a bad play." TIMON is not much better. CYMBELINE has quite recently been pronounced " a silly play." And even the claimants to " dramatic sense," who *ex cathedra* inform us that only Shakespeare could have planned RICHARD III, are found to confess that CORIOLANUS, surely a great play, is " intolerable " on the stage. In view of the singular inconsistencies of their position, then, it may suffice to point out to them that if they find *only* good stage work in the RICHARD plays they are distressingly uncritical of the grave dramatic blemish of such duplicated effects as the wooing of Anne and the wooing of Elizabeth for her daughter in RICHARD III, and the duplication of quarrel-scenes in RICHARD II. These may have been in their day effective ; for us they are fundamentally bad in art. And Shakespeare, we argue, does not of his own accord fault in *that* way— though in the LABOUR there are two masking scenes. For there, as Mr. Dover Wilson very convincingly argues[1], one scene was meant in the main to supersede the other, but the plan was not properly carried out in the MS. from which the play was printed.

[1] In the new Cambridge Univ. Press ed. of the play.

On a review of the whole problem, then, the argument that TITUS owes its stage effectiveness to a special faculty in the young Shakespeare for such effect, if advanced, cannot stand. That exiguous measure of credit may very well be given to the four hard-pressed play-makers whose hands we have seen in it. Earning their bread, they employed all the devices within their reach to draw crowds for the actors, where the young Shakespeare, putting an opening to the ERRORS and adding something here and there as he did in the TWO GENTLEMEN and in the RICHARD plays, or penning the DREAM, was so far concerned with higher things than the creation of raw and gross situations for the delectation of the groundlings. Had he not been so biassed, he would hardly have become the poet dramatist we know.

CHAPTER XII

SUMMARY

In such an inquiry, it is apt to be at times too " hard to see the wood for the trees " ; and a summary may avert some confusion. The argument may be succinctly stated thus :

1. The external evidence for Shakespeare's authorship of Titus, though it would be sufficient were it reconcilable with the internal evidence, is in itself quite inconclusive ; and the circumstantial evidence strongly contradicts that of literary record.

2. The publication of three editions of the play, evidently from a theatre copy or authorised transcript, in Shakespeare's lifetime, *without his name*, tells strongly on the other side ; and Ben Jonson's manner of reference to an early form of the play almost excludes the possibility that he held it for Shakespeare's.

3. The existing play bears to have been originally in the possession of a theatrical company with which Shakespeare had no known connection.

4. The principle of theatrical property in the play would suffice to account for its being claimed by Shakespeare's company as his, if he had merely revised the versification.

5. It is substantially proved that there was an old play on the same theme, and that that play was recast ; and there is even reason to guess that the present play is a revision of an earlier one which was a recast of the first.

6. The majority of those who affirm Shakespeare's authorship have dated the present play in or before 1589. Those who have really investigated its history, and still maintain that authorship, date it, in the present form, 1593.

478

7. In respect merely of the metrical phenomena, it must be years later than 1589, and cannot have been written by Shakespeare as early as 1593.

8. In respect of the plot and diction, it cannot conceivably have been written by him as late as 1593.

9. The whole mass of the internal evidence is overwhelmingly against the traditionist view. To the full extent to which æsthetic demonstration is possible, it is demonstrated by comparative evidence that much of the play is written by Peele ; and it is hardly less certain that much of the rest was written by Greene and Kyd, with some by Marlowe.

10. The probability is that Greene had collaborated with Kyd on the old play of TITUS AND VESPASIAN ; and in that play Peele may have had a share ; but in any case it was he who mainly recast it as TITUS ANDRONICUS, making it figure as a new play in 1593. Greene's share, on the other hand, may have been penned by way of an earlier collaboration ; while Marlowe, in view of the double-endings, is to be held to have worked at the later stage, whatever he may have done in the earlier.

11. There is abundant proof that Elizabethan plays were in this way frequently re-cast ; and that Peele and Greene in particular frequently collaborated, or eked out each other's plays. But it is only in working vigilantly through such a play as TITUS that we realise what a patchwork quilt an Elizabethan drama can be.

12. The argument from alleged internal evidence of Shakespeare's authorship breaks down at nearly every point, the proposed tests almost invariably recoiling against the thesis. But if at any points there be evidence for Shakespeare's touch, his authorship of the whole is only the more incredible.

13. There is no more evidence of structural revision or amendment by Shakespeare in TITUS than in LOCRINE. Any revision he gave it appears to have been limited to trimming the speeches, eliding the feeblest matter, " toning up " in respect of continuity ;

and making the lines scan ; and even this is not very carefully done.

The case is thus proved against his authorship independently of the extremely strong presumption that the most coarsely repulsive play in the entire Elizabethan drama cannot have been the work of the greatest and most subtle of all the dramatists of the age.

EPILOGUE

That such a discussion as this should have been necessary is, I think, a sufficient proof that the scientific criticism of literature in general and of Shakespeare in particular has not latterly gone forward among us. Shakespearean commentary, indeed, has never been so admirably done as by Professor A. C. Bradley : what I mean by scientific criticism is the quantitative and qualitative study of style, morphology, and authorship.[1] After a generation in which much was done to reach exactness of method and rationality of test, we seem to be in large part given over to the merest intuitionism. When Charles Knight justified his support of the traditionalist view concerning TITUS ANDRONICUS by passages of absurd æsthetic argumentation from Franz Horn, to the effect that, from a youth of genius so circumstanced and so slightly educated as Shakespeare, we were bound to have a first drama marked by " colossal errors,"[2] it did not seem that there was much danger of a general conversion of English opinion to the German doctrine. But we have seen latterly evolved among ourselves an æsthetic which reaches, à posteriori, less plausible results than Horn reached à priori, and this at even less philosophic cost. The explanation seems to be, not that the faculty for scientific thought is falling away, but that it is now being employed in other fields, leaving the survey of the æsthetic field to students not scientifically disposed.[3]

[1] I gratefully add, in 1919, that within the past year new pioneering work of high importance has been done on bibliographical lines by Mr. A. W Pollard and Mr. T. Dover Wilson.

[2] " Not merely single errors," the German philosopher goes on. " No, we should have a whole drama which is diseased at its very root, which rests upon one single monstrous error. Such a drama is this *Titus*."

[3] This judgment, penned in 1905, would seem to be supported by Mr. E. K. Chambers in his 1907 Introduction to *Titus*.

At a time when " higher criticism " is being zealously and successfully applied by a multitude of investigators in directions formerly blocked to such methods, the criticism of some developments of secular literature has reverted to pre-scientific forms. It is with some hope of promoting a revival of better methods that the foregoing investigation has been set about. If its shortcomings lead to its correction, so much the better : we shall be in the way of substituting argument and evidence for the mere dogmatisn which has latterly come in fashion. The first requisite is a return towards the analytic and comparative methods of the sciences. We have seen a number of Professors of literature, English and German, pronounce on a question of literary morphology without attempting any methodic comparison of the possible sources of type ; for even the painstaking Professor Schröer has but glanced at them. Professor Collins, for his part, avowed that he had not read Professor Schröer because, as he explained, " I abominate German academic monographs, and indulge myself in the luxury of avoiding them, wherever it is possible to do so ; being moreover insular enough to think that, on the question of the authenticity of an Elizabethan drama, an English scholar can dispense with German lights."[1] The trouble was that Professor Collins dispensed with all lights. On the one hand he dismissed the German critics as unreadable, though his special thesis may be said to have been " made in Germany " ; on the other hand the whole line of English critics who are against him were dismissed by him, without argument, as paradoxers, iconoclasts, and illegitimate practitioners. It had not occurred to him, in the exercise of his special functions, to collate TITUS critically with the contemporary Elizabethan drama, any more than he had thought of comparing Shakespeare's prose with the other prose of the time in pronouncing on its special merits.

It is true that German specialists have not advanced

[1] *Studies in Shakespeare*, pref., p. xii.

the study of Shakespeare in proportion to their admirable exertion of industry ; though it was left to Professor Sarrazin, after Fleay, to make the first careful investigation as to Kyd ; and German monographs on questions of English literature are generally helpful by their attention to detail. What is too often lacking in German work of this kind is the due operation of critical judgment. In the second edition of Schmidt's SHAKESPEARE-LEXIKON, revised and edited by Professor Sarrazin, there remain uncorrected the most monumental of the absurdities exposed by Richard Grant White a generation ago—the " squeaking Cleopatraboy," the explanation of the crocodile in Hamlet's rant as being a " mournful animal," and a score of other " howlers." If the circulation of such follies is persisted in as a propagation of scholarly knowledge, the hope of useful contribution by German experts to the deeper questions of English literary history will indeed dwindle.[1] But at present, in view of the contributions of Professor Collins and Mr. Baildon, it cannot be said that native criticism would be well advised to throw stones at the alien. The investigation seems quite as likely to be carried on elsewhere as in England. Professor Kellner, of Vienna, who knows English literature with peculiar intimacy, spontaneously recoils, in his comprehensive volume on Shakespeare,[2] from the belief that TITUS is of Shakespeare's invention. And German professors do at least work at their business. When Fleay in his edition of EDWARD II declared confidently in favour of Peele as main author of TITUS, he met with no countenance from native critics ; and Professor Schröer, having seen only his alternative theory naming Marlowe, dealt with that, which was at least more than his English fellow-students did. When Mr. Verity, in 1890, put on record as " worth a thought " his suggestion that TITUS was " precisely the type of work that Peele might have

[1] Written in 1905.
[2] *Shakespeare*, Berlin, etc., 1900, p. 24.

written," it seems to have met with almost no attention in England, being indeed entombed in an *édition de luxe* which no student was likely to handle. Dr. Grosart's thesis of Greene's authorship, in its turn, was published in the ENGLISCHE STUDIEN, apparently in the knowledge that no English periodical would print it. We are still without an English SHAKESPEARE YEAR-BOOK.

" On the whole," I wrote in 1905, " the position of Shakespeare-study appears to be most hopeful in the United States, whence have latterly come the only important contributions to the problem hereinbefore treated of. I can but trust that Professor Baker and his students will carry their scholarly investigations further. If only the field be scientifically examined, there will be plenty of work for another generation." Since then, though the main result from America has been the essay of Professor Parrott, which I have had to controvert, the movement in Shakespeare-study has been distinctly promising, both there and at home. The SHAKESPEARE (compendium) of Professor R. M. Alden of Stanford University must be helpful to many students ; and the new LIFE by Professor Quincy Adams usefully counters some obstinate myths, though, as we have seen, it introduces one of its own. To say nothing of the greatly enlarged edition of Sir Sidney Lee's standard LIFE, such books as the COLLECTANEA of Mr. Crawford, Mr. Dugdale Sykes's SIDELIGHTS, and Mr. E. H. C. Oliphant's studies, yield distinct gains to serious scholarship despite miscarriages of inference ; the studies of Mr. A. W. Pollard and Mr. Dover Wilson, on bibliographical lines, and the editorial work of Mr. Wilson on the new Cambridge Press Shakespeare, carry much new light ; and Professor Herford's SKETCH of RECENT SHAKESPEARE INVESTIGATIONS brings these and other results under the notice of all who care to look for them. The Shakespeare Association, established by Sir Israel Gollancz, is another sign of reviving zeal, and in the face of such movement the prospect must be called hopeful. I would venture the hope that Professor Parrott will again explore the ground as to TITUS, unswayed by his mistaken assumption as to the early versification of Shakespeare and his corrivals.

Should the foregoing results in the main stand criticism—as distinct from denunciation—they will, it is hoped, be to some extent applicable to the whole series of problems set up by the earlier plays ascribed to Shakespeare. With those problems, however, I have only incidentally dealt in this volume, preferring as far as possible so to limit the discussion as to avoid all appearance of an argument in a circle. The main thesis of this volume logically stands or falls by the main issues raised ; and those who find the survey of the single problem an undue demand on their time would not be likely to forgive the detailed handling of half-a-dozen more.

The great difficulty, indeed, is to induce the majority of people who " know their Shakespeare " to do any critical thinking on any Shakespeare problem. Challenged by the insane Bacon Theory, and the breed of kindred Chimæras generated by its decomposition, they comfortably decide that all innovating doctrines are alike visionary. Yet all the while the comfortable majority accept without a pretence of thought an idle falsism which has served as one of the bases of Baconism, to wit, the dictum that the vocabulary of the Shakespeare Plays is very much larger than that of any other English writer. An imposing assertion to that effect, once launched, is everywhere adopted and repeated, by essayists, by Professors, by commentators, by devout readers, though there has never been a semblance of an attempt to prove it by even a partial collation of the vocabulary of Shakespeare with that of Jonson, or Chapman, or Fox, or Hooker, or Bacon, or Browne, or Fletcher, or Spenser, or Holland, or Florio, to say nothing of moderns. A sham collation of the Shakespeare Concordance with a Milton Concordance which ignores Milton's prose is the only pretence of justification offered. The late Dr. H.

Bradley avowed that he could never discover how the figures propounded were arrived at. Yet he consented to accept the assertion as broadly probable.

I once more submit the proposition that it is false— false even if we ascribe to Shakespeare the whole vocabulary of the plays. The falsity will doubtless peacefully proceed upon its unimpeded way ; for the mass of professional Shakespeare scholars pay no heed whatever to the challenge. Were they to dismiss it on the score that the matter is of no great importance, they would indeed be within their rights. But what they mostly do is to repeat the falsism.[1] If here and there an open-minded reader can be induced to look into even that simple question for himself, some progress may be made towards the critical end of re-valuing Shakespeare for what he was, and dispelling the mist of delusion in which he is so confusedly conceived as what he was not.

[1] A fresh allusion to the "vast vocabulary" of Shakespeare comes before me as I read my final "proofs."

INDEX

A

Aaron, in *Titus*, character of, 18, 48, 108, 127, 241 sq.
Adams, Prof. J. Quincy, 79 *n.*, 196, 307 *n.*, 367, 378
Æsthetic criticism, fallacies in, 39, 45, 137, 378, 471 sq.
Agnosticism and criticism, 53
Ajax, the, of Sophocles, 465, 466
Alden, Prof, R. M., 484
Alliteration in Elizabethan drama, 177 sq., 204 sq., 417
Allot, R., 317
Anachronisms in Elizabethan drama, 455 sq.
Alleyn, E., 85 sq.
Alphonsus Emperor of Germany, 98, 154, 252 sq., 461, 465, 475 ; probably of Italian origin, 256
Alphonsus King of Arragon, 274, 316, 321, 357, 358
Animals, allusions to, 160 sq., 472
Antwerp, the siege of, 394 sq.
Archer, W., on *Edward III.*, 369 sq., 373, 375 ; on *Arden*, 370
Arden of Feversham, 16, 20, 27, 32, 38, 123, 338 sq., 370, 403 sq.
Aristotelian canon in tragedy, 293, 457 sq.
Arnold, Matthew, 136
Arraignment of Paris, The, 188, 473
Antigone, the, of Sophocles, 466
Antoine, Garnier's, 421

B

Baconian theory, 53, 142 *n.*, 170, 485
Baildon, H. B., on *Titus*, 49, 51, 112, 465 ; on " anti-Shakespeareans," 52 sq., 57 sq., 59 sq., 62 ; on the chronology of the problem, 54, 76 ; on Ravenscroft and Malone, 57, 58 ; on the evidence of Meres, 57, 59 ; on the date of *Titus*, 76, 177 *n.* ; on Grosart, 217, 218 ; on Shakespeare's anachronisms, 455 ; surrender of case by, 455 ; on the plot of *Titus*, 461, 466 ; on Lavinia, 458 *n.* ; on Fleay, 469 ; on dramatic ethics, 471

Baker, Prof., cited, 68, 76, 460
Battle of Alcazar, The, 64, 188, 200 n., 249 *n.*
Bathurst, C., on *Titus*, 44, 438
Bear-baiting, Shakespeare and, 244 sq.
Beaumont and Fletcher, verse of, 421
Bible, criticism of the, 53
Blank verse, grafted on old plays, 63 ; evolution of, 416 sq, 431 sq.
Boas, Prof., on *Titus*, 49, 472 ; on its date, 54, 79 ; on *The Spanish Tragedy*, 107 ; on Marlowe, 417 *n.* ; on Shakespeare's early work, 89
Boswell, A., on *Titus*, 239
Brabine, 80 *n.*
Bradley, Prof. A. C., 481
——, Dr. H., 485-6
Briggs, Dr. W. D., 16
Brown, Prof. J. M., cited, 365
Browning, R., on *Titus*, 45 *n.*
Buck, Sir George, 198
Bullen, A. H., cited, 188, 239, 281, 285, 404, 418 *n.*, 463
Burckhardt, 75
Burns, and Shakespeare, 167 *n.*
Byron, and Shakespeare, 167 *n.*

C

Cambyses, 189 *n.*, 238
Capell, 43
Catiline, cited, 164
Chambers, E. K., on *Titus*, 2 sq. ; on critical method, 3 sq., 481 *n.* ; on literary equations, 35 ; on the *Comedy of Errors*, 35 sq. ; on Shakespeare's first company, 61 ; on " Tito Andronico," 73 n.
——, R. W., on *Sir Thomas More*, 442
Chapman, legal language in, 117 ; not author of *Alphonsus of Germany*, 252 sq. ; early style of, 255
Chaucer, canon of, 52
Chettle, 77, 89, 410
Circumstantial evidence, 56 sq., 478
Classical allusions in Elizabethan drama, 108, 135 sq., 141 sq., 255 sq., 308, 465
Cohn, on *Titus*, 44
Coleridge, S. T., on *Titus*, 43, 46 ; on *Venus and Adonis*, 78 *n.*

Coleridge, Hartley, on authorship of *Titus*, 41, 44
Collaboration, early, 34, 90, 233 sq., 249, 266
Collier, J. P., on *Titus*, 43, 45 ; on *Locrine*, 198 ; on *Edward III*, 305 ; on double-endings, 422
Collins, Prof. J. Churton, on *Titus*, 3, 4, 24, 51, 52 *n*., 92 sq., 104 sq., 106 ; on German criticism, 49, 482 ; on opponents, 52, 77 ; contradicts himself, 54, 104 ; on Ravenscroft, 57 ; on chronology, 76, 77 sq. ; on the Folio, 81 ; on Shakespearean style, 91, 104 ; on *The Spanish Tragedy*, 107 ; on Shakespeare's classical knowledge, 108, 466 sq. ; on his legal knowledge, 116 sq.
Comedy of Errors, double-endings in, 29, 427 ; date of, 87 sq. ; 378, 435 ; E. K. Chambers' theory of, 35 sq. ; Prof. Quincy Adams' theory of, 79 ; authorship of, 88 ; style of, 371, 427
Congreve, 391 *n*.
Contention of York and Lancaster, 27, 103
Copyright, theatrical, 80, 161, 249
Coriolanus, 476
Cornélie, Kyd's trans. of Garnier's, 27 sq., 124, 164
Courthope, Prof., on Kyd, 107 ; on Greene, 357 *n*. ; on Peele, 358
Craig, W. J., on *Titus*, 84
Crawford, C., 4, 35, 484 ; on authorship of *Arden of Feversham*, 20, 338 *n*. ; on *Titus*, 41, 54, 170 sq. ; on Ravenscroft, 58 and *note* ; on Shakespeare's imitations, 177, 180 ; on *Locrine* and *Selimus*, 199 *n*., 312 sq.
Creizenach, Prof., on *Titus*, 48
Critical method, 2 sq., 168 sq., 243, 244, 245, 263, 272
Croce, on *Titus*, 32, 469 *n*.
Cunliffe, Prof., 74 *n*. ; cited, 75
Cymbeline, 93 *n*., 476

D

Daniel, Samuel, 136
Darley, G., cited, 421 *n*.
David and Bethsabe, 15, 64, 127, 271 sq., 358, 457
Dekker, 365 *n*.
Delius, on *Titus*, 47, 50
Devecmon, on law in Shakespeare, 117

Diction, test of, 444 sq.
Dido, 95 *n*., 157 *n*., 302
Doctor Dodypoll, 249 sq.
Donovan, T., cited, 475
Double-endings, evolution of, 27 sq., 122 sq., 130, 244, 272, 277, 284, 291, 302 *n*., 330 *n*., 408, 415 *n*., 416 sq. ; counting of, 421 *n*.
Dowden, Prof., 367 *n*.
Drake, 44
Drayton, 402
Dyce, on *Titus*, 44 ; on the *Dream*, 88 ; on *Locrine*, 200 ; on the old *King John*, 281 ; on *David*, 358 ; on *A 'Larum for London*, 393 ; on *Sir Thomas More*, 443

E

Earl of Huntington plays, 410
Edmund, character of, 107-8
Edward I, 305
Edward II, 91, 299 sq.
Edward III, 21, 90, 123, 305 sq., 326 sq., 343 sq., 352 sq., 368 sq., 381 sq., 424, 429, 430
Edwards, Richard, 188
Elizabeth as " mortal moon," 367 *n*.
Elze, on *Titus*, 47 ; on date of *Titus*, 79 ; on word-test, 174 *n*. ; on *Alphonsus of Germany*, 253 sq.
England's Parnassus, 313, 317
Euphues, 222, 358 *n*.
Euphuism in drama, 472
Euripides, 465, 466

F

Fairfax, cited, 94 *n*.
Farmer, 41
Ferrex and Porrex, 204, 209, 319 *n*., 417 sq.
Fidele and Fortunio, 189, 319 *n*.
Fleay, F. G., 4, 44, 76 *n*., 89 *n*. ; services of, 22 sq., 42 ; on *The Jealous Comedy*, 37 sq. ; on Peele's share in *Titus*, 41, 483 ; on *Locrine*, 63, 198 ; on *Henry VIII* and *Pericles*, 49 ; on Shakespeare's company, 60, 61 ; on chronology of the plays, 76 *n*., 428 ; on Marlowe's work, 90 *n*., 95 *n*. ; on *Edward III*, 90, 305 sq., 326 ; on *Sir Clyomon*, 189 *n*. ; on *Doctor Dodypoll*, 249 ; on *Jack Straw*, 251 ; on *Wily Beguiled*, 250 ; on *Alphonsus of Germany*, 252 sq., 316 *n*. ; on the old *King John*, 281 ; on

Selimus, 315 ; on *Arden of Feversham*, 338 sq. ; on *A 'Larum for London*, 395 ; on *A Warning for Faire Women*, 406, 411 ; on the *Shrew*, 413 ; on double-endings, 422 *n.*, 428

Fletcher, verse of, 421, 440 *n.*

" For-to," use of, 285, 291, 303 *n*, 316

" Fourteener " metre, the, 189

Friar Bacon and Friar Bungay, 358, 473

Fuller, H. de W., 68, 83, 458, 460

Furnivall, Dr., 45, 49, 79, 427 ; on chronology of the plays, 87 sq.

G

Gager, on Peele's trans. of Euripides, 466

Garnett, Dr. R., on *Titus*, 13 sq., 161 sq., 239

Gayley, Prof. C. M., 421 *n.*

George-a-Greene, 358, 423, 473

German criticism, 44, 46, 48, 138, 482, 483

Gervinus, on *Titus*, 46

Ghosts in Elizabethan drama, 459

Gollancz, Prof., 484 ; on *pathaires*, 342

Gosse, E., on *Titus*, 49

Greene, Robert, tags of, 25, 94 sq., 329 sq., 446 sq. ; unsigned work of, 311 sq. ; share of, in *Titus*, 45, 94 sq., 122, 130, 216 sq., 232 sq., 274, 446 sq. ; in *Arden*, 341 sq., 403 ; in *Locrine*, 210 sq., 312 sq. ; on Shakespeare, 77, 89, 103 ; and Marlowe, 313 sq., 312 ; in the old *Leir*, 387 sq. ; in *Henry VI* plays, 104, 311 ; in *Selimus*, 210 sq., 224, 234, 312 sq. ; legal phrases in, 120 ; repetitiveness of, 172 ; opinions of, 234, 314, 317 ; style of, 236, 357, 373 sq., 436 sq. ; character of, 326, 358 sq. ; merits of, 357 ; imitation of Marlowe by, 274 ; and Peele, 235 ; double-endings in, 422 sq. ; share of, in *Edward III*, 307, sq., 326 sq., 343 sq., 352 sq., 371 sq., 424 ; influence of Spenser on, 316 ; influence of, on Shakespeare and Dekker, 365 ; in *Soliman*, 350 sq., 361 sq. ; in the *Two Gentlemen of Verona*, 371 sq., 424 ; versification of, 236, 318, 363, 368 sq., 422 sq. ; evolution of, 357 sq., 359

Greenwood, Sir G. G., 117

Greg, Dr. W. W., 34, 60 *n.* ; on Meres, 62 ; on the German *Titus*, 70, 82 sq. ; on the history of *Titus*,

83 sq. ; on *Wily Beguiled*, 250 ; on *A 'Larum for London*, 397

Grosart, Dr., on Ravenscroft's testimony, 58 ; on Greene's share in *Titus*, 42, 58, 94, 216, 483 ; on *Selimus*, 210, 234

H

Hales, Prof. J. W., cited, 314

Hallam, on *Titus*, 44, 45

Halliwell-Phillipps on *Titus*, 46 and *note* ; on Meres, 59 *n.* ; on Shakespeare's first works, 60

Hamlet, 459, 462

Hart, H. C., 23, 267, 308

Hazlitt, on *Titus*, 44

——, W. C., cited, 198 *n.*, 246

Hecatompathia, Watson's, 213

Hecuba, the, of Euripides, 465 sq.

Heminge [variously spelt] and Condell, 10, 26, 43, 81

Henley, W. E., cited, 167 *n.*

1 and 2 *Henry IV*, 64, 65, 441

Henry V, 65, 328 *n.*

Henry VI trilogy, 26, 45, 49, 65, 80, 145, 306

1 *Henry VI*, 6, 65, 476

2 *Henry VI*, 103, 145

3 *Henry VI*, 103, 467

Henry VIII, Fletcher's share in, 49, 80, 440 *n.*

Henslowe's Diary, 60, 67, 76, 83 sq.

Herford, Prof., cited, 47 *n.*, 473

Hero and Leander, 274

Hertzberg, on *Titus*, 47, 48

Heywood, T., 67, 377, 470

Hieronimo and Titus, 226, 460

Higgins, John, 198

Higher criticism, the, 53

Historie of Error, 35 sq.

Hopkinson, A. F., cited, 201 *n.*

Horn, Franz, on *Titus*, 44, 46, 47, 481

Horrors in Elizabethan drama, 17, 135 sq., 167 sq., 457 sq., 471

Hubbard, Prof. F. G., on *Locrine* and *Selimus*, 325

Hughes, Thomas, 419

Hume, 53

Hunting, Shakespeare and, 160 sq.

I

Iago, character of, 107-8

Iconoclasm, charge of, 52

Imitation Theory, the, 46, 47, 91, 104, 111, 120, 176 sq., 177, 180, 183, 203, 242, 243, 245, 315, 378, 403, 439, 440, 454, 469

Ingleby, Dr., 44 ; cited, 50 n.
Italian drama, 33, 73 sq. ; influence of on English, 74 sq., 256 sq., 457 sq., 462

J

Jack Straw, by Peele, 23, 249 sq.
Jacobs, J., on Painter, 47 n.
James IV, 357, 374
Jealous Comedy, The, 36 sq.
Jests, hackneyed, in Elizabethan plays, 453 sq.
Jeronymo, 226, 460
Jew of Malta, The, 463
Jocasta, 163
John, Ivor B., cited, 281
Johnson, Dr., on Titus, 43, 58
Jonson, Ben, evidence of, on Titus, 69, 460 ; additions by, to the Spanish Tragedy, 398 ; versification of, 241 ; repetitions of, 172 ; legal language in, 117
Julius Cæsar, 102, 63 n., 410

K

Kant and criticism, 53
Kellner, Prof., on Titus, 48 n., 483 ; on Sir Clyomon, 189 n.
King John, the old, 266 sq., 278 sq., 400 sq.
King Leir and his Three Daughters. See Leir
Kittredge, Prof., 189 n.
Knight, Charles, on Titus, 43, 44, 56, 57, 481
Kreyssig, on Titus, 46-47
Kyd, Thomas, 75, 142 ; evolution of, 27 sq., 405 ; his authorship of Arden of Feversham, 20, 338 sq., 403 sq. ; share of, in Titus, 16, 63, 75, 131 sq., 141 sq., 223 sq., 448 ; double-endings in, 27 sq., 123-4, 408, 417, 426 ; trace of, in Richard III, 339 ; authorship of Soliman and Perseda, 20, 21, 341 ; realism of, 129, 131, 142, 289, 403 sq., 406 sq. ; style and versification of, 142, 229, 384, 418 ; classical allusions in, 141 sq. ; legal language in, 119 sq. ; trace of, in Edward III, 23, 310, 341, 381 sq. ; as plotter, 107, 131, 226, 292, 406 sq., 461 sq. ; author of the early Hamlet, 459 ; in the old Leir, 287 sq., 387 sq. ; in Alphonsus of Germany, 256 sq., 278 ; in A Warning for Faire Women, 406 sq.

L

Lamb, Charles, on Titus, 43 ; on the Spanish Tragedy, 399
'Larum for London, A, 392 sq.
Latimer, 172
Lavinia, character of, 127, 458
Lee, Sir Sidney, on " Tito Andronico," 73 n. ; services of, 484
Legal Allusions in Elizabethan drama, 108, 116 sq.
Leir, the old play on, 287 sq., 385 sq.
Lilly, imitations of, 94 n, 169, 172, 178 n., 211 n., 222, 451 n. ; work of, 258 n.
Lloyd, W. W., 53, 287 sq.
Llunggren, cited, 451 n.
Locrine, 44, 63, 113, 115, 198 sq., 288 sq., 312 sq., 322 ; compared with Titus, 198 sq., 459 ; authorship of, 41, 198 sq., 312 sq.
Lodge, 77, 282, 283, 385 ; in the old King John, 281 sq., 400 sq. ; in the old Leir, 386 sq. ; in the 'Larum for London, 395 sq. ; supposed share of, in Selimus, 234 ; supposed share of, in Edward III, 375 sq., 382 sq. ; unsigned work of, 385 sq., 411 sq. ; repetitiveness of, 172 ; style of, 383 ; imitated Greene, 246, 291, 319 n., 376, 454 n. ; and Marlowe, 301, 376, 395 ; vocabulary of, in Titus, 246 sq., 411 sq. ; romances of, 358 n. ; in Rosalynde, 386 ; his use of double-endings, 422 sq. ; supposed share of, in A Warning for Faire Women, 406, 411 ; in the Shrew, 413
London Prodigal, The, 62
Looking-Glass for London, A, 358
Love's Labour's Lost, 427, 432, 467, 475, 476 ; date of, 430
Loyalism in Elizabethan drama, 296
Lust's Dominion, 108
Lucrece, 136 sq., 306
Lyly. See Lilly

M

Macaulay, G. C., 421 n.
Macbeth, early traces of, 408 sq.
McCallum, Prof., cited, 2 n.
Machiavelli, 313, 317
Madden, Dr., on Titus, 158 sq., 160, 161
Madness in Elizabethan drama, 227
Malone, 36 sq., 438 ; on Titus, 43 ; on the old King John, 281
Margaret, character of, 108

Marlowe, and Greene, 313, 321 ; editing of, 90, 302 ; share of, in the *Henry VI* plays, 104, 145, 425 sq. ; double-endings in, 28, 133, 244, 284, 400, 440 ; share of, in *Richard III*, 104, 123, 380, 430 ; in *Henry V*, 380 ; in the Roses scene, 425 sq. ; share of, in *Titus*, 2, 14, 42, 45, 91, 150 sq., 239 sq., 274, 399 sq., 436 sq. ; vocabulary of, in *Titus*, 239 sq. ; initiated by Peele, Greene, Kyd, and Lodge, 301, 376, 395, 403, 423 ; repetitiveness of, 172 ; his literary evolution, 241, 244, 274, 379, 418 sq., 436, 462, 475 ; unsigned work of, 378 sq. ; in the *Comedy of Errors*, 79 *n.* ; influence of, on blank verse, 417 sq. ; versification of, 417 sq., 436 sq. ; share of, in *A 'Larum for London*, 393 sq.; in the old *Shrew*, 378-9 ; in *Richard II*, 439 ; in the old *Shrew*, 352 *n.* ; in *Arden of Feversham*, 403 sq. ; in *Edward III*, 22 sq., 306 sq., 377, 379 sq. ; in *Alphonsus of Germany*, 271 sq. ; in the old *King John*, 281 sq. ; supposed share of, in *Selimus*, 234 sq., 312 sq. ; style of, 274, 309, 436, 437, 462, 475 ; influence of Spenser on, 315 ; use of rhyme by, 382
Marston, 250, 251, 397, 421
Massacre at Paris, The, 90 sq., 296
Massinger, verse of, 421
Merchant of Venice, The, 131, 144
Meredith, George, 440 *n.*
Meres, evidence of, 3, 10, 56 sq., 59 sq., 62 sq., 65 sq.
Merry Wives of Windsor, 38
Metre and versification in Elizabethan drama, 30 sq., 138, 183, 189, 274, 368 sq., 416 sq. ; *See* Double-endings, and Rhythm
Middleton, 421
Midsummer Night's Dream, 87 sq., 430, 440, 475
Milton, verse of, 421
Mirror for Magistrates, The, 199
Misfortunes of Arthur, 163, 418
Moorman, Prof., 20, 21
More, Sir Thomas, 81
Mosely, 252-3
Mucedorus, 411
Mutiple-authorship of Elizabethan drama, 34
Munday, 410
Mythology in Peele and Greene, 201, 308

N

Nashe, 302
Nature, allusions to, in Elizabethan drama, 108, 473
Newman, Ernest 42
New Shakspere Society, the, 45, 49
Nicholson, Dr., 59 *n.*
Novel, the Elizabethan, 359

O

Oldcastle, Sir John, 44, 62
Old Wives Tale, 358 ; possible share of Greene in, 224
Oliphant, E. H. C., 23 *n.*, 403, 442, 484
Once-used words, test of, 174 sq.
Orbecche, 74
Orlando Furioso, 358, 473

P

Painter's *Palace of Pleasure*, 47, 306
Parallels in *Titus*, alleged and real, 92 sq., 121 sq.
Parrott, Prof. T. M., 484-5 ; on *Titus*, 12 sq., 24 sq., 121 sq., 242 sq. ; on evolution of double-endings, 27 sq., 122 sq. ; on history of *Titus*, 61 ; on the Folio, 81 ; on parallels in *Titus*, 121 sq., 220, 222, 242 sq. ; on *Alphonsus of Germany*, 255 sq. ; on Peele, 256, 273 ; critical method of, 243 sq., 257
Pathaires, the word, a misprint for *Pathemas*, 342
Pathos in *Titus*, 15, 109, 147
Peele, George, share of in *Titus*, 13, 41, 64, 92 *n.*, 126 sq., 176 sq., 190 sq., 240, 431 sq., 444 sq. ; in *Locrine*, 200 sq. ; style of, 14, 17, 140, 144, 156, 204 sq., 229, 236, 251, 273, 280, 303, 305, 307, 387, 437, 445 ; life of, 64, 86, 301 ; legal allusions in, 118 sq. ; double-endings in, 124 sq., 271, 422 sq. ; dramatic methods of, 127, 189, 457 sq., 460 sq. ; repetitiveness of, 172, 184, 200 sq. ; imitativeness of, 272, 297 ; mythological allusions in, 201, 308 ; alliteration in, 204 sq. ; versification of, 229, 236, 431 sq. ; unsigned work of, 249 sq. ; in *Jack Straw*, 251 ; in *Alphonsus of Germany*, 252 sq. ; in the old *King John*, 278 sq. ; in the old *King Leir*, 287 sq. ; in *Edward II*,

300 ; in the *Massacre*, 302 ; in *Edward III*, 305-310, 385 ; plagiarism in, 271 sq., 297, 323 ; versification of, 422 sq., 431 sq. ; scholarship of, 466 sq.

Pembroke, Lord, Company of, 60, 61

—— Countess of, 421

Pericles, E. K. Chambers on, 6 ; problem of, 23, 49, 80

Plagiarism, tests of, 244, 273

Plays within plays, in old drama, 459

Pollard, Prof. A. W., 70, 441, 442, 481 *n.*, 484

Polymnestor, story of, 465

Preston, Thomas, 189 *n.*

Property, theatrical, 80, 161, 249, 478

Protestantism in plays, 303 sq., 456

Puns in Shakespeare, 143, 160, 230

Q

Quartos, the, publication of, 64, 70

R

Raleigh, Prof., cited, 2 *n.*, 326 *n.*

Rants, duplicated, 224, 229, 250, 463 sq.

Rape of Lucrece, The, 136 sq., 306

Ravenscroft, testimony of, as to *Titus*, 46, 57 sq.

Re.d, E., on Bacon and Shakespeare, 142 *n.*

Realism in Elizabethan drama, 129, 131, 142, 289, 403 sq., 406 sq.

Return from Parnassus, The, 80

Revenge-motive in the Elizabethan drama, 199, 457 sq.

Rhymes, irregular, 391

Rhythm, test of, 368 sq., 404, 424, 431 sq.

Richard II, Saintsbury on, 22 ; authorship of, 89, 90, 145, 439 ; and *Titus*, 162 sq. ; date of, 440 ; Shakespeare in, 439 ; demerits of, 476

Richard III, 428 ; non-Shakespearean work in, 52 ; double-endings in, 430 ; Shakespeare's hand in, 437 ; demerits of, 476

——, the old play on, 279, 386

Richard Conqueror, 253

Richard Duke of York, 103, 292

Ritson, 41

Robinson, Crabb, cited, 43

Romeo and Juliet, 427 ; quartos of, 64 ; date of, 88 ; words and phrases in, 145 ; original authorship of, 64, 88, 145, 300

Roses scene, the, in 1 *H. VI*, 28, 424 sq.

Rosmunda, 74

Rucellai, 74

S

Sackville and Norton, 416 sq.

Sacrifice, human, in *Titus*, 93, 467

Saintsbury, Prof. G., on *Titus*, 17 sq., 51, 242 ; on *Richard II*, 22

Sarrazin, on *Titus*, 47 ; on *Arden*, 403 *n.* ; on Kyd, 483

Schelling, Prof., cited, 279

Schick, Prof., 107, 114

Schiller, 47

Schlegel, A, on *Titus*, 44 ; on Meres, 59 *n.*

Schmidt's *Shakespeare-Lexikon*, 483

Schröer, Prof., 4, 47 *n.*, 51, 56, 171, 174 *n.*, 427, 437, 462, 467, 482, 483

Schücking, Prof, 443-4

Scientific tests, 5, 7 sq. 46 *n.*, 168 sq.

Scilla's Metamorphosis, 77, 423

Seccombe and Allen, cited, 417 *n.*

Sejanus, 421

Selimus, 102 *n.*, 210 sq., 224 sq., 270 sq., 312 sq., 457, 459

Senecan influence, 74 sq., 457

Sentimentalism in criticism, 6

Seymour, E. H., on *Titus*, 43

Shakespeare, the Canon of, 1, 50, 87 sq. ; double-endings in, 27 sq., 124 sq., 138, 244 sq., 425, 427 ; alleged classical scholarship of, 466 ; style of, 50, 124, 135 sq., 155, 371 sq., 437, 439, 443 ; in the Chamberlain's Company, 60 ; early work of, 87 sq., 124 sq., 371 sq., 424 sq., 432 sq. ; revision of *Titus* by, 13 sq., 92 sq., 121 sq. ; æsthetic taste of, 137 sq., 468 sq. ; versification of, 138 sq, 368 sq., 371 sq., 432 sq. ; views of, on sport, 159 sq., 244 sq. ; repetitions in, 173 ; alleged imitation of Marlowe by, 243 sq., 439 ; presence of, in 2 *H. VI*, 424 sq. ; in *Richard III*, 437 ; in *Richard II*, 439 ; in *Sir Thomas More*, 442 ; in *The Two Noble Kinsmen*, 442 ; handwriting of, 441 ; politics of, 441 ; sanity of, 458 ; dramatic outset of, 475 sq., 477 ; prose of, 482 ; vocabulary of, 485-6 ; false valuations of, 486

Sidney, Sir P, cited, 96, 328 n.
Sidgwick, Prof. H., on *Titus*, 66-67 ;
on *Macbeth*, 67
Simpson, R., cited, 174 sq., 397, 406,
443
Sir Clyomon and Sir Clamydes, 188
sq.
Sir Thomas More, 441 sq.
Smith, Prof. Gregory, 20
—— G. C. Moore, 306, 328 n., 330 n.,
375 sq., 380, 381 n.
Soliman and Perseda, 27, 293 sq., 340,
341, 350 sq.
Sonnets, Shakespeare's, 366 sq.
Spanish Tragedy, The, 27, 41, 43, 69,
74, 75 ; plot of, 107, 459 ; mannerisms in, 209 ; hands in, 293 sq. ;
additions to, 398 sq.; double-
endings in, 417 ; touch of " nature"
in, 473
Spedding, on *Henry VIII*, 49
Spenser, words and phrases in, 100 n.,
111 n., 163, 181 n., 190 n., 199, 212,
213 n., 215, 222, 223 n., 225, 233 n.,
294, 312 n., 450 n., 451 ; imitations
of, in *Locrine* and *Selimus*, 312 sq ;
early work of, 314
Sport, Shakespeare and, 159 sq.,
244
Stanza-verse in drama, 234, 236, 318
sq.
Steevens, on *Titus*, 47 n., 176
Storojenko, Prof., cited, 357 n.,
423
Strange, Lord, company of, 60, 61
Style, the test of, 3 sq., 8 sq., 11 sq.,
50, 170, 243, 264, 271 sq., 283, 370,
438, 443 sq.
Sussex, Lord, company of, 60
Swinburne, on *Arden* and *Edward
III*, 32, 305 sq., 369 sq., 379 sq.,
404 ; on *Titus*, 45 n., 52 n. ; on
Marlowe, 393 sq. ; on *A Warning
for Faire Women*, 406 sq.
Sykes, H. Dugdale, 34, 196, 484 ; on
Peele's unsigned work, 285 sq.,
389 ; on tags, 264 sq., 280 sq.,
298 sq., 310, 389 ; on *Selimus*, 270 ;
on *A Warning for Faire Women*,
406
Symonds, J. A., cited, 75, 357,
417 n.
Symons, A., on *Titus* 33, 458 n.

T

Talbot scenes, in 1 *Henry VI*, 6 n.,
77 n., 424
Tamburlaine, 199, 436, 460 n.

Taming of the Shrew, The, 49, 66, 413,
467
Taming of A Shrew, The, 63, 352,
378-9, 413
Tamora, 22, 107, 436, 471
Tancred and Gismunda, 74, 209, 459,
463 n.
Tennyson, on *Edward III*, 23, 32,
305, 306, 370
Tests of authorship, scientific, 5,
7 sq., 46 n., 168
Theobald, on *Titus*, 43, 58
Thompson, Sir E. M., 441
Thomson, James, 15
" Thrice," use of, 308
Timon, Dr., on *Titus*, 48
Timon, E. K. Chambers on, 6 ;
problem of, 23 ; demerit of, 476
Tiraboschi, cited, 74
" *Tito Andronico*," a mystification,
73 n.
" *Titus and Andronicus*," 68, 69, 70,
84
Titus Andronicus, general opinion as
to authorship of, 2, 43 sq., 50, 58 ;
hands in, 2, 92 sq., 121 sq., 151 sq.,
176 sq., 239 sq., 274, 398, 436,
444 sq. ; plot of, 107, 457 sq. ;
horrors of, 135 sq., 167 sq., 457 sq. ;
chronology of, 54, 60, 61, 79 sq., 83
sq., 127, 430 ; summary of debate
on, 478 sq. ; external evidence as
to, 56 sq. ; the German version
of, 71 sq., 83 sq., 127 ; probable
Italian origin of, 73 sq. ; internal
evidence as to, 92 sq., 121 sq. ;
double-endings in, 121 sq., 149,
153, 154, 158, 243 sq., 447 ; stage
effectiveness of, 474 sq. ; alliteration in, 207 sq.
Titus and Vespasian, 35, 61, 62 sq.,
68, 70, 71 sq., 74, 82 sq., 86, 115,
127
Troilus and Cressida, 80, 476
*Troublesome Raigne of King John,
The*, 266 sq., 278 sq., 400 sq.
Troynovant, 210
Tucker-Brooke, C. F., on *Locrine*,
201, 312 ; on *Edward III*, 307 ; on
Selimus, 312
Two Italian Gentlemen, The, 189,
319 n.
Two Gentlemen of Verona, The, date
of, 31, 88, 427 ; words and phrases
in, 100 ; authorship of, 89, 100,
220, 367 n., 371 sq. ; double-
endings in, 31
Two Noble Kinsmen, The, 81
Tyler, T., 47 n., 367 n., 368
Tylney, Charles, 198

U

Ulrici, on *Titus*, 46 ; on *Edward III*, 305
United States, Shakespeare study in, 484
Universities, English, and literary science, 4, 438, 482

V

Venus and Adonis, date of, 77, 78, 88 ; parallels from, 123 sq., 220 sq.
Verity, A. W., on Peele's authorship of *Titus*, 41, 216 ; on Marlowe, 295, 298, 302, 418 *n.*, 483
Verplanck, on *Titus*, 45
Versification, Shakespeare's, 138, 183, 368 sq., 404, 431 sq.
Vespasian, in the old *Titus*, 70 sq.
Villains, in Elizabethan drama, 241, 244
Virginius, references to, 154, sq.
Vocabulary tests, 190 sq., 224, 328 sq.

W

Walker, Sidney, on *Titus*, 44, 438
Ward, Prof. A. W., cited, 45 *n.*, 92 *n.* ; on *Edward III*, 90, 305 ; on Peele, 249 ; on *Alphonsus of Germany*, 253, 257 ; on *Edward II*, 295 ; on Greene, 357

Warning for Faire Women, *A*, 406 sq.
Watson, 213
Webster, 171 sq.
Weckherlin, Rudolf, 257
White, R. G., on *Titus*, 42 *n.*, 45, 49-50, 104 sq., 216 ; on Schmidt's *Lexikon*, 483
Wiclif, 172
Wilmot, 74, 209
Wilson, T., Dover, 70, 441, 476, 481 *n.*, 484
Wily Beguiled, 249 sq.
Wolff, Max J., on *Titus*, 48, 73 *n.*
Women in Elizabethan drama, 357, 359
Wood and Winstanley, 253
Wounds of Civil War, 163, 246 sq., 301, 376
Wright, Aldis, on *Titus*, 84 ; cited, 339 *n.*

Y

Yorkshire Tragedy, The, 44, 62

Z

Zodiac, Peele on the, 179 sq.